Human Rights and the International Law of Military Operations

Human Rights and the International Law of Military Operations

Emmett Sloan

MURPHY & MOORE

www.murphy-moorepublishing.com

Murphy & Moore Publishing,
1 Rockefeller Plaza,
New York City, NY 10020, USA

ISBN: 978-1-63987-315-9

Cataloging-in-Publication Data

Human rights and the international law of military operations / Emmett Sloan.
    p. cm.
Includes bibliographical references and index.
ISBN 978-1-63987-315-9
1. Human rights. 2. Military law. 3. Intervention (International law).
4. Peacekeeping forces (International law). 5. Humanitarian law.
6. War (International law). I. Sloan, Emmett.
K3240 .H86 2022
341.48--dc23

For information on all Murphy & Moore Publications
visit our website at www.murphy-moorepublishing.com

Contents

Preface

The basic rights and freedom inherited by an individual at the time of their birth are called human rights. These can never be taken away and are possessed by them until his death. Human rights are applicable everywhere, for everyone, and at every time. Some of the basic human rights are protection against enslavement, right to education, and right to free speech. International military law is responsible for regulating the actions of armed individuals, groups, and states involved in hostilities. Law on military operations draws from different bodies of legal rules such as the international humanitarian law, targeting law, weapons law, etc. This legal framework attempts to counterbalance the fragmentations of different international laws. This book presents the complex subject of human rights and law of military operations in the most comprehensible and easy to understand language. Some of the diverse topics covered herein address the varied branches that fall under this category. The book is appropriate for those seeking detailed information in this area.

The information shared in this book is based on empirical researches made by veterans in this field of study. The elaborative information provided in this book will help the readers further their scope of knowledge leading to advancements in this field.

Finally, I would like to thank my fellow researchers who gave constructive feedback and my family members who supported me at every step of my research.

Emmett Sloan

Introduction

Erika de Wet & Jann Kleffner

1   Background

This publication resulted from a series of conferences and training sessions involving academics, government officials, military personnel and members of civil society. The series of events took place between August 2011 and June 2013 in the context of a collaborative partnership between the Institute for International and Comparative Law in Africa (ICLA) in the Faculty of Law of the University of Pretoria and the International Law Center of the Swedish National Defence College (SNDC) in Stockholm, with the financial support of the Swedish National Development Agency (SIDA).

The subject matter of convergence and conflicts of human rights and international humanitarian law in military operation was determined by the implications of increased interplay between international human rights law (IHRL) and international humanitarian law (IHL); interplay which at times implies convergence, while at other times conflict. These situations of convergences and/or conflicts are particularly acute in non-international armed conflicts, situations of belligerent occupation, detention and in the area of international peace operations. Non-international armed conflicts imply that individuals, including members of organised non-state armed groups and civilians that directly participate in hostilities, are 'within the jurisdiction' of the territorial state against whom they are fighting. IHRL hence applies as much as IHL does. In a similar vein, the control exercised by a detaining or occupying power entails an exercise of 'jurisdiction' and hence triggers the applicability of human rights norms. As far as peace operations are concerned, it becomes increasingly difficult to classify them as taking place in a context of 'peace' or 'armed conflict'. More often than not, the situation implies elements of both.

These realities in turn elevate the interplay between the fields of IHRL and IHL to a great practical significance, as these areas of law provide the most pertinent regulatory framework for the conduct of non-international armed conflicts, detention, belligerent occupation and peace operations. In some situations this interplay results in layers of protection, a better understanding of which can inform responses to the nature of contemporary organised armed violence. Moreover, the pervasiveness of non-international armed conflicts on the African continent makes it imperative that institutions on the continent – whether academic, governmental or humanitarian – further their understanding of the interplay between IHRL and IHL. In addition, given the growing demand for peace operations in Africa and South Africa's prominence as a regional power, the importance of in-depth knowledge of the regulatory framework applicable during peace operations is indispensable.

Before ICLA and the SNDC undertook the above mentioned collaborative partnership, there was no institution in South Africa (or elsewhere on the African continent) that explored the interplay between IHRL and IHL and its implications for the regulatory framework of military operations in any depth. As a result, the government, military and humanitarian organisations had to rely on foreign expertise for assistance with legislative reform in areas that affected military operations, training of military personnel, as well as training of humanitarian workers active in conflict areas.

The series of conferences and training events culminating in these conference proceedings contributes to filling a major gap in practical and scholarly relevance for the African region as a whole. The proceedings, which consist of chapters written by eminent scholars and practitioners in the fields of IHL and IHRL, serve as an important point of reference for all stakeholders working on the interface between these two areas. The publication focuses exclusively on issues of interplay between IHL and IHRL and attempts to unpack (if not necessarily resolve) some of the major challenges pertaining to such interplay. No other publication of its kind exists on the African continent and very few similar publications exist in other regions. The choice for Pretoria University Law Press, the peer reviewed publisher of the Faculty of Law of the University of Pretoria, is an obvious choice in light of its standing and distribution network on the African continent and the relevance of the topic for the African continent in particular.

2   Chapter overview

The topics covered in the proceedings reflect the approach followed during the conferences and training sessions, namely to combine theoretical, conceptual and practice oriented presentations. Given the breadth and depth of the current debate surrounding the interrelationship between IHL and IHRL during contemporary military operations, it would have been impossible to give the subject an exhaustive and comprehensive treatment.

Instead, a number of themes were selected that raise particularly intricate questions, be it on the foundational, practical, institutional or adjudicative level. Accordingly, the selected themes fall into four broad categories, that lie at the basis of the structure of the present book.

A first cluster (Part A) assembles some contributions that address foundational issues of a more theoretical or conceptual nature that underlie IHL and IHRL and their interrelationship. In Chapter 1, Iain Scobbie examines the fundamental question whether and to what extent the two fields of international law can be reconciled at all. He does so against the backdrop of a juxtaposition of the rights that IHL affords to those who do not or no longer participate in hostilities, on the one hand, and the rights that IHRL affords to combatants, on the other hand. Thereafter the focus of the first cluster of the book shifts to the conceptualisation of two aspects of the relationship between IHL and IHRL that are of particular relevance in the African context and because of the global trends and nature of contemporary organised armed violence. The first concerns the (lacking) gender perspective on the relationship between IHL and IHRL. In Chapter 2 Bonita Meyersfeld traces the trajectory of IHL and IHRL's responses to gender-based violence, identifies main areas of convergence that still ought to occur, as well as pleads for the change necessary for an appropriate response to the changing nature of conflict and its impact on women. In Chapter 3, Jann Kleffner examines whether and to what extent the two fields of IHL and IHRL are applicable to organised armed groups. Recalling that IHL is generally accepted to bind organised armed groups, while the binding nature of IHRL on such groups is subject to significant controversy, he subjects the explanations of why the two areas of law are purported to apply to a critical examination.

Part B then turns to five situations in which the interrelationship of IHL and IHRL poses particularly acute problems. In Chapter 4 Bruce Oswald explores the application of IHL and IHRL when taking and handling detainees. He examines, in particular: the phases of detention in military operations; the legal regimes that apply to detention; the approaches taken by some states, international organisations and tribunals to the interplay; and how the interplay impacts on the treatment of detainees.

In Chapter 5 Michelle Lesh examines the convergence and conflicts of the normative frameworks of IHL and IHRL during the conduct of hostilities. She illustrates the complexities of the relationship between the two regimes by assessing the extent to which the right to life in IHRL comes to play a role during military operations that are regulated by the rules on the conduct of hostilities under IHL. Central to her analysis is the role of the *lex specialis* doctrine as informed by the principles of military necessity and humanity.

Chapter 6, written by Andrea Carcano, analyses the relationship between the law of belligerent occupation and its relationship with IHRL. After first illustrating the legal basis on which one can argue that a state is required to comply with IHRL in the territory it happens to occupy, the chapter explores the extent to which IHRL has impacted on the authorities, responsibilities, and duties of an occupying power as framed by the law of occupation. It further examines the implications of the law of occupation as *lex specialis* for the applicability of IHRL during occupation, as well as whether adherence to IHRL standards could augment the normative powers of the occupying power.

In Chapter 7 Marten Zwanenburg illuminates the relationship between IHL and IHRL in peace operations, specifically multinational operations established or authorised by the United Nations to establish or maintain international peace and security. He explores the applicability of IHL and IHRL to these operations, paying particular attention to the question whether the law of international armed conflicts or that of non-international armed conflict would be relevant. He also explores the implications of the role of *lex specialis* in situations where both IHRL and IHL apply during peace operations.

Andre Smit deals with selected issues of IHL and IHRL in naval counter-piracy operations in Chapter 8. His chapter is situation specific in as far as it provides a South African perspective on the international law framework behind African driven counter piracy operations. It discusses the context of the Somali piracy, the international law on maritime piracy, alternative international crimes to maritime piracy, and analyses the application of IHL and IHRL to the combating, capturing, arrest and transfer of maritime pirates.

The subsequent four chapters constitute Part C, in which the focus is shifted from specific situations in which the interrelationship occurs to the perspectives of a number of central institutions on that interrelationship. Chapter 9, written by Daphna Shraga, focuses on the interplay between IHL and IHRL during United Nations operations. Although the chapter deals with questions that to some extent overlap with those dealt with by Marten Zwanenburg in Chapter 7, it takes a different perspective. It emphasises in particular the perspective of the United Nations on the applicability of IHL and IHRL to its operations, as distilled from the organisation's practice in the context of the administration of territories; the practicing of law and order functions (such as arrest and detention); the handing over of individuals on United Nations premises to national authorities for prosecution; and the responsibility of the organisation for violations of IHL and IHRL.

Chapter 10 addresses the interplay between IHL and IHRL from the perspective of the North Atlantic Treaty Organization (NATO). Peter Olson illuminates how NATO's mission, history and resulting structure directly shapes its approach to the interplay between IHL and IHRL. Since NATO is designed to function as a mechanism for common action by sovereign states rather than as an autonomous entity, it has not developed a single doctrine in this regard. Instead, it applies IHL and IHRL in NATO operations in a manner reflecting the individual national legal positions of the 28 Allies. The chapter examines the implications of this approach against the background of recent NATO practice.

In Chapter 11 James Ross elaborates on ways in which human rights organisations have sought to obtain better protections for civilians and captured fighters and populations at risk during armed conflict. The rational of the chapter is that the overlap between IHL and IHRL can provide better protection to those at risk without threatening the role of IHL in wartime situations.

Chapter 12 concludes part C with an analysis of the role of the legal advisor in applying IHL and IHRL during military operations. Taking a Canadian perspective, Blaise Cathcart discusses the impact of IHL and IHRL in the provision of legal advice by legal advisors of armed forces during armed conflict. He elaborates in particular on the extra-territorial application of IHRL during armed conflict, being one of the most challenging and controversial issues that legal advisors are confronted with.

Part D, which consists of four chapters, constitutes the final part of the book. It focuses on the role of the most prominent international judicial bodies in giving effect to the interplay between IHL and IHRL through their jurisprudence. In Chapter 13, Frans Viljoen explores the relationship between IHL and IHRL in the African human rights system. The chapter deals with the fledgling attempts as well as the future potential of the African Commission on Human and Peoples' Rights, the African Court on Human and Peoples' Rights and the African Committee of Experts on the Rights of the Child to apply IHL either indirectly through interpretation or in a more direct manner.

In Chapter 14 Karin Oellers-Frahm examines the extent to which the European Court of Human Rights (ECtHR), which has jurisdiction to interpret and apply the European Convention on Human Rights, has to consider IHL as *lex specialis* in cases that result from armed conflicts. This raises questions as to whether IHL can be directly applicable by the ECtHR *ratione materiae*; about the limits of the jurisdiction of the ECtHR *ratione personae*; and the manner in which IHL shapes the ECtHR's decisions on the merits.

In Chapter 15 Dinah Shelton illuminates how the Inter-American Commission and Inter-American Court of Human Rights have considered the relationship between IHRL and IHL. She outlines the (sometimes divergent) approaches of these bodies in relation to the scope of their jurisdiction to apply IHL; the threshold of violence that triggers application of IHL norms; and the content of the relevant norms.

Chapter 16, by Gentian Zyberi, concludes this part with an analysis of the jurisprudence of the International Court of Justice and international criminal courts and tribunals in the application of IHL and IHRL.

The editors have deliberately refrained from drawing any conclusions in a concluding chapter. Given the diversity of the topics addressed and the complexity of each of the issues at stake, the drawing of conclusion at this stage seems premature. Instead the sixteen chapter volume is intended to engender further debate and reflection on one of the major normative debates of our time.

PART A: Theories and Concepts

Protection of Human Rights

*Iain Scobbie**

1 Introduction

It is now commonplace to affirm that during hostilities the law of armed conflict and international human rights law lie in some sort of relationship, but the substantive contours of this remain unclear. Some might wish that this question no longer be discussed, on the assumption that both apply in tandem, perhaps basing themselves on an over-generous reading of the Human Rights Committee's General Comment 31 which affirms that the International Covenant on Civil and Political Rights applies in situations of armed conflict, and continues:

> While, in respect of certain Covenant rights, more specific rules of international humanitarian law may be specially relevant for the purposes of the interpretation of Covenant rights, both spheres of law are complementary, not mutually exclusive.[1]

Mapping the relationship between these branches of international law cannot be avoided. To ignore this issue is simply not an option as to do so would disregard too many questions, such as the extent to which this relationship is determined by the nature or classification of the conflict and the type of human rights that might be relevant to both the situation and the actors involved. At root, the difficulties inherent in mapping this substantive relationship appear to lie in the axiologies of these areas of law which are fundamentally incompatible, and also in the diversity of the legitimate expectations that may be directed at the state by its citizens, by those subject to its jurisdiction or effective control, and by those it places at risk.

* Professor of Public International Law, University of Manchester, and Visiting Professor in International law, SOAS, University of London. I should like to thank the editors for their patience and support.

1 Human Rights Committee, General Comment 31, *Nature of the General Legal Obligation on States Parties to the Covenant*, UN Doc CCPR/C/21/Rev.1/Add.13 (2004), para11.

This essay seeks to examine some of the under-discussed questions in the debate regarding human rights and the law of armed conflict. What are the implications of the classification of a conflict in mapping this relationship? This is principally a technical matter. More incisively, and more conceptually, to what extent does the state bear responsibility to protect the human rights of its combatants? Could this question be a test case, or a breaking point, in this debate?

As Professor Koskenniemi has argued, specialisation is a characteristic of contemporary international legal practice. Discrete sets of substantive issues are parcelled into categories such as trade law or environmental law or human rights law and so on. These specialisations 'cater for special audiences with special interests and special ethos'.[2] Each contains structural biases in the form of dominant expectations about the values, actors and solutions appropriate to that specialisation, which thus affect practical outcomes. The actors in these different fields conceptualise issues in ways which pull upon these preconceptions to reach solutions which are thought suitable for the specialisation.[3] In discussing the relationship between the law of armed conflict and human rights, Professor Garraway has underlined the importance of the analyst's own perspective and presuppositions:

> For human rights lawyers, human rights principles are those that provide the greatest protection to all by introducing a high threshold for any use of force and even if that threshold is crossed, a graduated use of force thereafter. On the other hand, international humanitarian lawyers see this as idealistic and impracticable. As they see it, it would become almost impossible to conduct hostilities legally to which many human rights lawyers would reply that that would be no bad thing! The difficulty is that such an attitude will not abolish armed conflict.[4]

Similarly, Professor Kretzmer notes that the post-WWII development of the law of non-international armed conflict and international human rights law 'advanced on parallel tracks' but that 'different personalities were involved ... [who] represented different State interests' and, when the various conventions were drafted, 'no serious consideration was given to the relationship between the two branches of law'.[5]

2　　M Koskenniemi 'The politics of international law – 20 years later' (2009) 20 *European Journal of International Law* 7 9.

3　　See also J Beckett 'The politics of international law – 20 years later: A reply' www.ejiltalk.org/the-politics-of-international-law-twenty-years-later-a-reply/#more-9 33 (accessed 11 October 2014); and I Scobbie 'On the road to Avila: A reply to Koskenniemi' www.ejiltalk.org/on-the-road-to-avila-a-response-to-koskenniemi/#mo re-1005 (accessed 11 October 2014).

4　　C Garraway '"To kill or not to kill"– Dilemmas on the use of force' (2010) 14 *Journal of Conflict and Security Law* 499 509.

5　　D Kretzmer 'Rethinking application of IHL in non-international armed conflict' (2009) 42 *Israel Law Review* 8 10.

At the 1974-1977 Diplomatic Conference which drafted Additional Protocols I (international armed conflict) and II (non-international armed conflict) to the Geneva Conventions, the majority of participating states emphasised that, in order to maintain the unity of international law, the law of armed conflict, or international humanitarian law, could not be isolated and self-contained but had to take into account the rules of general international law. In this connection, emphasis was placed on the need to adapt the law of armed conflict to conform with the principles expounded by the International Court of Justice in paragraph 53 of the *Namibia* Advisory Opinion,[6] namely that 'an international instrument must be interpreted and applied within the overall framework of the juridical system in force at the time of the interpretation'.[7] One of the implications of this approach is the increasing insistence that international human rights law is relevant in times of armed conflict.

This was a trend which was already apparent before the 1974-1977 Diplomatic Conference. As early as the late 1960s, United Nations bodies had affirmed that some substantive human rights remained relevant during an international armed conflict.[8] Thus, for instance, in resolution 237 (14 June 1967) on the situation in the Middle East, the Security Council noted that 'essential and inalienable human rights should be respected even during the vicissitudes of war' and in operative paragraph 1 of resolution 2675 (XXV) of 9 December 1970, *Basic principles for the protection of civilian populations in armed conflicts*, the General Assembly affirmed:

> Fundamental human rights, as accepted in international law and laid down in international instruments, continue to apply fully in situations of armed conflict.

By the mid-1990s, although it was generally accepted that both human rights instruments and the law of armed conflict were relevant in the regulation of non-international armed conflict, the idea that both could also be applicable during an international armed conflict was only emerging towards doctrinal consolidation.[9] The first authoritative ruling on the nature of the relationship between international humanitarian and

---

6   See Y Sandoz et al (eds) *Commentary on the Additional Protocols of 8 June 1977 to the Geneva Conventions of 12 August 1949* (1987) 51-52.

7   *Legal Consequences for States of the Continued Presence of South Africa in Namibia (South West Africa), notwithstanding Security Council Resolution 276 (1970)* Advisory Opinion ICJ Rep, 1971, 16 31, para 53.

8   For contemporary commentary see, for instance, GIAD Draper 'The relationship between the human rights regime and the law of armed conflicts' (1971) 1 *Israel Yearbook on Human Rights* 191; and G von Glahn 'The protection of human rights in time of armed conflicts' (1971) 1 *Israel Yearbook on Human Rights* 208.

9   See, for instance, HS Burgos 'The application of international humanitarian law as compared to human rights law in situations qualified as internal armed conflict, internal disturbances and tensions, or public emergency, with special reference to war crimes and political crimes' in F Kalshoven & Y Sandoz (eds) *Implementation of international humanitarian law* (1989) 1; CM Cerna 'Human rights in armed conflict: Implementation of international humanitarian norms by regional intergovernmental human rights bodies' in Kalshoven & Sandoz, *op cit*, 31; Y Dinstein 'Human rights in

human rights law in an international armed conflict was enunciated by the International Court of Justice in the *Legality of the Threat or Use of Nuclear Weapons* Advisory Opinion in 1996. It had to consider whether or not the International Covenant on Civil and Political Rights was applicable during an international armed conflict. The Court ruled:

> [T]he protection of the International Covenant on Civil and Political Rights does not cease in times of war, except by operation of article 4 of the Covenant whereby certain provisions may be derogated from in a time of national emergency. Respect for the right to life is not, however, such a provision. In principle, the right not arbitrarily to be deprived of one's life applies also in hostilities. The test of what is an arbitrary deprivation of life, however, then falls to be determined by the applicable *lex specialis*, namely, the law applicable in armed conflict which is designed to regulate the conduct of hostilities.[10]

In the *Legal Consequences of the Construction of a Wall in Occupied Palestinian Territory* Advisory Opinion, the Court reaffirmed this ruling in slightly different terms stating that it had to 'take into consideration both these branches of international law, namely human rights law and, as *lex specialis*, international humanitarian law'.[11] Some commentators see this as marking a subtle change in the Court's view, indicating that the *lex specialis* maxim should not be used to displace the application of human

armed conflict: International humanitarian law' in T Meron (ed) *Human rights in international law: Legal and policy issues* (1984) Vol II 345; L Doswald-Beck & S Vite 'International humanitarian law and human rights law' (1993) 293 *International Review of the Red Cross* 94; A Eide 'The laws of war and human rights – Divergences and convergences' in C Swinarski (ed) *Studies and essays on international humanitarian law and Red Cross principles in honour of Jean Pictet* (1984) 675; F Hampson 'Human rights and humanitarian law in internal conflicts' in A Meyer (ed) *Armed conflict and the new law* (1989) 55; PH Kooijmans 'In the shadowland between civil war and civil strife: Some reflections on the standard-setting process' in A Delissen & G Tanja (eds) *Humanitarian law of armed conflict: Challenges ahead: Essays in honour of Frits Kalshoven* (1991) 225; T Meron *Human rights in internal strife: Their international protection* (1987); AH Robertson 'Humanitarian law and human rights' in Swinarski, *op cit*, 793; and D Schindler 'Human rights and humanitarian law: Interrelationship of the laws' (1982) 31 *American University Law Review* 935.

10   *Legality of the Threat or Use of Nuclear Weapons* Advisory Opinion ICJ Rep, 1996 (1), 226, 240, para 25. The earlier ruling by the European Court of Human Rights which addressed aspects of the applicability of human rights norms in an international armed conflict, delivered in *Loizidou v Turkey, preliminary objections judgment* (23 March 1995), Series A, No 310 23-24, paras 62-64, is more restricted than that of the International Court in the *Nuclear Weapons* Advisory Opinion. In *Loisidou*, the European Court addressed only the extra-territorial applicability of the European Convention on Human Rights where a state party exercises effective control over foreign territory. It ruled (24, para 62):
>   'Bearing in mind the object and purpose of the Convention, the responsibilities of a Contracting Party may also arise when as a consequence of military action – whether lawful or unlawful ? it exercises effective control of an area outside its national territory. The obligation to secure, in such an area, the rights and freedoms set forth in the Convention derives from the fact of such control whether it be exercised directly, through its armed forces, or through a subordinate local administration.'

11   *Legal Consequences of the Construction of a Wall in Occupied Palestinian Territory*, ICJ Rep, 2004, 136, 178, para 106.

rights law, but rather that human rights norms should be interpreted in the light of the law of armed conflict.[12] Professor Schabas comments that in this ruling the Court 'seemed to withdraw from what may have been taken as a rather absolute statement in *Nuclear Weapons*'.[13]

In the *Armed Activities on the Territory of the Congo (Democratic Republic of the Congo v Uganda)* case, the Court recalled its ruling in the *Nuclear Weapons* Advisory Opinion and quoted the one delivered in the *Legal Consequences of the Construction of a Wall* Advisory Opinion, but it omitted the reference to *lex specialis* which some have taken to mean that the Court has abandoned this approach.[14] One would have wished, having dealt with the issue repeatedly, that the International Court might have been more candid and more specific. It has not provided a transparent account of the relationship between the law of armed conflict and human rights law in armed conflict. In fact, in the *Legal Consequences of the Construction of a Wall* Advisory Opinion, the Court made the trite and essentially vacuous observation that:

> As regards the relationship between international humanitarian law and human rights law, there are three possible situations: some rights may be exclusively matters of international humanitarian law; others may be exclusively matters of human rights law; yet others may be matters of both these branches of international law.[15]

The nature of the relationship between the law of armed conflict and international human rights law is complex, and its contours contested in academic literature. It must be acknowledged that there is a degree of substantive overlap between the two disciplines – for instance, both prohibit torture and inhuman treatment – but there are also some clear differences. The law of international armed conflict expressly contemplates that states may intern individuals without trial (for instance, as prisoners of war, or inhabitants of occupied territory for security reasons) while this would be prohibited under human rights instruments

---

12   See F Hampson & I Salama *Working paper on the relationship between human rights law and international humanitarian law*, UN Doc E/CN.4/Sub.2/2005/14 (21 June 2005) 15, para 57.

13   W Schabas '*Lex specialis*? Belt and suspenders? The parallel operation of human rights law and the law of armed conflict, and the conundrum of *jus ad bellum*' (2007) 40 *Israel Law Review* 592 596.

14   *Armed Activities on the Territory of the Congo (Democratic Republic of the Congo v Uganda)*, ICJ Rep. 2005, 168 242–243, para 216. For the claim that the Court abandoned the *lex specialis* approach, see N Prud'homme '*Lex specialis*: Oversimplifying a more complex and multifaceted relationship?' (2007) 40 *Israel Law Review* 355 385. The *lex specialis* maxim has been criticised as an impractical method to resolve normative conflicts because it is conceptually vague – see A Lindroos 'Addressing norm conflicts in a fragmented legal system: The doctrine of *lex specialis*' (2005) 74 *Nordic Journal of International Law* 27.

15   *Legal Consequences of the Construction of a Wall in Occupied Palestinian Territory* (n 11 above) 178, para 106.

unless the detaining state had made a derogation to the relevant treaty.[16] Indeed, the European Court of Human Rights has indicated that a state party which is involved in an international armed conflict must derogate from its obligations under the European Convention if it wishes to detain civilians using its power to do so under the Fourth Geneva Convention.[17] This is perhaps an example of the many broad, or over-broad, claims that have been made as to the extent that human rights law applies during an armed conflict, and has caused one commentator to argue that the *Al–Jedda* judgment 'will have a chilling effect on the ability of Council of Europe States to take part in multinational operations abroad that involve deprivation of liberty'.[18]

The debate tends to focus on human rights treaties, without adequately taking into account that some core rights, such as the right to life, are defined differently in different conventions, or that these contain different provisions which determine their applicability. States forming a coalition could easily bear different human rights obligations simply because they adhere to different treaties, posing a challenge to the inter-operability and cohesion of the force as a whole. The debate also often tends to ignore customary international law. My view is that there are no general axiological principles that can determine this relationship, and that the extent to which human rights apply during an armed conflict essentially depends on context and circumstances.[19] Nevertheless the rulings by the International Court of Justice have legally entrenched the idea that there is some normative relationship between these two branches of law.

2 The importance of the classification of a conflict

In the *Nuclear Weapons* Advisory Opinion, the International Court focused on the right to life and the parameters of a state's legitimate use of deadly force in an international armed conflict. It has been argued that of all the matters regulated by both the law of armed conflict and international human rights law, the greatest differences are found in the rules which govern the use of force.[20] This focus perhaps gave an unduly narrow cast

---

16 For a discussion of the different detention regimes under the law of armed conflict and international human rights law, see J Pejic 'Conflict classification and the law applicable to detention and the use of force' in E Wilmshurst (ed) *International law and the classification of conflict* (2012) 80 86-94.

17 See *Al–Jedda v United Kingdom* [2011] ECtHR 1092 (App No 27021/08, decided 7 July 2011) paras 99 and 107. For commentary, see J Pejic 'The European Court of Human Rights' *Al–Jedda* judgment: The oversight of international humanitarian law' (2011) 93 *International Review of the Red Cross* 837, who notes that the *lex specialis* argument was not raised by the UK in this case (at 850).

18 Pejic (n 16 above) 92.

19 See I Scobbie 'Principle or pragmatics? The relationship between human rights law and the law of armed conflict' (2010) 14 *Journal of Conflict and Security Law* 449.

20 Pejic (n 16 above) 110.

to the initial debate on the inter-relationship of the law of armed conflict and international human rights law during hostilities, with much relying on the textual exegesis of the Court's repeated rulings. But these rulings dealt with the position in an international armed conflict. The discussion must take into account that the operative rules of the law of armed conflict differ depending on whether the situation is classified as an international or non-international armed conflict. Further, within the latter category, it might be relevant to determine whether a given conflict should be classified as one which attracts the application of common article 3[21] of the 1949 Geneva Conventions alone, or whether it is of greater intensity and fulfils the requirements of article 1(1)[22] concerning the application of 1977 Additional Protocol II to the Geneva Conventions.[23]

It must be acknowledged that there is evidence of a degree of assimilation of the customary rules governing international and non-international armed conflicts, to the extent that the ICRC customary international humanitarian law study felt able to proclaim:

> This study provides evidence that many rules of customary international law apply in both international and non–international armed conflicts and shows the extent to which State practice has gone beyond existing treaty law and expanded the rules applicable to non–international armed conflicts. In particular, the gaps in the regulation of the conduct of hostilities in Additional Protocol II have largely been filled through State practice, which has led to the creation of rules parallel to those in Additional Protocol I, but applicable as customary law to non–international conflicts.[24]

It has been claimed that some of the rules, originating in the law governing international armed conflict, which the study alleges now also regulate non-international armed conflict, lack evidentiary support.[25] Further, this assimilation, like the ICRC study itself, is not comprehensive. In

---

21   Common article 3 simply provides that it applies '[i]n the case of armed conflict not of an international character occurring in the territory of one of the High Contracting Parties'.

22   Art 1(1) provides that the provisions of Additional Protocol II supplement and develop common art 3 and applies during armed conflicts 'which take place in the territory of a High Contracting Party between its armed forces and dissident armed forces or other organized armed groups which, under responsible command, exercise such control over a part of its territory as to enable them to carry out sustained and concerted military operations and to implement this Protocol'.

23   See D Akande 'Classification of armed conflicts: Relevant legal concepts' in Wilmshurst (n 16 above) 32 50-56; and S Sivakumaran *The law of non–international armed conflict* (2012) Chapter 5, but compare J Pelic 'Status of armed conflicts' in E Wilmshurst E & S Breau (eds) *Perspectives on the ICRC study on customary international humanitarian law* (2007) 77 85-89.

24   J-M Henckaerts & L Doswald-Beck *Customary international humanitarian law: Volume 1: Rules* (2005) xxix: see also Akande (n 23 above) 34-37.

25   See, eg, E Wilmshurst 'Conclusions' in Wilmshurst and Breau (n 23 above) 401 406-407. For assessments of the methodology employed in the study, see G Aldrich 'Customary international humanitarian law – An interpretation on behalf of the International Committee of the Red Cross' (2005) 76 *British Yearbook of International Law 503*; JB Bellinger III& WJ Haynes II 'A US government response to the International Committee of the Red Cross study *Customary International Humanitarian*

particular, rules regarding belligerent occupation, combatant status and entitlement to prisoner of war status on capture, simply do not exist in non-international armed conflict. Despite proposals to the contrary,[26] the distinction between the two types of conflict and the legal consequences of this distinction remain relevant.

The substantive interplay between the law of armed conflict and international human rights law depends, to some extent, on the classification of the conflict, and thus the identification of the armed conflict rules applicable. For example, in an international armed conflict, the treatment of captured combatants entitled to prisoner of war status would, obviously, principally be regulated by the provisions of the Third Geneva Convention. In contrast, in a non-international conflict, the treatment by the belligerent state of captured fighters belonging to a non-state armed group would be regulated by domestic law which, one hopes, would be compliant with that state's obligations arising principally under international human rights law and, where relevant, articles 5 and 6 of Additional Protocol II.

This substantive interplay also depends on the specific situation in which the actors find themselves. For example, in the *Legal Consequences of the Construction of a Wall* Advisory Opinion, the International Court ruled that a range of human rights treaties – the International Covenants on Civil and Political Rights, and on Economic, Social and Cultural Rights, and the Convention on the Rights of the Child – supplements the occupier's application of the Fourth Geneva Convention during a belligerent occupation.[27] In the *Armed Activities on the Territory of the Congo* case, the Court found that Uganda was the belligerent occupant of the bordering

---

Law' (2007) 89 *International Review of the Red Cross* 443; Y Dinstein 'The ICRC customary international humanitarian law study' in AM Helm (ed) *The law of war in the 21st century: Weaponry and the use of force* (2006) 99; TLH MacCormack 'An Australian perspective on the ICRC customary international humanitarian law study' in Helm, *op cit* 81; M MacLaren & F Schwendimann 'An exercise in the development of international law: The new ICRC study on customary international humanitarian law' (2005) 6 *German Law Journal* 1217; WH Parks 'The ICRC customary law study: A preliminary assessment' (2005) 99 *Proceedings of the American Society of International Law* 208; and I Scobbie 'The approach to customary international law in the Study' in Wilmshurst & Breau (n 23 above) 15. For the ICRC response to assessments of the study, see J-M Henckaerts 'Customary international humanitarian law – A rejoinder to Judge Aldrich' (2005) 76 *British Yearbook of International Law* 525; 'Study on customary international humanitarian law: A contribution to the understanding and respect for the rule of law in armed conflict' in Helm, *op cit* 37; 'Customary international humanitarian law: A response to US comments' (2007) 866 *International Review of the Red Cross* 474; and his 'Customary international humanitarian law: Taking stock of the ICRC study' (2010) 78 *Nordic Journal of International Law* 435v.

26   See, eg, E Crawford 'Unequal before the law: The case for the elimination of the distinction between international and non–international armed conflicts' (2007) 20 *Leiden Journal of International Law* 441; and her *The treatment of combatants and insurgents under the law of armed conflict* (2010) Chapter 5.

27   *Legal Consequences of the Construction of a Wall* Advisory Opinion, ICJ Rep, 1984, 177-181, paras 102-113.

Ituri region of Congo during the time relevant to the proceedings.[28] Accordingly, it ruled that in addition to the 1907 Hague Regulations, the Fourth Geneva Convention and its Additional Protocol I, Uganda as occupant was duty-bound to apply the International Covenant on Civil and Political Rights, the African Charter on Human and Peoples' Rights, the Convention on the Rights of the Child and its Optional Protocol on the Involvement of Children in Armed Conflict in Ituri.[29] It is doubtful, to say the least, that human rights treaties such as these should be seen to apply to the extra-territorial armed activities of a belligerent state during the invasion of its opponent's territory.

The identification of the substantive law of armed conflict norms which are applicable in a given situation presupposes that it may be clearly classified. This is generally not difficult in an international armed conflict which, in principle, is a conflict between states.[30] The problem of classification can, however, be acute when one is faced with a situation of conflict within a state. When is the threshold reached, that turns the violence into a non-international armed conflict? Common article 3 of the Geneva Conventions is silent on the matter, simply stating that '[i]n the case of armed conflict not of an international character occurring in the territory of one of the High Contracting Parties', the parties to the conflict must respect specified minimum humanitarian standards. Article 1(2) of Additional Protocol II is slightly more forthcoming and states that the Protocol:

> [S]hall not apply to situations of internal disturbances and tensions, such as riots, isolated and sporadic acts of violence and other acts of a similar nature, as not being armed conflicts.

This notion is reflected in the test set out by the International Criminal Tribunal for the former Yugoslavia in its jurisdiction decision in the *Tadić* case (1995) that 'an armed conflict exists whenever there is a resort to

28   *Armed Activities on the Territory of the Congo (Democratic Republic of the Congo v Uganda)*, ICJ Rep 2005, 231, para 178.
29   *Armed Activities on the Territory of the Congo* (n 28 above) 243-244, para 217.
30   For parties to Additional Protocol I, by virtue of article 1(4), international armed conflicts include those 'in which peoples are fighting against colonial domination and alien occupation and against racist régimes in the exercise of their right of self–determination'. The 'internationalisation' of a non-international armed conflict may also occur if a state recognises the belligerency of the non-state armed group which is fighting against it: see, eg, the Harvard Draft Convention on the Rights and Duties of Neutral States in Naval and Aerial War (1939) 33 *American Journal of International Law: Supplement* 204 209-211; H Lauterpacht *Recognition in international law* (1947) 193-199; YM Lootsteen 'The concept of belligerency in international law' (2000) 166 *Military Law Review* 109; and I Scobbie 'Gaza' in Wilmshurst (n 16 above) 281 301-305, which is also available at Oxford Public International Law's 'Debate map: Israel-Gaza wars 2008-2014' http://opil.ouplaw.com/page/israel-gaza-debate-map (accessed 13 October 2014). It must be acknowledged that some commentators argue that the doctrine of recognition of belligerency is an obsolete doctrine, see, eg, A Paulus & M Vashakmadze 'Asymmetrical war and the notion of armed conflict – A tentative conceptualization' (2009) 91 *International Review of the Red Cross* 95.

armed force between States or protracted armed violence between governmental authorities and organised armed groups or between such groups within a State'.[31] On the *Tadić* test, Professor Sivakumaran comments:

> [E]ven though the precise *Tadić* formulation was set out in 1995, its component elements are steeped in history. What the ICTY managed to do was to encapsulate in a brief sentence the core elements of a definition that had been recognized decades and centuries earlier.[32]

Any situation which falls beneath this threshold is not an armed conflict, and thus is regulated by domestic law which should conform with the state's obligations under international human rights law. It is, however, evident that there have been numerous situations of protracted internal violence which were not classified as non-international armed conflicts. One need only think of the 'Troubles' in Northern Ireland which lasted from the late 1960s until the 'ceasefire' reached between Republican and Loyalist armed groups in 1994. The United Kingdom never conceded that this amounted to a non-international armed conflict, although it is arguable that this threshold was surpassed for a period in the early 1970s.[33]

The nub of the problem is that the classification of internal violence is principally determined by the state concerned, which is generally loathe to admit that it is harbouring a non-international armed conflict on its territory, often for fear of giving legitimacy and status to an armed opposition group. In this it is aided by the abstract nature of the thresholds for the existence of a non-international armed conflict set out in Additional Protocol II and the *Tadić* ruling which leaves both open to interpretation. This discretionary power, however, cuts both ways. As Professor Kretzmer demonstrates, it might be in a state's interest to classify a situation as a non-international armed conflict in order to dislodge, at least to some extent, its obligations under human rights law in favour of the provisions of the law of armed conflict. The move is effectively one from a law-enforcement paradigm, in which the right to life is enshrined and thus severe restraints are placed upon the state's ability to employ force against criminals, to a conflict paradigm which countenances the use of deadly force by the state against its adversaries.[34] Classifying a situation as a non-international armed conflict quite simply loosens the normative shackles on state behaviour regarding the use of force.

Further, Professor Kretzmer points out that the doctrine of proportionality employed by the law of armed conflict differs from that

---

31　*Prosecutor v Tadić*, IT-94-1-AR72, Decision on the Defence Motion for Interlocutory Appeal on Jurisdiction (Appeals Chamber) 2 October 1995, para 70.
32　Sivakumaran (n 23 above) 166.
33　For a thorough analysis of this situation, see S Haines 'Northern Ireland 1968-1998' in Wilmshurst (n 16 above) 117, specifically 130-136.
34　See Kretzmer (n 5 above) 15-19.

employed by human rights law. Proportionality in the law of armed conflict concerns collateral damage, and thus permits civilian death and injury, an advance calculation which is an anathema to human rights law. He observes that Additional Protocol II makes no reference to proportionality, but that the International Committee of the Red Cross' customary international law study claims it is a principle which applies in non-international, as well as in international, conflicts.[35] Professor Kretzmer comments that this appears to assume that in an internal armed conflict proportionality protects potential victims, but its introduction could instead weaken the protection they might otherwise enjoy under a human rights regime because the armed conflict test of proportionality entrenches as a legitimate expectation that civilians, individuals taking no part in the hostilities, may be killed and injured. To put it bluntly, on this issue the law of armed conflict and human rights law have antithetical aims. Once an armed conflict exists, the use of lethal force by a state against members of the adversary's armed forces is legitimate and any incidental civilian death and injury which is not excessive in relation to the military advantage anticipated is justified, but where there is no armed conflict, any lethal use of force by the state must be justified and investigated.[36]

The principal practical problem raised by the classification of conflicts in delineating the relationship between the law of armed conflict and international human rights law is the malleability of standards involved in determining if a given situation reaches the threshold to qualify as a non-international armed conflict, and the discretion of the decision-maker in making that determination. The conceptual problem, the antithetical approaches of these branches of law to the use of deadly force, is, as Dr Pejic argues, an issue which they both regulate but where their rules differ. On other issues, there can be a degree of overlap or complementarity, but the problem of classification may impinge to make the substantive parameters of their relationship unstable or shifting, and dependent on the attitude adopted by the state concerned.

3   Whose human rights?

International human rights law offers protection to individuals who are under the jurisdiction or effective control of a state. In *Smith v The Ministry of Defence*[37] the United Kingdom Supreme Court unanimously held that members of the United Kingdom's armed forces serving outside its territory were within its jurisdiction for the purposes of article 1[38] of the

---

35   See Henckaerts & Doswald-Beck (n 24 above) 46-50. This is also available at www.icrc.org/customary-ihl/eng/docs/v1_rul_rule14 (accessed 13 October 2014).
36   See Kretzmer (n 5 above) 17-22.
37   [2013] UKSC 41, delivered 19 June 2013.
38   Art 1 provides: 'The High Contracting Parties shall secure to everyone within their jurisdiction the rights and freedoms defined in Section 1 of this Convention'.

European Convention on Human Rights.[39] In part this case concerned claims brought by the representatives of two soldiers killed in Iraq by improvised explosive devices when they were on patrol. They claimed that the United Kingdom was in breach of its obligation under article 2 of the European Convention (the right to life) as the Ministry of Defence had failed to take reasonable measures to safeguard soldiers on patrol given the real and immediate risks this entailed. The claim revolved around the adequacy of the equipment provided to the soldiers concerned.[40]

The Supreme Court's decision in relation to these claims dealt only with the jurisdictional point and did not deal with the merits. It noted that this issue was not directly answered by the Grand Chamber's judgment in *Al–Skeini v United Kingdom*,[41] but latched onto its ruling that where jurisdiction is exercised extra-territorially the package of rights contained in the European Convention can be divided and tailored to the particular circumstances of the act in question. Lord Hope commented that if the rights were indivisible then:

> It was always going to be difficult to see how, if that was to be the guiding principle, it could be possible to accept that a state's armed forces abroad in whatever circumstances were within [its] jurisdiction for the purposes of article 1 as its ability to guarantee the entire range of the Convention rights would in many cases be severely limited.[42]

He also relied on recommendation 1742 (2006) of the Council of Europe's Parliamentary Assembly, *Human rights of members of the armed forces*, which stated in paragraph 2 that:

> [M]embers of the armed forces are citizens in uniform who must enjoy the same fundamental freedoms ... and the same protection of their rights and dignity as any other citizen, within the limits imposed by the specific exigencies of military duties.

This recommendation was endorsed by the Committee of Ministers in February 2010 which stated that these principles should be applied in all circumstances, including in time of armed conflict.[43]

---

39   The leading judgment of the Court was delivered by Lord Hope: For his exposition of this point, in which the other Justices concurred, see paras 17-55 of his opinion.
40   See the opinion of Lord Hope, paras 10-13 for a succinct statement of the relevant claims. For a brief indication of the operational dilemma this set of claims could raise, see C Garraway 'Direct participation and the principle of distinction: squaring the circle' in C Harvey et al (eds) *Contemporary challenges to the laws of war: Essays in honour of Professor Peter Rowe* (2014) 169 185-186.
41   (2011) 53 EHRR 18 (App No 55721/07, delivered 7 July 2011).
42   Opinion of Lord Hope, para 48.
43   Opinion of Lord Hope, para 54. The text of recommendation 1742 is available at: http://assembly.coe.int/Main.asp?link=/Documents/AdoptedText/ta06/EREC17 42.htm (accessed 13 October 2014).

Consequently, there exists some authority to hold that states should actively protect the human rights of members of their armed forces during an armed conflict, even if this does not extend to the entirety of rights enjoyed by civilians during peace time. All depends on 'the specific exigencies of military duties'. But the question is, how far should this protection extend?

Consider the Kasher-Yadlin doctrine, which was 'developed by a team we have headed at the Israel Defense Force (IDF) College of National Defense'.[44] This doctrine starts from the eminently contestable proposition that fighting terror is a relatively new phenomenon:

> [T]he fight against terror has to be new because it cannot be carried out in a pure, proper and effective way, within any of the traditional paradigms of a state fighting familiar sources of public danger, first and foremost the paradigms of warfare and of law–enforcement.[45]

Relying essentially on social contract theory, Kasher and Yadlin argue that a democratic state ought to respect and protect human rights in a two-tier system. In the first place, it should respect and protect its citizens in their capacity as both citizens and human beings. In the second it should respect non-citizens in their capacity as human beings.[46] In fighting terror using military force, Kasher and Yadlin claim that the state's priorities should be that minimum injury should be caused to non-combatant individuals who are its citizens, and then to individuals who are outside its territory but under its effective control who are not involved in terrorism. Essentially, this latter category contemplates individuals in territory occupied by the state. The state's third priority should be to cause minimum injury to members of its armed forces involved in combat operations, and only after this category should attention be paid to the lives of those, outside its territory, who are not involved in terrorism, but who are not under the effective control of the state. They claim:

---

44   A Kasher A & A Yadlin 'Military ethics of fighting terror: An Israeli perspective' (2005) 4 *Journal of Military Ethics* 3; see also their 'Israel & the rules of war: An exchange' *The New York Review of Books* 11 June 2009, http://www.nybooks.com/articles/archives/2009/jun/11/israel-the-rules-of-war-an-exchange/ (accessed 13 October 2014), to which is appended a reply by Avishai Margalit and Michael Walzer. Most of the commentary on the Kasher–Yadlin doctrine has been from the perspective of just war theory: see, eg, N Fotion 'Transforming and expanding the Kasher/Yadlin theory on the ethics of fighting wars against terrorism' (2005) 4 *Journal of Military Ethics* 33; B Haydar 'The ethics of fighting terror and the priority of civilians' *ibid* 52; DL Perry 'Ambiguities in the "war on terror"' *ibid* 44; and A Kasher & A Yadlin, 'Military ethics of fighting terror: Response' *ibid* 60. See also Z Bohrer & M Osiel 'Proportionality in military force at war's multiple levels: Averting civilian casualties vs. safeguarding soldiers' (2013) 46 *Vanderbilt Journal of International Law* 747; and MA Khalidi '"The most moral army in the world": The new "ethical code" of the Israeli military and the war on Gaza' (2010) 39 *Journal of Palestine Studies* 6.

45   Kasher & Yadlin 'Military ethics' (n 44 above) 6-7.

46   Kasher & Yadlin 'Military ethics' (n 44 above) 9.

A state is responsible for the protection of human life and well-being of its citizens and of any other person who resides under its effective control. A state does not shoulder responsibility for regular effective protection of persons who are neither its citizens nor under its effective control.[47]

They simply reject 'the common conception of noncombatants having a preference over combatants' because a 'combatant is a citizen in uniform'.[48] They continue by noting that there are:

situations in which persons directly involved in terror are pursued or targeted by combatants in the vicinity of persons not involved in terror. Where the state does not have effective control over the vicinity, it does not have to shoulder responsibility for the fact that persons who are involved in terror operate in the vicinity of persons who are not. Injury to bystanders is not intended. On the contrary, jeopardizing combatants rather than bystanders during a military act against a terrorist would mean shouldering responsibility for the mixed nature of the vicinity for no reason at all.[49]

Note that according to Kasher and Yadlin, the state should privilege the human rights and lives of its citizen-soldiers over those of foreign non-combatants in a conflict zone over which, by definition, it does not exercise effective control because it does not bear the moral responsibility for distinguishing between terrorists and non-combatants, between dangerous individuals and harmless ones.

Margalit and Walzer reject this position, arguing that soldiers:

must reflect respect for innocent lives, whatever the political identity of those lives, and even when they are not under 'our' control. What risks we impose, and what risks we decide to accept, are always under our control ... [S]tates, democratic states most obviously, have special obligations to defend the lives of their citizens. Therefore they can decide to put soldiers at risk for that purpose, as Israel did in its Entebbe raid, without committing themselves to do the same for citizens of other states. But when soldiers are on the attack, when they are imposing risks on civilians, the citizenship of those civilians is morally irrelevant. Soldiers must do their best not to kill them, and their 'best' will sometimes involve some 'cost' to themselves.[50]

They continue that the risks imposed on combatants should be reflected in the strategy and tactics employed in the battle. Further, as Khalidi argues, at the operational level combatants intentionally undertake acts of violence and seek to endanger others and thus forfeit their right to security.

---

47 Kasher & Yadlin, 'Military ethics' (n 44 above) 16.
48 Kasher & Yadlin 'Military ethics' (n 44 above) 17; compare Garraway (n 40 above) 183-186.
49 Kasher & Yadlin 'Military ethics' (n 44 above) 18; see also A Kasher 'Operation Cast Lead and the ethics of just war' (2009) 37 *Azure* 43 65-67.
50 Margalit & Walzer (n 44 above); for commentary on Margalit & Walzer's views, see Bohrer & Osiel (n 44 above) 756-761. See also M Walzer 'Two kinds of military responsibility' in M Walzer *Arguing about war* (2004) 23.

Moreover, they are armed and capable of defending themselves which is 'why combatants are in a different moral category than noncombatants according to prevailing conceptions of just war theory and international law'.[51] Under the law of armed conflict, unlike civilians, combatants and those taking a direct part in hostilities are legitimate targets who have forfeited their immunity from attack, and if the question resolves to one of moral agency, even in a conscript army there is ultimately a choice not to serve.

It has been claimed that Israel implemented the Kasher-Yadlin doctrine during Operation Cast Lead, the war in Gaza in December 2008-January 2009.[52] It is difficult to conceive how this could be classified as anything other than an armed conflict.[53] Indeed, during Operation Cast Lead, a majority of states in debates before both the Security Council and General Assembly called upon Israel to apply the Fourth Geneva Convention in its dealings with Gaza.[54] This indicates that they did not see the situation as a novel one involving the use of armed force to suppress terror rather than the established category of armed conflict. Indeed, this view was shared by Israel itself which stated:

> At the end of the day, classification of the armed conflict between Hamas and Israel as international or non-international in the current context is largely of theoretical concern, as many similar norms and principles govern both types of conflict.[55]

This is not the place to debate the merits or demerits of the Kasher-Yadlin doctrine exhaustively, but to what extent is its emphasis on the moral responsibility of the state towards its combatants germane to the debate regarding the relationship between the law of armed conflict and human rights law? The Kasher-Yadlin doctrine is based on a social contract theory, but is this relevant when one is dealing with an external projection of armed force by a state? The law of international armed conflict, in broad terms, sets out what non-nationals may demand from a belligerent, not the treatment to be meted out to its own nationals. By denying any responsibility for foreign civilians in a combat area, the doctrine enunciated by Kasher and Yadlin arguably effaces a fundamental tenet of the law of armed conflict, namely the principle of distinction between those who take part in hostilities and those who do not. If so, it runs

---

51 Khalidi (n 44 above) 11.
52 See, eg, Khalidi (n 44 above) specifically 14-18; Public Committee against Torture in Israel *No second thoughts: The changes in the Israel Defense Forces' combat doctrine in the light of "Operation Cast Lead"* (2009) Chapter III, available on PCATI's website www.stoptorture.org.il/en (accessed 13 October 2014); and also A Kasher 'A moral evaluation of the Gaza war – Operation Cast Lead' 9/18 *Jerusalem Issue Briefs* (4 February 2010), available on www.jcpa.org (accessed 13 October 2014).
53 See Scobbie (n 30 above) 280.
54 See Scobbie (n 30 above) 293-294.
55 Government of Israel *The operation in Gaza: Factual and legal aspects* (July 2009) 11 para 30, available at: mfa.gov.il/MFA/ForeignPolicy/Terrorism/Pages/Operation_in_Gaza-Factual_and_Legal_Aspects.aspx (accessed 13 October 2014).

counter to the broad requirement that 'The civilian population and individual civilians shall enjoy general protection against dangers arising from military operations'.[56] Should a precept rooted in a doctrine of political philosophy which concerns the relationship between the citizen and the state over-ride an established norm which is at the core of the law of armed conflict? Quite simply, is it legitimate to argue that force protection, minimising injuries to one's own combatants, should take priority over the protection of foreign civilians in a combat area? Could it be argued that to do so is to prejudice civilians because of the actions of their government – or in the precise terms of Kasher and Yadlin's doctrine, for the actions of terrorists embedded within a civilian population? If so, does this mean that the situation should be seen as one where moral blame somehow attaches to a whole population? The notion of punishing whole populations dates back to classic publicists of international law such as Vitoria:

> *[T]he whole commonwealth may lawfully be punished for the sin of its monarch.* If a sovereign wages an unjust war against another prince, the injured party may plunder and pursue all the other rights of war against the sovereign's subjects, even if they are innocent of offence. The reason is that once the sovereign has been duly constituted by the commonwealth, if he permits any injustice in the exercise of his office the blame lies with the commonwealth, since the commonwealth is held responsible for entrusting its power only to a man who will justly exercise any authority or executive power he may be given; in other words, it delegates power at its own risk. In the same way, anyone may lawfully be condemned for the wrongdoings of his appointed agent.[57]

Although hardly a democrat – 'the best form of government is monarchy, just as the universe is controlled by a single Lord and Ruler'[58] – Vitoria is clear that moral blame should only devolve upon a population that has chosen, or allows itself to be led, by a prince who acts wrongfully. Ascribing moral blame surely postulates a failure to live up to defined standards of behaviour. Consequently, attributing moral blame to a population entails the judgement that a causal connection exists between that failure and the population's actions in terms of its abilities and opportunities to prevent that failure.[59] What would constitute this causal connection – would it be enough that the population acquiesced in the delicts of the government, whether or not that government was unrepresentative and perhaps repressive, or need there be evidence of the population validating or participating in the government's policies? Or when one is dealing not with the actions of government but those of a

---

56   1977 Additional Protocol I, art 51(1).
57   Vitoria *On civil power (De potestate ciuilli)* (1528), *Question 1, Article 9* in A Pagden & J Lawrance (eds) *Francisco de Vitoria: Political writings* (1991) 1 21: editorial footnote omitted.
58   *Question 1, Article 8* (n 57 above) 18-21: quotation at 20.
59   See, for instance, PA French 'Morally blaming whole populations' in V Held et al (eds) *Philosophy, morality, and international affairs* (1974) 266.

terrorist group, can civilians be blamed and consequently put at risk for the actions of others whom they might not support and cannot control?

The function of this discussion of the Kasher-Yadlin doctrine is simply to throw into relief the question of whose rights should take priority in an armed conflict. Combatants, apart from when they fall into protected categories such as prisoners of war, or the wounded, sick or shipwrecked – namely, soldiers who are *hors de combat* – do not feature much in the debate about the inter-relationship between the law of armed conflict and international human rights law. If it is now accepted that states owe human rights obligations to members of their armed forces even during an armed conflict, then can they legitimately privilege their soldiers' rights over those of non-combatants who find themselves mixed in or somehow associated with the opposing party? In particular, concerning combatants' right to life, does the state exhaust its duties by ensuring that they are properly equipped or by issuing rules of engagement which prejudices the interests of non-combatants? If the former, does this make a soldier's putative right to life dependent on economic considerations, namely, the extent to which the state can afford to equip its forces, which in turn would seem to make that right incapable of consistent application. At root here is an apparent clash not simply between rights but between disciplines. Apart from the protections afforded to soldiers who are *hors de combat*, if combatants have rights under human rights law in a conflict zone, where the attacking state does not exercise effective control, and the protection afforded to the non-combatant population arises under the law of armed conflict, then can these be reconciled or must we inevitably favour one over the other?

2

Human Rights Law and International Humanitarian Law: From the View of Gender

Bonita Meyersfeld

1 Introduction

There are few areas of law that are as compelling as the Law of Armed Conflict (LOAC). This area of law seeks to do that which is intuitively impossible: regulate chaos. It is the ultimate contradiction, where we import law and order into a context of deliberate violence.

The complexity of this area of law mirrors the complexity of humanity: we engage in violent chaos while we remain, simultaneously, committed to regulated order. In some senses, this contradiction is something of which we should be proud. Notwithstanding our species' propensity for conflict, we cling, perhaps naively, to the notion that rules and order will protect us at our most vulnerable – and control us at our most cruel.

One of the oldest manifestations of violence is gender-based violence. Gender-based violence is a form of violence that affects, either directly or indirectly, a person because of their gendered identity. General Recommendation 19 of the UN Committee for the Elimination of All Forms of Discrimination against Women defines gender-based violence as 'violence that is directed against a woman because she is a woman or that affects women disproportionately'.[1] Gender-based violence occurs in both conflict and non-conflict societies. It is therefore an important portal through which to analyse the similarities, intersection and differences between the LOAC and international human rights law.

The need for regulation during violence underscores both the LOAC and international human rights law (IHRL). The LOAC (or international humanitarian law or IHL) sanctions the use of deadly weapons but they must kill or injure *in a specific way*. Similarly, international human rights

---

1   UN Committee for the Elimination of All Forms of Discrimination against Women, 'General Recommendation 19: Violence against Women' UN Doc A/47/38 (1992) art 6.

law, for example, allows for the imprisonment of a person in a cell but regulates the specific way in which that person must be deprived of her freedom.

Both humanitarian and human rights law respond to the imperatives of dignity, accountability and the constraint of power.[2] Both areas of law demand some kind of common denominator of behaviour in circumstances where the violation of a person's autonomy is legitimised. And both areas of law regularly fail us. Neither area of law is the force we hope it will be. On their own, these legal systems do not change human behaviour; they do not stay the thrust of a violent fist or prevent the extra-judicial killing of civilians.[3] They do, however, change the way we *respond* to that violence; the way the state, authorities and the so-called international community regulate harm.

These two areas of international law reveal three converging characteristics: protecting and promoting human dignity in the context of the lawful violation of a person's physical and psychological autonomy; ensuring accountability; and, imposing constraints and restraints on people who are in a position to cause harm. These converging characteristics, namely, dignity, accountability and constraint of power, come clearly into focus through the lens of gender-based violence.

Both humanitarian and human rights law have seen a surge in gender-responsive jurisprudence. This upsurge in international women's rights law reveals a useful pattern of cross-fertilisation of specific norms from international human rights law to humanitarian law, and the reverse.[4] Gender-based violence has influenced the transfer of norms across humanitarian and human rights law and as such provides an important portal to analyse the points of convergence – and the conflicts – between these two areas of international law.[5]

The first part of the article traces the trajectory of IHL and IHRL's responses to gender-based violence. This analysis lays the foundation for a consideration of how the two areas of law have converged, either explicitly or implicitly.

2	T Meron 'The humanization of humanitarian law' (2000) 94 *American Journal of International Law* 239 241, noting that '[h]umanizing the law can and should temper the treatment of civilians and POWs'.
3	Meron (n 2 above) 241, noting that the humanisation of international humanitarian law does little to discourage the resort to war.
4	Meron (n 2 above) 244, refers to the 'process of osmosis or application by analogy', which causes international human rights law instruments to affect the interpretation and the status of 'parallel norms in instruments of international humanitarian law'.
5	For a discussion of the convergence of international human rights law and international humanitarian law in UN instruments, see I Siatitsa & M Titberidze 'Human rights in armed conflict from the perspective of the contemporary state practice in the United Nations: Factual answers to certain hypothetical challenges' (2011), available at: http://www.geneva-academy.ch/RULAC/pdf/HRL-in-AC.pdf (accessed 11 December 2014).

The second part identifies the many areas of convergence that I argue *ought* to occur. In other words, there are several human rights violations that ought to constitute a violation of international humanitarian law. The designation of sexual violence as a violation of the LOAC reflects only one narrow manifestation of gender-based harm in conflict. There is a myriad of ways in which women *qua* women endure harm in war.[6] This part of the article identifies the areas of harm endured by women during a conflict that ought to constitute violations of the LOAC but do not. These forms of harm are targeted and deliberate and their exclusion from the rubric of the LOAC is neither principled nor logical. Rather, it is a function of assumptions around women's roles in war and peace – the same assumptions, in my view, that precluded the prosecution of rape in post-conflict tribunals until the 1990s.

The final part of this chapter argues that a seismic change is necessary for a proper response to the changing nature of conflict and its impact on women. Similarly, it probes whether the principles of international humanitarian law could be used to better understand and address gender-based violence outside of conflict situations. This is appropriate not only because of a need for better responses to the practicalities of war; it is also theoretically consistent with the fact that the LOAC and IHRL share, at least, three clear common characteristics, namely, the need to protect dignity, enforce accountability and impose constraints in times of violence. These three characteristics are inherent in common article 3 of the 1949 Geneva Conventions and reflect, as the International Court of Justice articulated, 'elementary considerations of humanity'.[7]

2   Part one: The trajectory of gender-based violence through international human rights law and international humanitarian law: From peace to war and back

The focus on the well-being and rights of women in armed conflict is probably one of the best examples of the manner in which international human rights law has permeated and helped to shape principles of the LOAC.

---

6   RM Schott 'War rape, natality and genocide' (2011) 13 *Journal of Genocide Research* 5 5, noting that many of the harms committed in war and genocide are 'gender-skewed', for example, forced displacement and removals.

7   *Military and paramilitary activities in and against Nicaragua (Nicar v US)* Merits ICJ Rep (1986) 14 114.

Targeting women during a conflict is not new. The jurisprudential response, however, is, relatively speaking, new.[8] While the principle of non-discrimination is embodied in the LOAC, and the Geneva Conventions make specific reference to women, the elaboration of these principles was wanting.[9] Historically, principles of international humanitarian law have failed to fully address the specific ways in which women endure conflict.[10] Perhaps this is unsurprising given that the LOAC only recently (relatively speaking) developed principles relating to the rights and wellbeing of civilians in general.

Rather, the comprehensive development of women's rights in international law has been the preserve of international human rights law. The principle of equality between women and men was crystallised in 1948, in the UN's Universal Declaration of Human Rights (UDHR).[11] The UDHR, a declaration and not a treaty, became a reflection of customary international law, encompassing a list of mandatory norms that apply to all nations. The UDHR was followed by the two rights covenants, namely the International Covenant on Civil and Political Rights (ICCPR) and the International Covenant on Economic, Social and Cultural Rights (ICESCR), dealing with civil and political rights, and socio-economic and cultural rights respectively.[12] Based largely on the events of World War Two and the Holocaust, the rights articulated in these instruments reflect 'the inherent dignity and the equal and inalienable rights' of all people.[13]

This so-called International Bill of Rights contains several provisions relating to the rights of women. In the course of the last fifty years, however, individuals and women's groups have identified the ways in

---

8   For a discussion of the development of mass rape as a crime in international criminal law see: B Meyersfeld *Domestic violence and international law* (2010) 269-274; K Askin 'Prosecuting wartime rape and other gender-related crimes under international law: Extraordinary advances, enduring obstacles' (2003) 21 *Berkley Journal of International Law* 288 347; T Meron 'Rape as a crime under international law' (1993) 87 *American Journal of International Law* 424 425-427; JR Mchenry III 'The prosecution of rape under international law: Justice that is long overdue' (2002) 35 *Vanderbilt Journal of Transnational Law* 1269; and Schott (n 6 above) 6.

9   Common article 3, arts 12 of the first two Geneva Conventions of 1949.

10 This is not to say there was silence in respect of violence against women. There was an imperative that chivalry precluded violence against women, not for the sake of respecting the rights of individuals, but rather because of the violence done to the honour of the man to whom the victim 'belonged'. Schott (n 6 above) 6.

11 Universal Declaration of Human Rights, adopted 10 December 1948, UNGA Res 217 A(III) (UDHR).

12 International Covenant on Civil and Political Rights (adopted 16 December 1966, entered into force 23 March 1976) 999 UNTS 171 (ICCPR); International Covenant on Economic, Social and Cultural Rights (adopted 16 December 1966, entered into force 3 January 1976) 993 UNTS 3 (ICESCR).

13 UDHR (n 11 above) Preamble. For a brief discussion of the development of human rights in international law see MS McDougal et al *Human rights and the world public order: The basic policies of an international law of human dignity* (1980) 4-5 ('From demands for physical security and inviolability of the person, with freedom from cruel and inhuman treatment and freedom from arbitrary arrest and confinement, a progression may be noted to demands for freedom of conscience and religion, of opinion and expression, and of association and assembly.').

which the needs and rights of women have not been addressed by these instruments.[14] Theorists have argued that women are abused as a group, and endure a particular version of harm relating to their gender, which intersects with their ethnicity, race or religion. While the provisions of the UDHR arguably could be extrapolated to apply to gender-based violence and discrimination, many maintained that this was insufficient and did not provide the nuanced protection to meet the many realities in which women are hurt, both because of bodily and social imperatives.[15]

The call for precise and express rights for women[16] resulted in the development of international instruments, bodies and organisations, which address specifically the rights of women in international law.[17]

The development of gender-specific principles in international humanitarian law, however, fell sluggishly behind. The criminal accountability mechanisms of the International Military Tribunal in Nuremberg and its equivalent in Tokyo could have drawn far more on the LOAC imperatives around women's rights in their assessment of the conflict. This could have established a much more robust precedent for the application of the LOAC requirements vis-à-vis women in future conflict.[18] The London Charter did not mention rape although it was included in Local Council Law No 10.[19] While the Tokyo Tribunal included rape as a war crime in its mandate, acts of rape were not prosecuted. This is so notwithstanding the Rape of Nanking, during which Japanese forces raped over 20 000 women and Emperor Hirohito was well

14   RJ Cook 'Women's international human rights law: The way forward' (1993) 15
       Human Rights Quarterly 230 231 (stating that until 1993 international law did not
       effectively address the rights of women); H Charlesworth et al *Feminist approaches to
       international law*, (1991) 85 *American Journal of International Law* 613; EM Schneider
       'The violence of privacy' in MA Fineman & R Mykitiuk (eds) *The public nature of
       private violence: The Discovery of domestic abuse* (1994) 36; C Romany 'Women as aliens:
       A feminist critique of the public/private distinction in international human rights law'
       (1993) 6 *Harvard Human Rights Journal* 87 (confirming the male-centric structure and
       application of international law).
15   See SP Subedi 'Protection of women against domestic violence: The response of
       international law' (1997) 6 *European Human Rights Law Review* 587 592-593 (arguing
       that the accumulation of international human rights law does not 'contain specific
       measures for the protection of women against violence within the house and the
       community and violence during times of peace'). See also DQ Thomas & ME Beasley
       Esq 'Domestic violence as a human rights issue' (1993) 15 *Human Rights Quarterly* 36
       39 (describing the inadequacy of international law to prevent violence against women).
16   For a comprehensive discussion of the history of women's rights in international law,
       see AS Fraser *Becoming human: The origins and development of women's human rights*
       (1999) (originally published in (1999) 21 *Human Rights Quarterly* 853).
17   See McDougal et al (n 13 above) 612-652.
18   Meron (n 8 above) 425-427. See also C Chinkin 'Gender-based crimes' in *Max Planck
       Encyclopedia of Public International Law* (2011) para 5; B Bedont & K Hall Martinez
       'Ending impunity for gender crimes under the International Criminal Court' (1999) 65
       The Brown Journal of World Affairs 1.
19   Control Council Law No 10 'Punishment of persons guilty of war crimes, crimes
       against peace and against humanity' (20 December 1945) 3 Official Gazette Control
       Council for Germany (1946) 50-55. Art II (1)(c) includes rape in the definition of
       crimes against humanity.

aware of the atrocities. The so-called 'comfort women' who were forced into sexual services for the Japanese military during WWII were abandoned in the peace negotiations by all the governments involved, including their own, and, in 1965, with the signing of the Japan-South Korea Basic Treaty, they were legally foreclosed from the possibility of reparations.[20] Traditional views of chastity and morality prevented, and continue to limit, a national dialogue about the sexual exploitation and enslavement of women during WWII by the Japanese military (although non-judicial processes have developed in the form of the Women's International War Crimes Tribunal on Japan's Military Sexual Slavery).[21]

In 1994, the internationalisation of violence against women gained significant momentum with the adoption of the General Assembly's Declaration on the Elimination of Violence against Women.[22] DEVAW defined violence against women as 'any act of gender-based violence that results in, or is likely to result in, physical, sexual or psychological harm or suffering to women, including threats of such acts, coercion or arbitrary deprivation of liberty, whether occurring in public or private life'.[23]

20 The Treaty on Basic Relations between Japan and the Republic of Korea (22 June 1965) provided that South Korea agreed to demand no compensations, either at the government or individual level, after receiving $800 million in grants and soft loans from Japan as compensation for its 1910-1945 colonial rule in the treaty. For a discussion of the plight of the so-called 'Korean comfort women' during and after WWII see BL Yoon 'Imperial Japan's comfort women from Korea: History and politics of silence-breaking' (2010) 7 *The Journal of North-East Asian History* 5.

21 See Women's International War Crimes Tribunal on Japan's Military Sexual Slavery, a tribunal established and organised by non-governmental organisations, was held in Tokyo from 8 to 12 December 2000. Information about the Tribunal, its objectives and decisions, is available at: http://www1.jca.apc.org/vaww-net-japan/english/womenstribunal2000/whatstribunal.html (accessed 11 December 2014). For a discussion of the Tribunal, see R Sakamoto 'The Women's International War Crimes Tribunal on Japan's Military Sexual Slavery: A legal and feminist approach to the "comfort women" Issue' (June 2001) 3 *New Zealand Journal of Asian Studies* 49. The final paragraph of the judgment reads as follows: 'The Crimes committed against these survivors remain one of the greatest unacknowledged and unremedied injustices of the Second World War. There are no museums, no graves for the unknown "comfort woman", no education of future generations, and there have been no judgement days for the victims of Japan's military sexual slavery and the rampant sexual violence and brutality that characterized its aggressive war.' See also, SR Lee 'Comforting the comfort women: Who can make Japan pay?' (2003) 24 *University of Pennsylvania Journal of International Economic Law* 509.

22 Declaration on the Elimination of Violence against Women, UNGA Res 48/104 (20 December 1993) UN Doc A/RES/48/104 (DEVAW), defines violence against women as including public and private violence: 'For the purposes of this Declaration, the term "violence against women" means any act of gender-based violence that results in, or is likely to result in, physical, sexual or psychological harm or suffering to women, including threats of such acts, coercion or arbitrary deprivation of liberty, whether occurring in public or in private life.' Ibid, art 1. Art 4(k) requires states to '[p]romote research, collect data and compile statistics, especially concerning domestic violence, relating to the prevalence of different forms of violence against women and encourage research on the causes, nature, seriousness and consequences of violence against women and on the effectiveness of measures implemented to prevent and redress violence against women; those statistics and findings of the research will be made public'.

23 DEVAW (n 22 above) art 1.

DEVAW adopted the same principles as the CEDAW Committee's General Recommendation 19, identifying the need for 'a clear and comprehensive definition of violence against women, a clear statement of the rights to be applied to ensure the elimination of violence against women in all its forms, a commitment by States in respect of their responsibilities, and a commitment by the international community at large to the elimination of violence against women'.[24]

In the same year, the General Assembly of the Organization of American States (OAS) adopted the Inter-American Convention on the Prevention, Punishment and Eradication of Violence against Women, which became known as the Convention of Belem Do Para.[25]

In 1995 at the IV World Conference of Women in Beijing, violence against women was identified as one of the twelve areas of women's lives requiring urgent action.[26] The consequent Beijing Declaration and Platform for Action adopted the definition of violence against women in DEVAW and expanded it to include violence perpetrated against women in war.[27]

In 1994 the legal response to war-time violence against women began to change. The jurisprudence of women's international rights was augmented by the decisions of the International Criminal Tribunals for the Former Yugoslavia and Rwanda (ICTY and ICTR or collectively the ad hoc tribunals), which established the precedent and legal rationale that led to the criminalisation of mass rape as a weapon of war, a crime against humanity, and an instrument of genocide under the Rome Statute for the International Criminal Court.[28] Although the Additional Protocols to the Geneva Conventions included imperatives regarding the protection of

---

24 DEVAW (n 22 above) Preamble.
25 Inter-American Convention on the Prevention, Punishment and Eradication of Violence against Women (Convention of Belem Do Para) (adopted 9 June 1994, entered into force 5 March 1995) (1994) 33 *International Legal Materials* 1534.
26 'Beijing Declaration and Platform for Action' (15 September 1995) UN Doc A/CONF.177/20/Rev.1 (1995) and A/Conf.177/20/Add.1 (1995) (Beijing Declaration).
27 n 22 above para 101 (identifying domestic violence as one of the causes of ill health of women) and para 110(d) (urging governments to increase financial support to prevent and deal with domestic violence).
28 The International Criminal Tribunal for Rwanda was established by UNSC Res 955 (8 November 1994) UN Doc S/RES/955 (the ICTR). See also Statute of the International Criminal Tribunal for Rwanda, available at: http://www.ictr.org/ENGLISH/basicdocs/statute/2007.pdf (accessed 20 July 2009) (the ICTR Statute). The International Criminal Tribunal for the Former Yugoslavia was established by UNSC Res 808 (22 February 1993) UN Doc S/RES/808 (the ICTY). See also Statute of the International Criminal Tribunal for the Former Yugoslavia, available at: http://www.icty.org/sid/135 (accessed 20 July 2009) (the ICTY Statute). See *Prosecutor v Akayesu* (Judgment) ICTR-96-4-T, T Ch I (2 September 1998) para 597: 'Like torture, rape is used for such purposes as intimidation, degradation, humiliation, discrimination, punishment, control or destruction of a person. Like torture, rape is a violation of personal dignity, and rape in fact constitutes torture when it is inflicted by or at the instigation of or with the consent or acquiescence of a public official or other person acting in an official capacity.' See also *Prosecutor v Furundzija* (Judgment) (1999)

women's physical wellbeing, this prohibition had not made its way into a judicial response to conflict.[29]

The decisions of the ad hoc tribunals clearly superimpose a human rights framework over the armed conflicts falling within their jurisdiction. For example, in *Prosecutor v Akayesu*, the ICTR applied the definition and jurisprudence of torture to mass rape during the Rwandan genocide.[30] The ICTR identified the composite factors of rape that intend to destroy, in whole or in part, a group of people.[31] The ICTY followed suit in *Prosecutor v Kunarac*, cementing the *Akayesu* precedent and confirming that widespread rape constitutes a war crime and crime against humanity.[32] By combining the provisions of common article 3 of the Geneva Conventions and article 3 of the ICTY Statute, the ICTY established the requisite elements for certain conduct to constitute mass rape under international criminal law.[33] In *Prosecutor v Delalić et al* (otherwise known as the infamous *Celebici* case)[34] the ICTY, in keeping with *Akayesu*, employed the

---

ICTY- 95-17/1-T; 38 *International Legal Materials* 317 352-353 (indicating that although '[n]o international human rights instrument specifically prohibits rape ... [i]n certain circumstances ... rape can amount to torture ...'). Ibid, 353. See also *Prosecutor v Rutaganda* (Judgment) ICTR-96-3-T (1999) or 39 *International Legal Materials* 557 570 (ICTR 1999) (identifying, inter alia, rape and torture as crimes against humanity). Art 7 of the UN General Assembly *Rome Statute of the International Criminal Court* (last amended 2010), 17 July 1998, ISBN No 92-9227-227-6, defines crimes against humanity as conduct that is: 'widespread, systematic and focused on a segment of a population, including, rape, sexual slavery, enforced prostitution, forced pregnancy, enforced sterilisation, or any other form of sexual violence of comparable gravity ... [p]ersecution against any identifiable group or collectivity on political, racial, national, ethnic, cultural, religious, gender ... or other grounds that are universally recognized as impermissible under international law ... [o]ther inhumane acts of a similar character intentionally causing great suffering, or serious injury to body or to mental or physical health.' Ibid, art 7 § 1(k).

29   Art 27 of the Fourth Geneva Convention states that: 'Protected persons are entitled, in all circumstances, to respect for their person, their honour, their family rights, their religious conviction and practices, and their manners and customs. They shall at all times be humanely treated, and shall be protected especially against all acts of violence or threats thereof and against insults and public curiosity. Women shall be especially protected against any attack on their honour, in particular against rape, enforced prostitution, or any form of indecent assault.' *Geneva Convention (IV) Relative to the Protection of Civilian Persons in Time of War* 6 UST 3516, 75 UNTS 287. For a criticism of the link between the prohibition against violence and women's honour, see Bedont and Hall Martinez (n 18 above). Art 4(2)(e) of the Protocol Additional to the Geneva Conventions of 12 August 1949, and Relating to the Protection of Victims of Non-International Armed Conflicts (Protocol II), 8 June 1977, S Treaty Doc No 100-2, 1125 UNTS 609, provides that prohibited acts include 'outrages upon personal dignity, in particular humiliating and degrading treatment, rape, enforced prostitution and any form of indecent assault.'. See in general Chinkin (n 18 above).

30   n 28 above.

31   For a compelling philosophical analysis of the judgment, see Schott (n 6 above) 8.

32   *Prosecutor v Kunerac* (Judgment) ICTY-96-23-T (22 February 2001). See also Mchenry (n 8 above) 284.

33   Meyersfeld (n 8 above) 270. For an analysis of this process see Mchenry (n 8 above) 1290-96.

34   The Trial Chamber held that the rape of any person is a despicable act which strikes at the very core of human dignity and physical integrity and that the condemnation and punishment of rape becomes all the more urgent where it is committed by, or at the instigation of, a public official, or with the consent or acquiescence of such an official. *Prosecutor v Delalić* (Judgment) ICTY-96-21-T (16 November 1998).

language of torture in describing the severe pain and suffering, both physical and psychological, caused by rape. It also acknowledged that psychological suffering may be exacerbated by social and cultural conditions and can be particularly acute and long lasting.[35] The Tribunal concluded that it is difficult to envisage circumstances in which rape, by, or at the instigation of a public official, or with the consent or acquiescence of an official, could be considered as occurring for a purpose that does not, in some way, involve punishment, coercion, discrimination or intimidation.[36]

By accepting that mass rape and sexual violence may constitute the *actus reus* of war crimes, the ICTR and ICTY brought gender-specific harm into the jurisprudence of the law of war in the context of international criminal law. Prior to *Akayesu* there was no meaningful jurisprudence on violence committed against women as an unlawful act of war. In fact, *Akayesu* would not have contained a conviction for mass rape but for the fact that Judge Pillay, president of the ICTR at the time, insisted that the indictment include sexual violence.[37] This was contentious, partly because technically it is not the domain of a judge to determine the substance of an indictment and also because prosecutors were reluctant to bring cases for which there was no precedent and for which there were no established legal principles. Without this jurisprudence, however, it is unlikely that the Rome Statute would have included such robust provisions regarding the criminal elements of mass rape and sexual slavery, amongst others. The inclusion of women in the institutions of transitional justice, such as Louise Arbour, Carla del Ponte, Elizabeth Odio Benito, Gabrielle Kirk McDonald, Navanethem 'Navi' Pillay and Dorothee de Sampayo, has resulted in an expansion of the laws of war and international criminal law that will be felt for generations.[38] This jurisprudence culminated in the historic criminalisation of rape and gender-based harm in the Rome Statute of the International Criminal Court.[39]

At this stage, the jurisprudential response to violations against women in war had focused on mass rape. In a seminal expansion of the understanding of gender-based harm, the Special Court for Sierra Leone (SCSL) worked its way to the articulation of forced marriage as a crime against humanity. In 2008, the Appeals Chamber held that forced

---

35   As above.
36   As above.
37   Meyersfeld (n 8 above) 269-70.
38   As above.
39   For example, the crime of genocide includes the imposition of measures intended to prevent births within a group (art 6(d)) (although this was already a part of the definition of Genocide in the Genocide Convention itself); crimes against humanity include rape, sexual slavery, enforced prostitution, forced pregnancy, enforced sterilization, or any other forms of sexual violence of comparable gravity (art 7(1)(g)); war crimes include rape, sexual slavery, enforced prostitution, forced pregnancy, enforced sterilization or any other form of sexual violence constituting a grave breach of the Geneva Conventions (art 8(2)(b)).

marriage is a distinct, inhumane act of sufficient gravity to be considered a crime against humanity.[40] The SCSL defined the crime of forced marriage as

> a situation in which the perpetrator through his words or conduct, or those of someone for whose actions he is responsible, compels a person by force, threat of force, or coercion to serve as a conjugal partner resulting in severe suffering, or physical, mental or psychological injury to the victim.[41]

The Prosecutor of the SCSL had prioritised gender, with the result that ten of the thirteen accused from Sierra Leone were charged with crimes relating to gender-based violence.[42]

This development was particularly important as the crime encompasses an array of harm in addition to sexual violence, including a broad range of conjugal duties, abduction, unwanted pregnancies, enforced pregnancies, physical abuse, miscarriages, death threats, being forced to live with and be loyal to an individual whom one fears and despises, forced relocation, mental trauma and lasting stigma.[43] The Appeals Chamber identified that 'unlike sexual slavery, forced marriage implies a relationship of exclusivity between "husband" and "wife", which could lead to disciplinary consequences for breach of this exclusive arrangement'.[44]

The Security Council too has played an important role in the specification of international prohibitions against violence against women in conflict. Security Council Resolutions 1325 (2000), 1674 (2006), 1820 (2008), 1888 (September 2009), 1889 (2009) and 1894 (2009) have added both content and gravitas to the international prohibition on sexual and gendered violence.

UNSC Resolution 1325 calls 'all parties to armed conflict to take special measures to protect women and girls from gender-based violence,

---

40   *Prosecutor v Brima, Kamara & Kanu* Case No SCSL-04-16A, Appeals Chamber Judgment (22 February 2008) paras 181-185. For a discussion of the SCSL's approach to forced marriage see V Oosterveld 'Lessons from the Special Court for Sierra Leone on the prosecution of gender-based crimes' (2009) 17 *American University Journal of Gender, Social Policy & the Law* 407 414-424.

41   *Brima* Appeal (n 40 above) 196.

42   These accused were Charles Taylor, three Armed Forces Revolutionary Council (AFRC) accused, three Revolutionary United Front (RUF) accused, Sam Bockarie, Johnny Paul Koroma, and Foday Sankoh. See Oosterveld (n 40 above) 408.

43   *Prosecutor v Brima, Kamara & Kanu* Case No SCSL-04-16-T, Trial Chamber Judgment (20 June 2007) para 37-50 (Doherty J dissenting). Oosterveld (n 40 above) 409-410. See also CA MacKinnon 'Rape, genocide and women's human rights' in A Stiglmayer (ed) *Mass rape: The war against women in Bosnia-Herzegovina* (1994) 190; and Schott (n 6 above) 8.

44   *Brima* Appeal (n 40 above) 195. The Prosecutor of the ICC has also referred to forced marriage in the conflict in the Democratic Republic of Congo. *Prosecutor v Katanga & Ngudjolo Chui* Case No ICC-01/04-01/07, Prosecution's Submission of Public Version of Document Containing the Charges (24 April 2008) para 89.

particularly rape and other forms of sexual abuse, and all other forms of violence in situations of armed conflict'.[45] The 2006 UNSC Resolution 1674 confirmed that civilians account for the vast majority of casualties in situations of armed conflict and that deliberately targeting civilians in armed conflict is a flagrant violation of international humanitarian law.

These resolutions had an impact: in 2007, partly in response to Resolution 1325, India sent the first ever all-female police unit to participate in the UN peacekeeping operations in Liberia. In a country where more than 90 per cent of women have survived some form of sexual violence, the all-female police force was an important manifestation of the empowerment of women, greatly strengthening the transitional justice process.[46] This was unprecedented.

In 2008 the UN Security Council voted unanimously to classify rape as a tactic of war and a threat to international security.[47] UNSC Resolution 1820 notes that women and girls are 'particularly targeted by the use of sexual violence, including in some cases as a tactic of war to humiliate, dominate, instil fear in, disperse and/or forcibly relocate civilian members of a community or ethnic group'.[48]

Resolution 1888 specifically mandates peacekeeping missions to protect women and children from rampant sexual violence during armed conflict.[49] Importantly, this Security Council Resolution recognises that allowing peacekeeping forces to respond to and prevent acts of sexual violence can significantly contribute to the maintenance of international peace and security.[50] The importance of a gender-inclusive approach to peace was reiterated in UNSC Resolution 1889 (2009) and UNSC Resolution 1894 (2009), which once again confirmed that civilians account for the vast majority of casualties in armed conflict. UNSC Res 1960

---

45 Security Council Resolution 1325 (2000), adopted by the Security Council at its 4213th meeting, on 31 October 2000 S/RES/1325 (2000) para 10.
46 See 'Indian women police inspire Liberian women to join Liberia's police force' *New Liberian* 14 November 2008, available at http://newliberian.com/?p=470 (accessed 11 December 2014). See also Meyersfeld (n 8 above).
47 UN Security Council Resolution 1820 (2008) to end sexual violence in conflict, adopted by the Security Council at its 5916th meeting, on 19 June 2008 S/RES/1820 (2008).
48 Resolution to end sexual violence in conflict (n 47 above) Preamble.
49 UN Security Council Resolution 1888 (2009), adopted by the Security Council at its 6195th meeting, on 30 September 2009, S/RES/1888 (2009).
50 See art 1, which '[r]eaffirms that sexual violence, when used or commissioned as a tactic of war in order to deliberately target civilians or as a part of a widespread or systematic attack against civilian populations, can significantly exacerbate situations of armed conflict and may impede the restoration of international peace and security; affirms in this regard that effective steps to prevent and respond to such acts of sexual violence can significantly contribute to the maintenance of international peace and security; and expresses its readiness, when considering situations on the agenda of the Council, to take, where necessary, appropriate steps to address widespread or systematic sexual violence in situations of armed conflict'.

identified the sexual violence as a tactic, which exacerbates and prolongs situations of armed conflict.[51]

Most recently, in October 2013, the CEDAW Committee adopted General Recommendation No 30, obliging states to uphold women's rights before, during and after conflict.[52] This is the most recent articulation by a human rights body regarding the rights of women in conflict. Paragraph 16 incorporates common article 3 of the Geneva Conventions of 1949 and the Protocols additional to the Geneva Conventions.

The formal integration of LOAC is clear and international human rights law is brought keenly into focus in this instrument.

The combination of jurisprudence, Security Council Resolutions and academic writings have placed the prohibition on sexual violence in conflict at the foreground of a gendered approach to IHL.[53] This development, however, is one strand of a much larger network of gender-specific harm that is perpetrated during conflict.

A robust legal response to these forms of harm is an awaiting development.

3   Part two: Awaiting developments

3.1   Enhancing our understanding of gender-specific war-time harm

Women in conflict experience a range of harm, which is designed to, or results in, the depreciation of an aspect of women's lives, which is particular to their gender.[54] This harm continues to be perceived as a side-effect of war, much as rape was perceived prior to the shift in the 1990s, discussed above. These forms of harm which speak not only to the sexual violence perpetrated against women, but also the gender-specific impact of

---

51   UN Security Council Resolution 1960 (2010), adopted by the Security Council at its 6453rd meeting, on 16 December 2010, S/RES/1960 (2010).

52   Adopted by the CEDAW Committee on 18 October 2013 CEDAW/C/GC/30 (2013), available at: http://www.ohchr.org/Documents/HRBodies/CEDAW/GComments/CEDAW.C.CG.30.pdf (accessed 11 December 2014).

53   See, in particular, the historic work of K Askin (n 8 above) 347; and Meron (n 8 above) 425-427.

54   S McKay & D Mazurana *Where are the girls? Girls in fighting forces in Northern Uganda, Sierra Leone and Mozambique: Their lives during and after war* (2004) 91-93 (women and girls were recruited into fighting forces where they fulfilled roles of cook, porters, caretakers, labourers in diamond mines and as 'wives' of the combatants). MU Walker 'Gender and violence in focus: A background for gender justice in reparations' in R Rubio-Marin (ed) *The gender of reparations: Unsettling sexual hierarchies while redressing human rights violations* (2009) 19.

post-conflict poverty, which are deliberate tactics of war, are not categorised as violations of the LOAC. International human rights law, on the other hand, has recognised such forms of harm as legal violations, many of which, in times of conflict and under the LOAC, are not categorised as legal contraventions of military conduct.

What are these forms of harm and should these gender-specific human rights violations also be categorised as violations of the LOAC? This part of the article answers the first question.

3.1.1 The gendered nature of mass killing

In 2008, a former UN peacekeeping commander testified that '[i]t has probably become more dangerous to be a woman than a soldier in an armed conflict'.[55] The statistics underscore this: by the 1990s, nine out of ten people who died in war from direct and indirect effects were civilians (the majority of whom are women and children, particularly girl children).[56] This is due to a change in war technology and strategy. Aerial bombardment usually results in the destruction of infrastructures such as power plants, water works, hospitals, industrial plants and communications systems.[57] There are fewer face-to-face battles, with the result that warfare is located in civilian cities, towns, and villages – and the vast majority of civilians are women. In Rwanda, for example, an estimated 40 to 45 per cent of those killed in the genocide were women. This was so in large part because of the occurrence of the conflict in civilian villages and towns and also because of the genocidal intent to eradicate the Tutsi people.[58] In the war in Sierra Leone the killing of civilians was found to constitute a targeted campaign by the RUF and AFRC.[59]

One of the major contributors to civilian death is landmines.[60] Landmines have been used to target civilian populations (predominantly women and children) for decades. More than 100 million landmines and

---

55 'Rice: Rape shouldn't be war weapon' *abc NEWS* 13 July 2008, available at: http://abc news.go.com/GMA/rice-rape-warweapon/story?id=5364523. See also B van Schaack '"The grass that gets trampled when elephants fight": Will the codification of the crime of aggression protect women?' SSRN (September 2010), available at: http://works.bepress.com/beth_van_schaack/3/ (accessed 11 December 2014). See also B van Schaack 'The crime of aggression and humanitarian intervention on behalf of women' (2011) 11 *International Criminal Law Review* 477.
56 P Heynes 'War and women' 13 March 2003 (on file with author).
57 As above.
58 As above.
59 'Chapter three: Women and the armed conflict in Sierra Leone' in 'Witness to truth': Report of the Sierra Leone Truth and Reconciliation Commission Vol 3B' 152 para 259, available at: http://www.sierra-leone.org/Other-Conflict/TRCVolume3B.pdf (accessed 11 December 2014). 25.6% of victims of mass killings comprised women (the Commission has the testimony of 1149 individuals, para 201).
60 Convention on the Prohibition of the Use, Stockpiling, Production and Transfer of Anti-Personnel Mines and on their Destruction, Oslo, 18 September 1997, UNTS 2956 p.211 (Mine Ban Treaty).

unexploded ordnance lie dispersed and unmarked in fields, roadways, pasturelands, and near borders in 90 countries throughout the world.[61] From 15 000 to 20 000 people are maimed or killed each year by landmines and more than 70 per cent of the reported victims are civilians.[62]

The objective of landmines is to ensure the disruption of a community's life and livelihood without the presence of a military force. Landmines are deliberately placed in agricultural fields and along routes to water sources and markets. This impedes the production of food, inhibits the development and recovery of the community and extends the conflict into the non-combatant zone of civilians.[63] Women and children are common casualties in agrarian and subsistence-farming structures particularly. In Bajaur, Pakistan, thousands of landmines have been scattered on the Pakistan-Afghanistan border by the Soviet military during Soviet conflict. Women and girls constitute almost 35 per cent of mine victims, injured while fetching fodder for animals, crossing agricultural fields, and carrying out their daily activities. Yet mine awareness sessions are provided predominantly in mosques and schools to men and boys who are then relied upon to educate women and girls at home. Nearly one-half of land in Cambodia, where one in every 236 people is an amputee due to landmine injury, is unsafe for cultivation and human use.[64]

So as the recovery from war continues, it is likely that an even greater percentage of those injured and killed by landmines will be women and children as they return to peacetime sustenance activities, collecting firewood and water, tending animals and farming.[65] This is especially true in Africa where women are responsible for 80 per cent of agricultural production.[66]

The killing of women and civilians is certainly prohibited by the LOAC. However, it is not understood as a gendered harm, with constitutive elements that speak to the disproportionate impact on women. Female victims may well fall within the generic prohibition against such munitions but the absence of a gender-specific prohibition means that the

---

61   Heynes (n 56 above).
62   See Mine Ban Treaty (n 60 above) Preamble: 'Determined to put an end to the suffering and casualties caused by anti-personnel mines, that kill or maim hundreds of people every week, mostly innocent and defenceless civilians and especially children, obstruct economic development and reconstruction, inhibit the repatriation of refugees and internally displaced persons, and have other severe consequences for years after emplacement'. See also Heynes (n 56 above).
63   Heynes (n 56 above).
64   As above.
65   As above.
66   See USAID Fact Sheet 'Food security and gender', available at: pdf.usaid.gov/pdf_docs/PNADR706.pdf (accessed 11 December 2014). See also 'Women and sustainable food security' by the Women in Development Service (SDWW), FAO Women and Population Division, available at: http://www.fao.org/sd/fsdirect/fbdirect/FSP001.htm (accessed 11 December 2014). See also YI Ogunlela & AA Mukhtar 'Gender issues in agriculture and rural development in Nigeria: The role of women' (2009) 4 *Humanity & Social Sciences Journal* 19.

gendered experience is not caught within the net of post-conflict accountability.

3.1.2   Long-term economic hardship

Long-term economic hardship is one of the primary ways in which women suffer during and after war.[67] Policies of property destruction and laying waste target civilians specifically. Just as mass rape, this is not a side-effect of war but a deliberate component of conflict strategies. The disintegration of an enemy community is a great strength to combatants. And it is this disintegration of which women are the primary victims. For example, the burning of homes, towns and villages, the poisoning of food and water sources, and the destruction of livestock, buildings and other forms of property, are all methods of de-stabilising a community. Without such resources, the community is forced to scatter, losing solidarity, uniformity and strength.[68] Of course, the individual acts of laying waste, poisoning water supplies and targeting civilian structures, all constitute violations of the LOAC. The harm, however, is not understood in a gender specific way. Because of gendered structures, poisoned water will have the same – and different – impact on women and men. This differential is not captured in the understanding and punishment of violations of the LOAC. In order for the LOAC to be truly responsive to women, it cannot presume to apply to a homogenous group in a homogenous manner. And this understanding should not be limited to gender but includes an array of differential identities and experiences, including for example, disability, age, poor health, sexual orientation and national origin. This differential is similar to the differential identified by hate crimes, for example. In the case of rape, the crime of a man raping a woman is the same as, and different from, the crime of a man raping a woman who is lesbian in order to punish her for her sexual orientation. The latter comprises the same conduct but the nature of the harm and intent are different.

The same differential is required in the LOAC and, especially, in relation to the impact of extreme poverty on women. As with many violations, economic hardship is a harm, which operates on a continuum. It may begin during the conflict but its end perpetuates well beyond the

---

67   See The Inter-Agency Standing Committee Task Force on Gender and Humanitarian Assistance 'Guidelines for gender-based violence interventions in humanitarian settings focusing on prevention of and response to sexual violence in emergencies' (September 2005) 50. See also United Nations High Commissioner for Refugees 'Sexual and gender-based violence against refugees, returnees and internally displaced persons: Guidelines for prevention and response' (May 2003). The long-term consequences of war for women are discussed by J Ferril 'A call for new justice: Victims of sexual violence in Africa's internal conflicts' (2008) 4 *Florida International University Law Review* 333 336 and SS Mohan 'The battle after the war: Gender discrimination in property rights and post-conflict restitution' (2011) 46 *Yale Journal of International Law* 461 464.

68   For a more general discussion regarding the impoverishment of women in war see Walker (n 54 above) 41.

final handshake across the negotiating table. In communities where men are wage earners or are responsible for the income of the family, the deliberate killing of male community members will ensure the impoverishment of a community, especially where women are precluded from meaningful or gainful employment.

Women in agrarian economies are particularly exposed to post-conflict poverty. The larger percentage of farmers in Asia and Africa are women, where women are responsible for up to 80 per cent of food produced in many parts of Africa. The obligation of food production exists alongside and absence of property rights, forcing many women who head families into forms of indentured labour in post-conflict situations.[69] Seventy per cent of Rwandan children are supported solely by mothers, grandmothers, or oldest girl children. Girls in Rwanda are heads of family for an estimated 58 500 households.[70] In Kosovo alone, where an estimated 10 000 men died or disappeared, many widows who returned from refugee camps had no social safety nets or advocacy organisations and became indigent and socially marginalised.[71]

Sex work often becomes the only viable form of income. In regions such as Nepal and Bangladesh, where girls are trafficked into Indian brothels, the daughters of widows are more likely to be taken out of school to help their mothers and are particularly at risk of being trafficked into prostitution.[72] In former war-torn countries of Angola, Bosnia and Herzegovina, Kosovo, Mozambique, and Somalia, the majority of adult women are widows who, without the support of a male breadwinner, are required to provide an income in environments which may not be conducive to women in the work place.[73]

The feminisation of poverty occurs during times of conflict as well as peace. However, the normalisation of gendered poverty should not obscure the fact that impoverishment is a consequence, and often a deliberate one, of armed conflict. The constitutive elements of the harm of impoverishment may exist in the LOAC. The challenge is to identify its gendered nature, its disproportionate impact on a specific group and the implementation of the rules of LOAC that are responsive to this reality.

3.1.3 Displacement

The scale and nature of war in the late 20th century has resulted in unprecedented numbers of people fleeing conflict, such that the

---

69	Heynes (n 56 above). See also Mohan (n 67 above) 461.
70	As above.
71	As above.
72	As above.
73	As above.

displacement of people by war in the 1990s has had more severe public health impact, in many situations, than the conflict itself.[74]

Women are particularly vulnerable to, and bear significant consequences of, forced displacement.[75] The intersectionality between rape and displacement is also relevant: rape is an inexpensive weapon which is an 'instrument of forced exile' which 'make[s] you leave your home and never want to go back'.[76] Eighty per cent of the world's refugees and internally displaced persons are women and children.[77] In Sierra Leone 36,9 per cent of victims of forced displacement were women (the Commission has the testimony of 2941 individuals).[78] This is the most common violation recorded by the Commission and accounts for 23,5 per cent of the violations committed against women as opposed to only 19,3 per cent of the violations committed against men.[79]

In refugee camps women and girls are more exposed to contaminated water supplies and human waste than men.[80] Women and girls tend to be responsible for basic household needs, including procuring food, fuel, fodder, and water and for disposal of waste. This compels women to operate outside refugee camps, towns or cities, making them increasingly vulnerable to acts of harm and particularly rape.[81] It has been reported that refugee women and girls have a higher mortality rate than men and boys because systems of health services and food provision in refugee camps privilege men and boys over women and girls.[82] For example, Rwandan refugee families headed by women suffered more malnutrition than those headed by men in an eastern Zaire refugee camp.[83] In South Africa women generally endured displacement as a result of the Group Areas Act. Women were displaced or abandoned in unknown parts of the country where their association with political activism led to their social isolation.[84]

Sadly, women's rights are also violated by humanitarian aid workers in displacement camps.[85] They may be forced to barter sex for the aid to

---

74   As above.
75   Approximately 50% of the world's refugee population are women and girls. See UNHCR 'Refugee women', available at: http://www.unhcr.org/pages/49c3646c 1d9.html (accessed 11 December 2014).
76   CA MacKinnon 'Rape, genocide and women's human rights' in A Stiglmayer (ed) *Mass rape: The war against women in Bosnia-Herzegovina* (1994) 190.
77   Heynes (n 56 above).
78   Sierra Leone TRC Report (n 59 above) para 201.
79   Sierra Leone TRC Report (n 59 above) para 136.
80   Heynes (n 56 above).
81   See Guidelines for gender-based violence interventions (n 67 above) 58.
82   Heynes (n 56 above).
83   As above.
84   'Truth and Reconciliation Report Vol IV' 305, available at http://www.justice.gov.za/trc/report/finalreport/Volume%204.pdf (accessed 11 December 2014).
85   See 'Extensive abuse of West African refugee children reported' UNHCR Press Releases (26 February 2002), available at: http://www.unhcr.org/cgi-bin/texis/vtx/news/opendoc.htm?tbl=NEWS&id=3c7bf8094 (accessed 11 December 2014). See also Sierra Leone TRC Report (n 59 above) para 6.

which they are entitled. In February 2002, The United Nations High Commissioner for Refugees (UNHCR) and Save the Children released a report on their investigation into allegations of sexual abuse of West African refugee children in Guinea, Liberia, and Sierra Leone.[86] Their interviews with 1500 women, men and children refugees revealed that girls between the ages of 13 and 18 were sexually exploited by male aid workers, many of whom were employed by national and international non-governmental agencies and the UN, and also by UN peacekeepers and community leaders: 'They say "a kilo for sex"' reported a woman from Guinea about the rampant extortion of sex for food by aid workers.[87] A man interviewed stated that without a sister, wife or daughter to 'offer the NGO workers', one doesn't have access to oil, tents, medicines, loans, education and skill training, and ration cards.[88] The violation by peacekeepers and aid workers is particularly acute because of the enhanced and specialised responsibility and role of trust that accompanies such agents. Exploiting that role is a violation that is not currently captured by the specifics of international law, although it certainly triggered moral outrage. This is a peculiar crime which has occurred and which requires delineation – and redress – in order to ensure accountability.

3.1.4   Forced recruitment

Conflicts have seen women captured as 'property' of combatants and forced into the role of so-called 'bush wives' or members of 'harems'. Heyns identifies the root cause of the this phenomenon as governments and leaders, on all sides of a conflict, who initiate, accommodate, and tolerate 'military brothels under the aegis of "rest and recreation" for their soldiers, with the private admission that a regulated system of brothels will contain male sexual aggression, limit sexually transmitted diseases in the military, and boost soldiers' morale for war'.[89] This captivity allows for sanctioned mass rape by combatants. The period of slavery is prolonged and comprises multiple, at times innumerable, rapes. Women may become the property of individual combatants (this may also constitute forced marriage) or a group of combatants, whom they serve on an on-going basis.

In Sierra Leone captured women were scarred with the initials 'RUF' cut into their bodies, putting women further at risk if they were captured by government soldiers or allied militia, who would think they were

---

86   See Report of the Secretary-General on the activities of the Office of Internal Oversight Services 'Investigation into sexual exploitation of refugees by aid workers in West Africa' A/57/465.

87   As above.

88   See Heynes (n 56 above). In Sierra Leone girls and women were forced to pay aid workers for aid benefits – to which they were entitled – with sex or they and family members would not be able to obtain aid. Sierra Leone TRC Report (n 59 above) 86.

89   Heynes (n 56 above).

rebels.[90] Women in Sierra Leone were also forcibly recruited and compelled to take part in the hostilities.[91]

3.1.5 Forced marriage and abduction

The capture of women by combatants may not be exclusively, or even predominantly, sexual and as such is not encompassed in the crime of sexual slavery. It may also involve the imposition of the status of marriage and a conjugal association by force, or threat of force. The gravamen of the offence is the assertion of a claim of right and ownership by the 'husband' over the 'wife', which involves the right to demand a whole range of 'conjugal duties' (including, but not limited to, rape) in exchange for support and protection. This was recognised by the Sierra Leone Special Court, which defined the crime against humanity of forced marriage as involving 'forced conjugal association with another person resulting in great suffering, or serious physical or mental injury on the part of the victim'.[92]

3.1.6 Reproductive violence

Reproductive violence is a form of sexual violence and includes forced impregnation, enforced sterilisation, and the limitation or denial of reproductive freedom.[93] As is the case with economic hardship, the harm is not limited to the original act of rape but continues well after the conflict expires. Enforced pregnancy or sterilisation is a long-term and extreme violation of an individual woman's autonomy and bodily integrity.

It is also a deliberate tactic of war. The violence of enforced pregnancy or enforced sterilisation violates the individual, severs the connections between families and dismantles the community of which the families are a part. The linkages between the individual, the family and the community, are necessary for the survival of a group. Sever those links and one begins the destruction of the group.[94] As Joeden-Forgey notes, '[m]en are killed to expose women and children, women are raped to humiliate men, children are tortured to destroy parents – this relational logic is the core of genocidal violence against families'.[95]

This tactical nature of reproductive violence, however, has largely been overlooked by the LOAC and post-conflict measures. National

---

90   Sierra Leone TRC Report (n 59 above) paras 208-213 and 219.
91   Sierra Leone TRC Report (n 59 above) paras 214-217.
92   *Brima* Appeal (n 40 above) paras 181-185.
93   Chinkin (n 18 above) paras 14-15.
94   See Schott (n 6 above) 14. See also E von Joeden-Forgey 'The devil in the details: "Life force atrocities" and the assault ion the family in times of conflict' (2010) 5 *Genocide Studies and Prevention* 13.
95   Schott (n 6 above) 14. See also Joeden-Forgey (n 94 above) 13.

abortion laws and imperatives against access to safe abortion impede women's access to reproductive assistance and choice.[96] Such ideological reluctance may exacerbate the injury of the rape, extending the harm beyond the act itself. The Sierra Leone Truth Commission found that there were women who became pregnant and were not permitted by their rapist or another to obtain abortion.[97] There was also evidence of enforced sterilisation.

The ICC Elements define enforced sterilisation as follows: 'The perpetrator deprived one or more persons of biological reproductive capacity' and 'the conduct was neither justified by the medicine or hospital treatment of the person or persons concerned nor carried out with their genuine consent'.[98] According to the Sierra Leone Truth Commission, forced sterilisation 'includes acts committed upon women including during the war in Sierra Leone, such as the removal of foetus, uterus, castration, destruction of reproductive organs, as well as medical sterilisation without consent'.[99] Although not listed as a crime in the Sierra Leone Special Court Statute, the SCSL heard evidence of numerous acts of violence on pregnant women, including the cutting open of a pregnant woman's uterus and the removal of the foetus, the mutilation of her organs, enforced sterilisation, mutilation and cruel and inhuman treatment.[100]

The harm, again, is long-term. When victims of rape do give birth, the children may be viewed as 'enemy children' or 'children of rebels'. In the Former Yugoslavia, survivors of rape camps reported that as soon as they became visibly pregnant, they would be released to give birth to the new generation of Serb children.[101] As a result, both the mothers and their children are ostracised and continue to suffer the effects of the rape well after the culmination of the conflict. This in turn increases the risk of economic hardship.

Miscarriages may be intentionally triggered. Women also miscarry as an indirect result of beatings and maltreatment. The risk of miscarriage and maternal mortality increases as a result of a lack of access to health, either because such facilities are not available or because women may be denied access to health due to their ethnicity, language or another form of group

---

96 As above.
97 Sierra Leone TRC Report (n 59 above) para 185 and page 131.
98 See the ICC Elements, at art 7(1)(g)-5. The deprivation is not intended to include birth control measures, which have a non-permanent effect in practice. It is understood that 'genuine consent' does not include consent obtained through deception. Sierra Leone TRC Report (n 59 above) para 186.
99 Sierra Leone TRC Report (n 59 above) para 186.
100 As above.
101 Schott (n 6 above) 9.

membership. Sexual violence, poor sanitation and poor nutrition may lead to serious and life-threatening reproductive health complications.[102]

3.1.7   Long-term health impairment

The denial of access to health, especially gynecological health, which, in the context of food shortages, sexual violence and the spread of HIV, constitutes an element of conflict that thus far, has not been recognised as a specific, justiciable violation. Other forms of ill-health affecting women specifically caused by conflict include: vesico-vaginal fistula; uterine problems; scarring of the vagina; compromised reproductive health due to non-medical abortions or rape during pregnancy; denormalisation of all sexual activities; exacerbated pain in future childbirth; severe mental ill-health such as depression, trauma, post-traumatic stress disorder and suicide.

Domestic violence is also a major cause of ill-health for women and rises incrementally during and after conflicts, where violence becomes increasingly normalised. In addition, if DDR programmes (Disarmament, Demobilisation and Reintegration) are not implemented, arms, if not removed after a conflict, may be used against women in domestic or intimate contexts.[103]

These health risks are exacerbated by the lack of medical resources or the destruction of medical facilities during conflict and due to malnutrition. Gender roles may require an unequal distribution of food between men and women which, in times of conflict and food shortage, impairs women's immunity to disease and ill-health.

The deliberate infection of women with HIV AIDS or other sexually transmitted diseases is a more contemporary component of conflict that affects women specifically. Diseases may be spread as a result of the ability of combatants to command sexual services from women while moving from region to region. The movement of troops to different parts of the country and their ultimate return to their home areas after demobilisation present significant risks to women. In Rwanda, women survivors of violence started to feel unwell. After a range of medical tests, many found that they are HIV positive:[104] '[W]e saw that by 1999 many of the young

---

102   In the Sierra Leone conflict, miscarriages were common among the so-called 'bush wives' or victims of forced marriage, who received limited or no medical attention. See *Brima* Trial (n 43 above) para 30 (Doherty J dissenting).

103   For a general discussion on post-conflict harm, see B Meyersfeld 'Domestic violence, health and international law' (2008) 22 *Emory International Law Review* 61.

104   WHO 'Violence against Women Living in Situations of Armed Conflict' (October 2000) 8, available at: http://www.who.int/violence_injury_prevention/media/en/152.pdf (accessed 11 December 2014).

girls who had been infected by HIV during the mass rape, were occupying the hospital beds, dying of AIDS-related diseases'.[105]

3.2   Are these forms of harm contraventions of the LOAC?

It is arguable that a prohibition of many of these forms of harm exists or can be read into the provisions of the LOAC dealing with the protection of civilians. As matters stand, however, there has been very little jurisprudence interpreting economic or social harm as violations of the LOAC. The result is that, other than sexual violence, egregious and deliberate methods of war that lead to disproportionate forms of poverty, ill-health and long-term violations, are not penalised. Where the harm is utilised as a military strategy, a method of long-term destabilisation, there should be an appropriate approbation under the rubric of the LOAC. In order to achieve this type of specific regulation, however, a seismic conceptual shift is needed, both in how we understand gender and in how we view the operation of the LOAC.

4   Part three: Seismic shift in understanding how war – *and peace* – harms women

4.1   Enhancing our understanding of war-time harm

There are several ways in which women are involved in or experience conflict. Women may be combatants, direct victims of conflict and victims of post-unrest exigencies.[106] While the LOAC regulates the treatment of civilians and non-combatants, it does not create a legal framework that captures the array of gendered harm that targets women and men precisely because of their gender. Women suffer a range of harm that affects them precisely because they are women and because social constructs cast women with particular roles in different societies that enemy forces deliberately target.[107] Not all such harm violates the LOAC (nor should all forms of harm fall under an unlawful rubric), but many components are sufficiently egregious to warrant judicial elaboration. It is also important to note that women not only endure harm; they are also the perpetrators of

---

105   As above. For a discussion of the health disparities – both physical and mental – between women and men in detention, see: ICRC Interview 'Differences in the health needs of men and women in detention' (7 March 2013), available at: http://www.icrc.org/eng/resources/documents/interview/2013/03-07-health-men-women-detention.htm (accessed 11 December 2014).
106   For an extensive and still relevant account of women's diverse and unexpected experiences of war, see S Saywell *Women in war* (1985).
107   See Chinkin (n 18 above) paras 1-5.

harm.[108] This does not change the analysis, however, of how LOAC fails to map the forms of harm perpetrated *against* women.

As noted above, the deficiency is not necessarily in the black letter law of the LOAC. The content of this area of international law may well contain – or be interpreted as containing – reference to the harm described in the previous section. The challenge is in (i) identifying the gendered nature of this harm and (ii) finding the will to punish and remedy such harm. If many of these acts are already prohibited by the LOAC, why is there so little remediation of and response to gender-specific harm in conflicts?

There is an array of factors, which, traditionally, have excluded women from the protective structure of the LOAC. These have been explored extensively in the academic literature and one of the prominent explanations is the well-canvassed subject of gender discrimination and differentiation.[109] The distinction between men and women in many societies often demarcates women as subordinate to men, particularly in political or public contexts. In times of post-conflict peace-keeping, women's experiences tend to be subsumed into generic group experiences, such as religious or racial persecution, or sex-specific harm is deemed to be an unavoidable, tangential effect of war.

The reliance on gender stereotypes and hetero-normativity has also precluded women from post-conflict and post-oppressive regime prosecutions. The perpetuation of stereotypes tends to cast men as combatants and heroes and women as secondary participants, with the result that many forms of harm affecting women have not been categorised as legal wrongs. In many ways, the Rome Statue's criminalisation of sexual and reproductive violence against women reinforces such stereotypes. The harm that has been criminalised (correctly) is harm relating to the identity of women as sexual, virtuous and physical. To be clear: the criminalisation of such violence is seminal. However, that is only one component of harm experienced by women in and after conflict. The Rome Statute, therefore, has taken us a considerable distance in advancing women's rights jurisprudence in international law but international law is still not responsive to the full gamut of gender-specific harm.

As a result, the legal categorisation of wartime harm continues to suffer from a series of 'bad habits'. We are habituated to create laws that

108 *The Prosecutor v Pauline Nyiramasuhuko, Arsène Shalom Ntahobali, Sylvain Nsabimana, Alphonse Nteziryayo, Joseph Kanyabashi,* Élie *Ndayambaje* (2011) ICTR-98-42-T. See C Sperling 'Mother of atrocities: Pauline Nyiramasuhuko's role in the Rwandan Genocide' (2005-2006) 33 *Fordham Urban Law Journal* 637.
109 See Van Schaack (n 55 above). See also in general: Oosterveld (n 40 above) and Meyersfeld (n 8 above) 105-106.

reflect a culture, an order and a way of life.[110] An adherence to law in its current form may well be the continuation of a myth, which allows us to ignore the 'invisible pattern of order in law'.[111] Put plainly: our laws may not reflect the needs of all. Claudia Card, for example, provides an alternative understanding of genocide. She identifies the notion of a social death, where a community or ethnic group can be destroyed without physical destruction.[112] The harm exists in severing ties between families and generations and pulling apart the weave that constitutes a particular identity. It is this destruction, which the LOAC is yet to address.

During conflicts, women are violated in a way that may not be considered a violation of the LOAC either because the harm is invisible in that it takes place in private (for example, many women remain in isolation because of vaginal fistula, caused by violent rape), or because the harm is invisible in that it forms part of a system of post conflict poverty (for example enforced sex work due to indigence).[113] For these reasons the harm is deemed to fall outside the purview of the radar of judicial activity. The successful prosecution of sexual violence against women in war is a laudable development. It has not, however, put an end to the debate about the criminalisation of gender-specific harm in conflict and bias against the inclusion of such harm remains. Contexts of militarisation mobilise ideas of hetero-normativity to define military strength or depict enemy vulnerability and these assumptions tend to inform the legal categorisation of war-time harm. In other words, there are still very few gender-specific forms of harm that are categorised as acts contrary to the rules of the LOAC. To the extent that there have been post-conflict prosecutions of war-crimes committed against women, the focus has been on sexual violence, which is packaged with assumptions of universality – that all women have the same experience – and objectification.[114] The almost exclusive focus on sexual violence revives the perception of women as solely sexual and reproductive beings. Such focus also ignores the multi-faceted way in which women experience harm (particularly in Africa

---

110 See AV Alfieri 'Retrying race' (2003) 101 *Michigan Law Review* 1141 1145, noting that race 'colors law, crime, and community. It shadows the performance of public and private roles. It shades the meaning of relationships. And it stains the operating norms of institutions'. I propose that the same infiltrating tendency exists with respect to gender.

111 B Grossfeld & EJ Eberle 'Patterns of order in comparative law: Discovering and decoding invisible powers' (2003) 38 *Texas International Law Journal* 291 294 (maintaining that invisible phenomena that influence the path of law include a range of tangible, intangible, intuitional, or rational factors). See also PW Kahn *The reign of law: Marbury v Madison and the construction of America* (1997) xi.

112 C Card *Confronting evil: Terrorism, torture, genocide* (2010) 84.

113 For a discussion of the role of language in the understanding of international humanitarian law, see Meron (n 2 above) 244 and 246. Schott artfully identifies both the invisibility of harm caused by rape – often there are no scars – and the invisibility of the crime in under reporting or failure to include sexual violence in casualty statistics. Schott (n 6 above) 7.

114 See Oosterveld (n 40 above) 5 and 10.

where poverty, poor health and susceptibility to terminal infection affects women disproportionately to men).[115]

Today's conflicts are not battlefield-bound and military objectives are not limited to military entities; the conflict occurs in a multitude of locations and its objectives may include the destruction of a comprehensive group or community.

Given the contemporary nature of armed conflict, legal adaptation is necessary. One such adaptation is the inclusion of a crime of enforced impoverishment of women as a result of acts of war such as poisoning water supplies, forced displacement or destroying infrastructure. International law currently focuses on the political, the civil and the physical. It does not focus on the economic consequences of war, which have a disproportionate effect on women. The call for such reform is not without substantiation in the provisions of international human rights law. For example, it is quite clear that the right to water is a fundamental right in international law. Currently, international law obliges states to progressively realise this right. What happens, however, when a state or non-state actor takes steps to thwart the individual enjoyment of that right through military action that aims to, and destroys, water and sanitation infrastructure?

Is LOAC ripe for such reform? From a technical legal point of view, it is. For example, the rules relating to biological warfare are new, having been developed after the creation of bio-chemical compounds that could be used in conflict. Consider that it was only in 1994 that the wartime phenomenon of rape received an international definition: 'a physical invasion of a sexual nature committed on a person under circumstances which are coercive'.[116] Legal change is not an anathema to the LOAC. The question is whether there is political appetite for such change. We need an acknowledgment that the degradation caused by war is not only about the grey scale images of wounded soldiers bleeding inhumanely on stretches of beaches and fields; it is about the hauntingly raw reality of an amputee never being able to till her own fields or a survivor of rape facing a life of isolation due to fistula fibrosis.

Unless one has experienced war in this manner, can one possibly know and understand the need for its commensurate prohibition?

---

115   These factors are identified as impediments to justice in UN Women 'Progress of the world's women in pursuit of justice' (2011-2012) 53, available at: http://progress. unwomen.org/ (accessed 11 December 2014). See A Buchanan *Justice, legitimacy and self-determination* (2006) 79. See also MC Nussbaum *Women and human development* (2000) 1.
116   Schott (n 6 above) 7.

4.2   Enhancing our understanding of peace-time harm

The preceding discussion focuses on the inadequacies of the implementation of the LOAC in respect of gender. These inadequacies have been mitigated to some extent by the interlacing of LOAC, international criminal law and international human rights law.

The corollary also applies. What about the way humanitarian law bleeds into human rights law? Is there value in understanding violence against women in times of peace as a form of conflict, requiring an assessment of the problem that evokes the same notions of mass atrocity as the LOAC? And is this at all useful?

The conceptualisation of gendered harm in war can also influence the legal response to gender-based violence under IHRL. The European Court of Human Rights (ECtHR) in the case of *MC v Bulgaria* referred to the jurisprudence of the ICTY and ICTR in concluding that Belgium had deficient laws in respect of rape and the constitutive elements of coercion.[117]

In that case, the ECtHR cited developments in international criminal law in recognising that

> force is not an element of rape and that taking advantage of coercive circumstances to proceed with sexual acts is also punishable. The International Criminal Tribunal for the former Yugoslavia has found that, in international criminal law, any sexual penetration without the victim's consent constitutes rape and that consent must be given voluntarily, as a result of the person's free will, assessed in the context of the surrounding circumstances. While the above definition was formulated in the particular context of rapes committed against the population in the conditions of an armed conflict, it also reflects a universal trend towards regarding lack of consent as the essential element of rape and sexual abuse.[118]

The understanding of rape in war, fuelled the ECtHR's conclusion that often there is 'no physical resistance because of a variety of psychological factors or because they fear violence on the part of the perpetrator'.[119] As a result, 'any rigid approach to the prosecution of sexual offences, such as requiring proof of physical resistance in all circumstances, risks leaving certain types of rape unpunished and thus jeopardising the effective protection of the individual's sexual autonomy'.[120]

There is another way in which IHL can influence the reconceptualisation of human rights law. South Africa, for example, is

---

117   *MC v Bulgaria* App no 39272/98 ECtHR (4 March 2004).
118   *MC v Bulgaria* (n 117 above) para 163.
119   *MC v Bulgaria* (n 117 above) para 164.
120   *MC v Bulgaria* (n 117 above) para 166.

widely cited as having some of the highest rape statistics in the world.[121] Research indicates that one out of three women – a significant number of women living in South Africa – will be subject to some form of violence at one point in their lives. South Africa may not be at war, but does this constitute peace for those enduring this violence? There is clearly a significant wave of harm by one group, men, against another group, women. This is not to say that violence in South Africa does not have other delineated players; gender-based violence, however, is particularly segmented and particularly rife. The suggestion is not that the LOAC should apply in contexts of peace; rather, we should identify the *seriousness* of gender-based violence in contexts that are not designated as conflict zones but where the harm is equivalent to that experienced in conflicts. Are there useful lessons and principles that exist in IHRL that could enhance our understanding of, and response to, gender-based harm in general?

If we were to replace the group 'women' with the group 'Catholic', and replace the group 'men' with the group 'Protestant', we would have the following scenario: half the Catholics in the country will be subject to attacks by Protestants. This type of scenario, at the very least, would trigger an inquiry into the nature of the violence and whether this amounts to an internal conflict. The analogy is simplistic but it does force us to reconsider our notions of peace and conflict. It is debatable whether gender-based violence in South Africa constitutes a civil war. However, can we say that it constitutes peace? If not, is there a legal terrain somewhere between human rights law and humanitarian law that could better facilitate a legal intervention? This is the subject of another discussion but one that hopefully teases out the nuanced ways in which these two areas of law may converge.

5 Conclusion

The development of the LOAC in respect of sexual violence should be seen as an example of how legal constructions may be broadened to include violations that women endure as a result of a deliberate war policy. To date, the laws and legal categories of the LOAC tend to by-pass the factual harm committed against women in conflicts. It is therefore necessary to clarify the legal provisions to be applied to these identified forms of harm and, where necessary, implement the constitutive elements of the LOAC in a responsive manner.

The process of the criminalisation of forced marriage by the SLSC is informative. At the trial level, the majority of the Trial Chamber viewed

---

121   N Abrahams et al 'Every eight hours: Intimate femicide in South Africa 10 years later!' South African Medical Research Council Research Brief (August 2012), available at: http://www.mrc.co.za/policybriefs/everyeighthours.pdf (accessed 11 December 2014).

forced marriage as a sexual crime, which should be categorised as sexual slavery. It failed to engage the criminality of many other components of the crime of forced marriage. It was only on appeal that the Appeal Chamber embraced the broader notion of a 'forced conjugal association by the perpetrator over the victim'.[122]

The most abusive aspect of a human injury may not be captured by the act alone but emerges from the range of social attitudes and policy frameworks within which the act is embedded. In the same way as genocide and ethnic cleansing comprise individual acts of harm in the context of a system of eradicating a people, the system of violence against women constitutes the crime as much as the individual acts of harm. The question now is whether the points of convergence between IHRL and the LOAC will yield a stronger regulatory response to deliberate methods of war, which are often invisible, masked by the cloak of normalcy and accepted gender differentiation. And perhaps as compelling, whether the LOAC may influence a stronger and more robust response to violence against women outside of situations of armed conflict.

---

122 *Brima* Appeal (n 40 above). This was a statement made by Justice Doherty in her dissenting judgment in *Brima* Trial (n 43 above) para 33.

3

Armed Conflict and Human Rights Law

Jann K Kleffner* **

1 Introduction

It is a truism that there is hardly a contemporary armed conflict in which organised armed groups (hereafter OAGs) are not involved. The question whether and to what extent the law of armed conflict (LoAC) and human rights law (HRL) applies to them is therefore a question of utmost importance. In addressing that question, the two branches of international law differ in important respects. Most significantly, it is today generally accepted that the LoAC is binding on organised armed groups. Both conventional and customary LoAC make it abundantly clear that the LoAC applies to 'each Party' to a non-international armed conflict,[1] and that 'each party to the conflict must respect and ensure respect for international humanitarian law'.[2] However, the questions why that is so and how the binding force of LoAC on organised armed groups is to be construed remain controversial.

*   Professor Dr Jann K Kleffner, Head of the International Law Centre, Swedish Defence University. I would like to thank Zarah Abrahamsson for her research assistance.
**   Parts of the present chapter that address the applicability of the law of armed conflict to organised armed groups draw upon my earlier publication: 'The applicability of international humanitarian law to organized armed groups' (2011) 93 *International Review of the Red Cross* 443.
1   Common article 3 to the Four 1949 Geneva Conventions. Also cf art 1(1) AP II, which assumes that binding force in as much as it 'develops and supplements article 3 common to the Geneva Conventions ... without modifying its existing conditions of application', albeit with the caveat that AP II only applies to a specific type of organised armed groups, namely those that meet the high threshold of exercising control over territory as to enable them to carry out sustained and concerted military operations and to implement AP II.
2   J-M Henckaerts & L Doswald-Beck (eds) *Customary international humanitarian law,* Vol I: Rules (2005). Rule 139, applicable in both international and non-international armed conflicts.

In stark contrast, there is considerable controversy surrounding the question whether and to what extent HRL applies *at all* to OAGs. In other words, whereas in relation to the applicability of the LoAC the main questions are *why*, and *how* that applicability is to be construed, the main question in relation to HRL is *whether* that body of law applies to organised armed groups. Yet, beyond this radical difference on the fundamental level, there is a striking resemblance in the different ways how the binding nature – or purported binding nature – of the LoAC and HRL on OAGs is conceptualised.

In the following, these different constructions of the binding nature of both bodies of international law will be submitted to a critical analysis. The aim of this chapter hence is not to take position and defend any particular explanation of the binding nature of either the LoAC or HRL. Rather, the chapter endeavours to bring to the fore the respective strengths and weaknesses in these different explanations with the view to illustrate the difficulties that confront international law when faced with the reality of one of the constant features of contemporary armed conflicts: organised armed groups.

After briefly defining the concept of an 'organised armed group' in the following section (2), the chapter will address five different explanations. A first such explanation is to construe the binding nature of the LoAC and HRL on OAGs through the state (3). A second one is to rely on the fact that both bodies of law are binding upon the individual (4). Thirdly, it is being suggested that LoAC and HRL are binding OAGs because such groups exercise de facto governmental functions (5). Fourthly, it is argued that OAGs possess (limited) international legal personality which entails that the LoAC and HRL bind them as a matter of customary international law (6). Finally, the consent of an OAG is offered as the basis for the binding nature of LoAC and HRL (7).

2 Organised armed groups defined

For the purposes of the present chapter, 'organised armed groups' are understood to be those armed groups that are sufficiently organised to render them a party to an armed conflict. The ICTY has identified several indicative factors for an armed group to be considered sufficiently 'organised' in this sense, amongst which the existence of a command structure and disciplinary rules and mechanisms within the group; the existence of a headquarters; the fact that the group controls a certain territory; the ability of the group to gain access to weapons, other military equipment, recruits and military training; its ability to plan, coordinate and carry out military operations, including troop movements and logistics; its ability to define a unified military strategy and use military tactics; and its ability to speak with one voice and negotiate and conclude agreements such as cease-fire or peace accords.[3]

The aforementioned factors have been identified in the jurisprudence of the ad-hoc tribunals as being *indicative*. In other words, while they may point to the qualification of a non-state actor as an organised armed group, they are not regarded as being (necessarily) constitutive of such a group. The existence of an organised armed group is not dependent on the presence of *all* identified factors, nor is the existence of any one of them sufficient. Rather, the identified factors are seen as providing guidance in making the factual determination of whether or not a group of individuals is an organised armed group for purposes of the LoAC. Indeed, a closer look at these factors reveals a mixture of those whose absence do not preclude the existence of an organised armed group (such as territorial control), and those that, it is submitted, are quintessential preconditions for that existence, such as the presence of a command structure and disciplinary rules and mechanisms within the group, the ability of the group to gain access to military equipment and recruits and the ability to plan, coordinate and carry out military operations.

At the same time, it is clear from the identified factors and the degree to which they are present or absent in a given group that the resulting notion of an 'organised armed group' extends to a broad spectrum. It may include quasi-states and *de facto* regimes, such as those organised armed groups that exercise firm and stable control over parts of a state's territory so as to allow them to establish a parallel government and offer 'public' services. This would include, for example, the entity established by the Liberation Tigers of Tamil Eelam (LTTE) in north-eastern Sri Lanka in the late 1980's, with its own police, army, navy, air force, legal codes, courts, prisons, taxes, customs, immigration, administration, local government, planning, development programmes, social services, financial system, trades, shops, commercial ventures, medical services, and educational services.[4] On the other end of the spectrum, it also includes those organised armed groups that operate solely on the basis of guerilla tactics and do not exercise territorial control, although they fulfil the quintessential conditions of a command structure, access to military equipment and recruits and the ability to plan, coordinate and carry out military operations (for example, the Lord's Resistance Army (LRA) that is operating from temporary bases in Uganda, the Democratic Republic of Congo (DRC), and the Central African Republic).[5] Between these outer

---

3   See eg ICTY *The Prosecutor v Boskoski and Tarculovski* Trial Chamber judgment (10 June 2008) paras 194-205.
4   See AJV Chandrakanthan 'Eelam Tamil nationalism: An inside view' in A Jeyarantam Wilson (ed) *Sri Lankan Tamil nationalism: Its origins and development in the nineteenth and twentieth centuries* (2000) 168.
5   'Report of the Secretary General on the activities of the United Nations Regional Office for Central Africa and on the Lord's Resistance Army-affected areas' UN Doc S/2014/319 (6 May 2014), para 45.

bounds of the spectrum of what constitutes an 'organised armed group' for our purposes, an infinite diversity exists. Furthermore, an organised armed group is not a static entity, but evolves and is subject to change over time. The resulting variety in the generic concept of an 'organised armed group' needs to be borne in mind when turning to the following examination of the different ways that are being offered to explain why the LoAC and HRL apply.

3   Bindingness construed through the state

A first conceptualisation is to construe the binding nature of the LoAC and HRL on OAGs through the state.

In the field of *LoAC*, this conceptualisation manifests itself in the doctrine of legislative jurisdiction. According to this doctrine, LoAC is binding on OAGs by virtue of the fact that the 'parent' state has accepted a given rule of the LoAC. This is notwithstanding the fact that the state's legitimacy and monopoly of the use of force is challenged by the OAG. According to this construction, the capacity of a state to legislate for all its nationals entails that the state may impose obligations upon them that originate from international law, even if those individuals take up arms to fight that state or another organised armed group(s) within it.[6]

In the field of *HRL*, the construction of obligations of OAGs via the state manifests itself in the obligation of states to *protect* human rights, which features besides the obligation to *respect* and to *fulfil* human rights.[7] The positive obligation to protect human rights gives rise to the horizontal effect of human rights. In the words of the Human Rights Committee:

> [T]he positive obligations on States Parties to ensure Covenant rights will only be fully discharged if individuals are protected by the State, not just against violations of Covenant rights by its agents, but also against acts committed by private persons or entities that would impair the enjoyment of Covenant rights in so far as they are amenable to application between private persons or entities. There may be circumstances in which a failure to ensure Covenant rights as required by article 2 [of the ICCPR] would give rise to violations by States Parties of those rights, as a result of States Parties' permitting or failing to take appropriate measures or to exercise due diligence to prevent, punish, investigate or redress the harm caused by such acts by private persons or entities.[8]

---

6   For a recent defense of the doctrine of legislative jurisdiction, see S Sivakumaran 'Binding armed opposition groups' (2006) 55 *International and Comparative Law Quarterly* 369-394, 381-393.

7   On these three dimensions to respect, protect and fulfil human rights, see generally O De Schutter *International human rights law: Cases, materials, commentary* (2010) 280-283.

8   Human Rights Committee, General Comment No 31 [80] 'The nature of the general legal obligation imposed on states parties to the Covenant' Adopted on 29 March 2004 (2187th meeting), UN Doc CCPR/C/21/Rev.1/Add. 13 (26 May 2004) para 8.

In other words, OAGs incur human rights obligations by virtue of the fact that the state concerned is under an obligation to protect the human rights of those individuals that find themselves in its jurisdiction.[9] This obligation to protect generically entails that states must ensure that OAGs are not violating the human rights of individuals. Through this construction, OAGs thus incur human rights obligations, albeit indirectly. Where the state fails to protect the human rights of individuals against violations committed by an OAG, the latter will not be directly accountable from the perspective of international law.

The construction of the binding nature of LoAC and HRL via the state bears the significant advantage that it supplies a reason why organised armed groups are bound by all rules of the LoAC and HRL that the territorial state has consented to, despite the fact that organised armed groups themselves may not have consented to them.[10] One may add that such a construct, which considers the consent of OAGs to be irrelevant, is fully compatible with other areas of international law, through which states grant rights to, or impose obligations on, individuals and other legal persons. When a state consents to a given rule of international law, which criminalises a given conduct, for instance, the consent of individuals, who may be subject to criminal prosecution on the basis of that rule, is generally considered to be irrelevant. The same holds true for rights under international law, which states can grant to individuals by accepting a given treaty as binding or by not persistently objecting to a rule of customary international law, regardless of the position taken by individuals who are to benefit from such rights.

However, the lack of consent to rules of the LoAC or HRL by OAGs also entails important limitations regarding their propensity to accept the binding force of these bodies of law on the basis of the doctrine of legislative jurisdiction or the doctrine of indirect, horizontal effect. After all, it does not come as a surprise when an OAG rejects an explanation, which draws on the fact that the very state against whom that OAG is fighting has accepted a given rule of the LoAC or HRL.[11] Indeed, the fact that an organised armed group is a party to an armed conflict against the central government of a state suggests very strongly that it does not recognise even the most basic of laws of that state. The equation of members of an organised armed group with 'ordinary citizens' who can reasonably be assumed to be at least perceptible to the suggestion that they

---

9   For relevant jurisprudence confirming such an effect of human rights on organised armed groups, see L Zegveld *Accountability of armed opposition groups in international law* (2002) 166-173.
10   In the field of LoAC, see Sivakumaran (n 6 above) 382.
11   For a pertinent example, see the assertion of the National Liberation Front in Vietnam in the 1960's that 'it was not bound by the international treaties to which others beside itself subscribed', in ICRC 'External activities: Viet Nam' (1965) 57 *International Review of the Red Cross* 636.

are bound by the legal rules that the state has accepted or issued, appears to be somewhat strained, if not entirely neglecting the reality of OAGs.

Besides the aforementioned objection, the construction of the binding nature of LoAC and HRL on OAGs via the state also suffers from an important legal defect. As far as the doctrine of legislative jurisdiction in the realm of the LoAC is concerned, it rests on the argument that 'the government is competent to legislate for all its nationals'.[12] Thus understood, the doctrine should therefore better be called more precisely the doctrine of active nationality legislative jurisdiction, as opposed to other jurisdictional bases, such as territory or passive nationality, in as much as it limits the reach of the rules of the LoAC to the nationals of the consenting state. If considered in the light of recent developments relating to the concept of 'nationality', the doctrine loses much of its explanatory value. According to the ICTY, in particular in armed conflicts with ethnic, religious or similar connotations that are today the rule rather than the exception, the concept of nationality cannot be reduced to an exercise in formalism: its substantive dimension, that is the allegiance of a given individual (or lack thereof) to a given state or government also needs to be considered.[13] Put differently, individuals with allegiance to states or entities other than the state whose nationals they are as a matter of formality, should not be considered nationals of the former state as a matter of substance. Admittedly, it is at least doubtful that the finding of the ICTY has led to a general shift in the concept of 'nationality' as a matter of general international law. However, its reasoning in the specific context of the LoAC is quite compelling. If one transposed such an understanding of 'nationality' to the doctrine of active nationality legislative jurisdiction, it would mean that jurisdiction does not extend to members of organised armed groups, because they should not be considered 'nationals' of the state against whom they are fighting. After all, being a member of an OAG involved in a non-international armed conflict against the state is the quintessential expression of a lack of allegiance to that state.

Turning to the doctrine of indirect horizontal effect in the field of HRL, there is a resembling legal defect. While that legal defect does not emanate from a specific concept of 'nationality' as in the case of the doctrine of legislative jurisdiction, it flows from the potential legal consequences of the existence of an OAGs on a state's territory for that state's obligation to protect the human rights of individuals from acts of an OAG. The starting point here is that HRL applies, as a rule, in the territory

---

12   Sivakumaran (n 6 above) 381, emphasis added. Sivakumaran further recounts the opinion expressed by the Greek delegate at the Diplomatic Conference of 1974-1977 that also ties the binding nature of international humanitarian law on organised armed groups to the fact that their members 'were obviously nationals of some State, and were thereby bound by the obligations undertaken by the latter', id.

13   See ICTY *The Prosecutor v Tadić* Appeals Chamber Decision (15 July 1999) para 166.

of the state bound by the respective treaty or customary rule of human rights. However, parts of that state's territory may find itself under the control of an organised armed group in the course of a non-international armed conflict. While evidence exists to suggest that the state retains, as a rule, its obligation to protect individuals from such groups, the obligation is temporarily inoperative in such a scenario of a lack of territorial control on behalf of the state.[14] This is namely the case if, to the extent, and for such time that, such lack of territorial control meets the criteria for invoking force majeure as a ground precluding the wrongfulness of breaching its human rights obligations under the law of state responsibility.[15] In other words, if an OAG exercises such territorial control, the indirect effect of a state's human rights obligations is dormant as a matter of law. For as long as such a situation continues, the basis to construe the binding nature of human rights on OAGs via the state is unavailable.

In sum, in relation to both LoAC and HRL, the construction of their binding effect via the state fails to be entirely convincing. Indeed, that construction suffers from a number of important defects.

4   Bindingness through individual

A second way in which the binding nature of LoAC and HRL is construed is to rely on the fact that both bodies of law are binding upon the individual. Surely, as far as the LoAC is concerned, the very existence of the notion of war crimes – that is serious violations of the *LoAC* that entail the indvidual criminal responsibility of the perpetrator – epitomises that the LoAC is binding the individual directly as a matter of international law. Similarly, the fact that individuals, including individual members of OAGs,[16] can be punished for genocide and crimes against humanity – that is serious violations of *HRL* that are either committed in the context of a widepsread or systematic attack against a civilian population, or with the

---

14   See eg ECtHR, for eg *Ilascu and others v Moldova and Russia* App no 48787/99 EctHR (8 July 2004) paras 312, 330. Note, however, that the Court nevertheless held (para 331) that the positive obligation under art 1 of the European Convention to take the diplomatic, economic, judicial or other measures *that are in a State Party's power* and in accordance with international law to secure to individuals the rights guaranteed by the Convention.

15   Cf art 23 of the articles on Responsibility of States for Internationally Wrongful Acts (2001) UNGA Resolution 56/83 (12 December 2001) and corrected by document A/56/49 (Vol I)/Corr.4., which defines *force majeure* as 'the occurrence of an irresistible force or of an unforeseen event, beyond the control of the State, making it materially impossible in the circumstances to perform the obligation', and excludes the plea of *force majeure* if 'the situation of *force majeure* is due, either alone or in combination with other factors, to the conduct of the State invoking it; or the State has assumed the risk of that situation occurring'.

16   See eg ICTY *Prosecutor v Tadić* IT-94-1 Trial Chamber (7 May 1997) para 654; ICTY *Prosecutor v Kupreskic et al* IT-95-16 Trial Chamber (14 January 2000) para 551.

specific genocidal intent to destroy an ethnic, racial, religious or national group – presuppose that HRL is binding upon individuals.

At first sight, this way of construing the binding nature has an inherent appeal to it. It appears only logical that the body of secondary norms pertaining to individual criminal responsibility for war crimes, genocide and crimes against humanity is based on primary norms of LoAC and HRL that are binding upon the individual. At first sight it appears equally logic that such obligations of individuals under LoAC and HRL are transported into OAGs that are made up by these individuals.

Yet, both of these analytical steps are open to objection. While it is of course true that secondary norms presuppose the existence and binding nature of primary norms, the lack of the latter cannot be compensated by the former. To construe the binding nature of LoAC and HRL by relying on individual criminal responsibility amounts to the proverbial putting the cart before the horse. Indeed, it is somewhat discomforting that those courts and tribunals that have produced case law which addresses the criminal responsibility of members of OAGs have to a large extent shied away from addressing this issue. Admittedly, this may be less objectionable in the realm of the LoAC, where there is wide agreement that the law applies to members of OAGs. But it is undoubtedly problematic in the area of HRL whose applicability to OAGs and their individual members is shrouded in uncertainty.

A second objection is that the body of secondary norms governing war crimes, genocide and crimes against humanity only represent a fraction of the LoAC and HRL in the realm of primary norms. As is well known, not every violation of the LoAC entails individual criminal responsibility and amounts to a war crime under international law; nor does any violation of human rights amount to a crime against humanity or genocide. To construe the binding nature of LoAC and HRL on OAGs through the secondary norms of individual criminal responsibility would hence effectively mean that one would lose a plethora of norms in both fields.

Thirdly, to construe the binding nature of LoAC and HRL on OAGs via the individual fails to account for the collective dimension of OAGs. OAGs are not simply the mere sum of their individual members. Rather, OAGs (similar to states parties to an armed conflict) are identifiable entities, with political objectives (broadly conceived), which they pursue by violent means. They possess an organised military force and an authority responsible for its acts,[17] while the individual member concerned

---

17 Cf J Pictet (ed) *Commentary to the First Geneva Convention for the Amelioration of the Condition of the Wounded and the Sick in Armed Forces in the Field* (1952) 49, referring to the two criteria of possessing an organised military force and an authority responsible for its acts amongst several others, which can serve to indicate the existence of a non-international armed conflict in the sense of common article 3. For an elaboration of

acts on behalf of an OAG. Indeed, it is the collective nature of political violence and the organisation of a group of individuals engaged in such violence, which elevates a given situation to an armed conflict. Accordingly, the LoAC clearly distinguishes between individuals and OAGs as norm-addressees; the two are not the same. If we were to make a case for the applicability of HRL to OAGs, it is submitted that we should pursue the same route and distinguish between individuals and OAGs as collective entities. This is not the least so because it is hard, if not outright impossible, to make sense of some obligations under the LoAC and HRL, which presuppose the existence of a collective entity that alone is capable to implement and comply with these obligations. The due process guarantees in LoAC and HRL, for instance, presuppose that parties to an armed conflict (including OAGs) install judicial mechanisms, which satisfy the mentioned requirements. To do so is not the matter of individual members, but of the OAG as a whole.

In the light of the foregoing, it is not convincing to construe the binding force of the LoAC and HRL on OAGs by reference to its binding force on individuals.

5   Bindingness due to the exercise of *de facto* governmental functions

A third way of construing the binding nature of LoAC and HRL on OAGs is to tie it to the exercise of *de facto* governmental functions by such groups. In essence, this construction holds that if OAGs behave as if they were states, they should also be subject to the same rights and obligations under LoAC and HRL as states.

Such an approach certainly shifts the focus away from the binding force of LoAC and HRL on the individual to the collective entity of the OAG. To construe the binding force because of the exercise of *de facto* governmental functions also takes an important step towards understanding OAGs as autonomous actors. As such, the argument does not suffer from the same defects as the explanations examined previously.

At the same time, it is readily apparent that the argument is limited to only a certain type of OAG, namely to those that exercise relatively stable control over part of a state's territory and/or the control over persons, and possess organs which replace those of the state in the exercise of public power. However, as previously noted, such quasi-states and *de facto* regimes represent only a fraction of the entire spectrum of OAGs. Indeed, it would seem that not many of those OAGs that participate in today's non-international armed conflicts reach that threshold. When that

the required degree of organisation, see *Boskoski and Tarculovski* (n 3 above) paras 194-205.

threshold is not reached, the *de facto* governmental functions-argument fails to explain why OAGs are bound by LoAC and HRL.[18]

Such an outcome is perhaps less problematic in the realm of HRL as it is first and foremost designed to regulate the exercise of public power and hence befits much better a situation in which a given actor does exercise such powers. In contrast, to limit the binding nature of the LoAC to only a certain type of OAG clearly contradicts what the law suggests, namely that *all* OAGs are bound by the LoAC. Indeed, nothing in the law as it currently stands suggests that LoAC obligations of OAGs have to be approached in a more differentiated and contextual manner in a way that ties the extent of such obligations and their actual meaning to the OAG at hand. Quite to the contrary, the rudimentary differentiation between OAGs that satisfy the requirements stipulated under the 1977 Second Additional Protocol to the Geneva Conventions to 'exercise such control over part of [a High Contracting Party to the Protocol] as to enable [the OAG] to carry out sustained and concerted military operations and to implement [the Second Additional Protocol]'[19] and other OAGs seems to have gradually been abandoned. Article 8(2)(c)-(f) of the ICC Statute pertaining to war crimes in non-international armed conflicts epitomises this development. The provision sets forth 16 such war crimes, some of which find their bases in common article 3 (article 8(2)(c)), while others stem from primary norms that have been stipulated in the Second Additional Protocol, in addition to some that are derived from neither of these two treaty bases. Yet, none of these war crime provisions suggests a distinction between different types of OAGs.[20] Likewise, the ICRC Customary International Humanitarian Law Study does not distinguish

---

18 In this vein also Zegveld (n 9 above) 15.
19 Cf art 1(1) AP II.
20 Cf art 8(2)(c)-(f) ICC Statute. For the argument that the war crimes in non-international armed conflicts in art 8(2) of the ICC Statute are all subject to an identical minimum threshold of a non-international armed conflict under common article 3, see A Cullen 'The definition of non-international armed conflict in the Rome Statute of the International Criminal Court: An analysis of the threshold of application contained in article 8(2)(f)' (2007) 12 *J Conflict Security Law* 419. For the contrary view, holding that art 8 (2)(c) and (2)(e) establish different thresholds, see L Condorelli 'War crimes and internal armed conflicts in the Statute of the International Criminal Court' in M Politi & G Nesi (eds) *The Rome Statute of the International Criminal Court* (2001) 107, 112-113. The latter view is informed by the distinction between 'an armed conflict not of an international character' referred to in art 8 (2)(c) and 'protracted armed conflict between governmental authorities and organized armed groups or between such groups' referred to in art 8(2)(f). According to the ICC Trial Chamber, whatever the significance of this distinction, it does not imply a distinction between different types of OAGs: 'Article 8(2)(f) of the Statute only requires the existence of a "protracted" conflict between "organised armed groups". It does not include the requirement in Additional Protocol II that the armed groups need to "exercise such control over a part of [the] territory as to enable them to carry out sustained and concerted military operations" ... Furthermore, article 8(2)(f) does not incorporate the requirement that the organised armed groups were "under responsible command", as set out in article 1(1) of Additional Protocol II. Instead, the "organized armed groups" must have a sufficient degree of organisation, in order to enable them to carry out protracted armed violence'. *Prosecutor v Lubanga* Case No ICC-01/04-01/06 ICC Trial Judgment (14 March 2012) para 536 (footnotes omitted).

between different thresholds for non-international armed conflicts or types of OAGs in stipulating those rules that, in its opinion, apply in such armed conflicts. In other words, notwithstanding the potential value in differentiating *de lege ferenda* between different types of OAGs and in tailoring the extent of LoAC obligations to the actual capacity of a given OAG to comply with the imposed obligations,[21] the trend in the *lex lata* seems to point in the opposite direction.

The argument to derive LoAC obligations from the fact that a given OAG exercises *de facto* governmental functions would run counter to such a trend of consolidation, which suggests that *all* OAGs are subject to *all* rules of the law of non-international armed conflict. Instead, the argument suggests that an OAG either exercises *de facto* powers and is hence bound by LoAC and HRL in its entirety, or an OAG lacks such powers, in case of which it is not bound by either body of law.

6   Bindingness as a matter of customary international law because of international legal personality

Let us then turn to a fourth argument that is advanced to make the case for the bindingness of LoAC and HRL on OAGs: the argument that OAGs are bound by customary international humanitarian and HRL because of the limited international legal personality that they possess.

The main strength of this argument is that it does recognise OAGs as actors in their own right and does not reason via the state or, for that matter, via individual members of OAGs. At the same time, it needs to be acknowledged that OAGs remain excluded from the process of customary law formation. This is confirmed in the ICRC Customary Law Study[22] and it holds *a fortiori* true for the formation of customary HRL. Put differently, while the argument recognises OAGs as actors in their own right on the level of norm application, OAGs are not considered such actors on the level of norm creation.

Another persistent problem of the argument is that of the circularity of construing the binding nature of customary law on the basis of international legal personality, although that circularity is by no means limited to the fields of the LoAC and HRL. The circularity results from the

---

21   M Sassoli 'Introducing a sliding-scale of obligations to address the fundamental inequality between armed groups and states?' (2011) 93 *International Review of the Red Cross* 426.

22   While Henckaerts & Doswald-Beck (n 2 above) xxxvi, include practice of non-state OAGs, such practice is listed as 'other practice' (rather than state practice as one of the two constitute elements of customary international law), because the legal significance of such practice is unclear.

derivation of international legal personality from the fact that a given entity bears rights and/or obligations under international law,[23] while the question whether and to what extent such rights and obligations exist is conditioned by the international legal personality of the entity concerned. However, besides this logical defect that bugs international law more broadly, there are other more tangible problems, which the argument based on customary law entails.

In the realm of the LoAC, the argument fails to account for the binding nature of treaty law. Customary law of non-international armed conflict is not co-extensive to conventional law. The former lags behind the latter in certain respects.[24] To the extent that treaty law reaches beyond customary international law, the explanation based on international legal personality fails to account for the purported binding nature of conventional rules of the law of non-international armed conflicts vis-a-vis OAGs.

More fundamentally problematic, however, is the argument in the area of general HRL, when considering the very basis of the purported customary nature of human rights obligations of OAGs. By and large, that customary claim is based on the practice of the Security Council and some human rights bodies, such as the Human Rights Council and the Special Rapporteurs, to call upon parties to armed conflicts to respect IHL and HRL, or to document and denounce violations of the two bodies of law of both states and OAGs.[25] Yet, it would seem doubtful whether that practice is widespread, uniform and consistent enough to have crystallised into a

23 *Reparation for Injuries Suffered in the Service of the United Nations* Advisory Opinion, ICJ Reports (1949) 174, 178.
24 An example is the obligation to record the placement of landmines as envisaged in Amended Protocol II to the Convention on Prohibitions or Restrictions on the Use of Certain Conventional Weapons Which May be Deemed to be Excessively Injurious or to Have Indiscriminate Effects (CCW), Geneva (10 October 1980) art 1(2) and art 9, if compared to customary international humanitarian law as identified by the ICRC, see Henckaerts & Doswald-Beck (n 2 above) Rule 82 and Summary of the Rule, 284-285.
25 For the Security Council, see eg SC Res 2170 (15 August 2014) on threats to international peace and security caused by terrorist acts, which is ripe of references to human rights when addressing the acts of the Islamic State in Iraq and the Levant (ISIL) and other OAGs, see eg paras 1-3; SC Res. 1814 [15 May 2008] on the situation in Somalia, para 16, addressed to 'all parties in Somalia'; SC Res 1778 (25 September 2007) on the situation in Chad, the Central African Republic and the subregion, Preamble ('activities of armed groups and other attacks in eastern Chad, the north-eastern Central African Republic and western Sudan which threaten the security of the civilian population, the conduct of humanitarian operations in those areas and the stability of those countries, and which result in serious violations of human rights and international humanitarian law'). See also Human Rights Council, 22nd Special Session, Resolution S-22/1 (1 September 2014) 'The human rights situation in Iraq in the light of abuses committed by the so-called Islamic State in Iraq and the Levant and associated groups' UN Doc A/HRC/RES/S-22/1; Commission on Human Rights, UN Doc E/CN.4/2005/3 [7 May 2004] CHR, 61st Session, Item 4, Situation of Human Rights in the Darfur Region of the Sudan, where the Human Rights Commission stated that '[t]he rebel forces also appear to violate human rights and humanitarian law'; UN Doc E/CN.4/2006/53/Add.5 [27 March 2006] 'Report of the Special Rapporteur, Philip Alston, Addendum, 'Mission to Sri Lanka' (28 November to 6 December 2005) especially paras 24-27 and accompanying

norm of customary international law. For one, states do not seem to share the view of the mentioned bodies that HRL is binding upon OAGs. What is more, even the practice amongst human rights and other bodies is inconsistent. Some of them have expressly rejected the idea that HRL is binding upon OAGs;[26] others are more ambivalent. The Security Council, for instance, adopts at times the difference between violations of human rights – reserved to states – and 'human rights abuses'[27] that are committed by OAGs. While the significance, if any, of that linguistic distinction is unclear, it would seem to indicate an ambivalent attitude towards the idea that OAGs are bound by HRL in the same way as states are. Even if one were to dismiss the linguistic distinction as irrelevant, the lack of consistency between the Security Council and certain human rights bodies, on the one hand, and of other human rights bodies and states on the other hand, puts the conclusion that OAGs are generally bound by human rights as a matter of customary international law very much into doubt.

7   Bindingness because of consent by OAG

The last argument that is advanced in order to construe the binding effect of LoAC and HRL on OAGs is that the group concerned consents. In stark contrast to all of the aforementioned explanations, a consent-based conceptualisation stands and falls with the will of OAGs. Indeed, in the field of LoAC, common article 3 encourages the parties to a non-international armed conflict to conclude 'special agreements' through which all or part of the other provisions of the Geneva Conventions are brought into force. The provision thereby already contemplates that OAGs can bind themselves to rules of LoAC. In addition, it is by no means exceptional that OAGs unilaterally declare their acceptance of rules of the LoAC, for instance in the form of 'Deeds of Commitment' made under the auspices of Geneva Call.[28] Furthermore, national liberation movements – a distinct sub-species of OAGs that have gained express recognition and regulation in the First Additional Protocol[29] – only become subject to the rules of the First Additional Protocol if they express their consent to be

---

footnotes. For further relevant resolutions of the Security Council and the General Assembly pertaining to violations of human rights (as well as humanitarian law) committed in the Former Yugoslavia, Afghanistan, The Sudan, Sierra Leone, Ivory Coast, The Congo, Angola, Liberia and Somalia, and further discussion, see C Tomuschat 'The Applicability of Human Rights Law to Insurgent Movements' in H Fischer et al (eds) *Krisensicherung und Humanitärer Schutz – Crisis management and humanitarian protection: Festschrift für Dieter Fleck* (2004) 577-585.

26   For relevant examples, see Zegveld (n 9 above) 39-46.
27   See eg SC Res 2170 (n 25 above).
28   See generally, http://www.genevacall.org/ (accessed 2 December 2014) and for specific such Deeds and OAGs: http://www.genevacall.org/resources/documents/ (accessed 2 December 2014).
29   Cf art 1(4) of AP I.

bound.[30] While less widespread and less firmly rooted in the law, OAGs at times also consent expressly to HRL.[31]

On the one hand, a consent-based construction of the binding effect of LoAC and HRL brings with it a number of serious limitations. The first, and most obvious, limitation is that, taken to its logical conclusion, it would mean that no rule of the LoAC or HRL applies to an OAG that has failed to accept to be bound by the rule in question. That consequence is particularly rampant in the field of human rights, where consent of OAGs is comparatively sporadic.

In addition, on a very practical level, it may at times be difficult to establish who is competent to express the consent to be bound of a given OAG.

A further consequence of requiring consent by an OAG for it to be bound by LoAC and HRL is that it raises the issue of reciprocity and equality of belligerent parties before the law. For, if consent of the OAG is required, the question looms large whether the law applicable in a given non-international armed conflict is limited to those rules that all parties have accepted.[32] Or, alternatively, if the relationship between states and OAGs (or between several OAGs) has to be conceptualised in a way so that reciprocity in the realm of applicability is not required as a matter of law, and that the belligerent parties can be unequal before the law. The aspects of reciprocity and equality of belligerents before the law brings to the fore one of the fundamental differences between LoAC and HRL, as reciprocity in the realm of applicability and equality of belligerents are generally considered to be associated with the LoAC,[33] rather than with HRL.[34] When conceptualising consent as a basis for the binding nature of

---

30   Cf art 96(3) AP I.
31   See eg some peace agreements and some Deeds of Commitment under Geneva Call, such as the April 2012 Deed of Commitment by the JEM (Sudan), see http://www.genevacall.org/wp-content/uploads/dlm_uploads/2013/12/jem.pdf (accessed 2 December 2014). For unilateral declarations and agreements on human rights law, see also S Sivakumaran *The law of non-international armed conflicts* (2012) 123, 131 (with further references).
32   Cf *mutatis mutandis* common article 2 to the Four 1949 Geneva Conventions, according to which the conventions apply to all cases of declared war or of any other armed conflict which may arise 'between two or more of the High Contracting Parties'. Cf also art 1(3) of AP I.
33   See eg S Watts 'Reciprocity and the law of war' (2009) 50 *Harvard International Law Journal* 365. For a recent debate on the notion of belligerent equality, see Sassoli (n 21 above) and Y Shany 'A rebuttal to Marco Sassoli' (2011) 93 *International Review of the Red Cross* 432. It should be noted, however, that this reciprocity and equality chiefly pertains to the question whether the law is applicable, not with the question whether parties to an armed conflict are obliged to *comply* with applicable law. As far as compliance is concerned, reciprocity is not required in the LoAC, cf Rule 140 Henckaerts & Doswald-Beck (n 2 above). For the limited exception concerning belligerent reprisals, see Rules 145-148.
34   See S Sivakumaran (n 31 above) 95. For extensive analysis of the role of reciprocity in both fields of law, see R Provost *International human rights and humanitarian law* (2002) 121-238.

LoAC and HRL vis-à-vis OAGs, one would hence have to determine whether LoAC moves into the direction of HRL and abandons the notions of reciprocity and belligerent equality before the law, whether HRL moves into the direction of LoAC and incorporates these notions, or, indeed, whether the two bodies of law should be approached differently, leaving intact their distinct approaches regarding the notions of reciprocity and belligerent equality before the law. The answer to this question can reasonably be expected to have a bearing also on the degree of compliance with LoAC and HRL, since reciprocity and belligerent equality before the law are regularly advanced as important factors that induce compliance.[35]

At the same time, a consent-based approach to the applicability of LoAC and HRL can be reasonably expected to in and of itself generate a greater pull of compliance than the other constructions that impose obligations on OAGs against or irrespective of their will.[36] By taking ownership of the process of acceptance, the norms of LoAC and HRL can be endowed with a greater degree of legitimacy from the perspective of the OAG in question. That legitimacy in turn makes a process of norm-internalisation into the practice of an OAG more likely.[37] Furthermore, to allow an OAG to consent or to withhold consent to a given rule of the LoAC or HRL also bears the potential of identifying those rules that the OAG considers to be realistic for it.[38] Such a process of norm selection bears the potential of avoiding a normative overreach which undermines compliance because of unrealistic legal demands.

8   Conclusion

The lack of an entirely convincing and coherent explanation why and whether LoAC or HRL bind OAGs confirms the continued state of perplexity of international law in the face of non-state actors generally and OAGs more specifically. Admittedly, that is, of course, far from a revolutionary insight. International law remains deeply engrained in a state-centric paradigm. And yet, it seems hard to accept such an unsatisfactory situation, not because it may bug the academic in his or her quest for coherence, logic and systematicity. Rather, the lack of a convincing argument undermines the credibility and effectiveness of the law. As long as international law fails to convincingly argue why LoAC and HRL are binding OAGs, the potential of these two bodies of law is

---

35   Cf L Moir *The law of internal armed conflict* (2002) 86, 107-108; Provost, ibid, 236.
36   See further, M Sassòli 'Taking armed groups seriously: Ways to improve their compliance with international humanitarian law' (2010) 1 *International Humanitarian Legal Studies* 5 29-32.
37   For the parallel argument that legitimacy of a norm furthers its compliance by states, see in particular, T Franck 'Legitimacy in the international system' (1988) 82 *American Journal of International Law* 705 709-710; T Franck *The power of legitimacy among nations* (1990) 303; and T Franck *Fairness in international law and institutions* (1995) 500, especially 25-46.
38   In this vein, see Sassòli (n 36 above) 20-21.

bound not to be fully realised. The consequence of that weakness is born by those that the two bodies of law seek to protect and those that the two bodies of law seek to guide when they act. Surely, it would be outright naïve to expect that the conceptual deficiency be remedied in the foreseeable future. However, realising this deficiency should not be used as a pretext to abandon the idea of LoAC and HRL as restraints on the actions of OAGs. Instead, it allows us to manage our expectations and to develop a sense of realism.

PART B: Situational Perspectives on Human Rights and International Humanitarian Law

4

International Military Operations: Dealing with Detainees

Bruce 'Ossie' Oswald*

1 Introduction

This chapter explores the application of both international humanitarian law (IHL) and international human rights law (IHRL) when taking and handling detainees. The focus is on practical matters with the aim of explaining the interplay between those legal regimes as regards when military forces detain persons in international military operations[1] that are classified as non-international armed[2] and peace operations.[3] To that end, the chapter is divided into six parts and has an annex. Part 1 is the introduction. Part 2 describes the phases of detention in civilian operations and briefly explains some of the practical issues that arise during those phases. Part 3 outlines the legal regimes that apply to detention. Part 4 focuses on the interplay between IHL and IHRL by identifying the approaches taken by some states, international organisations and

*   Ossie is an Associate Professor at Melbourne Law School. He has served on military operations in Rwanda, East Timor (as it was then), Iraq and Afghanistan. In each of those operations he was involved with the law and policy concerning the taking and handling of detainees. An earlier draft of this paper was written while Ossie was a Jennings Randolph Senior Fellow at the United States Institute of Peace in 2012-2013. Ossie would like to acknowledge the editors and Gus Waschefort for their comments concerning this paper; and Ms Natasha Robbins for her editorial assistance. Ossie remains grateful to Ms Liz Saltnes for her ongoing support.

1   The term 'international military operations' refers to those operations that are conducted by states outside their territory and on the territory of another state.

2   The term 'non-international armed conflicts' refers to those armed conflicts that are protracted between the government of the state in which the armed conflict is occurring and the organised armed groups fighting with that government or between themselves. Non-international armed conflicts also include situations where international forces engage in armed conflict with the consent of the host state against non-state armed actors or organised armed groups.

3   The term 'peace operations' refers to those operations that are conducted to ensure, or maintain, international peace and security. Such operations might include non-international armed conflicts as well. This chapter does not deal with international armed conflict because the legal regime concerning those conflicts is relatively settled and uncontroversial for most states.

tribunals. Part 5 explains how the interplay impacts on the treatment of detainees by using both the law and examples of recent or extant practice. Part six is the conclusion.

Before addressing the substantive aspects of the interplay of IHL and IHRL in non-international armed conflicts and peace operations it is important to note that this chapter does not address detention in international armed conflicts, including occupation. The primary reason for not addressing international armed conflicts is because the interplay between IHL and IHRL in international armed conflicts is not as contentious as the interplay of those regimes in non-international armed conflicts and peace operations. It is generally accepted that IHL is the primary legal regime or *lex specialis* that determines the treatment of prisoners of war (PWs)[4] and internees in international armed conflicts.[5] The role of IHRL, such as the International Covenant on Civil and Political Rights (ICCPR), complements IHL and where there is a conflict between the two regimes with regard to a specific situation, IHL is the *lex specialis* is to be applied.[6] The International Committee of the Red Cross (ICRC) in October 2011, specifically referring to detention in international armed conflicts made a similar point by stating: 'that the interplay of IHL and human rights rules governing procedural safeguards in internment in IAC [international armed conflict] must be resolved by reference to the *lex specialis*, that is the relevant provisions of IHL that were specifically designed for it.'[7]

2   The context

The term 'detention' as used in this chapter refers to an international military force depriving a person of their liberty for reasons related to an

4   See Geneva Convention Relative to the Treatment of Prisoners of War, opened for signature 12 August 1949, 75 UNTS 135 (entered into force 21 October 1950) (GC III); and Protocol Additional to the Geneva Conventions of 12 August 1949, and Relating to the Protection of Victims of International Armed Conflicts, opened for signature 8 June 1977, 1125 UNTS 3 (entered into force 7 December 1979) (AP I) for determining who is a PW and the rights and duties of PWs and Detaining Powers.
5   See Geneva Convention Relative to the Protection of Civilian Persons in Time of War, opened for signature 12 August 1949, 75 UNTS 135 (entered into force 21 October 1950) (GC IV); AP I (n 4 above) for determining the basis for internment and the treatment of internees.
6   See eg *Legality of the Threat or Use of Force of Nuclear Weapons* ICJ Reports (8 July 1996) 226 para 25. See also P Alston 'Report of the Special Rapporteur on extrajudicial killing, summary or arbitrary executions: Study on targeted killings' A/HRC/14/24 Add. 6 (28 May 2010) para 29.
7   International Committee of the Red Cross 'International Humanitarian Law and the Challenges to Contemporary Armed Conflicts' prepared for the 31st International Conference of the Red Cross and Red Crescent, 31IC/11/5.1.2 (28 November-1 December 2011) 17.

international military operation.[8] The deprivation of liberty might be distinguished from situations where an individual's liberty is restricted such as when the individual is being searched, questioned or stopped at a road block.

Civilians are most likely to be detained when military forces are exercising powers of self-defence, undertaking military operations in the context of an armed conflict, or are authorised to use force to achieve their mandate or mission. When military forces detain they might do so as a part of a coalition under the command and control of a state or under command of an international organisation – such as the African Union, the United Nations (UN) or the North Atlantic Treaty Organisation (NATO).

The two main forms of detention that occur are the detention of a civilian suspected of, or found committing, a serious offence (criminal detainees); or the detention of a civilian believed to be a serious threat to the security of the mission (security detainees). Both criminal and security detainees can be taken during armed conflict and in peace operations.[9] Sometimes detention will be unplanned because members of a military force might detain a civilian during the course of their duties (such as patrolling); and at other times detention will be planned in the sense that the mission of the unit is to detain – as will be the case when military members set out to capture a high-value target. Regardless of whether a detainee is criminal or a security detainee, or the type of operation which led to their detention there are generally four phases of detention: (1) point of capture; (2) transfer; (3) ongoing detention; and (4) handover and monitoring.[10] In some peace operations, such as those conducted by the UN, the general practice of UN forces is to not hold detainees in ongoing detention, but to hand them over as soon as possible to the host state.

At the 'point of capture' a civilian is taken into custody either because the detaining authority believes that the civilian is a suspected criminal or a security threat. Depending on the circumstances, military personnel might use force, such as applying a restraint to the detainee's hands, to

---

8   See The Copenhagen Process on the Handling of Detainees in International Military Operations: Principles and Guidelines (CPPG) principle 1. Therefore this chapter is not concerned with the detention of military persons during armed conflict (ie, prisoners of war), detention of civilians by civilian police, or detention carried out by non-state armed actors.

9   For a more detailed discussion of, for eg, the taking of security detainees during peace operations see B Oswald 'The INTERFET Detainee Management Unit in East Timor' (2000) 3 *Yearbook of International Humanitarian Law* 347; and B Oswald 'Detention by United Nations Peacekeepers: Searching for definition and classification' (2011) 15 *Journal of International Peacekeeping* 119.

10 Not all detainees will go through all four phases of detention because, for example, a detainee might be released at the end of the first phase, or they might be handed over to the host state immediately after the first phase or even before reaching the third phase. These phases are based on the author's experience of taking and handling detainees on a range of military operations including those operations conducted by UN forces and 'coalitions of the willing'.

control the detainee. The detainee might also be questioned about, for example, their identity or the identity of others, searched, told the reasons for their detention, and what is going to happen next. If the detainee has been injured, and depending on the severity of the injury, the detainee might have to be provided with medical assistance. Where possible, the capturing unit might also inform the detainee's family or some other person from the community why the detainee has been captured and where the detainee is being taken to. The detainee's identity, the reasons for detention, and details of any contraband removed from the detainee or property found on the detainee will often be recorded.[11] This phase might end with the detainee being released (because the detaining force has no reason to hold the individual in custody) or it might continue into phase two – the transfer of the detainee. The first review concerning the release or transfer of the detainee will sometimes be carried out at the point of capture phase.

The 'transfer of the detainee' phase (phase two) is where the capturing unit passes the detainee to another unit or entity within the coalition force.[12] Transfer usually occurs to facilitate the movement of the detainee from the point of capture to a safe area where the detainee will be controlled by another unit. During the transfer phase the detainee remains in the control of the detaining force or coalition forces with whom the detaining force is engaged in operations with. The detainee might be further questioned and searched, and a more detailed record will be made concerning the detainee's background and the reasons for their detention. If required, the detainee will also be given further medical assistance. At this stage a range of issues regarding the conditions of detention are likely to arise. These include: the provision of adequate food, water and clothing; appropriate medical care; the sanitary conditions of the facility in which the detainee is held; and the detainee's access to the outside world including access to family members and organisations that are in a position to assist in protecting the rights of detainees (such as the ICRC). The transfer phase ends if the detainee is released or moved to a detention facility for ongoing detention. The transfer phase is another opportunity for the detaining authority to review whether ongoing detention is merited. At this stage it is also likely that the detainee's status as a criminal or security detainee will again be evaluated.

---

11   The United States Army describes the technique, or steps, expected of their soldiers at the point of capture as the '5 Ss and T': search, silence, segregate, safeguard, speed to safe area/rear and tag. For more details of what each step consists of see International Law and Operations Law Department 'Operations Law Handbook' (2012) 168.
12   It is sometimes the case that the terms 'transfer' and 'handover' are used interchangeably.

Phase three, or the 'ongoing detention phase', is where a detainee is held in custody for a period of time amounting to more than a few days.[13] Ongoing detention is most often undertaken in a more secure detention facility, which is usually subject to greater controls. Typically, a detainee will again be questioned; and detailed records will be made as to reasons for detention, the property in the possession of, or confiscated from the detainee, and the detainee's health. All detainees are likely to be subject to further medical examinations in this phase. Depending on the period for which the detainee is held, they will usually be given access to the ICRC and be permitted to receive visits, or establish and maintain contact with their families and sometimes the wider community. The ongoing detention phase is also when the detainee will most frequently have their ongoing detention reviewed by the detaining authority and another assessment might be made about their status. If ongoing detention is not warranted the detainee must be released. Apart from the conditions of detention, issues mentioned in the context of phase two above, a key matter that arises in phase three is the review of the detainee's status so as to ensure that the ongoing detention of the detainee is valid, lawful and in no way arbitrary. If the detainee is not released the detaining authority might handover the detainee to the custody of the host state or another entity that is not a part of the coalition force, such as the International Criminal Court (ICC).

The 'handover' phase is where the detaining authority ceases having direct or effective control over the detainee. Typically the physical handover of the detainee will be accompanied by a handover of all the relevant documentation justifying the detention, relevant medical documents, and notifications to the ICRC and the detainee's family. Traditionally, the responsibilities of the coalition force or detaining unit that had captured the detainee end once a detainee has been handed over. However, more recently, there has been considerable debate concerning the obligations of states and the rights of detainees during the handover phase and post-handover.[14]

A number of concerns arise in each of the above phases. These include whether the civilian has been detained lawfully; whether he or she is a security or a criminal detainee; the conditions of detention; which conditions must be met concerning the release, transfer, handover or ongoing detention of the detainee; standards of accountability against which detaining authorities will be held; and the rights that are, or should be, available to a detainee or their family if their rights have been abused. The ICRC has pointed out that, for example, 'lack of knowledge of the reasons for internment or how long it will last is one of the main causes for suffering for detained persons and their families, as well as the cause for

---

13   For the purposes of this chapter, ongoing detention refers to holding a detainee for more than 96 hours. For eg, ongoing detention in Afghanistan by ISAF forces was limited to 96 hours before the detainee had to be handed to Afghan authorities.
14   See the discussion below concerning handover in Part 5.2.

heightened tensions in many detention settings'.[15] In relation to handing over detainees, Amnesty International (AI) has argued that based on allegations of Afghan authorities abusing detainees handed to them by ISAF contributing states, those states must 'immediately declare a moratorium on any further ... [handovers] of detainees to the Afghan authorities'.[16] Human Rights First has noted that the detainees they interviewed had not been compensated for their wrongful detention, or for theft or damage to property.[17] In relation to handovers, two principal concerns arise. The first is the extent to which the detaining authority that is handing over the detainee continues to have responsibility for the detainee. Dealing with that issue includes considerations about ongoing access to the detainee, whether the original detaining authority might reclaim a detainee that has been handed over, and the extent to which the handing over authority can investigate any allegations made concerning the mistreatment of the detainee. The second issue is the extent to which the host state might refuse access to the detaining authority to visit or speak with the transferred detainee. Typically a detainee may be released once handed over or they might be held in ongoing custody.

These abovementioned concerns fit under the broader concern of ensuring there is an appropriate balance between detainees being treated humanely, with the competing need to ensure that military personnel are able to carry out their mission or mandate successfully. Put another way, humanitarian considerations 'in order to be realistic ... [must also take] into account military and political constraints'.[18] Each of these concerns is capable of being answered by law. The real question is: which law? It is to that question we now turn.

3 Applicable legal frameworks

There are three broad legal frameworks that apply to detention in military operations: international law; the law of the host state; and the law of the troop-contributing state. The legal regimes within international law that are relevant include IHL, IHRL, international criminal law (ICL),[19] and

---

15 International Committee of the Red Cross 'Strengthening legal protection for victims of armed conflict' prepared for the 31st International Conference of the Red Cross and Red Crescent, 31IC/11/5.1.1 (28 November-1 December 2011) 8 (31st ICRC Conference).
16 Amnesty International 'Afghanistan: Detainees transferred to torture: ISAF complicity?' ASA 11/011/2007 (13 November 2007) 36.
17 Human Rights First 'Detained and denied in Afghanistan: How to make US detention comply with the law' (May 2011) 21-22.
18 International Committee of the Red Cross *General Commentary on the Additional Protocols I and II of 8 June 1977, to the Geneva Conventions of 12 August 1949* (1987) xxxi (AP I Commentary).
19 In contemporary military operations the most relevant ICL treaty is the Rome Statute of the International Criminal Court (Rome Statute).

what one might describe in general terms as UN law.[20] The host state's domestic criminal law is likely to be relevant to detention in a number of ways. First, it is most likely to be the law that justifies the reasons for detaining a civilian on the grounds that they are suspected of, or have committed, a criminal offence. Second, the host state's criminal law process will determine the evidence that the military force will need to gather if they wish the detainee to be dealt with by the host state's law and order authorities. Third, the host state's laws might also govern the extent of accountability of the host state for the treatment of the detainee once the detainee is handed over to it. Fourth, the host state's laws might apply to the military force in the context of the powers that the military force has to deal with civilians in the host state or the extent to which the host state's laws will apply to the military force.[21] Of course in each of the above situations the host state's international law obligations in relation to IHL and IHRL will also come into play.

Depending on the troop-contributing nation's legal system, the reach of its law might be quite extensive in terms of its impact on its own personnel. Thus, military personnel might be subject to the extraterritorial application of their state's domestic criminal laws, military law, internal orders and directives, and instructions concerning a range of matters including their powers to take detainees, and their liabilities if they commit offences such as the mistreatment of detainees. In some cases the troop-contributing nation's international obligations, while not a part of its domestic law, might apply to its personnel as a matter of policy and, such policy might be translated into orders, directives and administrative instructions with which military personnel from that state must comply. The troop-contributing nation's international legal obligations in relation to IHL and IHRL will also come into play.

Where an international organisation is responsible for establishing and commanding a peace operation that organisation's international legal obligations, the legal obligations of states that agree to contribute troops to the operation, the host state's laws, and the internal legal framework of the organisation will impact on the norms applied to detainees taken during that operation. So, for example, in situations where a peace operation is established, and commanded and controlled by the UN: the Charter of the

---

20 For a more detailed discussion of UN law see the Chapter by Shraga in this book. Other normative frameworks that determine legal obligations, principles and standards concerning the taking and handling of detainees during military operations include international criminal law; the doctrines of state responsibility in international law; the law relating to privileges and immunities as stated in, for eg, status of forces agreements (SOFA); and privileges and immunities.

21 The extent of jurisdiction that host state law and order authorities will have over a military force conducting operations on the host nation's territory is most frequently governed by a SOFA entered into between the host nation and the troop – contributing nation or the host nation and the international organisation under whom the military forces are serving.

United Nations,[22] agreements entered into between the UN, the host nation; and agreements entered between the UN and the troop-contributing nations; legally binding IHL and IHRL norms; the doctrine of privileges and immunities; and any binding internal directives (such as the 'Secretary-General's bulletin: Observance by United Nation's forces of international humanitarian law')[23] will apply to the taking and handling of detainees.

Thus, when developing a detention policy for dealing with detainees the interplay between IHL and IHRL must be considered against the international legal obligations of the troop-contributing nation or international organisation conducting the operation, the troop-contributing state's domestic legal obligations, and the host state's legal obligations. However, as this chapter focuses only on the interplay between IHL and IHRL in relation to detention what follows is an outline of the specific treaty regimes or legal provisions that might apply either *de jure* or as a matter of policy to dealing with detainees.

3.1 The application of IHL[24]

In relation to detainees taken during non-international armed conflict where common article 3 applies the minimum IHL provisions which include the prohibitions against discrimination; murder, cruel treatment, torture, humiliating and degrading treatment; and fundamental judicial guarantees.[25] If the conflict is a non-international armed conflict to which Additional Protocol II (AP II)[26] applies there are more nuanced norms of humane treatment;[27] minimum standards of treatment for those whose liberty has been deprived;[28] and the prosecution and punishment of those accused of committing criminal offences[29] that come into play. Of particular note is the fact that AP II, article 4(3) makes special reference to the guarantees that are to be afforded to children. The AP II, article 5 developments include the distinction between those deprived of their

---

22　(26 June 1945) 59 Stat. 1031, TS No 993, 3 Bevans 1153 (UN Charter).
23　UN Secretary-General (UNSG) 'Secretary-General's bulletin: Observance by United Nations forces of international humanitarian law' ST/SGB/1999/13 (6 August 1999).
24　For further detail about the applicability of IHL to armed conflict and peace operations see the chapter by Zwaneburg in this book.
25　See common article 3(1)(a), (c) & (d) in Geneva Convention Relative to the Amelioration of the Condition of the Wounded and Sick in Armed Forces in the Field, opened for signature 12 August 1949, 75 UNTS 31 (entered into force 21 October 1950); Geneva Convention Relative to the Amelioration of the Condition of Wounded, Sick and Shipwrecked Members of Armed Forces at Sea, opened for signature 12 August 1949, 75 UNTS 85 (entered into force 21 October 1950); GC III (n 4 above); and GC IV (n 5 above).
26　Protocol Additional to the Geneva Conventions of 12 August 1949, and relating to the Protection of Victims of Non-International Armed Conflicts, opened for signature 8 June 1977, 1125 UNTS 609 (entered into force 7 December 1978) (AP II).
27　AP II (n 26 above) art 4.
28　AP II (n 26 above) art 5.
29　AP II (n 26 above) art 6.

liberty and those whose liberty has been restricted;[30] the rights of detainees to be medically examined;[31] the need to take into account the safety of detainees when they are released;[32] and providing detainees with safeguards concerning their health, safety and general well-being.[33] AP II, article 6 introduces due process protection for detainees found guilty of criminal offences, such as the right to be informed of the particulars of the offence,[34] the rights and means to mount a defence against the allegations,[35] and the presumption of innocence.[36] Therefore, taken as a whole, AP II adds further depth to the common article 3 protections afforded to detainees during all four phases of detention.

Even if not applicable as a matter of law to non-international armed conflict there are other IHL treaties that regulate international armed conflicts such as Geneva Conventions III and IV, and Additional Protocol I (AP I) that have much more extensive and developed provisions relevant to the treatment of detainees. Those provisions relate to equality before the law,[37] discipline in detention facilities,[38] access to the outside world,[39] accountability measures concerning investigating death or serious injuries,[40] release,[41] being informed of the reasons for detention,[42] and the protections that are to be afforded to detainees until they are released.[43] AP I, article 75 in particular, provides a number of rights for detainees. For example, article 75(3) requires the detaining authority to promptly inform any 'person arrested, detained or interned for reasons related to the armed conflict' the reason for those actions. Article 75(4) concerns those charged with criminal offences, and article 75(6) frames the protections given to those arrested, detained or interned as existing until their final release or repatriation. Article 75(5) concerns protecting the interests of women by separating their quarters from those of men and requiring that women whose liberty has been restricted to be supervised by women. As a matter of law there is no restriction to the provisions in GC III, IV and AP I being applied to non-international armed conflicts as a matter of policy.

30   AP II (n 26 above) art 5(3).
31   AP II (n 26 above) art 2(d).
32   AP II (n 26 above) art 4.
33   See eg AP II (n 26 above) arts 1(b), (c), (d), 2(c) & 2(e).
34   AP II (n 26 above) art 6 (2)(a).
35   As above.
36   AP II (n 26 above) art 2(e).
37   GC IV (n 5 above) art 80.
38   GC IV (n 5 above) art 100.
39   GC IV (n 5 above) arts 105-116.
40   GC IV (n 5 above) arts 129-131.
41   GC IV (n 5 above) art 132.
42   AP I (n 4 above) art 75(3).
43   AP I (n 4 above) art 75(6).

In its ongoing study entitled 'Customary International Humanitarian Law', the ICRC has identified a number of rules concerning fundamental guarantees[44] and the treatment of persons deprived of their liberty,[45] which they argue apply to both international and non-international armed conflicts. In relation to the rules that apply to fundamental guarantees the ICRC remarks that it is 'beyond the scope of ... [its] study to determine whether these guarantees apply equally outside armed conflict although collected practice appears to indicate that they do'.[46] It should also be noted that the ICRC has stated more recently that the relevant rules of customary law 'are by necessity formulated in general terms, and thus do not provide sufficient guidance to detaining authorities on how an adequate detention regime may be created and operated'.[47]

Moreover, the ICRC acknowledges there are at least five areas of 'specific humanitarian concerns related to the deprivation of liberty, some of which are not, or not sufficiently, addressed by'[48] IHL: conditions of detention, specific protection, procedural safeguards, ICRC access to persons deprived of their liberty, and transfers [specifically, handovers] of persons deprived of their liberty.[49] Furthermore, both common article 3 and AP II provisions concerning detention are limited to instances where detention occurs in the context of an armed conflict and therefore have very limited *de jure* application in other military operations that do not amount to armed conflict.

3.2   Application of IHRL[50]

Avoiding for the moment the debate about the *de jure* application of IHRL to military operations it is clear that there are a number of treaty and soft law norms that are relevant to the four phases of detention. Beginning with the Universal Declaration of Human Rights (UDHR),[51] it is now accepted that '[e]veryone has the right to life, liberty and security of person;[52] [n]o one shall be subjected to arbitrary arrest, detention or exile;'[53] that '[n]o one shall be subjected to torture, or to cruel, inhuman or degrading treatment or punishment;'[54] and '[e]veryone has the right to an effective remedy by the competent national tribunals for acts violating the

---

44   J-M Henckaerts & L Doswald-Beck (eds) *Customary international humanitarian law – Volume 1: Rules* (2005) ch 32.
45   Henckaerts & Doswald-Beck (n 44 above) ch 37.
46   Henckaerts & Doswald-Beck (n 44 above) 299.
47   31st ICRC Conference (n 15 above) 7.
48   As above.
49   31st ICRC Conference (n 15 above) 7-10.
50   For further detail about the applicability of IHRL to armed conflict and peace operations see the chapter by Zwaneburg in this book.
51   UN Doc A/RES/217A (III) (10 December 1948).
52   UDHR (n 51 above) art 3.
53   UDHR (n 51 above) art 9.
54   UDHR (n 51 above) art 5.

fundamental rights granted him by the constitution or by law'.[55] Article 11 of that Declaration provides for the rights of those charged with penal offences [that is, criminal offences] by encapsulating the presumption of innocence, guarantees necessary for mounting a defence, the requirement of the offence existing in law, and the requirement of penalties reflecting those that were applicable when the offence was committed.[56]

The fundamental protections dealt with in the UDHR have flowed to other international legal regimes as well. The International Covenant on Civil and Political Rights (ICCPR)[57] also deals with the prohibition of arbitrary and unlawful detention;[58] the prohibition regarding torture or cruel, inhuman or degrading treatment or punishment;[59] the rights of a person accused of committing a criminal offence;[60] and the requirement that all persons deprived of their liberty shall be treated humanely.[61] If a person has been detained or arrested unlawfully the ICCPR requires that they have an enforceable right to compensation.[62]

The Convention Against Torture and Other Cruel, Inhuman, or Degrading Treatment or Punishment (CAT)[63] has a number of provisions that relate to the treatment of detainees including the prohibition against torture,[64] cruel, inhuman and degrading treatment,[65] the prohibition against expelling, returning, surrendering or extraditing a person in situations where they might be tortured;[66] the requirement to carry out investigations that are prompt and impartial where there are reasonable grounds to believe that torture has been committed in any territory under that states jurisdiction;[67] and the need to ensure that a victim of torture 'obtains redress and has an enforceable right to fair and adequate compensation, including the means for as full rehabilitation as possible'.[68]

In situations where the International Convention for the Protection of All Persons from Enforced Disappearances (Enforced Disappearances Convention)[69] applies, the provisions relevant to dealing with detainees

---

55   UDHR (n 51 above) art 8.
56   UDHR (n 51 above) art 11.
57   Opened for signature 16 December 1966, 999 UNTS 171 (entered into force 26 March 1976).
58   ICCPR (n 57 above) art 9(1).
59   ICCPR (n 57 above) art 7.
60   ICCPR (n 57 above) art 14.
61   ICCPR (n 57 above) art 10.
62   ICCPR (n 57 above) art 9(5).
63   Opened for signature 10 December 1984, 1465 UNTS 85 (entered into force 26 June 1987).
64   CAT (n 63 above) art 2(1). Note that art 1 defines torture.
65   CAT (n 63 above) art 16.
66   CAT (n 63 above) art 3.
67   CAT (n 63 above) art 12.
68   CAT (n 63 above) art 14.
69   Opened for signature 20 December 2006, UN Doc A/RES/61/177 (2007) (entered into force 23 December 2010).

include the prohibition against holding anyone in secret detention;[70] the requirement to compile and maintain up-to-date details concerning the detainee;[71] the prohibition against expelling, returning, surrendering or extraditing a person 'to another State where there are substantial grounds for believing that he or she would be in danger of being subjected to enforced disappearances';[72] and that a 'disappeared victim' has 'the right to obtain reparation and prompt, fair and adequate compensation'.[73]

In relation to children, the Convention on the Rights of the Child (CROC),[74] the chapeau notion that '[i]n all actions concerning children ... the best interests of the child shall be a primary consideration'[75] means that any decisions concerning dealing with detainees who are under the age of 18, the interests of the child must be paramount. The CROC also limits detention of children by providing that 'detention [of children] ... shall be used only as a measure of last resort and for the shortest period of time'.[76]

Where a state is required to comply with regional treaty obligations when conducting military operations, those obligations will also impact on detention. Pursuant to, for example, the African Charter on Human and Peoples' Rights (ACHPR),[77] the American Convention on Human Rights (AmCHR),[78] and the European Convention of Human Rights (ECHR),[79] there are general prohibitions concerning when a person might be detained. All three Conventions recognise the right to liberty and security;[80] the prohibition against torture or inhuman or degrading treatment or punishment;[81] the right to be informed of the reasons for detention;[82] the right to a fair trial;[83] and the right to compensation.[84]

Other than treaty obligations there are also a number of IHRL principles and standards that are articulated in so-called soft norm

---

70   Enforced Disappearances Convention (n 69 above) arts 1 & 2.
71   Enforced Disappearances Convention (n 69 above) art 17(3).
72   Enforced Disappearances Convention (n 69 above) art 16.
73   Enforced Disappearances Convention (n 69 above) art 24. Reparation includes restitution, rehabilitation, satisfaction and guarantees of non-repetition (see art 24(5)).
74   Opened for signature 20 November 1989, 1577 UNTS 3 (entered into force 2 September 1990).
75   CROC (n 74 above) art 3(1).
76   CROC (n 73 above) art 37(b).
77   Opened for signature 27 June 1981, OAU Doc CAB/LEG/67/3 rev 5, 21 ILM 58 (1982) (entered into force 21 October 1986).
78   Opened for signature 22 November 1969, 1144 UNTS 123 (entered into force 18 July 1978).
79   Convention for the Protection of Human Rights and Fundamental Freedoms, opened for signature 4 November 1950, 213 UNTS 222 (entered into force 3 September 1953).
80   See ACHPR (n 77 above) art 6; AmChR (n 78 above) art 7(1); ECHR (n 79 above) art 5(1).
81   See ACHPR (n 77 above) art 5; AmChR (n 78 above) art 5; ECHR (n 79 above) art 3.
82   See AmChR (n 78 above) art 7(4); ECHR (n 79 above) art 5(3) in relation to arrests.
83   See ACHPR (n 77 above) art 7; AmCh (n 78 above) art 8; ECHR (n 79 above) art 6.
84   See AmChR (n 78 above) art 10; ECHR (n 79 above) arts 5(5), 10 & 41.

documents.[85] The two key non-binding instruments in the context of detention are the Standard Minimum Rules for the Treatment of Prisoners (Standard Minimum Rules);[86] and the Body of Principles for the Protection of All Persons under Any Form of Detention or Imprisonment (Body of Principles).[87] The Standard Minimum Rules are useful for setting guidelines for the treatment of prisoners and the management of penal institutions[88] and therefore, while not directly relevant to detention centres established in military operations, provide useful standards concerning establishing registers, accommodation, hygiene, clothing and bedding, and instruments of restraint. The Body of Principles apply broadly in that they 'apply for the protection of all persons under any form of detention or imprisonment'.[89] The Principles cover a wide range of issues including the right to information at the time of arrest, the matters that are to be recorded concerning the detainee, the right of notification at the time of transfer, the right to communicate with legal counsel, and the right to complain regarding treatment. Allied to those key instruments are a number of other non-binding instruments that deal with specific issues relevant to detention. These include: United Nations Rules for the Protection of Juveniles Deprived of their Liberty,[90] the Basic Principles and Guidelines on the Right to a Remedy and Reparation for Victims of Gross Violations of International Human Rights Law and Serious Violations of International Humanitarian Law.[91]

There have been a number of debates concerning the *de jure* application of IHRL during military operations. At one extreme is the view that IHRL provisions do not apply in military operations.[92] Another debate concerns obligations that members of the UN have under the UN Charter and the obligations they have under other treaty regimes. The essence of this debate is that where a state is acting pursuant to a binding UN Security Council (SC) resolution and that state has conflicting obligations with

---

85　For a more detailed discussion about what 'soft law' is, see eg A Boyle & C Chinkin *The making of international law* (2007) 212-214.

86　UN Doc A/CONF/611, Annex 1 (30 August 1955).

87　UN Doc A/RES/43/173, Annex (9 December 1988). See also the *Basic Principles for the Treatment of Prisoners* UN Doc A/ARES/45/111, Annex (14 December 1990), which supplement the Body of Principles.

88　Standard Minimum Rules (n 86 above) para 1.

89　Body of Principles (n 87 above) preamble.

90　UN Doc A/RES/45/113, adopted by the GA 14 December 1990.

91　UN Doc A/RES/60/147, adopted by the GA 16 December 2005. See also UN Children's Fund 'The Paris Principles: Principles and guidelines on children associated with armed forces or armed groups' (February 2007); ECOSOC 'Guidelines on justice in matters involving child victims and witnesses of crime' E/Res/2005/20 (22 July 2005); human rights reports such as the Final report of the Special Rapporteur, Mr Cherif Bassiouni 'Civil and political rights, including the questions of independence of the judiciary, administration of justice, impunity' UN Doc E/CN.4/2000/62 (18 January 2000); and the Commissions of Inquiry established by the UN.

92　See eg the discussion in Part 4 below where the approach taken by the United States is discussed. See also the discussion by Cathcart in this book for the Canadian Government's approach.

another treaty regime then its obligations to the UN shall prevail.[93] That debate, at least from the perspective of the European Court of Human Rights, seems to have been narrowed to an expectation that 'in the absence of clear provision to the contrary, the presumption must be that the Security Council intended States ... to contribute towards the maintenance of security [...] while complying with their obligations under international human rights law'.[94] Another debate concerning the application of IHRL provisions relates to the territorial and personal reach of the particular IHRL treaty. So, for example, the reach of the ICCPR is that it is to apply to 'all individuals within its territory and subject to its jurisdiction.'[95] The CAT on the other hand has a broader application because it provides that each state party 'prevent acts of torture in any territory under its jurisdiction.'[96]

4 The IHL and IHRL interplay

There is a breadth in the variety of views as to the interplay of IHL and IHRL with regard to detention in military operations. At one extreme is the view of the United States that detention is governed only by IHL. The US Detainee Program Directive, for example, states that detainees are to be afforded 'at a minimum the standards articulated in common article 3 and the protections afforded by Geneva Convention III'.[97] There is no express mention made in the Directive of the application of IHRL. That approach is reinforced by the broader US Directive concerning the application of IHL: 'Members of the DoD [Department of Defence] Components comply with the law of war [that is, IHL] during all armed conflicts, however such conflicts are characterised and in all other military operations'.[98] On one reading of both directives it would be reasonable to conclude that the US view is that, regardless of the type of military operation, the default position in regards to the treatment of detainees is that its military forces are only to apply IHL.[99]

---

93   UN Charter (n 22 above) art 103.
94   See *Al-Jedda v The United Kingdom* App no 27021/08 ECtHR (7 July 2011) paras 100 & 109 (*Al-Jedda* case). See also discussion concerning the *Al-Jedda* case accompanying the text to n 103 below.
95   ICCPR (n 57 above) art 1.
96   CAT (n 63 above) art 1.
97   Department of Defence Directive 'The Department of Defence Detainee Program' Number 2310.01E (5 September 2006) para 4.2, Enclosures 1 & 4.
98   The United States Department of Defence Directive 'DoD Law of War Program' Number 2311.01E, 9 May 2006 (certified current as of 22 February 2011) para 4.1.
99   The International and Operations Law Department *Operations law handbook* (2010) published by the US Army Judge Advocate General's Legal Centre and School, states that it is only IHRL found in customary international law (and not IHRL treaty law) that binds the US. The Handbook goes on to argue: 'there exists no authoritative source that articulates which human rights the United States considers to be CIL [customary international law].' See 43.

Australia's approach – at least as it was explained to the Human Rights Committee (HRC) in 2009 – recognises the role of the ICCPR but still emphasises the *lex specialis* nature of IHL:

> If Australia were exercising authority as a consequence of an occupation or during a consensual deployment with the consent of a Host State, in circumstances in which the principles of international humanitarian law are applied, Australia accepts that there is some scope for the rights under the Covenant to remain applicable, although in case of conflict between the applicable standards under the Covenant and the standards of international humanitarian law, the latter applies *lex specialis*. Further the existence of a UN mandate may also be relevant in determining the lawfulness of a particular action, such as detention ...[100]

Thus one might reasonably assume that Australia applies IHL as the principal regime when dealing with detainees.

The United Kingdom Ministry of Defence's stated view in relation to the treatment of detainees is that its forces will apply, as a minimum, common article 3 protections to detainees and that it 'is recommended that while detained in military custody, persons who have taken a direct part in hostilities should be given the same treatment as if they were prisoners of war'.[101] The Ministry further adds that detainees are also entitled to a number of judicial guarantees which are founded in both IHL and IHRL.[102] In relation to peace operations, the UK view is that 'the principles and spirit of the law of armed conflict remain relevant'.[103] After the *Al-Jedda*[104] decision by the European Court of Human Rights it is open to conclude that UK forces serving on military operations overseas will be expected to comply with their ECHR obligations unless the SC explicitly provides in a binding Chapter VII resolution that detention is authorised and that detaining UK forces were obliged by the resolution not to comply with their relevant ECHR obligations. Since the more recent UK High Court decision in *Serdar Mohammed*[105] concerning an individual detained by UK forces in Afghanistan it seems that UK High Court will not permit UK military forces to justify taking security detainees outside either the local criminal justice system or in violation of IHRL. The Court in that case emphasised that IHL does not displace the application of the UK

100 Human Rights Committee 'Replies to the list of issues' (CCPR/C/AUS/Q/5), to be taken up in connection with the consideration of the fifth periodic report of the Government of Australia (CCPR/C/AUS/5) [19 January 2009], 21 January 2009, 4-5.
101 United Kingdom Ministry of Defence *The manual of the law of armed conflict* (2004) paras 15.30 & 15.30.3.
102 UK Ministry of Defence (n 101 above) para 15.30.5.
103 UK Ministry of Defence (n 101 above) para 14.10.
104 n 94 above.
105 *Serdar Mohammed v Ministry of Defence and Mohammed Qasim, Mohammed Nazim, and Abdullah v Secretary of State for Defence* [2014] EWHC 1369 (QB).

Human Rights Act or article 5 of the European Convention on Human Rights for UK forces.[106] The Court further added that IHL does not provide a basis for detention in NIAC.[107] However the Court also stated that IHL would be relevant to provide fundamental guarantees to the detainee in situations where the UK had derogated from its article 5 obligations but as the UK had not derogated from the application of that article there was no real role for IHL in that case.[108]

The NATO position concerning the interplay between IHL and IHRL in relation to detentions carried out by ISAF members is that:

> Commanders at all levels are to ensure that detention operations are conducted in accordance with applicable international law and human rights standards and that all detainees are treated with respect and dignity at all times. It is ISAF policy that all detainees be treated in accordance with international law, applicable national law and the law of armed conflict. All persons subject to this policy [that is the standard operating procedures concerning detention of non-ISAF personnel] will observe the requirements of the law of armed conflict and at a minimum shall apply, without regard to a detainee's legal status; the standards articulated in common article 3 to the Geneva Conventions of 1949 in the treatment of all detainees until their final release or transfer out of ISAF control.[109]

In relation to taking detainees in counter-piracy operations off the coast of Somalia the NATO position was that IHRL was the core law that was applicable.[110] As reflected in Peter Olson's chapter, the approach taken by NATO concerning the interplay between IHL and IHRL is approached in a pragmatic manner and there is no 'NATO doctrine' on that interplay.

The UN's detention policy in situations where its peacekeepers are in situations of armed conflict and 'actively engaged therein as combatants, to the extent and for the duration of their engagement' is that any detainee taken by UN forces is to be 'treated in accordance with the relevant provisions of the Third Geneva Convention'.[111] In non-armed conflict situations the UN has a detention policy but that policy is not in the public domain. However, based on the general approach of the UN found, for example, in some Status of Forces Agreements (SOFA) entered into by the UN with the host nation, it would be reasonable to conclude that the start point for developing detention standards for UN peace operations would

106   *Serdar Mohammed* (n 105 above) para 277.
107   *Serdar Mohammed* (n 105 above) paras 239-251.
108   *Serdar Mohammed* (n 105 above) paras 288-292.
109   International Security Assistance Force 'Standard operating procedure 362: Detention of non-ISAF personnel' (20 April 2011) para 2.
110   For a more detailed discussion of NATO position concerning the counter-piracy operations see Peter Olson 'Piracy and NATO' in P Koutrakos & A Skordas (eds) *The law and practice of piracy at sea: European and international perspectives* (2014) and the Chapter by Smit in this book.
111   See Secretary-General's bulletin (n 23 above) sec 8.

be IHL. That conclusion is based on, for example, the United Nations Mission in Sudan (UNMIS) SOFA, which provides:

> The United Nations shall ensure that UNMIS shall conduct its operation in Sudan with full respect for the principles and rules of the international conventions applicable to the conduct of military personnel. These international conventions include the four Geneva Conventions of 12 August 1949 and their Additional Protocols of 8 June 1977 and the UNESCO Convention of 14 May 1954 for the Protection of Cultural Property in the Event of an Armed Conflict.[112]

The phrase 'applicable to the conduct of military personnel' in the above quote might also suggest that where particular IHRL norms apply as a matter of law to the conduct of military personnel that those norms would also apply. That interpretation is supported by the United Nations Peacekeeping Operations: Principles and Guidelines, which provides that UN 'peacekeeping operations should be conducted in full respect of human rights and should seek to advance human rights through the implementation of their mandates'.[113]

The HRC has argued that the application of IHL and the ICCPR are complementary and are not mutually exclusive. In General Comment 31, the Committee stated:

> The Covenant [ICCPR] applies also in situations of armed conflict to which the rules of international humanitarian law are applicable. While, in respect of certain Covenant rights, more specific rules of international humanitarian law may be especially relevant for the purpose of the interpretation of the Covenant rights, both spheres of law are complementary and not mutually exclusive.[114]

Adopting the complementary approach, a report to the UN Commission of Human Rights has argued that in relation to the situation of detainees at Guantanamo Bay that in the context of:

> ongoing non-international armed conflicts involving the United States forces, the *lex specialis* authorizing detention [pursuant to IHL] without respect for the guarantees set forth in article 9 of the ICCPR ... can no longer serve as the basis for that detention.[115]

---

112   *Agreement between the Government of Sudan and the United Nations concerning the status of the United Nations mission in Sudan* para 6(a).
113   Department of Peacekeeping Operations *United Nations peacekeeping operations: Principles and guidelines* (2008) 14.
114   Human Rights Committee 'General Comment 31: The nature of the general legal obligation imposed on states parties to the Covenant' (adopted on 29 March 2004) para 11.
115   UN Commission on Human Rights 'Situation of detainees at Guantanamo Bay' E/CN.4/2006/120 (27 February 2006) para 24. See also para 15.

The Inter-American Commission on Human Rights has addressed the interplay between IHL and IHRL in relation to detention in its 2002 report on Terrorism and Human Rights by emphasising that in some situations notwithstanding the application of IHL *de jure* there might be reasons to apply IHRL:

> Accordingly, where detainees find themselves in uncertain or protracted situations of armed conflict or occupation, the Commission considers that the supervisory mechanisms as well as judicial guarantees under international human rights law and domestic law, including habeas corpus and amparo remedies, may necessarily supersede international humanitarian law where this is necessary to safeguard the fundamental rights of those detainees.[116]

The European Court of Human Rights (ECHR) judgment in the case of *Al-Jedda* also appears to take an IHRL dominates over IHL stand in the context of detention. First, the Court in that case adopted an approach which focused on the presumption that if the SC intended for military forces to detain in breach of their international human rights obligations the Council would be expected to use 'clear and explicit language'.[117] The Court then determined that internment under IHL and more specifically the law of occupation did not displace the requirements of article 5(1) of the ECHR.[118] While it is true that the case focused on the application of IHL as a valid basis for detention in international armed conflicts, it is open to argue that the Court's view would be similar if reliance was placed on AP II for justifying detention in non-international armed conflicts, or SC resolutions in either non-international armed conflict or peace operations. In the more recent *Case of Hassan v the United Kingdom* the ECHR has reinforced that 'even in situations of international armed conflict, the safeguards under the Convention continue to apply, albeit interpreted against the background of the provisions of international humanitarian law'.[119] The Court went on to state that both IHL and the Convention, in relation to deprivation of liberty, 'should be accommodated, as far as possible'.[120] Put more simply the Court concluded that 'detention must comply with international humanitarian law and, most importantly, that it should be in keeping with the fundamental purpose of Article 5(1), which is to protect the individual from arbitrariness'.[121] It might be concluded therefore, that the Court view remains that both IHL and the *European Convention of Human Rights* continue to apply during international armed conflicts but are the question of whether IHRL has been breached will be determined by considering whether the powers granted to the detaining power under IHL.

---

116 Inter-American Commission on Human Rights 'Report on terrorism and human rights' OEA/SER.L/V/II.116 Doc 5 rev. 1 corr. (22 October 2002) para 146.
117 *Al-Jedda* (n 94 above) para 102.
118 *Al-Jedda* (n 94 above) para 107.
119 *Hassan v The United Kingdom* App no 29750/09 ECtHR (16 September 2014) para 104
120 As above.
121 *Hassan* (n 119 above) para 105.

Reinforcing that conclusion is the Court's explanation that the appropriate interpretation of periodic review of detention by a competent body (pursuant to articles 43 and 78 of GCIV) must be undertaken in light of obligations arising from the Convention (article 5(4)) – that is to say that the '"competent body" should provide sufficient guarantees of impartiality and fair procedure to protect against arbitrariness'.[122]

The International Court for the Prosecutions of Persons Responsible for Serious Violations of International Humanitarian Law Committed in the Territory of the Former Yugoslavia since 1991 (ICTY) has, at least in the context of torturing detainees, recognised the importance of the role of IHRL. In the case of the *Prosecutor v Anto Furundzija* the Trial Chamber argued that the convergence between IHL and IHRL in relation to torture demonstrates that the elements of torture, as articulated in article 1 of the CAT, apply in IHL situations as well.[123]

Another view concerning the interplay between IHL and IHRL is that they cannot apply simultaneously. As summarised after an ICRC expert meeting in 2008:

> The prevailing view is that IHRL continues to apply during armed conflict and is particularly relevant when addressing the issue of detention in NIAC [and other operations short of armed conflict]. However, when giving concrete substance to [the] interplay with IHL in practice, the different cultures of the two regimes need to be taken into account: 'IHL' is not equal to 'IHRL during armed conflict'. The two bodies of law – while similar in some of their purposes and on many points of substance – are designed to address very different contexts. Finally, while IHL imposes obligations on all parties to a conflict, including non-state actors, IHRL – in the current state of international law – can only be said to be directly binding on States.[124]

The ICRC has, since at least 1977 when it negotiated AP I and II, accepted the importance of IHRL in affording protections to detainees. Specifically in relation to standards of humane treatment, the ICRC acknowledged that it was inspired by the ICCPR.[125] The guarantees found in articles 4-6 in AP II 'underlie the whole system of human rights ... [and are] properly

---

122   *Hassan* (n 119 above) para 106.
123   ICTY Case IT-95-17/1-T (10 December 1993) paras 143-164.
124   Chatham House and International Committee of the Red Cross London 'Expert Meeting on Procedural Safeguards for Security Detention in Non-International Armed Conflict (22-23 September 2008)' (2009) 91(876) *International Review of the Red Cross* 859, 861. The footnote accompanying that quote went on to state:
>   The ongoing debate on this question was reflected in the different opinions of meeting participants. Without concluding on the issue, the discussion highlighted the need to take into account that even if IHRL can be said to be binding on non-State actors, some of its obligations are of a nature that allows implementation only by States (see footnote 5, 861).
125   International Committee of the Red Cross *General commentary to the Protocol Additional to the Geneva Conventions of 12 August 1949, and relating to the protection of victims of non-international armed conflicts (Protocol II), 8 June 1977* (1987) para 4509 (AP II Commentary).

adapted and supplemented to match the circumstances for which the Protocol is intended'.[126] It is also worth noting that the general commentary to AP II recognises that the 'rules of international law on human rights, and in particular the International Covenant on Civil and Political Rights, would be used as a point of reference to bring into focus the fundamental guarantees given in Protocol II for the way in which human beings should be treated'.[127] Furthermore, article 75(8) of AP II specifically states that:

[n]o provision of this Article [article 75] may be construed as limiting or infringing on any other more favourable provision granting greater protection, under any applicable rules of international law, to persons covered by paragraph 1 [which deals with the humane treatment of persons who are in the power of the Party to the conflict].

While the ICRC continues to believe that IHRL applies both in times of peace and armed conflict[128] it is also of the view that in relation to detention the interplay between IHL and IHRL still leaves a number of gaps which raise humanitarian concerns.[129]

Finally, to close this brief survey of approaches taken in navigating the interplay between IHL and IHRL in regards to detention it is relevant to briefly mention that the matter was discussed extensively by participants during the Copenhagen Process on the Handling of Detainees in International Military Operations.[130] The final document – The Copenhagen Process Principles and Guidelines (CPPG)[131] – which was welcomed by most of the states[132] attending the final workshop of the

126 AP II Commentary (n 125 above) para 4510.
127 AP II Commentary (n 125 above) para 4371.
128 31st ICRC Conference (n 15 above) 5.
129 31st ICRC Conference (n 15 above) 6-10.
130 For a brief discussion of the Copenhagen Process see eg B Oswald & T Winkler 'Copenhagen process: Principles and guidelines on the handling of detainees in international military operations' (2012) 16 *American Society of International Law Insights* 26 December 2012: http://www.asil.org/insights/volume/16/issue/39/copenhagen-process-principles-and-guidelines-handling-detainees (accessed 2 December 2014); J Horowitz 'Introductory note to the Copenhagen Principles and Guidelines on the Handling of Detainees in International Military Operations' (2012) 51 *American Society of International Law International Legal Materials* 1364.
131 The CPPG apply to 'handling detainees in international military operations in the context of non-international armed conflict situations and peace operations ...' See CPPG (n 8 above) preamble VII.
132 Representatives from the following governments attended the final conference: Argentina, Australia, Canada, China, Denmark (Host), France, Finland, Germany, Malaysia, the Netherlands, Norway, the Russian Federation, South Africa, Sweden, Turkey, Uganda, United Kingdom, and the United States. During the final session, the Chairman noted that delegations from Argentina, Australia, Canada, China, Denmark, France, Finland, Germany, Malaysia, the Netherlands, Norway, South Africa, Sweden, Turkey, Uganda, United Kingdom, and the United States welcomed the CPPG. Representatives from the African Union, the European Union, the ICRC, North Atlantic Treaty Organisation, and the United Nations were the observer organisations that attended the final conference. See Minutes (as recorded by the Chair) of the 3rd Conference on the Handling of Detainees in International Military Operations, Copenhagen (18-19 October 2012).

'Copenhagen Process on the Handling of Detainees in International Military Operations' reinforced that the principle of humane treatment of those detained required respect for applicable IHL and IHRL,[133] but noted the challenges 'of agreeing upon a precise description of the interaction between international human rights law and international humanitarian law'.[134] The importance of the CPPG in relation to the interplay of IHL and IHRL in regards to detention is that most of the participants, while accepting that IHRL has a role in dealing with detainees, appear to have taken an IHL perspective of the applicable norms particularly in relation to the distinction between 'deprivation of liberty' and 'restriction of liberty';[135] the distinction between 'security detainees' and 'criminal detainees';[136] the need for adequate conditions of detention;[137] and the transfer of detainees to another state.[138]

Following the above survey concerning the approaches taken regarding the interplay between IHL and IHRL in the context of detention in non-international armed conflicts and peace operations the following observations may be drawn. First, some states such as the US take a *lex specialis* approach, which leaves little room for the application of IHRL. Other states take a *lex specialis* approach but are willing to concede that in some circumstances IHRL will have a role – albeit a minimal one. States that fall in this category are arguably the UK and Australia. There is also a preference, most frequently expressed by international institutions to adopt a complementarity approach which recognises the role that both IHL and IHRL play in regards to detention. The HRC and the ICRC take that approach. Last but not least, it seems that in some cases institutions such as the Inter-American Commission on Human Rights and the European Court on Human Rights are willing to consider that IHRL will dominate IHL or that IHRL serves to fill gaps in the law, even if IHL applies as a matter of law.

It is worth noting that one influential journal article on detention takes the approach that neither the *lex specialis* nor the complementarity approaches reconcile the IHL and IHRL in relation to detention. In the context of undertaking reviews concerning the ongoing detention of detainees, John Bellinger and Vijay Padmanabhan argue that since IHL

---

133 CPPG (n 8 above) preamble V.
134 CPPG (n 8 above) preamble IV. Note that the delegation of Sweden indicated that the Swedish interpretation of the reference to international law in principle 16 is that it also includes human rights law, and that Sweden would have preferred if this had been explicitly stated in principle 16. The delegation of the Russian Federation welcomed the conclusion of the Copenhagen Process and took note of the CPPG. The Russian Federation further indicated that the Copenhagen Process could contribute more to the safeguarding of the humane treatment of detainees by placing greater emphasis on their inherent rights, which derive from IHRL and IHL.
135 See CPPG (n 8 above) principles 1 & 2.
136 See CPPG (n 8 above) principles 12 & 13.
137 See CPPG (n 8 above) principle 9.
138 See CPPG (n 8 above) principle 15. Also note that most of the other principles are inspired by IHL standards.

and IHRL 'have different presumptions about the context of detention, they have different, specific, but contradictory rules'.[139] They go on to argue that 'determining which set of rules applies requires a framework other than complementarity or *lex specialis* – a framework that needs to be developed'.[140] Daniel Bethlehem has also argued for developing a framework that goes beyond the *lex specialis* and complementarity approaches. He recommends focusing on scenarios or taking a provision-by-provision analysis to develop a framework that is more appropriate to deal with the complexity surrounding the relationship between IHL and IHRL.[141]

As we shall now see, when we seek to apply specific IHL or IHRL norms to particular situations described in the phases of detention presented in Part I, the interplay is rarely binary – that is IHL or IHRL – but rather an interplay between the two depending on such factors as the provisions involved, the facts to which those provisions are applied, and pragmatic issues arising from the conduct of military operations and the application of policy.

5   Identifying the precise interplay of IHL and IHRL

Taking into account the approaches outlined in Part III above it is worth considering the extent to which those approaches are relevant to specific aspects of detention. This Part considers three key detention issues so as to evaluate the precise – rather than general – interplay between IHL and IHRL: the detention of security detainees; the handover of detainees; and a detainee's right to reparations. Each of these issues raises particular issues concerning the interplay between IHL and IHRL and therefore demonstrates some of the tensions and challenges faced by those required to identify precisely which law applies and when it applies.[142]

---

139   JB Bellinger III & VM Padmanabhan 'Detention operations in contemporary conflicts: Four challenges for the Geneva conventions and other existing law' (2011) 105 *American Journal of International Law* 201 210. See also B Oswald 'Detention of civilians on military operations: Reasons for and challenges to developing a special law of detention' (2008) 32 *Melbourne University Law Review* 524.
140   As above.
141   D Bethlehem QC 'The relationship between international humanitarian law and international human rights law in situations of armed conflict' (2013) 2 *Cambridge Journal of International and Comparative Law* 180 194-195.
142   There are other issues relating to detention that pose challenges as well. For some other examples of challenges and how they should be addressed see eg J Pejic 'Procedural principles and safeguards for internment/administrative detention in armed conflict and other situations of violence' (2005) 87 *International Review of the Red Cross* 375.

5.1   Security detainees

Detention of a person suspected of being a security threat arises in situations where military personnel take custody of a person for reasons such as when the person is an imperative threat to the security of the force or the civilian population.[143] Whereas criminal detainees are usually detained on the basis of being suspected of committing a criminal offence, security detainees are detained on the basis that they are likely to be a security threat. The principle of depriving a civilian of their liberty for security reasons is envisaged in both international[144] and non-international armed conflicts;[145] and has arisen on numerous occasions in a variety of peace operations, including UN commanded and controlled operations.[146] However, the fact remains that while AP II implies that detainees may be taken in relation to military operations it does not provide security detainees with procedural protections concerning their ongoing detention. Thus there is no AP II provision that determines, for example, the right of a detainee to have their detention reviewed, the basis for exercising the right, the minimum requirements for review, the avoidance of indefinite detention, and the provision of legal assistance to the detainee subject to the review process.

As long as the detainee is not subjected to arbitrary detention there is no specific prohibition in the ICCPR to taking security detainees.[147] The procedural safeguards for security detainees pursuant to IHRL are also minimal. On a literal interpretation the ICCPR provisions concerning due process are limited to persons who are arrested and not those detained for security reasons.[148] The ECHR does not provide for taking security detainees unless a state subject to that treaty regime derogates pursuant to article 15 of that Convention on the basis of being in armed conflict facing a public emergency threatening its life. The Body of Principles provides a number of guidelines relevant to the treatment and rights of security detainees. For example, principle 11 provides for the procedural right for a detainee to be 'given an effective opportunity to be heard promptly by a judicial or other authority[149]... [and] a judicial or other authority shall be

---

143   Note that, as a matter of fact, on a number of military operations 'a threat to the successful accomplishment of the mission' is used to justify detention. See eg 'NATO/ISAF standard operating procedure 362: Detention of non-ISAF Personnel' (20 April 2011) para 6, which provides that one of the grounds for detention under ISAF ROE is if the detention is necessary to accomplish the ISAF mission.
144   See eg GC IV (n 4 above) arts 27, 42, 76-104.
145   See AP II (n 26 above) art 5.
146   See eg B Oswald 'Detention by United Nations peacekeepers: Searching for definition and categorisation' (2011) 15 *Journal of International Peacekeeping* 119-151.
147   See ICCPR (n 57 above) art 9.
148   On a plain reading of the ACHPR and AmCHR texts, it appears that taking security detainees is not prohibited under those conventions.
149   Body of Principles (n 87 above) principle 11(1).

empowered to review as appropriate the continuance of detention'.[150] Similarly principle 13 sets a useful benchmark concerning providing security detainees with information by providing:

> [a]ny person shall ... at the commencement of detention, or promptly thereafter, be provided by the authority responsible for his ... detention ... with information on and an explanation of his rights and how to avail himself of such rights.

Principle 16 provides further rights by stipulating that when a detainee is moved from one detention facility to another the detainee 'shall be entitled to notify or to require the competent authority to notify members of his family or other appropriate persons of his choice of his ... detention ... or of the transfer and of the place where he is kept in custody'.

Arguably some states have evolved their practices concerning the due process rights to be given to detainees in non-international armed conflicts by developing policies that go further than the IHL and IHRL norms. William Lietzau[151] has argued that the US detention review processes that existed during the initial phases of the wars in Afghanistan and Iraq had weaknesses and 'as a consequence, both have been discarded'.[152] Now the Detainee Review Board:

> comprised of three field grade officers [typically ranging in rank from Major to Colonel equivalents] review each individual's detention for both legality and necessity of continued detention. The detainee receives expert assistance from a U.S. officer who is authorized access to all reasonable information pertaining to the detainee. The review is repeated periodically after the initial hearing, which must take place within sixty days of arrival in the detention facility.[153]

The recently settled principle of review in the Copenhagen Process also demonstrates how states envisage security detainees being dealt with in non-international armed conflicts and peace operations. Principle 12 provides:

> A detainee whose liberty has been deprived for security reasons is to, in addition to a prompt initial review, have the decision to detain reconsidered periodically by an impartial and objective authority that is authorised to determine the lawfulness and appropriateness of continued detention.

In at least one peace operation – International Force for East Timor (INTERFET) – the review process undertaken for security detainees

---

150 Body of Principles (n 87 above) principle 11(3).
151 Until September 2013 William Lietzau was the Deputy Assistant Secretary of Defence, Rule of Law and Detainee Policy (USA).
152 W Lietzau 'Detention of terrorists in the twenty-first century' in Kenneth Watkin & AJ Norris (eds) *International law studies – Vol 88: Non-international armed conflict in the twenty-first century* (2012) 323-345, 336.
153 As above.

involved a military magistrate reviewing all detentions of civilians taken into custody.[154] The peace operation conducted by NATO forces in Kosovo – Kosovo Force (KFOR) – in 1999 used local courts, such as the Pristina district court, to review the continued detention of persons held by those forces.[155]

In regard to the interplay between IHL and IHRL, the situation of security detainees raises some interesting issues. First, there is the issue of whether IHL provides the more detailed and nuanced protections for security detainees by way of analogy – in relation to, for example, initial review and ongoing reviews. Second, is the fact that IHRL treaty law does little to add to the body of provisions found in IHL. Third, soft norm principles such as those found in the Body of Principles and in the Copenhagen Process add to IHL but because those norms are non-binding their effectiveness, similar to applying IHL by analogy, is based on adherence by policy rather than by obligation. It seems to be the case that most of the states that have detained security detainees during armed conflicts have, as a matter of legal interpretation and pragmatism, adopted an IHL focus when dealing with detention. Where issues concerning the rights of security detainees have arisen in the domestic courts of the UK the approach of those courts has also been to emphasise IHL over IHRL. However, if the UK government does not appeal *Serdar Mohammed*[156] it would seem that UK forces cannot imply that they have a power to take security detainees in NIAC pursuant to IHL and, therefore, must rely on domestic law to provide them with that power. Furthermore, even when there is a binding Security Council resolution, that case is authority for concluding that UK forces cannot detain in situations which would breach IHRL. In relation to the *European Convention on Human Rights* the ECHR continues to emphasise the dominance of IHRL but in its most recent case of Hassan it appears to be willing to accept that detention in international armed conflict which is consistent with IHL will be sufficient to demonstrate that article 5 of the *European Convention on Human Rights* has not been violated.

5.2   Handover

The second issue relates to the handover of detainees particularly in situations where there is a risk that the detainee might be subject to torture and other forms of cruel or ill-treatment upon being handed over to the receiving state. Historically, it was generally accepted that the detaining authority would as soon as reasonably practicable hand detainees to the host state. That practice was based on the simple presumption of accepting

---

154   Oswald (n 146 above).
155   See 'Report of the situation of human rights in Kosovo' FRY, E/CN.4/2000/10 (7 September 1999) para 113.
156   n 105 above.

that the host state has sovereignty over all persons within its territory. Since AP II was silent on the matter there was little reason to consider that practice as a violation of AP II. However, more recently, the CAT has been used as a basis for arguing that where the detaining authority has substantial grounds for believing that the detainee would be abused or ill-treated by the host state authorities, based on a view that those authorities have 'a consistent pattern of gross, flagrant or mass violations of human rights'[157] handover is prohibited.[158] While it has been argued that the prohibition expressed in the CAT does not apply to situations where a military force is carrying out operations in the host state (that is that article 3 of the CAT does not apply to extraterritorial situations) the reality is that, as a matter of policy, it is generally accepted that handovers in circumstances as stated in CAT would not occur.[159]

The tension between sovereignty and not handing over a detainee because of a belief that they might be subjected to torture or other forms of ill-treatment is reflected in the ISAF detention policy. That policy provides:

> ISAF cannot seek to constrain the freedom of action of the Afghan authorities. However, bilateral agreements may be concluded between TCN's [Troop Contributing Nations] and the Host Nation, according to national requirements ... Consistent with international law [however], persons should not be transferred [that is handed over] under any circumstances in which there is a risk that they be subjected to torture or other forms of ill-treatment.[160]

The ISAF benchmark of recognising the importance of the host state's sovereignty is also reinforced by the CPPG, principle 15, which provides in part:

> Where the transferring State or international organisation determines it appropriate to request access to transferred detainees or to the detention facilities of the receiving State, the receiving State or authority *should* [emphasis added] facilitate such access for monitoring of the detainee until such time as the detainee has been released, transferred to another authority, or convicted of a crime in accordance with applicable national law.

---

157 CAT (n 63 above) art 3(1).
158 For a more detailed analysis of the debate concerning the applicability of non-refoulement in the context of detainee transfers see eg C Droege 'Transfers of detainees: Legal framework, non-refoulement and contemporary challenges' (2008) 90 *International Review of the Red Cross* 669. See also *Amnesty International Canada and British Columbia Civil Liberties Association v Chief of Defence Staff for the Canadian Forces, Minister of National Defence and Attorney-General of Canada* (2008) FC 336, T-324-07; *Amnesty International Canada v Canada (Minister of National Defence)* (2007) FC 1147.
159 See eg J Bellinger 'Diplomatic assurances and rendition to torture: The perspective of the State Department's legal adviser' Hearing before the Subcommittee on International Organisations, Human Rights, and Oversight of the Committee on Foreign Affairs House of Representatives (10 June 2008) 2-3.
160 ISAF (n 109 above) annex D, para 3.

There are at least two comments that might be made about transferring or handing-over detainees. The first is that the rule prohibiting torture, cruel, humiliating and degrading treatment[161] is interpreted by a more developed IHRL treaty regime – the CAT. Further, it is that treaty that appears to set limitations on handovers. The second is that as a matter of pragmatic balancing of policy and politics, the trend is to avoid the opprobrium that detaining authorities are being wilfully blind about the risk of torture and other forms of ill-treatment. Clearly therefore IHRL has informed the interpretation of the IHL prohibitions of torture or ill-treatment by developing it in the context of expelling, returning, or extraditing a detainee and that has in turn evolved to a policy approach of using IHRL, even in situations where the CAT might not be considered to apply as a matter of law.

Two issues concerning handover remain unanswered. First, how does a detaining authority deal with a situation where the host state demands the return of a detainee on the basis of sovereignty? Second, what recourse is available to the state that handed over the detainee if it is subsequently found that the detainee was tortured some months or even years after the detainee was handed over and the state's forces have returned home? Can the detaining authority demand the detainee back? If yes, under what conditions might the detainee be returned to the state that initially detained the individual? Both IHL and IHRL are silent on those matters. If the matter could not be resolved through diplomatic negotiations it would be open for courts to take into account the reasons for demanding the return of the detainee against the security requirements of the detaining authority and the rights of the detainee. Developments in international law, particularly in relation to the rights of detainees, would suggest that international tribunals, particularly those that favour human rights, would emphasise the rights of the detainee over sovereignty. Domestic courts on the other hand might not only favour sovereignty but also take greater notice of the threat to the security of the state.

5.3   Reparations[162]

Increasingly, there is recognition that in armed conflicts and in situations such as peace operations there is a requirement to provide reparations for individuals who have been harmed by military operations.[163] The term 'reparations' is used here to deal with situations where a detainee, or their family, might be entitled to – as a minimum – restitution, compensation or

---

161 See eg, n 25 above, common article 3.
162 For a more detailed account of reparations in armed conflict see eg B Oswald & B Wellington 'Reparations for violations in armed conflict and the emerging practice of making amends' in R Liivoja & T McCormack (eds) *Routledge handbook of the law of armed conflict* (forthcoming).
163 For the work of the Civilians in Conflict see Centre for Civilians in Conflict: http://civiliansinconflict.org/ (accessed 24 December 2013).

satisfaction for serious harm, such as being unlawfully detained or being abused while detained. There is also a growing tendency to compensate individuals, for instance, in the form of ex gratia payments, for harm suffered or damages arising from lawful actions.

Historically there are two provisions in IHL that deal with compensation during armed conflict: the 1907 Hague Convention IV, article 3; and AP I, article 91. The traditional IHL approach in international armed conflicts has been to recognise that violations of the GCs or of AP I might give rise to the violating state paying compensation to the parties to the conflict;[164] and compensation only arises if there has been a loss or damage.[165] There are no treaty provisions concerning reparations in AP II.[166] Therefore, the article 91 provision is of limited benefit to detainees who have been unlawfully detained or abused in non-international armed conflicts. However, what rights does a detainee have if they do not wish to be compensated? Is there a right to non-repetition of the act of abuse, or the right to truth or, for that matter, rehabilitation of the injuries suffered?

The limited nature of compensation implied by article 91 is in stark contrast to the reparation provisions found in some IHRL treaties. For example, the CAT expects states to provide both substantive and procedural redress to victims as defined in that Convention. Consequently, a detainee tortured in situations where the CAT applies as a matter of law would be entitled to restitution, compensation, rehabilitation, satisfaction and the right to truth, and guarantees of non-repetition.[167] If a detainee 'disappears' in situations where the Enforced Disappearances Convention applies as a matter of law there will be a need to consider reparation in the sense of material and moral damages, as well as restitution, rehabilitation, satisfaction, and guarantees of non-repetition.[168] Thus both the CAT and the Enforced Disappearance Convention provide a much more comprehensive and developed form of reparations to deal with situations where detainees might be abused.

Clearly, therefore, where the CAT or the Enforced Disappearance Convention apply a detainee will be entitled to a much greater range of reparations than the narrow form of compensation envisaged by article 91 of AP I. However, putting aside the issue of whether AP I, article 91 is a rule that applies in non-international armed conflict as customary

---

164 AP I Commentary (n 18 above) para 3656.
165 AP I Commentary (n 18 above) para 3655.
166 The ICRC argues that the compensation principles found in Hague Convention IV, art 3; and AP II (n 26 above) art 91, is an international customary law rule and that it applies to non-international armed conflicts as well. See Hanckaerts & Doswald-Beck (n 44 above) rule 150. No state has publicly denounced the ICRC's view of the customary law status of that rule.
167 Committee Against Torture 'General Comment No 3' CAT/C/GC/3 (13 December 2012) paras 2-5.
168 Enforced Disappearances Convention (n 69 above) art 24(4).

international law the question arises whether increased sensibilities of the rights of victims of military operations has developed to the extent where the notion of reparations is as reflected in the CAT or Enforced Disappearance Convention. The answer would appear to be that recent IHL treaties concerning the use of weapons have arguably gone even further than the CAT or the Enforced Disappearance Convention. The 1997 Ottawa Treaty,[169] the 2003 Protocol on Explosive Remnants of War[170] and the 2008 Convention on Cluster Munitions[171] require state parties to assist civilians harmed, and to facilitate assistance for all civilian victims of these weapons, rather than predicating assistance on the commission of a violation of IHL.

Another factor that has influenced the notion of reparations in armed conflicts and peace operations is the role played by human rights tribunals such as the ECHR. The fact that individuals have the option to hold their state accountable for breaches of their rights through human rights tribunals means that victims' rights advocates are likely to seek remedies through human rights mechanisms.

The fact is that in practice there are a myriad of approaches taken by states and international organisations concerning reparations. Taking the armed conflict in Afghanistan as a case study, the US has legislation – the Foreign Claims Act – which facilitates payment of compensation to civilians who are injured.[172] Australia, Canada and the UK also have a system of ex gratia, or act of grace compensation practices, that could be used to pay Afghan detainees who are injured or killed by members of their forces. NATO also has a non-binding policy which seeks to encourage troop-contributing countries to '[p]roactively offer assistance for civilian casualty cases or damages to civilian property, in order to mitigate human suffering'.[173]

169 Convention on the Prohibition of the Use, Stockpiling, Production and Transfer of Anti-Personal Mines and on the Destruction, opened for signature 18 September 1997, 2056 UNTS 211(entered into force 1 March 1999) (Ottawa Treaty).

170 Protocol on Explosive Remnants of War (Protocol V to the 1980 Convention on Certain Conventional Weapons), opened for signature 28 November 2003, 2399 UNTS 100 (entered into force 12 November 2006).

171 Convention on Cluster Munitions, opened for signature 30 May 2008, 2688 UNTS (entered into force 1 August 2010) art 5.

172 For further discussion on the Foreign Claims Act and the distinction between combat and non-combat activities, see J Walerstein 'Coping with combat claims: An analysis of the Foreign Claims Act's combat exclusion' (2009-2010) 11 *Cardozo Journal of Conflict Resolution* 319.

173 'NATO Final Council approval of non-binding guidelines for payments in combat-related cases of civilian casualties' SG (2010) 0377 (9 June 2010) para 2; and Annex to SG (2010) 0377 (n 9) para 9. See also NATO 'NATO Nations Approve Civilian Casualty Guidelines' (6 August 2010). In March 2012, the UN Human Rights Council recommended these guidelines be applied by NATO in the Libyan conflict: 'Report of the 15th Special Session of the Council' UN Doc A/HRC/19/68 (25 February 2011) para 130(b).

In UN peacekeeping operations it is possible for detainees to claim compensation where the UN is liable as a result of the actions of its peacekeepers.[174] However, where the claim arises from, or is attributable to, acts of peacekeepers arising from 'operational necessity' the UN will not be liable. Thus, it would be possible for detainees or their relatives to claim from the UN where a detainee has been injured or killed due to, for example, the unlawful acts of peacekeepers.[175]

Three issues concerning reparations in regard to detention therefore arise. First, the notion of reparations in IHL is limited as a treaty obligation by and to situations where AP I applies as a matter of law. Second, in certain circumstances, such as where IHRL provisions of treaties like the CAT or the Enforced Disappearances Convention apply, the notion of reparations is more extensive than that found in article 91 of AP I. Third, it is possible to argue that developments in IHL treaties that deal with the use of weapons have broadened the concept of compensating individuals for the harm caused to them even where there has been no violation of IHL. From a pragmatic perspective, contemporary military commanders and planners could interpret the above legal developments in the context of counter-insurgency operations or trying to win the 'hearts and minds' of the civilian population and seek to balance those objectives with financial and other resources available to the operation they are responsible for. The overall result of taking the above legal and policy factors into account is that it is more likely than not that a reasonable military commander would be advocating for a policy of reparations that was more consistent with developments in IHRL and recent IHL weapon conventions than relying upon older IHL provisions.

6   Conclusion

The above exploration demonstrates that the interplay between IHL and IHRL with regards to detention remains uncertain in relation to non-international armed conflicts and peace operations. Notwithstanding that uncertainty, the following conclusions are suggested: First, there is a spectrum of approaches taken by states, international organisations and tribunals concerning the interplay between IHL and IHRL in regards to detention. Second, the difference in approaches is especially felt in coalition operations where differing legal cultures, traditions and obligations are likely to lead to the treatment of detainees varying in accordance with which state detains them. The US stance on the application of IHRL, for example, might lead to clashes concerning treatment obligations for those states that believe they have a legal

---

174   See GA Res 'Third party liability: Temporal and financial limitations' UN Doc A/RES/52/247 (17 July 1988).
175   For more detail concerning the General Assembly resolution see eg B Oswald et al *Documents on the law of UN peace operations* (2010) 323.

obligation to apply IHRL extraterritorially. Third, generally speaking, both IHL and IHRL co-exist at the very least as a matter of policy in relation to the taking and handling of detainees. In the main, that co-existence as demonstrated by the example of security detainees, handover and reparations is recognised as a matter of policy if not law and one might therefore conclude that such coexistence is useful both for military forces and for the detainees. Fourth, interpretations of the interplay between IHL and IHRL will vary over time and context. Thus it should come as no surprise that the US amended its detainee review process or that the CAT influences handover. Fifth, in relation to some rights, such as those concerning reparation, human rights treaties provide a more enforceable legal regime for individuals. One example of the effectiveness of human rights treaties is the result of *Al-Jedda* case before the ECHR. Sixth, in some cases such as torture and enforced disappearances, the more nuanced treaty regimes found in the CAT and the Enforced Disappearances Convention are likely to, either as a matter of law or policy, determine the approaches taken by states when dealing with detainees. For example, the influence of the CAT over handovers has led to states taking detainees in Afghanistan to be much more cautious about handing over detainees to the Afghan authorities.

Keeping the above points in mind, it is perhaps inevitable that practitioners must constantly seek to establish guarantees for the benefits of detainees while being 'realistic, taking into account military and political constraints'.[176]

---

176   AP I Commentary (n 18 above), xxxi.

5

Hostilities Conduct

Michelle Lesh

1 Introduction

This chapter will focus on the convergence and conflicts of the normative frameworks of IHRL and IHL during armed conflict and more specifically, on the use of force during the conduct of hostilities. The approach will be to examine the relationship between particular norms governing the two regimes rather than analysing the relationship between the regimes as a whole. Therefore, it will assess the extent to which the IHRL right to life comes into play during military operations that are regulated by the rules on the conduct of hostilities under IHL. This chapter will discuss potential restraints on the use of force during the conduct of hostilities imposed by both bodies of law, conflict between the two bodies of laws and whether they can be resolved, and areas where the bodies of laws converge and complement one an other.

Part two of this chapter will briefly set out the two legal regimes and outline the relevant provisions on restraints on the use of force. This brings into focus the way in which the regimes differ. It is important to establish that difference before reflecting on their relationship. Part three, the bulk of the chapter, will discuss the interaction between IHRL and IHL based on the doctrine *lex specialis*. It will explore this doctrine in the framework of the two underlying principles of IHL – military necessity and humanity – and whether they can be relied on as interpretive tools in understanding restraints on the use of force during the conduct of hostilities, in particular in relation to rules regulating precautions in attack and civilians directly participating in hostilities. Part four will offer some conclusions on the interplay of IHRL and IHL in relation to the use of force during the conduct of hostilities.

2   Background to the normative frameworks

IHRL is a distinct body of international law that focuses on individual rights. All persons enjoy these rights equally except for the limits of derogations and jurisdiction.[1] This can be contrasted to IHL, which is state-centric and whose application is limited to specific categories of persons in situations of armed conflict and occupation.[2] The term 'law enforcement' is often used interchangeably with IHRL to describe the normative paradigm. It is also used to describe the factual situation to which the normative framework applies: a state exercising its authority over individuals by imposing territorial and extra-territorial measures relating to security, law and order.[3] 'Law enforcement officials' who conduct such measures are all government officials who exercise police powers, including a state's military and security forces.[4]

Further preliminary points need to be made about how this chapter will approach IHL. In the analysis, the specific focus is on the conduct of hostilities, which includes the rules on distinction,[5] proportionality,[6] precautions in attack,[7] and superfluous injury and unnecessary suffering.[8] These rules regulate the means and methods of war during active combat.[9] While IHL is much broader, and includes law enforcement rules on the use of force (most notably in relation to the duties of the Occupying Power to maintain law and order),[10] this chapter will confine its discussion of IHL

---

1   See, eg, Universal Declaration on Human Rights, UN Doc A/810 (10 December 1948) art 2 (Universal Declaration).
2   ICRC, International humanitarian law and the challenges of contemporary armed conflicts, 31 October 2011 http://www.icrc.org/eng/resources/documents/report/31-international-conference-ihl-challenges-report-2011-10-31.htm14-15   (accessed 10 December 2013).
3   See N Melzer *Targeted killing in international law* (2008) 90.
4   UN Human Rights 'Basic Principles on the Use of Force and Firearms by Law Enforcement Officials' Preamble (1990) http://www.ohchr.org/EN/Professional Interest/Pages/UseOfForceAndFirearms.aspx (accessed 13 October 2014); P Alston 'The CIA and targeted killings beyond borders' (2011) 2 *Harvard National Security Journal* 303.
5   Protocol Additional to the Geneva Conventions of 12 August 1949, and relating to the Protection of Victims of International Armed Conflicts (1977) art 48 (API); JM Henckaerts & L Doswald-Beck *Customary international humanitarian law* (2005) rules 1-10. Parties to an armed conflict must at all times distinguish between civilians and civilian objects on the one hand, and combatants and military objectives on the other hand and direct their attacks only against the latter.
6   Art 51(5)(b) API.
7   Art 57 API.
8   Art 35(2) API.
9   ICRC 'Expert meeting: The use of force in armed conflicts: Interplay between the conduct of hostilities and law enforcement paradigms' 7, 15 November 2013 http://www.icrc.org/eng/resources/documents/publication/p4171.htm   (accessed 10 December 2013); LC Green *The contemporary law of armed conflict* (2008) 390.
10   Regulations annexed to *Hague Convention (IV) Respecting the Laws and Customs of War on Land* (1910) art 43. See also K Watkin 'Use of force during occupation: Law enforcement and conduct of hostilities' (2012) 94 *International Review of the Red Cross* 295-296.

to the conduct of hostilities regulating targeting operations against individuals.

The analysis applies to both international armed conflicts (IACs) and non-international armed conflicts (NIACs), however, the law regulating the conduct of hostilities is significantly confined during a NIAC because of the law enforcement imperative in this context.[11] It is generally accepted that IHRL applies to a greater extent in a NIAC than in an IAC.[12] One reason for this is that the IHL rules governing NIACs are not as comprehensive and are less clearly defined than the rules governing IACs.[13] While this has resulted in the growing trend of deferring to IAC rules on the conduct of hostilities during NIAC,[14] it has also resulted in a reliance on IHRL.

Coexistence of this kind between the two regimes is supported by the Preamble to Protocol Additional to the Geneva Conventions of 12 August 1949, and relating to the Protection of Victims of non-International Armed Conflicts which recalls that 'international instruments relating to human rights offer a basic protection for the victims'. In addition, the more control the state has over territory, the more probable it is that it can exercise forms of internal governance, and the more likely it is that IHRL continues to operate.[15] The 2010 Report of the UN Special Rapporteur on Extrajudicial, Summary or Arbitrary Executions (Extrajudicial Executions Special Rapporteur) stated that during a NIAC, when a 'state has control over the area in which a military operation is taking place,' it 'should use graduated force and, where possible, capture rather than kill'.[16] Thus, the application of IHRL to NIACs is relatively clear, provided territorial control is exercised by the state and it is not temporarily under the control

---

11   See, eg, D Kretzmer 'Rethinking the application of IHL in non-international armed conflicts' (2009) 42 *Israel Law Review* 8.

12   The same is also true for a situation of occupation. *Legal Consequences of the Construction of a Wall in the Occupied Palestinian Territory (Advisory Opinion)* (9 July 2004) (2004) ICJ Reports 136 (*Wall Opinion*); ICRC 'Experts meeting: Occupation and other forms of administration of foreign territory: Third meeting of experts: The use of force in occupied territory' April 2012 http://www.icrc.org/eng/assets/files/publications/icrc-002-4094.pdf (accessed 10 December 2013).

13   See M Sassòli & LM Olson 'The relationship between international humanitarian law and human rights law where it matters: Admissible killing and internment of fighters in non-international armed conflict' (2008) 90 *International Review of the Red Cross* 599 601–602.

14   See, eg, *Tadić Appeal on Jurisdiction* International Criminal Tribunal for the former Yugoslavia Case No IT-94-1-AR72 (2 October 1995) para 127; Rome Statute of the International Criminal Court (1998) art 8(2)(e) (Rome Statute). See also Henckaerts & Doswald-Beck (n 5 above); MN Schmitt et al (eds) *The manual on the law of non-international armed conflict: With commentary* (2006).

15   See *Abella v Argentina* Inter-American Commission of Human Rights, IAm Comm of HR (18 November 1997) Case 11.137. See, also, K Watkin 'Controlling the use of force: A role for human rights norms in contemporary armed conflict' (2004) 98 *American Journal of International Law* 26.

16   P Alston 'Report of the Special Rapporteur on extrajudicial, summary or arbitrary executions: Addendum: Communications to and from governments' UN Doc A/HRC/14/24/Add.6 (28 May 2010) para 77.

of an organised armed group.[17] Additionally, because NIACs takes place in a single territory such situations do not touch on the question of whether IHRL applies extraterritorially. Notwithstanding the continuing debate concerning extraterritorial application of IHRL,[18] the chapter adopts the view that IHRL does apply extraterritorially, during IACs, where a state exercises effective control over territory or persons.[19]

The differences between IAC and NIAC, as revealed in the opposing presumptions of effective control and jurisdiction in IACs and NIACs, indicates that the way the conflict is characterised and where it takes place will determine the extent to which the rules regulating the conduct of hostilities and law enforcement rules apply. Ultimately however, the determination of the applicable norms to a specific incident is context-dependent and a flexible approach is preferable. This approach more accurately reflects the realities on the ground than the blanket approach of broadly characterising the entire conflict and consequently the applicable

17   In this debate, there are however, those who argue that applying IHRL to NIACs creates an asymmetry between the state, that bears human rights obligations, and the armed groups, that are not bound by them. This gives to the armed groups a choice of means and methods not available to states due to the range of rules they must respect, thus undermining the concept of equality of belligerent parties. See F Bugnion 'Jus ad bellum, jus in bello and non-international armed conflicts' (2003) 6 *Yearbook of International Humanitarian Law* 174. On the question of the impact of territorial control on a state exercising its human rights obligations see, eg, *Ilascu v Moldova and Russia* (2004) EHRR 312.

18   For an in-depth analysis of the extraterritorial application of human rights law see N Lubell *Extraterritorial use of force against non-state actors* (2010); M Milanovic *Extraterritorial application of human rights treaties: Law, principles and policy* (2011). For the view that human rights has limited application in armed conflict see MJ Dennis 'Application of human rights treaties extraterritorially in times of armed conflict and military occupation' (2005) 99 *American Journal of International Law* 119. For a development in the US position see: US Department of State 'Fourth periodic report of the United States of America to the United Nations committee on human rights concerning the International Covenant on Civil and Political Rights' (30 December 2011) paras 506-507, http://www.state.gov/j/drl/rls/179781.htm (accessed 10 December 2013).

19   See *Wall Opinion* (n 12 above) paras 109–113; *Case Concerning Armed Activities on the Territory of the Congo (Democratic Republic of the Congo v Uganda)* (19 December 2005) (2005) ICJ Reports 168 paras 216-217; General Comment 31: Nature of the general legal obligation imposed on states parties to the Covenant, UNHR Committee (26 May 2004), UN Doc CCPR/C/21/Rev.1/Add.13, (2004) para 10; *McCann v United Kingdom* (1995) EHRR 161 paras 145–148; *Coard v United States of America* Inter-America Commission of Human Rights, IAm Comm of HR (29 September 1999) OEA/Ser.L/V/II.106 Doc 3 Rev para 37; M Nowak *UN covenant on civil and political rights, CCPR Commentary* (2005) 41–43; C Heyns 'Report of the Special Rapporteur on extrajudicial, summary or arbitrary executions' UN Doc A/68/382 (13 September 2013) paras 42-51; Turkel Commission: The Public Commission to Examine the Maritime Incident of 31 May 2010 'Second report: Israeli's mechanisms for examining and investigating complaints and claims of violations of the laws of armed conflict according to international law' (February 2013) 64-65: http://www.turkel-committee.gov.il/files/newDoc3/The%20Turkel%20Report%20for%20website.pdf (accessed 10 December).

norms to that conflict. To determine which norms are applicable to situations of violence, a case-by-case approach is preferable.[20]

2.1 IHL: Relevant treaty provisions

According to IHL, lethal force is permissible against legitimate military targets (namely, members of the armed forces of a party to an armed conflict and civilians directly participating in hostilities) provided the attack is proportionate and feasible precautions are taken.[21] 'Those who belong to armed forces or armed groups may be attacked at any time.'[22] However, it is always preferable when possible to arrest rather than kill. Operational concerns support this conclusion.[23] It is therefore important to determine whether, in the context of the conduct of hostilities, it is a requirement of the law to arrest in certain circumstances, or alternatively, whether its appeal is based on policy concerns or on moral grounds.[24]

The rule of IHL on 'denial of quarter' expresses the idea that: 'to give quarter to an enemy means to desist from further attack'.[25] In an IAC the option must be given to take the combatant as a Prisoner Of War (POW).[26] Although 'surrender' is irrelevant in a NIAC because combatant and POW status does not apply, non-state organised armed groups can give themselves up for 'capture'.[27] Some scholars rely on denial of quarter to support their position that there are restraints on the use of force under IHL.[28] Melzer explains that 'while traditional military operations have achieved their purpose once the targeted personnel are *hors de combat*, targeted killings are accomplished only once the targeted individual is

---

20 ICRC 'The use of armed drones must comply with laws' (10 May 2013): http://www.icrc.org/eng/resources/documents/interview/2013/05-10-drone-weapons-ihl.htm (accessed 10 December).
21 See Geneva Convention Relative to the Treatment of Prisoners of War (1949) art 4A ('GCIII'); arts 43, 44, 51, 57 API.
22 Y Sandoz et al (eds) *Commentary on the additional protocols of 8 June 1977 to the Geneva conventions of 12 August 1949* (1987) para 1453.
23 If captured, the individuals may become valuable sources of intelligence.
24 For policy reasons see G Blum & P Heymann 'Law and policy of targeted killing' (2010) 1 *Harvard National Security Journal* 145. The moral case relates to whether the principle of humanity can be relied on in interpreting the law. See pages 106-113 of this chapter.
25 See Program on Humanitarian Policy and Conflict Research at Harvard University *Commentary on the HPCR manual on international law applicable to air and missile warfare* (March 2010) rule 126.2: http://ihlresearch.org/amw/Commentary%20on%20the%20HPCR%20Manual.pdf (accessed 10 December 2013) (AMW Manual).
26 The prohibition of denial of quarter is a customary rule applying in IAC and NIAC and has been codified in Hague Regulations arts 22, 23(1)(e); API art 35(1)–(2). API, art 40: 'it is prohibited to order that there shall be no survivors, to threaten an adversary therewith or to conduct hostilities on this basis'.
27 AMW Manual (n 25 above) rule 125.6; rule 127.
28 See, eg, VJ Proulx 'If the hat fits, wear it, if the turban fits, run for your life: Reflections on the indefinite detention and targeted killing of suspected terrorists' (2005) 56 *Hastings Law Journal* 801 884; R Goodman 'The power to kill or capture enemy combatants' (2013) 24 *European Journal of International Law* 850.

dead'.[29] Denial of quarter, however, is not about failing to give a combatant an option to surrender. The prohibition is against an order that there shall be no survivors. The position that that denial of quarter includes removing the *option* to surrender rather than the rejection of the clear intention to surrender is inaccurate. It translates to the extreme conclusion that most targeting from the air is illegal. Furthermore, the treaty provision on denial of quarter indicates that the onus is on the enemy combatant to state his or her intention to surrender. One can therefore draw the conclusion that denial of quarter is much more limited than the requirement that the attacking combatant arrest a legitimate target regardless of whether he or she has expressed an intention to surrender.

The principle of superfluous injury and unnecessary harm is another area in IHL that concerns restraints on the use of force. Article 35(2) of Protocol Additional to the Geneva Conventions of 12 August 1949, and relating to the Protection of Victims of International Armed Conflicts (API) states that '[i]t is prohibited to employ weapons, projectiles and material and methods of warfare of a nature to cause superfluous injury or unnecessary suffering'.[30] The prohibition was discussed on a number of occasions in the expert process culminating in the ICRC 'Interpretive Guidance on the Notion of Direct Participation in Hostilities under International Humanitarian Law' ('ICRC Guidance')[31] and more specifically in the context of Section IX of the Guidance, which declares that IHL *requires* restraints on the use of force.[32] Section IX does not explicitly rely on the principle but its relevance can be inferred from the fact that the Section invokes Jean Pictet's famous statement made in the context of the work of experts on weapons causing superfluous injury:

> A State involved in a conflict will seek to destroy or weaken the enemy's war potential ... in three ways: death, wound or capture ... All three are equally capable of eliminating the enemy's strength. Humanitarian reasoning is different. Humanity demands capture rather than wounds and wounds rather than death; that non-combatants shall be spared as far as possible.[33]

---

29   n 3 above, 369.
30   Art 35(b), API.
31   ICRC 'Interpretive guidance on the notion of direct participation in hostilities under international humanitarian law' (2009).
32   See Fourth Expert Meeting on the Notion of 'Direct participation in hostilities under IHL' Geneva, 27/28 November 2006, Background Document, 47; Expert Meeting on the Notion of 'Direct participation in hostilities under IHL', Geneva, 5/6 February 2008, Background Document, 39 http://www.icrc.org/eng/resources/documents/article/other/direct-participation-article-020709.htm (accessed 10 December 2013); N Melzer 'Keeping the balance between military necessity and humanity: A response to four critiques on the ICRC's interpretive guidance on the notion of direct participation in hostilities' (2010) 42 *New York University Journal of International Law and Politics* 831 905-906. See pages 108-111 of this chapter for a discussion of section IX of the Guidance.
33   J Pictet 'Developments and principles of international humanitarian law' (1985) 62.

Discussion of this principle has also resurfaced in subsequent debate. For example, Goodman is a supporter of section IX but he attempts to strengthen its basis by securing it more firmly in the law through analysing treaty law, state practice, drafting history, Pictet's work and UN positions.[34] He enlists support for the Guidance's overall position on capture versus kill by contending that:

> In some circumstances, it is thus unlawful to use lethal force when a fighter could clearly be rendered *hors de combat* just as easily – and without endangering the attacking party – by injury or capture rather than death. This rule is embodied in the prohibition on superfluous injury and unnecessary suffering.[35]

Kleffner, by way of contrast, adopts a more restrained approach in his analysis of the principle of superfluous injury in the context of understanding section IX. He arrives at the conclusion that a case could conceivably be made that the prohibition has extended from covering weapons to also apply to methods of warfare. However, state practice does not reflect this interpretation.[36]

Like the law on denial of quarter, the principle of superfluous injury and unnecessary harm is much more limited than the requirement that the attacking combatant arrest a legitimate target. In conclusion, there is no *lex scripta* on arrest in IHL, and, according to the rules regulating the conduct of hostilities, capture does not constitute a legally required method of warfare.

2.2 IHRL: Relevant treaty provisions

One of the 'cardinal' human rights is the right to life. The right against arbitrary deprivation of the right to life has been described as *jus cogen*[37] and it is included in the Universal Declaration on Human Rights.[38] Its 'foundational status' is widely accepted.[39]

Article 6(1) of the ICCPR guarantees the right to life: 'every human being has the inherent right to life. This right shall be protected by law. No

---

34 n 28 above, 839-852. This should be read in conjunction with the other aspect of his argument, which focuses on the definition of *hors de combat*.
35 n 28 above, 822. For a critique of Goodman's thesis see: G Corn et al 'Belligerent targeting and the invalidity of a least harmful means rule' (2013) 89 *International Law Studies* 536.
36 JK Kleffner 'Section IX of the ICRC Interpretive Guidance on Direct Participation in Hostilities: The end of jus in bello proportionality as we know It? (2012) 45 *Israel Law Review* 44-45.
37 General Comment 6: The right to life (art 6), UNHR Committee (30 April 1982), UN Doc CCPR General Comment No 6 (1982).
38 Universal Declaration, art 3.
39 Heyns (n 19 above) para 30.

one shall be arbitrarily deprived of his life'.[40] Although the right to life is non-derogable (because it applies even in times of emergency), it is not absolute (in certain circumstances the right can be forfeited).[41] Only 'arbitrary' deprivations of life are prohibited. Thus, the legality of lethal force according to IHRL depends on the meaning of the term 'arbitrary'.[42] In assessing whether a killing was arbitrary, a number of factors are considered. They include the nature of the threat, whether the force was necessary or intentional, and whether all non-lethal measures were exhausted.[43] Ultimately, however, arbitrariness must be assessed on a case-by-case basis. In addition to the negative duty to abstain from arbitrarily depriving an individual of the right to life, there is also a positive duty to implement measures to preserve that right. The supervisory organ for the ICCPR, the Human Rights Committee, has indicated that there is a duty to train relevant personnel in order to minimise the chances of arbitrary killing.[44] Non-binding standards governing the use of force in law enforcement also exist, which clarify that the use of force may not exceed what is strictly or absolutely necessary to protect life.[45] In sum, the deprivation of the right to life is only permitted in exceptional circumstances under IHRL.

---

40   International Covenant on Civil and Political Rights, art 6 (1966). Similar provisions have been incorporated in Convention for the Protection of Human Rights and Fundamental Freedoms, (1950) art 2; African Charter on Human and Peoples' Rights (1981) art 4; American Convention on Human Rights (1969) art 4(1); The European Convention on Human Rights, (1950) ('ECHR') art 2. The wording of the ECHR differs from the right under the ICCPR, instead of 'arbitrary', art 2 sets out three circumstances in which the deprivation of life does not amount to a violation of the right to life because in the circumstances it is 'absolutely necessary'. See, eg, *McCann* (n 19 above) 49.

41   See ICCPR, art 4: '[i]n time of public emergency which threatens the life of the nation', states can take measures derogating from their obligations under the *Covenant*. For interpretations of the limits of state of emergency see D McGoldrick *The Human Rights Committee* (2003) 303; R Provost *International human rights and humanitarian law* (2002) 273.

42   The negotiations of the ICCPR resulted in controversy over whether exceptions to the right to life should be limited to an exhaustive list or whether the adjective 'arbitrary' was adequate. See Melzer (n 3 above) 92–93. For a detailed discussion of what constitutes 'arbitrary' deprivation under international human rights law, see P Alston 'Report of the Special Rapporteur on extrajudicial, summary or arbitrary Executions' UN Doc A/61/311 (5 September 2006) paras 33–45.

43   See S Joseph et al *The international covenant on civil and political rights: Cases, materials and commentary* (2005) 156; *Burrell v Jamaica*, Communication No 546/1993, UN Doc CCPR/C/53/D/546/1993 (1996) para 9.5.

44   *De Guerrero v Colombia*, Communication No 11/45, UN Doc A/37/40 (1979) 137. See General Comment No 6 (n 37 above) para 13.2.

45   Basic Principles on the Use of Force and Firearms (n 4 above) art 1; Principles on the Effective Prevention and Investigation of Extra-Legal, Arbitrary and Summary Executions, UN Doc E/RES/1989/65 (24 May 1989) art 1. See, also, *McCann* (n 19 above) paras 203-214; University Centre for International Humanitarian Law 'Expert meeting on the right to life in armed conflicts and situations of occupation' 8-14, 1-2 September 2005 http://www.adh-geneva.ch/docs/expert-meetings/2005/3rapport_ droit_vie.pdf (accessed 10 December 2013).

2.3 Concluding comments on normative frameworks

The above analysis has revealed that according to IHL there is no explicit legal provision to arrest a legitimate target and there is disagreement as to whether an implicit obligation can be read into the treaty provisions. In contrast, IHRL has many sources (both soft and hard law) that reinforce the principle that human life cannot be taken arbitrarily. Arrest is the common law enforcement measure employed in IHRL. Therefore, the legal regimes operate differently on the question of the use of force. Under IHL the conduct of hostilities permits the killing of legitimate targets provided the rules on proportionality and precautions in attack are fulfilled, and this body of law also tolerates incidental death of civilians, or 'collateral damage' in certain circumstances. Under IHRL, lethal force is permissible in much stricter circumstances: it may only be used as a last resort to protect life when other available means prove ineffective.

3   *Lex specialis*

There is increasing support for the claim that human rights, such as the right to life, continue to apply beyond peacetime,[46] including during IACs,[47] NIACs[48] and occupation.[49] This is based on the notion that IHL and IHRL share 'a common core of fundamental standards which are applicable in all times'.[50] The common legal reasoning used to understand the interplay between the paradigms has been that IHL constitutes the '*lex specialis*' and therefore prevails over the general paradigm of IHRL because its rules are specifically designed to address the realities of armed conflict.[51] According to the interpretive maxim *lex specialis derogat lex generalis*, also known as the principle of speciality, the specialised rule overrides the general rule.[52] The International Court of Justice (ICJ) in the

---

46   *Wall Opinion* (n 12 above) para 106.
47   *Legality of the Threat or Use of Nuclear Weapons (Advisory Opinion)* ICJ (8 July 1996) (1996) ICJ Reports 226, 256 para 240 (Nuclear Weapons Opinion).
48   *Abella v Argentina* (n 15 above) paras 151-171.
49   *Banković v Belgium* (2007) 44 EHRR SE5.
50   *Prosecutor v Delalić* International Criminal Tribunal for the former Yugoslavia, Appeals Chamber, Case No IT-96-21-A (20 February 2001) para 149.
51   *Nuclear Weapons Opinion* (n 47 above) para 25. See, also, FJ Hampson 'The relationship between international humanitarian law and human rights law from the perspective of a human rights treaty body' (2008) 90 *International Review of the Red Cross* 549 559; L Doswald-Beck 'International humanitarian law and the advisory opinion of the International Court of Justice on the legality of the threat or use of nuclear weapons' (1997) 316 *International Review of the Red Cross* 35.
52   The rationale behind this rule was expressed long ago by Grotius: 'Among agreements which are equal in respects to the qualities mentioned, that should be given preference which is most specific and approaches most nearly to the subject in hand; for special provisions are ordinarily more effective than those that are general'. See H Grotius *De Jure Belli Ac Pacis Libri Tris* (1646) trans F Kelsey (1925) 428. For a recent discussion of its meaning see International Law Commission *Fragmentation of international law: Difficulties arising from the diversification and expansion of international law*, UN Doc A/CN.4/L.682 (13 April 2006) paras 56-57.

Nuclear Weapons Advisory Opinion articulated this argument when it was presented with the question of whether the threat or use of nuclear weapons was in any circumstances permitted in international law and held that even during an IAC the right to life continues to apply.[53] The extent to which the right applies is determined by the *lex specialis* and therefore what is considered to be an arbitrary deprivation of life under IHRL is determined by IHL.

At the time it was handed down in 1996 the *Nuclear Weapons* opinion was considered a landmark in finding that IHRL continues to apply during armed conflict.[54] However, caution has been expressed about the value of the opinion (and the doctrine) because it provides little direction on how to apply the doctrine in practice.[55] Unclarity remains on to how to approach the interaction of the paradigms, particularly in NIACs where the interplay is most prominent. The ICJ has progressed beyond the *lex specialis* framework in its discussion of the interplay between IHL and IHRL.[56] Some scholars have reinterpreted the maxim based on the view that the *lex specialis* cannot always be the law pertaining to the conduct of hostilities, particularly in NIACs.[57] Moreover, there has been growing reference to the jurisprudence of regional human rights courts where the applicable framework is IHRL in assessing activities that occurred in conflict situations.[58]

Despite the limitations of this doctrine, it remains a sensible starting point because IHL offers the practical value of focusing on the status of the person, thereby framing the discussion in the realities of armed conflict. Targeting may be permissible against members of the armed forces, fighters and civilians directly taking part in hostilities and IHL provides detailed rules on such conduct. Considering that the analysis in this chapter is rooted in the conduct of hostilities, the status-based approach is the most natural way to begin assessing the use of force in armed conflict.

53 The ICJ acknowledged the application of IHRL in general to situations of armed conflict. See *Nuclear Weapons Opinion* (n 47 above) para 25. On the question before the Court, the ICJ did not make a clear finding on the legality of the use of nuclear weapons, para 95.
54 This was confirmed by the ICJ in subsequent decisions. See *Wall Opinion* (n 12 above) 178; *DRC v Uganda* (n 19 above) para 243-244.
55 Milanovic (n 18 above) 249-252; N Prud'homme 'Lex specialis: Oversimplifying a more complex and multi-faceted relationship?' (2007) 40 *Israel Law Review* 355 356.
56 *DRC v Uganda* (n 19 above) para 216. The Court referred to the *Wall Opinion*, where it held that 'both branches of international law, namely international human rights law and international humanitarian law, would have to be taken into consideration'. It did not describe IHL as the *lex specialis.*
57 See Sassòli & Olson (n 13 above) 599.
58 See the jurisprudence of the European Court of Human Rights, eg: *Gül v Turkey* (2000) EHRR 82; *Ogur v Turkey* (1999) EHRR; *Hamiyet Kaplan v Turkey* (2005) EHRR; *Mansuroglu v Turkey* (2008) EHRR; *Al Skeini v The United Kingdom* (2005) EHRR; *Hassan v the United Kingdom* (2014) EHRR. See W Abresch 'A human rights law of internal armed conflict: The European Court of Human Rights in Chechnya' (2005) 16 *European Journal of International Law* 741 746-748.

3.1   Assessing the meaning of 'arbitrary'

Although combatants/fighters[59] and civilians both enjoy the same fundamental right to life, interpreting the meaning of arbitrary deprivation of life will be informed by whether in fact a person is a legitimate target. This task is often made more challenging in many of the conflicts to which IHRL and IHRL apply simultaneously because it is often unclear whether an individual is a legitimate target:

> In a non-international armed conflict, when a State is using force against fighters, it may be considered as simultaneously conducting hostilities and maintaining law and order (since fighters are also frequently criminals under domestic law). Similarly, situations of civilian unrest (such as riots) may arise while combat operations against the adversary are taking place. Sometimes the two situations of violence may even intermingle, for instance when fighters are hiding among rioting civilians or demonstrators. In such cases, it may become difficult to distinguish fighters from rioting civilians and to identify the relevant applicable paradigm.[60]

Determining the meaning of arbitrary is difficult because it depends on whether the fighter is a legitimate target or a criminal/civilian rioter. The ICRC expert meeting on the use of force in armed conflict canvassed the logical approach that there can be circumstances where the two legal paradigms apply 'in parallel'.[61] This entails that in the one incident it may be legal to use lethal force against some individuals but illegal against others. The approach seems legally straightforward, however it places practical obstacles on the belligerent who is required to distinguish in real time between the kinds of use of force that is permissible against different individuals involved in the same incident.

In situations where it is clear that the rules regulating the conduct of hostilities apply, classifying the status of the individual poses a different set of challenges because the majority of conflicts in recent times do not reflect the traditional battlefield of state armies of the opposing sides fighting each other. Current debate has focused on the legal ramifications for individuals who are not traditional soldiers but nonetheless participate in hostilities. This debate (lead by the ICRC Guidance on the topic) has revolved around when and if it is legitimate to target individuals who fall in the category of

---

59   Combatant status is absent from NIAC treaty law, however, the term 'combatant' can be used descriptively in relation to those individuals who actively participate in hostilities. There has also been a trend to adopt the term 'fighters' in NIAC in order to avoid confusion with the meaning of 'combatant' in IAC. See art 3 GC; Henckaerts & Doswald-Beck (n 5 above), rule 1; Schmitt et al (n 14 above) rule 1.1.2. For an insightful analysis of applying the principle of distinction to NIAC see JK Kleffner 'From "belligerents" to "fighters" and civilians directly participating in hostilities – On the principle of distinction in non-international armed conflicts one hundred years after the Second Hague Peace Conference' (2007) 54 *Netherlands International Law Review* 315.
60   ICRC experts meeting: The use of force in armed conflict (n 9 above) 1.
61   n 9 above, 25.

'civilians directly participating in hostilities' ('DPH') because they have forfeited their civilian protection for the time that they participate.[62] The legal meaning of DPH is heavily disputed and this makes it difficult to interpret 'arbitrary'. Taking a broad or narrow interpretation of when civilian protection is forfeited will influence whether the targeting is legitimate under IHL or whether there is an obligation to arrest because such a killing would be arbitrary. For example, according to a narrow approach where DPH is limited to the duration of a specific act or function, in all other circumstances targeting would be arbitrary because the target is not posing an imminent threat and arrest would be required.[63] In contrast, a broad approach to DPH that considers loss of civilian immunity to continue for the duration of hostilities unless the individual actively opts out of participation targeting would not be arbitrary.[64]

In this context it is worth noting the Israeli Supreme Court *Targeted Killing* case, which, in its assessment of the legality of targeted killing, found civilians 'directly participating in hostilities' to be the relevant conduct for its analysis. The Court held that there is a 'less harmful means requirement', which states that where possible less drastic measures, such as arrest, should be used to stop a potential target posing a security threat.[65] The Court (which actually adopted a broad approach to DPH) did not, however, arrive at this conclusion based on its assessment of the meaning of 'arbitrary' according to the right to life.[66] The 'less harmful means requirement' is a rule called for by the principle of proportionality

---

62   ICRC Guidance (n 31 above); For critiques of the Guidance see: K Watkin 'Opportunity lost: Organized armed groups and the ICRC "Direct participation in hostilities" interpretive guidance' (2010) 42 *New York University Journal of International Law and Politics* 641; MN Schmitt 'Deconstructing direct participation in hostilities: The constitutive elements' (2010) 42 *New York University Journal of International Law and Politics* 641 697; B Boothby '"And for such time as": The time dimension to direct participation in hostilities' (2010) 42 *New York University Journal of International Law and Politics* 741; WH Parks 'Part IX of the ICRC "Direct participation in hostilities" study: No mandate, no expertise and legally incorrect' (2010) 42 *New York University Journal of International Law and Politics* 769; Melzer (n 32 above) 837. The author has addressed the debate more exhaustively elsewhere: M Lesh 'Loss of protection: Direct participation in hostilities' in T McCormack & R Liivoja *Routledge handbook of the law of armed conflict* (forthcoming 2015).

63   ICRC Guidance (n 31 above). See, also, Melzer (n 3 above); A Cassese 'Expert opinion on whether Israel's targeted killings of Palestinian terrorists is consonant with international humanitarian law' (2003) 8 http://www.stoptorture.org.il/files/cassese.pdf (accessed 10 December 2013); APV Rogers 'Direct participation in hostilities: Some personal reflections' (2009) 48 *Military Law and the Law of War Review* 143; D Akande 'Clearing the fog of war? The ICRC's interpretive guidance on direct participation in hostilities' (2010) 59 *International and Comparative Law Quarterly* 180 188.

64   See, eg, *Public Committee against Torture in Israel v Government of Israel* 13 December 2006 HCJ 769/02 (*Targeted Killing* case); WH Parks 'Air war and the law of war' (1990) 32 *Air Force Law Review* 134; MN Schmitt 'The interpretive guidance on the notion of direct participation in hostilities: A critical analysis' (2010) 1 *Harvard National Security Journal* 1; Watkin (n 62 above); C Garraway '"To kill or not to kill?" – Dilemmas on the use of force' (2010) 15 *Journal of Conflict and Security Law* 499.

65   *Targeted Killing* case (n 64 above) para 5.

66   n 64 above, para 40.

under Israeli domestic law.[67] This is based on an IHRL understanding of proportionality.[68] Proportionality is a key concept in both IHL and IHRL, yet their meanings are very different.[69]

Thus, the Court placed restraints on targeting a civilian directly participating in hostilities by appealing to the IHRL concept of proportionality. Because the content of proportionality under the two paradigms are incompatible, mixing them creates confusion. The *Targeted Killing* case has indeed been criticised for not clearly applying the rule of *lex specialis* to determine the arrest requirement.[70] The judgment needed to be more explicit in its approach. It was, nonetheless, accurate in its implicit application of *lex specialis* as evidenced by the attention to force protection. The arrest requirement cannot be implemented if it puts soldiers at too great a risk of harm. That is, the IHRL concept of proportionality, reflected in the less harmful means, cannot be implemented if it interferes with the IHL rule on proportionality, reflected in force protection.

Current day conflicts tend to involve multiple armed groups as well as foreign fighters (as, for example, in Syria) and the growing use of drone strikes (particularly by the United States)[71] challenges the geographical boundaries of war.[72] Moreover, military operations are often conducted amongst the civilian population where situations of civil unrest may unfold

---

67   As above. See, also, *McCann* (n 19 above) para 236.
68   A Barak 'Proportional effect – The Israeli experience' (2007) 14 (on file with the author). See also Y Shany 'Competing legal paradigms for fighting terror' in O Ben-Naftali (ed) *International humanitarian law and international human rights law: Pas de deux* (2011) 26–27.
69   Under IHL, proportionality does not cover the legitimate target of an attack but whether damage to surrounding civilians and civilian objects is excessive in relation to the concrete and direct military advantage anticipated in the attack. In contrast, under IHRL, when a state agent is using force against an individual, the proportionality principle assesses the risk posed by the individual as well as the potential harm to the individual and to bystanders. Such an assessment must result in the smallest amount of force necessary and restricting the use of lethal force. See N Lubell 'Challenges in applying human rights law to armed conflict' (2005) 87 *International Review of the Red Cross* 737 745-746.
70   See Milanovic (n 18 above) 256.
71   United States, Office of the President 'Fact Sheet: US policy standards on the use for force in counterterrorism operations outside the United States and areas of active hostilities' (23 May 2013) http://www.whitehouse.gov/the-press-office/2013/05/23/fact-sheet-us-policy-standards-and-procedures-use-force-counterterrorism (accessed 10 December 2013).
72   In recent years there has been an abundance of literature on the legal ramifications of drones and on the geographical scope of conflict. See, eg: ICRC 'The use of armed drones must comply with laws' (10 May 2013) www.icrc.org/eng/resources/documents/interview/2013/05-10-drone-weapons-ihl.htm (accessed 10 December 2013); Heyns (n 19 above) para 103; B Emmerson 'Report of the Special Rapporteur on the promotion and protection of human rights and fundamental freedoms while countering terrorism' UN Doc A/68/389 (18 September 2013); N Melzer 'Human rights implications of the usage of drones and unmanned robots in warfare' European Parliament, Directorate General for External Policies of the Union, Policy Department Study (Brussels, 2013); N Lubell & N Derejko 'A global battlefield?: Drones and the geographical scope of armed conflict' (2013) 11 *Journal of International Criminal Justice* 65; JD Ohlin 'Is *jus in bello* in crisis?' (2013) 11 *Journal of International Criminal Justice* 27.

at the same time as combat operations are occurring, making it difficult to distinguish between fighters and civilians. The factual situations therefore exacerbate the difficulty in applying two paradigms simultaneously. A context-dependent approach, which assesses the applicable law on the use of force on a case-by-case basis, has aided in navigating through these complex scenarios.[73] Some scholars even claim that on certain issues (drones) there has been growing agreement on the appropriate legal frameworks, allowing for a more sophisticated and constructive dialogue.[74] To repeat: according to the *lex specialis*, the starting point for assessing the use of force during the conduct of hostilities is IHL. IHRL may limit the kind of force otherwise permissible under IHL if that force is rendered arbitrary according to IHL. From this perspective, where the contours of the use of force under the two applicable paradigms often conflict, a lot depends on whether the meaning of 'arbitrary' can create workable convergence.

3.2   The principles of military necessity and humanity

One way of attempting to give added utility and value to the doctrine of *lex specialis* in determining the relationship between IHL and IHRL is through a reliance on the principles that underpin IHL. Often, IHRL is seen to be in accord with and to extend what is implicit in the principle of humanity that underpins IHL.[75] The growing acceptance that ideas of human rights should inform IHL is what Meron dubbed the 'humanization of humanitarian law'.[76] In this connection it is important to note that, the ICJ, in the *Nuclear Weapons* Advisory Opinion, emphasised the 'overriding consideration of humanity'[77] when interpreting the rules of IHL. It did not do so, however, in order to implant into the conduct of hostilities a *lex generalis* which, while complementary to the principle of humanity, might be *inconsistent* with military necessity. The principle of military necessity and the principle of humanity need not be inconsistent or even in tension. The doctrine of *lex specialis* therefore indicates the appropriate balance between the principles of military necessity and humanity, and limits the

---

73   *Wall Opinion* (n 12 above) para 106; *DRC v Uganda* (n 19 above) para 216.
74   MN Schmitt 'Narrowing the international law divide: The drone debate matures' (2014) 39 *The Yale Journal of International Law Online* 1 5-8. Schmitt argues that growing recognition that the three international law regimes governing drone operations are sovereignty, IHL and IHRL has put a stop to previous confusion in the drones debate caused by conflation of these distinct regimes. Moreover, Schmitt's analysis of relevant IGO and NGO reports concludes that all the reports 'illustrate the human rights community's acceptance of IHL as the prevailing legal regime for drone strikes during a conflict with an organized armed group, or "non-international armed conflict" (NIAC)' and that 'all parties to the debate agree that absent an armed conflict, IHRL rather than IHL applies, [however] the arbitrariness of a lethal attack under that law is judged by reference to IHL standards'.
75   See *Furundžija Trial Chamber Judgment* International Criminal Tribunal for the former Yugoslavia Case No 1T-95-17/1-T (10 December 1998).
76   T Meron 'The humanization of humanitarian law' (2000) 94 *American Journal of International Law* 239.
77   *Nuclear Weapons Opinion* (n 47 above) para 95.

extent to which IHRL is needed to restrain the imperatives of military necessity for the sake of humanitarian concerns. It is therefore an important question whether the principle of humanity and the recognition that the right to life is forfeited only in very special circumstances can coincide in their application to the use of force during the conduct of hostilities.

If it is accepted that when interpreting the law, particularly its vague provisions, the underlying principles of that law should guide our interpretation, then there is nothing novel about this approach to *lex specialis*. Moreover, in the light of the growing acceptance of the idea that IHRL continues to apply during armed conflict, this seems a fitting approach to determine the applicability of IHRL. In order to determine the extent to which restraints on the use of force apply to the rules regulating the conduct of hostilities, this approach will be applied to two vague provisions of IHL on direct participation in hostilities of civilians and on precautionary measures (articles 51(3) and 57 API). The application will draw on two scholars who take radically different approaches to the role of these principles. Thus, varied attitudes on the influence of the principles of humanity and necessity in interpreting and applying IHL and IHRL are critical to an adequate discussion of 'capture over kill'.

3.2.1 Article 57: Additional Protocol I

The focus of article 57 API is to take precautions in order to avoid incidental harm (that is, other than to the target).[78] Nonetheless, arresting the target can still be in keeping with the purpose of the provision and therefore a relevant precautionary measure when there is reason to believe

---

78 Art 57 (API):
'1. In the conduct of military operations, constant care shall be taken to spare the civilian population, civilians and civilian objects.
2. With respect to attacks, the following precautions shall be taken:
(a) those who plan or decide upon an attack shall:
(i) do everything feasible to verify that the objectives to be attacked are neither civilians nor civilian objects and are not subject to special protection but are military objectives within the meaning of paragraph 2 of article 52 and that it is not prohibited by the provisions of this Protocol to attack them;
(ii) take all feasible precautions in the choice of means and methods of attack with a view to avoiding, and in any event to minimizing, incidental loss of civilian life, injury to civilians and damage to civilian objects;
(iii) refrain from deciding to launch any attack which may be expected to cause incidental loss of civilian life, injury to civilians, damage to civilian objects, or a combination thereof, which would be excessive in relation to the concrete and direct military advantage anticipated;
(b) an attack shall be cancelled or suspended if it becomes apparent that the objective is not a military one or is subject to special protection or that the attack may be expected to cause incidental loss of civilian life, injury to civilians, damage to civilian objects, or a combination thereof, which would be excessive in relation to the concrete and direct military advantage anticipated;
(c) effective advance warning shall be given of attacks which may affect the civilian population, unless circumstances do not permit.

that fewer civilians would be placed at risk during an arrest operation than would be the case in a targeting operation.[79] The term 'feasible' is overly broad and the extent to which IHRL can aid in clarifying this provision is determined by the principles of military necessity and humanity. The nature of the violence and the level of control will influence the feasibility to arrest as part of the duty to take 'constant care' to asses the proportionate nature of means and methods of warfare and, therefore, the obligation to attempt to arrest.

Some IHL experts reject this proposed approach. For example, Schmitt adopts a black letter reading of article 57 and concludes that 'since enemy combatants and directly participating civilians constitute lawful targets under IHL until they surrender or are otherwise rendered *hors de combat*, it is lawful to kill them even when capture is feasible'.[80] Parks advocates a similar approach.[81] For Schmitt, the lawfulness of an act is not influenced by whether it is 'humane':

> The fact that a killing is lawful when capture might be feasible does not mean that killing is sensible operationally or from a policy perspective, or even that it is ethical. On the contrary, capture is usually preferable, whether to acquire a possible source of intelligence, avoid alienating the local population or emboldening the enemy, or maintain the high ground in the lawfare battlespace.[82]

---

3. When a choice is possible between several military objectives for obtaining a similar military advantage, the objective to be selected shall be that the attack on which may be expected to cause the least danger to civilian lives and to civilian objects.
4. In the conduct of military operations at sea or in the air, each Party to the conflict shall, in conformity with its rights and duties under the rules of international law applicable in armed conflict, take all reasonable precautions to avoid losses of civilian lives and damage to civilian objects.
5. No provision of this article may be construed as authorizing any attacks against the civilian population, civilians or civilian objects.'

79   For example, scholars have relied on art 57 (API) to argue that the duty to take 'feasible precaution' includes an investigation of potential violations of the principle of proportionality. See, eg, E Benvenisti 'The State of Israel's obligation to examine and investigate violations of the laws of war' Legal opinion submitted to the Turkel Commission   http://www.turkelcommittee.com/files/wordocs/Benvenisti_opinion. pdf (accessed 10 December 2013); A Cohen & Y Shany 'Beyond the grave breaches regime: The duty to investigate alleged violations of international law governing armed conflicts' (2011) 14 *Yearbook of International Humanitarian Law* 37 47:
>   'investigation of past incidents in which harm has occurred is arguably part of the "constant care" which parties are expected to demonstrate in order to assess on an ongoing basis the proportionate nature of the methods and means of warfare they employ'.

80   See MN Schmitt 'Investigating violations of international law in armed conflicts' (2011) 2 *Harvard National Security Journal* 31 54.
81   See WH Parks 'Memorandum of law: Executive order 1233 and assassination' (1989) *The Army Lawyer* 4 7 (fn 6).
82   MN Schmitt 'Wound, capture, or kill: A reply to Ryan Goodman's "The power to kill or capture enemy combatants"' (2013) 24 *European Journal of International Law* 855 861.

Interestingly, the US, a state that uses drones regularly, has stated that as a matter of *policy* it will not use lethal force when it is *feasible* to capture the individual.[83] A 2013 report by the Extrajudicial Executions Special Rapporteur, which focused on the use of drones, stated that 'whether or not they recognize this as a legal obligation, states *should* capture rather than kill during armed conflict where feasible'.[84] 'Should' implies *lex ferenda* rather than *lex lata* and hence does not suggest that there is a legal obligation to arrest based on the duty to take precautionary measures. However, a different way to approach the matter is to ask whether targeting (namely, killing) is *unlawful* if capture is *feasible*. The answer to that question depends, of course, on the circumstances and whether the arrest operation will foreseeably place fewer civilians at risk. This is not always the case, especially in 'clean' sniper operations.

3.2.2   Article 51(3): Additional Protocol I

Article 51(3) of API articulates the limits to the scope of protected civilian status: 'Civilians shall enjoy the protection afforded by this Section, unless and for such time as they take a direct part in hostilities'.[85] The legal consequence of DPH is the loss of civilian protection without becoming entitled to the rights given to combatants.[86] Defining DPH has proven to be problematic.[87]

The questions of 'capture over kill' and the role of the underlying principles of IHL in determining the meaning of article 51(3), bring to mind a much deeper debate, sparked by the ICRC Guidance and specifically section IX, which states that 'the kind and degree of force which is permissible against persons not entitled to protection against direct attack must not exceed what is actually necessary to accomplish a legitimate military purpose in the prevailing circumstances'.[88] This sentiment sounds reasonable and is, in a way, an obvious expression of humanity. The Guidance supports its position with reference to the principles of humanity and necessity.[89] This interpretation by the Guidance has received both support[90] and criticism.[91] The inclusion of

---

83   United States, Office of the President, Fact Sheet (n 71 above).
84   Heyns (n above 19) para 114 [emphasis added]. It is unclear what 'should' means in this context.
85   API, art 51(3). This notion is replicated in other embodiments of IHL. See GCI–IV, art 3; Rome Statute art 8.2(b)(i), 8.2(e)(i). See also UK Ministry of Defence *The manual of the law of armed conflict* (2004) para 5.3.2; Schmitt et al (n 14 above) rule 2.1.1.2.
86   Sandoz et al (n 22 above) para 1942.
87   Henckaerts & Doswald-Beck (n 5 above) practice to r 6.
88   ICRC Guidance (n 31 above) 77. The Guidance did nonetheless state that in practice, such considerations are likely to become more relevant where a party to the conflict exercises effective territorial control during occupation or during a NIAC. See 80–81. Parks (n 62 above) 788 (fn 64).
89   ICRC Guidance (n 31 above) 82.
90   See Alston (n 16 above) para 76. See also Melzer (n 3 above) 289, 286. Goodman (n 28 above).
91   See Parks (n 62 above); Garraway (n 64 above) 506–507; Kleffner (n 36 above).

this section in the Guidance is the main reason why approximately one-third of the experts (particularly those with military backgrounds) refused to put their name to a document they had spent five years working on.[92] The Guidance is therefore an 'expression solely of the ICRC's views'.[93]

There are two aspects to the controversy surrounding section IX of the Guidance. First, there is the claim by its critics that despite the fact that the Guidance calls its most important section 'Recommendations and Commentary', section IX is naturally read as (and, its critics' claim is intended to be read as) an interpretation of IHL rather than a recommendation to change the law. Second, it raises this important question: if it is taken as a recommendation, is it one that is plausibly an expression of the spirit of IHL as that spirit may be interpreted in times such as the present when there is arguably greater concern for the value of individual lives than was the case when the principle of humanity was formulated?

In regard to the first point Melzer (the author of the Guidance) rejects the criticism that section IX is an example of the Guidance going beyond its mandate and, in effect, making law:

> [T]he international community of States has provided the ICRC with a broad mandate to act as a promoter and guardian of IHL ... Accordingly, in exercising its mandate, the ICRC has repeatedly addressed questions relating to the conduct of hostilities.[94]

Defending the Guidance, Melzer provides examples of state practice that support section IX. He points to the adoption by the General Command of the Colombian Armed Forces of the new 'Manual de Derecho Operacional' and the Israeli *Targeted Killing* case.[95] Such state practice, in Melzer's view, demonstrates that the principle of humanity places restraints on the use of force. Melzer also argues that interpretation of existing treaty provisions within IHL[96] further supports the position of the Guidance that 'it would defy basic notions of humanity to kill an adversary or to refrain from giving him or her an opportunity to surrender where there manifestly is no necessity for the use of lethal force'.[97]

Schmitt is critical of the Guidance requirement on restraints on the use of force precisely because of the way it uses the principles of humanity and

---

92   See, eg, Parks (n 62 above) 783–785: For rebuttal see Melzer (n 32 above) 894–913.
93   See ICRC Guidance (n 31 above) 6; Melzer (n 32 above) 831.
94   Melzer (n 32 above) 893.
95   n 32 above, 910. See, also, See Decision of the German Federal Prosecutor, 20 June 2013: www.generalbundesanwalt.de/docs/drohneneinsatz_vom_04oktober2010_mir_ali_pakistan.pdf (in German) (accessed 10 December 2013); Goodman (n 28 above).
96   Melzer (n 32 above) 905–908. See, eg, Hague Regulations, art 22; API, arts 35, 48, 51(3), 52(2); *Nuclear Weapons Opinion* (n 47 above) para 257; Hague Convention II preamble (Martens Clause).
97   ICRC Guidance (n 31 above) 82.

military necessity as interpretive tools. He argues that it is only when positive law specifically cites either humanity or necessity that these principles come into play.[98] Schmitt's argument consists of three points. First, there is no state practice that supports the Guidance's approach that either of these principles applies as a 'separate restriction that constitutes an additional hurdle over which an attack must pass before mounting an attack'.[99] According to his second point, the Guidance requirement of restraints on the use of force is skewed too much in favour of humanity,[100] upsetting the delicate balance between the two underlying principles that already exist in IHL rules.

In connection with Schmitt's second point is should be noted that the debate is in part about what kind of considerations should determine what counts as 'too much' in favour of humanity. Melzer would say that Schmitt's belief that the Guidance requirement is skewed too much in favour of humanity is itself an expression of his failure to be, in this day and age, fully responsive to the spirit of the principle of humanity – to the need to 'humanise' it, as Meron put it. Schmitt, on the other hand, would say that in the name of being true to its spirit, Melzer's recommendation distorts the principle of humanity, whose sober interpretation demands that one be realistic about the requirements of military necessity. The principle of humanity is naturally taken to be, in part, a moral principle. If that is so, there seems to be no morally neutral way of understanding the principle and its applications that would resolve this dispute.

Schmitt's third point is that he accepts that the law can be interpreted by using the principles of military necessity and humanity so long as such interpretation is done by states.[101] The evolution of the balance achieved by states is through the process of codification or custom.

The five-year working group on DPH (the impetus behind the Guidance) is an example of an external factor interpreting the sufficiency of the law with respect to changing circumstances. Its interpretation was informed by its understanding of the balance between military necessity and humanity. Insofar as disagreements in the interpretation of the law on such matters have an inescapable moral dimension (which, in the case of IHL shows most clearly in differing interpretations of the principle of humanity and of its role), it is difficult to accept a reading of the law that maintains that the balance of military necessity and humanity has already been achieved in the legal provisions, and that when circumstances change it is only for states to decide how to adapt the law. This seems to neglect other important influences on the interpretation process and other

---

98   MN Schmitt 'Military necessity and humanity in international humanitarian law: Preserving the delicate balance' (2010) 50 *Virginia Journal of International Law* 795, 796, 805, 811–812, 798–799.
99   n 64 above, 41.
100   n 64 above, 7.
101   Schmitt (n 98 above) 796, 805, 811–812.

important factors that shape the formation of law – interpretations of vague provisions that are grounded in the principles that underpin the law. It is for this reason that we say that the law is reinterpreted in new ways while remaining 'true to its spirit'. The only way to remain true to the spirit of the law is to interpret it based on its underpinning principles. In the case of the principle of humanity, that will include interpretations of the moral attitudes that shaped it.

It is important to keep in mind that the section IX debate is about whether IHL imposes restraints on the use of force. The focus in this chapter is on whether the concept of *lex specialis* could be enlisted because there is a lack of clarity on the meaning of article 51(3). IHRL is arguably very suited to supplement IHL in just those cases. The meaning of DPH is far from clear. Therefore, the stricter IHRL obligation to arrest is an appropriate 'filler' when it is reasonable to apply it in the specific circumstances. It is impossible to avoid discussing the debate surrounding section IX of the Guidance when contemplating the relevance of the principles of humanity and necessity to interpreting the law. There is no explicit requirement in the law to arrest based on the meaning of civilians directly participating in hostilities. An arrest requirement cannot be construed as *lex lata*. To do so would render it unconvincing to use the principles as a legal basis for creating additional restraints on the use of force under IHL that do not already exist in positive law.

However, this is different from using the underlying principles as a way of determining whether the *lex generalis* can come into play to bring clarity to a vague provision of law given the acceptance that IHRL applies to armed conflict. The distinction between the interpretation that relies on the principles to create additional restraints on the use of force under IHL and the interpretation that relies on the principles to determine how IHRL comes into play to clarify provisions of IHL on the use of force, should not be dismissed as mere semantics on the basis that the end result is the same: namely, restraints on the use of force against legitimate targets. Relying on the underlying principles, as interpretive tools, reveal different approaches in the interpretation process. Some of these approaches become more important factors than others in shaping the formation of law, and some may not reflect *lex lata,* but perhaps indicate instead *lex ferenda.* The latter would be in keeping with the sentiment that the aim of armed conflict is to weaken the military potential of the enemy while preserving, as much as possible, the civilian population.[102] It would follow that arresting a 'civilian directly participating in hostilities' should be a preferred where feasible because that best protects the human dignity and life of the civilian population.

---

102   E Benvenisti 'Human dignity in combat: The duty to spare enemy civilians' (2006) 39 *Israel Law Review* 87. See also O Ben-Naftali & Y Shany 'Living in Denial: The application of human rights in the occupied territories' (2003) 37 *Israel Law Review* 17, 42; *Furundžija* (n 75 above) para 183.

3.3 Conclusions on *lex specialis*

This chapter proposes using the principle of humanity as a way to understand IHRL. This does not mean that the principle of necessity is disregarded. Military necessity sets the limits. The IHRL restraints on the use of force should be considered on the basis of the principle of humanity with the aim of minimising human suffering. *Lex generalis* should apply when appropriate to remedy the lack of clarity as to the meaning of DPH and feasible precautions. That, however depends on the assumption that arrest will bring about fewer casualties, which, it is important to note, is not always the case.[103]

The principle of military necessity informs the limits of the interaction between the *lex specialis* and the *lex generalis*. Therefore the requirement to arrest the target is determined by factors such as the nature of the threat, the intensity of violence, the level of control,[104] and other important elements that dictate whether military operations can be conducted effectively and contribute to the aim of weakening the military potential of the enemy. The principle of humanity is a point of convergence between the two regimes. Although some may regard this approach as merely substituting the term 'arbitrary' with 'inhumane' in order to determine the extent to which restraints on the use of force apply in the conduct of hostilities, the principle of humanity does seem conceptually more appropriate because it captures what it is that lies at the heart of this debate: human life. As a consequence it may bring about more practical and effective results in the interplay. However, as the debate between Melzer and Schmitt reveals there is also no morally neutral account of 'humanity': different interpretations that are at least implicitly morally committed will lead to different conclusion on what type of restraints are justified.

Ultimately, on the question of the use of force during the conduct of hostilities it is very difficult to come up with a fully satisfactory approach to the interplay between the two regimes. This can be demonstrated by comparing the application of the *lex specialis* doctrine to a different obligation. For example, if we look at the obligation to investigate under IHL, it lacks specificity, particularly in relation to the manner of conducting an investigation.[105] The trend has been to turn to the IHRL standards for conducting an investigation (independence, impartiality, effectiveness and thoroughness, promptness and transparency) and to apply those standards to the IHL duty to investigate. There has been wide

---

103 N Modirzadeh 'The dark side of convergence: A pro-civilian critique of the extraterritorial application of human rights law in armed conflict' (2010) 86 *US Naval War College International Law Studies (Blue Book) Series* 349.
104 Alston (n 16 above) para 77.
105 See GCIV, arts 146-147; API, arts 86-87.

agreement in this approach.[106] IHRL standards are more specific and therefore fill in a lacuna in IHL. The lack of consensus on the question of the use of force can be explained by two inter-connected reasons. The first is that in the use of force analysis the relevant provisions, such as 'feasible precautions' and 'direct participation in hostilities', are vague provisions that lend themselves to a variety of interpretations.[107] It is not the case that the law is silent, but that its terminology is ambiguous. The second more fundamental reason comes back to the contrasting approaches to the use of force. The problem lies not so much with the *lex specialis* doctrine but with the conflicting content of the rules regulating the use of force under to two regimes. Sometimes the conflict is unresolvable and there needs to be limits to methods of interpretation employed in order to prevent the dilution of the core of the two paradigms.[108]

4   Conclusion

It is often a challenge to distinguish between violence that is criminal in nature (and which therefore requires a law enforcement operation) and violence that is part of the armed conflict. A nuanced approach must be taken to interpreting the right to life both in the IHL and IHRL paradigms. It has been established that there 'is no single formula'[109] for *lex specialis* because it involves the weighing of different considerations. *Lex specialis* supports the idea that IHRL supplements IHL where there is lack of clarity. The principles of humanity and military necessity guide the way in which IHRL interprets broad IHL provisions. IHRL can aid in interpreting article 51(3) (the meaning of DPH) and to a lesser extent article 57 (the meaning of feasible precautions). It is hoped that this will bring about practical and effective ways of understanding the interplay between the two regimes. Nonetheless, in order to demonstrate fidelity to the position that IHL and IHRL operate in parallel during the conduct of hostilities, it must be acknowledged that there are limits to the attempts to create harmony between the two because often it is a relationship of conflict.

---

106   Goldstone Report 'UN fact-finding mission on the Gaza con?ict' UN Doc A/HRC/12/48 (25 September 2009); Report of the Secretary General, Israeli practices affecting the human rights of the Palestinian people in the Occupied Palestinian Territory, including East Jerusalem UN Doc A/68/502 (4 October 2013); Turkel (n 19 above); Schmitt (n 80 above); Cohen & Shany (n 79 above).
107   See Lubell (n 18 above) 245.
108   On the limits to harmony between the two regimes based on their markedly different approaches to jus ad bellum see: W Schabas '*Lex specialis?* Belts and suspenders? The parallel operation of human rights law and the law of armed conflict, the conundrum of *jus ad bellum*' (2007) 40 *Israel Law Review* 592.
109   Fragmentation of International Law (n 52 above) para 107.

6

Belligerent Occupation: Human Right and International Humanitarian Law

Andrea Carcano*

1 Introduction

As traditionally understood, a belligerent occupation (occupation) is a situation of fact involving the forcible control of a territory by a 'hostile army' belonging to a state, which occurs during or as a result of an international armed conflict[1] and is primarily governed by the law applicable *pendente bello*, that is international humanitarian law (IHL). Within the field of IHL, a specific set of norms and principles which international lawyers generally refer to as the 'law of occupation' have emerged over the years.[2] Though specific in the sense of having been designed to govern situations of occupation, the application of the law of occupation does not exclude the application of other norms of international law. The law of occupation is a planet within the galaxy, so to speak. The galaxy is international law: a polyhedric and multi-layered legal system. Hence, as part of the system of international law, the law of occupation must accommodate those other branches of international law which, depending on the rights and interests affected, may have a bearing on a situation of occupation, though they were not designed for that specific contingency. These include the principles of sovereignty and self-determination;[3] the resolutions of the Security Council and, though

* Andrea Carcano (PhD, University of Milan, 2008; LLM, NYU, 2005) is a Lecturer in International Criminal Law with the LLM Programme in International Crime and Justice (University of Turin and UNICRI) and an Adjunct Lecturer in Human Rights Law with the Faculty of Law of the University of Milan-Bicocca.

1   E Benvenisti *The international law of occupation* (2012) 43-67; Y Dinstein *The international law of belligerent occupation* (2009) 31-51; A Roberts 'What is a military occupation?' (1984) 55 *British Yearbook of International Law* 249.
2   Benvenisti (n 1 above) 1-12; Dinstein (n 1 above) 4-8; R Kolb & S Vité *Le droit de l'occupation militaire: Perspective historiques et enjeux juridiques actuels* (2010) 61-86.
3   *Legal Consequences of the Construction of a Wall in Occupied Palestinian Territory* (9 July 2004) (2004) ICJ Reports 136, paras 114-137 (*Wall* Advisory Opinion).

without binding force, those of the General Assembly; international human rights law[4] (IHRL); and the norms and principles of international criminal law. As these branches of international law may apply concomitantly to situations of occupation, this gives rise to the problem of coordination, both among them and between them and the law of occupation.

This paper discusses one of these relationships: that between the law of occupation and IHRL.[5] It seeks to understand whether these two regimes provide a coherent and clear framework to govern the conduct (acts and omissions) of an occupying power administering a state or a territory in the twenty-first century.

To this end this paper is structured as follows. It begins with a discussion of the reasons behind the determination that, in addition to its other obligations, a state is also required to comply with IHRL in the territory it happens to occupy. It then discusses the nature of the relationship between the law of occupation and IHRL by considering the situations in which (i) the norms of the two regimes apply in parallel to distinct matters; (ii) such norms converge in validating the same conduct; and (iii) such norms diverge on whether validating a particular conduct. With respect to this latter point, the paper examines whether the norms of the law of occupation, which are seen as the '*lex specialis*', should be given primacy over those of IHRL in any case of divergence. And, in contrast, it considers whether adherence to IHRL standards could influence the law of occupation to the point of justifying an expansion in the normative authority of an occupying power. Lastly, this paper concludes by asking whether the construction of a coherent and clear framework encompassing IHL and IHRL can be achieved only through interpretation by states, judicial institutions, human rights bodies and, on a different level, scholars, as it is currently done, or whether it would be better achieved through some form of codification.

Before turning to these arguments, however, two clarifications are in order. First, this paper adopts a '*jus in bello* perspective'.[6] It focuses on gauging how IHRL impacts on the authorities, responsibilities, and duties of an occupying power during an occupation. It does not tackle the *jus ad bellum* question of the legality of the existence of an occupation – that is, whether an occupying power has the right to remain within the occupied

---

4   See in this regard Dinstein (n 1 above) 68-88; Kolb & Vité (n 2 above) 303-336.
5   On the topic of the relationship between IHL and IHRL see, in particular, G Gaggioli & R Kolb (eds) *Research handbook on human rights and humanitarian law* (2013) 273-293; O Ben-Naftali *International humanitarian law and international human rights law* (2011) 13-304; M Milanovic *Extraterritorial application of human rights treaties* (2011) 229-261; T Meron *International law in the age of human rights: General course on public international law* (2004) vol 301, 60-85.
6   C Greenwood 'The relationship between *ius ad bellum* and *ius in bello*' (1983) 9 *Review of International Studies* 221.

territory – and how the legality or not of such presence may impact on the authorities and duties of an occupying power under IHRL. These issues, however, are not peregrine when one looks at international law as a coherent normative system and expects it to be so. At least one of them must be flagged here, although only for further reflection in specific studies, namely, whether the question of the illegality – which must be ascertained and cannot be presumed – of a situation of occupation affects the validity of the acts carried out by an occupying power in compliance with its human rights obligations.

By operation of the distinction between *jus in bello* and *jus ad bellum*, the general international law principle *ex iniuria ius non oritur* does not apply to the field of IHL. The authorities, responsibilities, and duties of an occupying power remain in place throughout the duration of an occupation, regardless of the legality of the use of force that brought the occupation about and perpetuates its existence. An occupation is not an illegal form of administration of territory *per se*. But, as any situation of fact governed by international law, it may be legal or not, depending on its adherence to the applicable norms and principles of international law, which include those governing the use of force, the principles of sovereignty and self-determination, and the right to self-defence.[7] What is to be clarified is whether the *jus ad bellum/jus in bello* rationale, which, for good reasons,[8] underlies the application of IHL, should also inform the application of IHRL during occupation, thereby making its application independent from the question of the legality of the presence of an occupying power within the occupied territory. In a domestic setting, though, of course, there could be differences from one system to another, the subsequent acts of an entity whose existence is found to be illegal would normally also be regarded as invalid. This argument, however, is not dispositive. International law proceeds on the basis of logical and structural premises that are different from those of national legal systems and it may therefore contemplate approaches that differ from those of domestic systems.

While the issue of the validity of the acts of an occupying power undertaken in the pursuit of human rights obligations from the perspective of the *jus ad bellum* has been somewhat neglected in the literature,[9] the practice of the International Court of Justice (ICJ), which is discussed in this paper, reveals the emergence of a rather consistent approach. The ICJ

7	O Ben-Naftali et al 'Illegal occupation: Framing the occupied Palestinian territory' (2005) 23 *Berkley Journal of International Law* 551.
8	M Sassòli '*Jus ad bellum and jus in bello*: The separation between the legality of the use of force and humanitarian rules to be respected in warfare: Crucial or outdated?' in M Schmitt & J Pejic (eds) *International law and armed conflict: Exploring the faultlines – Essays in honour of Yoram Dinstein* (2007) 241-264.
9	But see WA Schabas '*Lex specialis*? Belt and suspenders? The parallel operation of human rights law and the law of armed conflict, and the conundrum of *jus ad bellum*' (2007) 40 *Israel Law Review* 592 592-593, 606-613.

did apply norms of IHRL to an occupation regardless of the question of the legality of the presence of an occupying power in the occupied territory – an issue, which it neither touched upon, nor discussed, albeit making findings that human rights norms had indeed been violated. This could be taken as a *sui generis* expansion to the field of IHRL of the rationale underlying the distinction between *jus ad bellum* and *jus in bello* and may be justified as ensuring a continuous protection of human rights as long as an occupation lasts. On the other hand, the related question of whether, in so doing, there is a risk of implicitly conferring legitimacy upon an illegitimate occupying power, should not be disregarded either.

Second, this paper does not discuss the question of an occupying power's compliance with IHRL indirectly, that is through adherence to the laws in force in an occupied territory, which could well happen when the legislation of the occupied state conforms to human rights standards. If the occupied state is a human rights abiding state, respecting the local law could be, in fact, the most immediate way of ensuring respect for the human rights of the occupied people. However, when the occupied state is not a human rights abiding state (or, perhaps, only in part), which is not a remote possibility, adherence to the local laws by an occupying power is not sufficient. It becomes necessary to insist that an occupying power, regardless of the content of the local laws, is bound, for the reasons discussed in the next section, to comply with applicable human rights norms.

2 The applicability of human rights law to a belligerent occupation

As a result of an interpretative process carried out by a number of international actors, such as international and regional courts and human rights bodies, there is a growing consensus that contemporary international law has come to recognise the duty on the part of states to comply with their human rights obligations in territories that are placed under their jurisdiction by consequence of military occupation.[10] Some of the key steps of this process may be briefly recalled here.

As early as 1967, the Security Council adopted Resolution 237 in connection with the Six-Day War, which stressed that 'essential and inalienable human rights should be respected even during the vicissitudes

---

10   Observing that 'control, rather than territorial sovereignty, defines the outer limits of human rights law obligations' see OA Haathaway et al 'Which law governs during armed conflict? The relationship between international humanitarian law and human rights law' (2012) 96 *Minnesota Law Review* 1883. See also T Ferraro 'The law of occupation and human rights law' in G Gaggioli & R Kolb (eds) (n 5 above) 273-293.

of war'.[11] Shortly after, and having taken stock of the Teheran United Nations Conference on Human Rights,[12] the General Assembly called for the respect of human rights in the 'Occupied Territories', and set up a 'Special Committee' to investigate any such violations.[13] Since then, the General Assembly has consistently upheld the applicability of human rights to situations of armed conflict and occupation.[14] In 1976, Thomas Buerghental called for the application of the International Covenant on Civil and Political Rights (ICCPR)[15] in territories where a state 'maintains actual civil or military control over a given territory ... irrespective of whether it has formally annexed the territory or has a legal right to occupy or control it'.[16] Other international lawyers have followed suit.[17] In the *Nuclear Weapons* Advisory Opinion, the ICJ found that, while certain provisions of the ICCPR were subject to derogations in wartime, article 4 of the ICCPR (the right to life) was not one of these, and that it could therefore, in principle, be applied in a wartime situation.[18] Although the ICJ went on to conclude that this provision should be interpreted in light

---

11   UNSC Res 237 (14 June 1967) UN Doc S/RES/237, Preamble; see also UNSC Res 271 (15 September 1969) UN Doc S/RES/271 calling upon 'Israel scrupulously to observe the provisions of the Geneva Conventions and international law governing military occupation'; UNSC Res 366 (17 December 1974) UN Doc S/RES/366; UNSC Res 605 (22 December 1987) UN Doc S/RS/605; and the report of the UN Secretary-General 'Respect for human rights in armed conflicts: Report of the Secretary General' (1969) UN Doc A/7720 para 16.

12   See Resolution I 'Respect for and implementation of human rights in occupied territories' Teheran United Nations Conference on Human Rights (7 May 1968), reprinted in (1969) 63 *American Journal of International Law* 674 677-678. See R Kolb 'Human rights law and international humanitarian law between 1945 and the aftermath of the Teheran Conference of 1968' in Gaggioli & Kolb (n 5 above) 45; see also in the same collection of studies H-J Heintze 'Theories on the relationship between international humanitarian law and human rights law' 54-55; N Prud'homme '*Lex specialis*: Oversimplifying a more complex and multifaceted relationship?' (2007) 40 *Israel Law Review* 355 356-362.

13   UNGA Res 2443 (XXIII) (19 December 1968).

14   See among others, UNGA Res 2675 (XXV) (9 December 1970); UNGA Resolution 2727 (XXV) (15 December 1970); UNGA Res (XXIX) (14 December 1974). See the annual resolutions entitled 'Report of the Special Committee to investigate Israeli practices affecting the human rights of the population of the occupied territories'. See also, among others, UNGA Res 32/91 (13 December 1977); UNGA Res 33/113 (19 December 1978); UNGA Res 34/90 (12 December 1979); UNGA Res 35/122 (11 December 1980); UNGA Res 36/147 (16 December 1981); UNGA Res 37/88 (10 December 1983); UNGA Res 46/135 (17 December 1991). See further, Haathaway et al (n 10 above) 1884-1885. YA Takahashi *The law of occupation: Continuity and change of international humanitarian law, and its interaction with international human rights law* (2009) 403.

15   International Covenant on Civil and Political Rights (adopted 16 December 1966, entered into force 23 March 1976) 999 UNTS 171.

16   T Buerghental 'To Respect and to Ensure, State Obligations and Permissible Derogations' in L Henkin (ed) *The International Bill of Human Rights* (1984) 74.

17   See also T Meron 'Human rights in time of peace and in time of armed strife: Selected problems' in T Buerghental (ed) *Essays in honor of Louis B Sohn* (1984) 1-21.

18   The ICJ put it thus: 'In principle, the right not arbitrarily to be deprived of one's life applies to hostilities. The test of what is an arbitrary deprivation of life, however, then falls to be determined by the applicable *lex specialis*, namely, the law applicable in armed conflict which is designed to regulate the conduct of hostilities. Thus, whether a particular loss of life, through the use of a certain weapon in warfare, is to be considered an arbitrary deprivation of life contrary to article 6 of the Covenant, can only be decided by reference to the law applicable in armed conflict and not deduced

of IHL as *lex specialis*, its conclusion demonstrated that an international human rights instrument was applicable to a context governed by IHL.

In a similar vein, the Human Rights Committee (HRC), in the two reports it published concerning Israel in 1998 and 2003 respectively, found that the ICCPR applied to occupied Palestinian territories.[19] According to the HRC, Israel could be held accountable for human rights violations because the occupied territories fell 'within the ambit of State responsibility of Israel under the principles of public international law',[20] and because IHL did not impede the concomitant application of international humanitarian law and human rights treaties.[21]

Building on the *Nuclear Weapons Opinion* and on the practice of the HRC, the ICJ in the *Wall* Advisory Opinion[22] held that the ICCPR was applicable in the occupied territories for three reasons: (i) Israel's exercise of jurisdiction over these territories and their citizens;[23] (ii) that such a conclusion was justified based on the practice of the HRC;[24] and (iii) a

---

from the terms of the Covenant itself.' *Legality of the Threat or Use of Nuclear Weapons* (8 July 1996) ICJ Reports 226, paras 25, 134-137 (*Nuclear Weapons* Advisory Opinion). In commenting on this passage, Vera Gowlland observed that the Advisory Opinion served: 'to reinforce the consistent trend in human rights case law that the individual is entitled to both human rights and humanitarian law protection in complementary fashion in time of armed conflict.' V Gowlland 'Human rights and humanitarian law: Are there some individuals bereft of all legal protection? The relevance of paragraph 25 of the ICJ's Advisory Opinion on Nuclear Weapons' in *Mapping new boundaries, Proceedings of the American Society of International Law* (98th Annual Meeting, Washington DC, 2004) 359.

19   See UNCHR 'Concluding observations of the Human Rights Committee' (18 August 1998) UN Doc CCPR/C/79/Add.93; UNCHR 'Concluding observations of the Human Rights Committee: Israel' (21 August 2003) UN Doc CCPR/CO/78/ISR (2003 HRC Report).

20   2003 HRC Report (n 19 above) para 11. Furthermore, in an earlier report the HRC pointed 'to the long-standing presence of Israel in these territories, Israel's ambiguous attitude towards their future status, as well as the exercise of effective jurisdiction by Israeli security forces therein', UNCHR 'Concluding observations of the Human Rights Committee' (18 August 1998) UN Doc CCPR/C/79/Add.93, para 10.

21   The HRC expressed its view thus: 'The Committee reiterates the view, previously spelled out in paragraph 10 of its concluding observations on Israel's initial report (CCPR/C/79/Add.93 of 18 August 1998) ... that the applicability of the regime of international humanitarian law during an armed conflict does not preclude the application of the Covenant, including article 4 which covers situations of public emergency which threaten the life of the nation. Nor does the applicability of the regime of international humanitarian law preclude accountability of States' parties under article 2, paragraph 1, of the Covenant for the actions of their authorities ... ' 2003 HRC Report (n 19 above) para 11. See also CESCR, 'Concluding observations of the Committee on Economic, Social and Cultural Rights: Israel' (31 August 2001) UN Doc E/C.12/1/Add.69, paras 11 and 12. The HRC reverted to these issues in its General Comment No 31 (May 2004), where in respect to the responsibility of a state for its conduct towards the population of the occupied territories, it held that: 'States Parties are required by article 2, paragraph 1, to respect and to ensure the Covenant rights to all persons who may be within their territory and to all persons subject to their jurisdiction'. UNCHR 'General Comment No 31 'Nature of the general legal obligation imposed on state parties to the Covenant' (26 May 2004) UN Doc CCPR/C/21/Rev.1/ADD.13, para 10.

22   *Wall* Advisory Opinion (n 3 above) para 106.

23   *Wall* Advisory Opinion (n 3 above) para 109.

24   As above.

detailed analysis of the *travaux préparatoires* of the ICCPR.[25] The Court also determined the applicability of the CESCR[26] based on the practice of the Committee on Economic, Social and Cultural Rights and the fact that 'the territories occupied by Israel have for over 37 years been subject to its territorial jurisdiction'.[27] Likewise, the ICJ found in favour of the applicability of the Convention on the Rights of the Child (CRC) during an armed conflict.[28]

This approach was continued in the *Armed Activities* case, where the ICJ, relying on its earlier jurisprudence, considered that both branches of international law, namely IHRL and IHL, would have to be 'taken into consideration in occupied territories'.[29] The ICJ concluded that international human rights instruments are applicable 'in respect of acts done by a State in the exercise of its jurisdiction outside its own territory',[30] particularly in occupied territories, and held Uganda 'responsible for [several] violations of international human rights law and international humanitarian law in the occupied territory'.[31] The Inter-American Court of Human Rights[32] and the European Court of Human Rights (ECtHR)

---

25   In discussing the *travaux preparatoires* of the ICCPR, the ICJ found that the expression 'within their jurisdiction' contained in article 1 was not intended to 'allow States to escape from their obligations when they exercise jurisdiction outside their national territory. They only intended to prevent persons residing abroad from asserting vis-à-vis their state of origin, rights that do not fall within the competence of that State, but of that of the State of residence.' *Wall* Advisory Opinion (n 3 above) para 109.

26   International Covenant on Economic, Social and Cultural Rights Rights (adopted 16 December 1966, entered into force 3 March 1976) 993 UNTS 3 (CESCR).

27   *Wall* Advisory Opinion (n 3 above) para 112.

28   *Wall* Advisory Opinion (n 3 above) para 113.

29   *Case Concerning Armed Activities on the Territory of the Congo (Democratic Republic of the Congo v Uganda)* (Merits) (19 December 2005) (2005) ICJ Reports 168, para 216 (*Armed Activities*).

30   As above.

31   *Armed Activities* (n 29 above) 220, Uganda was found in breach of the provisions of the ICCPR, the African Charter on Human and People's Rights, the CRC, and the Optional Protocol to this latter Convention, para 219.

32   In the *Coard* case, which concerned the detention of an individual by US military forces during the 1983 US invasion of Grenada, the Inter-American Commission of Human Rights held that: '[W]hile international humanitarian law pertains primarily in times of war and the international law of human rights applies most fully in times of peace, the potential occupation of one does not necessarily exclude or displace the other. There is an integral linkage between the law of human rights and humanitarian law because they share a 'common nucleus of non-derogable rights and a common purpose of protecting human life and dignity,' and there may be a substantial overlap in the application of these bodies of law. Certain core guarantees apply in all circumstances, including situations of conflict and this is reflected, inter alia, in the designation of certain protection pertaining to the person as peremptory norms (*ius cogens*) and obligations *erga omnes*, in a vast body of treaty law, in principles of customary international law, and in the doctrine and practice of international human rights bodies such as this Commission. Both normative systems may thus be applicable in the situation under study.' *Coard v United States* IACHR (29 September 1999) Case No 10.951, Report No 109/99, para 39.

have adopted a similar approach.[33] In the recent *Al Skeini* judgment, the ECtHR recalled its own settled jurisprudence, inaugurated in the *Loizidou* case,[34] proscribing that 'when, as a consequence of lawful or unlawful military action, a Contracting State exercises effective control of an area outside that national territory' which includes the case of belligerent occupation, then:

> The controlling State has the responsibility under article 1 to secure, within the area under its control, the entire range of substantive rights set out in the Convention ...[35]

Quite recently, the United States (US), traditionally reluctant to recognise the applicability of IHRL in armed conflicts,[36] appeared to go in this direction with its Fourth Periodic Report (2011) to the HRC stating that: 'a time of war does not suspend the operation of the Covenant to matters within its scope of application'.[37] The US government provided two examples of its stance on human rights during war, stating that a 'State Party's participation in a war' would (i) 'in no way excuse it from respecting and ensuring rights to have or adopt a religion or belief of one's choice'; or (ii) allow it to deny 'the right and opportunity of every citizen to vote and to be elected at genuine periodic elections'.[38] From the somewhat ambiguous language used in the Report, it may be excessive, however, to draw the conclusion that the US went as far as reversing its

---

33   *Loizidou v Turkey* (Preliminary Objections) App no 15318/89 ECHR (23 March 1995) para 62. *Banković v Belgium and 16 Other Contracting States* App no 52207/99 ECtHR (9 December 2001) para 80. It stated: [T]he case-law of the Court demonstrates that its recognition of the exercise of extra-territorial jurisdiction by a Contracting State is exceptional: it has done so when the respondent State, through the effective control of the relevant territory and its inhabitants abroad as *a consequence of military occupation* or through the consent, invitation or acquiescence of the Government of that territory, exercises all or some of the public powers normally to be exercised by that Government' (emphasis added).
34   As above.
35   *Al-Skeini v The United Kingdom* App no 55721/07 ECtHR (7 July 2011) para 138.
36   In a document encompassing the Second and Third Periodic Reports submitted to the HRC which covered the years of the occupation of Iraq (2003–2004), the United States did not make any reference to the human rights situation in Iraq. Instead, the document referred to the 'continuing difference of view between the Committee and the United States concerning certain matters in relation to the importance and scope of provisions of the Covenant'. See US Department of State, 'Second and Third Periodic Report of the United States of America to the UN Committee on Human Rights Concerning the International Covenant on Civil and Political Rights' (21 October 2005) para 3, available at http://www.state.gov/j/drl/rls/55504.htm (accessed 10 December 2013) (US Second and Third Periodic Report). See also, in the same document, 'Annex I: Territorial application of the International Covenant on Civil and Political Rights' para 2.
37   Fourth Periodic Report of the United States of America to the United Nations Committee on Human Rights Concerning the International Covenant on Civil and Political Rights (30 December 2011) para 506 (Fourth Periodic Report).
38   As above.

previous stance as to the inapplicability of IHRL in times of belligerent occupation.[39] In fact, the argument that such a change of policy did not occur can be made in light of the subsequent exchanges between the HRC and the US. Upon receiving the US fourth periodic report, the HRC asked the US to clarify its position as concerns the 'State party's understanding of the scope of applicability of the Covenant with respect to individuals under its jurisdiction both outside its territory; in times of peace, as well as in times of armed conflict'.[40] The US responded only by drawing the attention of the HRC to the relevant section of its Fourth Period Report without adding any word of clarification.[41] In its 'Concluding Observations on the fourth periodic report of the United States of America', the HRC took the US response as a confirmation that the US had not changed its view. It put it thus:

> The Committee regrets that the State party [US] continues to maintain the position that the Covenant does not apply with respect to individuals under its jurisdiction, but outside its territory, despite the interpretation to the contrary of article 2, paragraph 1 of the ICCPR, supported by the Committee's established jurisprudence, the jurisprudence of the International Court of Justice and State practice.[42]

In the same way, the government of Israel has contested the applicability of human rights treaties to situations of occupation.[43] Responding to the 'Concluding Observations on Israel's Initial Report' in which 'the Committee [HRC] questioned Israel's position regarding the applicability of the Covenant to the West Bank and the Gaza Strip', the government of Israel stated that it had 'consistently maintained that the Covenant does not apply to areas that are not subject to its sovereign territory and jurisdiction' and that the HRC's mandate 'cannot relate to events in the

---

39　In the Fourth Periodic Report (n 37 above) para 505, the US recognised the developments within the practice of the ICJ stating: 'The United States is mindful that in General Comment 31 (2004) the Committee presented the view that "States Parties are required by article 2, paragraph 1, to respect and to ensure the Covenant rights to all persons who may be within their territory and to all persons subject to their jurisdiction. This means that a State party must respect and ensure the rights laid down in the Covenant to anyone within the power or effective control of that State Party, even if not situated within the territory of the State Party." *The United States is also aware of the jurisprudence of the International Court of Justice ("ICJ"), which has found the ICCPR "applicable in respect of acts done by a State in the exercise of its jurisdiction outside its own territory," as well as positions taken by other States Parties.*' (emphasis added) See also MJ Dennis 'Application of human rights treaties extraterritoriality in times of armed conflict and military occupation' (2005) 99 *American Journal of International Law* 119.

40　HRC 'List of issues in relation to the fourth periodic report of the United States of America' (CCPR/C/USA/4 and Corr 1), adopted by the Committee at its 107th session (11-28 March 2013) (29 April 2013) CCPR/C/USA/Q/4, para 1.

41　In 'Replies of the United States of America to the list of issues' (12 September 2013) CCPR/C/USA/Q/4/Add. 1, para 2, the US wrote 'With respect to the scope of applicability of the ICCPR, the United States refers the Committee to 504-510 of its Fourth Periodic Report'.

42　'Concluding observations on the Fourth Periodic Report of the United States of America' (23 April 2014) CCPR/C/USA/CO/4, para 4.

43　For a detailed analysis see O Ben-Naftali & Y Shany 'Living in denial: The application of human rights in the occupied territories' (2003-2004) 37 *Israel Law Review* 17.

West Bank and the Gaza Strip, inasmuch as they are part and parcel of the context of armed conflict as distinct from a relationship of human rights'.[44] In its Fourth Period Report to the HRC, Israel (re-) affirmed the inapplicability of the ICCPR in the occupied Palestinian territory. While recognising that 'there is a profound connection between human rights and the Law of Armed Conflict, and that there may well be a convergence between these two bodies-of-law in some respects', Israel took the view that 'in the current state of international law and state-practice worldwide', IHL and IHRL 'which are codified in separate instruments, remain distinct and apply in different circumstances' also because 'Israel believes that the Convention, which is territorially bound, does not apply, nor was it intended to apply, to areas beyond a state's national territory'.[45]

3 The relationship between the law of occupation and IHRL

3.1 The case of convergence

As a result of the above analysis, the conclusion that IHRL is binding on an occupying power either as treaty law or customary law within an occupied territory can be regarded as generally accepted, even though it is far from universal due to the opposition of some of the states who have been occupying powers in recent years. While it may be unlikely that this opposition will impact on the prevailing view in the near future, it may be unwarranted to dismiss it summarily. As it is true that IHRL has not been created to govern a situation of occupation, the opposition manifested by the US and Israel could instead be taken as a useful reminder of the opportunity to reflect on the suitability of a given norm of IHRL in the context of an occupation rather than accepting its application uncritically. After all, the ideals that IHRL norms are meant to serve can only be achieved if their application in occupied territory is feasible.

Once it has been determined that the law of occupation and IHRL apply concomitantly during a given occupation, the question that arises is how to articulate their relationship and define the criteria governing it. This is what the ICJ sought to do in the following passage of the *Wall* Advisory Opinion:

---

44   'Second Periodic Report' (4 December 2001) CCPR/C/ISR/2001/2, para 8. In its 'Concluding observations of the Committee on Economic, Social and Cultural Rights' (16 December 2001) E/C.12/ISR/CO/3, para 8, the Committee on Economic, Social and Cultural Rights (CESCR) regretted the 'absence in the State party's third period report as well as in its replies to the list of issues of information related to the enjoyment of economic, social and cultural rights as ensrhined in the Covenant in the Occupied Palestinian territory'.

45   Israel 'Fourth periodic reports of states parties due in 2013: Israel' (12 December 2013) CCPR/C/ISR/4, paras 47-48. The conclusion of the HRC on this latter report has not, as yet, been issued.

As regards the relationship between international humanitarian law and human rights law, there are thus three possible situations: some rights may be *exclusively* matters of international humanitarian law; others may be *exclusively* matters of human rights law; yet others may be *matters of both these branches of international law.* In order to answer the question put to it, the Court will have to take into consideration both these branches of international law, namely human rights law *and, as lex specialis, international humanitarian law.*[46] (emphasis added)

Because the law of occupation is part of IHL, this paragraph is to be interpreted as also applying to the relationship between the law of occupation and IHRL. This deduction is reinforced by the circumstance that this paragraph is contained within an opinion discussing the normative framework applicable to a situation of occupation.

Leaving the discussion of the *lex specialis* rule to the next section, it is the first part of this paragraph that calls for immediate attention. What is somewhat puzzling is the consideration that there are matters under the 'exclusive' purview of IHL and others that are the 'exclusive' purview of IHRL. It is difficult to identify with a reasonable degree of precision – something the ICJ did not do – which norms fall within one category and which under the other. If one undertakes a perusal of the text of relevant treaties, it could be said that the ICJ is right to speak of matters falling under the purview of one regime but not that of the other.[47] When the conduct of an occupying power is governed only by one legal regime and not by the other, there may not be a problem of coordination for the obvious reason that only one legal regime would govern a given matter.

However, given the breadth of the two regimes, it is difficult to draw clear demarcation lines. On the one hand, article 43 of the Hague Regulations enables an occupying power to take measures to maintain and ensure 'public order and safety' within a territory, which also includes, by extension, measures that protect its own security. Evidently, this status and function as the *de facto* government of an occupied territory enables an occupying power to legitimately take legislative and administrative measures on a wide number of issues. On the other hand, IHRL contains

---

46   *Wall* Advisory Opinion (n 3 above) para 106.
47   As examples of the norms of the law of occupation that may be regarded as concerning IHL matters only see, inter alia, the following norms of the Hague Regulations: the notion of occupation (art 42); the normative powers of an occupant (art 43); the prohibition against forcibly furnishing information against the other belligerent (art 44); the prohibition against compelling the swearing of allegiance (art 45); the prohibition against pillage (art 47); the taxation of the occupied territory (art 49); the right to requisition (art 52); the administration of property and territory (art 55) and others. As examples in the field of IHRL see, among others, the norms of the ICCPR concerning the prohibition against slavery (art 8), the treatment of accused juvenile persons (art 10(2)); the prohibition against imprisonment for debts (art 11); the right to recognition (art 16); the right to freedom of thought (art 18); the right to hold opinions without interference (art 19); freedom of association (art 22), the right to marriage (art 23); and the rights of children (art 24).

detailed norms concerning numerous rights that may well be affected by the conduct of an occupying power.

Hence, the *dictum* of the ICJ ought to be treated with circumspection. This is not because there could be no matters in which IHL could apply quite independently from IHRL and *vice-versa*. It is rather because, once the law of occupation (IHL) and IHRL apply to the same factual framework, the boundaries between the areas covered by the two regimes may be more blurred than the approach of the ICJ suggests, and the number of matters that in one way or another fall under the purview of both regimes may end up being rather extensive.

Consider the case of the *Wall* Advisory Opinion. What emerges from this Opinion is the scenario that the conduct of the occupying power, namely the construction of a wall in occupied Palestinian territory, amounted to breaches of the norms of both regimes.[48] These breaches included the violation of the prohibition on the building of settlements[49] as well as those concerning the destruction or requisition of properties which contravened 'the requirements of articles 46 and 52 of the Hague Regulations of 1907 and of article 53 of the Fourth Geneva Convention'.[50] As for IHRL, the breaches identified in the *Wall* Advisory Opinion concerned various rights and values expressed in the ICCPR, CESCR and CRC,[51] such as 'the right to liberty of movement and freedom to choose [one's] residence',[52] the 'right to work, to health, to education and to an adequate standard of living',[53] and the right to self-determination.[54]

Other examples where the same conduct may be in breach of more than one legal regime may be found in the practice of the UN Secretariat and of human rights bodies. For example, while the prohibition against settlements is covered by the law of occupation, as provided for under article 49 of the Geneva Convention IV, it is difficult to say that it is an IHL matter only. In fact, it may also constitute a human rights matter so that the construction and presence of settlements in the occupied territory may breach norms belonging to this legal regime.[55] In his 2012 Report concerning the 'Situation of Human Rights in the Palestinian Territories Occupied Since 1967', the UN Special Rapporteur found that the establishment of the settlements (and the associated infrastructure) breached both the law of occupation and norms of IHRL:

---

48   *Wall* Advisory Opinion (n 3 above) paras 102-135.
49   *Wall* Advisory Opinion (n 3 above) para 120.
50   *Wall* Advisory Opinion (n 3 above) para 132.
51   *Wall* Advisory Opinion (n 3 above) paras 133-6.
52   *Wall* Advisory Opinion (n 3 above) para 129.
53   *Wall* Advisory Opinion (n 3 above) para 134.
54   *Wall* Advisory Opinion (n 3 above) para 122.
55   See, by way of example, the human rights violations that are caused by the settlements (and associated infrastructure) in Palestinian occupied territory as described in Report of the UN Secretary-General 'Situation of human rights in the Palestinian territories occupied since 1967' (19 September 2012) A/67/379, para 11.

The establishment of the settlements is a flagrant violation of international humanitarian law as set forth in the Geneva Convention relative to the Protection of Civilian Persons in Time of War (Fourth Geneva Convention) and the Regulations annexed to the Hague Convention IV of 1907 ... In building settlements and associated infrastructure, Israel further violates international law through the appropriation of Palestinian property not justified by military necessity, and by imposing severe movement restrictions on Palestinians. Such restrictions *violate those human rights dependent on freedom of movement, including rights to health, education, family life, work and worship.*[56] (emphasis added)

On the same lines, the 2012 'Report of the Special Rapporteur on the situation of human rights in the Palestinian territories occupied since 1967' concluded:

[T]hat Israel's policies in occupied Palestinian territory concerning demolition and displacement of Palestinians constitute both human rights, including the right to an adequate standard of living, right to housing, and the right to non-discrimination, and humanitarian law violations.[57]

The Advisory Opinion and these latter two examples show that the law of occupation and IHRL may not merely coexist and operate in parallel, that is independently of each other as when they apply to different matters, but that they could converge towards the same objectives by complementing each other in governing aspects of the same conduct in one way or another.[58]

Secondly, the ICJ's view that there are matters in which IHL and IHRL may operate exclusively needs to be qualified by recalling the possibility that the conduct of an occupant may extend to matters that *prima facie* fall under the exclusive purview of IHRL. This would happen

---

56 As above.
57 'Report of the Special Rapporteur on the situation of human rights in the Palestinian territories occupied since 1967' (25 May 2012) A/HRC/20/32, para 32. See also the 2014 Report of the UN Secretary General 'Human rights situation in the Occupied Palestinian Territory, including East Jerusalem' (22 August 2013) A/HRC/24/30 para 57, stating that: 'According to UNICEF, ill-treatment of Palestinian children in the Israeli detention system is widespread, systematic and institutionalized. There are serious concerns that such treatment and combination of practices may, in some cases, amount to torture, as defined by article 1 of the Convention against Torture and Other Cruel, Inhuman or Degrading Treatment or Punishment. *Such practices would also violate the Convention on the Rights of the Child (art 37) and international humanitarian law.*' (emphasis added).
58 See C Droege 'Elective affinities? Human rights and humanitarian law' (2008) 90 *International Review of the Red Cross* 501 521. The US government recognised the complementarity between IHL and IHRL in its Fourth Periodic Report (n 37 above) para 507 when it stated that: 'Under the doctrine of *lex specialis*, the applicable rules for the protection of individuals and conduct of hostilities in armed conflict are typically found in international humanitarian law, including the Geneva Conventions of 1949, the Hague Regulations of 1907, and other international humanitarian law instruments, as well as in the customary international law of armed conflict. In this context, it is important to bear in mind that international human rights law and the law of armed conflict are in many respects complementary and mutually reinforcing. These two bodies of law contain many similar protections ...'

when it uses its normative authority under article 43 of the Hague Regulations and article 64 of the Geneva Convention IV. Those provisions define the normative competence of an occupant in terms of objectives to be reached and broad areas to be managed, but they do not contain a detailed list of matters on which legislation is possible.[59] The absence of such demarcation enables an occupying power to legislate on a variety of issues which can, therefore, also cover areas where IHRL would normally play a significant role. While declaring that there are matters that pertain only to IHRL, the ICJ did not indicate on which 'human rights' issues the occupant would, as a result, be barred from 'legislating'. The normative powers of an occupant are certainly limited *ratione temporis* to what is required for the administration of a territory for the duration of an occupation.[60] But the limits *ratione materiae* are difficult to identify, because an occupying power exercises no less than *de facto* government of a territory and consequently it may be involved in legislating on quite a variety of issues. It could be argued, for instance, that rights such as freedom of expression, political and economic rights[61] are 'human rights matters' only, in the sense of the ICJ's case-law. And yet it cannot be excluded that an occupying power may 'legislate' on these issues on the basis that, for instance, such legislation would be justified for reasons of security or for ensuring the orderly administration of territory, as article 43 of the Hague Regulations and article 64 of the Geneva Convention IV allow. If, as a result, the two normative regimes diverge in prescription, it is possible to speak of the existence of a 'conflict' of norms. The question arises of determining whether such conflict can be resolved, and if so how.

3.2   The case of divergence: The function(s) of the *lex specialis* rule

The problem of coordination between the law of occupation and IHRL emerges in all of its complexity when IHL and IHRL, while applying to the same matters, do not march in the same but rather in divergent directions because the state that is charged with applying such laws is left in a state of doubt about the conduct expected.[62] The jurisprudence of the ICJ makes it clear that the mechanism through which a case of conflict between

---

59   See in this regard Expert Meeting Report 'Occupation and other forms of administration of foreign territory' (ICRC 2012) 69 (ICRC Expert Report on Occupation) 56-59.

60   See generally Kolb & Vité (n 2 above) 304-314; Benvenisti (n 1 above) 55-57 and 89-103.

61   For further analysis see S Vité 'The interrelation of the law of occupation and economic, social and cultural rights: The examples of food, health and property' (2008) 90 *International Review of the Red Cross* 629.

62   M Sassòli 'Le droit international humanitaire, une *lex specialis* par rapport aux droits humains?' in A Auer et al (eds) *Les droits de l'homme et la constitution, études en l'honneur du Professeur Giorgio Malinverni* (2007) 381.

norms of IHL and norms of IHRL can be tackled is through the application of the *lex specialis derogat legi generali* rule.[63]

The *lex specialis* rule may be construed in two ways. One is the case where the 'specific rule should be read and understood within the confines or against the background of the general standard' namely as an 'elaboration, updating or a technical specification' of the general rule.[64] The other is as a mechanism of conflict resolution to be used when 'two legal provisions that are both valid and applicable' but provide 'incompatible direction on how to deal with the same set of facts'.[65] In such cases, instead of the (general) rule, one should apply the (specific) exception.[66] In both cases, however, priority falls on the provision which is 'special', that is, the rule with a more precisely delimited scope of application. The latter case may suggest 'different ways of dealing with a problem'.[67] In the latter case, the *lex specialis* rule could be construed as an interpretative criterion that, while not impeding the concomitant application of the two regimes, may help 'to reconcile conflicting norms through a balancing interpretation'.[68]

In the *Nuclear Weapons* Advisory Opinion, the ICJ determined that IHL was *lex specialis* because it was 'the law applicable in armed conflict which is designed to regulate the conduct of hostilities'.[69] This approach has been reiterated in the *Wall* Advisory Opinion.[70] Being part and parcel of IHL and following the same rationale, the law of occupation may also be considered *lex specialis*, having been expressly designed to regulate situations of belligerent occupation. As a result, it could be deduced that the norms of the law of occupation may prevail over those of IHRL as *lex specialis* in any case of conflict with the corresponding norms of IHRL. The

---

63   See also J Frowein 'The relationship between human rights regimes and regimes of belligerent occupation' (1998) 28 *Israel Yearbook on Human Rights* 1. *Nuclear Weapons* Advisory Opinion (n 18 above) para 25. For further analysis see A Guellali 'Lex specialis, droit internationale humanitaire et droits de l'homme: Leur interaction dans les nouveaux conflicts armés' (2007) 111 *Revue générale de droit international public* 539.

64   International Law Commission, Fifty-eighth session (Geneva, 1 May-9 June and 3 July-11 August 2006) 'Fragmentation of international law: Difficulties arising from the diversification and expansion of international law' Report of the Study Group of the International Law Commission, finalised by Martti Koskenniemi, UN Doc A/CN.4/L.682, paras 56. (Report of the Study Group on Fragmentation)

65   Report of the Study Group on Fragmentation (n 64 above) para 57.

66   As above.

67   Report of the Study Group on Fragmentation (n 64 above) para 25.

68   Arguably, this is what the ICJ did in the *Nuclear Weapons* Advisory Opinion in the following passage: 'In principle, the right not arbitrarily to be deprived of one's life applies to hostilities. The *test of what is an arbitrary deprivation of life, however, then falls to be determined by the applicable lex specialis, namely, the law applicable in armed conflict which is designed to regulate the conduct of hostilities.* Thus, whether a particular loss of life, through the use of a certain weapon in warfare, is to be considered an arbitrary deprivation of life contrary to article 6 of the Covenant, can only be decided by reference to the law applicable in armed conflict and not deduced from the terms of the Covenant itself' (emphasis added) *Nuclear Weapons* Advisory Opinion (n 18 above) para 25.

69   As above.

70   *Wall* Advisory Opinion (n 3 above) para 106.

approach adopted by the ICJ may be excessive, however, if it ends up according to the law of occupation an almost mechanic prevalence over norms of IHRL, and would impede the construction of IHRL as a regime on the same footing and capable of, because of the detail of its provisions, complementing the law of occupation when necessary. The reasons for this concern are articulated in the next section.

3.3   Interpreting the *lex specialis* rule in the context of a belligerent occupation

Underlying the technical nature of the *lex specialis* rule, Martti Koskenniemi's Report of the Study Group on Fragmentation speaks of the *lex specialis* as a 'widely accepted maxim of legal interpretation and technique for the resolution of normative conflicts',[71] and defines it as an 'informal part of legal reasoning that is of the pragmatic process through which lawyers go about interpreting and applying formal law'.[72] For Anjia Lindroos, '*lex specialis* is not a substantive rule of international law that might help determine which rule is special in relation to a more general rule', but 'a descriptive principle that has little independent normative force'.[73] While it is true that the *lex specialis* is a 'technical' rule in the sense that it 'does not provide any criteria to guide the decision whether one area of law is generally more important than another',[74] it is equally true that the application of the *lex specialis* rule to a given context carries significant normative consequences and involves passing a value judgment. Therefore, what is, and may appear, neutral *in abstracto* is not necessarily neutral *in concreto*. This is because, in concomitance with the application of the *lex specialis* rule, the interpreter undertakes a substantive determination of which is the *lex specialis* in a specific case. Thus the *lex specialis* rule becomes the tool through which the substantive determination made by the interpreter as to which of the two norms or principles should apply in a given context is given effect. Describing the *lex specialis* as a merely technical rule presents the risk, I believe, of underestimating the value judgment that accompanies its application to a specific case and of paying little attention to the criteria for choosing one body of law over the other, which should instead be discussed as a distinct question in a transparent manner so as to be open to scrutiny.

As noted by Marco Sassòli, the decision of which normative framework is to be given priority is a 'highly value-based decision',[75] which should take into account 'des buts systémiques du droit international dans son ensemble, ce qui ouvre la porte a des jugements de

71   Report of the Study Group on Fragmentation (n 64 above) para 56.
72   A Lindroos 'Addressing norm conflicts in a fragmented legal system: The doctrine of *Lex Specialis*' (2005) 74 *Nordic Journal of International Law* 27 36.
73   Lindroos (n 72 above) 66.
74   Lindroos (n 72 above) 44.
75   Lindroos (n 72 above) 42.

valeur, subjectifs'.[76] In the *Nuclear Weapons* Advisory Opinion, the ICJ defined IHL as *lex specialis* because of it being 'the law applicable in armed conflict which is designed to regulate the conduct of hostilities'.[77] As this sentence reveals, the reason why the ICJ considered IHL as *lex specialis* was the scope for which IHL had been designed. There is nothing inherently wrong with the determination made by the ICJ, but if this approach is automatically transposed to the field of the law of occupation, it could be tantamount to a rather abstract determination of an entire area of law as being more specific towards another area of law. A more balanced approach that takes into account the shift towards the applicability of IHRL norms also in cases of occupation, would be to undertake an *in concreto* case-by-case determination as to whether a given norm should be considered *lex specialis* in respect of IHRL. Hence, the qualification of a norm or a legal regime as *lex specialis* should involve a determination that those rules have been created for a specific situation or that they are more suited than the alternatives to regulate a given matter. This determination should be based on the logical understanding that the suitability of a given norm or set of norms to tackle a given factual situation that arises in a contemporary occupation cannot be derived only from the purpose the regime to which it belongs is meant to serve. It must be assessed *in concreto* in relation to the circumstances in which it applies and in light of more recent normative developments on the kind of issues that emerge in the context of a contemporary occupation.

While it may certainly be presumed that the law of occupation being drafted specifically for situations of occupation is, in a case of conflict amongst specific norms, the most obvious norm to be qualified as *lex specialis*, such presumption cannot be regarded as absolute. There is more than one indicator to qualify a norm as *specialis*. These indicators could include, for instance, 'the precision and clarity of a rule and its adaptation to the particular circumstances of the case.' As put in the International Committee of the Red Cross (ICRC) Expert Report on Occupation, *lex specialis* is a:

> [P]rinciple according to which, in choosing between two rules, the one that was more specific and most *pertinent* should be given precedence, since a special rule would usually give a *clearer* answer to the question at hand than a general one.[78] (emphasis added)

Along this line, the International Law Commission's Study Group on the Fragmentation of International Law[79] stated that 'special law has priority

---

76 Sassòli (n 62 above) 395.
77 See full quotation above *Nuclear Weapons* Advisory Opinion (n 18 above).
78 ICRC Expert Report on Occupation (n 59 above) 63.
79 See 'Conclusions of the work of the Study Group on the Fragmentation of International Law: Difficulties arising from the diversification and expansion of international law' (A/61/10) *Yearbook of the International Law Commission*, 2006, vol II, Part Two, para 7.

over general law' because 'such special law, being more concrete, often takes better account of the particular features of the context in which it is to be applied than any applicable general law'.[80]

Next, in order to define the law of occupation as *lex specialis*, it is necessary to qualify another set of norms and principles as *lex generalis*. Although at times qualified as *lex generalis*, it is not axiomatic that IHRL can be defined as *lex generalis* in times of occupation. Even less convincing is the idea that the drafters of the law of occupation intended to create a system in derogation from IHRL as *lex generalis*. The *lex specialis* rules finds its justification in the widely accepted notion that parties may 'contract out' rules of international law. As put by the ICJ: 'It is well understood that, in practice, rules of international law can by agreement, be derogated from in particular cases or as between particular parties'.[81] It is not possible, however, to say that the law of occupation is *specialis* in the sense of having being contracted out from existing norms of IHRL. When the law of occupation had reached its maturity, IHRL was still in its infancy,[82] with the consequence that 'IHL and international HRL largely ignored each other in the formative stage of the 1940s and 1950s'.[83] At the time of its drafting, for instance, the law of occupation did not, and could not consider all the issues that would be later covered by IHRL.

The exception in this regard, which, arguably, confirms the thesis advanced here, is the case of Additional Protocol I. Drafted after the adoption of the ICCPR, Additional Protocol I incorporates, in its article 75, a conspicuous number of human rights norms based on the ICCPR.[84] The incorporation into Additional Protocol I of certain human rights norms, which follows the norms on fair trial already contained in the Geneva Convention IV (see in particular articles 65-73), may be taken as an indication that the law of occupation, or at least some parts of it, was not necessarily meant to operate independently of, or in derogation to, human rights standards. Arguably, where it did not incorporate such standards, it could be suggested that such an approach owed more to the objective circumstance of the limited numbers of the rules and principles of international law in matters of human rights available at the time of

---

80   As above.
81   *North Sea Continental Shelf Cases (Federal Republic of Germany v Denmark; Federal Republic of Germany v Netherlands)* (20 February 1969) (1969) ICJ Reports 1969, para 72.
82   For a comparative historical evolution of IHL and HRL see R Kolb 'Human rights law and international humanitarian law between 1945 and the aftermath of the Teheran Conference of 1968' in Gaggioli & Kolb (n 5 above) 41-47.
83   Kolb (n 82 above) 43.
84   On art 75 of Additional Protocol I see, among others, F Pocar 'To what extent is Protocol I customary international law?' in AE Wall (ed) *Legal and ethical lessons of NATO's Kosovo Campaign* (2002) 337. Pointing to arts 4-6 of Additional Protocol I for an additional example of incorporation of human rights standards within IHL, see G Gaggioli & V Gowlland 'The relationship between international human rights and humanitarian law: An overview' in Gaggioli & Kolb (n 5 above) 79.

drafting the law of occupation than to a systematic policy aimed at creating a regime in derogation to human rights norms.

The concepts of fair trial and the protection of human rights in criminal proceedings are, for instance, matters that have developed considerably in recent years, in particular because of the practice of international courts and tribunals. On these issues, IHRL should, in case of conflict, be construed as the *lex specialis* – as being more pertinent and adequate than the traditional law of occupation to ensure respect for human rights during trials held during occupations.[85] This means that IHRL could be used to fill the gaps that an earlier normative framework could not take into account so as to offer solutions to problems not covered, or only partially covered, by IHL.[86] According to Tristan Ferraro 'Occupation law is indeed the body of law specifically dealing with occupation and, therefore, has taken the specific characteristics of this situation for all its norms'.[87] As such, it should obtain an 'interpretative dominance' and shape the application of the other applicable bodies of law as well, in particular HRL with the consequence that 'HRL would need to adjust to the specific situation of occupation'.[88] But the suggested interpretative dominance must take into account the limits of the law of occupation as quite a succinct body of law drafted for, and belonging to an earlier phase of international law than IHRL. As such, the law of occupation, far from being comprehensive, requires updating and amending in order to reflect the conspicuous developments of international law in recent decades and to be equipped to tackle the problems that may emerge in contemporary occupations. This is not to suggest the application of the *lex posterior derogat legi priori* rule, which, it is submitted, would apply only when a subsequent law is intended to replace

---

85   Andrea Bianchi pointed out that there are certain provisions that are more specific in human rights law than under international humanitarian law. In this regard, he remarked that: '[T]he notion of inhumane treatment or the right to protection from arbitrary detention under international humanitarian law do not enjoy the same degree of specificity that they have acquired in human rights law, due to more detailed regulation and judicial interpretation.' According to this author, the two regimes should be complementary and mutually supportive, rather than being considered in contradistinction with each other. See A Bianchi 'Dismantling the Wall: The ICJ's Advisory Opinion and its likely impact on international law' (2005) 47 *German Yearbook of International Law* 343 370-373.

86   See the analyses of: Andrea Bianchi (n 85 above) 370-373; A Gioia 'The Role of the European Court of Human Rights in monitoring compliance with humanitarian law in armed conflict' in O Ben-Naftali (ed) *International humanitarian law and international human rights law* (2011) 201, 214-215 and in the same volume, see also M Milanovic 'Norm conflicts, IHL and IHRL' 99-101; A Orakhelashvili 'The interaction between human rights and humanitarian law: Fragmentation, conflict, parallelism or convergence' (2008) 19 *European Journal of International Law* 162-168. JA Pastor Ridruejo 'Droit international des droits de l'homme et droit international humanitaire: Leurs rapports à la lumière de la jurisprudence de la Cour internationale' in M Kohen (ed) *Promoting justice, human rights and conflict resolution through international law* (2007) 399-408; C Tomuschat 'Human rights and international humanitarian law' (2010) 21 *European Journal of International Law* 15.

87   T Ferraro (n 10 above) 275.

88   As above.

or eventually complement a precedent law operating in the same field. It is not possible to speak of a formal replacement of a rule of IHL by a rule of IHRL when the two normative regimes continue to apply concomitantly and are both equally valid and no intention to the contrary has been shown by the states, their creators. What may be possible is to argue in favour of an interpretation that seeks to ensure that the substantive content of the law that is binding on an occupying power be as up to date and as comprehensive as possible as to provide adequate guidance and protection in contemporary contexts. This can be obtained by a determination directed at emphasising the adequacy of the content of a given norm or set of norms, rather than its formal status.

Therefore, not only should the criterion of *lex specialis* be interpreted in a manner less formalistic than has been the practice of the ICJ – by examining whether IHLR is adequate to perform the function assigned to it in a given occupation context – but room should also be made for an evolving interpretation that will enable the incorporation, within the international law applicable to an occupation, of developments in the field of IHRL. This is not to say that IHRL should automatically trump the norms of the law of occupation so that IHRL would be the *lex specialis* in any case of conflict. This expansive approach would be excessive as dogmatically favouring one regime over the other. More realistically, IHRL may then be considered *lex specialis* in the sense that it could place limits on the conduct of an occupying power authorised by the law of occupation and help 'to reconcile conflicting norms through a balancing interpretation' and thus enable the concomitant application of the law of occupation and IHRL not only when they converge but, most importantly, also when they diverge, so as to increase the level of protection of human rights within the occupied territory.

In light of these considerations, it is submitted that, contrary to what the practice of the ICJ seems to suggest, it should be open to the interpreter to challenge the assumption that the law of occupation is *ipso facto* the *lex specialis*, with the consequence of impeding the application of IHRL norms rather than seeking to reconcile the two regimes. In matters of fair trial, for instance, there is no question that 'the more pertinent, precise, concrete, and suitable rule for a given context may not be found within the law of occupation but may be obtained by applying norms of IHRL'.[89] This determination, however, should not be considered as a mere technical determination. As discussed above, what is suitable in a given context depends also on an interpreter's value judgment of what human rights standards should be regarded as 'non-negotiable' from a contemporary perspective.

---

89   F Hampson 'The relationship between international humanitarian law and human rights law from the perspective of a human rights treaty body' (2008) 871 *International Review of the Red Cross* 561.

3.4   Complementing and interpreting the law of occupation in light of IHRL

Adopting a rather innovative approach, the ICJ, in the *Armed Activities* case, interpreted article 43 of the Hague Regulations as comprising the:

> [D]uty to secure respect for the applicable rules of international human rights law and international humanitarian law, to protect the inhabitants of the occupied territory against acts of violence, and not to tolerate such violence by any third party.[90]

As a result of this interpretation, the ICJ found that Uganda, as an Occupying Power, was under the duty to comply with applicable rules of IHRL and 'to take measures to ensure respect for human rights and international humanitarian law in the occupied territories'.[91] The ICJ also determined that Uganda's responsibility was engaged 'both for any acts of its military that violated its international obligations and for any lack of vigilance in preventing violations of human rights and international humanitarian law by other actors present in the occupied territory, including rebel groups acting on their own account'.[92]

Interpreting article 43 of the Hague Regulations as encompassing the duty to secure respect for the applicable rules of IHRL reveals the understanding on the part of the ICJ that even in a situation that would traditionally fall under the purview of the law of occupation, such as the maintenance of public order and security, IHRL may have a role to play because it could pursue goals that, while different from those of IHL, may not be mutually exclusive or conflicting. This is an important example of complementarity between the law of occupation and the field of IHRL: not in the sense of sharing the same goals, but of operating a division of labour whereby the law of occupation may define the general authorities and objectives of an occupying power, and IHRL would shape the parameters within which such authorities may be exercised, or, as the case may be, reinforce prohibitions that already exist within the law of occupation, such as those concerning the physical treatment of individuals. Despite this theoretical perspective, however, the practical application of this approach remains difficult and requires the development of a more normative detailed framework than the one currently available. Arguably, therefore, the application of the rule of *lex specialis* should be accompanied by the *lex specialis compleat legi generali* rule (the special rule completes the general rule). IHRL may, on a case-by-case basis, upon an examination of the content and detail of the relevant applicable provisions, fill the gaps within IHL as a more specialised and advanced normative regime than the law of

---

90   *Armed Activities* (n 29 above) para 178.
91   *Armed Activities* (n 29 above) para 211.
92   *Armed Activities* (n 29 above) para 179.

occupation.[93] Reliance on the *lex specialis compleat legi generali* rule would be consistent with article 31(3)(c) of the Vienna Convention on the Law of Treaties, which stipulates that, in interpreting a norm, 'any relevant rules of international law applicable in the relations between the parties' shall be taken into account. Encompassing the idea that international law is to be understood as a coherent system,[94] this provision offers an avenue through which the law of occupation may be interpreted in an evolutive manner, so that developments within the field of IHRL may enrich it. While not providing general criteria, international practice contains examples of how IHRL may appropriately limit and complement the law of occupation.

Take the case of the practice of 'administrative detention' provided for by article 78 of the Geneva Convention IV. This norm authorises the deprivation of an individual's freedom for an undefined period of time on grounds of security.[95] The rationale for this norm may be found in the need for an occupying power to protect its own security in a situation of occupation. However, when seen from a human rights perspective, it may be considered to be in breach of article 9 of the ICCPR, which requires stricter parameters, defined in advance, for legitimately depriving an individual of his freedom, including the maximum duration of the length of detention without charge. Israel has often resorted to this practice in the course of its occupation of Palestinian territory, but neither the UN Secretary-General nor the HRC censured it as such. They could not do so, it is submitted, because they could not deny the validity of what was authorised by IHL, but they could, and therefore did, seek to circumscribe this practice in light of IHRL. In so doing, they avoided granting article 78 undue primacy as *lex specialis* and rightly placed the relevant norms of IHRL on an equal footing. In one of its reports on the human rights situation in the Palestinian territory, seeking to balance considerations of IHL with IHRL, the UN Secretary-General stated 'administrative detention should be used only in the most exceptional cases and only for imperative reasons of security. It should not be used as an alternative to criminal proceedings'.[96] Likewise the UN Special Committee investigating human rights violations in the Palestinian territory did not state that the practice of administrative detention was illegal *per se*; it reviewed and criticised it in light of IHRL. In a 2012 Report, the Committee stated:

---

93   Ferraro (n 10 above) 275.
94   C McLachlan 'The principle of systemic integration and article 31(3)(c) of the Vienna Convention' (2005) 54 *International and Comparative Law Quarterly* 279. On the principle of systemic integration see also Report of the Study Group on Fragmentation (n 64 above) paras 410-423.
95   See text of article 78 in A Roberts & R Guelff *Documents on the laws of war* (3rd ed, 2000) 328.
96   HRC 'Report of the Special Committee to Investigate Israel Practices Affecting the Human Rights of the Palestinian People and Other Arabs of the Occupied Territories' (2 November 2012) A/67/550, para 21.

The Committee nonetheless expresses concern at the *frequent* and *extensive* use of administrative detention, including for children, under Military Order No 1591, as well as the Emergency Powers (Detention) Law.[97]

And it went on to criticise the practice of administrative detention on the following grounds:

In fact Administrative detention infringes detainees' rights to a fair trial, including their right to be informed promptly and in detail, in a language which they understand, of the nature and cause of the charge against them, to have adequate time and facilities for the preparation of their defence and to communicate with counsel of their own choosing, to be tried in their presence, and to defend themselves in person or through legal assistance of their own choosing (arts. 4, 14 and 24).[98]

On the same lines, the HRC could blame Israel's practice 'of demolishing property and homes of families whose members were or are suspected of involvement in terrorist activities', not because it was necessarily illegal, but because Israel had acted 'without considering other less intrusive measures'.[99]

Concerned by the response of Israeli Forces to 'regular demonstrations' that 'have been taking place to express grievances against the practices of occupation by Israel', the UN Secretary-General remarked that Israel's forces had used 'Military Order 101', which concerns the 'Prohibition of Incitement and Hostile Propaganda Actions', to restrict Palestinians' rights to freedom of expression and assembly.[100] Without considering it illegal *per se*, which would have been difficult to do because it could be justified as a security measure, the UN Secretary-General went on to censure it on the grounds that one of the main problems with the order was 'the sweeping prohibition of expression deemed to be "political", which is vague and subject to interpretation', and the use of the expression 'required degree of force', which left 'considerable room for discretion and the potential for excessive use of force'.[101]

3.5   The use of force in occupied territory

Furthermore, an example of how IHRL can supplement IHL, based upon an evaluation of the factual circumstances, and also be the *lex specialis* on certain matters, is the case of the use of force in occupied territory. As

---

97   As above.
98   HRC 'Concluding observations of the Human Rights Committee' (3 September 2010) CCPR/C/ISR/CO/3, para 7.
99   Concluding observations of the Human Rights Committee (n 98 above) para 17.
100 'Report of the Special Rapporteur on the promotion and protection of the right to freedom of opinion and expression' (11 June 2012) A/HRC/20/17, para 77.
101 'Report of the Special Rapporteur on the promotion and protection of the right to freedom of opinion and expression' (n 100 above) para 78.

noted in the recent ICRC Expert Report on Occupation,[102] the law of occupation does not spell out when and how force may be used in occupied territory.[103] Thus, a central question that characterises the debate on the use of force in occupied territory is whether such use should be governed by 'the law-enforcement model' or by the so-called 'conduct of hostilities model'.[104] According to a majority of the experts whose opinions are reported in the ICRC Expert Report on Occupation, 'the application of the law enforcement model should be presumed in occupied territory'.[105] This model, which would be carried out within the framework of article 43 of the Hague Regulations, imposes stricter standards on the occupying power, which is authorised to use lethal force – while exercising its policing functions – only when this is strictly unavoidable in order to protect life and when 'less extreme means are insufficient for achieving that objective'.[106] As noted by the Secretary General:

> Primarily based on human rights norms, the application of the law-enforcement model would essentially amount to the introduction of a peacetime model in a situation of occupation, which would apply when the occupying forces were engaged in police operations aimed at enforcing the law against criminal acts not linked to the armed conflict[107]... In the West Bank, Israeli forces act in a law-enforcement capacity and are therefore bound by article 6 of the International Covenant on Civil and Political Rights and article 43 of the Hague Regulations, in addition to general principles on the use of force by law enforcement officials, including the principles of necessity and proportionality contained in the Basic Principles on the Use of Force and Firearms by Law Enforcement Officials, 1990,[11] and the Code of Conduct for Law Enforcement Officials, 1979 (see General Assembly resolution 34/169, annex).[108]

In light of this passage, it could be suggested that in situations concerning law and order operations, IHRL would prevail as *lex specialis* in cases of divergence and be the framework of reference, while it is only in 'conduct of hostilities' situations that IHL would be the *lex specialis*.[109]

To give some examples of how IHRL may substantiate the application of the law-enforcement model, it may be appropriate to recall the wording of the UN Secretary-General in his 2011 Report concerning the respect of

---

102 ICRC Expert Report on Occupation (n 59 above) 109.
103 ICRC Expert Report on Occupation (n 59 above) 110. See also Ferraro (n 10 above) 284.
104 As above.
105 ICRC Expert Report on Occupation (n 59 above) 116.
106 ICRC Expert Report on Occupation (n 59 above) 109.
107 As above.
108 Report of the UN Secretary-General 'Israel practices affecting the human rights of the Palestinian people in the Occupied Palestinian Territory, including East Jerusalem' (14 September 2012) A/67/372, para 17.
109 Sassòli (n 62 above) 394.

human rights in the occupied Palestinian territory.[110] Censuring the excessive use of force against unarmed Palestinians in the West Bank and emphasising that the conduct of the occupying powers should follow the law-enforcement model, the Report stated that:

> The use of firearms against unarmed persons raises serious concerns with regard to the open-fire regulations and training received by the Israeli security forces. In the West Bank, occupying forces act in a law-enforcement capacity. They are bound by article 6 of the International Covenant on Civil and Political Rights and should act in accordance with the Basic Principles for the Use of Force and Firearms by Law Enforcement Officials. In this context, the use of firearms is authorized in extremely limited circumstances, namely, self-defence or defence of others against imminent threat of death or serious injury and only if less extreme means are insufficient.[111]

And speaking of the attitude towards the demonstrators, the Report stressed that:

> The use of firearms is not an appropriate means of riot control against unarmed demonstrators, and their use in this context is not in conformity with international standards on the use of firearms by law enforcement officials. The use of excessive force against demonstrators has a negative impact on the rights of Palestinians to freedom of expression and freedom of assembly, rights which are guaranteed by the International Covenant on Civil and Political Rights. (emphasis added)

This presumption for the applicability of the law enforcement model to an occupation could, however, be rebutted in favour of the 'conduct-of-hostilities' model when, based on analysis of the factual circumstances, the conditions for the application of this latter model are fulfilled.[112] The occupying power – which is one of the parties to an international armed conflict – would be entitled to use the 'conduct-of-hostilities' model when active hostilities persist or resume within the framework of the original international armed conflict. An insurgency could be considered the continuation of the original international armed conflict when the insurgents could be associated in one way or another with the occupied state, unless of course the dislodged sovereign would not declare its indifference to the hostilities.[113] Last but not least, it should not be excluded that both models may apply concomitantly in the same territory or quickly change from one to another, depending on the facts at hand. For example, it is absolutely possible that in the same city there could be a group of fighters that seek to overthrow the occupation administration as well as a group of thieves that try to take advantage of the resulting confusion to steal, and the occupying power may have recourse to force in both situations, though under quite different criteria. This double function

---

110   Report of the UN Secretary-General (n 108 above) para 15.
111   As above.
112   Report of the UN Secretary-General (n 108 above) 112-116.
113   ICRC Expert Report on Occupation (n 59 above) 252.

requires an occupying power to have the ability to switch from a conduct-of-hostilities to a law-enforcement model, at least as concerns the attitude towards the civilian population. Admittedly, this is a difficult task, which requires foresight and flexibility on the part of civilian and military leaders. It can be achieved only if a state that is likely to become an occupying power in the course of an armed conflict or has become one, puts as its first order of business the provision to its soldiers of adequate instructions and rules concerning the treatment of the civilian population.

4   A pro-human rights expansion of the normative authority of an occupying power?

Another aspect through which IHRL can influence the authorities and duties of an occupying power is through an enlargement of its normative authorities. This is still a matter of debate amongst scholars, but the idea that protecting the human rights of the persons under occupation by introducing human rights-oriented legislation has gained considerable attention in recent years, particularly in connection with the transformative efforts by the occupying powers in Iraq in 2003.[114] According to Tristan Ferraro, 'HRL is essentially an agenda for social reform, the contradiction between the conservationist principle and the implementation of this body of law in occupied territory could become quite problematic'.[115] Adam Roberts, in a seminal study on transformative occupation, contemplated the possibility of an occupying power being justified in carrying out 'transformative policies' on the basis that 'these are the best way to meet certain goals and principles enshrined in international human rights law, including the right to self-determination'.[116] On a similar note, Gregory Fox has observed that – at first glance – the conservationist principle may be thought of as 'regressive and even anachronistic' when confronted with the possibility of ensuring 'greater protection of human rights and the introduction of democratic politics'.[117] On the other hand, Fox has also, rightly, stressed that it is 'one thing to say that occupiers should refrain from neglecting or mistreating inhabitants. It is quite another to grant them licence to become agents of constitutional revolutions'.[118]

Eyal Benvenisti seems to be open to the possibility of a pro-human rights occupation when he argues that 'human rights law may strengthen

114   See in this regard G Fox 'The occupation of Iraq' (2005) 36 *Georgetown Journal of International Law* 195; M Sassòli 'Legislation and maintenance of public order and civil life by occupying powers' (2005) 16 *European Journal of International Law* 661.
115   Ferraro (n 10 above) 277.
116   A Roberts 'Transformative military occupation: Applying the laws of war and human rights' (2006) 100 *American Journal of International Law* 580 620.
117   G Fox 'Transformative occupation and the unilateralist impulse' (2012) 94 *International Review of the Red Cross* 237 241.
118   As above.

the law-making function of occupants'[119] and 'enlarge' it.[120] In the ICRC Expert Report on Occupation, a majority of the experts agreed that some changes could be effected in an occupied territory to meet human rights standards and that while there exists a 'certain amount of flexibility' to implement human rights law in occupied territory, it 'should not be interpreted as giving [the occupying power] a blank cheque to change legislation and institutions in the name of human rights' in order to make them accord with the legal and institutional ideas of the occupying power.[121] Accordingly, 'human rights law should not be invoked in order to justify transformative occupation'.[122] The argument that an occupant should act as a kind of protector of the human rights of a people from previous or future abuses by the local government, which is dislodged or disbanded during an occupation, by setting aside, amending, or introducing new legislation, is a noble aspiration. But from the perspective of the inhabitants of the occupied territory, it could already be a meaningful step if the occupant itself would take all possible precautions to protect their security from its own conduct, which during an occupation is probably the one most likely to infringe their human rights. The problem remains, however, of clarifying the specific content and nature of the human rights reforms an occupant should be introducing in the occupied territory, and whether its authority/duty to do so should be limited to taking measures having effect solely during the occupation or also after it. It is one thing to protect human rights during an occupation, which could be done by suspending or declaring as inapplicable discriminatory norms for the duration of the occupation and passing legislation mandating respect for human rights on the part of occupation forces; it is quite another to try to impose the protection of human rights on the sovereign coming (or returning) to power after the end of the occupation by amending local laws.

Gregory Fox has aptly summarised that human rights treaties may impose three distinct sets of obligations on occupying states, namely to: (i) refrain from violating protected rights; (ii) ensure that others within their jurisdiction refrain from such violations; and (iii) act affirmatively to ensure that procedures for the protection of rights exist.[123] Regarding the first two sets of obligations, it can be argued that throughout an occupation, an occupying power should be entitled to 'legislate' interstitially in order to create the conditions for its own adherence to applicable human rights norms and to take measures to protect the inhabitants of the occupied territory against acts of violence,[124] including

---

119   Benvenisti (n 1 above) 102.
120   Benvenisti (n 1 above) 104.
121   ICRC Expert Report on Occupation (n 59 above) 69.
122   As above.
123   Fox (n 117 above) 259.
124   N Lubell 'Human rights obligations in military occupation' (2012) 94 *International Review of the Red Cross* 326.

in situations of detention,[125] as well as to address and deal with such violence by any third party,[126] and to prevent its occurrence.[127] The adoption of these kinds of measures would also demonstrate the occupant's efforts to comply with its obligations under international treaties such as the ICCPR and the ICESCR in occupied territory.[128] Moreover, compliance with human rights during an occupation would require ensuring the right to food, the right to work,[129] and ensuring that the 'health, education, and employment situation' of the inhabitants of the occupied territory 'continue in as uninterrupted a manner as possible'.[130] At times, such interstitial legislation may overlap with legislation that is permissible under the law of occupation. Furthermore, from a contemporary perspective, the protection of human rights in occupied territory may be regarded as essential to ensure security within the occupied territory and to achieve an 'orderly government of territory', as provided under article 64 of the Geneva Convention IV. To give an example, an occupying power may legitimately intervene under the law of occupation to prevent the stoning of a woman for adultery on the basis that, in its view, it is necessary for reasons of public order and safety.[131] Moreover, an occupying power, in accordance with its duty to ensure the non-discrimination of all 'individuals within its territory and subject to its jurisdiction' under article 2(1) of the ICCPR, could suspend all discriminatory legislation in place in a given territory. Acting under article 10 of the ICCPR, it should also enact norms to ensure that 'all persons deprive[ed] of their liberty' be treated by the occupation forces 'with humanity and with respect for the inherent dignity of the human person' throughout the occupation.[132]

That said, it is a different issue whether an occupant should be accorded an additional and autonomous normative authority, based on the advancement and protection of human rights and the eventual introduction of a democratic system, which would enable the occupant to amend or replace local laws with new legislation directed to have effect also, or rather principally, beyond the end of the occupation.[133] Under this hypothesis, while claiming to protect human rights, an occupant could not only suspend or repel a given applicable law so as to prevent the harming of individual rights during an occupation, it could go as far as replacing existing local laws and institutions with new norms and/or institutions of its own making and design, having effect well beyond the occupation and

125 Lubell (n 124 above) 328.
126 As stated by the ICJ in the *Armed Activities* case (n 29 above) para 178. See also quotation in § 3.5.1 above.
127 *Armed Activities* (n 29 above) para 179.
128 ICRC Expert Report on Occupation (n 59 above) 65.
129 *Wall* Advisory Opinion (n 3 above) paras 130, 133 and 134.
130 Lubell (n 124 above) 330.
131 But taking a different approach on this issue see Milanović (n 74 above) 121-123.
132 International Covenant on Civil and Political Rights (adopted 16 December 1966, entered into force 23 March 1976) 999 UNTS 171, article 10 (ICCPR).
133 Lubell (n 124 above) 330.

thus resulting in an alteration of the relationship between the indigenous government gaining power after the occupation and its citizens. The occupant would, then, be acting as a legislator in the same way, but not with the same authority, as an indigenous parliament. Once incorporated into domestic law, human rights-oriented legislation issued by the occupant would remain in force after the end of the occupation unless and until the returning (legitimate) sovereign opts to remove it. However, the returning sovereign would not automatically be able to make the necessary reforms in a timely and comprehensive manner. Hence, reforms introduced under the guise of protecting human rights during an occupation may interfere with the jurisdiction of the incoming sovereign, cementing a force-based transformation in the relationship between the legitimate sovereign over that territory and its people. Furthermore, a danger with such expansive legislation, despite its apparent attractiveness, is that it would elevate to the rank of law what is, at best, a sort of 'amateur' legislation, resulting from the work (and opinions) of a few foreign officials operating with urgency and secrecy in the 'cubicles' of an occupation administration, rather than arising in the halls of a parliament on the basis of an informed and transparent legislative process participated in by the citizens of the territory concerned.

In view of the foregoing, it is suggested that for human rights-oriented legislation adopted by an occupant to be considered valid, it must be anchored to, and justified by compliance with, applicable human rights norms binding the occupant, or brought under one of the fields in which an occupant is recognised as having the authority to legislate under the law of occupation and be within the limits of such authority. If, outside of these parameters, an occupant were to adopt human rights legislation, or any other legislation, directed at displaying the bulk of its effects after the end of the occupation by incorporating them into the domestic laws of the occupied country, it would be acting *ultra vires* – unless specifically authorised to act in this way by the Security Council – exercising a role which is not its own.[134] While IHRL may certainly be a basis for reforms that are required during an occupation in order to protect the civilian population from the occupant or, for instance, from courts or enforcement agencies of the dislodged regime that may still operate during the occupation, it cannot become a justification for long-lasting transformative policies which the local population has not asked for and with which it may not agree.

Last but not least, it may be argued that the relevance of human rights law for the governance of an occupied territory largely depends on the duration of the occupation.[135] Yoram Dinstein considers it 'almost axiomatic that the military government must be given more leeway in the

---

134 Fox (n 117 above) 262.
135 As above.

application of its law-making power if the occupation endures for many years'.[136] While in short-term occupation, the core of human rights obligations would correspond to the obligations set out under IHL, during longer periods of occupation, human rights law would become increasingly important and provide for more detailed answers than IHL norms. That being so, however, a situation of prolonged occupation does not justify conferring on an occupying power a broader normative authority, because, otherwise, the occupying power would be rewarded by receiving in the long term that legitimisation to shape the future of a country, which, for good reasons, it did not have in the short term.[137]

5   Concluding thoughts

Identifying IHL, and hence the law of occupation as *lex specialis* in respect of IHRL, as the case-law of the ICJ does, is a timely reminder that adapting a field of law to a context for which it was not created should be done with caution and flexibility.

On the one hand, treating the law of occupation as the only possible *lex specialis* in times of occupation would be a crystallisation rather than a necessary development of the international law applicable to an occupation. IHL can be interpreted in light of IHRL and the two could join forces to provide concrete solutions to the problems that are emerging in the rather complex governance of occupied territory in the twenty-first century and to ensure respect for rights that had not been recognised when the law of occupation was drafted and developed. Speciality, in the sense of having been codified for a specific factual situation, is not necessarily synonymous with suitability or pertinence, let alone desirability, when a body of law has not undergone any process of revision and updating for a considerable number of years.[138] For this reason, although not specifically drafted for situations of occupation, IHRL can be *lex specialis* either as prevailing over the law of occupation when, for instance, the situation in the occupied territory is one of law-enforcement, or of shaping it, as in some of the examples discussed, by delimiting the otherwise legal conduct of an occupying power. This requires the adoption of a more nuanced and less formalistic interpretation of the term *specialis* than that used by the ICJ, while also taking into account and highlighting the intrinsic limitations of the law of occupation.

---

136   Dinstein (n 1 above) 120.
137   Arguing that the 'influence of the prolonged character of an occupation over the application of IHL and IHRL should not, as such, be overestimated' because 'More than the time factor, it is other characteritics of prolonged occupations that have an impact on the rules of IHL and IHRL, namely the existence or not of hostilites in the occupied territory' see V Koutrolis 'The application of international humanitarian law and international human rights law in situation of prolonged occupation: Only a matter of time?' (2012) 94 *International Review of the Red Cross* 164.
138   See in this regard the thorough analysis conducted in KE Boon 'The future of the law of occupation' (2009) *Canadian Yearbook of International Law* 107-142.

But paving the way for a stronger role for IHRL is not the same as providing adequate guidance. From this perspective, it seems possible to suggest that we are still far from a comprehensive set of rules and principles that can offer reasonably adequate and clear guidance to all those called to simultaneously implement both the law of occupation and IHRL. The examples discussed in this paper constitute important interpretative attempts to reconcile the two regimes, but it would be somewhat presumptuous to suggest that this effort can always provide viable and generally accepted interpretations. Even though the studies dedicated to the topic are certainly not in short supply, the formulation of concrete and clear directives is yet to emerge. Intended to perform a different function, the scholarly publications that are available cannot easily replace the need to agree on what is actually required in relation to issues governed, in whole or in part, by both IHL and IHRL and to clarify these issues for the benefit of the law enforcers, who may not be professional lawyers. More clarity may enable those who apply the law of occupation, whether military or civilian personnel, to perform their duties more effectively and thus, ultimately, more fairly.

Perhaps, in addition to the important interpretative effort undertaken by international courts, UN bodies and academics, it is time to undertake the effort to update the law of occupation, codifying within it the numerous developments that have occurred in the field of IHRL in recent years. This could start with proposals submitted to the consideration of states from professional associations of international lawyers and scholars. The task is admittedly rather daunting. But some inspiration could be drawn from the Preamble of the Manual on the Laws of War on Land, which the *Institut de droit international* adopted on 9 September 1880 during its Oxford session (Oxford Manual). Already at that time, the *Institut* was mindful, as noted in the Preamble of the Oxford Manual, of the difficulty of adopting a new treaty, stating that:

> The Institute, too, does not propose an international treaty, which might perhaps be premature or at least very difficult to obtain but it believes that it was 'fulfilling a duty in offering to the governments a "Manual" suitable as the basis for national legislation in each State' which was in accord with both the progress of juridical science and the needs of civilized armies [...][139]

Nevertheless, the *Institut* insisted on outlining a rationale for preparing the Manual as follows:

> The Institute has not sought innovations in drawing up the 'Manual'; it has contented itself with stating clearly and codifying the accepted ideas of our age so far as this has appeared allowable and practicable. By so doing, it believes it is rendering a service to military men themselves. In fact so long as

---

139　See the text in the Preamble of the Oxford Manual published in D Schindler & J Toman (eds) *The laws of armed conflicts: A collection of conventions, resolutions and other documents* (3rd ed, 1988) 35-47.

the demands of opinion remain indeterminate, belligerents are exposed to painful uncertainty and to endless accusations. A positive set of rules, on the contrary, if they are judicious, serves the interests of belligerents ... it also ennobles their patriotic mission in the eyes of the soldiers by keeping them within the limits of respect due to the rights of humanity.[140]

If we consider that the *Oxford Manual* served as a basis for the Hague Regulations as attested to, inter alia, by the circumstance that several of the Regulations recall formulations used in the *Oxford Manual*,[141] the latter can be regarded as a case of a successful cooperation between international lawyers and states. Thus, it may be fitting to close this paper by drawing to the attention of scholars – notwithstanding the obvious and numerous difficulties associated with such an approach – the example already set by the *Institut de droit international* in 1880. Perhaps, assuming that the subject matter is ripe for codification and without ignoring the fact that the difficulties of so doing have probably been augmented today because of the increase in the number of actors involved, it could be submitted that no less is what international lawyers owe to those they expect to comply with an increasingly complex set of international norms and principles.

140   As above.
141   Comparare for instance the text (in brackets I added the subject-matter of the article) of the following articles of the *Oxford Manual*: Arts 41 (definition), 43 (Rules of conduct with respect to persons), 44 (maintenance of the law of force in a country), 45 (dismissal of public officials), 47 (prohibition to swear allegiance), 49 (famously honour and rights), 52 (occupant ad provisional administrator), 53 (public property), 54 (private property), 56 (taxation) with arts 42,43, 45, 46, 48, 49, 52, 55, 56 of the Hague Regulations. See text of the *Oxford Manual* in Schindler & Toman (n 139 above) 35-47 and of the Hague Regulations in A Roberts & R Guelff *Documents on the laws of war* (3rd ed, 2000) 80-82.

7

Role of Human Right and International Humanitarian Law in Peace Operations

*Marten Zwanenburg**

1   Introduction

On 30 July 2013, the United Nations peacekeeping mission in the Democratic Republic of the Congo (MONUSCO) announced that it would use its recently established intervention brigade to enforce a security zone around the flashpoint city of Goma in the eastern part of the country, giving rebels 48 hours to disarm. A statement issued by the mission said that any individuals in the area of the North Kivu province that includes Goma and Sake who are not members of national security forces would be given 48 hours to hand in their weapons. Failing which, they would be considered to pose an imminent threat of physical violence to civilians and MONUSCO would take all necessary measures to disarm them, including by the use of force in accordance with its mandate and rules of engagement.[1] It must be assumed that before issuing this statement, MONUSCO had considered in detail the measures that could and would be taken against persons found not to have complied with the ultimatum. For the MONUSCO legal advisers involved, one of the most pressing questions this raises is the legal regime governing such measures. In particular, are such measures regulated by international humanitarian law (IHL) and if so, by the IHL regime of non-international or of international armed conflicts? Are they governed by international human rights law (IHRL)? Or do both regimes apply simultaneously, and if this is the case,

---

*   martenzwanenburg@yahoo.com. Marten Zwanenburg is a legal counsel with the Ministry of Foreign Affairs of the Netherlands. This contribution was written in a personal capacity. The opinions presented herein do not necessarily reflect the opinions of the Ministry of Foreign Affairs of the Netherlands or any other part of the government of the Netherlands.

1   United Nations 'UN mission sets up security zone in eastern DR Congo, gives rebels 48 hour ultimatum':http://www.un.org/apps/news/story.asp?NewsID=45535&Cr=democratic&Cr1=congo#.Uf4Oho6ChUR (accessed 4 August 2013).

which one takes precedence when the two regimes provide different outcomes in a specific situation? Legal advisers in peace operations are increasingly confronted with such questions concerning the convergence and conflicts of IHL and IHRL. There are a number of reasons for this. One of these is that it is increasingly argued that IHRL obligations of a state continue to apply when a state acts outside its own territory. A body of non-binding statements and case law has emerged from human rights monitoring bodies holding that in certain circumstances a state is bound by human rights extraterritorially, including when it contributes personnel to a peace operation. The clearest statement in this sense was made by the Human Rights Committee in its General Comment No 31, in which it stated that:

> [A] State party must respect and ensure the rights laid down in the Covenant to anyone within the power or effective control of that State Party, even if not situated within the territory of the State Party ... This principle also applies to those within the power or effective control of the forces of a State Party acting outside its territory, regardless of the circumstances in which such power or effective control was obtained, such as forces constituting a national contingent of a State Party assigned to an international peace-keeping or peace-enforcement operation.[2]

Another reason is that contemporary peace operations are frequently authorised to use force beyond self-defence to achieve their mandate. If they make use of such authorisation, this may lead them to become a party to an armed conflict and make IHL applicable.

As a consequence, practice in peace operations increasingly calls for an answer to questions concerning the convergence and conflicts of IHL and IHRL. This contribution will address a number of these questions. To this end, it will start by looking at the applicability of IHL and IHRL to peace operations. With respect to the applicability of IHL, it will discuss which of the different IHL regimes, that of international armed conflicts or that of non-international armed conflicts, is relevant. Having concluded that there are situations where both IHL and IHRL apply, some observations will be made on the interplay between these two regimes, in particular in respect of the principle of *lex specialis*. The contribution will then focus more specifically on the specificities of the interplay between the two regimes in peace operations.

For the purposes of this contribution, the term 'peace operation' refers to multinational operations established or authorised by the United Nations to establish or maintain international peace and security. This includes operations referred to by the UN as 'peacekeeping operations' as

---

2   General Comment No 31, UNHR Committee (26 May 2004), UN Doc CCPR/C/21/ Rev.1/Add.13 (2004), para 10.

well as 'peace enforcement operations'.[3] These operations have in common that they do not aim at the destruction or defeat of an enemy, but rather to achieve a particular mandate in an impartial manner. This distinguishes them from so-called 'enforcement actions' which imply the use of force for the purpose of imposing the will of the enforcer on the addressee of the action.[4] Peace operations may be led by the UN, like MONUSCO referred to above. They may also be led by another international organisation (like the International Security Assistance Force (ISAF) in Afghanistan, which is led by the North Atlantic Treaty Organization (NATO)) or by one or more states.

This definition of peace operations highlights that such operations are frequently led by an international organisation, be it the UN or another organisation. This contribution will not address questions related to the involvement of an international organisation in the operation, however.[5] It will take the obligations of individual troop contributing states under IHL and IHRL as a starting point, under the assumption that these remain applicable to the troops that states contribute to a peace operation. From an international law perspective, such an assumption is open to criticism. It could be argued that for the conduct of troops that are placed at the disposal of an international organisation with international legal personality, the international obligations of that organisation are of primary relevance and not those of the sending states. Nevertheless, as mentioned above human rights treaty bodies have held that troop contributing states' human rights obligations continue to apply to a state's troops in a peace operation. In addition, personnel contributed to a peace operation normally continue to be bound by the law of the sending state, including its criminal law. The IHL and IHRL obligations of that state will be implemented in its domestic law. For example, the Netherlands has criminalised the crimes in the Rome Statute of the International Criminal

---

3   United Nations 'United Nations peacekeeping operations: Principles and guidelines' *(Capstone Doctrine)* (2004) 18. The document defines peacekeeping and peace enforcement operations as follows: Peacekeeping is a technique designed to preserve the peace, however fragile, where fighting has been halted, and to assist in implementing agreements achieved by the peacemakers. Over the years, peacekeeping has evolved from a primarily military model of observing cease-fires and the separation of forces after inter-state wars, to incorporate a complex model of many elements – military, police and civilian – working together to help lay the foundations for sustainable peace. Peace enforcement involves the application, with the authorisation of the Security Council, of a range of coercive measures, including the use of military force. Such actions are authorised to restore international peace and security in situations where the Security Council has determined the existence of a threat to the peace, breach of the peace or act of aggression. The Security Council may utilise, where appropriate, regional organisations and agencies for enforcement action under its authority.

4   M Bothe 'Peacekeeping forces' in R Wolfrum (ed) *Max Planck encyclopedia of public international law* (2010) http://opil.ouplaw.com/home/EPIL (accessed 5 August 2013).

5   See on this question O Engdahl 'Multinational peace operations involved in armed conflict: Who are the parties?' in KM Larsen et al (eds) *Searching for a 'principle of humanity' in international humanitarian law* (2013) 233.

Court in the International Crimes Act, which applies under all circumstances to Dutch nationals.[6] The conduct of the personnel in a peace operation will be judged by prosecutorial and judicial authorities against those standards of domestic law. This justifies taking the international obligations of troop contributing states as a point of departure.

2   Applicability of international humanitarian law and international human rights law in peace operations

2.1   International humanitarian law

IHL is not one single set of norms but consists of different regimes. The principal distinction that can be made is between international armed conflicts and non-international armed conflicts. International armed conflicts are mainly regulated by the four Geneva Conventions of 1949 as well as by the first Additional Protocol to those Conventions of 1977 (API). The Geneva Conventions provide in their common article 2 that they apply to:

> [A]ll cases of declared war or of any other armed conflict which may arise between two or more of the High Contracting Parties, even if the state of war is not recognized by one of them.

The article adds that the Conventions also apply to all cases of partial or total occupation of the territory of a high contracting party, even if the said occupation meets with no armed resistance. IHL treaty law does not provide a definition of the term armed conflict. The statement by the International Criminal Tribunal for the former Yugoslavia (ICTY) in the *Tadić* case that 'an armed conflict exists whenever there is a resort to armed force between States' is considered as an authoritative clarification.[7] It does not resolve all possible controversy, however. For example, there is debate whether or not the armed force used must reach a minimum level of intensity. State practice suggests that it does.[8]

Non-international conflicts are covered by common article 3 to the Geneva Conventions and by Additional Protocol II to those Conventions (APII). Non-international armed conflicts are conflicts in which at least one of the parties is not a state. IHL treaties do not define what a non-

---

6   International Crimes Act (Wet Internationale Misdrijven) 19 June 2003.
7   *The Prosecutor v Dusko Tadić*, ICTY, Decision on the Defence Motion for Interlocutory Appeal on Jurisdiction, IT-94-1-A, 2 October 1995, para 70 (ICTY).
8   See eg International Law Association Committee on the Use of Force *Final report on the meaning of armed conflict in international law* (2010) (ILA).

international armed conflict is. The Appeals Chamber of the ICTY in the *Tadić* case held there is a NIAC when there is 'protracted armed violence between governmental authorities and organized armed groups or between such groups within a State'.[9] In subsequent case law, the ICTY has developed two main criteria for determining whether there is a NIAC. These are a minimum level of organisation of the parties involved as well as a minimum level of intensity of the fighting. These criteria are now broadly regarded as determinative of the question whether there is a NIAC.[10] The threshold for application of APII is higher than that for common article 3. Article 1 of APII provides that the Protocol applies to all armed conflicts not covered by API and:

> [W]hich take place in the territory of a High Contracting Party between its armed forces and dissident armed forces or other organized armed groups which, under responsible command, exercise such control over a part of its territory as to enable them to carry out sustained and concerted military operations and to implement this Protocol.

Consequently, in addition to the above-mentioned criteria for a NIAC, APII requires that the non-state actor exercises control over territory.

The applicability of IHL was controversial when the first peace operations were established. Some commentators argued that forces mandated or authorised by the UN could not be subject to the same rules as their opponents.[11] They should be considered as international policemen, not as just another party in a conflict. This point of view now has very few supporters. One reason is that it is recognised that reciprocity remains an important mechanism in IHL if this branch of law is to remain relevant.[12] As Sir Hersch Lauterpacht stated:

> [I]t is impossible to visualize the conduct of hostilities in which one side would be bound by rules of warfare without benefiting from them and the other side would benefit from rules of warfare without being bound by them.[13]

Related to this idea is the point of view that the determination of whether IHL applies must depend on the factual circumstances and not the objectives pursued by the parties. This idea is reflected in the preamble to API, in which the drafters reaffirmed that the Geneva Conventions and the Protocol must be applied without any adverse distinction based on the

---

9   ICTY (n 7 above) para 70.
10   ILA (n 8 above).
11   See eg WJ Bivens et al 'Report of the Committee on the Study of the Legal Problems of the United Nations: Should the laws of war apply to United Nations enforcement action?' (1952) *American Society of International Law Proceedings* 216 217.
12   See generally on reciprocity in IHL, S Watts 'Reciprocity and the law of war' (2009) 50 *Harvard International Law Journal* 365.
13   H Lauterpacht 'The limits of the operation of the law of war' (1953) 30 *British Yearbook of International Law* 206 212.

nature or origin of the armed conflict or on the causes espoused by or attributed to the parties to the conflict.

As a matter of principle, it is now broadly accepted that the use of force by peace operations may cross the threshold of an armed conflict and make IHL applicable.[14] The application of this principle in practice however demonstrates that states are still uneasy with accepting the application of IHL in concrete cases. Accepting that the law of war applies does not sit well with the moral superiority associated with taking part in a peace operation. It may also make it more difficult for governments to 'sell' an operation to political parties or to the general public.

In many cases, this is not a problem because IHL by its own terms is not applicable to a peace operation. Although the threshold for an armed conflict is notoriously vague, in many cases it is clear that there is no armed conflict or at least that the peace operation is not a party to the conflict. For example, it is uncontroversial that the United Nations Force in Cyprus (UNFICYP) is not a party to an armed conflict. In other cases, the situation is not so clear. One reason for this may be that on the basis of the available facts, reasonable minds can come to different conclusions as to whether there is an armed conflict to which a peace operation is a party. For example, in the DRC MONUSCO personnel have on a number of occasions become involved in exchanges of fire with members of the M23 rebel movement.[15] It could be argued that taken together, these incidents cross the threshold of intensity required to establish an armed conflict between MONUSCO and M23. Even if this is not the case at present, the establishment of an intervention brigade with a mandate of 'neutralising' is likely to lead MONUSCO to become party to an armed conflict. Yet the UN has never publicly admitted that its peacekeepers are parties to the conflicts in which they engage, including in the case of MONUSCO.[16]

The latter state of affairs undoubtedly has to do with the fact that international organisations and troop contributing states involved in a peace operation are often reluctant to conclude that such an operation has become party to an armed conflict.[17] An illustration of this is the position of Germany on the application of IHL to its forces participating in the UN-

14   D Shraga 'The Applicability of international humanitarian law to peace operations from rejection to acceptance' in GL Beruto (ed) *International humanitarian law, human rights and peace operations* (2009) 90.
15   See eg 'Secretary-General Ban regrets death of UN peacekeeper in eastern DR Congo clashes' *UN News Centre* 6 July 2012; 'MONUSCO warns M23 against repeated attacks on UN helicopters' *MONUSCO* 28 December 2012; 'DRC troops, UN forces attack rebel positions' *Agence France Presse* 13 July 2012.
16   B Oswald 'The Security Council and the Intervention Brigade: Some legal issues' (2013) 17 *American Society of International Law Insights* http://www.asil.org/insights/volume/17/issue/15/security-council-and-intervention-brigade-some-legal-issues (accessed 5 August 2013).
17   See also C Greenwood 'International humanitarian law and United Nations military operations' (1998) 1 *Yearbook of International Humanitarian Law* 3 24.

authorised and NATO-led ISAF in Afghanistan. For a long time the German government denied that its forces were involved in an armed conflict. In an interview with a German magazine in November 2009, the German defence minister maintained that there was no armed conflict but was willing to accept that there were circumstances resembling war ('Kriegsähnliche Zustände').[18] Only in February 2010 did the German government accept that in north Afghanistan there was an armed conflict in the sense of IHL.[19] The original position of Germany may be contrasted with that of Canada. In litigation before its domestic courts concerning the detention by Canadian forces in ISAF, the Canadian government argued that IHL applied to detainees taken by Canadian forces in ISAF.[20] It should be noted that Germany is certainly not the only state contributing troops to ISAF that is reluctant to accept that it is a party to an armed conflict. Indeed, how ISAF should be characterised in terms of the applicable law has led to debate elsewhere in practice and academia.[21]

In case it is accepted that a peace operation has become a party to an armed conflict, the question arises how this conflict should be classified. It is generally accepted that if the opposing side is a state, the conflict should be qualified as an international armed conflict. There is some debate on the regime that applies when there is an armed conflict with an organised armed group. As regards UN-led operations, opinions in the literature are more or less equally divided between those who consider that an armed conflict between a UN force and an armed group is a non-international armed conflict, and those who consider that a UN operation by definition 'internationalises' the conflict.[22] The practice in UN operations in any event offers little clarity, because as mentioned above the UN has never publicly admitted that its peacekeepers are parties to the conflicts in which they engage. In peace operations not led by the UN, there is support for the application of the regime of NIAC to a conflict in which a peace operation and a non-state armed group are involved. State practice generally

18   Interview by Defense Minister zu Guttenberg with 'Bild' magazine, 3 November 2009: http://www.bundesregierung.de/Content/DE/Interview/2009/11/2009-11-03-interview-guttenberg-bild.html (accessed 16 August 2013).
19   Statement by Minister of Foreign Affairs Westerwelle in Parliament, 10 February 2010: http://www.auswaertiges-amt.de/DE/Infoservice/Presse/Reden/2010/1002 10-BM-BT-Afghanistan.html (accessed 16 October 2014).
20   See *Amnesty International Canada v Canada (Chief of Defence Staff)* 2008 FC 336, [2008] 4 FCR 540.
21   See CD Mortopoulos 'Could ISAF be a PSO? Theoretical extensions, practical problematic and the notion of neutrality' (2010) 15 *Journal of Conflict & Security Law* 573.
22   G Porretto & S Vité 'The Application of International Humanitarian Law and Human Rights Law to International Organisations' (2006) 1 Geneva University Centre for Humanitarian Law Research Paper: http://www.geneva-academy.ch/docs/projets/ CTR_application_du_DIH.pdf. (accessed 18 August 2013).

considers the conflict in which ISAF is involved in Afghanistan to be of a non-international character.[23]

2.2   International human rights law

The applicability of human rights to peace operations as a matter of principle is more controversial than is the case for IHL. This does not have to do so much with peace operations specifically, but more with the extraterritorial application of human rights obligations generally.[24] The extent of such application of human rights beyond the territory of the state is controversial. With respect to the International Covenant on Civil and Political Rights (ICCPR), the view of the United States is at one extreme end of the spectrum. That state rejects such extraterritorial application in principle.[25] The view of the Human Rights Committee is closer to the other end of the spectrum. The Committee holds a very broad view of when the ICCPR applies extraterritorially. In the view of the Committee:

> States Parties are required ... to respect and to ensure the Covenant rights to all persons who may be within their territory and to all persons subject to their jurisdiction. This means that a State party must respect and ensure the rights laid down in the Covenant to anyone within the power or effective control of that State Party, even if not situated within the territory of the State Party ... This principle also applies to those within the power or effective control of the forces of a State Party acting outside its territory, regardless of the circumstances in which such power or effective control was obtained, such as forces constituting a national contingent of a State Party assigned to an international peace-keeping or peace-enforcement operation.[26]

There are an increasing number of court decisions concerning this question, including in the context of peace operations. In the Netherlands, for example, the court of appeal of The Hague in July 2011 issued

---

23   See on the UK position D Turns 'Jus ad pacem in bello? Afghanistan, stability operations and international law relating to armed conflict' (2009) 39 Israel Yearbook on Human Rights 236. See on the German position the press release of the German Public Prosecutors Office of 19 April 2010: http://www.generalbundesanwalt.de/de/showpress.php?newsid=360 (accessed 22 August 2013). The ICRC also considers the conflict to be non-international. See ICRC 'International humanitarian law and the challenges of contemporary armed conflicts: Document prepared by the ICRC for the 30th Conference of the Red Cross and Red Crescent' (2009) 89 International Review of the Red Cross 719 725.

24   See eg M Milanovic Extraterritorial application of human rights treaties: Law, principles, and policy (2011); M Gondek The reach of human rights in a globalising world: Extraterritorial application of human rights treaties (2009).

25   See UN Commission on Human Rights 'Situation of Detainees at Guantánamo Bay' 27 February 2006, UN Doc E/CN.4/2006/120: 'The United States has made clear its position that ... the International Covenant on Civil and Political Rights, by its express terms, applies only to "individuals within its territory and subject to its jurisdiction".'

26   General Comment No 31 (n 2 above) para 10.

important judgments in relation to the Netherland's contingent in the UN operation in the former Yugoslavia in Srebrenica.[27] The court held that persons present on the compound of the Netherland's contingent benefited from the protection of the European Convention on Human Rights. This conclusion was upheld by the Supreme Court in its judgment of 6 September 2013.[28] There are a number of other domestic judgments relating to the extraterritorial application of human rights, not to mention by international courts and tribunals. In the framework of the European Convention on Human Rights, the European Court of Human Rights (ECtHR) issued a landmark judgment on 7 July 2011 in *Al-Skeini v UK*.[29] This is only one example of the fact that questions of the application of human rights in peace operations are increasingly placed before the courts. The problem is that court judgments are often very fact-specific, so that it is difficult to derive general principles from them that can easily be applied to different factual constellations. As Judge Bonello stated in his concurring opinion in *Al-Skeini*, the ECtHR's case-law on extraterritorial application 'has, so far, been bedevilled by an inability or an unwillingness to establish a coherent and axiomatic regime, grounded in essential basics and even-handedly applicable across the widest spectrum of jurisdictional controversies'.[30]

Certain human rights treaties provide for the possibility of derogation.[31] Derogation means that a state may temporarily adjust its obligations under the treaty. Both the ICCPR and the ECHR provide for such a possibility. Derogation is only possible in respect of some of the rights guaranteed by these treaties. Other rights are so-called 'non-derogable' rights. These notably include the right to life, although article 15 (2) ECHR makes an exception for 'deaths resulting from lawful acts of war'. Derogation is only possible if certain requirements are met, and under strict conditions.[32] The ICCPR for example requires in article 4 that there must be a 'time of public emergency which threatens the life of the nation and the existence of which is officially proclaimed'. In such circumstances a state party to the ICCPR may take measures derogating from its obligations under the Covenant to the extent strictly required by the exigencies of the situation, provided that such measures are not inconsistent with its other obligations under international law and do not involve discrimination solely on the ground of race, colour, sex, language, religion or social origin. The Human Rights Committee has elaborated on

---

27   *Mustafic v the Netherlands and Nuhanovic v the Netherlands* Appeals Court of the Hague (5 July 2011).
28   *Mustafic v the Netherlands and Nuhanovic v the Netherlands* Supreme Court (6 September 2013).
29   *Al-Skeini v UK* Appl No 55721/07, ECtHR (7 July 2011).
30   *Al-Skeini* (n 29 above) concurring opinion of Judge Bonello, para 4.
31   See generally E Hafner-Burton et al 'Emergency and escape: Explaining derogation fom human rights treaties' (2011) 65 *International Organization* 673.
32   For the ECHR see A Greene 'Separating normalcy from emergency: The jurisprudence of article 15 of the European Convention on Human Rights' (2011) 12 *German Law Journal* 1764.

these requirements in its General Comment 29, making it clear that it considers that measures derogating from the provisions of the Covenant must be of an exceptional and temporary nature.[33] In the same document the Committee also lists a number of rights as being non-derogable, although they are not included in the list of non-derogable rights in article 4. One of these is the right to take proceedings before a court to enable the court to decide without delay on the lawfulness of detention.[34]

2.3   Simultaneous application of IHL and IHRL

The discussion of the scope of application of IHL and IHRL in paragraphs 2.1 and 2.2 implies that there are situations where norms from both regimes are, at least a priori, applicable simultaneously. It also suggests that, due to the controversy concerning the question when human rights apply extraterritorially and surrounding the determination of an armed conflict, the demarcation of such situations is not always clear. Nevertheless, it is possible to point out a number of scenarios where the facts would entail simultaneous application. One is a scenario in which a peace operation is involved as a party to an armed conflict in which it makes detainees amongst the opposing forces. Such detainees are held in a detention facility run by troops of a state that is party to the ICCPR. The Human Rights Committee would almost certainly consider that in such a situation that state exercised power or effective control over the detainees, making the ICCPR applicable. One concrete example of such a scenario is ISAF. If it is accepted that UNOSOM II was a party to a NIAC in Somalia, as has been suggested, this is another example.[35] Another scenario which entails simultaneous application is where a peace operation engaged in an armed conflict has taken control of a city and is carrying out certain public functions there, which includes carrying out security operations. In such a case it is highly likely that both the Human Rights Committee and the ECtHR would consider that the operation exercises effective control over the city, making the ICCPR and the ECHR applicable.

To say that in a particular situation IHL and IHRL both apply begs the question which specific norms of IHL and IHRL are then applicable. The answer to this question will depend on a number of factors. One of these is whether the state concerned is bound by a particular norm. For example, not all states are parties to API. Only those that are, will be bound by a norm in that treaty, except to the extent that the norm also has a customary law nature. Another factor is whether the state concerned has derogated

33   General Comment No 29, States of Emergency (article 4), UNHR Committee (31 August 2001), UN Doc CCPR/C/21/Rev.1/Add.11 (2001), para 2.
34   General Comment No 29 (n 33 above) para 16.
35   S Sivukumaran *The Law of non-international armed conflict* (2012) 326.

from its obligations under IHRL. So far, no state has done so in respect of its participation in a peace operation.[36]

3   The interplay between IHL and IHRL

3.1   The interplay between IHL and IHRL in general

The previous paragraph illustrated that there are scenarios in which IHL and IHRL apply simultaneously. This paragraph will address the interplay between the two. It will first look at this interplay in general, focusing in particular on the situation where an IHL and an IHRL norm conflict. It will then zoom in on the interplay in peace operations in particular.

Broadly speaking, in case a situation is covered by a norm of IHL as well as a norm of human rights, there are three possible situations.[37] The first is a case where both a norm from IHL and the overlapping norm of human rights can be applied without any difficulty. This is the case for the prohibition of torture for example.

The second case is where an IHL and a human rights norm appear to conflict, but can be reconciled through interpretation of one of them. Such a complementary reading will often require that one of the two norms must be 'read down' from what its ordinary meaning would initially suggest or from how it is ordinarily applied.[38] In the case of an apparent conflict between norms of IHL and human rights, it is submitted that the norm that must be read down will usually be the human rights norm. This is necessary for the human rights norm to be capable of realistic application in time of armed conflict. A good example is the obligation to investigate in case of a death. This procedural obligation is not found in express terms in any human rights treaty. It has been found by the Human Rights Committee and the ECtHR as implied by the substantive right to life. In *McCann v UK* the Court noted that:

> [A] general legal prohibition of arbitrary killing by the agents of the State would be ineffective, in practice, if there existed no procedure for reviewing the lawfulness of the use of lethal force by State authorities. The obligation to

---

36   There is a question whether derogations are possible at all in respect of extraterritorial conduct. Human rights monitoring bodies have not had to deal with this question yet. This author's view is that the possibility for making derogations should be concomitant with the extraterritorial application of the treaty concerned. See also F Naert *International law aspects of the EU's Security and Defence Policy, with a particular focus on the law of armed conflict and human rights* (2010) 577-580.

37   See generally JK Kleffner 'Human rights and international humanitarian law: General issues' in TD Gill & D Fleck (eds) *The handbook of the international law of military operations* (2010) 51.

38   M Milanovic 'Norm conflicts, international humanitarian law and human rights law' in O Ben-Naftali (ed) *International humanitarian law and international human rights law* (2011) 95 106.

protect the right to life under this provision (art 2), read in conjunction with the State's general duty under article 1 of the Convention to 'secure to everyone within their jurisdiction the rights and freedoms defined in [the] Convention', requires by implication that there should be some form of effective official investigation when individuals have been killed as a result of the use of force by, *inter alios*, agents of the State.[39]

The ECtHR in particular has further developed this procedural obligation in its case-law.[40] It has held inter alia that for an investigation to be considered effective:

> In particular, the authorities must take the reasonable steps available to them to secure the evidence concerning the incident, including, *inter alia*, eyewitness testimony, forensic evidence and, where appropriate, an autopsy which provides a complete and accurate record of injury and an objective analysis of clinical findings, including the cause of death (see, concerning autopsies, for example, *Salman v Turkey* [GC], no 21986/93, § 106, ECHR 2000- VII; concerning witnesses, for example, *Tanrıkulu*, cited above, § 109; and concerning forensic evidence, for example, *Gül v Turkey*, no 22676/93, § 89). Any deficiency in the investigation which undermines its ability to establish the cause of death or the person responsible may risk falling foul of this standard.[41]

The Court has held that the procedural obligation under article 2 continues to apply in difficult security conditions, including in a context of armed conflict.[42] It is clear however that not all of the requirements developed by the court for peacetime situations can be implemented during an armed conflict in all circumstances.[43] The Court has accepted this. In its judgment in the *Al-Skeini* case it stated that:

> It is clear that where the death to be investigated under article 2 occurs in circumstances of generalised violence, armed conflict or insurgency, obstacles may be placed in the way of investigators and, as the United Nations Special Rapporteur has also observed, concrete constraints may compel the use of less effective measures of investigation or may cause an investigation to be delayed. Nonetheless, the obligation under article 2 to safeguard life entails that, even in difficult security conditions, all reasonable steps must be taken to ensure that an effective, independent investigation is conducted into alleged breaches of the right to life.[44]

---

39 *McCann v UK* ECHR (27 September 1995) Ser A 324, para 161.
40 See J Chevalier-Watts 'Effective investigations under article 2 of the European Convention on Human Rights: Securing the right to life or onerous burden on a state?' (2010) 21 *European Journal of International Law* 701.
41 *Kerimova v Russia* Application nos 17170/04, 20792/04, 22448/04, 23360/04, 5681/05 and 5684/05 (3 May 2011) para 264.
42 See eg *Al-Skeini* (n 29 above) para 164.
43 See eg K Watkin 'Controlling the use of force: A role for human rights norms in contemporary armed conflict' (2004) 98 *American Journal of International Law* 1 33.
44 *Al-Skeini* (n 29 above) para 164 (internal references omitted).

In this respect, reference may be made for example to the use of forensic evidence that has been referred to by the ECtHR as an example of what may be required for an investigation to be 'effective'. Clearly, in a situation of armed conflict it may not be possible to obtain forensic evidence because of the security situation.

In its judgment in *Varnava v Turkey*, the ECtHR appears to have interpreted the obligation to conduct an effective investigation in the light of IHL, in this way reconciling IHL and IHRL. The Court stated that:

> Article 2 must be interpreted in so far as possible in light of the general principles of international law, including the rules of international humanitarian law which play an indispensable and universally-accepted role in mitigating the savagery and inhumanity of armed conflict. The Court therefore concurs with the reasoning of the Chamber in holding that in a zone of international conflict Contracting States are under obligation to protect the lives of those not, or no longer, engaged in hostilities. This would also extend to the provision of medical assistance to the wounded; where combatants have died, or succumbed to wounds, the need for accountability would necessitate proper disposal of remains and require the authorities to collect and provide information about the identity and fate of those concerned, or permit bodies such as the ICRC to do so.[45]

The ECtHR went even further in its judgment in *Hassan v UK*.[46] This case concerned a person who was detained as a security detainee by the UK in Iraq, a situation in which the UK had not derogated from its obligations under the ECHR. Article 5 ECHR does not provide for security detention as a lawful ground of detention. The respondent government argued that article 5 of the ECHR was displaced by IHL as *lex specialis*, or modified so as to incorporate or allow for the capture and detention of actual or suspected combatants in accordance with the Third and/or Fourth Geneva Convention. The ECtHR rejected the first argument but accepted the second. It relied on article 31(b) and (c) of the Vienna Convention on the Law of Treaties, which provide for taking into account subsequent practice of states parties and any relevant rules of international law applicable in the relations between the parties in interpreting a treaty provision. The ECtHR took into account that the practice of High Contracting Parties is not to derogate from their obligations under article 5 in order to detain persons on the basis of the Third and Fourth Geneva Convention. It also held that article 5 ECHR should be interpreted in so far as possible in the light of the general principles of international law, including IHL. The Court considered that:

> even in situations of international armed conflict, the safeguards of the Convention continue to apply, albeit interpreted against the background of the

---

45   *Varnava v Turkey* Application nos 16064/90, 16065/90, 16066/90, 16068/90, 16069/90, 16070/90, 16071/90, 16072/90 and 16073/90 (18 September 2009) para 185.
46   *Hassan v UK* Appl no 29750/09, ECtHR (16 September 2014).

provisions of international humanitarian law. By reason of the co-existence of the safeguards provided by international humanitarian law and by the Convention in time of armed conflict, the grounds of permitted deprivation of liberty set out in subparagraphs (a) to (f) [of article 5] should be accommodated, as far as possible, with the taking of prisoners of war and the detention of civilians who pose a risk to security under the Third and Fourth Geneva Conventions.[47]

The Court applied the same approach to article 5(4) ECHR, concerning review of detention. In doing so, it went quite far in accommodating IHL, to such an extent that it was prepared to read things into article 5 that are not in the text of that article. Although the wording of article 5(4) quite clearly requires review of detention by a court, the ECtHR held that in the course of an international armed conflict this might not be practicable and that review by a 'competent body' as provided for by articles 43 and 78 of the Fourth Geneva Convention suffices. It nevertheless considered that if the contracting state is to comply with article 5(4):

> the "competent body" should provide sufficient guarantees of impartiality and fair procedure to protect against arbitrariness. Moreover, the first review should take place shortly after the person is taken into detention, with subsequent reviews at frequent intervals[48]

In this way the Court superimposed a number of requirements on what the text of articles 43 and 78 of the Fourth Geneva Convention provide for.

The third case is where an IHL and an IHRL norm conflict, without there being any reasonable interpretation to avoid this conflict. Where courts are willing to go very far in interpreting human rights to take into account provisions of IHL which might seem *a priori* irreconcilable, as the ECtHR did in *Hassan v UK*, these cases would seem to be few if any.[49] Where they occur, however, it is generally recognised that the principle of *lex specialis derogat legi generali* can help resolve the norm conflict, by providing a standard for deciding which norm must be given precedence.

3.2   Lex specialis

Lex specialis can be seen in terms of legal regimes or in terms of legal norms. In other words, does the principle allow for one legal regime such as IHL to take precedence over another, such as human rights? Or does the principle apply between particular norms, so that in one situation a norm from regime X can take precedence over a norm from regime Y, while in

---

47   *Hassan v UK* (n 46 above) para 104.
48   *Hassan v UK* (n 46 above), para. 106.
49   It may be noted that in such cases the distinction between the second and third case described seems to more or less fall away. The question then becomes, to what extent the fact that human rights still apply, be it in the foreground or background, leads to further requirements being superimposed on IHL norms.

another situation the reverse applies? A number of states have argued that the former is the case.[50] The better view however appears to be that the principle must be seen in terms of specific norms.[51] In international jurisprudence courts have in general applied the maxim to the conflict of two specific norms and not as a general guideline for the relations between two specialised regimes.[52] In addition, the principle of lex specialis has a 'contextual character': it is applied to a particular set of facts. As a rule of precedence, it only comes into play when in a particular situation two norms that conflict are applicable: IHL and human rights as legal regimes cannot a priori be said to conflict. It is in relation to the specific facts of that situation that a determination needs to be made which norm is more specific.[53]

It is easy to state the lex specialis principle, but much harder to apply it in practice. What are the standards to determine whether one norm is more specific than the other?[54] In general, the lex specialis is the rule which is more to the point, or approaches more nearly the subject in hand, than a general one and it regulates the matter more effectively than general rules do.[55] This is a quite general statement and not easy to apply to specific facts. A number of factors have been suggested that aid in determining which norm is more relevant to a given situation.[56]

The first is the wording and content of norms. When the norm uses terms that make it uniquely relevant to the conduct at hand, that rule may become the lex specialis. Examples are norms in IHL that refer to prisoners

---

50   Eg Colombia. See Inter-American Commission on Human Rights 'Report No 112/10: Inter-State petition IP-02: Admissibility: Franklin Guillermo Aisalla Molina, Ecuador – Colombia' OAS Doc OEA/Ser.L/V/II.140, para 114. Russia has argued that international human rights law is of extremely limited application in periods of armed conflict and of no application at all in a situation of international armed conflict. *Georgia v Russia (II)* ECHR Decision on Admissibility of 12 December 2011 para 69.

51   M Koskeniemmi 'Fragmentation of international law: Difficulties arising from the diversification and expansion of international law' Report of the Study Group of the International Law Commission, UN Doc A/CN.4/L.682 (2006), para 112; H Krieger 'A conflict of norms: The relationship between humanitarian law and human rights law in the ICRC customary law study' (2006) 11 *Journal of Conflict & Security Law* 265 269; Kleffner (n 37 above) 72.

52   Krieger (n 51 above); see eg *Asian Agricultural Products Ltd v Sri Lanka*, final award on merits and damages of 21 June 1990, ICSID Case No ARB/87/3; IIC 18 (1990).

53   See eg C McCarthy 'Legal conclusion or interpretative process? *Lex Specialis* and the applicability of international human rights' in R Arnold & N Quenivet (eds) *International humanitarian law and human rights law: Towards a new merger in international law* (2008) 101 109-110.

54   It may be pointed out that there are several different contexts in which the lex specialis principle may be employed. For example, the principle may be applied to different norms within the same legal instrument or between norms from different instruments. This contribution focuses on the latter situation.

55   M Koskeniemmi 'Study on the function and scope of the lex specialis and the question of self-contained regimes' UN Doc ILC(LVI)/SG/FIL/CRD.1 of 7 March 2004 4.

56   The list of factors below is largely based on O Hathaway et al 'Which law governs during armed conflict? The relationship between international humanitarian law and human rights law' (2012) 96 *Minnesota Law Review* 1883 1917-1923.

of war. The category of prisoner of war only exists in IHL and is narrower than 'detention' or 'deprivation of liberty' as used in IHRL.

The second is the level of control exercised by the state. Human rights norms have developed largely based on a presumption that a state exercises effective control in its own territory. The demands that human rights place on a state presuppose that that state exercises a minimum level of control. This is reflected in the fact that being in effective control of an area or individual is seen as a requirement for the extraterritorial application of human rights. In contrast, IHL takes into account the limited control that states can exercise in the midst of hostilities. The exigencies of armed conflict expand the scope of permissible action while chaos, fear and timing limit the capacity of states to meet obligations reasonably expected of them in other contexts.[57] This suggests that the more control a state exercises in a particular situation, the stronger the argument that the IHRL norm is the *lex specialis*.

A third factor is state practice. As Pauwelyn states, the *lex specialis* principle is a practical measure in the search for the 'current expression of consent'. The principle is a consequence of the contractual freedom of states, grounded in the idea that the 'most closest, detailed, precise or strongest expression of state consent' ought to prevail.[58] This reflects the fact that states are still the principal lawmakers in the field of international law. Indeed, it is still exclusively states that are parties to treaties of IHL and human rights law.[59] States' understanding of the relationship between their international obligations is an important factor to be taken into account. This argument is buttressed by the fact that article 31(3)(b) of the Vienna Convention on the Law of Treaties (VCLT) provides that in treaty interpretation 'any subsequent practice in the application of the treaty which establishes the agreement of the parties regarding its interpretation is to be taken into account'. The principle of *lex specialis*, although not expressly codified in the VCLT, is another principle of treaty interpretation. These different principles are not isolated, and must be read in their relationship to the other principles. In accordance with article 31 (3)(b) VCLT, subsequent state practice may imply that the states parties to a treaty regard a particular norm as *lex specialis* in relation to another. This aspect appears to be rarely, if ever, part of the operative use made by courts and tribunals of the *lex specialis* principle.[60] This is surprising, given that it is states that entered into treaty obligations. It would therefore seem to make sense to take into account their views on the proper interpretation of the obligations they consented to be bound by and often helped draft.

---

57   As above.
58   J Pauwelyn *Conflict of norms in international law* 388 (2003).
59   Although the European Union is in the process of becoming a party to the ECHR.
60   But note the ECtHR judgment in *Hassan v UK* (n 46 above).

3.3   Interplay in peace operations

This paragraph will address the interplay between IHL and IHRL specifically in peace operations. Characteristics of peace operations have a number of consequences for this interplay. 'Characteristics' is used here in a loose sense. In early peace operations, consent, impartiality and the minimum use of force were considered as basic principles applying to peace operations. Over the years, some of these principles have come to be considered as less important in certain operations and some have been interpreted broadly. Nevertheless, these principles are still considered as important touchstones for peace operations.[61] Although not considered as a basic principle of peace operations, in practice a characteristic of peace operations is that they are multinational. They are made up of troops that have been contributed to the operation by different states. These characteristics will be taken as the starting point for analysis.

3.3.1   Consent

In peace operations consent plays an important role. Unless there is an authorisation under Chapter VII of the UN Charter from the UN Security Council, consent of the host state is a legal requirement for the presence of the operation. From a practical perspective, consent to the activities of the operation by the local (non-state) actors is also an important factor. For this reason there is a strong motivation for a peace operation to preserve consent, and to limit as much as possible those actions that might lead to the loss of consent. As the doctrine that the UN has developed for peace operations states:

> In the implementation of its mandate, a United Nations peacekeeping operation must work continuously to ensure that it does not lose the consent of the main parties, while ensuring that the peace process moves forward.[62]

One consequence is that, when a peace operation is able to choose between different courses of action, it will often choose the course that is least likely to upset any of the parties. In practice, this will often mean a course of action that is within the bounds of IHRL and does not make use of permissions under IHL.[63] One example would be to search houses only with a warrant from the local authorities, or only in assistance of local authorities.

---

61   See eg Report of the Special Committee on Peacekeeping Operations, UN Doc A/66/19, para 25.
62   United Nations Department of Peacekeeping Operations & Department of Field Support *United Nations peacekeeping: Principles and guidelines (Capstone doctrine)* (2008) 32.
63   There is a parallel with so-called counterinsurgency (COIN) doctrine. See ID Pedden 'Lex lacunae: The merging laws of war and human rights in counterinsurgency' (2012) 46 *Valparaiso University Law Review* 803.

Consent also plays a role in another way. Largely because of the importance attached to consent of the host state, if a peace operation becomes involved in an armed conflict this is almost invariably on the side of government forces. For example, MONUSCO cooperates frequently with the armed forces of the DRC.[64] To the extent that this has led the peace operation to become a party to an armed conflict, it was seen above that states appear to view such a conflict as a non-international armed conflict. This means that the law applicable to non-international armed conflicts would become applicable, which is much less detailed than the law applicable to international armed conflicts. In such a case there will be more potential for the application of norms of IHRL due to the absence of norms of IHL that can operate as *lex specialis*.

3.3.2 Impartiality

Impartiality is another basic principle of peace operations.[65] It means that the operation should remain detached from the conflict in the sense that it should never become partisan, helping one side or hindering the other. This principle was traditionally seen as closely linked to a limited use of force, in particular by UN peace operations. As such, it served as a restraining factor on the use of force and thus on IHL becoming applicable to a peace operation. In recent years, impartiality has been somewhat redefined. It has been stressed that impartiality is not the same as doing nothing. The UN Capstone doctrine explains (at 33) that:

> The need for even-handedness towards the parties should not become an excuse for inaction in the face of behavior that clearly works against the peace process. In this context, reference is often made to the distinction that must be made between neutrality and impartiality.

Notwithstanding this distinction, impartiality still serves as a restraint on the use of force. This means that a peace operation is less likely to become involved in hostilities, making IHL applicable. In cases where IHL arguably has become applicable, the desire to be seen as impartial may lead to a reluctance to acknowledge the application of IHL. This is because the notion of impartiality is difficult to reconcile with being a 'party to an armed conflict'. As a consequence, in such a situation a peace operation will less easily invoke a norm of IHL than a norm of IHRL, because the former could be seen as acknowledging that the operation has become a party to the conflict.

---

64   See eg 'UN gunships battle rebels in east Congo' *CNN* 27 October 2008 http://edition.cnn.com/2008/WORLD/africa/10/27/congo.united.nations/index.html (accessed 16 August 2013).

65   See generally S Vohra 'Impartiality in United Nations peace-keeping' (1996) 9 *Leiden Journal of International Law* 63.

3.3.3   Minimum use of force

Minimum use of force is another basic principle of peacekeeping. It is closely related to the principle of impartiality.[66] In UN peace operations, the minimum use of force was traditionally understood to mean that use of force was prohibited except where necessary for self-defense. The UN as well as NATO have come to make a distinction between peacekeeping operations and peace enforcement operations. UN doctrine provides that:

> Although on the ground they may sometimes appear similar, robust peace-keeping should not be confused with peace enforcement, as envisaged under Chapter VII of the Charter. Robust peacekeeping involves the use of force at the tactical level with the authorization of the Security Council and con- sent of the host nation and/or the main parties to the conflict. By contrast, peace enforcement does not require the consent of the main parties and may involve the use of military force at the strategic or international level.[67]

Nevertheless, in both types of operations the principle is that restraint should be exercised when applying force. Against this background, states seem uneasy with the notion that peace enforcement operations should apply all or most of international humanitarian law during their missions as standard operating procedure. For political leaders, this may reflect unease at the prospect of telling the public that their armed forces are engaged in combat.[68]

The principle of minimum use of force in peace operations is generally understood to include the requirement that all use of force must be necessary and proportional. This is normally 'operationalised' by inserting a requirement that all use of force must be necessary and proportional in the Rules of Engagement for the operation. Importantly, the term 'proportionality' in this context is not understood in the sense in which that term is understood in IHL. It is closer to the way in which that term is understood in IHRL, although in practice the standard applied by peace operations is not as rigorous as that employed by human rights monitoring bodies. The UNOSOM II Rules of Engagement may be taken as an example. These provide that minimum force is to be used at all times, which must be read to mean that whenever force is used no more than minimum force may be used. The term 'minimum force' is defined as '[t]he minimum authorized degree of force which is necessary, reasonable and lawful in the circumstances'.[69] This formulation of the principle of proportionality includes harm to the target of the use of force by the operation as a factor to be taken into account, which is different from the

66   S Vohra (n 65 above) 82.
67   *Capstone doctrine* (n 62 above) 34.
68   M Hoffman 'Peace-enforcement actions and humanitarian law: Emerging rules for interventional armed conflict' (2000) 82 *International Review of the Red Cross* 193.
69   Rules of Engagement for UNOSOM, II reproduced in T Findlay *The use of force in UN peace operations* (2002) 423-424.

way proportionality is understood in IHL. In this way, a norm that is based on IHRL is introduced into the legal framework for an operation to which arguably IHL applied.

3.3.4 *Multinational*

In practice, peace operations are almost invariably multinational in character. This is to say that they are composed of troops from different troop contributing states. These states may have different obligations under IHL and human rights. For example, of the 49 states contributing troops to the International Security Assistance Force in Afghanistan (ISAF), 37 have ratified the ECHR.[70] In the field of IHL, the largest troop contributing state by far, the United States, is not a party to Additional Protocol I to the Geneva Conventions, unlike many of the other troop contributing states. Even if troop contributing states are parties to the same treaty they may have different interpretations of that treaty. The consequence is that in a multinational operation, different legal frameworks may apply to troops from different troop contributing states. This does not have direct consequences for the interplay between IHL and IHRL. Indirectly, however, it does. This is because the more differences there are in the legal framework that applies, the more difficult it becomes for troops from different states to effectively cooperate. For example, if one state considers that it is involved in an international armed conflict whereas another does not, the former cannot transfer a civilian that has been detained to the latter. This is because article 45 of Geneva Convention IV provides that protected persons may be transferred only to a Power which is a party to the Convention and after the Detaining Power has satisfied itself of the willingness and ability of such transferee Power to apply the Convention. To avoid such consequences, one method that is used in peace operations is for some troop contributing states to apply specific norms as a matter of policy, or at least to fashion their conduct in a way in which it is compatible with those norms. One example of such an approach is the Copenhagen Process on the Handling of Detainees in International Military Operations.[71] This process involved the elaboration by a number of states of guidelines and principles on the treatment of detained persons in international military operations. One of the declared aims of the process was to contribute to the effectiveness of international military operations. It was considered that achieving agreement on a set of principles that will be applied to international military operations in the context of non-international armed conflicts and peace operations would be such a contribution. The document that resulted from the process

---

70   NATO: International Security Assistance Force 'Key facts and figures': http://www. isaf.nato.int/images/stories/File/Placemats/2013-08-01%20ISAF%20Placematfinal. pdf; and Council of Europe: Treaty Office website: http://www. conventions.coe.int/ (accessed 2 September 2013).
71   See generally B Oswald 'The Copenhagen Principles, international military operations and detention' (2013) 17 *Journal of International Peacekeeping* 116.

contains principles that are sometimes clearly based on IHL, and sometimes contain language that is taken from provisions in IHRL treaties.[72]

3.3.5   State practice: Evidence of lex specialis?

The paragraphs above discussed a number of characteristics of peace operations that influence the conduct of those operations. In most situations they provide incentives for a peace operation to take action that is in conformity with a norm of IHRL, where a norm of IHL that is applicable in the situation is more permissive. As was discussed in paragraph 3.2 above, state practice is one factor that can assist in determining which norm is the *lex specialis* in a particular situation. This could lead to the conclusion that in those cases in which state conduct is in accordance with IHRL, this is evidence that states consider an IHRL norm to be the *lex specialis*. In some cases this will indeed be the case. In many cases such a conclusion may not be warranted, however. Peace operations may also not take advantage of more permissive IHL norms for other reasons than that they consider an IHRL norm to be the applicable *lex specialis*. One of these reasons is the desire to ensure legal interoperability. Another may be because although they do not consider IHRL to be applicable *de jure*, they use it as a useful reference. This is particularly the case in non-international armed conflicts, in which there may not be a norm of IHL that regulates the situation at hand. In such a case a state may choose to use a norm of IHRL as inspiration although it does not consider that norm to be applicable *de iure*.[73] A third reason may be to increase the acceptability and legitimacy of the operation.

There are various examples of states applying IHRL norms in cases in which they formally do not accept the *de iure* application of IHRL. One example is the practice of a number of states participating in ISAF of seeking assurances from Afghan authorities that detained persons transferred to those authorities by ISAF forces will not be mistreated. These states include the United Kingdom and the Netherlands. If the ECHR applies to persons detained by UK or Netherlands forces, such assurances would arguably be an important element in ensuring that the transfer does not violate article 3 of the ECHR.[74] The same is the case for article 3 of the Convention against Torture. There are indications however that the UK does not consider these conventions to be applicable to (some

---

72   See for the text of the Principles; 'Copenhagen process on handling detainees in international military operations: Introductory note by Jonathan Horowitz' (2012) 51 *International Legal Materials* 1364.

73   The current author has on a number of occasions used IHRL norms as inspiration when drafting instructions for troops involved in an armed conflict. One example is the drafting of instructions for interrogators. In these situations the Netherlands did not necessarily accept that human rights applied *de iure*.

74   See eg *Othman (Abu Qatada) v UK*, Application no 8239/09, ECHR (17 January 2012).

or all) persons detained by its troops in Afghanistan.[75] The Netherlands stated in 2005 that it did not consider that the ECRM applied to its troops in Afghanistan, because the Netherlands did not exercise 'effective control' there.[76]

3.3.6 Feasibility

In some cases applying the doctrine of *lex specialis* may lead to an outcome that does not seem realistically feasible. Detention in a non-international armed conflict provides an example. IHRL requires a prompt judicial review of such a detention. IHL in non-international armed conflict does not regulate procedural guarantees for detained persons. This being the case, it would seem clear that in accordance with the *lex specialis* principle, human rights should step in to fill the gap. It is doubtful however whether it is realistic to expect states and non-state actors, possibly interning thousands of people, to bring all internees before a judge without delay during armed conflict.[77] This may be less of an obstacle in peace operations than in full-blown wars, as in the former the number of persons detained is generally smaller and detained persons tend to be transferred quickly to local authorities. In addition, it may be recalled that states may derogate from many IHRL provisions. With particular reference to the right to judicial review of detention, neither the ICCPR nor the ECHR refer to this right as non-derogable.[78] In addition, it is open to states to agree on a new rule of IHL that would function as *lex specialis*. Although it would be novel for states to draft new IHL rules for the specific purpose of limiting the application of IHRL norms to which they are already bound, there is nothing in general international law standing in the way of this possibility. It may be noted however that it is unlikely that this would be accepted by the ECtHR in the specific context of the ECHR. Already in 1956 the European Commission on Human Rights held in *X v Germany* that:

---

75   See eg the following statement by the UK during the consideration of the fifth periodic report by the United Kingdom to the Committee against Torture, UN Doc CAT/C/ SR.1139, 15 May 2013: 'The Government did not accept that the activities of members of its armed forces in Afghanistan meant that Afghanistan had become a territory under the jurisdiction of the United Kingdom'. In response to the European Court of Human Rights judgment in *Al-Skeini* in which the Court found that the UK has jurisdiction over certain detained persons in Iraq, the UK Government has taken the view that the *Al-Skeini* judgment relates to the particular circumstances of the past operations in Iraq and it has no implications for its current operations elsewhere, including in Afghanistan, where the legal basis for UK operations is materially different from that which pertained in Iraq. See UK Ministry of Justice 'Responding to Human Rights Judgments: Report to the Joint Committee on Human Rights on the Government Response to Human Rights Judgments 2011-2012' (2012) 29.

76   Kamerstukken (Parliamentary papers) II 2004-2005, 27925, B, 10.

77   M Sassoli & LM Olson 'The relationship between international humanitarian law and human rights law where it matters: Admissible killing and internment of fighters in non-international armed conflicts' (2008) 90 *International Review of the Red Cross* 599 622.

78   Although the Human Rights Committee has posited that it is non-derogable nevertheless. General Comment No 29 (n 33 above).

[W]hen a Member State, having submitted itself to contractual obligations, concludes a later international agreement that does not allow for further observation of its obligations under the earlier Treaty, the State still is responsible under that preceding Treaty.[79]

4   Conclusion

Many of the issues discussed in this contribution deserve a more detailed analysis that is beyond the ambit of this contribution. It is nevertheless possible to draw a number of conclusions from the preceding analysis.

There will be situations where both IHL and IHRL apply to a peace operation. The precise boundaries of the overlap are difficult to determine. There is some controversy over the exact threshold at which IHL starts to apply and the debate over the application of IHRL during armed conflict and its extraterritorial application has not crystallised. The ICJ as well as human rights monitoring bodies have however made clear that there are situations where they consider both IHL and IHRL to apply. This is something that states have to take into account, in particular those states that have accepted the binding jurisdiction of such bodies in individual complaints procedures.

In cases in which both an IHL and an IHRL norm apply to the facts, three situations can be distinguished. The first is a case where both a norm from IHL and the overlapping norm of human rights can be applied without any difficulty. This is in fact the case in many situations. There are many examples of corresponding IHL and IHRL norms.[80] The second case is where an IHL and a human rights norm appear to conflict, but can be reconciled through interpretation of one of them. Such a complementary reading will often require that one of the two norms must be 'read down' from what its ordinary meaning would initially suggest or from how it is ordinarily applied. The third case is where an IHL and an IHRL norm conflict, without there being any reasonable interpretation to avoid this conflict.

In the latter situation the *lex specialis* maxim can assist in resolving the question which norm should take precedence. There is much controversy surrounding the proper application of this maxim. This contribution has suggested that at least three factors can help to give it substance in a specific case. These are the wording and content of the norms, the level of control exercised by the state, and state practice.

---

79   *X v Federal Republic of Germany* European Commission of Human Rights (4 September 1958) Ser A 256.

80   D Bethlehem 'The relationship between international humanitarian law and international human rights law in situations of armed conflict' (2013) 2 *Cambridge Journal of International and Comparative Law* 180 191.

The interplay between IHL and IHRL specifically in peace operations is influenced by a number of characteristics of such operations. These characteristics have consequences for how peace operations function that, in case of conflicting norms of IHL and IHRL, will often lead to conduct that is in conformity with human rights norms. This is not necessarily because states consider that in such situations human rights norms are the *lex specialis*, however. Unfortunately states rarely make public statements concerning the legal regime that applies to their conduct in a peace operation. This makes it very difficult if not impossible to determine whether in case they act in conformity with human rights norms this is out of a sense of legal obligation or rather for policy reasons. For reasons of legal certainty as well as for the purpose of further clarifying the interplay between IHL and IHRL in peace operations, it would be a positive development if states would be more transparent in this respect. It is also in their self-interest, because if states are not transparent their conduct may be taken as evidence of state practice even if it was not intended as such.

The questions discussed in this contribution have a relatively high level of abstraction. The main challenge in peace operations is to convert such complex questions of law and policy into clear instructions for commanders and troops on the ground. This requires legal advisors in ministries of foreign affairs and ministries of defence to thoroughly consider scenarios that may arise in an operation already during the planning phase. As was mentioned in the introduction, it must be assumed that this was done by the legal advisers of MONUSCO when planning for operations following the ultimatum of 30 July 2013. In this case, it will remain unclear to which instructions this led in that particular case. The ultimatum expired with some weapons handed over and without any fighting.[81] Unfortunately, it is likely that there will be other cases in which the outcome will be different. This underlines the importance of further clarifying the interplay between IHL and IHRL in peace operations.

---

81   United Nations 'MONUSCO Ultimatum Expires, Situation Remains Calm' 1 August 2013   http://www.unmultimedia.org/radio/english/2013/08/monusco-ultimatum-expires-situation-remains-calm/ (accessed 22 August 2012).

8

Naval Counter Piracy Operations: Human Rights and International Humanitarian Law*

*André R Smit***

1   Background

Maritime piracy was a global issue in the 16th and 17th centuries. The period stretching from 1660 to 1725 was known as the golden age of pirates when approximately 2 000 pirates roamed the oceans on between 20 and 30 ships.[1] All states (friend and foe) generally cooperated to eradicate it, although the diplomatic landscape was also marked by political rivalry that prevented effective and coordinated actions against pirates at times. Those engaged in piracy were subjected to laws that included a penalty such as being hung from the yardarms of the ships of sail. Special trials and rules were created to make it easier to prosecute pirates, and to facilitate speedy execution.[2] The Peace of Westphalia (that ended the 30 and 80 year wars) outlawed piracy in 1648 and the infamous pirate captain Blackbeard was captured in 1718. It is in the context of piracy that the phrase *hostis humani generis* (referring to foes of all mankind) was especially apt.[3]

Contrary to the present legal position, in the golden age of piracy, pirates were fought in a *sui generis* conflict where a zone between what we would today classify as 'law enforcement' and 'armed conflict' was straddled. In times past it may have veered closer to armed conflict than

---

*   This paper is based on a lecture presented in Pretoria during 2012 at the Winter School of the Institute for International and Comparative Law in Africa on the convergence and conflict between international humanitarian law and human rights law in military operations.
**   BComm LLB LLM (International Law), Legal Adviser and Staff Officer with the South African Department of Defence, Attorney of the High Court of South Africa. This paper does not necessarily represent the views of the government of the Republic of South Africa, nor that of the South African Department of Defence.
1   I Shearer 'Piracy' in R Wolfrum *Max Planc Encyclopaedia of Public International Law* (2010).
2   S de Bondt 'Prosecuting pirates and upholding human rights law: Taking perspective' (2010) *One Earth Future Working Paper* 13.
3   B Pemberton '"Pirate jurisdiction": Fact, fiction, and fragmentation in international law' (2011) *One Earth Future Working Paper* 11.

law enforcement as armed forces were allowed to use deadly military force in combating piracy. The mere fact that a person was a confirmed pirate was sufficient justification for attacking with military force.[4] The concept of privateering was also engaged in during this time where a private ship was issued with an official (state sanctioned) letter or marquee to attack foreign ships in wartime on behalf of the issuing state, creating a unique state sponsorship for violence by a private vessel.[5] Around the 1600s British sponsored privateers were active against the Spanish in the new world and it was a very lucrative endeavour for privateers. The Barbary pirates in the Mediterranean were not eliminated until the 1830s. The last remnants of ancient pirates held out as late as 1870, and it was in this historical context that the international crime of piracy was defined.[6]

With regard to the modern maritime piracy encountered off the Horn of Africa, incidents reached out to 165 nm from the Somali coastline in 2005, extending to 1 300 nm in 2011. Some of the furthest tentacles of the Somali piracy extended well into the Mozambican channel, reaching approximately 1 100 km from the South African Maritime borders. This was significant at the time as up to 30 per cent of all maritime traffic in the world, and 90 per cent of South African bound or originated maritime traffic passed through the Mozambican channel.

Shifting the 'spyglass' to sea lanes around the Horn of Africa (especially the Red Sea, Gulf of Aden, Arabian Sea and Gulf of Oman) it is estimated that approximately 20 per cent of the world's shipped goods pass through waters plagued by Somali pirates. More than 3.2 million barrels of oil transit the Bab-el-Mandeb strait between the Gulf of Aden and the Red Sea daily.[7] The cost of Somali piracy to the maritime industry is calculated to exceed $13 billion per year, including insurance increases, ransom, security measures and delays.[8] Attacks mounted steadily and 127 attacks were recorded in 2010 (of which 47 were successful), and 151 in 2011 (of which 25 were successful). As at February 2012, ten vessels and 159 hostages were still held by Somali pirates. Average earnings for pirates amounted to approximately $146 million in 2011 (at almost $5 million per ship). It is estimated that 3 000 to 5 000 pirates are presently active worldwide. Over 1 000 have been captured and prosecutions have taken place in 21 states. Somali piracy appears to be a sophisticated operation akin to a stock market, complete with money counting machines to combat counterfeiting by those who pay ransom.[9]

---

4   E Kontorovich 'Piracy and international law' (2009) *Global Law Forum.*
5   Shearer (n 1 above); Privateering was only abolished in 1856.
6   See JA Wombwell 'The long war against piracy: Historical trends' Occasional Paper 32, Combat Studies Institute Press, US Army Combined Arms Center (2010) for a very comprehensive study of the history of maritime piracy.
7   L Ploch et al 'Piracy off the Horn of Africa' (2011) *Congressional Research Service* 12.
8   Ploch et al (n 7 above) 1; A Bowden et al 'The economic cost of maritime piracy' (2010) *One Earth Future Working Paper* as referenced in Ploch et al (n 7 above) 13.
9   Ploch et al (n 7 above) 11; Annex III of the Report of the Monitoring Group on Somalia pursuant to UNSC Resolution 1853 (2008), S/2010/91.

In the Southern African sphere of interest there is an Eastern and Southern African – Indian Ocean (EAS-IO) Strategy to Combat Piracy. The region is currently grappling with the issues created by the piracy and is yet to come up with a comprehensive, integrated and joint strategy that is workable. The South African National Defence Force (SANDF) is engaged in counter-piracy operations through its Operation COPPER. This is a joint, multinational operation that involves Mozambique and Tanzania, and is focussed on the Mozambican channel.[10]

This paper is aimed at providing a South African perspective on the international law framework behind African driven counter piracy operations. It discusses a background to Somali piracy, the international law on maritime piracy, alternative international crimes to maritime piracy, and analyses the application of international humanitarian and human rights law to the combating, capturing, arrest and transfer of maritime pirates before concluding. It does not specifically address the wider and specific human rights issues faced by states from other regions, although some examples from foreign jurisdictions provide guidance on the interpretation of human rights issues for the region. This paper also does not extend to issues around private security involvement, the rights of pirates while being prosecuted, or the exercising of jurisdiction over other crimes committed parallel to the acts of piracy.

2   Somali piracy and the nature of the conflict in Somalia[11]

Somalia has seen war continuously for 23 years despite the fact that its population is almost all Sunni Muslim, and shares a uniform culture and language. The people are divided into clans who used to be nomadic. Colonisation divided Somalia into administrative regions and wars were fought against the Italians and British, with independence and unification following in 1960. In 1969 Major General Mohamed Siad Barre staged a successful coup and created a revolutionary council to rule the country. Military spending rose and conflict with Ethiopia broke out followed by civil war in 1991. The civil war degenerated into a disorganised power struggle between various 'warlords'. All central government control was lost and Somalia became known as the foremost example of a failed state wherein certain regions are attempting to restore some local government control.

---

10   The term 'joint' is used herein to refer to the involvement of more than one 'service' of the SANDF (with the services consisting of the Army, Air Force, Navy and Military Health Service), whereas the term 'multinational' is used to refer to the involvement of the armed forces of more than one state.

11   M Meredith *The state of Africa* (2005) 209-210, 464-484, 505; see also B Rudloff & A Weber 'Somalia and the Gulf of Aden' in S Mair (ed) 'Piracy and maritime security' German Institute for International and Security Affairs Research Paper (2011) 34-41 for a useful summary of the history of Somali piracy.

The largely unrecognised Somaliland still attempts to operate independently from the rest of Somalia in the north, and the semi-autonomous Puntland region in the north-east remains beyond TFG authority. As at 2012, the conflict in Somalia was one between the internationally supported Transitional Federal Government (TFG) that controlled Mogadishu, and Al-Shabaab that controlled southern Somalia.

Somalia has the longest coastline in Africa and is composed of 18 regions that are subdivided into districts. The Somali navy, police and air force are in the process of being re-established and a new Somali National Army of 10 000 men (with African Union backing in the form of AMISOM that includes substantial Kenyan presence) continues the fight against Al-Shabaab. The Puntland government is also actively attempting to curb piracy.[12]

European Union Naval Forces (EU NAVFOR) operate off the Somali coast in Operation ATLANTA alongside the North Atlantic Treaty Organisation's (NATO) Operation OCEAN SHIELD and the United States of America (US) led Combined Task Force 151.[13] Add to this the United Nations Security Council (UNSC) Resolutions on the issue of piracy off the Somali coast and multiple other navies involved,[14] and it becomes clear that there is a major international military presence off the coast of Somalia.

What must also not be forgotten are the alleged origins of modern Somali piracy. The pirates initially claimed to protect their natural environment against illegal toxic dumping and the decimation of Somali fishing stocks by foreign vessels that took advantage of the non-existence of an effective national Somali government. This was to some extent 'law enforcement' by private citizens whose lives (dependent on fishing) were severely and negatively affected by illegal activities of foreign flagged vessels in their maritime zones, and whose rights and interests could not be protected by a functioning government as there was none.[15]

A disturbing recent development has also been unconfirmed murmurings of closer cooperation between Al-Shabaab and the pirates, although there is no evidence of permanent and organised ties between the groups. In an ironic twist of fate, it is reported that Al-Shabaab kidnapped some of the most notorious pirate leaders and forced them to agree on a 20 per cent cut on all income from the pirate activities in exchange for non-interference in their affairs.[16]

---

12   Ploch et al (n 7 above) 6; International Expert Group on Piracy off the Somali Coast 'Final report' (2008).
13   Ploch et al (n 7 above) 3.
14   Ploch et al (n 7 above) 3, 25.
15   Ploch et al (n 7 above) 9.
16   Ploch et al (n 7 above) 16-17.

The brief facts stated above interplay in the analysis of the type of conflict that Somalia is facing, the effect that it has on the combating of piracy or the status of pirates, whether international humanitarian law is applicable to counter piracy operations, and the identification of applicable international human rights law and its parameters.

3   International law on maritime piracy

3.1   Piracy as an international crime

Tracing the origins of a crime that is regarded as a classic example of an international crime, uncovers records of pirate activity that are more than 4 000 years old. The first known written law against piracy is found in the Hammurabi code. Pirates plagued the Persian Gulf, the Nile and Ancient Greece, and piracy is often cited as the earliest international crime with the Roman Empire devoting much resources to combat piracy in the Mediterranean.[17] Being classified as an international crime signifies that piracy threatens the good order of the international community as a whole, and that all states have an interest in the suppression thereof.

3.2   Definition of piracy

Piracy is defined in article 101 of the United Nations Convention on the Law of the Sea (LOSC) of 10 December 1982[18] as follows:

> Piracy consists of any of the following acts:
> (a) any illegal acts of violence or detention, or any act of depredation, committed for private ends by the crew or the passengers of a private ship or a private aircraft, and directed:
> (i)   on the high seas, against another ship or aircraft, or against persons or property on board such ship or aircraft;
> (ii) against a ship, aircraft, persons or property in a place outside the jurisdiction of any State;
> (b) any act of voluntary participation in the operation of a ship or of an aircraft with knowledge of facts making it a pirate ship or aircraft;
> (c) any act of inciting or of intentionally facilitating an act described in subparagraph (a) or (b).

3.3   Qualifiers to the definition of piracy

The qualifiers to the definition of piracy that are most relevant to the issue of Somali piracy are that the acts committed must be for 'private' ends,

17   J Dugard *International law: A South African perspective* (2011) 157.
18   http://www.un.org/depts/los/convention_agreements/texts/unclos/unclos_e.pdf (accessed 29 July 2012).

must be committed on the 'high seas' or 'a place outside the jurisdiction of any State' and be committed by the passengers or crew of a 'ship'. These qualifiers are important because questions have been raised regarding whether Somali piracy is committed for private ends, are sometimes committed outside the high seas, and may sometimes not involve more than one ship as the vessels used are technically boats.

3.3.1 Private ends

In the context of the piracy witnessed off the Horn of Africa, there were initial indications that Somalis justified their 'piracy' as an act of self-defence against the plundering of their marine living resources by foreign states in the absence of a functioning Somali government that could protect it. One may then argue that such acts are not committed for 'private' ends but in the public interest. However, such actions have not been state sanctioned, and in the absence of a functioning government it could not be state sanctioned. There is also an argument to be made for the fact that any purpose that is not state sanctioned could only be regarded as for 'private ends'.[19]

Despite debate that may take place regarding the limits of the definition of 'private ends', and notwithstanding the origin of the acts of piracy off the Somali coast, the evidence seems to suggest that the current acts of piracy are indeed committed for private ends in the ordinary meaning of the words as there are no state interests involved anymore, no state sanction for the actions, and gains (in the form of ransom) is used by private persons for private reasons. The only persons who are benefiting from the current acts of piracy are the pirates themselves, the organised criminals masterminding, coordinating and funding their operations, and the community surrounding piracy activities who receive the benefit of an influx of foreign currency.

3.3.2 Location of piratical acts

The requirement of the LOSC that the piratical acts be committed on the high seas requires the investigation of whether acts committed in the territorial sea or other maritime zones will also qualify as piracy in accordance with the LOSC. Of importance is the territorial sea that reaches up to a maximum of 12 nm from baselines, and the exclusive economic zone or EEZ that reaches to a maximum of 200 nm from the baselines in accordance with the LOSC.

---

19   Report of the Special Adviser to the UN Secretary-General on Legal Issues Related to Piracy off the Coast of Somalia (English Translation) dated 20 January 2011 11 quoting the *Rapid environmental desk assessment Somalia* UNEP (March 2005); De Bondt (n 2 above) 8-9.

The territorial sea (including archipelagic waters, internal waters and ports) is not part of the high seas and an act that would otherwise qualify as piracy is regarded as a criminal act subject to the municipal[20] law of the coastal state, or other international instruments that may be applicable if committed in the territorial sea.[21] The LOSC does not bar states from calling the same acts piracy and declaring it a crime in accordance with the domestic laws of that coastal state, even if committed in territorial waters. However, in the absence of domestic laws to that effect, the piratical acts could only be regarded as piracy under the LOSC if they were committed on the high seas (and not inside the territorial sea of coastal states).[22]

Article 100 of the LOSC determines that the high seas regime applies to all parts of the sea that are not included in the EEZ, territorial sea, internal waters or archipelagic waters. Although there is some debate as to what exactly constitutes the high seas (as opposed to international waters or any place outside the jurisdiction of any state), the EEZ[23] is subject to LOSC provisions on piracy because article 58(2) explicitly makes the greater part of the LOSC regime on the high seas (articles 88 to 115) applicable to the EEZ as well. Therefore, the piracy regime as contained in articles 101 and further is applicable in the EEZ notwithstanding article 100. Practically, piratical acts constitute piracy for the purposes of the LOSC if committed in the EEZ of a coastal state or on the high seas.

This may impact on the jurisdiction over a suspected pirate as the exercise of jurisdiction in the territorial sea is then primarily determined by the municipal law of that state. In the instance of Somalia that is regarded as a failed state (with a concomitant impact on the effectiveness of domestic legislation), the acts committed in the territorial sea of Somalia do not qualify as piracy under the LOSC. Such acts will only qualify as piracy if Somali domestic law determines that they do.

As a further example, the SANDF is engaged in a counter piracy operation off the coast of Mozambique with Operation COPPER. In the context of Operation COPPER the SANDF may operate within the territorial waters of Mozambique as well as the high seas, the EEZ of

---

20 In the present document, references to 'municipal' law are to be understood as references to 'domestic' or 'national' law as opposed to international law.
21 Such as the 1988 Rome Convention for the Suppression of Unlawful Acts against the Safety of Maritime Navigation (SUA Convention) or the municipal law of the coastal state, if the municipal law provides for the relevant acts to be criminalised in those circumstances; art 2.A.1(c) of the Republic of Somaliland Law on Combating Piracy (Piracy Law) Law No 52/2012 relies on the LOSC definition of piracy and makes it a crime to commit such acts in the territorial waters of the Republic of Somaliland.
22 In accordance with arts 3 and 4 of LOSC, the territorial sea is a maritime zone to be claimed by a coastal state that may not extend beyond 12 nm from the baselines of the coastal state.
23 In accordance with arts 55 and 57 of LOSC, an area adjacent to the territorial sea that is to be claimed by the coastal state to a maximum of 200 nm from the baselines of the coastal state.

Mozambique and Madagascar, and the Mozambican territorial sea while straddling the maritime zones of Tanzania.

Most importantly, if acts that would otherwise have constituted piracy are committed in the territorial sea of Mozambique, it would not technically constitute the international law crime of piracy, and must be criminalised by Mozambican domestic law if the suspects are to be prosecuted, or be prosecuted under other international instruments.

3.3.3   A ship

There is no exact legal definition for a 'ship'. In the maritime domain, there is a clear distinction between a 'boat' and a 'ship', and a boat (with the exception of large submarines) will usually be a maritime vessel that is much smaller than a ship.[24] LOSC requires that the act of piracy be committed by the passengers or crew of a 'ship', yet many piracy acts are committed from small powered 'boats'.[25] While the definition of a pirate ship as found in article 103 of LOSC does not take the matter further, no evidence has been found that has been regarded as an obstacle in any case.[26]

3.4   Piracy jurisdiction and due process in the Law of the Sea Convention

Despite codification of piracy in the 1958 Geneva Convention on the High Seas[27] and LOSC,[28] piracy is generally also regarded as a customary international law crime, resulting in the crime existing and states being allowed to exercise universal jurisdiction over the crime notwithstanding whether the state concerned is a signatory (signed but did not ratify or acceded) or a party (ratified or acceded) to the relevant treaty.

Even though LOSC is silent on the rights that are to be afforded to persons arrested on suspicion of having committed piracy, it does provide for a pirate ship or aircraft, or a ship or aircraft taken by piracy and under the control of pirates to be seized, for the property on board to be seized and for the persons on board to be arrested. It is left to the courts of the state which carried out the seizure to decide upon the penalties to be imposed

---

24   Also see Wombwell (n 6 above) for a useful expose of the different types of ships and boats at 189-193.
25   Art 101(a).
26   This aspect was also raised by T Treves 'Piracy, law of the sea, and use of force: Developments off the coast of Somalia' (2009) 20 *European Journal of International Law* 399 at 402; It is interesting to note that art 2.B of the Republic of Somaliland Law on Combating Piracy (Piracy Law) Law No 52/2012 defines 'ship' as 'any sea vessel including ship, boat, speed boat, launch, canoe or any other sea vessels which are used for acts of piracy'.
27   Art 15.
28   Art 101.

and to determine the further action to be taken with regard to objects seized (subject to the rights of third parties acting in good faith).[29]

In affording the right to decide upon penalties to be imposed to the courts of the state which carried out the seizure, the LOSC deviates from the norm for customary international law crimes where a particular *nexus* such as being the state that carried out a seizure is not required. Notwithstanding, states are *obliged* to cooperate but *permitted* to exercise jurisdiction.[30]

If a state other than the seizing state wishes to exercise jurisdiction, it would have to argue that the *nexus* required in the LOSC is not related to the arrest of a suspect (as opposed to the seizure of objects), or that the LOSC has not amended the right of states to exercise universal jurisdiction over customary international law crimes. As a final option, a state may exercise jurisdiction on any other recognised ground, provided that the particular action is criminalised in the domestic law of the state concerned.[31]

There are other provisions of LOSC that also deal explicitly with other piracy related aspects such as the definition of a pirate ship, the retention or loss of the nationality of a pirate ship, liability for seizure without adequate grounds, and the ships that are entitled to exercise the right of seizure on account of piracy.[32]

Very importantly, article 293 of LOSC indicates applicable law:

(1) A court or tribunal having jurisdiction under this section shall apply this Convention and other rules of international law not incompatible with this Convention.
(2) Paragraph 1 does not prejudice the power of the court or tribunal having jurisdiction under this section to decide a case *ex aequo et bono*,[33] if the parties so agree.[34]

Thus, human rights obligations when jurisdiction is exercised are not specified in LOSC, but competencies and obligations are determined with

29　Art 105 uses the word 'may' with reference to seizure, arrest, deciding on penalties and determination of further action by the flag state that carried out the seizure.
30　Art 100 provides that all states 'shall cooperate to the fullest extent possible'.
31　Save for universal jurisdiction, the other recognised grounds for states to exercise jurisdiction are territoriality, subjective territoriality, objective territoriality, protection of the state, nationality (or active personality) and passive personality; see also Pemberton (n 3 above) 8, and in general for the argument that piracy is not truly an international crime and is not subject to universal jurisdiction; E Anderson et al 'Suppressing maritime piracy: Exploring the options in international law' One Earth Future, Academic Council on the United Nations System and American Society for International Law Workshop Report 8 (2009); De Bondt (n 2 above) 5.
32　Arts 100-107.
33　According to right or equity and good or conscience.
34　Also referred to in art 38(2) of the ICJ Statute where parties may dispense with the law altogether upon agreement.

reference to domestic or municipal law and international human rights law.

4　Alternative crimes to international maritime piracy

4.1　Rome Convention on the Suppression of Unlawful Acts against the Safety of Maritime Navigation

The definition of piracy requires that the acts be committed for private ends, and that the actions of piracy by the crew or passengers of one ship be directed against another ship. Conversely, the LOSC definition of piracy does not cover instances where the unlawful acts are committed for political purposes by some of the passengers, or where only one ship is involved – for example, the high jacking of the Santa Maria in 1961 and the Achille Lauro in 1985. In response to such situations the Rome Convention for the Suppression of Unlawful Acts against the Safety of Maritime Navigation (SUA Convention) was created in 1998.[35]

The SUA Convention must immediately be distinguished from LOSC in that it is not regarded as a codification of international customary law or of any particular customary international law crime. In contrast to LOSC (and the crime of piracy as defined therein) the SUA is only applicable between parties thereto, does not distinguish between locations/maritime zones where crimes may be committed, is not limited to private ends, does not require the involvement of more than one ship, and makes the taking of measures to establish jurisdiction compulsory. LOSC is permissive and not prescriptive with respect to establishing jurisdiction.[36] Article 3(1) of the SUA Convention defines the main SUA crimes as follows:

Any person commits an offence if that person unlawfully and intentionally:
(a) seizes or exercises control over a ship by force or threat thereof or any other form of intimidation; or
(b) performs an act of violence against a person on board a ship if that act is likely to endanger the safe navigation of that ship; or
(c) destroys a ship or causes damage to a ship or to its cargo which is likely to endanger the safe navigation of that ship; or
(d) places or causes to be placed on a ship, by any means whatsoever, a device or substance which is likely to destroy that ship, or cause damage to that ship or its cargo which endangers or is likely to endanger the safe navigation of that ship; or
(e) destroys or seriously damages maritime navigational facilities or seriously interferes with their operation, if any such act is likely to endanger the safe navigation of a ship; or

---

35　treaties.un.org/doc/db/Terrorism/Conv8-english.pdf (accessed 29 July 2012).
36　De Bondt (n 2 above) 7.

(f) communicates information which he knows to be false, thereby endangering the safe navigation of a ship; or

(g) injures or kills any person, in connection with the commission or the attempted commission of any of the offences set forth in the preceding paragraphs.

The SUA Convention contains provisions on the minimum rights to be afforded by states in the territory of which the alleged offender is found and requires the state to submit the case to competent authorities without delay or extradite the person.[37] In addition, any person regarding whom proceedings are being carried out in connection with any of the offences in the SUA Convention must be guaranteed fair treatment at all stages of the proceedings, including enjoyment of all the rights and guarantees provided for such proceedings by the law of the state in the territory of which he is present.[38] Note that Somalia is not a party to the SUA Convention.

4.2 Other treaty crimes

It is of course possible that (depending on the facts) the acts committed may also qualify as crimes under other international instruments such as the International Convention Against the Taking of Hostages of 1979,[39] the 2000 United Nations Convention Against Transnational Organized Crime of 2000[40] or instruments relating to international terrorism but these instances fall outside the scope of the present paper.

4.3 Codes and practices

Although not constituting an act that creates international criminal liability, the International Maritime Organisation (IMO) adopted a Code of Practice for the Investigation of the Crimes of Piracy and Armed Robbery against Ships.[41] This code defines armed robbery against ships as 'any unlawful act of violence or detention or any act of depredation, or threat thereof, other than an act of "piracy" directed against a ship or against persons or property on board such a ship within a State's jurisdiction over such offences'.

The Regional Cooperation Agreement on Combating Piracy and Armed Robbery against Ships in Asia of 28 April 2005[42] and in IMO-sponsored Code of Conduct Concerning the Repression of Piracy and

---

37   Secs 6 and 7.
38   Sec 7.
39   Available   at   www.un.org/en/sc/ctc/docs/conventions/Conv5.pdf   (accessed 16 October 2014).
40   www.unodc.org/documents/.../TOC%20Convention/TOCebook-e.pdf   (accessed 29 July 2012).
41   IMO Res A 922(22) of 29 November 2001.
42   44 ILM (2005) 829; see art 1(2).

Armed Robbery against Ships in the Western Indian Ocean and the Gulf of Aden of 19 January 2009[43] repeats this definition almost verbatim.

These definitions may be seen as an attempt to widen the scope of activities to be countered, as the international law crime of maritime piracy does not cover all aspects of the criminal activities that accompany piracy. It will be up to states to enact laws that criminalise the relevant acts in order to exercise jurisdiction effectively.

5 The application of international humanitarian law in maritime counter piracy operations[44]

The general question is whether international humanitarian law is applicable in Somalia. The more specific question is whether international humanitarian law is applicable to counter piracy operations by neutral states in Somalia and off the Somali coast. As the two questions are related, both aspects need to be considered together.

For the whole of the four Geneva Conventions of 1949 (GCI-IV) and Additional Protocol I of 1977 (API) to be applicable, a declared war or other international armed conflict (between two or more states), or a military occupation of the territory of one state by another, or peoples fighting against colonial domination, alien occupation, or against racist regimes in the exercise of their right to self-determination is required.[45] Additional Protocol II of 1977 (APII) is applicable where an armed conflict occurs in the territory of a state between the armed forces of that state and dissident armed forces or other organised armed groups (namely non-international armed conflicts), and the party fighting the state armed forces must be under responsible command, and exercise such control over a part of the territory of the state as to enable them to carry out sustained and concerted military operations, and to implement APII.[46]

There is no international armed conflict to be found in Somalia and none of the other stated requirements are satisfied so as to trigger the international armed conflict applicability of GCI-IV or API between the Somali government and Al-Shabaab, or between neutral states countering

---

43 www.imo.org/OurWork/Security/PIU/Documents/DCoC%20English.pdf (accessed 4 November 2014).
44 The website of the International Committee of the Red Cross provides a comprehensive database of all treaties relating to international humanitarian law at www.icrc.org and the texts of the 1949 Geneva Conventions and the 1977 Additional Protocols can be found there.
45 Common art 2; art 2(4) of API expands common art 2 to include armed conflicts which peoples are fighting against colonial domination and alien occupation and against racist regimes in the exercise of their right of self-determination. Somalia is not a party to API, but is bound thereby to the extent that customary international law requires it.
46 Art 1(1) of APII.

piracy and pirates. Also, the presence of African Union or other military forces supporting the Somali government against Al-Shabaab does not constitute military occupation by a foreign state, and therefore does not trigger the applicability of international humanitarian law in the international armed conflict context.[47]

Somalia is indeed experiencing a non-international armed conflict between the Somali government (initially a transitional and temporary government and now an elected government) and organised armed groups in the form of Al-Shabaab within Somalia's territory. The existence of an armed conflict between the Somali government and Al-Shabaab is borne out by the authoritative jurisprudence of the International Criminal Tribunal for the former Yugoslavia that has extensively clarified the factors to take into account to establish the existence of an armed conflict[48] as well as the existence of a non-international armed conflict.[49] In the non-international armed conflict between the Somali government and Al-Shabaab, parts of international humanitarian law are applicable as a matter of customary international law, and the Somali government and Al-Shabaab are to apply common article 3 of the GCI-IV as a minimum as well as applicable customary aspects of APII despite Somalia not being a party to APII.[50]

However, neither the Somali government, nor Al-Shabaab is a party to the counter piracy operations under scrutiny despite the fact that the Somali government has given permission for such operations in its territory. The parties to the counter piracy operations are pirates and neutral (to the conflict between the Somali government and Al-Shabaab) states utilising their military forces. There are no provisions in international humanitarian law that either party can invoke to ensure its applicability to counter piracy operations.

There are credible doubts as to whether Al-Shabaab is under responsible command as well as whether they are able to implement APII, and even if Al-Shabaab did comply with all requirements laid down in APII and Somalia was a party to APII, the pirates still constitute a separate entity from Al-Shabaab. The pirates are not a party to the armed conflict between the government and dissident armed forces or other organised armed groups.

---

47   Common art 2.
48   *Prosecutor v Tadić*, ICTY, Decision on the defence motion for interlocutory appeal on jurisdiction, Appeals Chamber, Case IT-94-1 (02 October 1995) paras 70 and 127.
49   *Prosecutor v Limaj*, ICTY, Judgment Trial Chamber II, Case IT-03-66-T (30 November 2005) paras 84-92 for the tests to be applied and 94-170 where the intensity of the conflict and organisation of the parties were used as determining factors; *Prosecutor v Haradinaj*, ICTY, Judgement Trial Chamber I, Case IT-04-84-T (3 April 2008) paras 37-62 on the tests to be applied and paras 63-100 on the application using various factors.
50   Art 1(4) of API.

Thus, notwithstanding the applicability of international humanitarian law to the conflict between the Somali government and dissident armed forces or other organised armed groups, the pirates are not a party to that conflict, and their status as pirates remain unaffected by international humanitarian law.

Another factor that points toward the non-applicability of international humanitarian law in counter piracy operations is the fact that only one UNSC Resolution of the nine important Resolutions available at the time of writing refers to applicable international humanitarian law.[51] All others refer to applicable international human rights law. The adoption of Res 1851 (2008) followed the French pursuit of pirates on the Somali mainland and the reason for the exception made in this Resolution may be the unconfirmed possibility that pirates could form part of the insurgency against the Somali government, thereby raising the spectre of attacks by neutral states on a party to a non-international armed conflict. Res 1851 (2008) cannot be regarded as an acknowledgement by the UNSC that the counter piracy actions are to be regarded as an armed conflict, and the references to 'applicable humanitarian law' was added as a cautionary measure only.[52]

The states and regional organisations that are combating piracy off the Somali coast are neutral with regard to any armed conflict raging in Somalia between the Somali government and dissident armed forces or other armed groups. Thus, these neutral states combating piracy have no relation to the armed conflict. The acts of piracy can be classified as criminal acts unrelated to the conflict in Somalia or the parties thereto.[53] Pirates do not form part of the armed entities fighting the government and do not meet the requirements to be regarded as combatants/prisoners of war or any other special category of persons in armed conflict. Neutral states are not obliged to act any differently than they would have against pirates in the absence of an armed conflict.

International humanitarian law is not applicable to the combating of piracy by the international armed forces positioned off the Somali coast.[54] This leaves the option of human rights law only to answer questions relating to status, rights and duties of the persons and parties involved.

---

51 Res 1851 (2008).
52 D Guilfoyle *Shipping interdiction and the law of the sea* (2009) 69-70; D Guilfoyle 'The laws of war and the fight against Somali piracy: Combatants or criminals?' (2010) 11 *Melbourne Journal of International Law* 1 7.
53 Kontorovich (n 4 above).
54 This conclusion is supported by Treves (n 26 above) 409.

6 Application of international human rights law in maritime counter piracy operations

6.1 Treaties and state obligations[55]

In the African context the rights, including the right to life and physical integrity, to be afforded to a person arrested, or otherwise apprehended and detained, on suspicion of having engaged in piracy is mostly to be found in instruments other than those already mentioned. Of course, substantive human rights can be found in municipal laws, but temporarily sidestepping municipal provisions, the sources for human rights norms in the current context is the 1955 Standard Minimum Rules for the Treatment of Prisoners (SMR), the 1966 International Covenant on Civil and Political Rights, the 1981 African Charter on Human and Peoples Rights, the 1984 Convention Against Torture and Other Cruel Inhuman or Degrading Treatment or Punishment (CAT) and possibly the 1989 Convention on the Rights of the Child (in light of the young age of persons involved in piracy in the context). Much has been written on the application of the European Charter of Human Rights (ECHR) from the perspective of EU members, but only the most important of the applicable instruments from an African perspective will be discussed further.[56]

Although due process rights are very relevant to the issue of the prosecution of pirates, this paper's scope is limited to the rights and duties relevant in the period leading up to, and including, capture and detention as these are relevant in military counter piracy operations. The issue of prosecution and due process rights after capture, initial detention and handing over to civilian authorities do not concern the operational commander, and is only referred to incidentally herein.

6.1.1 *1966 International Covenant on Civil and Political Rights (ICCPR)[57]*

States undertake to respect the human rights of persons and take steps to enact laws to realise those rights as contained in ICCPR as well as create effective mechanisms for persons whose rights have been violated to obtain redress. Of paramount importance (amongst many other rights mentioned) is the right to life, a prohibition on cruel, inhuman or degrading treatment or punishment, the right to liberty and security of a person, a prohibition

---

55   Most leading international human rights treaties can be accessed through the website of the office of the UN High Commissioner for Human Rights at www2.ohchr.org/ English/law/ (accessed 17 October 2014), besides the wide availability thereof on the internet; De Bondt (n 2 above) 12.
56   DeBondt (n 2 above) 12-13.
57   www2.ohchr.org/English/law/ccpr.htm (accessed 29 July 2012).

on arbitrary arrest or detention as well as deprivation of liberty outside the norms laid down by law, the right to be informed at the time of arrest of the reasons and charges, to be brought before a court promptly and be tried within a reasonable time, to challenge detention pending trial in a court and of course to be treated with dignity.[58]

The ICCPR provides that parties thereto undertake to respect and ensure to all individuals within its territory and subject to its jurisdiction, the rights recognised in ICCPR.[59] Articles 6 and 9 contain the most important rights to take note of. These are quoted in full for ease of reference:

> Article 6
> (1) Every human being has the inherent right to life. This right shall be protected by law. No one shall be arbitrarily deprived of his life.
>
> Article 9
> (1) Everyone has the right to liberty and security of person. No one shall be subjected to arbitrary arrest or detention. No one shall be deprived of his liberty except on such grounds and in accordance with such procedure as are established by law.
> (2) Anyone who is arrested shall be informed, at the time of arrest, of the reasons for his arrest and shall be promptly informed of any charges against him.
> (3) Anyone arrested or detained on a criminal charge shall be brought promptly before a judge or other officer authorized by law to exercise judicial power and shall be entitled to trial within a reasonable time or to release. It shall not be the general rule that persons awaiting trial shall be detained in custody, but release may be subject to guarantees to appear for trial, at any other stage of the judicial proceedings, and, should occasion arise, for execution of the judgement.
> (4) Anyone who is deprived of his liberty by arrest or detention shall be entitled to take proceedings before a court, in order that that court may decide without delay on the lawfulness of his detention and order his release if the detention is not lawful.
> (5) Anyone who has been the victim of unlawful arrest or detention shall have an enforceable right to compensation.

Parties to the ICCPR are to apply ICCPR provisions over all persons subject to their jurisdiction and that leaves no space for states involved in Operation COPPER to avoid having to respect the provisions of the ICCPR in the conduct of the operation.[60]

The ICCPR also contains many rights that are relevant to a person being tried in a court, but those provisions exceed the scope of the present focus, and are not scrutinised herein.

---

58   Arts 6, 7, 9, 10 and 14.
59   Art 2.
60   BJ Bill 'Human rights: Time for greater judge advocate understanding' (2010) *The Army Lawyer* 54 56-57, 60.

6.1.2   1981 African Charter on Human and Peoples Rights (Banjul Charter)[61]

The Banjul Charter declares that every individual shall be entitled to the enjoyment of the rights and freedoms recognised and guaranteed therein.[62] The salient rights in the Banjul Charter are: that every individual shall be equal before the law; entitlement to respect for life and integrity of a person; the right to have a person's human dignity respected; a prohibition on torture, cruel, inhuman or degrading punishment and treatment; the right to liberty and security of the person; the right not to be arbitrarily deprived of freedom or arbitrarily arrested or detained; to have one's cause heard (particularly if there has been a violation of rights); and the right to be tried within a reasonable time by an impartial court or tribunal.[63]

The most important right to take note of is contained in article 6 which provides that every individual shall have the right to liberty and to the security of his person, and that no one may be deprived of his freedom except for reasons and conditions previously laid down by law. In particular, no one may be arbitrarily arrested or detained.

6.1.3   Other regional human rights instruments

In the context of the piracy of the Horn of Africa, there are European naval task forces, NATO naval task forces, Indian naval task forces and various other states such as China and Russia are involved in combating piracy. The European Human Rights Framework and the Inter-American System for the Protection of Human Rights are two examples of international human rights regimes that may be applicable in the context to states subject to those regimes and who are operating naval forces in the area. These regimes are an important interpretative aid to determine rights and duties, even if not directly applicable or enforceable against the African or SANDF forces employed.

6.2   Examples of the enforcement of human rights

Depending on the region of origin and the international human rights regime applicable to the actor, there may be different obligations on different states. The enforcement of the obligations may be dependent on the enforcement mechanisms available under the relevant regional system.

---

61   http://www.achpr.org/files/instruments/achpr/banjul_charter.pdf (accessed 29 July 2012).
62   Art 2.
63   Arts 3-7.

For the African context, it is useful to take note of some examples from other jurisdictions.[64]

In 1999, the *Rigopoulus* matter came before the European Court of Human Rights (ECtHR). Spain arrested suspects on a Panamanian flagged vessel in relation to the suppression of the illegal drug trade with authorisation of the flag state. Measured against the right to be brought promptly before a court, the suspects only appeared before a Spanish court 16 days (to cover approximately 5 500 km) after arrest. The court found that there was no violation of article 5(3) of the ECHR – the right to be brought promptly before a court.[65]

In 2010, the *Medvedyev* matter also came before the ECtHR. The complaint related to an incident wherein France interdicted Cambodian flagged vessels with authorisation of the flag state in order to suppress the trade in illegal drugs. The persons arrested were brought to a French port after a 13 day (approximately 5 500 km) voyage. The question was again whether France violated article 5(3) of the ECHR. The ECtHR again ruled that there was no violation of article 5(3) in the circumstances, although there were issues with jurisdiction under article 5(1).[66] In both the *Rigopoulus* and the *Medvedyev* matters, the court indeed confirmed that the time lapse between arrest and appearance before a court was in principle incompatible with the requirement of promptness, but that exceptional circumstances could (and did in the instances) justify the detention. It was materially impossible to bring the suspects before the court sooner and allowance was made for the peculiar circumstances of maritime law enforcement.[67]

Although both the *Medvedyev* and *Rigopoulos* matters initially seem incompatible with the right to be brought before a court promptly, there were exceptional circumstances in both matters that justify the period that elapsed between arrest and appearance before a court. It was materially impossible to bring the applicants before a court sooner, and thus there was no violation of article 5(3). It may also be noted that article 5(1) provides that no one may be deprived of liberty except in specified cases, two of which are maritime piracy, or where other treaties provide for it.

On 18 November 2008, a Royal Navy warship transferred eight suspected pirates to Mombasa in Kenya after seven days in detention. The suspects were captured on 11 November 2008 in the Gulf of Aden. In this example, an African state obtained effective control over the suspects, and as such, the African regime concerning human rights should have become

---

64 C Schaller 'Prosecuting pirates' in Mair (n 11 above) 81-90, also discusses this issue at 86.
65 *Rigopoulos v Spain* ECHR (21 January 1999) Application No 37388/97.
66 *Medvedyev v France* ECHR (29 March 2010) Application No 3394/03.
67 T Treves 'Human rights and the law of the sea' (2010) 28 *Berkeley Journal of International Law* 1 7-8.

relevant from the moment that Kenya received the suspects. To answer whether this is a violation of article 9 of ICCPR or article 6 of the Banjul Charter, one may be assisted by the ECtHR interpretation of article 5 of the ECHR.

The African Court on Human and Peoples' Rights has only recently commenced is work and it remains to be seen how effective it is to be. However, in principle, it is possible for the African Court on Human and Peoples' Rights to adjudicate matters where a suspected pirate complains about rights violations by African states. Prior to suspension, the South African Development Community (SADC) Tribunal was empowered to hear human rights disputes, and it has done so. However, the nature of the powers and functions of the SADC Tribunal remains unclear pending the suspension and review attempts. It may be reconstructed in a format that does not allow individual access anymore.

What may result in violation of human rights is where, in accordance with the common practice of the patrolling navies to release Somali pirates ashore in Somalia, pirates are detained for a period of time aboard a ship while the states that have effective control are undecided on whether to prosecute, transfer or release. Where a suspect is not brought before a court but released, a violation of rights relating to the freedom and security of the person is possible. An example thereof may again be the January 2009 capture and detention for more than a month of five pirates by the Danish warship *Absalon* while authorities deliberated.[68] The 2007 incident involving the *Absalon* where the pirates were released ashore in Somalia after capture may also lead to potential violations as the detention was ultimately not for the purposes of bringing the suspects before a court.[69]

6.3 Regional cooperation and extra territorial application of human rights

Article 100 of the LOSC places a duty on all states to cooperate to the fullest possible extent in the repression of piracy on the high seas or in any other place outside the jurisdiction of any state. Unfortunately there is not as many explicit attempts to secure human rights concerned as there are to establish jurisdiction and cooperative measures.

In January 2009 the International Maritime Organisation (IMO) hosted a sub-regional meeting on maritime security, piracy and armed robbery against ships for Western Indian Ocean, Gulf of Aden and Red Sea States in Djibouti. The meeting resulted in the adoption of a Djibouti Code of Conduct Concerning the Repression of Piracy and Armed Robbery against Ships in the Western Indian Ocean and the Gulf of Aden

---

68   De Bondt (n 2 above) 22.
69   De Bondt (n 2 above) 23.

(DCoC),[70] as well as agreement on technical cooperation and training. It also lays the groundwork for cooperation between participants in the form currently exercised by South Africa and Mozambique.

South Africa is a signatory to the DCoC that is aimed at the cooperation and establishment of jurisdiction over maritime crimes, and not specifically on the advancement of human rights. There are a number of contact groups that have been established in order to facilitate closer cooperation. The International Chamber of Commerce International Maritime Bureau is also involved (from an industry interest perspective) and besides the International Contact Group on Piracy off the Coast of Somalia (CGPCS), coordination/information centres have also been established parallel to three regional facilities namely the Maritime Rescue Coordination Centre in Mombasa, the Sub-Regional Coordination Centre in Dar-es-Salaam, and a new regional maritime information centre in Sana'a. These support the information sharing components of the DCoC.[71]

The concept of 'shipriders' is also mentioned in the DCoC.[72] Because it is the international trend to prefer that the coastal state exercise jurisdiction over acts of piracy committed off their coast, a ship combating piracy may be temporarily accompanied by a duly authorised government law enforcement official of a state other than the flag state of the vessel. If an incident of piracy should occur while such official of the foreign state (then referred to as a 'shiprider') is present on board the vessel, it allows the foreign state to exercise *de jure* jurisdiction immediately, even though any *de facto* control will be exercised by persons other than that of the state of nationality of the shiprider.

The TFG, Somaliland and Puntland agreed in January 2010 to form a three-member technical committee to coordinate their efforts. This committee coordinates the efforts of members and is known as the Somali Contact Group on Counter-Piracy or the Kampala Process. The members also agreed on a draft anti-piracy law and began to work on laws related to the transfer of prisoners. They signed a memorandum of understanding to cooperate on counter-piracy issues in April 2010.[73] Both Puntland and Somaliland have interdicted and arrested suspected pirates and accepted them for trial, while the Somaliland piracy law has been enacted.[74]

---

70   http://www.imo.org/OurWork/Security/PIU/Pages/DCoC.aspx (accessed 17 October 2014). The Djibouti Code of Conduct is not a Treaty but a non-binding framework.
71   Ploch et al (n 7 above) 23.
72   Ploch et al (n 7 above) 28-29; see also UNSC Resolution 1851.
73   Another comparative initiative is the Straits of Malacca Regional Cooperation Agreement on Combating Piracy and Armed Robbery against ships in Asia (ReCAAP).
74   The Republic of Somaliland Law on Combating Piracy (Piracy Law) Law No 52/2012 was passed by the Somali House of Representatives on 21 February 2012, and the Somali House of Elders on 15 March 2012. It was signed into law on 21 March 2012.

The wording of LOSC on who has jurisdiction to try pirates has created some debate on the issue of transfer of suspects between states. The argument is that although article 105 of LOSC provides that any state may arrest pirates on the high seas or any place outside the jurisdiction of any state, the courts of the state which carried out the seizure of pirates or their ships may decide upon the penalties to be imposed. Thus, it is argued, a state other than the state who arrested the pirates is not empowered to prosecute.[75] This argument is not supported by state practice or *opinio juris* though.[76] Where states wish to exercise jurisdiction over pirates that they have not captured themselves, reliance is placed on universal jurisdiction over the crime of piracy, another recognised ground for a state to exercise jurisdiction, or shipriders.[77]

South Africa and Mozambique as well as South Africa, Mozambique and Tanzania have concluded Memoranda of Understanding that regulate their cooperation in the combating of piracy. South Africa, Mozambique and Tanzania (although Tanzania reportedly signed later) appended their signatures to a Memorandum of Understanding (MOU) dated 13 December 2011, that deals with maritime security cooperation. Its first purpose is to regulate the conduct of combined maritime operations in the territorial waters of the participants, and also foresees operations conducted in order to search and interdict pirate bases and maritime criminals. It deals with issues such as entry into each other's territorial waters for the purpose of implementing the MOU as well as the rights of the parties to conduct law enforcement operations, cease goods and arrest suspects in particular maritime zones.

South Africa and Mozambique also signed an MOU on 01 June 2011 on the conduct of combined maritime patrols within the territory of the Republic of Mozambique. It regulates the provision of personnel and equipment for the purposes of conducting law enforcement patrols and operations in and off Mozambican territorial waters, the right to retain custody of goods seized, and the prosecution of all suspects arrested during combined patrols. This agreement will be supplemented by classified 'Rules of Conduct and Engagement' (ROCE) provided by the military command to the deployed forces. These ROCE will further amplify the procedures regarding arrest and handover to appropriate civilian authorities (usually as soon as possible) of suspected pirates.

It was reported in the press on 24 September 2011 that two inmates in Mozambican prisons were beaten to death. Reportedly, the perpetrators were the Mozambican authorities. Such a report raises the spectre of suspected pirates that have been handed over to Mozambican authorities in violation of their rights. In the context of the arrangements entered into

---

75   De Bondt (n 2 above) 7-8.
76   Pemberton (n 3 above) 13-15.
77   Treves (n 26 above) 408-412; De Bondt (n 2 above) 5 and 7-8.

between South African and Mozambique, it is quite probable that an arrested suspect may challenge his/her transfer by South Africa to Mozambique. Once South Africa (whether *de facto* or *de jure*) has effective control over a person suspected of committing acts of piracy, and then hands that person over to Mozambique, the protection of the human rights of that suspect must be considered on a case-by-case basis, depending on the possible charges and sanctions.

In practical terms, Operation COPPER is a situation where the South Africans will have *de facto* control (interception, stopping, boarding, overcoming resistance to arrest, arrest and initial detention) while Mozambique is intended to have *de jure* control and exercise jurisdiction (being present or close by throughout and accepting the suspects when the South Africans hand them over, either formally on-board or at a Mozambican port). There can be little debate about whether South Africa has effective control over the suspects despite the presence of Mozambicans. While Mozambican officials may easily claim jurisdiction over suspects who are actually under the physical control of the South Africans, the question remains as to how an African court would view the same issue of the violation of international human rights norms by handing the person over to Mozambican authorities.

In *Mohamed v President of the Republic of South Africa (Society for the Abolition of the Death Penalty in South Africa and Another Intervening)* an extradition (rendition) to the United States without requisite assurances regarding the treatment of the accused was regarded as a breach of the Constitution of the Republic of South Africa, 1996.[78] In accordance with section 7(2) of the Constitution, it was confirmed that the state must respect, promote and fulfil the rights contained in the Bill of Rights, and in particular the rights to dignity, life, and freedom and security of the person.[79] The recent South African judgment in *Minister of Home Affairs v Tsebe; Minister of Justice and Constitutional Development v Tsebe* that was decided on 27 July 2012 further clarified the South African legal regime in this regard.[80] This matter related to two Botswana nationals who were suspected of having committed heinous crimes in Botswana. The suspects fled across the border into South Africa and Botswana requested the extradition of the suspects. While the South African Department of Home Affairs deals with issues of illegal aliens, the Department of Justice and Constitutional Development deals with extradition requests. The Department of Justice and Constitutional Development was initially unwilling to process the extradition if Botswana did not provide assurances that the suspects would not be handed the death penalty. In Botswana, the death penalty is a very probable sentence if the suspects are to be convicted, but Botswana refused to give such assurances. On the other hand, the

---

78   2001 (3) SA 893 (CC).
79   Secs 10, 11 and 12.
80   2012 (5) SA 467 (CC).

Department of Home Affairs was eager to repatriate the illegal Botswana nationals based on their illegal presence in South Africa.

To summarise, the Constitutional Court unequivocally reaffirmed that if South Africa:

> [A]s a society or the State hand somebody over to another State where he will face the real risk of the death penalty, we fail to protect, respect and promote the right to life, the right to human dignity and the right not to be subjected to cruel, inhuman or degrading treatment or punishment of that person, all of which are rights our Constitution confers on everyone. This Court's decision in *Mohamed* said that what the South African authorities did in that case was not consistent with the kind of society that we have committed ourselves to creating. It said in effect that we will not be party to the killing of any human being as a punishment – no matter who they are and no matter what they are alleged to have done.[81]

The implication is that suspected pirates captured by the SANDF may be able to raise exactly the same argument before South African courts to prevent their transfer to Mozambique, Somalia, or a host of other states if the facts are comparable.

A further complication may be the exact location of the arrest. If the suspected pirates are arrested in the territorial waters of Mozambique after having engaged in piratical acts there, there is technically no piracy for the purposes of LOSC. In these circumstances, South Africans would have to rely on Mozambican law and the role of the Mozambican officials in exercising jurisdiction becomes so much more important in the absence of international law grounds for South Africans to exercise jurisdiction.

In the context of multi-national cooperation, and when faced with an international crime and universal jurisdiction, the principle of *aut dedere aut judicare* must be considered. It means that the state who finds itself in control of a person who has committed an international crime must try or extradite the accused. The 'try or extradite' principle in international criminal law has been the cause of much frustration for the Danish and British governments. On 17 September 2008 the Danish naval vessel *Absolon* captured ten Somali pirates. They were detained for six days, their equipment confiscated, and released on a Somali shore. The Danes were concerned that the suspects may face torture or death if handed over to Somali authorities, and if they were returned to Denmark and convicted, would pose a problem upon completion of their sentences or acquittal. The reason is that Denmark would not be able to return them to Somalia based on the Somali human rights record, and they would probably end up as refugees or asylum seekers in Denmark. In 2008 the British Foreign Office warned against taking of pirates as that may raise the issue of asylum

---

81　Para 68; see also paras 42, 43, 45, 46, 67, 71 and 74.

claims.[82] Those with the means and will to capture the pirates do not have the will to prosecute them. Those willing to accept and prosecute them do not have the human rights capabilities and track records of those capturing them.

The issues of 'effective control', extradition and *non-refoulement* are topics that have been discussed more comprehensively elsewhere and these issues are intentionally not revisited in detail herein. It is settled practice before the ECtHR that where a member state arrests and detains a suspect outside their own territory, that person is within the 'effective control' or 'within the authority and control' of the state who has contracted with another to perform functions of a state, and the suspect should be able to hold that state liable if it should transfer the suspect to a third state in circumstances where the suspects' human rights are sure to be violated.[83] The Human Rights Committee has determined that states are obliged to give effect to the ICCPR extra territorially, but this is not accepted by all states, with the United States being a notable objector. The African view on the extra-territorial application of human rights treaties in the context of arrest and detention of pirates as well as the use of force against them will hopefully be influenced by the ECtHR.

All naval forces operating off the Horn of Africa (including those of China, India, Russia, the EU and NATO) may potentially face the same issues, although their human rights obligations may be less informed by the African Charter than by the particular regional human rights regimes applicable to them. In one example, Russia handed suspects over to Yemen. The suspects were captured by the crews of the Russian cruiser *Peter the Great* and the destroyer *Admiral Panteleyev* in 2009, and of obvious implication may be the Convention against Torture as well as the European Convention on Human Rights in the context of the Yemeni human rights record and the issue of *non-refoulement*.[84] Also, the return of any suspect to Somalia raises the spectre of torture or other cruel, inhuman or degrading treatment and punishment, and that is a common problem for all states in which pirates have served their prison terms or who have been found not-guilty, and then have to be sent somewhere else or retained as a refugee or under some other status.[85]

The states that have shown willingness to accept transfer of suspected pirates for the purposes of prosecution and punishment include Yemen,

82 Pemberton (n 3 above) 6.
83 *Al-Jedda v The United Kingdom* ECHR (07 July 2011) Application No 27021/08 84-85; *Al-Skeine vThe United Kingdom* ECHR (02 March 2010) Application No 55721/07 108 referring to *Al-Sadoon & Mufdhi vThe United Kingdom* ECHR (02 March 2010) Application No 61498/08 178.
84 De Bondt (n 2 above) 33.
85 De Bondt (n 2 above) 24-31.

Oman, Somaliland, Puntland, Somalia, Seychelles and Kenya.[86] Kenya entered into an agreement to receive and try suspected pirates with the US, UK, Denmark, Canada, China, and the EU, while the Seychelles entered into such an agreement with the EU.[87] The agreement between the UK and Kenya specifically indicate that the conditions of transfer are to be agreed. Unfortunately, after some successful prosecutions and convictions, Kenyan courts have recently refused to exercise jurisdiction and a moratorium was placed on accepting further suspects for trial.[88] Despite these successes, Kenya has been criticised for its human rights record in light of election violence and conditions of detention.[89]

Some UNSC Resolutions nevertheless encourage the handing over for prosecution of suspected pirates captured off the Horn of Africa to states willing to exercise jurisdiction. It is also specifically linked to the issue of shipriders as a means of ensuring that states willing to accept suspects are certain that they are able to exercise jurisdiction.[90]

The EU is taking the lead with respect to ensuring that the human rights of suspects are respected. An EU Joint Action Statement[91] makes provision for transfer to third states from the capturing state, but then insists that:

[N]o person ... may be transferred to a third State unless the conditions for the transfer have been agreed with that third State in a manner consistent with relevant international law, notably international law of human rights, in order to guarantee in particular that no one shall be subjected to the death penalty, to torture or to any cruel, inhuman or degrading treatment.[92]

The agreement concluded with Kenya on 06 March 2009 regarding the prosecution of pirates captured by EU forces in Kenya consequently contains detailed provision on treatment of persons handed over.[93]

---

86   Ploch et al (n 7 above) 27-28; RC Mason 'Piracy: A legal definition' (2010) *Congressional Research Service* 6.
87   JT Gathii 'Jurisdiction to prosecute non-national pirates captured by third states under Kenyan and international law' (2009) 31 *Loyola of Los Angeles International and Comparative Law Review* 363; De Bondt (n 2 above) 11.
88   Ploch et al (n 7 above) 35; Pemberton (n 3 above) 7.
89   Ploch et al (n 7 above) 28; De Bondt (n 2 above) 27-28.
90   See UNSC Resolutions 1846 and 1851.
91   (2008/851/CSFP OJ (2008) L301/33).
92   Pemberton (n 3 above) 6.
93   Schaller (n 64 above) 87.

6.4   United Nations Security Council Resolutions relevant to Somali piracy[94]

The UNSC issued a number of resolutions on the topic of piracy of the coast of Somalia being UNSC Resolutions 1816, 1838, 1846, 1851, 1897, 1918, 1950, 1976, 2015, 2020 and 2039. A number of issues are relevant.

The UNSC Resolutions reaffirm that there exists an international legal framework within which to combat piracy and armed robbery at sea and finds that the situation off the coast of Somalia constitutes a threat to international peace and security in the region.[95] Action is authorised under Chapter VII of the UN Charter (subject to certain requirements including advance consent of the Transitional Federal Government in Somalia if done inside Somali territorial waters) to 'use all necessary means' to repress piracy and armed robbery.[96]

The Resolutions call upon states to actively take part in the fight against piracy by deploying naval vessels in accordance with international law. The Resolutions also affirm that any action taken must be in conformity with the international legal obligations of states and calls on states to act in conformity with applicable international human rights law multiple times. It also calls on states to act in conformity with applicable international humanitarian law once.[97]

The UNSC Resolutions are careful to point out that the authorisations granted to third states (by the TFG and confirmed by the UNSC) must not be seen to be applicable to any other situation outside the Somali piracy phenomenon, and in particular does not relate to the granting of access to territorial waters of any other state than Somalia in the conduct of counter-piracy operations. Importantly, Res 1816 refers to a letter of 27 February 2008 wherein TFG advance consent is provided to foreign states to combat maritime piracy in Somali territorial waters, and that is often interpreted as the underlying basis for the authorisations under Chapter VII. Technically, the letter removes the legal necessity for Chapter VII authorisation for foreign states to enter Somali territorial waters as coastal state consent is sufficient for foreign states to enter territorial waters.[98] However, the TFG still requires advance notification to the UNSC when foreign warships will be present in Somali waters for the purpose of combating piracy. This system that is based on the consent of the TFG is repeated in subsequent resolutions. Three important objectives can be

---

94   Resolutions of the Security Council of the United Nations can be accessed through www.un.org/Docs/sc/unsc_resolutions.html (accessed 17 October 2014) and can be sorted in accordance with many parameters.
95   Res 1816, 1838, 1846, 1851.1897, 1950, 1976, 2015, 2020; Treves (n 26 above) 401.
96   See Res 1816 in particular.
97   Res 1851 (2008).
98   Treves (n 26 above) 412.

attached to the consent required of Somalia namely strengthening the sovereignty of Somalia, strengthening the legitimacy and power of the TFG, and limiting foreign presence in territorial waters of Somalia.[99]

As a related aspect, Somalia claimed a 200 nm territorial sea in 1972 and continued to do so despite signature of LOSC in 1989. A 200 nm territorial sea would mean that most of the piracy incidents would not qualify as piracy under LOSC. Although the present Somali position on the extent of their territorial sea is uncertain, it would be unacceptable to foreign states to allow a 200 nm territorial sea, and foreign states are sure to accept that the Somali territorial sea does not extend beyond 12 nm in accordance with LOSC. Notwithstanding the extent of the territorial sea of Somalia, the fact that UNSC Resolutions provide authority to enter into it makes the problems that it may have created regarding access irrelevant to foreign navies.[100]

The UNSC Resolutions also specifically encourage the handing over of suspected pirates to states willing to exercise jurisdiction for the purposes of prosecution despite the wording of article 105 of LOSC.[101]

6.5 Human rights limited by the right of states to use force

The right of a state to seize a pirate ship in accordance with LOSC implies the use of force (especially when the seizure is resisted by pirates).[102] However, the use of force in this context is not to be equated with the use of force during an armed conflict as international humanitarian law is not applicable here. The nature of force used must be measured against the standards of normal law enforcement in course of stopping, boarding and arresting a ship.[103]

Superimposed on this issue are the UNSC Resolutions that contain the authorisation to use 'all necessary means for repressing piracy and armed robbery'. Operation ATLANTA directives explicitly include the use of force, and so will Operation COPPER directives. But these guidelines

---

99   Treves (n 26 above) 402-408 provides a detailed explanation as to the background for the precise wording of the relevant Resolutions.
100 See E Kontorovich 'International legal responses to piracy off the coast of somalia' (2009) 13 *American Society for International Law Insights*, for a discussion of unique legal considerations for the UNSC in drafting Resolutions on Somali piracy.
101 Also see UNSC Resolution 1851.
102 Treves (n 26 above) 412-413; Refer to art 293 of the LOSC which confirms that court or tribunal having jurisdiction under this shall apply the LOSC as well as other rules of international law not incompatible with the LOSC Convention.
103 PJ Kwast *Maritime interdiction of weapons of mass destruction in international legal perspective* (2007) 31-32; Kwast also refers to IA Shearer 'The development of international law with respect to the law enforcement roles of navies andcoast guards in peacetime' (1998) 71 *International Law Studies* 437 and IA Shearer 'Problems of jurisdiction and law enforcement against delinquent vessels' (1986) 35 *International and Comparative Law Quarterly* 341; De Bondt (n 2 above) 14.

cannot rely on the principles from international humanitarian law of military necessity, distinction, proportionality, and avoiding unnecessary suffering as international humanitarian law is not applicable. On the contrary, warships deployed to combat Somali piracy have mostly used force only in self defence (for themselves or third parties).

The matter of the *MV Saiga* that served before the International Tribunal on the Law of the Sea (ITLOS) is cited as confirming the principles to be adhered to when force is used to stop and board a vessel in maritime law enforcement operations.[104] ITLOS provided clear guidelines on the use of force when stopping and boarding a vessel, and international law guidelines are so much more relevant where regional cooperation implies that resort cannot be had to the law of only one state in this regard. The *MV Saiga* ruling elaborated on the *I'm Alone* Arbitration[105] and the Commission of Inquiry on the *Red Crusader*,[106] and explained the position as follows:

> [I]nternational law ... requires that the use of force must be avoided as far as possible and, where force is inevitable, it must not go beyond what is reasonable and necessary in the circumstances. Considerations of humanity must apply in the law of the sea, as they do in other areas of international law.[107]

The *MV Saiga* matter and the *Nicaragua* case were also quoted and relied upon in the 2007 arbitration ruling between Guyana and Suriname.[108] In the context of a Suriname naval vessel threatening a Guyana oil drilling platform, the arbitration ruling accepted the argument that in international law force may be used in law enforcement activities provided that such force is unavoidable, reasonable and necessary.[109]

UN SC Res 1816, 1846 and others require states to act consistent with applicable international law, and this concept of the use of minimum force is a part of the law to be respected by states in the context of counter piracy operations. The requirements thereof will have to be met if the violation of human rights during counter piracy operations is to be justified.

---

104 *M/V Saiga* (*Saint Vincent and the Grenadines v Guinea*) (*No 2*) ITLOS Rep 1999 10 120 ILR 143; In particular, see paragraphs 153 to 159; Also see Treves (n 26 above) 413-414.

105 SS 'I'm alone' (Canada, United States) 30 June 1933 to 05 January 1935 Vol III United Nations Reports of International Arbitral Awards 1609-1618.

106 'Investigation of certain incidents affecting the British trawler *Red Crusader*': Report of 23 March 1962 of the Commission of Inquiry established by the government of the United Kingdom of Great Britain and Northern Ireland and the government of the Kingdom of Denmark on 15 November 1961 Vol XXIX, United Nations Reports of International Arbitral Awards 521-539 or (1962) 35 *International Law Review* 485.

107 *M/V 'Saiga' (No 2)* (n 104 above) 155.

108 Award of the Arbitral Tribunal Constituted Pursuant to article 287 and in Accordance with Annex VII of the United Nations Convention on the Law of the Sea paras 405, 419 and 440; Award of 17 September 2007, 47 ILM (2008) 66.

109 Treves (n 26 above) 414.

In practical terms, a ship being attacked by pirates may have a 15-30 minute warning of attack.[110] For warships travelling at anything between 20 to 30 knots, that warship must be relatively close to the vessel being attacked if it is to render timely assistance. Some examples where force was used in counter piracy operations are mentioned hereafter.

On 06 May 2010 the Russian anti-submarine warfare vessel *Marshal Shaposhnikov* captured ten pirates that hijacked the crude oil tanker *Moscow University* with 23 crewmembers on 05 May 2010. The attack was launched 350 nm east of the Gulf of Aden and the warship knew that the crew were secured in a safe room aboard the tanker. In a 22 minute operation the tanker was retaken by the Russians. Pirate equipment was seized and 1 suspected pirate died during the operation. It was reported that the pirates were disarmed, transferred to a small inflatable boat and released at sea. No one knows what became of them and it is reasonable to assume that they may have drowned.[111]

The US flagged and crewed *Maersk Alabama* was the subject of multiple attacks.[112] First attacked in April 2009, thereafter again but unsuccessfully in 2010, and a third time in March 2011. By 2011 the owners of the *Alabama* had hired armed security guards and had trained the crew on defensive manoeuvres. In 2009, the *Alabama* was delivering World Food Programme aid to Somalia. On 08 April 2009, approximately 250 nm east of Eyl, the 20 member crew overpowered their Somali captors but were unable to free their captain, Richard Phillips. The *USS Bainbridge*, an Arleigh Burke-class destroyer, monitored the situation and Federal Bureau of Investigation (FBI) officials conducted negotiations with the pirates. Upon determining that the captain's life was in immediate danger, United States Special Forces attempted to rescue the captain. Three pirates were killed by snipers and a fourth – Abdiwali Abdiqadir Muse – was captured.[113] It seems that the repeated attacks on the Alabama were in response to the pirates that were killed aboard it in 2009.

In February 2011 *the Quest*, a US flagged sailboat, was intercepted approximately 200 nm from Oman after it was captured by pirates.[114] An American aircraft carrier, a guided missile cruiser, and two destroyers were involved and during the interception the pirates fired rocket propelled grenades at the *USS Sterrett*. Again, the FBI attempted to negotiate with the two pirates who were taken aboard the *USS Sterrett* for that purpose, but

110 Ploch et al (n 7 above) 10.
111 De Bondt (n 2 above) 1.
112 Ploch et al (n 7 above) 1, 15-16.
113 Abduwali Abdiqadir Muse was a Somali national involved in the 2009 hijacking of the *Maersk Alabama*. A US court sentenced him in February 2011 to 34 years in prison on charges of hijacking, kidnapping, and hostage taking, but did not convict him of piracy. Of particular importance was the fact that the age of Muse was an initial point of dispute. Being unable to conclusively determine the age of a suspected pirate may put some minors at risk of being tried as adults; Ploch et al (n 7 above) 35.
114 Ploch et al (n 7 above) 2.

after negotiations broke down *The Quest* was boarded by US Special Forces. Two pirates were killed during the boarding and 13 were captured (suspected of being Somalis and a Yemeni national).

In April 2009 a French rescue operation to free family aboard small sailboat off Somalia resulted in death of the owner. In January 2011, South Korean commandos successfully rescued the crew of the tanker *Samho Jewelry*, but the tanker's captain was shot in the stomach.[115] In November 2008, the Indian Navy vessel *Ins Tabar* sunk a vessel suspected of being a mother ship, only to find that the 14 persons killed during the action were innocent Thai fishermen taken hostage when *Ekwat Nava 5* was hijacked.

Whether the force used in the examples mentioned was lawful can be answered with reference to the principles enumerated above, and international law provides ample guidance on the use of force in counter piracy operations. Despite the employment of military forces to conduct counter piracy operations, the guidance on the use of force is informed solely by international human rights norms and not international humanitarian law.

7   Conclusion

Presently, pirates may not necessarily deserve the name *hostes humani generis*, and there certainly are more serious crimes that deserve the attention of the world. Despite this fact, the international law defining piracy and regulating the measures of states to combat it rely on a legal framework that was created in the context of the time when piracy was indeed a threat to all mankind.

As piracy has developed in nature, international human rights law developed too. The reach of international human rights law stretches so far as to reach into the territory of a failed state to bring humanity into the ancient fight against piracy. Despite the significant impact that piracy off the coast of Somalia has on the major shipping activities that take place in that area, the world has yet to come up with an effective solution to address the root cause of the piratical acts, namely the absence of a functioning state and government in Somalia.

Even if progress to address the root cause is slow, there is significant cooperation between states of all regions of the globe to 'treat' the 'symptoms' through maritime patrolling in multinational operations, the arrangements entered into to accept transfer of pirates and to bring them to justice. It is precisely at the point of contact between states, when one state hands a pirate to another, that international human rights law is most

---

115   Ploch et al (n 7 above) 11.

relevant. It is going to assist the pirate in ensuring that, notwithstanding the state under whose power the pirate may be, it is expected of that state to adhere to minimum standards for treatment. It is also empowering states to ensure that the full might of the law can be brought to bear on those who commit piracy, even though the pirate leader, financiers, supporters and beneficiaries may still evade the law for now.

From a South African and African perspective there are many lessons to be learnt from the EU experience in the transfer of suspects to other states. It is hoped that a paper such as this will assist decision makers to act proactively in identifying human rights issues and to implement measures that will avoid the violation of human rights in African driven counter-piracy operations.

In conclusion, and in the words of the Constitutional Court of the Republic of South Africa, if a person is handed over to a state where he will face the real risk of the violation of human rights, we fail to protect, respect and promote the right to life, the right to human dignity and the right not to be subjected to cruel, inhuman or degrading treatment or punishment of that person. Let states stop, arrest, and try to punish pirates to the full extent of the law without being a party to human rights violation – no matter who they are and no matter what they are alleged to have done.

PART C: Institutional Perspectives on Human Rights and International Humanitarian Law

9

UN Operations

Daphna Shraga

1 Introduction

A discussion of the interplay between international humanitarian law (IHL) and human rights law (HRL) in UN peacekeeping operations must be prefaced by a few introductory comments.

First, a clear distinction should be made between pronouncements of the UN political organs, judicial decisions and legal instruments of all kinds, on the applicability of IHL and HRL in armed conflict – which is little more than a re-affirmation of an existing international law principle and an appeal for states – and a recognition (yet to be articulated) of the mutually inclusive applicability of these bodies of law in UN operations.

Second, for the United Nations to recognise the complexity of the inter-relationship between IHL and HRL in its military operations there must first be recognition that both bodies of law, independently of each other, are applicable to the Organisation. The Secretariat's recognition in 1999 of the applicability of IHL to UN forces, however, was not followed by a similar recognition of the applicability of HRL to UN operations, whether by the Secretariat or by any of the UN political organs.

And third, a discussion of the interplay between IHL and HRL in UN operations is a discussion also about the interplay between these and other bodies of law, notably international criminal law, privileges and immunities and responsibility of international organisations, as well as more generally, between law and politics.

In an empirical approach to the question of their inter-relationship, this paper will examine a number of seemingly unrelated cases at the meeting points between HRL and IHL. It will begin, however, with an observation on the legal basis and scope of application of IHL and HRL, respectively, to United Nations operations.

2 The applicability of IHL and HRL to UN operations

After a decade-long debate over the applicability of IHL to peacekeeping operations, the UN Secretary-General promulgated in 1999 the Secretary-General's 'Bulletin on the observance by United Nations forces of international humanitarian 'law'.[1] In circumscribing the scope of application of the bulletin (and therefore also of IHL) to peacekeeping operations, it provided in section 1 for a 'double-key' test, or a so-called 'conflict-within-a-conflict'. Accordingly, IHL would apply to UN forces when two cumulative conditions are met: (i) the existence of an armed conflict in the area of their operation, and (ii) their actual engagement therein as combatants. The applicability of IHL is further limited in time and space, and ceases to apply with the end of active engagement of the force, regardless of the continuation of the armed conflict in the area of its deployment.

Understanding the scope of application of international humanitarian law to peacekeeping operations is understanding the dual nature of peacekeepers as both – though not simultaneously – civilians and combatants. The duality of peacekeeping operations is premised on the assumption that in the circumstances of multi-dimensional operations deployed in conflict situations, the military component of the operation, in the conduct of its *non-military* or routine operational activities is entitled to protected civilian status.[2] A distinction between peacekeepers as civilians and as combatants, challenging though it may be in the realities of peacekeeping operations, is necessary for the determination of whether and for how long the UN operation becomes a 'party to the conflict', and whether an attack against it is a crime or a lawful act of combat.[3]

In Somalia,[4] Côte d'Ivoire,[5] and more recently in the DRC, UNOSOM II, UNOCI and MONUSCO, respectively, have been intermittently engaged in combat action, during which IHL would have

---

1 ST/SGB/1999/13 of 6 August 1999.
2 A distinction reaffirmed in art 8(e)(iii) of the ICC Statute.
3 The *1994 Convention on the safety of United Nations and associated personnel* General Assembly resolution 49/59 (9 December 1994) Annex (2051 *UNTS* 363).
4 In response to the attack on the Pakistani troops on 5 June 1993 by forces of General Mohammed Farah Aideed, the United Nations Operation in Somalia (UNOSOM II) mounted a military offensive against General Aideed's forces. In the view of the Security Council the 5 June 'unprovoked' attack against UNOSOM II was a criminal act for which those responsible should have been arrested, prosecuted, tried and punished (Security Council resolution 837 (1993) of 6 June 1993, paras 1 and 5).
5 Pursuant to Security Council resolution 1975 (2011) of 30 March 2011, the UN Operation in Côte d'Ivoire mounted an offensive operation against President Gbagbo's forces to prevent the use of heavy weapons against civilian population and UNOCI Headquarters and patrols (para 6; see also the Twenty-eighth report of the Secretary-General on the United Nations Operation in Côte d'Ivoire, S/2011/387 of 24 June 2011 (paras 4-6)).

been applicable to the UN operation as a 'party to the conflict'. In the particular case of the Intervention Brigade, established as an offensive military force under MONUSCO's operational command with the sole mission of 'neutralizing' rebel forces and other armed groups in the Eastern DRC,[6] the question is not whether it is a 'party to the conflict' when actively engaged in combat – as few would argue otherwise – but whether members of the Intervention Brigade should qualify *at all times* as combatants, or as part of MONUSCO, they may, while not in combat mission, qualify for a civilian protected status. A further, not less important question is whether qualifying the Intervention Brigade as a 'party to the conflict' implies that MONUSCO as a whole becomes a 'party' by association.[7] In the realities of the DRC, however, and regardless of the theoretical debate, the Security Council was acutely aware of the virtual impossibility of distinguishing between the Intervention Brigade and MONUSCO's military component – itself mandated to use all necessary measures against same armed groups to protect civilians[8] – and of the risks for the safety and security of MONUSCO's personnel that any such military offensive by the Intervention Brigade might entail.[9]

The principle of duality or distinction between peacekeepers as civilians and as combatants was the basis for the prosecution of attacks against peacekeepers before three international criminal jurisdictions. In the Special Court for Sierra Leone (SCSL), the International Criminal Tribunal for the former Yugoslavia (ICTY) and the International Criminal Court (ICC), respectively, members of armed groups of all kinds were prosecuted for the crime of abducting and detaining hundreds of UNAMSIL's peacekeepers, for hostage-taking and holding UN military observers of UNPROFOR as human shields, and for intentionally directing attacks against personnel and installation of UNAMID. In all three jurisdictions, it was held that at all relevant times including at the time of the attack, members of the military component of the respective UN operation took no part in hostilities; they were, therefore, deemed civilians and entitled to same protection.[10]

6　Security Council resolution 2098 (2013) of 28 March 2013, paras 9-10; Special Report of the Secretary-General on the Democratic Republic of the Congo and the Great Lakes Region, S/2013/119 of 27 February 2013 (paras 60-63).

7　B Oswald 'The Security Council and the intervention brigade: Some legal issues' (2013) 17 *American Society of International Law, Insights.*

8　Security Council resolution 2098 (2013), para. 12.

9　Security Council resolution 2098 (n 8 above) para 34(b)(vi); see, Secretary-General's reports on the United Nations Organization Stabilization Mission in the Democratic Republic of the Congo, S/2013/581 (30 September 2013) paras 66-68, and S/2013/757 (17 December 2013) paras 17, 20 and 73; Report of the Secretary-General on the implementation of the peace, security and cooperation framework for the Democratic Republic of the Congo and the region, S/2013/773 (23 December 2013), para 8.

10　*Prosecutor against Issa Hassan Sesay, Morris Kallon, Augustine Gbao* Case No SCSL-04-15-T Special Court for Sierra Leone, Trial Chamber I (2 March 2009) para 233; *The Prosecutor v Radovan Karadzic, Prosecution's Marked-up Indictment* Case No IT-95-5/18-PT International Criminal Tribunal for the former Yugoslavia, Trial Chamber III (19 October 2009); *Case of the Prosecutor v Bahar Idriss Abu Garda, Public Reduction Version,*

Unlike the debate over the applicability of IHL to peacekeeping operations which challenged the United Nations almost from the start, the debate over the applicability of human rights law to same operations has only recently begun. In an era when the obligation to respect, protect and fulfil human rights was considered 'territorial', and incumbent upon states alone, it would have been inconceivable to suggest that the United Nations – having no territory of its own and in no position to affect, in either act or omission, the human rights of individuals – would be subject to human rights obligations enshrined in treaties to which it was not even a party. But with the evolution in the 1990s in the size, nature and mandates of peacekeeping operations, and their growing potential to affect the human rights of individuals in areas of their deployment, the question of the applicability of human rights to UN operations, its legal basis, 'trigger point' and scope, could no longer be avoided.

In the search for a legal basis for the application of human rights law to UN operations, an analogy was drawn from states' military operations in areas beyond their jurisdiction. It was, like all analogies, imperfect. While for states, the applicability of human rights norms to the conduct of their military operations beyond their territories was a question of 'jurisdiction' re-defined, or extra-territorial application of human rights conventions to which they were parties,[11] for the United Nations, a non-party to any of these conventions, the legal basis for the applicability of human rights obligations in the territories of its deployment, had to be found elsewhere.

In making the case for the application of human rights norms and standards to UN operations other than on the basis of conventional international law, it was argued that human rights norms form part of the constitutional order of the United Nations, and that the Charter's foremost purpose of promoting human rights binds constitutionally the Organisation and enjoins it to act in accordance with the human rights norms it was established to promote. It was also argued that the United Nations is bound by the same human rights obligations by which states are bound, and to the same extent. Suggesting otherwise would have allowed states to evade their international law obligations by establishing international organisations and act collectively through them. While conceptually appealing, both arguments are legally flawed. The first disregards the fact that the duty to act in conformity with the Charter is

---

Decision on the Confirmation of Charges No ICC-02/05-02/09 International Criminal Court, Pre-Trial Chamber I, Situation in Darfur, Sudan (8 February 2010) paras 77-84 and 126-132.

11   In a series of cases, of which the following are the most notable, the European Court of Human Rights established the principle of extra-territorial application of the European Convention on Human Rights to states' military operations conducted beyond their territories, yet within their 'jurisdiction'. See, *Banković v Belgium* (Admissibility Decision) App no 52207/99 ECtHR (Grand Chamber) (12 December 2001) para 71; and *Al Skeini v the United Kingdom* App no 55721/07 ECtHR (7 July 2011) paras 137-138.

imposed on states rather than on the United Nations, whose purpose remains to promote, not, strictly speaking, to adhere. The second disregards the legal status of the UN as an independent subject of international law, having a legal personality distinct from its member states, and therefore not necessarily subject to the same obligations.

It was finally, and most convincingly, argued that the UN is bound by the same customary international human rights standards by which states are bound, not simplistically because its member states are bound by them, but because when, like states, it exercises governing authority over territory and population, the UN should be bound by the same customary international law rules applicable to the exercise of such authority.[12] In this connection, the question of whether an international organisation which had not participated in the formation of a customary international law rule, should nonetheless be bound by it once it has been crystallised into a customary international law rule, has never been seriously challenged. In the application of both IHL and HRL to UN operations, it has been the assumption of the UN Secretariat that what is customarily applicable to states should also be considered applicable *mutatis-mutandis* to the United Nations as a consequence of its international legal personality.[13]

But whatever may have been the legal basis for the applicability of human rights to military operations, what triggers their application in any given case is the 'effective control' of either states or the United Nations over a territory or its population. In either case, it is premised on the assumption that the capacity to impact human rights creates for them both a potential for abuse and an obligation to respect.

3   The meeting points between IHL and HRL in the practice of UN operations

The exercise of the following mandates and operational activities presumes a UN control over territory and population, and thus by implication, the applicability of core human rights law, international humanitarian law and international criminal law obligations, as appropriate.

---

12   F Mégret & F Hoffmann 'The UN as a human rights violator? Some reflections on the United Nations changing human rights responsibilities' (2003) 25 *Human Rights Quarterly* 314; A Devereux 'Selective universality? Human-rights accountability of the UN in post-conflict operations' in B Bowden et al (eds) *The role of international law in rebuilding societies after conflict* (2009) 198.

13   E de Brabandere 'Human rights accountability of international administrations: Theory and practice in East Timor' in J Wouters et al (eds) *Accountability for human rights violations by international organisations* (2010) 331 337-338.

3.1 The UN Interim Administration Mission in Kosovo (UNMIK) and the UN Transitional Administration in East Timor (UNTAET)

The UN Administrations in Kosovo and East Timor were entrusted under Security Council resolutions 1244(1999) and 1272(1999), respectively, with overall authority and responsibility for the administration of their territories, and were mandated to exercise therein legislative and executive authority, including in the administration of justice. They are, as such, the foremost example of UN 'effective/overall control' over a territory and its population; control which imposed on the UN Administrations an obligation to respect and protect a full range of human rights norms and standards,[14] and entailed for them international responsibility for their violation. But while as the 'virtual governments' in the territory under their administration, UNMIK and UNTAET were bound by the quasi-totality of human rights obligations, as UN organs, they were immune not only from any judicial process[15] (both local and international), but also exempted from treaty-based human rights monitoring mechanisms, except for those to which they might have voluntarily submitted, and to the extent of such submission.[16] To compensate for the lack of judicial review in the field of human rights UNMIK established in 2000 an independent Ombudsperson empowered to monitor, promote and protect the rights and freedoms of individuals and legal entities,[17] and in 2006, a Human Rights

14 The respective UNMIK and UNTAET Regulations on the Applicable Law in Kosovo and East Timor incorporated into the local legislation a core international human rights instruments, binding upon all office-holders in the performance of their public duties. They include, the Universal Declaration on Human Rights, the European Convention for the Protection of Human Rights and Fundamental Freedoms, the International Covenant on Civil and Political Rights, the International Covenant on Economic, Social and Cultural Rights, the Convention on the Elimination of All Forms of Racial Discrimination, the Convention on Elimination of All Forms of Discrimination against Women, the Convention Against Torture, and the International Convention on the Rights of the Child (UNMIK Regulation 2000/59 of 27 October 2000, Amending UNMIK Regulation No 1999/24 on the Law Applicable in Kosovo).

15 By Regulation 2000/47 on the Status, Privileges and Immunities of KFOR and UNMIK and their Personnel in Kosovo, 'UNMIK, its property, funds and assets shall be immune from any legal process' (UNMIK/REG/2000/47 of 18 August 2000).

16 Thus, for example, in the Agreement between UNMIK and the Council of Europe on Technical Arrangements related to the Framework Convention for the Protection of National Minorities (2004) UNMIK has agreed to abide by the principles contained in the Framework Convention in the exercise of its responsibilities, and be subject in the implementation of the Framework Convention to the reporting and monitoring mechanisms of the Committee of Ministers of the Council of Europe. UNMIK's undertakings to respect international human rights standards notwithstanding, the Administration has been criticised for its human rights record, whether in the protection of minorities or, most notoriously, in its 'executive detention' practice in breach of *habeas corpus* guarantees under the European Convention on Human Rights, and the 1966 ICCPR. C Stahn 'Justice under transnational administration: Contours and critique of a paradigm' (2005) 27 *Houston Journal of International Law* 311.

17 Regulation 2000/38 on the Establishment of the Ombudsperson Institution in Kosovo (UNMIK/REG/2000/38 of 30 June 2000), superseded by Regulation 2006/6 on the Ombudsperson Institution in Kosovo (UNMIK/REG2006/6 of 16 February 2006).

Advisory Panel to examine complaints from any person or group of individuals claiming to be the victim of a violation by UNMIK of the human rights, as set forth in the core international human rights instruments.[18]

But the question of what law governs the administration of the territory is a much wider debate than the obligation of the UN Transitional Administration under international human rights standards. It is within this broader context of exercising all-inclusive administrative and legislative powers in circumstances that resemble the most those of an occupied territory that the laws of occupation and international human rights law converged to provide a normative framework.

In the debate over the applicability of the laws of occupation to the UN Administrations, it was the view of the UN Secretariat that the conditions of article 42 of the Hague Regulations (defining an 'occupied territory' as a territory 'actually placed under the authority of a hostile army') have not been met, that the source of authority of the UN Administration has been the UN mandate and not the Hague Regulations, and that consequently the laws of occupation are not applicable *de jure*, although its principles will be guiding the UN Administration, by analogy, however imperfect it may be. In the circumstances of both Administrations principles analogous to the laws of occupation applied to questions of: respect for the applicable law to the extent of its consistency with international human rights standards, the administration of State's movable and immovable property, and the immunity of the UN Administration from local jurisdiction – both as a principle of UN law and one drawn by analogy from the laws of occupation.[19]

3.2   Arrest and detention by peacekeeping operations in the exercise of 'executive mandates' or 'law and order' functions

Another form of control, not necessarily over a territory, but one which likewise triggers for the UN operation human rights obligations, is control over persons, particularly those finding themselves in the hands of the operation, whether as detainees or refuge seekers. But unlike the UN Administration where overall territorial control entailed for the

---

18   Regulation 2006/12 on the Establishment of the Human Rights Advisory Panel (UNMIK/REG/2006/12 of 23 March 2006).

19   D Shraga 'Military occupation and UN transitional administrations – The analogy and its limitations' in MG Kohen (ed) *Promoting justice, human rights and conflict resolution through international law* (2007) 479; see also, E de Wet "The direct administration of territories by the United Nations and its member states in the post cold war era: Legal bases and implications for national law' in *Max Planck Yearbook of United Nations Law*, Vol 8 (2004) 291; SR Ratner 'Foreign occupation and international territorial administration: The challenges of convergence' (2005) 16 *European Journal of International Law* 695.

Administration conventional HRL/IHL obligations, in the case of control over persons, the legal regime of detention in peacekeeping operations had to be established first.

In the practice of peacekeeping operations detention has been the almost inevitable consequence of their engagement in non-international armed conflict, or in exercising law and order functions. Persons taking part in hostilities and other civilians have been detained in the course of the operation whether pursuant to a Security Council mandate (explicit or implicit), in self-defence (for posing a threat to the security of the Force) or for committing crimes (when the Force has been entrusted with law and order functions). Persons have also been held on UN premises on their own volition and for their own protection ('refuge seekers') albeit under a different legal regime.[20]

In regulating internment by UN peacekeeping operations in non-international armed conflict or other situations of violence, IHL rules provided little guidance. The legal regime of detention applicable in international armed conflict or belligerent occupation under the Third and Fourth Geneva Conventions and Additional Protocol I is, with rare exceptions,[21] largely irrelevant to the realities of peacekeeping operations. Deployed in places and situations of non-international armed conflict, or other situations of violence, where IHL is either inapplicable or contains too few and largely inadequate provisions on detention, importing from human rights law, norms and standards to supplement or substitute for a virtually non-existent regime has been crucial in developing a coherent legal framework for detention in peacekeeping operations.

Such human rights standards include: the principle of legality (a legal basis for detention, or detention in accordance with procedures under the domestic or international law (article 9(1) of the ICCPR)); judicial guarantees (judicial review of the lawfulness of the detention (article 9(4) of the ICCPR)); procedural guarantees (the right to be informed of the reasons for the detention (ICCPR, article 9(2)) and the Body of Principles for the Protection of All Persons under any Form of Detention); the right to be registered, to challenge the lawfulness of one's detention, to legal counsel, to have contact with one's own family, and to make complaints

---

20 For a cluster of articles which framed the issues for the debate on the detention regime in peacekeeping operations, see B Oswald 'The law on military occupation: Answering the challenges of detention during contemporary peace operations?' (2007) 8 *Melbourne Journal of International Law* 311; 'Detention of civilians on military operations: Reasons for and challenges to developing a special law of detention' (2008) 32 *Melbourne University Law Review* 524, and 'Detention by United Nations peacekeepers: Searching for definition and categorization' (2011) 15 *Journal of International Peacekeeping* 119.

21 In declaring itself bound by the laws of occupation (including the detention regime) in the area of its operation, the Australian contingent in UNTAET and INTERFET in Somalia and East Timor, respectively, was the exception. It is recalled, however, that the two operations were UN authorised operations conducted under national, not UN, command and control.

relating to his or her treatment or conditions of detention; conditions of detention (the right to be held in a recognised place of detention, the right to adequate food, water, shelter, clothing and medical treatment, and facilities for personal hygiene); and finally, the principle of accountability of individual peacekeepers, their states of nationality and the Organisation for their actions or omissions.[22]

In 2010 the UN Secretariat has issued an Interim Standard Operating Procedures (SOP) on Detention in United Nations Peace Operations. Designed to ensure that 'persons detained by United Nations personnel in United Nations peace operations ... are handled humanely and in a manner that is consistent with applicable international human rights, humanitarian and refugee law, norms and standards', it combined HRL and IHL rules to create a single legal regime applicable across operations and situations. The Interim SOP, however, is a framework detention regime adapted to the specificities of peacekeeping operations, which, with the exception of detention in non-international armed conflicts, is limited to 48 hours, or more, until such time as handing over the detainee to the national authorities for prosecution is made possible.[23] The end of the detention period, however brief, does not end the HRL/IHL obligations of the UN operation, as a new series of HRL/IHL obligations relating to the terms and conditions of such transfer will have emerged.

3.3   Hand-over of detainees or 'refuge seekers' on UN premises to national authorities for prosecution

In the realities of UN peacekeeping operations, hand-over of detainees to national authorities is the logical, most immediate consequence of arrest and detention by UN forces. Deployed in the territory of the host state and having no criminal justice system of its own, the UN force has neither the mandate, nor the power to prosecute the detainee. The obligations of the UN operation for the safety and well-being of the detainee do not end, however, with the end of the detention or hand-over to his national authorities. The decision to hand-over, its modalities and its aftermath, including ill-treatment of the detainee by the authorities to which he was transferred, may entail for the UN operation international responsibility

---

22   J Pejic 'Procedural principles and safeguards for internment/administrative detention in armed conflict and other situations of violence' (2005) 87 *International Review of the Red Cross* 375.

23   In its resolution 2124 (2013) of 12 November 2013, the Security Council underlined the need for the African Union Mission in Somalia (AMISOM – a Security Council authorised operation under regional command and control), 'to ensure that any detainees in their custody, including disengaged combatants, are treated in strict compliance with applicable obligations under international humanitarian law and human rights law, including ensuring their humane treatment, and further *requests* AMISOM to allow appropriate access to detainees by a neutral body, and to establish Standard Operating Procedures for the handover of any detainees, including children, who come into their custody during a military operation'.

within the limitations of the customary international law principle of *non-refoulement*. Borrowed, by analogy, from international refugee law, the principle of *non-refoulement* enjoins the UN operation to condition handover on guarantees that subsequent detention and legal proceedings be conducted in accordance with the state's obligations under IHL and HRL, that the death penalty not be imposed, and that the UN and the ICRC representatives be granted access for the purpose of verifying compliance with the state's international obligations.[24]

Adapted to the specificities of multinational and UN operations, the principle of *non- refoulement* applies within the same territory between two authorities – the military operation and the host country – and between the different contingents of the same operation when the final destination of the hand-over remains the host country (a so-called secondary *refoulement*).[25]

Persons seeking refuge on UN premises are not covered by the legal regime of detention, yet the principle of *non-refoulement* guides their handover to national authorities, and conditions it on similar guarantees of humane treatment, due process and, in case of prosecution and subsequent trial, on the non-imposition of the death penalty. It was this last condition which in the practice of UN operations has proven the most difficult to obtain, and where the objection of the host country has led to prolonged periods of stalemate.

Long before the principles and procedures for hand-over of detainees were established in the SOP on Detention,[26] it has been the policy of the United Nations not to transfer refuge-seekers on UN premises to local authorities without assurances given for the non-imposition of the death penalty. In the two most recent cases of the DRC (2007-2011) and the Sudan (2010), UN insistence on the non-imposition of the death penalty

---

24 The principle of *non-refoulement* prohibits the expulsion, extradition, repatriation and transfer of a person to a situation, territory or authority, where he may be at a serious risk of persecution, torture, ill-treatment or other forms of abuse. Applied originally in respect of asylum seekers (art 33(1) of the 1951 Convention Relating to the Status of Refugees), the principle of *non-refoulement* has expanded to other areas of law and all situations where 'effective control' is exercised over a person – effective enough to compel his hand-over. As a principle of both HRL and IHL, *non-refoulement* is established in the Third and Fourth Geneva Conventions with respect to the transfer of Prisoners of War (art 12), and protected persons (art 45(4)), respectively. It is considered part of the absolute prohibition on torture, and explicitly prohibited in art 3(1) of the Convention Against Torture, the 1966 International Covenant on Civil and Political Rights (arts 6 and 7), the 2006 International Convention for the Protection of All Persons from Enforced Disappearance (art 16(1)), and regional human rights conventions: the American Convention on Human Rights (art 22(8), and the European Convention on Human Rights (art 3)).

25 See generally, D Cordula 'Transfers of detainees: Legal framework, non-refoulement and contemporary challenges' (2008) 90 *International Review of the Red Cross* 669; EC Gillard 'There's no place like home: States' obligations in relation to transfer of persons' (2008) 90 *International Review of the Red Cross* 703.

26 Arts 80 and 82 of the Interim Standard Operating Procedures, Detention in United Nations Peace Operations.

has paid off. In the case of the DRC, some 400 combatants affiliated with the Détachment de protection présidentielle (DPP) and their families sought refuge in MONUC's premises, and remained there until, four years later, an agreement was reached with the Government of the DRC on their release against assurances of non-imposition of the death penalty, if prosecuted. In the case of the Sudan, 5 leaders of the Kalma IDP's camp in Darfur, sought protection in UNAMID community policing centre for fear of possible reprisals from opposing factions and mistreatment by the Government for crimes allegedly committed. They were sheltered for over a year, until in August 2011 they were amnestied by the Governor of South Darfur and allowed to return home.[27]

3.4   Responsibility for violations of IHL and HRL obligations – Sexual exploitation and abuse (SEA)

While the responsibility of the United Nations for violations of IHL committed by its forces in conflict situations has been established since the Congo operation in the 1960s, its responsibility for human rights violations committed by its peace-keeping operations has rarely been attributed to or otherwise assumed by the Organisation with any consequence. The case of 'sexual exploitation and abuse' by peacekeepers – a phenomenon that shocked the United Nations not only because of the seriousness of the allegations, but for their long duration and geographic scope cutting across countries and operations – was no exception.

3.4.1   The context

In the early 2000s, allegations of sexual exploitation and abuse by UN peacekeepers in West Africa have emerged. But while sexual exploitation – where sex was 'bartered' for money, work and food and in many cases was nothing short of 'rape in disguise' – was known to exist in Bosnia and Herzegovina, Kosovo, Haiti, East Timor and Cambodia throughout the 1990s, and in Burundi, Cote d'Ivoire, Sierra Leone, and Liberia – since the early 2000s, it was the revelation of the seriousness and scope of the phenomenon in the DRC in 2004 (the worst case yet of sexual exploitation by peacekeeping operations) that compelled the UN political organs to act.

3.4.2   The crime of sexual exploitation and its prevention

Broadly conceived, sexual exploitation and abuse – as rape, forced prostitution and sexual violence of all kinds, or as a form of inhumane treatment, wilfully causing great suffering or serious injury to body or

---

27   Reports of the Secretary-General on the African Union-United Nations Hybrid Operation in Darfur (UNAMID), S/2010/543 of 18 October 2010, paras 8-10 and S/ 2011/643 of 12 October 2011, para 43.

health – constitutes a serious violation of international humanitarian law or human rights law, or both. Somewhat less broadly, 'sexual exploitation' is defined in the Secretary-General's bulletin on measures to protect from sexual exploitation and abuse, as 'any actual or attempted abuse of a position of vulnerability, differential power, or trust, for sexual purposes ...'[28]

A criminal offence under the national law of the host state, the state of nationality – and that of virtually all states – 'sexual exploitation' may amount to a war crime, or a crime against humanity under IHL and the Statute of the ICC. From the vantage point of the United Nations, however, 'sexual exploitation' was considered misconduct or a criminal act performed outside the 'official functions' of the organ or the agent and thus not attributable to the Organisation. Sexual exploitation of whatever nature, therefore, remained the responsibility of those who had committed it, namely, the peacekeepers, officials or experts on mission, and subject, within the legal limitations imposed (that is, privileges and immunities of the operation and its personnel), to the jurisdiction of their host state or the state of nationality.[29] The possibility that the United Nations as the parent organ of the peacekeeping operation might be attributed responsibility for this long-standing and widespread practice of sexual abuse has never been seriously considered.

In its attempt to prevent further abuse and introduce a measure of accountability, the UN has adopted scores of General Assembly and Security Council resolutions condemning the practice, calling upon the Secretary-General and all states to prevent sexual abuse by all categories of personnel, and enforce UN standards of conduct.[30] A Secretary-General's

---

28   'Secretary-General's bulletin on special measures for protection from sexual exploitation and sexual abuse' (ST/SGB/2003/13 of 9 October 2003) sec 1.

29   Art 6 of the ILC 'Articles on responsibility of international organizations' attributes responsibility to the Organisation for conduct of its organ or agent done '*in the performance of functions of that organ* or agent'. In its commentary on this article the ILC noted:
    'The requirement ... that the organ or agent acts "in the performance of functions of that organ or agent" is intended to make it clear that conduct is attributable to the international organization when the organ or agent exercises *functions that have been given to that organ or agent, and at any event is not attributable when the organ or agent acts in a private capacity...*'. ILC 'Articles on responsibility of international organizations' International Law Commission, Report on the Work of its Sixty-Third Session (26 April-3 June and 4 July-12 August 2011), General Assembly, Official Records, Sixty-Sixth Session, Supplement No 10 (A/66/10 and Add.1) 52 84.

30   Most notably, General Assembly resolution 57/306 (15 April 2003), on Investigation into sexual exploitation of refugees by aid workers in West Africa, requesting the Secretary-General to take measures to prevent sexual exploitation and abuse in UN operations, which led to the promulgation in 2003 of the Secretary-General's bulletin on special measures for protection from sexual exploitation and sexual abuse, setting out standards of conduct by staff and managers for preventing and addressing SEA (ST/SGB/2003/13 of 9 October 2003). General Assembly resolution 62/63 (6 December 2007), on Criminal accountability of United Nations officials and experts

commissioned report, known as the 'Zeid Report' was the single most comprehensive report ever produced on the scope of the phenomenon.[31] The legal regime proposed in the report was a combined structure of a Secretary-General's Bulletin, a revised model Memorandum of Understanding between the United Nations and troop contributing states, and a proposed draft convention on the criminal accountability of United Nations officials and experts on mission. It has remained, however, largely inadequate to combat SEA in all its aspects, categories of personnel and offences.

The military component of peacekeeping operations – the largest component by far – remained outside the scope of application of the convention. The draft convention itself remained a dead letter, as the majority of states were unconvinced that the scale of the problem (that is among officials and experts on mission) is such as to warrant the conclusion of an international treaty.[32] The absolute immunity of military personnel from legal process has left them outside the jurisdiction of the host state, and the exclusive jurisdiction of their states of nationality in respect of extra-territorial offences is yet to be fully exercised, or reported on.[33] For the states of nationality, exercising jurisdiction over the civilian component of UN operations would have required specific legislation to allow for the extra-territorial application of their laws. For the United

on mission, urging states to ensure that crimes by UN officials and experts on mission do not go unpunished, and that jurisdiction is established over the crimes perpetrated by their nationals serving abroad. Presidential Statement S/PRST/2005/21 condemning the practice, recognising states' responsibility for the prosecution of the offenders but also the shared responsibility of states and the UN Secretariat to take every measures to prevent SEA by all categories of personnel.

31   A comprehensive strategy to eliminate future sexual exploitation and abuse in United Nations peacekeeping operations, A/59/710 (24 March 2005).

32   Draft convention on the criminal accountability of United Nations officials and experts on mission, in the 'Report of the group of legal experts on ensuring the accountability of United Nations officials and experts on mission with respect to criminal acts committed in peacekeeping operations' (A/60/980 of 16 August 2006, Annex III). See generally, R Murphy 'An assessment of UN efforts to address sexual misconduct by peacekeeping personnel' (2006) 13 *International Peacekeeping* 531; M O'Brien 'Issues of the Draft convention on the criminal accountability of United Nations officials and experts on mission' in N Quénivet & S Shah-Davis (eds) *International law and armed conflict: Challenges in the 21st century* (2010) 57.

33   Art 7 quinquiens of the Revised Memorandum of understanding between the United Nations and [participating State] contributing resources to [the United Nations Peacekeeping Operation], provides, in part, that:
  'Military members and any civilian members subject to national military law of the national contingent provided by the Government are subject to the Government's exclusive jurisdiction in respect of any crimes or offences that might be committed by them while they are assigned to the military component of [United Nations peacekeeping mission]. The Government assures the United Nations that it shall exercise such jurisdiction with respect to such crimes or offences.'
Manual on policies and procedures concerning the reimbursement and control of contingent-owned equipment of ttroop/police contributors participating in peacekeeping missions (COE Manual), UN Doc A/C.5/66/8 (27 October 2011) chap 9; Z Deen-Racsmány 'The amended UN model memorandum of understanding: A new incentive for states to discipline and prosecute military members of national peacekeeping contingents?' (2011) 16 *Journal of Conflict & Security Law* 321.

Nations and its member states their possible responsibility for lack of 'due diligence' to avert the crimes[34] has remained outside the international debate, and for the many hundreds and thousands of victims no remedy of any kind has ever been made available.

4   Conclusion

The debate of the last decades over the interplay between international humanitarian law and human rights law in situations of armed conflict found little echo in the United Nations. While the applicability of IHL to peacekeeping operations had long been acknowledged, the approach to the applicability of human rights law has been ambivalent. To begin with, the UN Secretariat has never declared the applicability of human rights law to UN operations in the same way that it acknowledged the applicability of international humanitarian law to said operations. On its part, the Security Council has never called upon UN peacekeeping operations to comply with IHL and HRL in the conduct of their operations in the same way that it has almost routinely called upon state-led authorised operations – such as, the Intervention Brigade in the DRC[35] and AMISOM in Somalia[36] – to do the same. That notwithstanding, the Council was keen to ensure that the UN operation is not implicated, or be seen to be implicated in the commission of human rights violations by national military forces assisted by the UN operation pursuant to a Security Council mandate. A 'conditionality policy' conditioning UN assistance to government-led forces on their IHL and HRL compliance was first adopted for MONUSCO in the DRC. Endorsed by the Security Council, it was later re-named United Nations Human Rights and Due Diligence Policy

---

34   J Murray 'Who will police the peace-builders? The failure to establish accountability for participation of United Nations civilian police in the trafficking of women in post-conflict Bosnia and Herzegovina' (2003) 34 *Columbia Human Rights Law Review* 475; M Ndulo 'The United Nations responses to the sexual abuse and exploitation of women and girls by peacekeepers during peacekeeping missions' (2009) 27 *Berkeley Journal of International Law* 127; R Burke 'Attribution of responsibility: Sexual abuse and exploitation, and effective control of blue helmets' (2012) 16 *Journal of International Peacekeeping* 1.

35   Security Council resolution 2098 (2013) authorised MONUSCO, through the Intervention Brigade, to carry out targeted offensive operations 'in strict compliance with international law, including international humanitarian law and with the human rights due diligence policy on UN-support to non UN forces (HRDDP) ...' (para 12(b)).

36   Security Council resolution 2124 (2013) of 12 November 2013, underlined 'the importance of AMISOM abiding by all requirements applicable to it under international human rights and humanitarian law', and further underlined 'the need for AMISOM to ensure that any detainees in their custody ... are treated in strict compliance with applicable obligations under international humanitarian law and human rights law ...'. (para 12).

(HRDDP) and made applicable across UN operations in all cases of support to non UN forces.[37]

Ambivalent though the UN position may have been, in reality, international humanitarian law and human rights law have converged to create a legal framework for peacekeeping operations in contexts as diverse as transitional administrations, detention and hand-over of detainees, and criminal accountability of UN personnel. Circumscribing the scope of application of human rights law to UN operations, and the core human rights obligations applicable in any given operation to the extent of its control over territory and population, remains, however, the Secretariat's greatest challenge.

37　The 'Human Rights due diligence policy on United Nations support to non United Nations security forces' is contained in the Identical Letters dated 25 February 2013 from the Secretary-General addressed to the President of the General Assembly and to the President of the Security Council, A/67/775-S/2013/110 (5 March 2013). See in particular, Security Council resolution 2098 (2013) para 12(b) and Security Council resolution 2124 (2013) (paras 14-16). In authorising the United Nations Support Office for AMISOM (UNSOA) to support the Somali National Army (SNA), the Security Council underlined 'that such … must be in full compliance with the United Nations Human rights and Due Diligence Policy (HRDDP)' (para 15), and 'that all forces supported by UNSOA shall act in compliance with Secretary-General's Human Rights and Due Diligence Policy (HRDDP) … ' (para 16).

10

Convergence Conflicts: A Military Perspective

*Peter M Olson**

1   Introduction

As the world's most experienced organisation with respect to training for, planning and conducting multilateral military operations, the North Atlantic Treaty Organization (NATO) places a high value on compliance with the dictates of both international humanitarian law (IHL) and, as applicable, human rights law (HRL).

NATO's approach towards IHL and HRL is directly related to its mission and history and resulting structure. As a political as well as military alliance, Allies' common values drive both its political and its military actions. NATO is designed to be and functions as a mechanism for common action by sovereign states rather than as an autonomous, empowered entity, and thus does not have a developed body of legal doctrine; rather, it applies IHL and HRL in NATO operations in a manner reflecting the individual national legal positions of the 28 Allies. The implications of the resulting pragmatic approach to applying IHL and HRL in military operations are discussed in the context of three current or recent NATO operations.

2   Bases of NATO policy on IHL and IRL

In a very real sense, NATO was founded in order to organise and carry out multilateral military operations, and doing so remains NATO's principal purposes and function today. NATO has gained extensive experience in planning for and conducting such operations over more than six decades,

*   Former Director of Legal Affairs and Legal Adviser, NATO Headquarters, Brussels. The author was from 2010 through early 2014 the principal legal adviser to then-Secretary General Anders Fogh Rasmussen, and the Organization's senior legal officer.

starting with coordination amongst Allied armed forces in western Europe in the 1950s and extending through a series of major military operations over the past two decades in the Balkans, Afghanistan, the Indian Ocean and Libya. Participants in these operations have included Allies, European states that are members of the Partnership for Peace, global partners that have participated in multiple NATO operations and other states from outside the NATO area that have participated on an operation-specific basis. In Afghanistan, personnel from over fifty states have operated under NATO command in the UN-mandated International Security Assistance Force (ISAF) mission.[1]

Other intergovernmental organisations, notably including the United Nations (UN) and the European Union (EU), have great experience in conducting multilateral peacekeeping operations. None, however, has experience comparable to NATO's in planning and carrying out multilateral military and combat operations. This experience is amongst the reasons that NATO has so often been called on to contribute military resources to achieving the common goals of the international community.[2]

Another is the seriousness with which Allies take their obligations to abide by the spirit and letter of applicable principles of international humanitarian law and human rights law in planning and carrying out Alliance military operations. It is important in this regard to appreciate that NATO includes many of the states that have over many years been the most active in advancing human rights on the international plane, and in particular in developing the international legal instruments which are at the core of HRL. The Allies do not set aside those policies when they enter NATO meeting rooms; rather, respect for and adherence to the requirements of HRL, as well as those of IHL, are an essential element of NATO policy discussions and operations. NATO has as a result long seen itself as setting the standard for the lawful conduct of military operations. The members of the Alliance fully appreciate the importance for the Alliance's credibility and the perceived legitimacy of its actions of meeting

---

1   ISAF 'Placemat' http://www.isaf.nato.int/images/stories/File/20131014_131001-
     ISAF-Placemat.pdf (accessed 17 October 2014). In addition to the 49 states listed
     there, Singapore and Switzerland were formerly ISAF participants.
2   See, UN Security Council Resolutions mandating or authorising NATO action in
     Bosnia (eg, UNSCR 1088 (12 December 1996)), Kosovo (eg, UNSCR 1244 (10 June
     1999)), Afghanistan (eg, UNSCRs 1386 (20 December 2001) and 1510 (13 October
     2003)), the Indian Ocean (eg, UNSCR 1816 (2 June 2008)) and Libya (UNSCR 1973
     (17 March 2011)).

a high standard in complying with international legal rules applicable to its operations.[3]

2.1   History of NATO operations

Understanding NATO's perspective on and operational approach toward the interrelationship of these two bodies of law requires an appreciation of core structural elements of the Organization.

NATO was created in 1949 to carry out a single, very large mission: to prepare for, and if necessary to fight, an apocalyptic war in the event the Soviet Union and its Warsaw Pact allies launched a land invasion of Western Europe.[4] It carried that mission out with notable success over some four decades, over which period it put in place and implemented a highly articulated system of policies, procedures and structures for coordinating Alliance militaries, but conducted no military operations.

Much changed with the fall of the Berlin Wall, dissolution of the Warsaw Pact and, shortly thereafter, the breakup of the Soviet Union. NATO's overarching purpose to ensure the security of the North Atlantic area remained, but its primary operational mission directed to that end disappeared with those events. Since that time, NATO's principal operational focus has been on crisis management and response operations.[5]

The newly-fluid situation in Eastern Europe – most notably in the Balkans in conjunction with the violent breakup of the Yugoslav state – gave rise to new sources of instability following the end of the Cold War. One NATO response was political, as the Allies adopted a series of

---

3   See, eg, 'Allied joint doctrine for non-article 5 crisis response operations: AJP-3.4(A)' (October 2010) (NA5CRO AJP), para 0210: 'NATO commanders at all levels must be aware of the relevance of the proper use of force on the perceived credibility and legitimacy of operations ... The use of force in NA5CRO depends upon a complex mixture of rights and obligations which are provided by international and national mandates, the UN Charter, applicable international rules, regulations and agreements, the law of armed conflict, international law, and by national laws and rules'. See also NATO's 2010 Strategic Concept, 'Active engagement, modern defence: Strategic concept for the defence and security of the members of the North Atlantic Treaty Organization: Adopted by heads of state and government at the NATO summit in Lisbon, 19-20 November 2010' (2010 Strategic Concept): http://www.nato.int/ nato_static/assets/pdf/pdf_publications/20120214_strategic-concept-2010-eng.pdf (accessed 20 October 2014). Para 2 provides: 'Our 2010 Strategic Concept continues to guide us in fulfilling effectively, and always in accordance with international law, our three essential core tasks – collective defence, crisis management, and cooperative security – all of which contribute to safeguarding Alliance members.'

4   NATO 'A treaty for our age': http://www.nato.int/history/nato-history.html (accessed 20 October 2014); US Department of State: Office of the Historian 'Milestones: 1945-1952: North Atlantic Treaty Organization (NATO), 1949': http:// history.state.gov/milestones/1945-1952/NATO (accessed 20 October 2014).

5   See, eg, 2010 Strategic Concept (n 3 above) paras 4, 20-26 ('Security through crisis management').

initiatives that paved the way for newly-independent countries to expand cooperation with NATO and then seek and obtain NATO membership as a first step in integrating themselves into what were called 'Euro-Atlantic institutions.'[6] First the Alliance and, as a second stage of integration, the EU have now welcomed most East European and many Balkan states into their ranks; almost all other European states, including states that once formed part of the Soviet Union as well as neutral states such as Finland, Sweden and Switzerland, work closely with NATO through the Partnership for Peace. A second response was through military operations, including monitoring, enforcement, combat and peacekeeping operations, in Bosnia-Herzegovina and in Serbia and Kosovo, in the context of the breakup of Yugoslavia.[7] These were the first military operations in NATO's history.

These responses marked a decisive turn in the Alliance's focus, from static territorial defense against a specific known threat to a more fluid focus on management of and response to crises presenting potential threats to Allied security outside its original west and southern European area of Allied focus. Allied crisis response has included, since the turn of the century, operations in Afghanistan,[8] in the Indian Ocean off Somalia[9] and in 2011 in Libya.[10] Most recently, NATO has deployed Patriot batteries to defend Turkey against possible attack from Syria.[11]

6   NATO 'Be careful what you wish for': http://www.nato.int/history/nato-history.html (accessed 20 October 2014).
7   NATO's operations in the Balkans include Operations Maritime Monitor, based on UNSCRs 713 (25 September 1991) and 757 (30 May 1992), Sky Monitor (UNSCR 781 (9 October 1992)), Maritime Guard (UNSCR 787 (16 November 1992)), Sharp Guard (above as well as UNSCRs 820 (17 April 1993) and 943 (23 September 1994)), Deny Flight (UNSCR 816 (31 March 1993)) and Deliberate Force, based on UNSCRs 836 (4 June 1993) and 958 (19 November 1994); implementation of the Dayton Accords based on UNSCRs 1031 (15 December 1995)(IFOR) and 1088 (1996) (SFOR); Operation Allied Force; and KFOR, based on UNSCR 1244 (1999).
8   International Security Assistance Force (ISAF), based on UNSCR 1386 (2001) and subsequent UNSCRs.
9   Operations Allied Provider (October-December 2008), Allied Protector (March-August 2009) and Ocean Shield (from 2009). The first two operations were undertaken at the request of the UN Secretary General for protection of World Food Program shipments to Somalia; Ocean Shield's actions within Somali territorial waters and on Somali territory derive from the authorisations for such action first set forth in UNSCRs 1846 (2 December 2008) and 1851 (16 December 2008), and extended by UNSCRs 1897 (30 November 2009), 1950 (23 November 2010), 2020 (22 November 2011), 2077 (21 November 2012), 2125 (18 November 2013) and, most recently, 2184 (12 November 2014).
10   The North Atlantic Council's mandate for Operation Unified Protector was based on the mandate to UN member states contained in UNSCR 1973 (2011), which built on UNSCR 1970 (26 February 2011).
11   NATO Press Release 'NATO foreign ministers' statement on Patriot deployment to Turkey' 4 December 2012: http://www.nato.int/cps/en/SID-F353D5C6-C6FFCFBC/natolive/news_92476.htm (accessed 20 October 2014).

2.2   NATO structures

Central to understanding NATO is that it is an alliance of sovereign states with both a political and a military character. Its members are united by shared core political values and interests – notable amongst them mutual defense – which they broadly agree are best protected and advanced through common action. The Alliance has two sets of structures through which it addresses these issues.

On the political side, NATO develops coordinated positions in the North Atlantic Council, made up of permanent representatives of all Allies supported by national delegations located at NATO headquarters in Brussels. The Council is chaired by the Secretary General, who is responsible for its agenda and operation but has no vote of his own; he is supported by a civilian international staff. On the military side, in addition to the Military Committee which advises the Council at NATO headquarters in Brussels, NATO has a set of command structures. The Supreme Commander in charge of all Allied operations, known as SACEUR, is head of the principal operational headquarters, Allied Command Operations (ACO), also located in Belgium. Under him is a series of standing military headquarters located in Europe, as well as the NATO headquarters in Kabul. The NATO integrated military structure also includes Allied Command Transformation (ACT), located in the United States. All these structures and commands are staffed largely by military personnel contributed by the Allies.

2.2.1   Roles of Allies and NATO Secretariat

NATO's functions relate to defence and national security, amongst the most sensitive and jealously-guarded aspects of national sovereignty. Two central and related features of NATO derive from this fact:

First, NATO decisions are made by consensus of the 28 Allies: there are no procedures for a vote, and any member state can block action by refusing to join consensus on a proposed way forward. By the same token, even when the Alliance has taken a decision no Ally can without its consent be required to take specific actions to implement it.

Second, the Organization as separate from the Nations – specifically, the Secretary General and Supreme Commanders and their staffs – has virtually no autonomous or devolved authorities. NATO has legal personality but, unlike the UN and most other inter-governmental organisations, has no 'charter' through which the members of the Organization permanently empower the Secretary General and secretariat to take decisions in specific areas in their name or that are binding on them.[12] The Secretary General has a very large political role in proposing actions and policies to be adopted by the Alliance, and the Allies expect him to play that role with energy. Nonetheless, virtually all decisions are taken directly by the member states themselves, through the Alliance's principal decisionmaking body, the North Atlantic Council or through a variety of subordinate committees. The Council is in practice more actively involved in the daily work of the civilian side of the Organization than in that of the military headquarters, but in principle exercises the same control over all aspects of the Organization.

NATO as an Organization should thus be understood as essentially a tool through which the Allies choose to advance their broad national security ends or particular objectives when they consider it desirable and feasible to do so. NATO accordingly has no foreign or security policy of its own, but only policies adopted by the Allies in common and pursued through NATO structures.[13] Similarly, while it has highly developed and effective military command structures, the terms under which those structures can be used in active operations, and the command over them exercised by SACEUR as supreme operational military commander, are separately defined and granted by the Council in the case of each operation, and the forces to be used in those operations are generated by participating Allies and operational partners on a case-by-case basis.

2.3   Changing perspectives on IHL and HRL

Human rights law as a separate body of law barely existed in the formative years of the Alliance, and at that time its scope was both narrower and differently understood than it is today.[14] There was little reason to consider that HRL as it then existed had any direct relevance in situations of armed conflict; in the event of war; whatever protections there might be for

---

12   The legal personality of the Organization is established in Art IV of the 'Agreement on the status of the North Atlantic Treaty Organization, national representatives and international staff' done at Ottawa 20 September 1951, entered into force 18 May 1954 (Ottawa Agreement). Consistent with Art II of the Ottawa Agreement, the two Allied Supreme Headquarters (now ACT and ACO) gained separate legal personality under Art X of the 'Protocol on the Status of International Military Headquarters Set Up Pursuant to the North Atlantic Treaty', done at Paris 28 August 1952, entered into force 10 April 1954 (Paris Protocol).

13   Key current strategies are summarised and addressed in the 2010 Strategic Concept (n 3 above).

14   In 1949, the principal document relating to protection of human rights at the international level was the Universal Declaration of Human Rights, adopted at Paris, 10 December 1948, giving effect to the general principles stated in the UN Charter (Preamble, art 55). Important foundational treaties (eg, the Convention on the Prevention and Punishment of the Crime of Genocide, adopted at New York 9 December 1948, entered into force 12 January 1951; the Convention Relating to the Status of Refugees, adopted at New York 28 July 1951, entered into force 22 April 1954; and the Convention for the Protection of Human Rights and Fundamental Freedoms, done at Rome 4 November 1950, entered into force 3 September 1953, as amended (European Convention on Human Rights)) were concluded in the late 1940s and 1950s, but had little immediate impact on the conduct of armed conflict.

civilians would be found in provisions of IHL aimed at that end that had been developed separately.[15]

The legal framework applicable in NATO's first decades was thus fairly simple: the law with which the Alliance needed to be concerned was the law of armed conflict, including IHL – and questions of its application would in any case arise only in the event of a World War III that happily never broke out. NATO forces trained and exercised extensively together, and common understandings of legal obligations regarding the conduct of combat operations developed over many years of such shared endeavours.[16] Because NATO conducted no combat operations at any point during the four decades of the Cold War, during those years the Alliance had no occasion actually to apply IHL in the first place, much less to consider whether other bodies of law such as HRL might also bear on the conduct of its operations.

2.4   Legal autonomy of participating states

In this context, and of fundamental relevance to the question of how NATO approaches issues of IHL and HRL, it is important to understand that NATO military operations are conducted by the national forces of Allies and other states that may accept an invitation to join in a NATO-led operation. Those forces are voluntarily committed by the troop-contributing Allies and operational partners, and remain under NATO command only so long as those states choose to leave them there. Moreover, as discussed further below, the troop-contributing states retain ultimate and at times substantial daily operational control over their forces even when they are under NATO command.

And this brings us to a key point: the law applicable to NATO operations is essentially the collection of individual legal frameworks of each the 28 Allies and any other states participating with them.

There is of course considerable overlap amongst those 28 legal environments. All Allies are party to key 'universal treaties' at the heart of both IHL and HRL, including the Geneva Conventions and the International Covenant on Civil and Political Rights.[17] There is, moreover, general agreement on certain basic propositions with respect to the applicability of these two bodies of law, including that the standards of HRL are generally applicable to non-armed conflict operations. In addition, while IHL is *lex specialis* applicable to situations of armed conflict,

15   In particular, the 'Fourth Geneva Convention relative to the Protection of Civilian Persons in Time of War', done at Geneva 12 August 1949, entered into force 21 October 1950.
16   See also NA5CRO AJP (n 3 above).
17   International Covenant on Civil and Political Rights, adopted at New York 16 December 1966, entered into force 23 March 1976.

IHL and HRL may in certain circumstances both be applicable to the same operation.

Allies agree as well that other bodies of law may apply in some cases. This is most obviously so in the case of operations built on UN Security Council Resolutions – and virtually all NATO operations have been based on such resolutions – but could also include other special bodies of law such as the law of the sea (in the case of counter-piracy or other maritime operations), or the national law of host countries when operations are being conducted in support of and within the territory of such countries.

But there are also important differences. While 26 Allies are parties to the European Convention on Human Rights (ECHR) and subject to the supranational jurisdiction of the European Court of Human Rights in Strasbourg established under that Convention,[18] the two North American allies – who have historically been amongst those most likely to participate in NATO military operations – are not, and in fact may have national legal positions that are at odds with those applicable to the European Allies. And every Ally has its own domestic law and national legal doctrines that may lead to significantly different results in different states.[19]

Unsurprisingly given this general context, NATO addresses legal questions, including issues of the relationship of IHL and HRL pragmatically rather than doctrinally. Once Allies agree in principle to undertake a military operation, NATO planners develop an Operations Plan (OPLAN) and associated Rules of Engagement (ROE) that will permit the operation to succeed and which all agree are lawful. If they have agreed on the OPLAN and ROE, whether or not Allies or other participating states agree on the exact legal justification or explanation underlying them is in principle of little interest to NATO as an organisation. Thus, rather than requiring adherence to a single common body of law, the Alliance's expectation is that all states participating in a NATO or NATO-led operation will act lawfully within the legal framework applicable to them.[20]

18　(n 14 above) http://www.conventions.coe.int/Treaty/Commun/ChercheSig.asp?NT=005&CM=8&DF=01/08/2013&CL=ENG (accessed 20 October 2014).

19　In the legal systems of some Allies, including the United Kingdom and United States, unless otherwise specifically provided treaties are given domestic legal effect through implementing legislation rather than directly.

20　The variety of legal approaches that may be relied on is reflected in the Security Council debate on Operation Allied Protector in Kosovo, UN Doc S/PV.3988 (24 March 1999), and in Belgium's presentation before the International Court of Justice in *Yugoslavia v Belgium* (Legality of use of force) (10 May 1999): http://www.icj-cij.org/docket/files/105/4515.pdf (accessed 20 October 2014).

3 NATO approach to application and interaction of IHL and HRL

Allies' basic views of the applicable law and its content are thus generally consistent so there are few fundamental conceptual clashes. Equally importantly, however, the NATO culture – going back to its beginnings – has long been oriented toward practical solutions. Doctrinal differences are unlikely to be a matter of serious discussion in deciding whether to undertake an operation. A principal reason is that the consensus rule allows any Ally to block any decision for whatever reason it considers sufficient, and an operation will therefore not even be proposed for NATO action if it is known that a consensus to pursue it will not be possible. The 28 Allies interact intensively and continuously, and are thoroughly familiar with each other's political and legal positions. If the basis for a consensus is not available, that political fact is accepted and those favouring action may consider other options; if it does, then – as in the case of Kosovo[21] – differences of opinion over the legal basis will not preclude a mandate for and conduct of the operation in question. The fact that most NATO operations potentially involving use of force have been built on the foundation of a UN Security Council Resolution authorising the taking of 'all necessary measures' normally makes the question of international lawfulness a relatively easy one to resolve.[22]

With respect to any particular operation or proposed operation, the question of applicable law will be addressed pragmatically, in the specifics of the OPLAN and the ROE. What the planners prepare and SACEUR, through the Military Committee, presents for Council approval takes national positions into account., but in practical terms – proposing specific rules and approaches for particular anticipated circumstances – rather than by offering conceptual views on the applicability of one or another legal doctrine or body of law.

Any such differences are in any event likely to be relatively minor, and susceptible to being addressed at the level of implementation. Moreover, no Ally is required to participate in any NATO operation, thus in many cases domestic political or legal issues need not prevent joining consensus to approve an operation that will be carried out by others. In the case of Libya, for example, Germany was able to join consensus on the mandate for Operation Unified Protector despite having abstained on Security Council Resolution 1973 of 11 March 2011, the basis for the NATO operation, and being unprepared to participate in the operation itself.

---

21   As above.
22   See, eg, UNSCRs cited in n 2 above.

Participating states are also able to limit their participation in other ways that may resolve, for them individually, any questions relating to their specific legal obligations. They may choose to participate in only parts of an operation. Or they may choose to participate with 'caveats' reflecting national legal or political concerns. At the limit, participating states can play a 'red card' and decline to carry out particular missions about which they may for one or another reason have reservations.

NATO's approach to differences in legal and political views thus involves applying a highly flexible and accommodating methodology to designing and conducting its operations. This method can obviously be frustrating but permits the Alliance to function effectively even when there are differences in perspective amongst the participating states.

4   Three illustrative NATO operations

Specific operations provide the context in which NATO's approach to balancing IHL and HRL is manifested. NATO's military operations involve a broad spectrum of potential activities, including armed conflict, law enforcement, counter-piracy, humanitarian and disaster relief – and any given operation may well include a mix of such activities.

The following discussion briefly discusses two operations illustrating the fundamentally pragmatic approach that NATO follows in applying differing bodies of law to its operations, then examines in some detail aspects of a third operation where NATO was called on to address more directly the question of the relationship between IHL and HRL.

4.1   Operation Ocean Shield

Operation Ocean Shield is NATO's counter-piracy operation off the coast of Somalia. The key point of reference for NATO in identifying the applicable legal framework has been Security Council Resolutions, and in particular Security Council Resolution 1851 (2008).[23]

The Somalia resolutions present a complex legal picture: They identify the law of the sea, and in particular the UN Convention on the Law of the Sea (UNCLOS)[24] as setting the legal framework for counter-piracy operations. UNSCR 1851, in particular, authorises the taking of 'all necessary measures that are appropriate in Somalia' to counter piracy, thus contemplating and allowing use of force; permits the taking of counter-

---

23   See, eg, UNSCRs 1816 (2008), 1838 (7 October 2008), 1846 (2008), 1851 (2008) and 1897 (2009).
24   United Nations Convention on the Law of the Sea, done at Montego Bay 10 December 1992, entered into force 16 November 1994. Preambular para 14 of UNSCR 1851 (2008).

piracy action on land in Somalia – although the law of the sea is not applicable on land – and indicate that such actions must be consistent with 'applicable international humanitarian and human rights law.'[25]

Unpacking these complex provisions is not easy. In particular, the references to IHL and the authorisation of 'all necessary measures', and the contemplation of such measures in areas to which the UNCLOS framework is clearly inapplicable, are puzzling. Happily, however, for NATO's purposes it has not been necessary to untangle these knots – at least to date. The reason is that Ocean Shield is framed in essentially law enforcement terms – in essence a legal lowest common denominator on which all Allies can agree.[26] From the beginning, the operation was built on the assumption that captured pirates would be tried as criminals in courts applying national law.

The prudence of this approach has been confirmed by decisions of the European Court of Human Rights and national courts applying its jurisprudence that have treated the terms of the ECHR, notably including its procedural requirements, to the counter-piracy operation – and in so doing effectively determining that the core law applicable to the participation of 26 Allies is HRL.[27] These decisions are in practice treated as binding by parties to the Convention; while having no such status for Canada and the United States, the ECHR's decisions are thus an inescapable factor in the context of a NATO operation. Because many Allies are reluctant to pursue national prosecutions in Europe, the operational consequence is that many participants in Ocean Shield follow a so-called 'catch and release' approach in which pirates are captured and briefly detained, but in the end released rather than being prosecuted.[28]

4.2   Operation Active Endeavor

It is instructive in this context also to consider another and less well known NATO maritime operation, Operation Active Endeavor (OAE). OAE was adopted in the aftermath of 9/11 as a counter-terrorism mission. It is the

---

25   UNSCR 1851(2008), operative para 6.
26   NATO OPLANs and ROE, including those governing Operation Ocean Shield, are classified.
27   *Medvedyev v France*, Application No 3394/03 (29 March 2010), discussed in, eg, Douglas Guilfoyle 'ECHR Rights at Sea: *Medvedyev and others v France*' (19 April 2010):http://www.ejiltalk.org/echr-rights-at-sea-medvedyev-and-others-v-france/ (accessed 20 October 2014). See also, 'Judgment case Somali pirates' *de Rechtspraak* 17 June 2010 http://www.rechtspraak.nl/Organisatie/Rechtbanken/Rotterdam/ Nieuws/Pages/Judgemen-tcase-Somali-pirates.aspx (accessed 20 October 2014), applying ECHR art 5 in the case of a pirate apprehended off Somalia.
28   Suspected pirates could in principle be transferred to a regional state with which is party to an applicable prisoner transfer agreement, but NATO is not yet a party to any such agreement.

only NATO operation ever authorised under article 5, the mutual self-defence article at the heart of the North Atlantic Treaty.[29] While it might seem evident that a self-defence operation necessarily implies an armed conflict paradigm – and with it the application of IHL – in fact the operation has from the beginning been implemented essentially as a law enforcement mission, with search and boarding rules and practices consistent with those applicable in any maritime law enforcement action.[30] This approach is consistent with the fact that the Mediterranean Sea, the principal area in which OAE is conducted, is not a combat zone, and that more extreme use of force is not necessary to conduct search activities in that environment.

These two examples reflect the pragmatism with which NATO designs and carries out its operations. The missions can be carried out effectively without reference to IHL, and thus there is no requirement to consider applying that body of law despite the existence of plausible arguments for doing so.

4.3   Operation Unified Protector

A third case, the NATO operation in Libya, Operation Unified Protector (OUP), was mandated by Allies to implement Security Council Resolution 1973, which authorised UN member states to take a range of actions to address the repression of protests by the Qaddafi regime.[31]

OUP had three elements. The first was a maritime arms embargo to be conducted on the high seas. The Security Council Resolution built on the earlier Resolution 1970, which barred the transfer of arms to Libya, but

29   The core of art 5 – and arguably of the Alliance itself – is the Parties' agreement that 'an armed attack against one or more of them in Europe or North America shall be considered an attack against them all'.
30   NATO 'Operation Active Endeavour': http://www.nato.int/cps/en/natolive/topics_7932.htm (accessed 20 October 2014).
31   UNSCR 1973 (2011). Operative para 4 of UNSCR 1973: 'Authorizes Member States ... acting nationally or through regional organizations or arrangements ... to take all necessary measures ... to protect civilians and civilian populated areas under threat of attack in [Libya].' In operative para 6, the Security Council '[d]ecides to establish a ban on all flights in the airspace of [Libya] in order to help protect civilians' and in operative para 8 '[a]uthorizes Member States ... acting nationally or through regional organizations or arrangements, to take all necessary measures to enforce compliance' with this no-fly zone; operative para 7 excludes certain categories of flights, including those 'whose sole purpose is humanitarian'. Operative para 13, finally, '[c]alls upon all Member States, acting regionally or through regional organizations or arrangements ... to inspect ... on the high seas, vessels and aircraft bound to or from [Libya]' on the basis of information providing reasonable grounds for belief that the arms embargo established in UNSCR 1970 (2011) was being violated, and 'authorizes Member States to use all measures commensurate to the specific circumstances to carry out such inspections'.

only through actions taken within national jurisdiction.[32] Resolution 1973 permitted more robust action, but cautiously – allowing inspections only if there were reasonable grounds to suspect the presence of embargoed goods,[33] and authorising (in an odd phrase) enforcement by the taking of 'all measures commensurate with the situation'.[34] While it was possible that implementation of the embargo could involve armed conflict, this element of the resolution clearly did not anticipate such a development. And in fact, NATO implemented this aspect of OUP essentially as a law enforcement action, rather than as armed conflict, and thus under HRL rather than IHL.

The second element of OUP, the no-fly zone preventing flights over Libyan territory other than those for humanitarian assistance purposes or as authorised by states enforcing the no-fly zone, was a somewhat closer call. The stated purpose of the no-fly zone was to protect civilians from aerial attack and to this end the resolution authorised the taking of 'all necessary measures', a phrase conventionally implying use of military force.[35] This was appropriate, as it was unknown how the regime would respond to what was a far more intrusive and aggressive action than the maritime embargo. In principle, this element of the operation was at the margin of armed conflict, and could have gone either way depending on the reaction of the regime. Since there was in fact no significant challenge to the no-fly zone, no question arose in practice as to the legal standard that would have been applicable in the event an aircraft had been shot down and lives lost.

The third and by far most important element of the operation was the mission to protect civilians and civilian-populated areas from land attack.[36] It may have been hoped that Colonel Qaddafi would respond to so robust a mandate by immediately standing down his military attacks on Benghazi and other civilian areas, but the general situation in Libya was already one arguably constituting a non-international armed conflict.[37] The wording of this element left no doubt implementation of this mission,

---

32   UNSCR 1970 (2011). Operative para 11 of UNSCR 1970 (before its amendment by operative para 13 of UNSCR 1973 (2011)) called on all states to inspect 'consistent with international law, all cargo to and from [Libya], in their territory, including seaports and airports' to enforce an arms embargo on Libya. It did not authorise use of force.

33   '[I]f the State concerned has information that provides reasonable grounds to believe that the cargo contains items the supply, sale, transfer or expeort of which is prohibited by ... resolution 1970 (2011) ...' Operative para 13, UNSCR 1973 (2011).

34   '[A]uthorizes Member States to use all measures commensurate to the specific circumstances to carry out such inspections.' Operative para 13, UNSCR 1973 (2011).

35   n 31 above.

36   As above.

37   Human Rights Council 'Report of the International Commission of Inquiry to investigate all alleged violations of international human rights law in the Libyan Arab Jamahiriya' A/HRC/17/44, Human Rights Council 17th session (12 January 2012) (First ICIL Report), Chap II, Sec D, and in particular para 55, which provides: 'While the Commission lacks full information concerning several aspects of the opposition

if necessary, would entail the use of military force against the regime's armed forces – and that the authorisation to take 'all necessary means' contemplated the application of military force.

In this context, it was evident that the relevant legal construct was IHL, and the NATO OPLAN and ROE for the protect-civilians element of OUP were drafted on that basis. Amongst the fundamental elements of IHL are the principles of necessity and proportionality, both aimed in significant part at minimising harm to civilians. In addition, the express purpose of Resolution 1973 and of the Council's mandate in OUP[38] was to protect civilians, further underscoring the importance of avoiding civilian casualties to the extent possible. In fact, immense care was taken to avoid harm to civilians both in the weapons used – virtually every weapon used was a precision-guided one – and in the 'zero civilian casualties' standard adopted by the targeters.[39] In the event, in over 7000 strikes there were credible reports of no more than 70 civilian deaths – a literally unprecedented performance for a major military operation.[40]

4.3.1 International Commission of Inquiry on Libya

Nonetheless, questions were raised after the operation regarding those deaths and the way NATO had dealt with them. In particular, the International Commission of Inquiry on Libya (ICIL or Commission) established by the Human Rights Council in March 2011 to investigate violations of HRL by the regime[41] posed a series of questions to NATO (including the Allies and any other participating states) relating to

forces organization, it has reached the preliminary view that by or around 24 February, a sufficient non-international armed conflict had developed to trigger the application of Protocol II and common article 3 of the Geneva conventions.' (Footnote omitted.)

38   Operative para 1 of UNSCR 1973 '[d]emanded ... a complete end to violence and all attacks against, and abuses of, civilians'. NATO Press Release 'NATO Secretary General's statement on Libya no-fly zone' (24 March 2011): http://www.nato.int/cps/en/natolive/news_71763.htm?mode=pressrelease (accessed 20 October 2014), Secretary General Rasmussen stated: 'We are taking action as part of the broad international effort to protect civilians against the attacks by the Gaddafi regime'.

39   Letters from NATO Legal Adviser to Judge Philippe Kirsch, Chair, International Commission of Inquiry on Libya (ICIL), 23 January 2012 (First NATO Letter) and 15 February 2012 (Second NATO Letter), reproduced as Human Rights Council 'Annex II to Report of the International Commission of Inquiry on Libya, Advance Unedited Version' A/HRC/19/68, Human Rights Council 19th session (2 March 2012) (Second ICIL Report) 3, 5 (unnumbered pp 204 and 206 of Second ICIL Report) and 2 (unnumbered p 211 of Second ICIL Report). See also Second ICIL Report, 18, para 89; 197, para 812.

40   First NATO Letter 4-5 (pp 205-206 of Second ICIL Report). Human Rights Watch alleges deaths of 'at least 72 civilians' in the campaign. Human Rights Watch 'Unacknowledged deaths: Civilian casualties in NATO's air campaign in Libya' (May 2012) (Human Rights Watch Report) 4. Human Rights Watch reported Libyan claims of 1108 civilian deaths. Ibid, 21.

41   HRC Resolution S-15/1 (25 February 2011). Para 11 of that Resolution directed the Commission 'to investigate all alleged violations of international human rights law in [Libya], establish the facts and circumstances of such violations and of the crimes perpetrated and, where possible, to identify those responsible, to make recommendations, in particular, on accountability measures, all with a view to

allegations of deaths of civilians, including allegations of deliberate targeting of civilians. The Commission's communications to NATO, and later its formal recommendations, urged NATO to conduct investigations into any such deaths.[42]

Mandate of the Commission

NATO had serious doubts that the mandate of the Commission to investigate violations of HRL by Libyan factions could legitimately be extended to include inquiries into the legality of NATO's use of force in implementation of a Security Council resolution. The Human Rights Council mandate was motivated by '*deep concern* at the deaths of hundreds of civilians and rejecting unequivocally the incitement to hostility and violence against the civilian population made from the highest level of the Libyan Government', concluded that the Libyan regime had engaged in 'gross and systematic abuses of human rights' and referred exclusively to repressive actions against civilians in Libya.[43] While the Commission stated that this extension of its mandate was required in order to fully investigate the actions of the Qaddafi regime, it offered no substantive reason for considering a need to further extend that inquiry to include actions by NATO.[44]

ensuring that those individuals responsible are held accountable'. The Commission subsequently interpreted its mandate to include also investigation into possible violations of international humanitarian and international criminal law, and as applying to the non-international armed conflict that developed shortly after adoption of Resolution S-15/1 as well as to the actions of NATO and states participating in Operation Unified Protector which it characterised as an international armed conflict. First ICIL Report, 14 para 4.

42 'The Commission calls upon NATO to: (a) Conduct investigations in Libya to determine the level of civilian casualties ...' Second ICIL Report, 24 para 130.

43 HRC Resolution S-15/1 (25 February 2011), 4th preambular para and operative paras 1-3, 5-7 and 11. '[NATO] retain[s] concerns about some aspects of the Commission's application of its mandate from the Human Rights Council (HRC), which was given in the specific context of gross repression and manifest human rights violations committed by and against Libyans in the context of political protests in that country ... We are not ... persuaded that examination of conduct of the parties to the Libyan internal conflict implies expansion of the Commission's work to include "investigation" of NATO's actions giving effect to the mandate contained in UN Security Council Resolution 1973.' Second NATO Letter, 1 (201, Second ICIL Report).

44 'When an armed conflict developed at the end of February, and with it the commission of violations of international humanitarian law on the part of the Gadhafi regime, the Commission determined it would be artificial to ignore such extensive new violations, and indeed that it was its responsibility to cover all violations perpetrated'. Letter from Judge Philippe Kirsch, Chair, ICIL, to NATO Legal Adviser, 20 December 2011. The Commission's chair asserted that it was 'imperative for the Commission to investigate allegations of violations of international humanitarian law against the Gadhafi forces, and that therefore it had to apply a similar treatment to all such allegations'. Letter from Judge Philippe Kirsch, Chair, ICIL, to NATO Legal Adviser, 3 February 2012 (unpublished; in NATO archives). The First ICIL Report, issued 12 January 2012, cast serious doubt on the veracity of Libyan regime allegations of NATO IHL violations: 'Despite the reports received, while in Tripoli, the authorities did not show to the Commission any evidence of civilian areas targeted by NATO forces ... The Commission also notes that the Libyan Government did not provide the details of or

The Commission's conclusion was thus an extremely broad interpretation of the original mandate, and one which implicitly equated the character – including the legality – of actions of UN member states in enforcing a Security Council-authorised enforcement action with those of the Libyan regime against which that enforcement was directed. It had, moreover, been created by a UN body, and it could be expected that its report would be considered in the context of Resolution 1970's reference of the situation in Libya to the International Criminal Court (ICC).[45]

NATO's response to the Commission

It was important, in NATO's view, to underscore that the applicable body of law in this case was IHL, including in particular with respect to the legal implications of deaths or injury to civilians in the context of a military campaign, as well as to counter any implication that NATO's lawful actions could be equated morally to the regime's violations of HRL and IHL.[46] NATO thus considered it important to respond to the Commission's inquiries, and that it was preferable if possible that the response be made collectively by NATO rather than by individual Allies or participating states.

NATO therefore felt called upon to clarify its position with respect to the application in this case of IHL and HRL, and their proper interaction. In designing and conducting OUP, NATO planners, targeters and commanders complied fully with all requirements of IHL, and more; it was in NATO's view not humanly possible to have conducted an effective military operation with any greater care to avoid civilian casualties or greater success in avoiding them.[47] IHL accepts, however, the reality that civilian casualties occur in armed conflict,[48] and that such casualties are not inherently suspect or presumptively unlawful. In this regard it differs from HRL, which recognises a right to life, and with it increasingly an obligation to individually investigate and justify each case in which life is

---

show concrete evidence of alleged incidents, such as civilian objects which had been destroyed (eg schools)', and stated in that context that it had 'not ... seen evidence to suggest that civilians or civilian objects had been intentionally targeted by NATO forces, nor that it has engaged in indiscriminate attacks'... First ICIL Report, paras 233 and 235.

45 UNSCR 1970 (2011), operative para 4. See also First ICIL Report, 14 para 4.
46 'We would be concerned ... if "NATO incidents" were included in the Commission's report as on a par with those which the Commission may ultimately conclude did violate law or constitute crimes.' Second NATO Letter, 2 (211, Second ICIL Report).
47 First NATO Letter, 4 (unnumbered 203 of Second ICIL Report).
48 See, eg, Second ICIL Report, 163 para 615: '[I]ncidental injury to civilians – so-called "collateral damage" – ... does not in itself render an attack unlawful according to the laws of war; rather the damage is to be weighed in proportion to the significance of the military advantage that would be achieved in a successful attack.'.

lost as a result of state action.[49] This thus presented a case in which the standards of IHL and HRL regarding what was legally permissible and what unlawful differed fundamentally, and in a manner requiring a clear determination as to which body of law governed.

For purposes of ensuring the future ability to conduct military operations of NATO, its members, or any other state which takes its IHL obligations seriously, it was thus important to establish both the level of protection afforded to civilians by strict compliance with the letter and spirit of IHL requirements, and that in a situation of armed conflict there is no obligation to investigate or justify civilian casualties that may unfortunately occur despite such efforts. In this case, moreover, any suggestion that the fact of civilian deaths during OUP, however few they might have been, was legally questionable was fundamentally at odds with the fact that the Security Council had authorised the use of force precisely to authorise the military operations that NATO carried out.

As a result, the Alliance took a firm and unusually clear position in its response to the Commission's questions. Its position was in essence that the relevant standard for addressing questions relating to civilian deaths was that of IHL, and that the requirements of IHL had been fully complied with in the conduct of each strike, including all those that had been reported as resulting in civilian casualties.[50] Although no specific or credible allegations of illegality had been made, NATO military and civilian personnel closely reviewed each of those strikes, including the basis for and specific content of targeting decisions and all information available to NATO regarding the results of each.[51] Based on that review, NATO advised the Commission that every feasible effort had been made to avoid civilian casualties.[52] In NATO's view, absent any credible allegation of grave breaches of IHL, no further investigation was required.

---

49   The European Court of Human Rights, for example, has consistently ruled that the right to life enshrined in art 2 of the Convention implies an obligation to conduct an effective official investigation in cases in which a life had been taken by state agents. See, eg, *Al-Skeini and Others v the United Kingdom* Application no 55721/07 (7 July 2011).

50   'We agree with the Commission that international humanitarian law is the *lex specialis* applicable to armed conflict ... NATO believes that its attentiveness during the course of OUP to a rigorous implementation of the rules of that body of law – and indeed to a standard exceeding what was required under international humanitarian law – contributed significantly to an extraordinarily low incidence of harm to civilians and civilian property.' First NATO Letter, 2 (unnumbered 202, Second ICIL Report).

51   First NATO Letter, 5-8 (unnumbered 208-210, Second ICIL Report), Second NATO Letter, 3-5 (unnumbered 214-215, Second ICIL Report).

52   'Not one of the targets struck ... was approved for attack, or in fact attacked, if either those designating and approving the target or the pilot executing it had any evidence or other reason to believe that civilians would be injured or killed by a strike ... [T]he targeting and strike methods employed in OUP were as well-designed and as successfully implemented to avoid civilian casualties as was humanly and technically possible.' First NATO Letter, 3-4 (unnumbered 202 and 203, Second ICIL Report).

In its final report, the Commission did not assert that NATO had violated either HRL or IHL,[53] nor did Human Rights Watch and Amnesty International in their separate reports.[54] Based on the ICIL's report, the ICC found no evidence or information indicating violations by NATO of crimes falling within its mandate.[55] From this it appears that both the Commission and, by implication, the ICC's Office of the Prosecutor essentially accepted the position asserted by NATO – that compliance with the requirements of IHL, as the *lex specialis* applicable to armed conflict, is legally sufficient with respect to any asserted contrary obligation under HRL associated with 'right to life' obligations.

5   Conclusion

The Alliance was founded on respect for rule of law, and respect for applicable law has been a hallmark of its training and operations. Amongst the Allies are states that have long been world leaders in developing and applying human rights law; many of the same states have long led in developing and applying IHL as well. It is important to both groups, and indeed, to the Alliance and its members as a whole, that NATO operations be carried out in a manner fully respecting and consistent with both bodies of law. NATO has long seen itself as setting the standard for the effective and lawful conduct of military operations, and is aware of the importance for its own credibility and the perceived legitimacy of its actions of meeting a high standard in complying with international legal rules.

However similar their basic legal obligations and perspectives may be, the Allies are sovereign and do not view all legal questions identically. NATO is an alliance, not an institution – and it has no mandate or ability to enforce a common view. There is thus no systematic 'NATO doctrine' on the relationship between IHL and HRL.

As an alliance of sovereigns, NATO approaches issues relating to the legal framework for its military operations in a pragmatic manner. An operation will not even be proposed if it is known that it cannot command consensus. The primary point of reference for deciding what kind of actions are legally available and appropriate within an operation will be the underlying UN Security Council Resolution, where there is one. ROE and other governing documents will be drafted with a focus on operational

---

53   See Second ICIL Report, 197 para 812; see also 170 paras 649-655.
54   Human Rights Watch Report (n 40 above); Amnesty International 'Libya: The forgotten victims of NATO strikes' (19 March 2012) Conclusion: http://www. amnesty.org/en/library/info/MDE19/003/2012 (accessed 20 October 2014).
55   ICC: The Office of the Prosecutor 'Third Report of the Prosecutor of the International Criminal Court to the UN Security Council Pursuant to UNSCR 1970 (2011)' (16 May 2012) paras 51, 55-57. Although it did not identify any credible allegations of violations of applicable law, the Office of the Prosecutor noted the responsibility of individual states to determine whether their own forces had engaged in criminal activities in the event of such allegations, para 58.

effectiveness and ensuring a high legal 'comfort level' on the part of all participating states rather than on any *a priori* view of the law.

One consequence of this approach is a considerably more cautious approach to the law than might be the case in certain national operations. Another is that there is more than a little 'blurriness' when it comes to articulating a 'NATO view' on legal issues.

There are, however, exceptions to this blurriness – notably in the position NATO has taken with respect to the applicability of certain elements of HRL to the Libyan air campaign. In that case, Allies were concerned to draw a firm line defending the primacy of IHL and to do so on terms articulated by the Alliance rather than leaving unanswered the suggestion that NATO's actions had been of questionable legality or worse.

The decision to take a firm Alliance position was driven in part by awareness of the potential consequences of silence. Although arriving at common positions on doctrine will never be easy for NATO, it may be that NATO will have to face this question increasingly in future, with the development of such phenomena as international commissions of inquiry and the ICC and the growing activism of NGOs. Allies may or may not wish to respond collectively on future occasions – but if they choose not to, they will need to find another way to ensure that NATO's silence in such a case is not taken as implicitly conceding a proposition damaging to its views and interests.

11

NGOs, International Law and Civilian Protection

*James Ross**

1 Introduction

It has been said that where you stand depends on where you sit.[1] That has often been the case for academics, military lawyers and human rights activists who are addressing wartime legal issues that may – or may not – invoke international human rights law. It might be surmised that state-centric observers, government policymakers and military officers are content to view the battlefield solely in terms of international humanitarian law (IHL), the laws of war, while the human rights activists wish to replace IHL and its acceptance of bloodletting with international human rights law.

The reality is not so simple. The influence of human rights law on IHL has long been recognised. Common article 3 to the Geneva Conventions of 1949[2] speaks of trials 'by a regularly constituted court affording all the judicial guarantees which are recognised as indispensable by civilized peoples', a phrase recognised to mean consistent with international human rights standards.[3] More explicitly the First Additional Protocol of 1977 to the 1949 Geneva Conventions (Protocol I),[4] in its article 75 on the treatment of persons in custody, draws directly from the International Covenant on Civil and Political Rights (ICCPR).[5] And whereas human

* Legal and Policy Director, Human Rights Watch. A special thanks to Maria Carolina Aissa de Figueredo, Legal and Policy Coordinator, Human Rights Watch, for her research assistance.
1 See, eg, GT Allison (ed) *Essence of decision: Explaining the Cuban missile crisis* (1971) 176.
2 See article 3 common to the four Geneva Conventions of 1949 (common article 3).
3 Common article 3(1)(d). See, eg, HJ Steiner et al *International human rights in context: Law, politics, morals* (2008) 432.
4 Protocol Additional to the Geneva Conventions of 12 August 1949, and Relating to the Protection of Victims of International Armed Conflicts (Protocol I), adopted 8 June 1977, 1125 UNTS 3, entered into force 7 December 1978, art 75.
5 International Covenant on Civil and Political Rights (ICCPR), adopted 16 December 1966, GA Res 2200A (XXI), 21 UN GAOR Supp (no 16) 49, UN Doc A/6316 (1966), 993 UNTS 3, entered into force 3 January 1976.

rights organisations traditionally considered IHL to be outside of their mandate – or even conflicting with a pro-peace policy – today many domestic and international human rights organisations have added IHL to their advocacy repertoire.

Still, it is evident that many governments involved in military operations consider human rights law to be an encroachment on their ability to act in wartime situations. This seems to be true both for major powers involved in military actions abroad and embattled governments in the midst of civil war. The United States government, especially since the attacks of 11 September 2001, has re-emphasised both the primacy of IHL to the exclusion of human rights law in its military operations abroad, but has also pressed to deny the extraterritorial reach of human rights law.[6] In its December 2011 submission to the United Nations Human Rights Committee,[7] the US did not repeat the strong anti-extraterritoriality language of past administrations, but nonetheless did not reverse the prevailing policy, which has become increasingly untenable.[8] And governments involved in civil wars continue to hold captured enemy fighters without legal process, refusing to apply even the more flexible human rights standards available to states under a state of emergency.[9]

This paper will explore the ways in which human rights organisations have sought to obtain better protections for civilians and captured fighters and populations at risk during armed conflict. The argument is not that human rights law can or should replace IHL. Rather, it is that the overlap between the two bodies of law can provide better protection to those at risk without threatening the role of IHL in wartime situations. Where most effective, human rights organisations have pressed for certain understandings of human rights law in armed conflict situations, but in a manner that does not undermine the protections offered by IHL itself. Trying to do otherwise would not get the attention of most militaries – and would ignore existing IHL protections.

6   See, eg, *Coard et al* case, IACHR (29 September 1999) case 10.951, report no 109/99; JB Bellinger III & WJ Haynes II 'A US government response to the International Committee of the Red Cross study *Customary International Humanitarian Law*' (2007) 46 *International Legal Materials* 514; LA Steven 'Genocide and the duty to extradite or prosecute: Why the United States is in breach of its international obligations' (1999) 39 *Virginia Journal of International Law* 425 450-461; Restatement (Third) of the Foreign Relations Law of the United States (1987) sec 702.

7   US Department of State 'Fourth periodic report of the United States of America to the United Nations Committee on Human Rights concerning the International Covenant on Civil and Political Rights' (30 December 2011).

8   See, eg, ICJ *Legal consequences of the construction of a wall in the occupied Palestinian territory* (9 July 2004).

9   See, eg, Human Rights Watch ' "Just don't call it a militia": Impunity, militias, and the "Afghan local police"' (2012) http://www.hrw.org/reports/2011/09/12/just-don-t-call-it-militia-0 (accessed 1 March 2013); Amnesty International 'Locked away: Sri Lanka's security detainees' (2012) http://files.amnesty.org/archives/asa3700320 12eng.pdf (accessed 1 March 2013).

2   Role of human rights organisations in promoting IHL

The expansion of domestic and international nongovernmental human rights organisations in the 60 years since the Universal Declaration of Human Rights was adopted in 1948 has not been matched by a similar explosion of nongovernmental organisations dedicated to promoting compliance with international humanitarian law. Perhaps this is because IHL long had its authorised champion, the Geneva-based International Committee of the Red Cross.[10] Nonetheless, organisations have been established to address specific IHL issues, such as the International Campaign to Ban Landmines,[11] which played a leading role in pressing for the adoption of the Land Mine Convention,[12] and Geneva Call,[13] to encourage IHL compliance by non-state armed groups. Many of the groups that get involved in this area are coalitions of organisations traditionally devoted to human rights law. The creation of the ad hoc international tribunals and the International Criminal Court has also resulted in organisations designed to apply international criminal law, looking at war crimes, crimes against humanity and genocide, such as the International Center for Transitional Justice.[14]

A parallel development has been that more traditional human rights organisations established to monitor and promote respect for human rights have also taken up investigating violations of IHL. While this process dates back to the early 1980s, it was neither preordained nor inevitable. Human rights organisations such as Amnesty International, organised in 1961, were intended from the start to ensure that governments met their international obligations under human rights law. Armed conflict was outside the self-defined mandate. It was a technical legal area inhabited by military lawyers and a small coterie of law professors that did not lend itself to the mass letter-writing campaigns and Soviet Bloc focus that was the bread and butter of international human rights work in those early years.[15]

In the early 1980s America's Watch – one of the 'Watch Committees' that became Human Rights Watch in 1988 – became the first international

---

10 Common article 3(2) states that 'an impartial humanitarian body, such as the International Committee of the Red Cross, may offer its services to the Parties to the conflict'.
11 International Campaign to Ban Landmines http://www.icbl.org/intro.php (accessed 1 March 2013).
12 Convention on the Prohibition of the Use, Stockpiling, Production, and Transfer of Anti-Personnel Mines and on their Destruction (Mine Ban Treaty), opened for signature 3 December 1997, 2056 UNTS 211, entered into force 1 March 1999.
13 Geneva Call http://www.genevacall.org/ (accessed 1 March 2013).
14 International Center for Transitional Justice http://ictj.org/ (accessed 1 March 2013).
15 There was also hostility from within the human rights community to taking on IHL issues when the subject was broached by Human Rights Watch in the early 1980s.

human rights organisation to routinely address IHL violations. This was more out of practical necessity than any strategic refocus. While its colleague entity Helsinki Watch was using information gathered largely from dissidents to report on torture and violations of free expression rights in the Soviet Union and its satellites, Americas Watch faced massacres of civilians by all sides in Latin America's 'dirty wars'.

A traditional human rights approach – reporting only on violations by the government – would have been hopelessly ineffectual in embattled places such as El Salvador. The United States government, which was strongly backing the Salvadoran leadership, was adept at discrediting organisations that pointed blame only at the government security forces, even when such forces were responsible for most atrocities. Aryeh Neier, then director of Americas Watch, recognised the necessity of reporting on and condemning abuses by government soldiers and rebels alike, wherever the chips fell. While only states are formally bound by human rights law, IHL was binding on all parties to a conflict, including rebel groups.[16] The Watch Committees began reporting on killings and torture by all sides to the conflicts in El Salvador and Nicaragua and later the Philippines and elsewhere.[17] This approach proved very powerful, making it much harder for the government and its foreign backers to discredit the information as being biased in support of the rebels.

Other human rights organisations, particularly at the local level, did not necessarily appreciate this new balance in reporting. In countries engaged in civil wars, some domestic rights groups tacitly supported or were at least sympathetic to rebel forces, even if very abusive. They preferred an advocacy strategy that allowed them to criticise the government but not have to worry about rebel atrocities. Under the model pioneered by Human Rights Watch, but particularly after its adoption by Amnesty International, the unwillingness of local rights groups to report on rebel abuses threatened to expose any lack of neutrality.

Over the years, however, more and more organisations have added investigation of, and reporting on, IHL violations into the mix of their human rights work. While some groups have not given this topic the attention it requires – both the nature of the research and the legal analysis can be complex – some organisations, such as Palestinian and Israeli nongovernmental organisations that have covered the armed conflicts in

---

16   Common article 3 states: 'In the case of armed conflict not of an international character occurring in the territory of one of the High Contracting Parties, each Party to the conflict shall be bound to apply, as a minimum, the following provisions'.
17   See, eg, Americas Watch (now Human Rights Watch) 'As bad as ever: A report on human rights in El Salvador' (1984); Americas Watch 'Violations of the laws of war by both sides in Nicaragua, 1981-1985' (1985); Americas Watch 'With friends like these: The Americas Watch Report on human rights and US policy in Latin America' (1985); Human Rights Watch 'Bad blood: Militia abuses in Mindanao, the Philippines' (1992).

the Occupied Palestinian Territories, have shown themselves to be capable at fact-gathering and IHL analysis.[18]

In addition, the various modes of advocacy with governments and inter-governmental institutions that have emerged in the human rights field have also touched on IHL. In recent years, this has spawned new kinds of efforts by organisations that engaged in traditional 'naming and shaming' human rights advocacy, such as Human Rights First, and more recent entrants, such as the Human Rights Program at Harvard Law School, to use these techniques to promote adherence to IHL.[19] As will be seen, all of these factors have focused greater attention to the overlap of – and gaps between – international human rights law and IHL.

3   Avenues of advocacy

Domestic and international human rights organisations have become more sophisticated at advocacy methods in the 50 years since Amnesty International founder Peter Berenson urged concerned individuals to write to the Greek junta to release detained student activists.[20] Of course they needed to: during those years, abusive governments around the world, as well as some public-relations savvy rebel groups, have likewise become more sophisticated in deflecting allegations of abuse.[21]

These new advocacy methods include targeting influential media and third governments using in-depth reports, timely news releases, public and private letters, opinion pieces in local and international newspapers and magazines, and multimedia. Combined with technological advances such as the Internet, World Wide Web and, most recently, social media like Facebook and Twitter, such methods have been crucial in helping to

---

18   See, eg, Al-Haq 'Four years since the beginning of the Intifada: Systematic violations of human rights in the occupied Palestinian territories' (2004) http://www.alhaq.org/publications/publications-index/item/four-years-since-the-beginning-of-the-intifada-systematic-violations-of-human-rights-in-the-occupied-palestinian-territories?category _id=1 (accessed 1 March 2013); B'Tselem 'Human rights in the occupied territories: 2011 annual report' (2012) http://www.btselem.org/sites/default/files2/2011_annual_report_eng.pdf (accessed 1 March 2013); Physicians for Human Rights (Israel) '"Humanitarian minimum" - Israel's role in creating food and water insecurity in the Gaza Strip, December 2010' (2011) http://www.phr.org.il/default.asp?Page ID=111&ItemID=799 (accessed 1 March 2013).
19   The International Human Rights Clinic at Harvard Law School 'Crimes in Burma' (2009) http://www.law.harvard.edu/programs/hrp/documents/Crimes-in-Burma. pdf (accessed 1 March 2013).
20   See J Power *Like water on stone: The story of Amnesty International* (2001).
21   C Lynch 'Can K Street save Teodoro Obiang Nguema Mbasogo's good name' *Foreign Policy* 24 June 2010 http://turtlebay.foreignpolicy.com/posts/2010/06/24/can_k_ street_save_teodoro_obiang_nguema_mbasogo_s_good_name (accessed 1 March 2013). See also, F Roberts 'Is this the hardest PR job in the city? Gaddafi tries to hire New York public relations firm in bid to improve image' *The Daily Mail* 1 August 2011 http://www.dailymail.co.uk/news/article-2020805/Libyan-dictator-Muammar-Gadd afi-tries-hire-NYC-public-relations-firm-improve-image.html (accessed 1 March 2013).

protect individuals, groups and populations at risk – or at least minimising the overall harm incurred.

Long-established human rights organisations have added these new advocacy methods to their arsenals, while new groups devoted to IHL issues have sprung up specifically to make the best of new opportunities. Most human rights groups still 'name and shame' by reporting on IHL violations employing largely the same methodologies used for reporting on human rights violations (though IHL investigations on recent battlefields are typically much more complicated in terms of fact-gathering and security risks). Coalitions of nongovernmental organisations have tried to jumpstart advocacy opportunities by pressing for international treaties, such as on anti-personnel landmines, cluster munitions, and, recently, small arms. These groups also work to make existing mechanisms effective in protecting those harmed and their families.

As is discussed below, far from muddying their message, the often confusing overlap between IHL and human rights law has given impetus for greater public debate of issues that previously were merely hidden behind the fog of military field manuals and scholarly analysis.

3.1   Reporting on armed conflicts

Reporting on IHL issues often demands fact gathering that is extremely difficult and dangerous. This is particularly the case where there are non-state armed groups involved. Not only are they more likely to operate in a lawless environment, but any kind of interaction with them might get treated as an unlawful act by the state.[22] Pro-government militias tend to get used for a government's 'dirty work'.[23] No less than governments, armed groups may react badly to reporting they consider hostile.[24]

Too often, discussions in the pages of scholarly journals and at conferences reflect the viewpoints and practices of the most modernised armed forces of the world, which are usually the most able and willing to abide by the laws of war. The role played by such armies in developing IHL is important, particularly as the more modern armies not

---

22   See CNN Wire Staff 'Swedish journalists receive 11 years in jail' *CNN* 28 December 2011   http://www.cnn.com/2011/12/27/world/africa/ethiopia-swedish-journalists/index.html (accessed 1 March 2013).

23   See Human Rights Watch 'Paramilitaries' heirs: The new face of violence in Colombia' (2010) http://www.hrw.org/reports/2010/02/03/paramilitaries-heirs-0 (accessed 1 March 2013).

24   See University Teachers for Human Rights (Jaffna) 'A tribute and reflections by the UTHR(J) upon the 20th Anniversary of the passing of Dr Rajani Thiranagama: Rajani's vision for Lanka' (18 September 2009) http://uthr.org/Rajani/Tribute_Reflections.htm (accessed 1 March 2013).

unexpectedly have the more sophisticated international lawyers.[25] But they do not always bring to the table the conduct of warfare in the grimmer, more brutal armed conflicts around the world. Even then, the more modern armies may be sophisticated about targeting and after-action reports to measure military success, but that does not always or even often translate into after-action investigations into possible laws-of-war violations.[26]

The void in IHL reporting tends to be left to opposing armed forces whose credibility will be suspect, journalists whose knowledge of the laws of war may be limited, and nongovernmental organisations. Of course, relatively few NGOs consider themselves competent or wish to conduct battlefield investigations into IHL violations. The International Committee of the Red Cross (ICRC), the most knowledgeable and experienced in this regard, normally does not report publicly, so their excellent reporting will be directed privately towards the warring party in question.[27] At the same time, humanitarian relief agencies will be found in the most dangerous places with staff whose long-term presence will develop exceptional knowledge of a situation – but humanitarian workers rarely have the investigative background and, more importantly, will understandably focus on the more immediate task of saving lives, whether it is caring for the wounded or feeding and housing the displaced. Furthermore, their very long-term presence on the ground that makes them unsurpassed witnesses to abuse also makes them most vulnerable to retaliation or deportation.[28]

As a result, in a typical wartime situation there will be limited resources for proper monitoring of possible IHL abuses. This often leaves human rights organisations as the best placed to gather information on laws-of-war violations that can be disseminated in a credible and compelling manner. Such groups will have to demonstrate that they understand the situation on the ground, that they have a developed

25 See Institute for Peace Studies 'Legality of targeted killings by drone attacks in Pakistan' (February 2011) http://harvard.academia.edu/AkbarNasirKhan/Papers/366658/Legality_of_Targeted_Killings_by_Drone_Attacks_in_Pakistan (accessed 1 March 2013).
26 See Second Report of the Independent Public Commission to Examine the Maritime Incident of 31 May 2010 (Turkel Commission), February 2013, 49-50 http://www.turkel-committee.gov.il/files/newDoc3/The%20Turkel%20Report%20for%20website.pdf (accessed 1 March 2013); Human Rights Watch 'Rain of fire: Israel's unlawful use of white phosphorus in Gaza' (2009) http://www.hrw.org/sites/de fault/files/reports/iopt0309web.pdf (accessed 1 March 2013).
27 See International Committee of the Red Cross (ICRC) 'Confidentiality: Key to the ICRC's work but not unconditional' (2010) http://www.icrc.org/eng/resources/documents/interview/confidentiality-interview-010608.htm (accessed 1 March 2013).
28 See Médecins Sans Frontières 'Grounds for divorce? MSF and the International Criminal Court' podcast series (2009) http://www.msf-crash.org/en/rencontre-debats/2010/10/01/393/grounds-for-divorce-msf-and-the-international-criminal-court/ (accessed 1 March 2013).

knowledge of the laws of armed conflict, and that they are unbiased monitors and reporters.

The first step for international human rights groups covering an armed conflict is to get the researchers as close as to the combat zone as is safely possible. Doing so while the bullets are still flying is often a nonstarter from a security perspective, and in any case the ability to do effective research under such situations is usually sharply constrained. However, wars are not static situations – fighting in one area may have moved on to another place, permitting relatively safe investigations in a previously unsafe area. People fleeing the fighting are no substitute for direct investigations of the battlefield, but can be extremely valuable nevertheless.[29]

Security for researchers and those they interview is just one consideration, albeit the most important one. Militaries and armed groups often try to keep human rights investigators and journalists out of areas of recent hostilities. In cases where they welcome investigators – officials in Libya during the 2011 war were happy to take journalists and foreign rights investigators to alleged spots of NATO bombing, complete with planted civilian artefacts – but it may mean that the evidence has been tampered with – even where opposing forces actually were responsible for the abuses – making findings unreliable. Physical evidence – bullet holes in walls, bloodstains, shrapnel and unexploded ordnance – can all be important determining what occurred. But it will almost always be necessary to talk to victims and witnesses – and those that are likely to provide accurate information. That means conducting interviews in private, asking often traumatised people questions that might disturb them, and getting all perspectives on a situation; witnesses will talk about the bombs dropping on them, but they also need to be able to speak about the deployment and wrongdoing of fighters from their side. And where possible it is important to talk to the fighters on both sides to get their views of what was happening on the ground.[30]

Human rights investigators must then be able to put together many pieces of eyewitness testimony, available forensic evidence, and their wider understanding of the nature of the conflict to present an impartial and credible picture of possible laws-of-war violations.

Each of these steps will be even more complicated in a situation that straddles the boundaries between IHL and international human rights law, as it could mean looking at cases through the prism of different bodies of

29   See, eg, Human Rights Watch 'No place for children: Child recruitment, forced marriage, and attacks on schools in Somalia' (2012) http://www.hrw.org/sites/default/files/reports/somalia0212ForUpload.pdf (accessed 1 March 2013).

30   See, eg, D Groome *The handbook of human rights investigation* (2011); K English *The human rights handbook: A practical guide to monitoring human rights* (1995); Office of the High Commissioner for Human Rights 'Training manual on human rights monitoring' (Index: E.01.XIV.2, 2001).

law.[31] Witnesses to armed violence are not likely to understand the legal distinctions, but supporters of one side are more likely to say that the belligerent forces were using military force in a situation where it was not needed – 'there were no rebel fighters'. Even neutral witnesses will often dismiss, for instance, the presence of an armed group out of fear of retribution. That said, the experience of Human Rights Watch has been that investigators who demonstrate empathy, patience and impartiality usually can gather testimony that can be corroborated. And it is that corroborated information that forms the basis for reporting and advocacy on IHL issues.[32]

Providing detailed and impartial accounts of hostilities is essential for bringing attention to violations of the laws of war. But even where violations are not found, or the information is too unclear to draw conclusions about legality, it can nonetheless be of significance. Reports that contradict assertions that no civilians were harmed, or can confirm or deny that enemy soldiers were present, can all impact a military's conduct of hostilities. This was evident in Afghanistan where reporting by local and international human rights groups on bombings of villages by NATO and US forces did not often find clear evidence of laws-of-war violations – but they confirmed that civilian deaths and injuries were much higher than NATO and the US reported. This, along with public criticism of allied bombing practices by Afghan President Hamid Karzai, contributed to decisions by NATO and the US to take major steps to reduce civilian casualties in air operations.[33]

As discussed below, the more details that can be presented about particular incidents, such as a raid on a suspected insurgents home or a shooting at a checkpoint, the easier it is to sort out how a situation plays out according to IHL – and those areas where international human rights law remains applicable.

31 See, eg, Amnesty International 'Will I be next?': US drone strikes in Pakistan' (2013) http://www.amnesty.org/en/library/asset/ASA33/013/2013/en/041c08cb-fb54-47b3-b3fe-a72c9169e487/asa330132013en.pdf; Human Rights Watch 'Between a drone and Al-Qaeda': The civilian cost of US targeted killings in Yemen' (October 2013) http://www.hrw.org/reports/2013/10/22/between-drone-and-al-qaeda-0 (both accessed 20 October 2014).
32 See Human Rights Watch 'Civilians under assault: Hezbollah's rocket attacks on Israel in the 2006 War' (2007) http://www.hrw.org/sites/default/files/reports/iopt08 07.pdf (accessed 1 March 2013).
33 See Human Rights Watch '"Troops in contact": Airstrikes and civilian deaths in Afghanistan' (2008) http://www.hrw.org/sites/default/files/reports/afghanistan09 08webwcover_0.pdf (accessed 1 March 2013); 'Letter from Human Rights Watch to US Secretary of Defense Robert Gates on US Airstrikes in Azizabad, Afghanistan' *Human Rights Watch News* 14 January 2009 http://www.hrw.org/news/2009/01/14/letter-secretary-defense-robert-gates-us-airstrikes-azizabad-afghanistan (accessed 1 March 2013).

3.2 Supporting adoption of new treaties

Treaty law on the conduct of hostilities is largely found in two multinational treaties – the Hague Regulations of 1907[34] and Protocol I to the 1949 Geneva Conventions.[35] As noted below, litigation by the international criminal courts has begun to provide greater nuance to the meaning of these treaties, but the words on paper remain unchanged. But while treaty law on the methods of armed conflict have largely been frozen since 1977, there have been important developments in how that law is interpreted.

Perhaps more than any other developments of IHL in recent years, nongovernmental organisations have played a key role in pressing for important changes with respect to outlawing certain weaponry that poses a special risk to civilians. Coalitions of NGOs played a crucial role in pressing for, negotiating and obtaining broad acceptance of the Mine Ban Treaty, which prohibits the production, transfer and use of anti-personnel land mines. This coalition helped produce a treaty in a relatively short time, garner broad adherence, even by countries that have not ratified the treaty, such as the US, and have undoubtedly saved many lives by doing so.[36]

NGOs made a similar successful effort with the Clusters Munitions Treaty, which outlaws bombs and shells that release numerous dangerous bomblets. The Clusters Munitions Treaty was passed quickly and with broad if not universal international support.[37]

Future treaties are being considered regarding the use of heavy artillery in densely populated areas and fully-autonomous weapons ('killer robots').[38]

The overlap of treaties that ban weapons and the role of international human rights law is less obvious. Regulation of military weapons on the grounds that they are fundamentally indiscriminate is very much *lex specialis* of international humanitarian law. However, one argument that has increasingly resonated in the debates over weapons such as anti-

---

34   Hague Convention (IV) 'Respecting the laws and customs of war on land and its annex: Regulations concerning the laws and customs of war on land' (adopted 18 October 1907) http://www.unhcr.org/refworld/docid/4374cae64.html (accessed 1 March 2013).

35   ICRC 'Protocol additional to the Geneva Conventions of 12 August 1949, and relating to the protection of victims of international armed conflicts (Protocol I)' adopted 8 June 1977, 1125 UNTS 3, entered into force 7 December 1978.

36   Landmine and Cluster Munitions Monitor http://www.the-monitor.org/ (accessed 1 March 2013).

37   Convention on Cluster Munitions (adopted 30 May 2008) CCM/77.

38   'UN: Nations agree to address "killer robots"': Conventional weapons process should lead to total ban' *Human Rights Watch News* 13 November 2013 http://www.hrw.org/news/2013/11/15/un-nations-agree-address-killer-robots (accessed 20 October 2014).

personnel landmines and cluster munitions has been their long-term impact on the general civilian population, rather than just their immediate effect. That is, while one can show that such weapons are indiscriminate in that they cannot distinguish between civilians and combatants, one can also make the case that the killings and injuries they cause over many years makes their use invariably disproportionate as well.[39]

Land mines and cluster submunition duds left behind in a populated area can create a serious harm for farmers, cattle-herders, and others for decades. This harm can have an important human rights component, depriving residents of their ability to grow food and obtain a livelihood. Such considerations of the long-term human rights impact of a cluster munitions attack would therefore have to be taken into account in a proportionality analysis. So would, for example, dropping cluster munitions in an area be expected to cause long-term harm to the civilian population – even in an area that had been evacuated – was disproportionate to the anticipated military advantage of the attack.

States parties to the Convention on Conventional Weapons (CCW) have adopted this approach to the proportionality test. The preamble to the final declaration of the CCW's Third Review Conference states that 'the foreseeable effects of explosive remnants of war on civilian populations as a factor to be considered in applying the international humanitarian law rules on proportionality in attack and precautions in attack'.[40]

Since 11 September there have been calls from various quarters to revise the laws of war to address what is perceived to be a gap in so-called asymmetric armed conflicts – in which modern armies are said to be hamstrung by rules that are ignored or purposefully not followed by terrorist groups or other non-state armed groups.[41] Some of these issues will be addressed below.

Suffice it to say that while there have been various governments and think tanks that have put forward proposals for substantially revising the laws of war to address this issue, the human rights community, along with the ICRC and others from IHL community, have not. While one can certainly make amendments to the Geneva Conventions to make them

---

39   See Human Rights Watch 'Civilians under assault' (n 32 above) 23-28; see also Human Rights Watch 'A dying practice: Use of cluster munitions by Russia and Georgia in August 2008' (2009).
40   Third Review Conference of the High Contracting Parties to the CCW 'Final Document, Part II, Final Declaration' CCW/CONF.III/11 (Part II) (7-17 November 2006) 4. See also Human Rights Watch and Harvard Law School International Human Rights Clinic 'Cluster munitions and the proportionality test: Memorandum to delegates of the Convention on Conventional Weapons' (2008).
41   See, eg, WC Banks *New battlefields/old laws: Critical debates on asymmetric warfare* (2011); MN Schmitt 'Asymmetrical warfare and international humanitarian law' (2008) 62 *Air Force Law Review* 1 http://www.afjag.af.mil/shared/media/document/AFD-090302-047.pdf (accessed 1 March 2013).

more effective and precisely worded legal documents that would better protect civilians and those *hors de combat*, there seems to be a general recognition amongst human rights advocates (and the ICRC) that the most pressing problem is in the implementation of the law, not the law as it currently exists on paper or customary law understandings. Moreover, any state effort that appears designed to create disparities in the application of international law to states and non-state armed groups is unlikely to work in practice, serving only to drive non-state actors away from implementing even current law. Instead, the push from human rights organisations has been to find ways to encourage non-state armed groups to abide by IHL, but also abide by human rights law in the areas that they control.[42]

3.3   New opportunities in new interpretations of the law

An important phenomenon in developing IHL has been the rise of international criminal courts. Prior to the creation of the ad hoc international tribunals for the former Yugoslavia and Rwanda in the 1990s, international criminal law relating to war crimes, crimes against humanity and genocide effectively stagnated. Without any international court to regularly consider cases on such matters, it was hard for the law to develop. Concepts such as indiscriminate attacks or the meaning of intent to commit a war crime might be discussed and debated in the war colleges and the law journals and at times be litigated before domestic courts martial, but without a court to rule on the issues, the law remained mired in the language in which it was set out, in the limited 1949 Geneva Conventions and the broader but at times problematic language of the 1977 Protocols Additional.[43]

The ad hoc international courts, and to a lesser extent the special national and mixed courts set up in Sierra Leone, Iraq, East Timor, and Cambodia, were to change this. In prosecuting offenders of grave crimes in violation of international law, meat was put on to the bare-bone treaties guiding military conduct that would have interpretative value globally. The International Criminal Tribunal for the former Yugoslavia, for instance, took on such issues as the needed nexus between the armed conflict and the alleged offense, the requirements needed for convicting someone of torture, and the definition of command responsibility.[44] As a

---

42   See, eg, Human Rights Watch 'Harsh war, harsh peace: Abuses by al-Shabaab, the Transitional Federal Government, and AMISOM in Somalia' (2010) http://www.hrw.org/reports/2010/04/13/harsh-war-harsh-peace (accessed 1 March 2013).

43   The ICRC tried to address the ambiguity with the concept of 'direct participation in hostilities'. See ICRC 'Interpretative guidance on the notion of direct participation in hostilities under international humanitarian law' (2009).

44   See Human Rights Watch 'Genocide, war crimes and crimes against humanity: Topical digests of the case law of the International Criminal Tribunal for Rwanda and the International Criminal Tribunal for the former Yugoslavia' (2004) http://www.hrw.org/sites/default/files/reports/digest.pdf (accessed 20 October 2014)

result, there is a much fuller understanding of the criminal side to the laws of war – as well as a greater sense of its shortcomings.

The Rome Statute of the International Criminal Court went even further in setting out the criminal law and procedure underlying war crimes, as well as crimes against humanity and genocide.[45] While some revisions were made in existing law in order to entice greater ratification by states – for instance, the definition of disproportionate attacks was narrowed from what is stated in Protocol I[46] – in general the Rome Statute mirrors current understanding of existing international law.[47] As increasing numbers of cases go through the system, from the pre-trial phase to trial to appellate review, there will eventually be a large body of case law that will increase our understanding and hopefully lead to the progressive development of IHL.

This should create real opportunities for nongovernmental organisations seeking to protect the rights or obtain redress for victims of war crimes. This has already been the case with respect to the regional human rights courts, namely the European Court of Human Rights (ECHR) and the Inter American Commission and Court of Human Rights. Each has taken on cases involving violations committed during wartime.[48] The fact that these courts, which conduct civil adjudications of matters arising from violations of regional human rights treaties, provide an important venue for addressing wartime violations under human rights law.

For instance, the Russian Justice Initiative, a nongovernmental organisation based in Moscow, has brought dozens of civil actions against the Russian government on behalf of the victims and families of individuals forcibly disappeared or tortured in Chechnya and, more recently, cases from the 2008 Russian-Georgian war. [49] Since 2006, the Russian government has lost more than 100 cases in the ECHR, and has been mandated to pay over seven million euros in compensation to applicants from the North Caucasus.[50] These cases have demonstrated

45   UN General Assembly, Rome Statute of the International Criminal Court (last amended January 2002), 17 July 1998, A/CONF. 183/9 http://www.unhcr.org/refworld/docid/3ae6b3a84.html (accessed 1 March 2013).
46   See O Triffterer (ed) 'Commentary on the Rome Statute of the International Criminal Court: Observers notes – Article by article' (2008) para 2(b)(iv), 338-341.
47   See 'Introduction to the second edition' in Triffterer (no 46 above) XXXIII-XXXV.
48   *Al-Skeini v United Kingdom* Application no: 55721/07, ECHR(7 July 2011); *Banković v Belgium* Application no 52207/99, ECHR (12 December 2001); *Juan Carlos Abella v Argentina* IACHR (Case no 11.137) 30 October 1997, Report No 55/97, OEA/Ser.L/V/II.95 Doc 7, 271.
49   See Russian Justice Initiative http://www.srji.org/en/about/ (accessed 1 March 2013).
50   T Parfitt 'European Court of Human Rights reforms could have "devastating" effect in Russia', *The Telegraph* 17 April 2012 http://www.telegraph.co.uk/news/worldnews/europe/russia/9207908/European-Court-of-Human-Rights-reforms-could-have-devastating-effect-in-Russia.html (accessed 1 March 2013).

how a human rights treaty can be effectively used to bring redress in at least certain kinds of cases related to an armed conflict situation, if not the full range of war crimes.

Cases regarding the death in British custody of detainees in Iraq have been brought before the ECHR. The British government argued that the deaths of four of the detainees were a result of military operations in the field, and therefore did not fall within the United Kingdom's jurisdiction under article 1 of the Convention. The court rejected this argument, holding instead that British forces were liable under the European Convention on Human Rights for the treatment of prisoners under their effective control. The ruling was upheld on appeal; in a stirring endorsement of human rights law in a wartime setting, Judge Giovanni Bonello stated that:

> The founding members of the Convention, and each subsequent Contracting Party, strove to achieve one aim, at once infinitesimal and infinite: the supremacy of the rule of human rights law. In article 1 they undertook to secure to everyone within their jurisdiction the rights and freedoms enshrined in the Convention. This was, and remains, the cornerstone of the Convention. That was, and remains, the agenda heralded in its preamble: 'the universal and effective recognition and observance' of fundamental human rights. 'Universal' hardly suggests an observance parceled off by territory on the checkerboard of geography.[51]

Under these circumstances, bringing elements of international human rights law into the cases before the ICC seems inevitable. Particularly on questions regarding the treatment of prisoners, including the definition of torture and other ill-treatment, enforced disappearance and the right to a fair trial, existing human rights case law is much richer than currently exists under the international war crimes courts. So it would only be expected that litigators and judges look to that body of law to assist in adjudicating alleged war crimes.

It also seems likely that the greater role for victim participation under the ICC statute[52] will encourage involvement by domestic human rights groups. This will encourage them to develop expertise on laws-of-war issues in order to provide assistance to victims seeking to interact with the court.

---

51   *Al-Skeini* (n 48 above). Concurring Opinion of Judge Bonello, 78 para 9.
52   The Rome Statute specifically states in article 68(3) that: 'where the personal interests of the victims are affected, the Court shall permit their views and concerns to be presented and considered at stages of the proceedings determined to be appropriate by the Court and in a manner which is not prejudicial to or inconsistent with the rights of the accused and a fair and impartial trial. Such views and concerns may be presented by the legal representatives of the victims where the Court considers it appropriate, in accordance with the Rules of Procedure and Evidence'.

3.4   Current issues: NGOs and impact

The overlap of IHL and international human rights law is not of course just of theoretical interest. At a minimum, characterisations of the applicable law will affect the nature of the debate. Determination of the applicable body of law can also mean the difference between whether a specific policy is lawful or not. Overlap will not necessary remain static but shift over time given circumstances and the political context. In recent years, the intersection of IHL and human rights law has been most pronounced on issues relating to (1) detention in non-international armed conflicts, (2) humanitarian access, and (3) targeted killings.[53]

All too often commentators on these issues adopt one or the other body of law to bolster a sought legal conclusion. As a result, they often find themselves talking past each other. This section does not try to explain or resolve the above issues. Rather it looks at the path human rights organisations that consider both IHL and human rights law have taken to address the issues raised by these situations. Such an approach generally seeks to maximise protections for civilians and combatants, but also needs to be consistent with existing law. Presenting arguments that are satisfying to a particular constituency but not legally compelling to those in a position to bring about changes in policy and practice are unlikely to get very far. From a human rights advocacy perspective, the aim is to win over those who are in the opposing camp or at least sitting on the fence – winning debating points or cheering those already in agreement is of little added value.

3.5   Detention in non-international armed conflicts

A longstanding source of disagreement between governments and NGOs has concerned the applicable law regarding detention of both rebel fighters and civilians during non-international armed conflicts. In the past this usually meant classic civil wars but since 11 September has frequently been invoked in transnational operations involving a state actor and one or more non-state armed groups.

International humanitarian law on detentions is straightforward for international armed conflicts: the Third and Fourth Geneva Conventions set out relatively detailed rules for the detention of prisoners-of-war and the internment of civilians who pose a security risk.[54] During a non-international armed conflict, common article 3 to the Geneva Conventions

---

53   See generally ICRC 'International humanitarian law and the challenges of contemporary armed conflicts' (October 2011).
54   Geneva Convention relative to the Treatment of Prisoners of War (Geneva III) (adopted 12 August 1949) 75 UNTS 135, entered into force 21 October 1950; Geneva Convention relative to the Protection of Civilian Persons in Time of War (Geneva IV) (adopted 12 August 1949) 75 UNTS 287, entered into force 21 October 1950.

and other sources of international law makes clear that parties to the conflict are not prohibited from taking individuals into custody.[55]

The longstanding point of contention concerns the rules under which those being held must be treated. During civil wars since the Second World War, governments have frequently detained captured rebels and civilians deemed a security risk and held them under real or virtual administrative detention laws that would not require the government to bring them to trial.[56] When the conflict ended, those not tried for a particular crime would eventually be released without ever having been charged.

Unlike during international armed conflicts, rebel fighters have no combatant privilege and can be prosecuted, at least for violating domestic law. At the same time, except under extraordinary circumstances, a country's criminal justice system will continue to function. So while human rights law does not prohibit administrative detention, it places restrictions on the practice that almost invariably results in frequent illegal detentions. Detainees are held without even the minimum of due process or are detained – not for an actual role in the violence – but for exercising their rights to free expression and association. The removal of political detainees from a legal process – denying them access to lawyers and families – also facilitates other abuses, such as torture and enforced disappearance. As a result, human rights groups typically contend that individuals picked up during non-international armed conflict should be fully protected by international human rights law. This means in practice trying them for criminal offenses – rebellion, murder, weapons' possession and the like – rather than holding them indefinitely without trial.

This central disagreement on the applicability of IHL or human rights law during non-international armed conflicts was to get new attention post-11 September as a result of US military alliances with newly installed governments in Afghanistan and Iraq.

There should have been little doubt that the Geneva Conventions applied to members of the Taliban captured by Northern Alliance forces during the US-led invasion of Afghanistan in 2001. But just as US forces in 2002 began holding and accepting responsibility for the treatment of Taliban prisoners, contending that provisions of the Fourth Geneva Convention on the treatment of civilians at least be applied by analogy, the legal situation changed. The Geneva Conventions require there be two or more high contracting parties for there to be an international armed

---

55 Common article 3; ICRC *Customary international humanitarian law* (2005) rules 118-128.
56 See, eg, Human Rights Watch 'Sri Lanka – Return to war: Human rights under siege' (2007) http://www.hrw.org/reports/2007/08/05/return-war-0; Human Rights Watch 'Collective punishment: War crimes and crimes against humanity in the Ogaden area of Ethiopia's Somali Region' (2008) http://www.hrw.org/reports/2008/06/11/collective-punishment (both accessed 20 October 2014).

conflict.[57] After the Taliban government was defeated in late 2001, and certainly after the establishment of the Karzai government in 2002, there was no basis for saying that fighting existed between two governments.[58] Instead the armed conflict, which expanded in scope and intensity since the mid-2000s, has been between a national government and its allies on one side and a non-state armed group on the other – a non-international armed conflict under the Geneva Conventions.

Similarly in Iraq, the insurgency that continued after the defeat of the Saddam Hussein regime in 2003 made the law of occupation – found in The Hague Regulations of 1907 and the Fourth Geneva Convention – applicable law. In 2005, after the formation of an Iraqi government and the end of the occupation, however, the conflict would be characterised as a non-international armed conflict.

In both situations US forces were ostensibly fighting on behalf of a sovereign state – the laws of those states and the protections they offered criminal suspects still applied. With respect to Iraq, Security Council Resolution 1483 gave US forces authority to apprehend insurgents.[59] However, the resolution did not otherwise transfer to the US the authority hold detainees under IHL. In Afghanistan, no agreement on the law applicable to detainees was worked out between the US and Afghan governments.[60] In both places, US forces engaged in military operations took into custody opposition fighters as well as civilians considered to be supporting those fighters.

The US government's approach to the treatment of detainees was to selectively apply the Geneva Conventions by analogy to all detainees. That is, it adopted the position that it was lawful to detain anyone who was a security risk under Geneva IV, articles 42 and 78, and hold them until the end of the armed conflict, under Geneva III, article 118, or until they are no longer a security risk under Geneva IV, article 132.[61] But the US did not go further than this, such as providing captured combatants the protections and privileges afforded to prisoners of war, such as those the US gave to captured Viet Cong during the Vietnam War.[62] It also adopted other provisions, such as providing security detainees a review of their case

57   See art 1 common to the four Geneva Conventions of 1949.
58   See Human Rights Watch '"Enduring freedom": Abuses by US forces in Afghanistan' (2004)   http://www.hrw.org/reports/2004/03/07/enduring-freedom   (accessed 1 March 2013).
59   UN Security Council, Resolution 1483 (2003), S/RES/1483 (2003).
60   In April 2012 a Memorandum of Understanding was signed between the US and Afghanistan detailing the transfer of detainees in US custody to Afghan authorities. White House Memorandum 'Memorandum of understanding between The Islamic Republic of Afghanistan and the United States of America on Afghanization of special operations on Afghan Soil' (Afghan US MOU) 8 April 2012 http://president.gov.af/en/news/8453 (accessed 1 March 2013).
61   See Geneva IV, arts 42, 78, 132; Geneva III, art 118.
62   See MACV Directive 20-5 'Inspections and Investigations, Prisoners of War – Determinations of Status' (17 May 1966) para 4.a.(2) and 4.b.(5).

twice a year on an aspirational basis, but not as a legal obligation. Consistent with the Bush administration's objection and the Obama administration's unwillingness to apply international human rights law extraterritorially,[63] the US simply ignored that body of law.

Human Rights Watch and other human rights organisations countered that Iraqi and Afghan criminal law still applied in both countries and the mere presence of foreign troops fighting insurgents did not deprive the population the protections of their own law. These domestic laws had to meet the requirements of international human rights law. A person could not lose these protections simply because they were taken into custody by a foreign force operating in their country rather than the forces of their own state. The US perspective essentially disregarded the sovereign authority of the new government, US public support for them notwithstanding.

This meant that all persons captured in connection with the internal armed conflicts in Iraq and Afghanistan were entitled to the criminal law protections of human rights law. They should have been charged with criminal offences and prosecuted. While both countries could have – but did not – declare states of emergency that would have allowed for them to have derogated from some requirements of the ICCPR – such as the right to a speedy trial – fundamental protections would have remained in place.[64] These include the right to be brought before a judicial authority and told the specific basis for one's arrest, have the opportunity to contest the detention, and have access to legal counsel and family members.[65]

The US reluctance to consider the application of human rights law to detainees was not shared by other NATO governments that were supplying troops to the Afghan effort.[66] They sought to transfer captured Afghans to Afghan civil authorities – but appreciated that this was problematic given the lack of protections against torture and the dysfunctional state of the Afghan criminal justice system.[67] Increasingly the US recognised the need, if not the legal requirement, of treating those taken into custody in Iraq and Afghanistan in accordance with

---

63   White House Memorandum 'Humane treatment of Taliban and Al Qaeda detainees' (7 February 2002) http://www.pegc.us/archive/White_House/bush_memo_2002 0207_ed.pdf (accessed 20 October 2014); Fourth periodic report (n 7 above).
64   ICCPR, art 4.
65   UN Human Rights Committee 'General comment no 29: States of Emergency (article 4)' UN Doc CCPR/C/21/Rev.1/Add.11 (2001).
66   This eventually resulted in a number of governments drafting 'The Copenhagen process on the handling of detainees in international military operations', which was announced on 20 October 2012 http://um.dk/en/~/media/UM/English-site/ Documents/Politics-and-diplomacy/Copenhangen%20Process%20Principles%20and %20Guidelines.pdf (accessed 1 March 2013).
67   In 2007, representatives from the UK Ministry of Defence justified these transfers by stating that: '[T]he UK takes human rights obligations very seriously. Procedures are in place to ensure that any detainees transferred from British forces to Afghan government authorities are not mistreated or tortured'. 'NATO Chided over Detainees' BBC News 13 November 2007 http://news.bbc.co.uk/2/hi/7091928.stm (accessed 1 March 2013).

fundamental human rights. Well prior to the US pull out of Iraq in December 2011, US forces increasingly provided certain due process protections to Iraqi detainees and transferred them to Iraqi civil authorities.[68] Likewise in Afghanistan, the US made significant progress in providing Afghan detainees more protections, though the major shortcomings in the criminal justice system continued to hinder treatment in line with international human rights law.[69] The April 2012 Memorandum of Understanding between the US and Afghanistan is something of a setback, however, as it evokes a commitment from the Afghan government to promulgate an administrative detention law, something the Karzai government had long resisted and may become the source of numerous rights abuses in the future.[70]

Human rights organisations did have some success over several years in raising these concerns with the US and other governments, if not in changing their position about the applicable law, but in improving due process protections for detainees. Key here was getting access to information on specific cases of individuals wrongfully held or held without the most basic of protections. Public statements and, perhaps more importantly, serious working meetings with relevant military officials were important in this regard.

Nongovernmental organisation efforts were hindered by the failure of the Iraqi and Afghan governments to address, despite significant international donor support, the major shortcomings in their own justice systems. So long as torture and unfair trials were the norm, it made it much more difficult for human rights groups to insist on the primacy of human rights law in these jurisdictions or administrative detention.

That said, the practical problems raised by detention issues in these two armed conflicts should not deflect from the overall need to ensure that persons apprehended during non-international armed conflicts receive the protections they are due under international human rights law, and not promises of analogous protections under the laws of war.

3.6 Access to humanitarian assistance

There is a tendency to view human rights law as more protective of civilians than IHL. This partly explains why human rights activists press for its inclusion in more traditional IHL situations – and why some

---

68   See J Deshmukh 'US transfers control of notorious Abu Ghraib prison' *AFP* 2 September 2006.
69   See JA Bovarnick 'Detainee review boards in Afghanistan: From strategic liability to legitimacy' *The Army Lawyer* (2010) 9 http://www.loc.gov/rr/frd/Military_Law/pdf/Bovarnick-Detainee.pdf (accessed 1 March 2013).
70   Afghan US MOU (n 60 above) 'Section two: Terms of Afghanization of special operations'.

governments and militaries try to resist this. There is an obvious truth to that assertion – killing is an accepted component of the laws of war in a way that human rights law, which gives the right to life primacy, could never condone.

But it is wrong to infer that human rights law is always more protective than IHL. Most obviously, while human rights law formally only places limits on governments, IHL also places restrictions on non-state groups that are parties to the conflict.[71]

Human rights organisations frequently address complex humanitarian emergencies – that is, situations in which civilians are at grave risk because of armed conflict or other mass violence. The need will be for humanitarian agencies to rush into the fray to provide the necessary food, medical care and shelter.

Human rights law is not particularly helpful in this context. There is no right to enter another country even in the midst of a grave emergency. And the right to freedom of movement has severe limitations. Article 12 of the ICCPR provides that: 'Everyone lawfully within the territory of a State shall, within that territory, have the right to liberty of movement ... The above-mentioned rights shall not be subject to any restrictions except those which are provided by law, are necessary to protect national security ... and are consistent with the other rights recognised in the present Covenant'.[72]

While national security restrictions on movement need to have a legal basis and be narrowly defined and not disproportionate given the threatened harm, they are derogable in a state of emergency.[73] During a situation of armed conflict, a state is likely to be able to make compelling arguments on such national security grounds. In practice that means that little or no assistance is likely to find its way to areas under the control of enemy forces, or to areas where government forces are committing abuses.

International humanitarian law, by contrast, provides far more leeway for humanitarian organisations to reach populations at risk. Parties to a conflict must allow and facilitate the rapid and unimpeded access of humanitarian assistance to civilians in need, so long as it is impartial in character and conducted without any adverse distinction. Parties to a conflict may require consent but such consent must be given if the aid is offered by an impartial humanitarian agency to a threatened population.[74]

71 See, eg, common art 3.
72 ICCPR, art 12.
73 ICCPR, art 4(2).
74 Protocol I, arts 68-71; ICRC 'Protocol additional to the Geneva Conventions of 12 August 1949, and relating to the protection of victims of non-international armed conflicts (Protocol II)' 1125 UNTS 609 (entered into force 7 December 1978) art 18; see also ICRC 'Commentary to Protocol II' (1987) paras 4883-4885.

Human rights law does provide for a right to food,[75] as well as to health,[76] and efforts to starve a population would clearly fall under those.[77] However, IHL specifically prohibits the use of starvation of the civilian population as a method of warfare in both international and non-international armed conflicts.[78]

These distinctions in the law are crucial for humanitarian agencies seeking access to a population during wartime, but they are also important for human rights organisations reporting on a situation on the ground and seeking to press for humanitarian access. Arguments based on the human right to freedom of movement will have less traction than those based on IHL, particularly if the armed forces are an advocacy target. They also allow for greater recognition that the civilian population under the control of opposition forces is entitled to access humanitarian assistance and that opposition armed forces are likewise obligated to ensure that assistance reaches those in need.

3.7   Targeted killings and the end of armed conflict

Since the Bush administration pronounced a 'war on terror' following the 11 September attacks by al-Qaeda on the United States, perhaps no other issue has challenged the boundaries between IHL and human rights law as the practice of so-called targeted killings. In recent years the phrase 'targeted killing' has commonly been used to refer to a deliberate lethal attack by government forces against a specific individual not in custody under the colour of law.

The concept of targeted killings is by no means new. In a World War II case often cited by US commentators to justify current attacks on specific individuals, US fighter planes tipped off by decoded radio intercepts shot down the airplane transporting Japanese General Isoroku Yamamoto over the Pacific Ocean on 18 April 1943.[79] But that was a wartime attack against an enemy combatant, no different from a sniper shooting an opposing general on the battlefield.

The issue received much more thorough analysis, as a result of the Israeli government's targeted killing campaign against alleged Palestinian

---

75   International Covenant on Economic, Social and Cultural Rights (CESCR) (adopted 16 December 1966) GA Res. 2200A (XXI), 21 UN GAOR Supp (No 16) 52, UN Doc A/6316 (1966), 993 UNTS 3 (entered into force 3 January 1976), art 11.
76   CESCR, art 12.
77   UN Committee on Economic, Social and Cultural Rights 'General comment no 12: Right to adequate food' (Twentieth session, 1999), UN Doc E/C.12/1999/5 (1999), reprinted in 'Compilation of general comments and general recommendations adopted by human rights treaty bodies', UN Doc HRI/GEN/1/Rev.6 at 62 (2003).
78   See Protocol I, art 54(1); Protocol II, art 14.
79   See EH Holder Jr 'Remarks on targeted killings' Speech at the Northwestern University School of Law, Evanston, Illinois (5 March 2012) http://www.justice.gov/iso/opa/ag/speeches/2012/ag-speech-1203051.html (accessed 1 March 2013).

terrorist suspects from 2001-2004. The Israel Defence Forces (IDF) carried out a number of aerial missile strikes against targets in Gaza and the West Bank, which often resulted in high numbers of civilian casualties. For instance, the 2002 IDF aerial attack on Hamas military chief Sheikh Salah Shehadeh's left at least 11 civilians dead, including 7 children, and wounded 120 others.[80]

The general issue of targeted killings eventually went to the Israeli Supreme Court, which to its credit did not shy away from addressing the complexities of the situation as they related to the boundaries between IHL and human rights law. While finding that IHL applied because of the Israeli occupation, the court concluded that it was necessary to obtain well-founded and verifiable information about civilians allegedly taking part in hostilities before they could be attacked and that they could not be attacked if less harmful means could be used against them, such as arrest and criminal prosecution. The court also ruled that an independent investigation be undertaken after each attack to determine whether the targeted killing was lawful, and to compensate civilians not taking part in hostilities who were harmed. But the court did not declare the targeted killing policy unlawful, finding that the lawfulness of a killing had to be determined according to the particular circumstances of the case.[81]

In November 2002, a missile – the first reported US Central Intelligence Agency aerial drone strike – killed Qaed Salim Sinan al-Harethi, a Yemeni suspected of masterminding the bombing of the USS *Cole,* which had claimed the lives of 17 US sailors two years earlier.[82]

Through various public statements – though not formal legal analyses – by President Barack Obama and other senior officials, the Obama administration has provided an outline of its legal authority for conducting targeted killings.[83] The fullest articulation of that position came from

80   See S Goldenberg '12 dead in attack on Hamas: Seven children killed as Israelis assassinate military chief' *The Guardian* 22 July 2002 http://www.guardian.co.uk/world/2002/jul/23/israel1 (accessed 1 March 2013).
81   *The Public Committee against Torture in Israel et al v The Government of Israel et al* Supreme Court of Israel (14 December 2006) http://elyon1.court.gov.il/Files_ENG/02/690/007/a34/02007690.a34.HTM (accessed 1 March 2013).
82   SM Hersh 'Manhunt: The Bush Administration's new strategy in the war against terrorism' *The New Yorker* 23 December 2002 66 http://www.newyorker.com/archive/2002/12/23/021223fa_fact#ixzz1rrjVnMp9 (accessed 1 March 2013).
83   State Department legal adviser Harold Koh told the American Society of International Law in March 2010 that the United States was in an ongoing armed conflict with al-Qaeda, and so has the authority under the laws of war to use lethal force against al-Qaeda members and associated forces. He noted that whether a particular individual will be targeted in a particular location would depend upon specific considerations, including 'the willingness and ability of those states to suppress the threat the target poses'. Koh said that in targeted killings and other operations against al-Qaeda and its affiliates: '[G]reat care is taken to adhere to [laws of war] principles in both planning and execution, to ensure that only legitimate objectives are targeted and that collateral damage [civilian casualties] is kept to a minimum'. HH Koh 'The Obama Administration and international law' Speech at the Annual Meeting of the American

Attorney General Eric Holder in March 2012. Holder basically argued that the US Constitution and the laws of armed conflict permitted targeted attacks against individuals outside the United States who have a senior operational role with al Qaeda or an al Qaeda-associated force, who is involved in the plotting of attacks targeting the United States. In addition, the threat posed by the individual must be 'imminent' in the sense that is it is the last clear window of opportunity to striker, and that there is no feasible option for capture without undue risk. Finally the strike needs to comply with the IHL principles of necessity, distinction, proportionality, and humanity.[84] A state department 'White Paper' leaked to the media in February 2013 repeated many of these arguments, but particular with respect to targeted attacks against US citizens, which has been the primary concern raised by the US public.[85]

On 23 May 2013, in a speech at the National Defence University, Obama outlined steps that he said his administration was undertaking or would take before targeting someone.[86] Simultaneously the White House released a fact sheet that summarised the classified Presidential Policy Guidance on targeted killings that the president had signed a day earlier.[87]

The speech and fact sheet fell short of providing a legal rationale for the targeted attacks it did also not respond to allegations that specific strikes were unlawful.[88] However, the policies enunciated by the president – if implemented – suggest a policy approach more along the lines of using lethal force under international human rights law than under the lower threshold of IHL. As described the standards demand near-certainty of no civilian casualties, 'capture instead of kill' when feasible, and that the

Society of International Law, Washington DC, 25 March 2010 http://www.state.gov/s/l/releases/remarks/139119.htm (accessed 1 March 2013). John Brennan, the administration's counterterrorism advisor, expanded on these arguments in a speech at Harvard University in September 2011. He argued for 'a more flexible understanding of "imminence"' to justify a military response to the threat posed by terrorist groups. He said that being at war with al-Qaeda 'does not mean we can use military force whenever we want, wherever we want'; respect for a state's sovereignty and the laws of war also restrict the way force is used abroad. JO Brennan 'Strengthening our security by adhering to our values and laws' Speech at Harvard Law School, Cambridge, Massachusetts, 16 September 2011 http://www.whitehouse.gov/the-press-office/2011/09/16/remarks-john-o-brennan-strengthening-our-security-adhering-our-values-an (accessed 20 October 2014).

84   See, eg, ICRC (n 55 above) rules 1-10 (distinction), rules 1-13 (indiscriminate attacks), rule 14 (proportionality in attack), rules 53-56 (access to humanitarian relief).

85   US Department of Justice 'White Paper: Lawfulness of US operation directed against a citizen who is a senior operational leader of al-Qa'ida or an associated force' (undated) http://msnbcmedia.msn.com/i/msnbc/sections/news/020413_DOJ_White_Paper.pdf (accessed 1 March 2013).

86   The White House 'Remarks by the President at the National Defense University' (23 May 2013) http://www.whitehouse.gov/the-press-office/2013/05/23/remarks-president-national-defense-university (accessed 23 August 2013).

87   The White House 'Fact sheet: US policy standards and procedures for the use of force in counterterrorism operations outside the United States and areas of active hostilities' Targeted Killing Fact Sheet (23 May 2013): www.whitehouse.gov/sites/default/files/uploads/2013.05.23_fact_sheet_on_ppg.pdf (accessed 23 August 2013).

88   See Human Rights Watch (n 31 above).

target most pose an imminent threat. However, an attack in December 2013 on alleged AQAP militants that may have killed 12 civilians – whether lawful or not under IHL – does not appear to have been carried out in accordance with the administration's stated policy.[89]

Reporting on targeted killings by Human Rights Watch and other human rights organisations has been severely hindered by the difficulty of access to the areas where most of the attacks have taken place, namely the Orakzai and Waziristan territories of Pakistan, remote Yemen, and war-torn Somalia. It is not known to what extent the strikes are hitting military targets in battle zones, causing disproportionate civilian loss compared to the expected military gain, or using unjustified lethal force in what are more properly law enforcement situations. Human Rights Watch reported on a US airstrike in central Yemen in September 2012 – drones were involved though it is not clear if the missile or bomb came from a drone or airplane. The Yemeni government admitted that all 12 people killed were civilians and provided some compensation to the victims' families.[90]

These are dangerous and difficult places to place a researcher and, even with access, the risks to witnesses would deter them from speaking or providing fully accurate information. The ability of drones to conduct surveillance for hours has increased the likelihood of killings being used in inaccessible places and makes them less reliant on ground-based intelligence sources often needed by manned aircraft and cruise missiles.[91]

These difficulties in conducting research contrasts with the situation in Afghanistan where Human Rights Watch and other groups, including Afghan NGOs, were able to investigate aerial bombings. During the fighting in Afghanistan, the US had been providing inadequate or outright inaccurate information regarding incidents in which large numbers of civilian casualties were reported. In a number of cases US forces had

---

89   'US/Yemen: Investigate civilian deaths from airstrikes: Four years on, no justice for 41 Bedouins killed by US cruise missiles' *Human Rights Watch News* 17 Dec 2013 http:// www.hrw.org/news/2013/12/17/usyemen-investigate-civilian-deaths-airstrikes (accessed Dec 30, 2013).
90   L Tayler 'Anatomy of a drone strike gone wrong: In rural Yemen a botched attack on terror suspects kills 12 civilians and destroys a community' *Foreign Policy* 26 Dec 2012 http://www.foreignpolicy.com/articles/2012/12/26/yemen_air_attack_civilians_dead (accessed 1 March 2013).
91   The use of drones for targeted killings does not directly affect the legal analysis of a particular attack. Drones themselves and their weaponry of missiles and laser-guided bombs are not illegal weapons under the laws of war – they can be used lawfully or unlawfully depending on the circumstances. When used appropriately, drones offer certain advantages over manned aircraft or cruise missiles that can help to minimise civilian casualties in combat operations. Drones have enhanced surveillance capabilities that allow them to linger with a view of the target for long periods without risk to human operators. Drone operators are thus in theory better equipped to distinguish valid military targets from civilians who are immune from attack. As with other aerial attacks, drone operations may be hampered by poor intelligence or local actors' manipulation, especially when operating outside of areas where reliable ground forces can direct them.

claimed immediately – before there could be any serious investigation of the incident – that all those killed in an airstrike were Taliban militants. But here information gathered on the ground by human rights organisations and journalists reached US authorities, which had the effect to push the US Defence Department to conduct more credible investigations.[92] In Afghanistan, the situation will more clearly be covered by IHL, and so there is less of a need to address human rights law issues in air attacks.

Without access to the sites of the attacks, it has been difficult for Human Rights Watch and other organisations to determine the nature of the target beyond US government claims and the numbers of civilian casualties. This is also has made it difficult to reach conclusions about the applicable law – whether it is an armed conflict situation covered primarily by the laws of war or a law enforcement situation that falls only under the realm of human rights law. Of course the applicable law is not dispositive as to whether an attack is lawful or not – a targeted killing can be unlawful because the target was not a genuine military objective or there was disproportionate loss of civilian life. A killing under law enforcement rules can be lawful when the individual targeted was imminently engaged in carrying out attacks and there was no realistic means of apprehension.[93]

So instead of focusing on the legality of specific attacks, as would normally be part of monitoring, NGOs have addressed government mechanisms to ensure respect for the applicable law. For instance, Human Rights Watch has argued that so long as the US government does not demonstrate a readiness to hold the CIA to international legal requirements for accountability and redress, only the US armed forces should have command responsibility to conduct attacks using drones. The organisation also repeatedly called upon the US government to clarify fully and publicly its legal rationale for conducting targeted killings and the legal limits on such strikes; explain why its attacks are in conformity with all applicable international law and make public information, including video footage, on how particular attacks comply with those standards; and conduct investigations of targeted killings where there is credible evidence of wrongdoing, provide compensation to all victims of unlawful attacks, and discipline or prosecute as appropriate those responsible for conducting or ordering illegal strikes.[94]

As the technology becomes cheaper and more readily available, the use of drones in targeted killings will become more prevalent around the world, testing the ability of human rights organisations to monitor their

92   Human Rights Watch (n 33 above).
93   See K Roth 'What rules should govern US drone attacks' *New York Review of Books* 4 April 2013 http://www.nybooks.com/articles/archives/2013/apr/04/what-rules-should-govern-us-drone-attacks/?pagination=false (accessed 15 March 2013).
94   'Q & A: US targeted killings and international law' *Human Rights Watch News* 19 December 2011 http://www.hrw.org/news/2011/12/19/q-us-targeted-killings-and-international-law (accessed 1 March 2013).

lawfulness. More than 70 countries now possess aerial drones.[95] Those drones are primarily used for surveillance. China, France, Germany, India, Iran, Israel, Italy, Russia, Turkey, the United Kingdom and the United States either have or are currently seeking drones with attack capacity.[96] The lines between armed conflict and law enforcement – and thus IHL and international human rights law are certainly going to become more entangled, not less.

4 Conclusion

Protecting a population from harm was long thought to be neatly divided into rules for armed conflict situations and rules for peacetime. However, parallel to that distinction being disavowed – or at least muddled – has been the increasing role played by human rights organisations in areas where IHL is applicable. Human rights organisations have increasingly added IHL to their work. More and more have taken on conducting field investigations in battle zones, advocating for treaties on weapons such as anti-personnel landmines and cluster munitions, and playing an active role in proceedings before the international criminal courts.

In doing so they have had to develop research and advocacy skills on IHL. At the same time, they have been able to bring to the debates on IHL issues, more in-depth understandings of international human rights law. This has been particularly useful in those areas where the boundaries of IHL and human rights law intersect or overlap. Often these have been issues where IHL has been vague, such as the rules for the treatment of detainees in non-international armed conflicts. On other issues, such as humanitarian access, IHL rules are more protective than those of human rights law. And on particularly vexing issues such as 'targeted killings', the jury remains out as to the best way to apply international law to ensure civilians the best protection from wrongful attack.

The influx of human rights organisations into an arena that was previously the monopoly of a small number of military lawyers and academics has not always been well received. Such problems were

---

95   P Bergen & J Rowland 'A dangerous new world of drones' *CNN* 1 October 2012 http://newamerica.net/publications/articles/2012/a_dangerous_new_world_of_drones_72125 (accessed 1 March 2013).

96   According to *The Washington Post*, more than 50 countries have purchased surveillance drones, and many have started developing armed models. W Wan & P Finn 'Global race on to match US drone capabilities' *The Washington Post* 4 July 2011 http://www.washingtonpost.com/world/national-security/global-race-on-to-match-us-drone-capabilities/2011/06/30/gHQACWdmxH_story.html (accessed 1 March 2013). See also The Fellowship of Reconciliation 'Convenient killing: Armed drones and the "Playstation" mentality' (2010) 11-12 http://www.for.org.uk/files/drones-conv-killing.pdf (accessed 1 March 2013).

exacerbated by human rights groups that jumped into the fray of IHL without a solid grounding in this area of law and its long history. The post-11 September challenges posed to IHL, advances in weapons' treaties and the creation of international and hybrid criminal courts has created an impetus for human rights organisations to get more involved – and to raise their level of competence. They are here to stay.

International Humanitarian Law and International Human Rights: Military Operations

Blaise Cathcart

1   Introduction

Military legal advisors (usually uniformed military legal officers) are deployed to some of the most dangerous and austere places in the world. In those places and, indeed, in national or multinational headquarter locations, they are frequently called upon to give legal advice under extreme conditions, on very short notice, with very little time to respond to serious issues. The most important involving matters of life and death. In fact in some cases, those dedicated and skilled legal advisors, half way around the world on a warship, in a command post or in an air operations centre, have only enough time to give a hand signal – a thumbs up or a thumbs down – before the commander they advise has to make a decision. Such is the solemn responsibility of the legal advisor of an armed force, particularly during an armed conflict. While the legal issues involved will often be complex, ambiguous and open to debate, the legal advisor is responsible for knowing when the time for legal debate is over. Advice must be provided. The mission must be completed or aborted.

Imagine the immense challenges for current military legal advisors as they attempt to explain and advise planners, commanders and civilian decision makers, often under urgent, grave and stressful circumstances, on the interaction of international humanitarian law (IHL) (frequently

*   Major General Blaise Cathcart, OMM, CD QC, Judge Advocate General of the Canadian Armed Forces. I am grateful to Colonel (ret'd) Kirby Abbott and Colonel Rob Holman of the Canadian Armed Forces Office of the Judge Advocate General, for their personal comments and suggestions. The views of the author do not necessarily reflect those of the Canadian Armed Forces, the Department of National Defence or the Government of Canada.

referred to as the law of armed conflict (LOAC))[1] and international human rights law (IHRL),[2] this may include:

(1) If an armed conflict exits, is it an international armed conflict (IAC) or a non-international armed conflict (NIAC)?
(2) What are the implications of the existence of a United Nations Security Council Resolution?
(3) Do human rights law treaties such as the International Covenant on Civil and Political Rights (ICCPR) or the European Convention of Human Rights (ECHR) apply extra-territorially to militaries operating beyond their national borders?
(4) Is IHL/IHL the *lex specialis* (law governing the specific subject matter) of armed conflict? If yes, what does this mean?
(5) What use of force is authorised for mission accomplishment? Is there a difference between combat use of force and law enforcement use of force?
(6) Does the force have to capture the enemy if possible, or is it lawful to kill him/her?
(7) What is the process for targeting the enemy? Who can be targeted?
(8) What weapons can the force use? Drones? Cyber? Autonomous systems?
(9) Can the force take detainees? If yes, what is their legal status? What rights must they be afforded?
(10) Does the force have to conduct investigations of all uses of force?

This chapter will not address all of these important issues in depth. Instead it will focus, from the perspective of a Canadian military legal advisor, on the impact of the convergence and conflicts of IHL and IHRL in the provision of legal advice by legal advisors of armed forces during armed conflict. In particular, the emphasis will be placed on the most challenging issue, namely, the question of the extra-territorial application of IHRL during armed conflict. The debate surrounding this issue today is seemingly endless and gives rise to much confusion for legal advisors, military commanders and decision-makers alike.

Accordingly, Part 2 will address the roles and responsibilities of a professional military legal advisor concerning issues arising from armed

---

1   In this chapter 'IHL' refers primarily the four 1949 Geneva Conventions (GCs), the two 1977 Additional Protocols (APs) to the GCs and the 1907 Hague Convention IV and Regulations (HR). The GCs and HR are considered reflective of customary law and have attained virtual universal recognition. The APs have less states parties and only some of their provisions are considered reflective of customary law.
2   In this chapter 'IHRL' refers primarily to the rights and obligations codified in Universal Declaration of Human Rights (UDHR), the International Covenants on Civil and Political Rights (ICCPR) and on Economic, Social and Cultural Rights (1966), Convention on Genocide (1948), Convention on Racial Discrimination (1965), Convention on the Discrimination Against Women (1979), Convention Against Torture (1984) and Convention on the Rights of the Child (1989). The regional human rights instruments: the European Convention for the Protection of Human Rights and Fundamental Freedoms (1950), the American Declaration of the Rights and Duties of Man (1948), the American Convention on Human Rights (1969), and the African Charter on Human and Peoples' Rights (1981). Generally, given the relative newness and variety of IHRL treaties, it is difficult to determine what, if anything, might constitute the customary law of IHRL.

conflict. The primary example will be the Judge Advocate General (JAG) of the Canadian Armed Forces (CAF). Part 3 will examine the critical debate concerning the extra-territorial application of IHRL during armed conflict and the significant confusion and challenges arising therefrom. Part 4 concludes by noting that in reality, both IHL and IHRL frameworks offer similar, if not identical, protections to persons in armed conflict. A type of convergence of the two bodies of law on the battlefield already exists in a practical, pragmatic and realistic sense. They both focus on ensuring respect and protection for fundamental rights and humane treatment. However, when the debate focuses more on formalistic, technical and, sometimes, politicised analysis (judicial, institutional and academic) about which framework applies, rather than simply trying to protect humans in the always terribly real and often unfair circumstances of armed conflict, then unconstructive divergence occurs.

2   The role of the military legal advisor[3]

21st century military operations are dynamic, incredibly complex and highly scrutinised. At a time when military actions and their effects can be transmitted instantaneously around the world and immediately analysed by the public and the media, mission success and legitimacy are judged in large part on a nation's adherence to the rule of law. As demonstrated during the last decade, the law is increasingly being used to either achieve or undermine strategic or operational effects.[4] In this complicated environment, the role of professional military legal advisors, as a source of

---

3   For other perspectives of the role of the legal advisor to the armed forces see LC Green *The role of legal advisers in the armed forces: Essays on the modern law of war*(1985) 73-82; APV Rogers & D Stewart 'The role of the military legal advisor' in TD Gill & D Fleck (eds) *The handbook of the international law of military operations* (2010) 537-564; APV Rogers 'The military lawyer's perspective' in APV Rogers *Law on the battlefield* (2004) 239-248; R McLaughlin 'Giving operational legal advice: Context and method' 2012 50 *Military Law and the Law of War Review* 99; Sir D Bethlehem QC 'The secret life of international law' (2012) 1 *Cambridge Journal of International and Comparative Law* 23; HH Koh 'The State Department Legal Adviser's Office: Eight decades in peace and war' (2012) 100 *The Georgetown Law Journal* 1747; SR Tully 'Getting it wrong or being ignored: Ten words on advice for government lawyers' (2009) 7 *The New Zealand Yearbook of International Law* 51; LA Dickinson 'Military lawyers on the battlefield: An empirical account of international law compliance' (2010) 104 *American Journal of International Law* 1; K Anderson 'The role of the Unites States military lawyer in projecting a vision of the laws of war' (2003) 4 *Chicago Journal of International Law* 445; CJ Dunlap Jr 'It ain't no TV show: JAGs and modern military operations' (2003) 4 *Chicago Journal of International Law* 479; Col LA Libman 'Legal advice in the conduct of operations in the Israel Defense Forces' (2011) 50 *Military Law and the Law of War Review* 67; MA Newton 'Modern military necessity: The role & relevance of military lawyers' (2006-2007) 12 *Roger Williams University Law Review* 877.

4   This is true whether one is discussing major procurement projects and compliance to established bidding processes, the transfer of detainees, use of force or the participation in armed conflict. In Canada, in the events surrounding the Somalia affair (primarily focused on the 1993 torture and killing of a young Somali detainee by CAF members), the role of the rule of law was a central theme. Moreover, in the US the term 'lawfare' has appeared in the last 10 years. Generally, 'lawfare' is often expressed as 'the strategy of using or misusing law and legal processes as a substitute for traditional instruments

independent and objective legal advice, has evolved and taken on greater importance.

Importantly, IHL requires states to ensure that legal advisers are available to advise military commanders on IHL.[5] Notably, the requirement is generally applicable at all times, not just during armed conflict. The main underlying rationale for this article, like much of Protocol I, is to enhance compliance with IHL and, consequently, achieve a better balance between humanitarianism and military necessity. Interestingly, there is no similar express obligation to have legal advisors under IHRL.

The implementation of the obligations under article 82 API can take different forms. Generally, most states have appointed legal advisors in their armed forces. While some legal advisors are civilians working in a Ministry or Department of Defence, most are members of the armed forces. Uniformed legal advisors have the distinct privilege and perspective of being members of both the profession of arms and the profession of laws. This combination of professions creates a military legal advisor who is uniquely qualified to effectively, independently and credibly analyse and synthesise the complexities and realities of military operations and the law, particularly during armed conflict.

While there are several models for how states may appoint military legal advisors, it is reasonable to say that western democratic states have had the most experience with the creation, development and employment of such advisors.[6] No one state has instituted the perfect model. Nonetheless, large western military powers such as the United States (US) and the United Kingdom (UK) have often set the example and the 'best practice' for the role and responsibilities of a military legal advisor, both in the armed forces and in government. Another similar useful example, but likely lesser known, is the role of the Judge Advocate General of the Canadian Armed Forces.

---

of power to achieve either strategic or operational effects' (from Colonel LL Turner 'The detainee interrogation debate and the legal policy process' (2009) 54 *Joint Force Quarterly* 40).

5   Art 82 API 1977; A Roberts & R Guelff *Documents on the laws of war* (2003) 469-470 states: 'The High Contracting Parties at all times, and the Parties to the conflict in time of armed conflict, shall ensure that legal advisers are available, when necessary, to advise military commanders at the appropriate level on the application of the Conventions and this Protocol and on the appropriate instruction to be given to the armed forces on this subject.'

6   Note 1 above describes different models amongst the US, the UK, Australia, Israel and New Zealand.

2.1 The Judge Advocate General of the Canadian Armed Forces

The JAG for the CAF is a key strategic participant in the decision-making processes within both the military chain of command and the government. Essentially, the JAG fills this role by providing independent legal advice to the Government of Canada (GoC), the Minister of National Defence (MND) and the Chief of the Defence Staff (CDS). All of these decision makers are entrusted with profound responsibilities. The most critical of which engage issues of life, death and liberty of CAF members, citizens, opposing forces and foreign civilians in the achievement of CAF mission success and the advancement of GoC interests. In fulfilling these responsibilities CAF leaders require access to candid, honest, and transparent legal advice. Furthermore, in an environment of heightened accountability and responsibility, GoC, CAF and departmental leaders rely increasingly on legal officers to deliver analysis and advice that advances goals and objectives within a clear rule of law framework.

More specifically, under the authority of the National Defence Act, RSC 1985, c N-5 (the NDA), the JAG for the CAF is appointed by the Governor in Council (the Cabinet) and reports to the Minister of National Defence (MND). The JAG serves as legal advisor to the Governor General (the Queen's representative in Canada), the MND, the Department of National Defence (DND) and the CAF in matters relating to military law.[7] Interestingly, 'military law' is not defined, but, through practice, it has crystallised as the broad legal discipline encompassing all international and domestic law relating to the CAF, including its governance, administration and activities.

Apart from this advisory role, the JAG also has a statutory mandate to superintend the administration of military justice in the CF.[8] It should be noted that 'military justice' is a sub-set of 'military law', and is concerned primarily with the maintenance and enforcement of discipline in the CAF.

The JAG is a military officer who holds a rank that is not less than Brigadier-General and is a barrister or advocate with at least ten years standing at the bar of a Canadian province.[9] In providing that the JAG must be an officer, the Canadian Parliament reaffirmed that the military law advisory function requires current military knowledge and expertise to effectively deliver operationally relevant military law advice to the chain of command. However, Parliament also recognised that in a hierarchical military command structure there was a real or perceived risk that a uniformed JAG would be unable to assert and maintain the independence

---

7   Sec 9 of the NDA.
8   As above.
9   As above.

required by both law and practice when carrying out the military law responsibilities imposed by Parliament. To mitigate this risk, the NDA states the JAG serves at the pleasure (of the Government) for a term not exceeding four years, is responsive to the military chain of command for the provision of legal services in the CAF, and is responsible to the MND in the performance of his duties. In this latter sense, the CAF JAG is unique amongst his western uniformed legal advisor counterparts because he reports directly to the political level, namely the MND.

All CAF legal officers are fully qualified professional lawyers, members in good standing of their respective Canadian provincial or territorial law societies, and are commissioned officers in the CF, ranging in rank from Captain/Lieutenant (Navy) to Colonel/Captain (Navy). Importantly, legal officers who provide legal services to the CAF or DND are under the command of the JAG, and in respect of the performance of their established duties, a legal officer is not subject to the command of an officer who is not a legal officer.[10] This reinforces the perceived and real independence of legal advice as legal advisors are not, strictly speaking, under the operational chain of command.

2.2   Importance of having professional lawyers providing independent legal advice in military operations

Why is independent legal advice delivered by a professional lawyer so critical in the context of military operations? The underlying rationale for independent, objective and candid legal advice is often recognised at a superficial level but the underlying rationale is rarely discussed, not well understood or consistently respected.

It is widely recognised that professional lawyers working as 'in-house counsel' or as government/military lawyers' must be vigilant in guarding against the erosion of full professional independence. This erosion can arise through self identification with the objectives and goals of the organisation (usually the military chain of command), as the result of subtle pressures such as professional advancement,[11] or through deference to chain of command or organisational imposed structures and processes that limit, shape or restrict a legal advisor's access to key commanders or decision makers. There is always the possibility for some military commanders and senior leaders to try to pressure the shaping of certain legal opinions and to short circuit established processes resulting in the marginalisation of legal advice.

---

10   Pursuant to the Queen's Regulations and Orders for the Canadian Forces (QR&O) 4.081, the JAG has command over all officers and non-commissioned members posted to a position established within the Office of the JAG, and whose duty it is to provide legal services to the CF. See http://www.admfincs.forces.gc.ca/qro-orf/vol-01/chapter-chapitre-004-eng.asp#cha-004-081 (accessed 1 September 2013).
11   BG Smith *Professional conduct for Canadian lawyers* (1989) 225.

There are many examples of operational and, often, consequential political crises arising, in large measure, as a result of independent legal advice being eroded either by design or by a lack of understanding as to why advice must be independent.[12] Failure to safeguard the legal advisor's independence places the effective provision of legal advice and mission success at risk. It is, therefore, essential, from a Canadian legal and military perspective, that the military legal advisor be both a professional lawyer and independent in the execution of the provision of legal services while, at the same time, advancing the goals and mission of the armed forces. In other words, the mission for the professional legal advisor must align with the mission of the armed forces and the government within the parameters of the law.

2.3   Operational law advice

Operational law is a subset of the broader definition of military and international law. Generally, operational law is that body of domestic and international law that applies to the conduct of all phases of a military operation at all levels of command (strategic, operational and tactical).[13] The particular bodies of law that will be relevant to the operational legal advisor and commander will vary depending upon the nature of the mission (international or national). It is often the largest area of practice for military legal advisors. While some military legal advisors may be uniformed and others civilian, all will practice operational law in some form. The role of an operational legal advisor is unique in legal practice. There is no equivalent role in private practice or in government service.

For example, when elements of the CAF are deployed on operations across Canada or around the world, legal officers deploy with those elements in order to provide dedicated legal support to commanders and staff on the ground or onboard ship. As uniformed members of the CAF,

12   The 1993 CAF mission in Somalia and the US issues related to torture in Iraq, Afghanistan and Guantanamo Bay are recent examples of when things 'go off the rails'. Consequently, post Somalia revisions to the NDA statutorily defined the role of JAG and it was the US torture cases which saw the elevation of US JAGs to Lieutenant General rank with added buffers enhancing their independence. This also occurred in Australia in 2004, when the court denied a claim for legal professional privilege advanced by the Chief of the Royal Australian Air Force. While the decision was overturned on appeal, the appeal court noted that in order for the advice of government lawyers to be protected by solicitor/client privilege steps had to be taken to ensure that legal advisors provided the advice independently. As a result, the Australian Defence Force (ADF) legal branch was significantly transformed to ensure greater independence for legal advisors and, more significantly, to better protect the ADF's confidentiality and credibility.
13   See CAF JAG website at http://www.forces.gc.ca/en/about-org-structure/judge-advocate-general-office.page (accessed 18 April 2014). For a United States definition of international and operational law see US Army *FM 104: Legal support to the operational army* (2009) 53 para 514: 'International law is the application of international agreements, US and international law, and customs related to military operations and activities. Operational law is the body of domestic, foreign, and international law that directly affects the conduct of military operations.'

legal officers are trained and equipped to live and work in any operational environment. This flexibility means that they can provide the chain of command with direct and independent legal advice during the actual conduct of operations.

Normally, operational legal advice will address, though not be limited to, the following:

(1) legal basis for the operation (international and national);
(2) international law issues (for example, applicability of treaties such as UNCLOS or the Chicago Convention on Aviation, or customary international law);
(3) international humanitarian law or the law of armed conflict;
(4) international human rights law;
(5) use of force/rules of engagement;
(6) targeting;
(7) detainees;
(8) use of specific weapons (for example, prohibition on the use of anti-personnel mines, particularly in the context of coalition or allied operations and the use of riot control agents); and
(9) enforcement of the law (for example, investigations, military justice and discipline).

Legal advice is provided during all phases of the mission, that is, pre-deployment training, deployment and post-deployment. Importantly, legal advisors must be part of any planning that occurs at each phase of the mission. This not only meets a state's obligations under article 82 API,[14] but also makes practical and operational sense. Legal advice during all planning phases will better ensure compliance with the rule of law and mission success.

While commanders and their staffs must recognise the requirement for a legal advisor to be able to provide independent legal advice, practicalities dictate that a legal advisor will be a fully integrated member of the mission and of the commander's staff. This is a reality given that the key role of an operational legal advisor is to facilitate the commander's ability to successfully complete the mission in accordance with the rule of law. There is no doubt that when legal advisors are deployed on missions, they are subject to orders and instructions issued by or on behalf of the commander. However, no such order or instruction should result in any situation that would interfere substantially or conflict with the legal advisor's professional duties as a legal officer. As previously noted, in the Canadian military context, the independence of the legal advisor from the chain of command is recognised and established in orders which clearly state that the JAG retains command over all legal advisors at all times.[15]

---

14 n 5 above.
15 See (QR&O) 4.081 (n 10 above).

With this overview of the role and responsibilities of the professional legal advisor and, more specifically, the operational legal advisor in the armed forces (exemplified primarily by the CAF JAG), it would be useful to consider several current legal issues that pose significant challenges for such advisors in dealing with the convergence and conflicts of IHL and IHRL in armed conflict; the most important issue being the question of the extra-territorial application of IHRL during armed conflict.

3 The convergence and conflict of IHL and IHRL in armed conflict: Extra-territorial application of IHRL

The issue of the interrelation of IHL and IHRL is relatively new and has developed since the end of the Second World War.[16] However, today, the interrelationship, convergence and conflict of IHL and IHRL are the most immediate and significant challenges facing military operational law advisors within the context of armed conflict, both international and non-international.[17] Currently, there are immense practical difficulties for operational law advisors as they attempt to explain and advise planners, commanders and civilian decision-makers, often under pressing and serious circumstances, on the interaction of IHL and IHRL.

This chapter is not the place for an extensive analysis of all the issues. The following sections will, therefore, focus on the current fundamental concern for military legal advisors: namely, how to address and advise on the legal tension and confusion created by the growing, often impractical,

16   See LC Green 'Human rights and the law of armed conflict' in Green (n 3 above) 83; GIAD Draper "The relationship between the human rights regime and the law of war' (1971) 1 *Israel Yearbook on Human Rights* 191; T Taylor et al 'Human rights and armed conflict: Conflicting views' (1973) 67 *American Journal of International Law* 141; and T Meron 'The humanization of humanitarian law' (2000) *American Journal of International Law* 239, which all discuss the evolution of human rights and human rights law post World war Two on IHL, particularly in the negotiation of the 1977 Additional Protocols I & II to the Geneva Conventions.

17   Colonel DK Abbott, Office of the Canadian JAG, and a recent senior legal advisor at NATO Supreme Headquarters Allied Powers Europe, articulated challenges for military legal advisors in a paper delivered at the Bruges Colloquium on International Humanitarian Law, 18-19 October 2012 (publication of conference papers forthcoming) as follows: 'From my perspective-emphasizing throughout my presentation that approach the topic for the perspective of a North American lawyer working within NATO – *clearly place the legally ambiguous inter relationship and tension between IHRL and IHL as above and beyond all other issues as the number one challenge facing IHL within situations of IAC. I should say that I also view this as an even more pressing issue within the context of a NIAC.'* (emphasis mine). He noted 7 significant sub-issues in the context of armed conflict: (1) The absence of a methodology which allows for the practical application of the *lex specialis* doctrine; (2) The interaction between ECtHR jurisprudence and the *lex specialis* doctrine when advising on the conduct of military operations during IAC; (3) Jurisdiction – the extra territorial scope of HR treaties; (4) Security Council resolutions as a source of legal authority to engage IHL; (5) Detention para 100 Al Jedda; (6) Right to life; and (7) Investigate cases where force was lawful under IHL-ICC.

ambiguous and unhelpful debate on the extra-territorial application of IHRL during armed conflict.

3.1   The application of IHL and IHRL in armed conflict

Starting at first principles, does human rights law even apply in times of armed conflict? The short answer is – maybe. IHRL treaties, the majority being regional treaties, continue to exist during armed conflict. However, the key threshold question is often overlooked, that is, does the treaty apply as a matter of law to the factual situation of an armed conflict? In other words, does an IHRL treaty bind all the parties in an armed conflict? It is clear that no IHRL treaty applies to or binds non-state actors. They only bind states, at least those states parties to a specific IHRL treaty.

The source of main debate and controversy today is whether IHRL treaties apply extra-territorially during an armed conflict. The current state of the law and academic commentary are ambiguous, uncertain and confusing on the issue of the extra-territorial application of IHRL in the context of armed conflict. State practice seems to indicate that many states do not immediately accept that human rights treaties apply extra-territorially. Accordingly, it is reasonable to say the IHRL may or may not apply. Moreover, if IHRL does apply during armed conflict, then the question becomes how does it interact with the *lex specialis* of IHL?

3.2   Extra-territorial application of IHRL

A crucial legal issue impacting current military operations during armed conflict is the question of the extra-territorial application of IHRL. Most often the issue focuses on the application of the ICCPR and the ECHR. In recent years there has been a relative explosion of analysis and commentary on this issue. Much of it has been inspired by jurisprudence from the European Court of Human Rights (ECtHR) and commentary by the United Nations (UN) Human Rights Committee.[18] The view that IHRL, specifically human rights treaties, apply to international military operations has caused much uncertainty, confusion and ambiguity for states and military commanders, particularly for commanders of multinational forces. Accordingly, as a result, states and military commanders are at greater risk of mission failure, including risk of legal liability. Equally important, civilians are at greater risk of loss of life and

---

18   *Al-Skeini v United Kingdom*, Application no 55721/07, ECHR (7 July 2011); *Behrami v France & Seramati v France*, (Admissibility) App no 71412/01, ECHR (2 May 2007); *Issa v Turkey*, Application no 31821/96, ECHR (16 November 2004); *Ocalan v Turkey*, App No 46221/99, ECHR, (12 March 2003); *Banković v Belgium*, (Admissibility) App no 52207/99, ECHR 2001-XII, [2001] 890; *Loizidou v Turkey*, App no 15318/89, ECHR (18 December 1996); HRC 'General Comment No 31: Nature of the general legal obligation on state parties to the Covenant' UN Doc CCPR/C/21/Rev.1/Add.13 (2004): http://www1.umn.edu/humanrts/ gencomm/hrcom31.html.

liberty. Such uncertainty, confusion and risks are significantly reduced, even eliminated, if greater clarity is generated and achieved.

The apparent trigger to the extra-territorial application of human rights treaties, at least the ICCPR and ECHR, is the concept of 'effective control'. ECtHR jurisprudence and UNHRC commentary have determined that if a state's military is in 'effective control' of foreign territory or individuals in foreign territory, then the ECHR and the ICCPR, as the case may be, apply as a matter of law, even during an armed conflict. For example, the judgment of the ECtHR in *Al-Skeini v The United Kingdom* has caused much confusion in addressing the issue of human rights in armed conflict. In *Al-Skeini*, the ECHR was found to be applicable to actions taken by British troops in Basra, Iraq, where the UK assumed the exercise of some of the public powers normally exercised by a sovereign government. The Court's decision was noteworthy in its breadth and scope. The Court expanded the concept of jurisdiction to include 'effective control of the individual', not just 'effective control of the territory'; this, combined with its view that Convention rights could be 'divided and tailored',[19] have caused much confusion for academics, legal advisors and commanders alike. Moreover, the Court conducted its analysis with a methodology that completely avoided the *lex specialis* of IHL. In other words, the Court assessed the legality of a state's use of force in armed conflict (in killing combatants or in detaining individuals) solely on the basis of a regional human rights treaty (the ECHR). The same was true of the more recent case of *Jaloud v The Netherlands*.[20] Although some have viewed this approach as being appropriate given that states have not invoked the derogation clause,[21] the Court itself has subsequently held, in the case of *Hassan v The United Kingdom*, that while a lack of derogation does not preclude it 'from taking account of the context and provisions of [IHL]' in interpreting and applying the provisions of the ECHR during armed conflict, such an approach will only be employed where it is clearly pleaded.[22] It is notable that, another regional human rights body, the IACHR did apply IHL in the *Abella* case. Perhaps the ECtHR will further

---

19   *Al-Skeini* paras 136 & 137.
20   *Jaloud v Netherlands* Application No 47708/08 ECHR (2008).
21   ECHR art 15 states in part: 'In time of war or other public emergency threatening the life of the nation any High Contracting Party may take measures derogating from its obligations under this Convention to the extent strictly required by the exigencies of the situation, provided that such measures are not inconsistent with its other obligations under international law... No derogation from article 2, except in respect of deaths resulting from lawful acts of war, or from articles 3, 4 (paragraph 1) and 7 shall be made under this provision. For analysis of the competence of the ECtHR to apply IHL with or without a derogation under art 15 ECHR see the chapter in this book by Dr Karin Oellers-Frahm 'Convergence and conflicts of human rights (IHRL) and international humanitarian law (IHL) in military operations regional perspectives: The European Court of Human Rights'.
22   *Hassan v UK* Application No 29750/09, ECHR (2009) paras 103 & 107.

clarify its approach to the application of IHL in its upcoming decision in the case of *Georgia v Russia*.[23]

While the methodology of the ECtHR (like that of UN Committees) in determining the interplay of IHL and IHRL remains obscure if not non-existent, the jurisprudence and commentary nevertheless confirm that rights such as the right to life and the right to liberty must be protected for every person in the 'effective control' of its armed force. It is not clear whether or how all the other rights in the treaties may apply or not. Such interpretations seem to have been formulated in a vacuum where state practice, the realities of armed conflict and the *lex specialis* of IHL are largely ignored. State practice, particularly that of the Unites States (US), indicates that the ECtHR's 'effective control' test for jurisdiction is not universally widely accepted.[24]

How, then, does a state's military legal advisor make sense of such confusion for the military commander? How does the legal advisor explain the ambiguous law to a military commander who is charged with achieving mission success within the rule of law?

Again, in the Canadian context, the military legal advisor's role is to facilitate the commander's ability to successfully execute the mission within the rule of law. Canada is not a party to the ECHR and, therefore, not bound by the jurisprudence of the ECtHR. Canada is a party to the ICCPR. Canadian courts have addressed the issue of the extra-territorial application of the *Canadian Charter of Rights and Freedoms*, which is considered, in part, a type of national implementation of the ICCPR. As some view the judgments of the ECtHR and the commentaries of UN Committees as the leading and binding statements on the extra-territorial application of IHRL treaties, it is important and useful to examine other jurisprudence, such as Canadian jurisprudence. Such other jurisprudence

---

23 *Georgia v Russia (no 2)* App No 38263/08, ECHR (2011). The case concerns the armed conflict between Georgia and Russia at the beginning of August 2008 following an extended period of mounting tension, provocations and incidents. Georgia lodged an application with the ECtHR alleging that Russia allowed, or caused to develop, an administrative practice through indiscriminate and disproportionate attacks against civilians and their property in the two autonomous regions of Georgia – Abkhazia and South Ossetia – by the Russian military forces and the separatist forces under their control. Of note, Russia argued, in part, that the events of August 2008 had to be examined under the rules of IHL and not the Convention provisions, because the armed conflict between Georgia and Russia had been an international one.

24 See MJ Dennis 'Non-application of civil and political rights treaties extraterritorially during times of international armed conflict' (2007) 40 *Israel Law Review* 453 456, in which he notes that: '[I]n practice, it would appear that most states generally do not apply the human rights recognized in the core international human rights treaties extra-territorially during times of international armed conflict and military occupation.'. The US recently reiterated before the UN Human Rights Committee its position that the ICCPR does not apply extra-territorially see C Savage 'US, rebuffing UN, maintains stance that rights treaty does not apply abroad' *NY Times* 13 March 2014: http://mobile.nytimes.com/2014/03/14/world/us-affirms-stance-that-rights-treaty-doesnt-apply-abroad.html?_r=2&referrer= (accessed 18 April 2014).

is equally binding (where applicable) and can be informative and practical in its analysis.

The question before the Federal Court of Canada in the case of *Amnesty International Canada (AI) v Canada (Chief of the Defence Staff)*[25] was whether, as a matter of law, the *Canadian Charter of Rights and Freedoms* (the Charter) applied extra-territorially to the detention and transfer of non-Canadians captured by the CAF in Afghanistan. The question of law arose against a backdrop of allegations brought by the applicants (Amnesty et al) that such transfers resulted in serious human rights violations (abuse and torture of detainees by Afghan authorities).

The applicants (AI) argued that the Charter applied extra-territorially to CAF military operations in the armed conflict in Afghanistan. It appeared the applicants focused on the Canadian Charter rather than the ICCPR because there were no express territorial limits on the application of the Charter. Nonetheless, the applicants and the Court noted that international law, including the ICCPR, informed the interpretation of the jurisdictional reach and limits of the application of the Charter. Accordingly, the interpretation of the application of the ICCPR was a prominent part of the case.

One of AI's primary arguments was that jurisdiction of the Canadian Charter extended to foreign soil in the context of military operations based on a 'military control of the person' test. Specifically, AI submitted that once an individual was arrested by CAF personnel, was detained at a facility controlled by the CAF, and was subject to ongoing detention or release at the sole discretion of the Canadian Forces, that individual was within the effective control of Canada and should enjoy the protections of the Charter and of Canadian courts.

Importantly, in support of their argument that 'effective military control of the person' should be the appropriate test to be applied in cases of the exercise of military force, AI relied on jurisprudence from the House of Lords, from the United States Supreme Court, and from the Court of Appeal for the District of Columbia. They argued this jurisprudence confirmed that domestic human rights legislation applies to individuals detained by military forces in Iraq and at Guantanamo Bay by citing *Al-Skeini v Secretary of State for Defence* [2007] UKHL 26, *Rasul v Bush* 542 US 466 (2004), and *Omar v Secretary of the United States Army* 479 F. 3d 1 (DC Cir 2007).

AI cited jurisprudence of the European Court of Human Rights, including the decisions in *Banković v Belgium* (2001) 11 BHRC 435, 2001–XII Eur Ct HR 333 (GC) and *Issa v Turkey* (2004) 41 EHRR 567. Finally,

---

25   *Amnesty International Canada v Canada (Chief of the Defence Staff)* (FC) 2008 FC 336, [2008] 4 FCR 546.

AI cited commentaries of the United Nations Human Rights Committee (General Comment 31) and of the United Nations Committee Against Torture (General Commentary No 2: Implementation of article 2 by States Parties (23/11/2007, CAT/C/GC/2/CRP.1/Rev.4)), both of which advocated the use of a test of *de facto* or *de jure* control over persons in detention as a basis for exercising extra-territorial human rights jurisdiction.

Conversely, the Government of Canada (GoC) argued the challenged transfer activities of the CAF in Afghanistan cannot be said to be within the authority of Parliament' of Canada as that phrase in section 32(1) of the Charter had been interpreted previously by the Supreme Court of Canada (SCC).[26] The detention and transfer of those captured by the CAF in Afghanistan occurred pursuant to Afghan and international law, including the UN Charter, applicable UN Security Council Resolutions (UNSCRs) and IHL. The application of the Charter to CAF detention and transfer activities pursuant to Afghan and international law would have been an impermissible exercise of Canadian jurisdiction as understood under Canadian law and would be an impermissible interference with Afghan sovereignty.

This issue is separate and distinct from whether the CAF detention and transfer activities in Afghanistan were authorised by the GoC. Domestic authorisation was necessary in order for CAF detention and transfer activities to occur. However, as such activities take place beyond the borders of Canada, domestic authority is not enough. Canada must have international law authority for such activities. This authority is contained in the three interrelated international legal bases for Canada's operations in Afghanistan: UNSCRs, state consent, and exercise of collective self-defence. During the duration of CAF operations in Afghanistan the prominence of the three legal bases varied depending on the facts on the ground, including whether the operations were under Operation Enduring Freedom (OEF) or NATO's International Security Assistance Force (ISAF). For example, collective self-defence was the sole legal basis during the start of operations in 2001 against the Taliban and Al-Qaeda. Twelve years later with different facts, including the existence of an allied Afghan government, the presence of NATO ISAF and significantly weakened Taliban and Al-Qaeda forces, the legal authority for operations shifted more towards Afghan consent and UNSCRs. Nevertheless, individual and collective state self-defence still existed from a Canadian perspective.

Canada's operations in Afghanistan, which derived their authority from these three international law bases, were governed by international law, most importantly the *lex specialis* of IHL. Whereas international

---

26 See GoC (Argument of Law) at: http://bccla.org/wp-content/uploads/2012/06/20010118-Afghan-Detainees-Factum-Crown.pdf (accessed 31 August 2013).

human rights law was *lex generalis*. In the circumstances, it was neither appropriate, nor necessary, for the Charter to apply.

In addressing AI's argument on the applicability of a 'military control of the person' test, the GoC rejected such a test. It submitted that Canada was not an occupying power in Afghanistan. The CAF controlled neither the military nor civilian administration of any part of the territory of Afghanistan. In fact, the CAF was one of several NATO forces operating in the territory as part of the UNSC mandated ISAF. The mere use of military force was not sufficient to establish effective control of territory. Therefore, it could not create the basis for the enforcement of the foreign state's law. A state cannot ensure respect for human rights if it is not effectively in control of the territory. Enforcement of law without consent or effective control of territory is largely unworkable as demonstrated in this case. While the government of Afghanistan consented to the presence of the CAF to conduct operations against the Taliban and Al-Qaeda, it did not consent to the application of the Charter or the entirety of Canadian law on its territory. Under a Technical Arrangement document, Afghanistan did agree that all Canadian personnel would, under all circumstances and at all times, be subject to the exclusive jurisdiction of their Canadian authorities in respect of any criminal or disciplinary offences which may be committed by them. This was the only significant exception that Afghanistan made to the exercise of its sovereignty regarding CAF operations.

Importantly, the GoC argued that if mere use of military force in Afghanistan would be sufficient to establish 'effective control of the person' then the sovereign country would become a patch-work of various foreign national laws and norms. For example, Dutch law would apply to detainees taken by Netherlands forces, Danish law to detainees taken by the Danes and so on. The result would be a hodgepodge of different foreign legal systems, imposed within the territory of a state whose sovereignty the international community has committed itself to uphold, and applicable on a purely random-chance basis. This impractical result result would significantly hinder a multi-national or coalition military operation such as ISAF which depended upon unity of command and legal clarity to ensure mission success. For example, the imposition of national law, largely through HR law, would cause much confusion on the standards and procedures to be followed when detaining and/or transferring an individual. The varying legal frameworks may or may not require a 'charge-or-release' approach or it may require states to offer more procedural rights, such as the right to counsel, to unlawful combatants or unprivileged belligerents that they would have to to lawful combatants. Conversely, IHL provided not only full protections but also the necessary coherence and legal certainty for military commanders.

The Federal Court of Canada agreed with the position of the GoC. The Court held that Canadian Charter of Rights and Freedoms did not apply extra-territorially to non-Canadians detained and transferred by CAF to Afghan authorities. The Court decided that Canadian law can only be applied in the territory of another state with that state's consent. There were potential exceptions to the requirement for host nation consent to the application of foreign laws. For example, the Court noted that there was a specific basis under international law for the exceptional extra-territorial jurisdiction accorded to states in relation to their embassies, consulates, vessels and aircraft. However, the Court rejected the argument the 'effective control of the person' test was a potential exception to the requirement for state consent.

The Court noted that a close reading of the cases and commentaries relied upon by the applicants (AI), suggested that the current state of international jurisprudence on the extra-territorial application of human rights treaties pursuant to the 'effective control' test was somewhat uncertain. The weight of authority did not support a different result with respect to the application of the Charter in this case. It found the jurisprudence of the ECtHR to be divergent. Moreover, the Court dismissed the UN Committees' commentaries on the same issue noting the commentaries were recommendations made by groups with advocacy responsibilities. The court stated:

> While they [the commentaries] clearly reflect the views of knowledgeable individuals, they do not reflect the current state of international law, but more the direction that those groups believe the law should take in the future.[27]

Significantly, the Court remarked on the practical realities of applying the 'effective control of the person' test on the ground in Afghanistan. It stated:

> Whatever its appeal may be, however, the practical result of applying such a 'control of the person' based test would be problematic in the context of a multinational military effort such as the one in which Canada is currently involved in Afghanistan. Indeed, it would result in a patchwork of different national legal norms applying in relation to detained Afghan citizens in different parts of Afghanistan, on a purely random-chance basis.

> That is, an Afghan insurgent detained by members of the Canadian Forces in Kandahar province could end up having entirely different rights than would Afghan insurgents detained by soldiers from other NATO partner countries, in other parts of Afghanistan. The result would be a hodgepodge of different foreign legal systems being imposed within the territory of a state whose sovereignty the international community has pledged to uphold.[28]

The Court remarked on the problematic results of applying the 'control of the person' test in Afghanistan and determined the appropriate legal framework would be IHL as follows:

---

27   Para 239.
28   Paras 274-275.

This would be a most unsatisfactory result, in the context of a United Nations-sanctioned multinational military effort, further suggesting that the appropriate legal regime to govern the military activities currently underway in Afghanistan is the law governing armed conflict – namely international humanitarian law ...

The application of international humanitarian law to the situation of detainees in Afghanistan would not only give certainty to the situation, but would also provide a coherent legal regime governing the actions of the international community in Afghanistan.[29]

The Court did not limit its practical approach to the question of whether the Charter applied or not. It also considered that if the Charter were to apply extra-territorially, how it would actually work on the ground. It stated:

Surely Canadian law, including the *Canadian Charter of Rights and Freedoms*, either applies in relation to the detention of individuals by the Canadian Forces in Afghanistan, or it does not. It cannot be that the Charter will not apply where the breach of a detainee's purported Charter rights is of a minor or technical nature, but will apply where the breach puts the detainee's fundamental human rights at risk.

That is, it cannot be that it is the nature or quality of the Charter breach that creates extra-territorial jurisdiction, where it does not otherwise exist. That would be a completely unprincipled approach to the exercise of extra-territorial jurisdiction ...

Moreover, to assert extra-territorial Charter jurisdiction based on a qualitative analysis of the nature or gravity of the breach would surely lead to tremendous uncertainty on the part of Canadian state actors 'on the ground' in foreign countries.[30]

While the Court concluded that detainees did not possess rights under the Canadian Charter, it did observe that they did enjoy rights under the Afghan Constitution and under international law, particularly under IHL. The Federal Court of Appeal upheld the judgment of the Federal Court and the Supreme Court of Canada refused to consider the appeal. Accordingly, it stands as the leading case on the issue of the extra-territorial application of the Canadian Charter to CAF military operations abroad. It is noted the case was decided prior to the ECtHR's judgment in *Al-Skeini*.[31] However, it is questionable, given the nature of the Federal Court's analysis of the 'control of the person' test, that it would have arrived at a different conclusion.

As Canadian law, this case is binding upon the CAF and its military legal advisors. The case is equally important in the broader context of international law. AI did not specifically argue the application of ICCPR

---

29   Paras 276 & 280.
30   Paras 310-311 & 314.
31   n 18 above.

in this case. Accordingly, it is open to question whether the Canadian courts will adopt a different view of the extra-territorial application of the ICCPR. However, it is reasonable to conclude the courts will likely adopt the same analysis of the issues of host nation consent and the 'effective control of the person' test. Unlike the Canadian Charter, the ICCPR has express limits on its application.[32] Therefore, Canadian courts are likely to interpret its application even more narrowly in an extra-territorial context. Moreover, the courts would probably arrive at the same conclusion regarding the 'effective control of the person' test in relation to the ICCPR. That is, the extra-territorial application of the ICCPR to military operations would result in a 'hodgepodge' of different foreign legal systems being imposed within the territory of a state whose sovereignty the international community has pledged to respect. Such a situation would be very problematic for military commanders and military legal advisors as the existence of multiple legal norms would cause much confusion and impact negatively on operational effectiveness. In addition, it would be unacceptable to have differing and conflicting national legal frameworks that would result in the weakening of human rights protections. Again, conversely, the application of IHL provides fuller protections, greater coherence and legal certainty because of common standards and procedures.

The case highlights that there are significantly different perspectives on the issue of the extra-territorial application of HRL instruments, especially in the possible application of the 'effective control of the person' test. Many advocates of the application of human rights instruments, principally the ICCPR[33] and the ECHR, to international military operations, rely almost exclusively on the jurisprudence of the ECtHR (particularly the judgment in *Al-Skeini*) and the commentaries from UN Committees (particularly General Comment 31 of the HRC regarding the application of the ICCPR). While the ECtHR jurisprudence and UN commentaries are important, they are not universally accepted. Indeed an analysis of state practice, including the 47 Council of Europe States, reveals varying interpretations of and reactions to of the jurisprudence of the EctHR,[34] the

---

32   ICCPR art 2(1) states: 'Each State Party to the present Covenant undertakes to respect and to ensure to all individuals *within its territory and subject to its jurisdiction* the rights recognized in the present Covenant, without distinction of any kind, such as race, colour, sex, language, religion, political or other opinion, national or social origin, property, birth or other status.' (emphasis mine) http://www.ohchr.org/en/professionalinterest/pages/ccpr.aspx (accessed 19 April 2014).

33   See n 26 above indicating the US position that the ICCPR does not apply extra-territorially.

34   For ECtHR jurisprudence see n 20-23 above.

ICJ[35] and to the UN HRC's General Comment 31. For example, most states have not derogated from any of the IHRL treaties and few militaries, particularly those major professional forces frequently deployed abroad in armed conflicts, have not accepted nor implemented General Comment 31. It is reasonable to interpret such state practice as at least a hesitation to adopt the jurisprudence and commentaries during armed conflict as they seem confusing and impractical given the realities of armed conflict and the existence of IHL.

3.3   The *lex specialis* of IHL

Generally, IHL does not apply in peacetime with the exception of certain state obligations to implement and enforce IHL. IHRL may or may not apply in situations of armed conflict. Human rights law would likely continue to apply domestically but there is uncertainty about their extra-territorial application. The ICJ addressed the issue of the possible application of human rights during armed conflict in the 'Legality of the threat or use of nuclear weapons' Advisory Opinion. In commenting on the argument that the use of nuclear weapons in war violates the right to life under article 6 of the ICCPR, the ICJ noted that the protection of the ICCPR does not cease in times of war, except by operation of article 4 of the Covenant whereby certain provisions may be derogated from in a time of national emergency.[36] It further noted that the test of what is an arbitrary deprivation of life must be determined by the applicable *lex specialis*, namely, IHL.[37]

This is an important qualifier that the Court places on the application of human rights law in times of armed conflict. More recently the ICJ in its Advisory Opinion on the *Legal Consequences of the Construction of a Wall in the Occupied Palestinian Territory*,[38] in its judgment in the *Case concerning armed activities on the territory of the Congo*[39] and in its Order regarding the application of the CERD in *Georgia v Russian Federation* [40] addressed the issue of human rights during situations of armed conflict. However, it is fair to say that its analyses were even more ambiguous than in the *Nuclear*

---

35   For ICJ jurisprudence see ICJ *Legality of the Threat or Use of Nuclear Weapons* Advisory Opinion (8 July 1996): http://www.icj-cij.org/docket/files/95/7495.pdf (accessed 20 April 2014); ICJ *Legal Consequences of the Construction of a Wall in the Occupied Palestinian Territory* Advisory Opinion (9 July 2004): http://www.icj-cij.org/docket/files/131/1671.pdf (accessed 20 April 2014); the *Case Concerning Armed Activities on the Territory of the Congo (Democratic Republic Of The Congo v Uganda)*: http://www.icj-cij.org/docket/files/116/10455.pdf (accessed 20 April 2014); and the *Case Concerning Application of the International Convention on the Elimination of All Forms of Racial Discrimination (Georgia v Russian Federation): Request for the Indication of Provisional Measures* Order of 15 October 2008: http://www.icj-cij.org/docket/files/140/14801.pdf (accessed 20 April 2014) regarding, in part, the extra-territorial application of the CERD.
36   (n 35 above) para 25.
37   As above.
38   n 35 above, paras 105-107.
39   n 35 above.
40   n 35 above, paras 108-109.

Weapons case and have provided little clarity for legal advisors or commanders.

The issue has also been broadly considered by the UN High Commissioner for Human Rights (UNHCR),[41] the UN Human Rights Committee (HRC) in its General Comment 31 on article 2 of the ICCPR[42] and the Inter-American Commission on Human Rights (IACHR).[43] Conceptually, it is very desirable, as noted in the jurisprudence and commentaries, that the two bodies of law operate in times of armed conflict, as they both promote the protection of humans and the preservation of humanitarian values. Nonetheless, such broad and rather imprecise comments on interaction of the *lex specialis* of IHL and IHRL are of very little practical use when military legal advisors are counseling commanders at all levels of operations on what law actually controls their activities, especially those dealing with the use of force and the detention of persons.[44]

In practical terms, if human rights law does operate during an armed conflict, it must be applied in the context of the realities of the conflict and the *lex specialis* of IHL.[45] For example, Canada views the *lex specialis* principle as meaning a state's international human rights obligations, to the

---

41 'Statement of High Commissioner for Human Rights on Detention of Taliban and Al Qaida Prisoners at US Base in Guantanamo Bay' Cuba, 16 Jan 2002 http://www.pegc.us/archive/State_Department/diplomatic_comments.txt (accessed 20April 2014)

42 See n 18 above.

43 *Abella v Argentina* IACHR Report 55/97 (1997), paras 158& 159 and the *Provisional Measures Decision* (n 35 above) 730.

44 See Sir D Bethlehem QC 'The relationship between international humanitarian law and international human rights law in situations of armed conflict' (2013) 2 *Cambridge Journal of International and Comparative Law* 180. In referring to the ICJ *Wall* case, the author notes: 'Given the high level of generality of the Court's statement on the relationship between IHL and HRL, and the absence of any subsequent analysis of the interaction of these two bodies of law at an operational level, there is little useful guidance to be had from this opinion on the detail of the relationship between IHL and HRL apart from the Court's bottom line conclusion that certain specified provisions of the ICCPR applied in the circumstances of Israel's (then) 37 year belligerent occupation of the West Bank.' (at 185). In his conclusion, he states: 'The debate [IHL & IHRL] to this point, however, has too often been characterised by a high level of generality, a lack of judicial rigour, a failure by those in government to engage actively in public discussion, overly expansive claims on the part of non-governmental commentators, and anxiety on the part of the military that these developments are hampering the flexibility to act effectively to keep society safe.' (at 195).

45 Other chapters in this book address the issue of the interrelationship of IHL an IHRL, particularly the effect of the *lex specialis* of IHL. Generally most jurisprudence and academic commentary accept that IHL is the *lex specialis* of armed conflict. For example see n 1 above; C Greenwood 'Rights at the frontier-protecting the individual in time of war' in BKA Rider *Law at the centre: The Institute of Advanced Legal Studies at fifty*, (1999) 227-293. Bethlehem (n 3 above); F Hampson 'The relationship between international humanitarian law and human rights from the perspective of a human rights treaty body' (2008) 871 *International Review of the Red Cross* 549; C Droege 'The interplay between international humanitarian law and international human rights law in situations of armed conflict' (2007) 40 *Israel Law Review* 310 322. For an academic perspective that is not adopted or reflected in state practice see, N Prud'homme '*Lex specialis*: Oversimplifying a more complex and multifaceted relationship?' (2007) 40

extent that they have extra-territorial effect, are not displaced during armed conflict. However, the relevant human rights principles can only be determined by reference to the *lex specialis* of IHL.[46] For example, for much of the recent armed conflict in Afghanistan, it was the policy of the Government of Canada to transfer those detained by the CAF to Afghan authorities. Both IHL and IHRL required humane treatment of he detainees during capture and after transfer to Afghan authorities. To this extent there was convergence of the two legal frameworks and, essentially, no conflict as they both provided the same basic fundamental protections for humane treatment. However, when some, such as Amnesty International Canada, argued that the Canadian Charter of Rights and Freedoms (which reflected the human rights delineated in the ICCPR) applied, this cause much concern for the government, commanders and military legal advisors. Why? Outside of the fact that the Charter did not apply extra-territorially in such circumstances, there was still much uncertainty in trying to determine how exactly the Charter rights might or could apply during an armed conflict in a sovereign state. Conversely, IHL was already a well-established, practical and effective framework. While IHL by no means provided for every eventuality during the transfer process, it did address the basic issues and allowed the CAF to successfully conduct detainee operations while respecting Afghan host nation law to the extent it did not conflict or contravene IHL/human rights standards of humane treatment. Moreover, the application of IHL as *lex specialis* by all of the major Allies in Afghanistan, better ensured consist application of the law across the entirety of Afghanistan rather than, as noted by Canadian

Israel Law Review 356 in which the author questions the ability of *lex specialis* to provide a coherent framework capable of clarifying the interplay between IHL and IHRL, rejects the idea that the *lex specialis* theoretical model facilitates the co-application of the disciplines. Finally, she suggests that the theory of *lex specialis* should give way to a different theoretical model, a model based on multiple pre-determined criteria balancing the reality of conflict with the respect for humanity and the protection of individuals; M Milanovic 'Norm conflicts, international humanitarian law, and human rights law' O Ben-Naftali (ed) *Human rights and international humanitarian law* (2010), in which the author refers to the 'lex specialis mantra' as legalese Latin which is descriptively misleading, vague in meaning, and of little practical use in application. It should be discarded as a general matter, and in particular it should not be used to describe the relationship between IHL and IHRL as a whole. The challenge with these interesting legal theory arguments rejecting the *lex specialis* of armed conflict is that they do not reflect state practice nor offer no real or practical solutions for military commanders. State practice, as exemplified below in n 25 above (Canada) and n 24 above (US), is convincing evidence that states continue to accept the *lex specialis* of IHL during armed conflict.

46   See Government of Argument of Law (Factum) at n 26 above. In support of this position the Factum quotes H Duffy *The war on terror and the framework of international law* (2005) 300: 'Critically, in the event of an apparent inconsistency in the content of the two strands of law, the more specific provisions will prevail: in relation to targeting in the conduct of hostilities, for example, human rights law will refer to more specific provisions (the lex specialis) of humanitarian law. In such circumstances, it is not that human rights law ceases to apply, but that it must be interpreted in light of the detailed rules of IHL. As such, the protection from arbitrary deprivation of life and arbitrary detention are non-derogable human rights that continue to apply in armed conflict; but targeting or detention is not arbitrary and the rights are not violated where permitted under IHL.'

Courts,[47] creating a 'patch work' of differing, and likely conflicting, national legal frameworks based on HR law.

IHL was designed primarily for conflicts between states, though it has more recently developed rules for non-international armed conflicts. It is a detailed code of conduct that has emerged over hundreds of years. It has been the product of judicious compromises between considerations of military necessity and humanitarianism (the protection of the victims of armed conflict). It also reflects the considerable experience, not just of states, but also of the International Committee of the Red Cross and non-governmental agencies (NGOs) gained from various conflicts. It would, therefore, be simply incorrect to claim that human rights laws must override IHL simply because they appear to provide greater protection for civilians during a conflict. IHL and human rights law are distinct branches of international law. There are important differences, conceptually, legally and practically, between them in the context of armed conflict.

The divergence of IHL and IHRL, based largely on theoretical arguments of the application of the law, has unquestionably created confusion and uncertainty. However interesting the theoretical debates may be, they are of little practical assistance to legal advisors who counsel decision-makers during armed conflict. In truth, both IHL and IHRL offer similar, if not identical, protections to persons in armed conflict.[48] The challenge for a military legal advisor is trying to manage the real divergences and conflicts that arise between IHL and IHRL largely in the area of applying procedural human rights safeguards (for example, obligation to charge or release a detainee – the right to counsel while detained – and is there an obligation to capture rather than kill?), and in the conduct of investigations (do all deaths during armed conflict need to be investigated? What is an 'independent' investigation in the context of military operations?). For a Canadian military legal advisor during armed conflict, the application of the *lex specialis* of IHL is the starting point in addressing such challenges. IHL can then, if required, be informed by HR normative frameworks. This is a more workable solution. It is clearer, practical, effective and fair. Moreover, the approach is more likely to result

47   See n 25 above.
48   See Bethlehem (n 44 above) 191 & 192 in which he notes that in considering how the ICCPR might apply in armed conflict that: 'An article-by-article review also discloses that in many cases ICCPR provisions find detailed corresponding expression in some form in IHL and that: "While, in practice, circumstances [in armed conflict] in which the substantive content of overlapping IHL and HRL provisions will be materially divergent *are likely to be relatively limited*, where there are such material divergences it will be important that the law develops an appropriate methodology of hierarchy, presumption, reconciliation and interpretation."' (emphasis mine). Also, see K Watkin 'Controlling the use of force: A role for human rights norms in contemporary armed conflict', (2004) 98 *American Journal of International Law* 1, in which the author notes that: 'Despite the differences between international humanitarian law and human rights law, they exhibit a commonality of content that causes them to converge' (at 10) and 'Like the human rights framework governing the use of force, international humanitarian law has an accountability structure' (at 22).

in clarity for commanders and in better human rights protections for civilians during armed conflict.

4   Conclusion

Today, the interrelationship, convergence and conflict of IHL and IHRL in armed conflict are the most immediate and important challenges facing legal advisors in the armed forces. While the two bodies of law promote the protection of humans and the preservation of humanitarian values, there are important differences, conceptually, legally and practically, between them. Often, the apparent convergence, or the desire for the convergence, of the two bodies is viewed as an important evolution of the humanisation of armed conflict. However, such views or sentiments seem to ignore the real risks and conflicts to the very goals and aspirations of human rights – the protection of humans.[49]

In drawing together some threads from the preceding analysis, the following conclusions can be made. Firstly, most states have appointed uniformed legal advisors in their armed forces. Such advisors have the distinct privilege and perspective of being members of both the profession of arms and the profession of laws. From the perspective of a Canadian military legal advisor, it is critical that legal advisors be professional lawyers. In other words, legal advisors should be practicing lawyers who are accountable and obligated to comply with rules and ethics of a regulating law society or equivalent.[50] This combination of professions creates a military legal advisor who is uniquely qualified to analyse and synthesise the complexities and realities of military operations and the law. Moreover, this approach better reinforces the perceived and real independence of legal advice, as legal advisors are not, strictly speaking,

---

49   See, NK Modirzadeh 'The dark sides of convergence: A pro-civilian critique of the extraterritorial application of human rights law in armed conflict' *US Naval War College international law studies (Blue Book) Series* (2010) 349 in which the author notes: 'This transformation, this much-touted shift in the field of international law, is often referred to as the "humanization of humanitarian law" and, morally, the "convergence" of international human rights law (IHRL) and international humanitarian law. Yet in the current headlong approach into convergence, rights and rights institutions may carry risks to the very goals many humanitarian-minded international lawyers seek to achieve ... The tone of the many articles and commentaries on the topic of "convergence" suggests that if only the views of various UN treaty bodies and forward-thinking courts were applied fully by the military, it is obvious that the experience of civilians caught up in armed conflict would be improved, that detention would be more humane, that accountability for violations would be increased – that, in short, outcomes would be more *humanitarian*. I aim to question that assumption, and to raise questions about whether even the full realization of the aspirations of human rights scholars and advocates would actually be better for civilians in war.' (at 350)

50   For example, in Canada, the JAG must be an officer who is a barrister or advocate with at least ten years standing at the bar of a province (see n 7 above) and those legal officers under JAG's command must be admitted to the Bar of a Canadian province or territory, and be a member in good standing of a provincial or territorial law society; see CAF: 'Browse jobs: Legal officer': http://forces.ca/en/job/legalofficer-64 (accessed 21 April 2014).

under the operational chain of command. An operationally focused, professionally knowledgeable, accountable and independent legal advisor will be better positioned to understand and explain the convergence and conflicts of IHL and IHRL to commanders. This can only help to lessen uncertainty and confusion and to reinforce applicable protections for those involved in armed conflict.

Secondly, IHL is the *lex specialis* of armed conflict. This is a fact for military legal advisors and commanders. It is the primary body of law that they will apply during armed conflict. It is troubling that the relevant jurisprudence of the ECtHR, the ICJ and the commentaries of UN Committees have largely avoided detailed analyses of the *lex specialis* of IHL in their methodologies for reviewing human rights violations in the context of armed conflict. Consequently, the jurisprudence of the ECtHR, ICJ and the commentaries of UN Committees regarding the application of IHRL during armed conflict are often shortsighted, fragmented, ambiguous and unpersuasive. In practice, it is of little assistance to the military legal advisor or the commander. Nonetheless, military legal advisors and commanders will continue to apply the *lex specialis* of IHL in a practical, meaningful and reasonable way, in order to balance military necessity and humanitarianism. Not only are they are obliged to do so, but, also, it makes the most sense in achieving mission success within the rule of law.

Thirdly, human rights law, particularly treaties, may or may not apply extra-territorially during armed conflict. The issue of the extra-territorial application of human rights instruments will continue to cause confusion and uncertainty. In particular, applying the expansive concept of 'effective control of the person' test to international military operations, particularly to armed conflict, will be very problematic. As the Federal Court of Canada has recognised, the result of applying one or more regional/national human rights instruments would create a 'hodgepodge of different foreign legal systems being imposed within the territory of a state' whose sovereignty is respected by the international community and under international law.

Fourthly, there is growing concern particularly amongst military legal advisors that the application of IHRL in armed conflict will make activity, which is lawful under IHL, unlawful under IHRL or HR norms. For example, there is suggestion that combatants should be captured rather than killed in armed conflict.[51] Also, there is view that the non-criminal detention of persons in armed conflict (for example, prisoner of war)

51	See R Goodman 'The power to kill or capture enemy combatants' NYU School of
	Law, Public Law Research Paper No 13-02 (February 2013) in which the author argues
	in certain well-specified and narrow circumstances in armed conflict, the use of force

would be in violation of human rights law, at least the ECHR.[52]

Fifthly, the jurisprudence of the ECtHR and the commentaries of UN Committees will likely have a distracting effect on the conduct of multinational military operations involving European Forces. It will be difficult for European Forces to reconcile their obligations under the ECHR with those non-European allies who will be largely regulated by IHL.

In reality, both IHL and IHRL offer similar, if not identical, protections to persons in armed conflict. A type of convergence of the two bodies of law on the battlefield already exists in a practical, pragmatic and realistic sense. They both focus on ensuring respect and protection for fundamental rights and humane treatment. Conflict, uncertainty and confusion arise when the analysis moves beyond the practical and

should instead be governed by a least-restrictive-means (LRM) analysis. He contends that the modern law of armed conflict (LOAC) supports the following maxim: if enemy combatants can be put out of action by capturing them, they should not be injured; if they can be put out of action by injury, they should not be killed; and if they can be put out of action by light injury, grave injury should be avoided ... However, the general formula – and its key components – should be understood to have a solid foundation in the structure, rules and practices of modern warfare; the ICRC *Interpretive guidance on the notion of direct participation in hostilities under international humanitarian law* (2009) that includes a controversial section on the restraints on the use of force (RUF). The ICRC declares its support for the following proposition: 'The kind and degree of force which is permissible against persons not entitled to protection against direct attack must not exceed what is actually necessary to accomplish a legitimate military purpose in the prevailing circumstances.' These are astonishing new perspectives on the use of force in armed conflict. They are interesting in that they do not argue the direct application of IHRL in place of IHL. Rather more inventively, they argue that IHL itself obliges forces to use lesser force, ie capture rather than kill enemy combatants. However, when the veil is lifted on such a perspective, it is, essentially, an IHRL interpretation. For persuasive arguments against such a novel application of IHL see GS Corn et al 'Belligerent targeting and the invalidity of a least harmful means rule' (2013) 89 *International Law Studies* 536 and JD Ohlin 'The Capture-Kill Debate: Lost Legislative History Or Revisionist History?' Cornell Legal Studies Research Paper No 13-80 (2013) (countering the Goodman perspective); WH Parks 'Part IX of the ICRC "Direct participation in hostilities" Study: No mandate, no expertise, and legally incorrect' (2010) 42 *New York University Journal of International Law & Politics* 769; JD Ohlin 'The duty to capture' (2013) 97 *Minnesota Law Review* 1268; JK Kleffner 'Section IX of the ICRC Interpretive Guidance on Direct Participation in Hostilities: The end of *jus in bello* proportionality as we know it?' (2012) 45 *Israel Law Review* 35; G Blum 'The dispensable lives of soldiers' (2010) 2 *Journal of Legal Analysis* 69 143,163-164; WJ Fenrick 'ICRC Guidance on Direct Participation in Hostilities' (2009) 12 *Yearbook Of International Humanitarian Law* 287 (countering the ICRC Interpretive Guidance on RUF).

52   See *Al-Jedda v United Kingdom*, App No 27021/08, ECHR (7 July 2011) para 100: 'It has long been established that the list of grounds of permissible detention in article 5 § 1 *does not include internment or preventive detention where there is no intention to bring criminal charges within a reasonable time* (see *Lawless v Ireland (no 3)*, 1 July 1961, §§ 13 and 14, Series A no 3; *Ireland v the United Kingdom*, cited above, § 196; *Guzzardi v Italy*, 6 November 1980, § 102, Series A no 39; *Ječius v Lithuania*, App No 34578/97, §§ 47-52, ECHR 2000-IX).' (emphasis mine).

pragmatic convergence to the theoretical and political debate.[53] In other words, when the debate focuses more on formalistic, technical and, sometimes, politicised analysis (judicial, institutional and academic) about which framework applies, rather than simply trying to protect humans in the always terribly real and often unfair circumstances of armed conflict, then unconstructive and risky divergence occurs. This type of divergence is unhelpful for military commanders, the very persons states call upon to make life-or-death decisions often under highly stressful, time-limited and disturbing circumstances, because it obscures how law actually works in armed conflict. This, in turn, inevitably puts humans at greater risk of deprivation of life and liberty.

---

53   See Modirzadeh (n 49 above) 400 where the author notes: '[S]uch an approach [emphasizing pragmatism over formal legal rules] would necessarily mean getting involved with the ugly realities of military decision making, accepting that not all legal rights–holders will be granted protections in the same way, and that military security will likely always trump policy-based rights and protections ... Rather than engaging in an adversarial conversation mediated by courts or human rights bodies, this approach would ask that human rights advocates envision rights through the prism of armed conflict, and from the perspective of the military. This raises a number of serious concerns about the extent to which this would still be human rights advocacy as we know it, but it may also pave the way for actual and significant changes in on-the-ground decisions, and in the ability of individuals caught in armed conflict to lead more dignified lives.'

PART D: Judicial Perspectives on Human Rights and International Humanitarian Law

13

African Human Rights System

Frans Viljoen

1   Introduction

This contribution covers the relationship between human rights law (HRL) and international humanitarian law (IHL) in the African human rights system. It deals with the way in which the African human rights system has treated the convergence of and potential conflict between human rights and IHL, and aims to contribute to the very sparse literature on this topic.[1] The term 'African human rights system', as it is used here, comprises three institutions. The first is the African Commission on Human and Peoples' Rights (African Commission), the main quasi-judicial institution in the system, comprising eleven part-time Commissioners, with its Secretariat in Banjul, the Gambia. The second is the African Court on Human and Peoples' Rights (African Human Rights Court), comprising eleven judges, with the Registry located and President of the Court permanently residing at its seat in Arusha, Tanzania. The third is the African Committee of Experts on the Rights and Welfare of the Child (African Children's Rights Committee), another quasi-judicial body comprising eleven members, with its seat in Addis Ababa, Ethiopia. This Committee functions as a self-standing body mandated under a separate treaty, the African Charter on

---

*   Professor of Law, Centre for Human Rights, Faculty of Law, University of Pretoria.

1   On the one hand, most texts about the African human rights system do not deal with this issue at all. On the other, most academic writing dealing with the convergence of IHRL and IHL and extra-territorial application of IHRL make sparse reference to the African Charter and its interpretation. See, for example, R Wilde 'The extraterritorial application of international human rights law on civil and political rights' in S Sheeran & N Rodley (eds) *Routledge handbook of international human rights law* (2013) 635, in which the author makes reference to the African Charter on Human and Peoples' Rights only in so far as it has been interpreted by the International Court of Justice in the *Case Concerning Armed Activities on the Territory of the Congo* 2005 ICJ 116 (19 December 2005) (*DRC v Uganda*) (and not by the African Commission). See also R Provost *International human rights and humanitarian law* (2002); and O Ben-Naftali (ed) *International humanitarian law and international human rights law* (2011), where scant if any reference is made to the African Charter and African Commission.

the Rights and Welfare of the Child (African Children's Charter). By focusing on the African Commission, African Human Rights Court and African Children's Committee, this contribution adopts an institutional approach, interrogating how each of the three institutions has dealt and may in future deal with the issue under discussion.

IHL applies under conditions of armed conflict. A distinction should therefore be drawn between armed conflict, whether of an international or non-international nature, on the one hand, and civil disturbances or turmoil, on the other. While armed conflict resulting from international armed conflict is relatively rare though not absent from the African continent, non-international armed conflict is much more common. Briefly stated, the 1949 Geneva Conventions apply when there is a 'declared war' or other form of international armed conflict between states ('an undeclared war').[2] The First Additional Protocol to the Geneva Conventions also applies during international armed conflict directed 'against colonial domination and alien occupation and against racist régimes in the exercise of their right of self-determination'.[3] The Second Additional Protocol applies during situations of non-international armed conflict ('armed conflict not of an international character').[4] The dividing line between 'armed conflict', during which IHL applies, and situations of internal conflict falling short of 'armed conflict', such as internal disturbances, is drawn with reference to the extent of organisation, command and control of those groupings opposing the state's armed forces: The term 'armed conflict' (and IHL, in the form of the Second Additional Protocol) applies when 'organized armed groups' with a clear command structure are involved; IHRL applies when this threshold has not been met.[5] As this contribution explores the relationship between IHL and IHRL, the focus here does not fall on internal disturbances and similar situations, in which IHL finds no application at all. The contribution therefore covers an 'organized armed group' such as the Lord's Resistance Army, while the conflict related to a more loosely structured terrorist 'organisation' such as Boko Haram does not enter the discussion, as IHL arguably is not relevant to its activities.[6] Still, there is a sense of ambiguity

---

2   Common article 2 to the 1949 Geneva Conventions.
3   Art 1(4) of First Additional Protocol of 1977.
4   Common article 3 to the 1977 Protocols.
5   See art 1(2) of the Second Additional Protocol of 1977: 'This Protocol shall not apply to situations of internal disturbances and tensions, such as riots, isolated and sporadic acts of violence and other acts of a similar nature, as not being armed conflicts.'
6   See, in this regard, the Commission's resolutions on Nigeria, in which it at times acknowledges that Nigeria is a state party to IHL treaties (Resolution 70 on Nigeria, 4 June 2004), and identifies the presence and conduct of 'armed groups', 'the Nigerian military' causing a threat to the 'civilian population' (Resolution 214 on the Human Rights Situation in the Federal Republic of Nigeria, 2 May 2002; and Resolution 267 on the Human Rights Situation in the Federal Republic of Nigeria, 14 March 2014); however, all these resolutions call on the government to abide by and ensure observance of human rights standards, obligations and treaties. See, however, the UN Security Council, Presidential Statement (S/PRST/2015/4), 19 January 2015, in

and artificiality to the distinction that reveal the inadequacies of the applicable legal regime.

Taken together, the jurisprudential record of the three institutions constituting the African human rights system is sparse, compared to the other two well-established regional human rights systems, the European and Inter-American. Consider that the African Commission has finalised less than 250 cases in the 25 years of its existence; that the African Court has between 2006 and 2013 decided only a single case on the merits; and the African Children's Rights Committee has by mid 2014 only finalised one case on the merits.[7] Given the dearth of concrete African case-law, in general, and in this thematic area, in particular, this contribution may tend towards the tentative and the speculative, and will for this reason draw on the comparative experience of the other two regional human rights systems.

Divided into three substantive sections, this paper examines the contribution of the African Commission, the African Human Rights Court and the African Children's Rights Committee in shedding light on the relationship between IHL and the human rights provided for under the African regional human rights system. The paper ends with a brief conclusion.

2 African Commission on Human and Peoples' Rights

This section of the paper analyses the provisions of the African Charter and the practice of the African Commission in so far as they relate to situations of armed conflict. The first sub-section interrogates the applicability of the Charter rights during such situations. The related issue of the Charter's extra-territorial application is considered in the second sub-section. The third sub-section shows that the Commission has at least in one prominent instance placed indirect interpretive reliance on IHL to animate and give concrete content to Charter rights in situations of armed conflict. The fourth sub-section takes stock of the potential for the expanded application of and reliance on IHL by the Commission, brought about by the explicit reference to IHL standards in subsequent treaties, in particular the Protocol to the African Charter on the Rights of Women in Africa (African Women's Protocol) and AU Convention for the Protection and Assistance of Internally Displaced Persons in Africa (IDP Convention). In the last

---

which Boko Haram is condemned for committing human rights violations and 'where applicable', violations of IHL.

7   F Viljoen 'From a cat into a lion? An overview of the progress and challenges of the African human rights system at the African Commission's 25 year mark' (2013) 17 *Law, Democracy and Development* 298.

sub-section, the Commission's role in facilitating reliance on article 4(h) of the AU Constitutive Act is touched upon.

2.1 Applicability of human rights under the African Charter during armed conflict

Even if its practice has been limited, the African Commission does, in its interpretation and application of the African Charter on Human and Peoples' Rights (African Charter), shed some light on the relationship between IHL and IHRL. The African Commission has taken the position that there is a close link between the human and peoples' rights in the African Charter and IHL, and found that all rights in the African Charter apply at all times, that is, during peace, war and other situations of armed conflict.[8] It has expressed relevant views in the exercise of both its promotional and protective mandate. Under its promotional mandate, the Commission examines state reports, undertakes promotional visits to state parties, adopts thematic resolutions and establishes and oversees the work of its special procedures. Under its protective mandate, the Commission considers and makes findings on individual and inter-state complaints ('communications') and undertakes on-site fact-finding missions or visits. A major difference in the two aspects of the Commission's mandate is that the output of its protective mandate remain confidential until its publication has been approved by the AU Executive Council/ Assembly of Heads of State and Government.[9]

In one of its first resolutions, adopted under its promotional mandate, the Commission called on states to adopt 'appropriate' domestic measures to 'ensure the promotion of the provisions of international humanitarian law and human and peoples' rights'.[10] In making this call, it departed from the starting point that there is a clear overlap in the objectives of the two 'systems' of law (IHL and IHRL), in that both protect 'human beings and their fundamental rights'.[11] However, this resolution is not targeting the protective mandate of the Commission, as such, but is rather aimed at training of and dissemination to relevant domestic actors. Even so, it foregrounds the Commission's understanding of the close co-operation between these two fields.

The position that the Charter rights are applicable in situations of armed conflict was first articulated as part of the Commission's protective

---

8   *Commission Nationale des Droits de l'Homme et des Libertés v Chad* (2000) AHRLR 66 (ACHPR 1995) (*Chad Mass Violations* case) para 21.
9   Under art 59 of the African Charter.
10   Resolution on the Promotion and Respect of International Humanitarian Law and Human and Peoples' Rights, adopted by the African Commission on Human and Peoples' Rights, meeting at its Fourteenth Ordinary Session in Addis Ababa, from 1-10 December 1993.
11   As above, preamble.

mandate in a case concerning a situation of civil war involving the security forces and other groups in Chad. The Commission found Chad in violation of the Charter for failing to provide security and stability to its nationals, and thus allowing 'serious and massive' human rights violations.[12] Both the government's duty to respect and protect came into play, in that its agents ('the national armed forces') were both 'participants' in the 'civil war', and failed to intervene to prevent 'other parties' from killing 'specific individuals'.[13] Although the Commission referred to the situation as one of civil war, it did not make any reference to IHL. This omission may be explained with reference to two factors. First, it is likely that the complainant did not place any reliance on IHL in its arguments – given the lack of any academic attention to this issue at that time, and the lack of any government response to the complaint.[14] Second, it should be pointed out that the Commission did not, in its earlier jurisprudence, including in the period during which this matter was decided, elaborate much on its conclusions, leaving its findings as terse and concise as possible.

In *Amnesty International v Sudan*, the Commission adopted a slightly different approach, in that it explicitly mentions that the state is under an obligation to treat 'civilians in areas of strife' during situations of non-international armed conflicts 'in accordance with international humanitarian law' due to their specific vulnerability.[15] However, beyond this very general reference to IHL, no further reliance is placed on any IHL norm.

This starting point – namely, that the regional treaty governs state conduct also in times of (international or non-international) armed conflict – is shared by the other two regional systems. Under the European Convention of Human Rights, states may derogate from the Convention 'in time of war',[16] leading to the conclusion that in the absence of such derogation, all treaty provisions remain applicable. The position under the American Convention is similar.[17]

---

12   *Chad Mass Violations* case para 22.
13   As above.
14   No mention is made of IHL in the Commission's 'summary of the facts', *Chad Mass Violations* case, paras 1-6.
15   *Amnesty International and Others v Sudan* (2000) AHRLR 297 (ACHPR 1999).
16   Art 15(1) of the European Convention of Human Rights, but the derogation may only be 'to the extent strictly required by the exigencies of the situation, provided that such measures are not inconsistent with its other obligations under international law'. Under art 15(2), certain Convention rights may not be derogated from, including the right to life, 'except in respect of deaths resulting from lawful acts of war'. See also K Oellers-Frahm 'Convergence and conflicts of human rights (IHRL) and international humanitarian law (IHL) in military operations regional perspectives: The European Court of Human Rights' in this volume, para 2.2.
17   Art 27(1) of the American Convention of Human Rights. See also D Shelton 'Humanitarian law in the Inter-American human rights system' in this volume, para 1.

In the first (and only) inter-state communication to be decided by the African Commission, *Democratic Republic of Congo v Burundi, Rwanda and Uganda* (*DRC* case),[18] the Commission for the first (and thus far, only) time explicitly referred to specific IHL standards in its finding. In a situation characterised by the Commission as 'undeclared war' between the DRC and its three neighbours,[19] the Commission observed that activities of the armed forces of the three state parties on the territory of the DRC, including their support of the rebels, fall 'not only within the province of international humanitarian law, but also within the mandate of the Commission'.[20] While this formulation underscores that both IHL and IHRL may apply to one set of circumstances, it also suggests a definite dividing line between the 'province' of IHL, on the one hand, and the human rights 'mandate' of the Commission, on the other. As is more fully explored below, the Commission, in line with the approach of the other two regional systems, held that it is not mandated to find violations of IHL standards. However, it took the view that it was entitled to, and did in fact, refer to IHL to guide and inform its interpretation of rights that fall under its mandate.

Faced with a number of cases in which states justify human rights violations on the basis of states of emergency or non-international armed conflict, the Commission concluded that states are never allowed to invoke derogations from human rights.[21] The Commission therefore implies that all Charter rights are applicable in times of war and peace, and that these rights may not be derogated from.

Its reasoning for disallowing any form of derogation is both textually and contextually based. As far as the text is concerned, the Commission's conclusion is based on the absence of a derogation clause in the African Charter.[22] The Charter contains neither a general limitation nor a derogation clause. In the latter respect, the Charter differs from the other two regional human rights systems, and is at odds with the position under the ICCPR. However, it is not unique in this respect. In fact, the International Covenant on Economic, Social and Cultural Rights (ICESCR) and all subsequent core UN human rights treaties, including the

18   *Democratic Republic of Congo v Burundi, Rwanda and Uganda* (2004) AHRLR 19 (ACHPR 2003) (*DRC* case). For a discussion of the IHL aspect of the finding (albeit only a small part of the article) see JD Mujuzi 'Case commentary: Interstate communications under the African Charter on Human and Peoples' Rights: Confirming the dwindling divide between international humanitarian law and human rights law? An appraisal of *the Democratic Republic of Congo v Burundi, Rwanda and Uganda* (Communication 227/99)' (2007) *African Yearbook of International Humanitarian Law* 139 153-156.
19   *DRC* case, para 61.
20   *DRC* case, para 64.
21   *Chad Mass Violations* case, para 21. See also *Media Rights Agenda and Others v Nigeria* (2000) AHRLR 200 (ACHPR 1998) (*Media Rights Agenda* case) para 67.
22   *Media Rights Agenda* case, para 67.

widely ratified Convention on the Rights of the Child (CRC)[23] and the Convention on the Elimination of All Forms of Discrimination against Women (CEDAW), also do not contain derogation clauses.

While the Commission does not countenance the legality of derogations under the Charter, as such, it has adopted the approach that all rights may be limited, and that the legality of the limitation must be assessed with reference to the proportionality between the harm emanating from the restriction imposed and the 'legitimate interest' or advantage it seeks to achieve.[24] As far as the (political) context is concerned, the conclusion reached by the Commission is informed by an apprehension about the likelihood of abuse of any possibility allowing for derogation from Charter rights. In the case against Chad, for example, the Commission noted the state should not be allowed, even during a civil war, to use the possibility of derogation as an 'excuse' to justify the commission of human rights violations.[25]

One may criticise this approach as unrealistic.[26] It does beg the question: What if a state with an appropriate domestic derogation clause, possibly combined with a list of non-derogable rights, derogates from particular provisions in accordance with its own domestic law? Also, what if such a state complies with the requirements set out in article 4(3) of the International Covenant on Civil and Political Rights (ICCPR)? It should be considered that all African states except the Comoros, Saõ Tomé and Príncipe and South Sudan are party to the ICCPR. If derogation is allowed under domestic constitutional law, and under the ICCPR, should the position in the African Charter enjoy override?[27]

The Commission's answer seems to be that all limitations or restrictions of rights, including derogations, must be assessed according to a similar standard.[28] Accordingly, limitations and derogations all have to meet the requirements of article 27(2) of the Charter, which the Commission in a sense elevated to a 'general limitations clause'.[29] According to the Commission's interpretation this provision has to be understood as imposing a proportionality test. A state seeking to justify both limitations to and derogations from rights must show that it acted under the authority of a general law, and that the restriction (limitation or

---

23 In her discussion of this omission G van Bueren *The international law on the rights of the child* (1998), dismissed criticism that this omission is a 'fatal flaw', arguing that such a clause would not 'necessarily have resulted in greater protection for the rights of the child', adding that it may present an opportunity 'for a new approach' (at 399).
24 See eg *Media Rights Agenda* case, para 67.
25 *Chad Mass Violations* case, para 22.
26 See eg F Ouguergouz *La Charte africaine des droits de l'homme et des peuples. Une approche juridique des droits de l'homme entre tradition et modernité* (1993) 479.
27 L Sermet 'The absence of a derogation clause from the African Charter on Human and Peoples' Rights: A critical discussion' (2007) 7 *African Human Rights Law Journal* 142.
28 *Media Rights Agenda* case.
29 *Media Rights Agenda* case, para 68.

derogation) serves an aim (need or interest) that is of overriding importance in the society and that it outweighs the extent to which the restriction violates, impedes or suspends the rights concerned. In respect of any derogation, a state would first have to invoke the clear legal competence to derogate under national law, conforming to the international standards of certainty, publicity, necessity and proportionality, and then would have to show that an external threat leading to a situation of armed conflict is of compelling national interest, and that the derogation-limitation is strictly required to attain the societal objective of peace, stability and human flourishing.

A proportionality inquiry is likely to favour the state only if a state of emergency has formally been declared, and a clearly articulated and very compelling justification is presented, given the far reaching effects of the suspension of rights. However, Ali argues that the limitations inquiry cannot be 'taken as a substitute for a derogation clause' because derogations and limitations are fundamentally different in that derogations 'eliminate' a right – even if this is just temporary.[30] While this is a fair comment, it should be possible for the Commission to develop its jurisprudence on limitations to take this complexity into consideration, taking into account principles such as non-discrimination, non-regressive measures and the existence of non-derogable rights.

In *Article 19 v Eritrea*,[31] it was alleged that the arbitrary arrest and prolonged and *incommunicado* detention of former government officials and journalists violated various provisions of the African Charter, including the right to a trial within a reasonable time. In an attempt to justify the detainees' prolonged detention without trial, the government argued that their detention was undertaken 'against a backdrop of war when the very existence of the nation was threatened' and that it was 'duty bound to take necessary precautionary measures (and even suspend certain rights).[32] On the one hand, the Commission responded by restating its position that the African Charter does not allow derogation from its provisions. On the other, it pointed out, for the sake of argument, that even if it was accepted that disallowing derogation 'goes against international principles', Eritrea would not be entitled, in the particular case, to derogate from the relevant rights because they are non-derogable.[33] According to the Commission, one such right is the right to a fair trial. The other non-derogable rights the Commission lists, without explaining the basis for identifying these rights as non-derogable, are the right to life, and the right to be free from torture and cruel, inhuman and degrading treatment. This

---

30　AJ Ali 'Derogation from constitutional rights and its implication under the African Charter on Human and Peoples' Rights' (2013) 17 *Law, Democracy & Development* 78 93.
31　(2007) AHRLR 73 (ACHPR 2007).
32　Para 87.
33　Para 98.

lack of substantiation of further explanation is unfortunate because not all elements of at least the right to a fair trial are generally accepted as being non-derogable.[34]

Although international law does not provide a definitive list of non-derogable rights, it has been argued that at least the four rights listed as non-derogoble in both the European and American Conventions of Human Rights would be very strong candidates. These rights are: the right to life; the right not to be subjected to torture and other forms of inhuman or degrading treatment or punishment; the right against forced labour or slavery; and the guarantee against the application of retroactive criminal sanctions.[35]

Eritrea's invocation of the context ('background') of war, without any indication that a formal state of emergency had been declared, or specifying which rights are specifically derogated from, to justify the derogation from rights, is clearly disingenuous. The significance of the *Article 19* case is the admittedly obiter remarks of the Commission that underscore the importance of non-derogable rights, an aspect which I argue should be part of the Commission's limitations inquiry.

It is also of particular relevance that the African Charter entitles the African Commission to make findings of massive and serious violations of human rights. However, under the legal framework of the Charter, a distinction is drawn between 'ordinary' communications and 'a series of serious or massive violations'. In respect of the second category, the Commission is, according to the Charter, only competent to 'draw the attention' of the AU Assembly of Heads of State and Government to the existence of these violations.[36] It should then await a request by the Assembly mandating it to undertake 'an in-depth study' and report back to the Assembly.[37] It can be safely assumed that many of the potential

---

34   The right to a fair trial is not non-derogable under the ICCPR (see art 4(2)); under the Constitution of the Republic of South Africa, 1996, only certain aspects of the right to a fair trial (of 'accused persons') are non-derogable (see sec 37). See, however, the International Committee of the Red Cross (ICRC) study: J-M Henckaerts & L Doswald-Beck *Customary international humanitarian law: Vol I: Rules* (2005) 352-371, in which fair trial rights are extensively covered as part of customary international humanitarian law http://www.icrc.org/eng/assets/files/other/customary-inter national-humanitarian-law-i-icrc-eng.pdf (accessed 22 October 2014). In respect of each aspect of the right to a fair trial, the study in the main looks at the three major regional human rights systems, in addition to relevant UN human rights treaties and humanitarian law standards. In respect of the right to examine witnesses, for example, the study notes the following (at 365): 'While the African Charter on Human and Peoples' Rights does not explicitly provide for this right, the African Commission on Human and Peoples' Rights has specified that it is part and parcel of the right to fair trial.'
35   J Oraa 'The protection of human rights in emergency situations under customary international law' in GS Goodwin-Gill & S Talmon (eds) *The reality of international law* (1999) 413.
36   African Charter, art 58(1).
37   Compare arts 55 and 56, on the one hand, with art 58 of the Charter, on the other.

situations of 'serious or massive violations' may occur within the context of armed conflict. The position in the Charter seems to depart from the acceptance of a dichotomy between law and politics, with the Assembly positioned to play a more prominent role in more politicised matters, where systemic issues – including armed conflict – arise. Although the Commission as a quasi-judicial body is mandated to find violations of human rights standards only, the Assembly may take into account IHL in its political resolution of the issue. However, despite a number of such referrals by the Commission, the Assembly never authorised an in-depth study under article 58. This failure to some extent explains the Commission's apparent reluctance to explicitly find 'massive or serious violations' of Charter provisions.

Because serious or massive human rights violations often occur as a result and in the context of armed conflict, the role of the African human rights system (and of the Assembly, under article 58 of the Charter) may overlap with that of the AU's Peace and Security Council (PSC), which came into being some 20 years subsequent to the drafting and adoption of the African Charter. The PSC aims to anticipate and prevent conflicts. One of its objectives is to promote respect for IHL,[38] and one of the principles that guide its operation is 'respect for' IHL.[39] Under its explicit mandate to 'bring to the attention' of the PSC information relevant to the PSC's mandate, the African Commission may refer matters more squarely dealing with armed conflict to the PSC, allowing it (rather than the Commission) to deal with the root causes of the violations and seek long-lasting political solutions.

In 2003, the Commission postponed *sine die* a communication pertaining to the international armed conflict between Ethiopia and Eritrea, starting in 1998, which led to the expulsion of Eritreans from Ethiopia, and Ethiopians from Eritrea.[40] One of the reasons that may explain why the Commission postponed its final decision by opting to leave the resolution of the dispute to the Ethiopia-Eritrea Claims Commission was the inclusion within the Claims Commission's mandate of claims for loss or damage resulting from the violation of IHL.

In summary, similar to the rights under the two other regional human rights systems, African Charter rights apply irrespective of whether a situation of international or non-international armed conflict prevails. The African Commission confirmed this position explicitly in a number of findings, including the *Chad Mass Violations* case, the *DRC* case and the case of *Article 19 v Eritrea*. One of the main reasons for this position is the absence from the Charter of a derogations clause, from which the

38   Art 3(f) of the Protocol on the PSC.
39   Art 4(c) of the Protocol on the PSC.
40   *Interights (on behalf of Pan African Movement and others) v Eritrea and Ethiopia* (2003) AHRLR 74 (ACHPR 2003).

Commission deduced that Charter rights remain operational during armed conflict. The Commission's view that all restrictions on Charter rights (including derogations during armed conflict) must be justified with reference to the proportionality principle needs to be further developed and clarified. In respect of massive violations during armed conflict, possible duplication between the African Commission and the AU PSC should be avoided, for example by allowing the PSC to address and seek solutions for the root causes of conflict.

2.2   Extra-territorial application of Charter rights

Military action resulting in the occupation by the forces of one state of the territory of another, and other forms of international armed conflict having an impact on the rights of persons in other states highlight the relevance of the extra-territorial application of human rights for the interaction between IHL and IHRL. In the exercise of its communications mandate, the African Commission has held, in the context of an international armed conflict, that the Charter applies extra-territorially. In the *DRC* case, the African Commission accepted without question that state parties to the African Charter can incur international responsibility for acts of their forces on the territory of another state. The alleged rape, pillage, murder and other forms of exploitation committed against the 'people' of the DRC by armed forces of Burundi, Rwanda and Uganda in the eastern provinces of the DRC gave rise to this conclusion. In its finding, the Commission accentuates the fact that the forces of these three countries were actually present in and effectively occupied these parts of the DRC.[41]

The Commission accepted, without elaborating on this issue, that the three state parties could be held accountable extra-territorially, that is, for the actions of its armed forces outside the territory of the state party, in this case, inside the territory of another state party, the DRC. Even if it does not stipulate that effective control is a prerequisite for the extra-territorial applicability of the Charter, this finding relates to and thus provides authority only for the extra-territorial application of the Charter in circumstances where the agents of a respondent state are physically present and in effective control of the part of the territory of another state where its agents are responsible for human rights violations.

Although the Commission does not elaborate on the legal basis of its finding, such a finding is consistent with the African Charter. The Charter does not explicitly stipulate that the African Charter applies only in the

---

41   The Commission 'finds' that the relevant human rights abuses were committed 'while the respondent states' armed forces were still in effective occupation of the eastern provinces' of the DRC (*DRC* case, para 79). The decision of the International Court of Justice (ICJ) related to this matter, *DRC v Uganda*, is discussed more fully below (note 61 below).

territory of member states,[42] leading to the inference (based on the facts and finding in the *DRC* case) that the Charter applies spatially to areas over which the state party vests effective control. Extra-territorial application therefore finds at least implicit textual support in the African Charter. It can further be inferred that the Charter also applies to state conduct in respect of individuals over whom the state has effective control, irrespective where the alleged violations occurred.

2.3   Commission's indirect application of IHL through interpretation

In respect of a situation where both international human rights and IHL potentially applies, the African Commission has found only violations of human rights law, but in so doing, has sought interpretive guidance from IHL. This approach could be described as the indirect enforcement of IHL. It amounts to the application of *lex specialis derogat generali* as 'nothing more than a rule of interpretation'[43] to 'assist in the interpretation of general terms and standards' in IHRL 'by reference to more specific norms' from IHL.[44]

In the *DRC* case, the Commission found that that the occupation of the DRC by forces of the three neighbouring countries itself constituted a violation of the African Charter, in that the occupation seriously undermined the right to national and international peace and security and to self-determination of the 'peoples' of the DRC, guaranteed under articles 23 and 20 of the Charter, respectively. The Commission did not make specific reference to IHL in this context. Instead, it referred to the Declaration on Principles of International Law Concerning Friendly Relations and Cooperation among States in accordance of the Charter of the United Nations,[45] and the OAU Charter.[46]

As far as the consequences of the occupation and its effects on the rights of the civilian population are concerned, the Commission engaged more explicitly with IHL. However, in its finding on the substance, the Commission only found violations of the African Charter, as such. At the same time, it acknowledged that the alleged violations committed by the armed forces 'fall within the province of humanitarian law'.[47] It therefore

---

42   Art 1 of the African Charter, which contains the overarching obligation of states to 'give effect to' and 'recognise' the rights in the Charter does not limit the Charter's application to the territory of the state.
43   M Akehurst 'The hierarchy of the sources of international law' (1975) 47 *British Yearbook of International Law* 273 410.
44   M Milanovic 'Norm conflicts, international humanitarian law, and human rights law' in Ben-Naftali (ed) (n 1 above) 95 115-116.
45   UN General Assembly Resolution 2625(XXV); see *DRC* case, para 73.
46   OAU Charter, art 3, referring in particular to the principle of peaceful settlement of disputes; see *DRC* case, para 74.
47   *DRC* case, para 69.

follows, the Commission held, that these events are covered by the four Geneva Conventions and the two Additional Protocols thereto, dealing with armed conflict.

Article 60 and 61 of the African Charter are often cited as allowing the Commission to draw interpretive inspiration from human rights treaties adopted outside the ambit of the African Union (and its predecessor, the OAU).[48] However, a distinction should be made between the two provisions. Article 60 allows the Commission to draw on a number of sources dealing with 'human and peoples' rights'. A strict interpretation of this phrase would exclude the Geneva Convention and Additional Protocols thereto. Apparently (but not explicitly) departing from such an understanding of the scope of article 60, the Commission finds its mandate to place reliance on humanitarian law treaties in article 61. This provision allows the Commission to also 'take into consideration', in order to determine the principles of law applicable in a particular case, a number of subsidiary sources.

The Commission locates the referenced humanitarian law treaties in two sources, both listed in article 61. The one source is 'other general or specialised international conventions laying down rules expressly recognised' by AU member states. 'Other conventions' here refers to treaties not dealing with 'human and peoples' rights'. The Geneva Conventions and Additional Protocols are referred to on this basis, in the words of the Commission, as 'special international conventions'.[49] Although the Commission does not use the term, it in effect categorises these treaties as *lex specialis*. The second source under article 61 that entitles the Commission to place reliance on humanitarian law texts is 'general principles of law recognised by African states'. The fact that the Commission did not engage with the issue whether the relevant treaties are 'expressly recognised' by member states, and did not endeavour to explain or substantiate how they have come to be recognised as 'general principles' by African states may be unfortunate, but can be explained by the prevailing situation that all African states, with the exception of Eritrea, Somalia and Angola, have become state party to all six treaties under discussion.[50]

Having located the six humanitarian law treaties within the scope of article 61, the Commission 'holds' that the provisions of these treaties will be taken into consideration in the 'determination' of the case.[51] Their role is thus to influence or guide the resolution (decision or finding) in the case, by shedding light on or animating the provisions of the Charter. In line

48   See eg the Commission's decision in *Legal Resources Foundation v Zambia* (2001) AHRLR 84 (ACHPR 2001).
49   Para 78.
50   Eritrea and Somalia have not accepted any of the two Additional Protocols, while Angola has not accepted the First Additional Protocol.
51   Para 70.

with this understanding, the Commission analysed the facts, and found a number of Charter violations. However, in each instance, it used the specific formulations under humanitarian law to breathe life into the much more general and open-ended Charter provisions.

The choice of the Commission to use the lens of article 61 to focus on the four Geneva Conventions and their two Optional Protocols may have been informed also by the fact that both the applicant and the three respondent states are party to these instruments. However, ratification of an instrument is not a prerequisite for interpretive reliance by the Commission. Relying on some scholarly writing, Mujuzi notes that the relevant humanitarian law standards 'are believed to have acquired the status of customary international law'.[52]

Three findings of Charter violations by the Commission in the *DRC* case illustrate this approach, thus also demonstrating the added benefit of it placing reliance on IHL.

First, in respect of the act by the respondent states' forces to besiege a hydroelectric dam in the DRC, the Commission found a violation of the right to national and international peace and security under article 23 of the Charter. This provision, quite predictably, does not deal with anything as detailed as dams. This open-endedness leaves obvious room for the interpretive guidance of humanitarian law, which the Commission found in the First Protocol Additional to the Geneva Conventions of 1949, which provides that 'dams ... shall not be made [an] object of attack'.[53]

Second, the Commission found that the rape of women and girls by members of the armed forces constituted a violation of articles 2 (the right not to be discriminated against on the basis of national origin) and article 4 (the right to life and personal integrity) of the Charter. As part of a general human rights treaty, it is unsurprising that the Commission locates the violation in generally framed provisions of general application. Again, the Commission substantiated its finding of Charter violations with reference to more specific and detailed IHL provisions.[54] In this instance, reliance is placed on the First Protocol Additional to the Geneva Conventions of 1949, which stipulates that women must be 'the object of special respect' and must be 'protected in particular against rape';[55] and on the Fourth Geneva Convention of 1949, which stipulates that 'protected

52　　Mujuzi (n 18 above) 155; see also the ICRC study on customary international humanitarian law (n 34 above).

53　　Art 56 of the 1977 First Protocol Additional to the Geneva Conventions of 1949.

54　　*DRC* case, paras 86 and 89.

55　　Art 76 of the 1977 First Protocol Additional to the Geneva Conventions of 1949. This Protocol (in art 49(2)) defines the term 'attack' as acts of violence against the adversary and it is at least debatable that mere besieging amounts to such acts. Certainly in the context of the protection of works and installations containing dangerous forces, the primary concern is with these works and installations not being damaged with a view to prevent a release of dangerous forces (see art 56 of the Protocol).

persons' are entitled, 'in all circumstances, to respect for their persons, their honour, their family rights' and that women 'shall be especially protected against any attack on their honour, in particular against rape, enforced prostitution, or any form of indecent assault'.[56]

The third example concerns the factual circumstances of the dumping of bodies and mass burials. These circumstances led the Commission to find a violation of article 22 of the African Charter, the right to cultural development, but through the prism of article 34 of the First Protocol Additional to the Geneva Conventions of 1949, which places a much more specific obligation on states to respect human remains. This very detailed provision requires state parties to respect the 'remains of persons who have died for reasons related to occupation or in detention resulting from occupation or hostilities' and to respect, maintain and mark 'the gravesites of all such persons'. Again, it is the specificity of this provision that gives concrete content to the rather abstract notion of 'cultural development' in article 22 of the Charter.

This approach mirrors that of the Inter-American Court of Human Rights. In the *Case of the Ituango Massacres v Colombia*,[57] the Inter-American Court found a violation of the right to property, provided for under the American Convention of Human Rights, while making specific reference to the Second Protocol Additional to the 1949 Geneva Convention. The Court found that the theft of livestock in the context of an internal armed conflict constituted a violation of the right to property by using IHL – particularly, the prohibition against destroying or rendering useless 'objects indispensable to the survival of the civilian population'.[58]

In its *DRC* judgment, the Commission on occasion used the term 'civilian population'.[59] However, this need not be problematic or lead to the conclusion that the Commission applies or enforces international humanitarian law. Here the question whether a situation constitutes an armed conflict (that is, implying the existence of 'combatants', on the one hand, and 'non-combatants' or 'civilians', on the other) is a threshold question, not for the application of international humanitarian law as source of law, but for the use of international humanitarian law as an interpretive source. As the concept of 'armed conflict' is left undefined, and as no institutional mechanism has been established to provide guidance, it is up to bodies such as the African Commission to determine whether the threshold has been met in the concrete cases upon which it adjudicates.

---

56 Art 27 of the 1949 Geneva Convention relative to the Protection of Civilian Persons in Time of War (Fourth Geneva Convention).
57 Series C No 148, Inter-American Court of Human Rights (IACrtHR) (1 July 2006); see D Shelton 'Humanitarian law in the Inter-American human rights system' in this volume, para 5.3.
58 Protocol II to the 1949 Geneva Convention, art 14.
59 Para 88.

In the *DRC* case the circumstances revealed that the threshold of an international armed conflict had been met. While the Commission refers to the situation as an 'undeclared war', thus bringing the 1949 Geneva Conventions into play, it also observed that the events are 'covered by' the two Protocols additional to the Geneva Conventions.[60] As indicated above, the Commission in fact placed reliance on both the Geneva Conventions and the two Protocols in the process of arriving at findings that the three states had violated the African Charter. This broadening of scope may be attributed to the provisions of article 61 of the Charter. It is on these provisions, rather than a determination that a particular yardstick has been met, that the Commission based its reliance on IHL norms in the process of interpreting Charter rights.

The approach in the *DRC* case should be contrasted with that of the International Court of Justice (ICJ). Based on essentially the same set of factual circumstances as the *DRC* case, the ICJ decided the case of *DRC v Uganda* in December 2005.[61] In this decision, the ICJ observes that the territory is 'occupied' when it is 'actually placed under the authority of the hostile army'.[62] Having established that Uganda was the 'occupying power' in the relevant part of the DRC's territory, the Court found that one set of factual circumstances gave rise to findings of violations of both international human rights law and humanitarian law. Uganda was held responsible for both the actions of its own forces in the territory and for its 'lack of vigilance' to prevent violation of IHL and IHRL by non-state actors perpetrated in the territory.[63]

It should be pointed out that such a broad finding is clearly allowed for and justified by the broad ambit of article 38(1) of the ICJ Statute, which provides the ICJ with a very expansive material jurisdiction. As a court of potentially unlimited global and substantive scope, the ICJ has jurisdiction over all treaties ('international conventions') recognised by the states concerned and over 'international custom' irrespective whether the 'convention' or 'custom' deals with IHRL or IHL. After concluding that the facts prove the responsibility of and may be attributed to Uganda, the Court finds that IHL standards (the 1907 Hague Regulations and the Fourth Geneva Convention of 1949) and IHRL norms (in the ICCPR, the African Charter, the Convention on the Rights of the Child and the Optional Protocol thereto on Child Soldiers) had been violated.[64]

In contrast, the jurisdictional scope of the African Commission is much more narrow, as determined by its founding treaty, the African Charter. Principally, the Commission's jurisdiction relates to the African

---

60   *DRC* case, para 69.
61   n 1 above. See FZ Ntoubandi 'The *Congo/Uganda* case: A comment on the main legal issues' (2007) 7 *African Human Rights Law Journal* 162.
62   Para 172.
63   Para 179.
64   Para 219.

Charter.[65] Although the Commission has on rare occasions based its finding on treaties other than the African Charter,[66] these treaties were all still adopted within the auspices of the OAU/AU. It is unlikely that the Commission has the competence to make findings that the Geneva Conventions or other IHL treaties or, for that matter, customary IHL, had been violated.

The *DRC* decision should be contrasted with the Commission's decision in a subsequent case against Sudan, dealing with forced displacement, destruction of property, extra-judicial executions and bombing of populated areas by the militias (in particular, the Jahjaweed), with the support of Sudanese government forces.[67]

In its finding of numerous violations, the Commission did not refer at all to IHL. It also largely steered clear of characterising the situation as one of serious or massive human rights violations, perhaps because it wants to avoid any controversy about the need to refer the matter to the AU Assembly as required under article 58 of the Charter. Although reliance on IHL was possible, for example, in respect of the bombing of civilians and the destruction of their property, the Commission opted to frame the case as one of human rights violations, and did not draw interpretive guidance from the relevant IHL standards. One explanation for this approach is that the complainants framed the case as one of human rights violations and did apparently not place reliance on humanitarian law.[68] Still, by not exploring the resonance of humanitarian law treaties, the Commission deviated from its approach in the *DRC* case and has allowed an opportunity to pass by to further expand on its understanding of the relationship between international human rights and humanitarian law. The potential for such an exploration is clear from the Commission's own characterisation of the state's response as targeting 'the civilian population' and not 'the combatants' 'while fighting the armed conflict'.[69]

However, despite the lack of any explicit reference to IHL, the Commission's approach here reinforces its point of departure that human rights are fully applicable in situations of armed conflict. Although it does not in so many words describe the situation as a non-international armed

65 One of the admissibility criteria for individual communications is that they must be 'compatible with' the African Charter.

66 See eg *African Institute for Human Rights and Development (on behalf of Sierra Leonean refugees in Guinea) v Guinea* (2004) AHRLR 57 (ACHPR 2004) (*Guinea* case), discussed more fully below.

67 *Sudan Human Rights Organisation v Sudan* (2009) AHRLR 153 (ACHPR 2009) (*Darfur* case).

68 Although the complainants refer to bombings by 'military fighter jets', 'militia', 'armed rebellion' and 'civilian population', according to the summary of facts, no explicit reliance is placed on IHL either as a source of interpretive guidance or as the source of a remedy (*Darfur* case, paras 1-16).

69 *Darfur* case, para 223.

conflict, the facts clearly show that this is what obtained in Darfur at that time.

The Commission's approach in the *Darfur* case is also at odds with the findings and recommendations in its on-site (fact-finding) protective mission, undertaken to Sudan in July 2004.[70] Although its mandate only refers to 'serious or massive human rights violations', it makes repeated reference to international humanitarian law in its report. It describes the situation as 'all out civil war',[71] describe the victims as 'the civilian population'[72] and find that war crimes had been committed.[73] In its recommendations, the mission report urged the government to investigate violations of human rights and *international humanitarian law,*[74] to stop the bombardment of the civilian population[75] and to abide by its obligations under both international human rights and *humanitarian law.*[76]

International humanitarian law may also be raised as part of the state reporting process, either by the state in the report itself, or by the African Commission in its Concluding Observations on the report. Reporting in 2011, in the context of the conflict between itself and Morocco, the Sahrawi Arab Democratic Republic made very limited reference to IHL, invoking only restrictions in freedom of movement as a violation of IHL, without specifying the particular provision relied on. Other aspects covered in the report, such as mines, indicate that more reliance could have been placed on reinforcing Morocco's obligations under IHL, especially since it is not a party to the African Charter, but to the Geneva Conventions and – since 2011 – to both Additional Protocols of 1977. In a resolution on the situation, adopted in 2014, the African Commission focused on issues of widespread violations in the occupied Western Sahara, such as crackdown on peaceful demonstration and arbitrary detentions, and on the right to self-determination.[77] It did however mention the 'continuing source of danger for the population' of anti-personnel mines in the area, but made no reference to IHL, as such.

From the above analysis, the Commission's reluctance to find violations of IHL is textual rather than principled. It appears that the African Commission did not articulate a principled position against

70 Report of the African Commission on Human and Peoples' Rights' fact-finding mission to the Republic of Sudan in the Darfur Region (8 to 18 July 2004) (Darfur report).
71 Darfur report, para 24.
72 Darfur report, para 122.
73 Darfur report, para 124.
74 Darfur report, para 138(a) (emphasis added).
75 Darfur report, para 140.
76 Darfur report, para 152 (emphasis added).
77 Resolution 282 on the situation in the Sahrawi Arab Democratic Republic, adopted at its 55th session, 28 April 2014, Luanda Angola. See also Resolution 45 on the Western Sahara, adopted by the African Commission on Human and Peoples' Rights, at its 27th Ordinary Session held in Algiers, from 27 April-11 May 2000.

making findings that IHL has been violated. Rather, the Commission has excluded this body of law as a basis on which it makes findings because the Commission's foundational text, the African Charter, does not include IHL in its jurisdictional scope. At least occasionally, the Commission has indirectly applied IHL by placing interpretive reliance on the more detailed provisions of IHL to reach the conclusion that states have violated the often vaguely formulated provisions of IHRL (in the form of the African Charter).

2.4 Expanded jurisdiction through explicit references to IHL in other OAU/AU human rights treaties

To be sure, the African Commission's material jurisdiction extends further than the African Charter. On occasion, the Commission has found a violation of the OAU Convention Governing the Specific Aspects of Refugee Problems in Africa (OAU Refugee Convention).[78] This broadening of the substantive basis of findings is possible because the Charter does not prescribe, as an admissibility requirement, that a communication must allege a violation of the African Charter. Instead, the relevant provision on admissibility stipulates that the communication must be 'compatible with' the Charter.[79] Arguably, the requisite compatibility is served if the Commission adjudicates on a violation of another OAU/AU treaty, particularly if such a treaty does not establish its own treaty monitoring body. However, on this basis, the Commission still lacks the jurisdictional competence to found findings of violation on IHL treaties such as the Geneva Conventions.

On this basis, the African Commission also has the competence to adjudicate on the 2003 Protocol to the African Charter on the Rights of Women in Africa (Women's Protocol), which entered into force in 2005; and the 2009 AU Convention for the Protection and Assistance of Internally Displaced Persons in Africa (IDP Convention), which entered into force in 2012. As the Women's Protocol supplements the substantive provisions of the Charter without establishing a new treaty body, logic dictates that the African Commission is the appropriate forum for the adjudication of violations of the Women's Protocol.[80] Although the IDP Convention is not a protocol to the African Charter, it adds to the AU landscape of substantive human rights standards without establishing a new treaty monitoring body. Logic therefore also impels the conclusion that it is 'compatible with' the African Charter to allow the African Commission to adjudicate complaints based on this treaty.[81]

---

78   See eg *Guinea* case (n 66 above), final (operative) paragraph, in which the Commission found a violation of art 4 of the OAU Refugee Convention.
79   Art 56(2) of the African Charter.
80   See the argument on this issue in F Viljoen *International human rights law in Africa* (2012) 313.
81   See also art 20(3) of the IDP Convention.

Different to the African Charter, these two treaties make specific reference to IHL. The Protocol on the Rights of Women, in article 11, requires state parties to respect the rules of international humanitarian law that affect the population, 'particularly women'.[82] This formulation incorporates the corpus of IHL – both treaty-based and customary law, at least as far as it relates to women – into the Women's Protocol, and thus brings those provisions under the jurisdiction of the African Commission. In addition to this general formulation, the provision also stipulates that women should be protected against all forms of violence, including rape, and that such acts should be considered as 'war crimes'; and requires states to ensure that girls, in particular, do not take part in direct hostilities.[83]

In the IDP Convention, the link between armed conflict and displacement is clearly recognised. From this acknowledgment flows the general obligation on states to 'respect and ensure respect for international humanitarian law regarding the protection' of IDPs.[84] One of the specifically mentioned categories of prohibited displacement is 'displacement intentionally used as a method of warfare or due to other violations of international humanitarian law in situations of armed conflict'.[85] In fact, the Convention stipulates that the particular provision 'shall be governed by international law and in particular international humanitarian law'.[86] The IDP Convention also stipulates that members of armed groups 'shall be prohibited' from various actions, including the recruitment of children and the violation of the 'civilian character' of places where IDPs are sheltered.[87] It is however clarified that the obligation to ensure that armed groups act in a particular way lies with state parties.[88] From the above, it appears that humanitarian law is incorporated into the treaty, and that the body mandated to make findings of violations on the basis of this treaty – arguably the African Commission – will in all likelihood make findings that international humanitarian law standards as set out in the relevant treaty have been violated – on the basis that IHL standards had been enacted into the IDP Convention.

If violations of these treaties are invoked before the African Commission, it may well find a violation of international humanitarian law, as incorporated into that particular treaty. In this way it is clearly possible that the African Commission may find it imperative to proceed, on the basis of *lex specialis*, to find specific humanitarian law violations, in the sense that these particular provisions have been codified in the relevant texts.

82　Art 11(1) of the Women's Protocol.
83　Art 11(3) of the Women's Protocol.
84　Art 3(1)(e) of the IDP Convention.
85　Art 4(4)(c) of the IDP Convention.
86　Art 7(3) of the IDP Convention.
87　Arts 7(5)(e) and (i) of the IDP Convention.
88　Art 5(11) of the IDP Convention.

2.5 Commission's role in ensuring article 4(h) intervention

One of the great innovations of the AU Constitutive Act, compared to its predecessor, the OAU Charter, is the inclusion of article 4(h), which allows the AU, multilaterally, by way of an Assembly decision, to intervene in a member state where crimes against humanity, genocide and war crimes have occurred, and the state is unable and unwilling to deal satisfactorily with the situation.[89] While genocide and crimes against humanity fall within the realm of human rights law, war crimes clearly bring IHL into the picture. In order for the Assembly to arrive at a decision, the AU's PSC must make a recommendation.[90] The African Commission should use its collaborative relationship with the PSC, provided for under the PSC Protocol,[91] to inform this recommendation and decision. Although such a role is not explicitly provided for, the Commission should use its competence to 'bring to the attention' of the PSC any information relevant to its objectives and mandate,[92] to provide a reliable factual and legal basis on which the PSC may base its recommendations in respect of article 4(h) to the AU Assembly.

3 African Human Rights Court

In the first sub-section, the question is posed to what extent IHL forms part of the substantive jurisdiction of the African Human Rights Court. The extent of actual reliance by the Court on IHL in one relevant case, the *Libya Provisional Measures* case, is considered in the second sub-section. In the third, the implications for IHL of the Court's future evolution into a two-chambered court (with two separate chambers dealing respectively with general affairs and human rights) and the extension of its jurisdiction to international criminal justice are investigated. A last brief sub-section deals with the Court's role in galvanising article 4(h) of the AU Constitutive Act.

3.1 IHL as part of the African Court's jurisdiction *ratione materiae*

As for the African Human Rights Court, its jurisdiction is not limited to the African Charter but extends to all other relevant 'human rights' treaties.[93] Questions about the application of IHL to some extent therefore hinge on the interpretation of the term 'human rights treaty'. A narrow

---

89 See in general D Kuwali & F Viljoen (eds) *Africa and the responsibility to protect: Article 4(h) of the African Union Constitutive Act* (2014).
90 Art 7(1)(e) of the PSC Protocol.
91 Art 19 of the PSC Protocol.
92 As above.
93 Art 3(1) of the Court Protocol.

interpretation of this term, departing from the premise that 'human rights treaties' are instruments that articulate clearly defined rights holders and duty bearers, would justify a conclusion that IHL instruments do not fall under the auspices of the African Human Rights Court. However, a broader and more purposive approach would lead to a different conclusion. According to such a more teleological approach, a 'human rights treaty' is any treaty that aims to protect aspects of human life and dignity. Using this understanding as the yardstick for what constitutes a 'human rights treaty', international humanitarian law treaties qualify as 'human rights treaties'. In any event, the term 'human rights treaty' needs not be applicable to a treaty as a whole, but should rather be understood as relating to particular provisions (those imposing rights and duties) within a treaty. From this perspective, the decisive factor in determining whether a matter falls under the Court's jurisdiction *ratione materiae* should be whether a particular treaty provision, which inevitably forms part of a treaty, meets the requirements of either the narrow or broad tests. In other words, even if one of the Geneva Conventions, for example, is not considered to be a 'human rights' treaty as such (that is, as a whole), some of its provisions may still fall under the Court's article 3(1) jurisdiction.

Another approach would be to identify whether, *in the main*, a treaty is a 'human rights treaty'. Once this determination is made, it follows that all its provisions fall under the Court's jurisdiction. Adopting this reasoning, African human rights treaties containing some IHL standards should therefore fall under the jurisdiction of the African Human Rights Court. For example, the Women's Rights Protocol clearly is a human rights treaty. On this basis, it falls within the jurisdictional scope of the Court. The explicit incorporation of IHL into one of its provisions, article 11, therefore brings that particular provision into the jurisdictional scope of the African Human Rights Court.

The fact that the IHL standards are not 'African' (in the sense of having been adopted by the OAU or AU) is not of importance, because article 3(1) does not stipulate that only *African* treaties fall under the Court's jurisdiction. The African Court's jurisdiction seems to correspond with that of the European Court, which arguably also has the competence not only to rely on IHL as a means of interpretation, but also as 'a direct source of normative standards applicable in times of armed conflict'.[94] This is so because article 15 of the European Convention allows derogation in times of war provided that the derogation does not constitute a violation of the state's 'other obligations under international law'.[95] These other obligations include those under IHL, a fact that opens 'the

---

94 A Gioia 'The role of the European Court of Human Rights in monitoring compliance with humanitarian law in armed conflict' in Ben-Naftali (ed) (n 1 above) 201 216.
95 Art 15(1) of the European Convention.

way for the Court to review whether violations under the Convention are justified by IHL and thus to apply IHL'.[96]

3.2 *Libya Provisional Measures* case

In a case against Libya, the African Human Rights Court ordered provisional measures during a situation of armed conflict.[97] This case relates to the events during the early stages of the conflict in Libya, specifically to the impending bombing of the civilian population from 16-19 February 2011 in Benghazi. The facts of the case relate to the early stages of what later took on the nature of an undeniable non-international (and eventually an international) armed conflict in Libya. The facts before the Court relate to the situation as it stood at around 20 February 2011, which concern mainly the detention of government opponents and the violent suppression of demonstrations. However, mention is also made of aerial bombardments and other types of attacks.[98] Despite the potential for (at least partially) contextualising the case within this armed conflict, the Court focuses only on the human rights dimension of the situation.

On the basis of a referral by the African Commission, the Court found that there was a situation of extreme gravity and urgency based on the violation of the rights to life and physical integrity of the population. The Court steered clear of any IHL-related language and focused on and framed the violations within the language of human rights, ordering the state to refrain from violating the African Charter and other international human rights law.

Since the Commission's request for further postponement in preparing its submissions on the merits of this case has been denied, the case was struck off the role. This is a pity, as it leaves unanswered the question whether IHL may have been used to deal with this case, particularly as the merits decision may have necessitated a factual enquiry broader than the events of the first few days in February 2011, which could still have been described as a situation of insurrection or internal turbulence rather than fully fledged non-international armed conflict. If the temporal scope of the factual enquiry was enlarged or broadened to include subsequent events, the relevance of IHL would have increased significantly in this case, and the case could even have extended to a situation of international armed conflict.

Still, even the situation prevailing at 20 February 2011 could also have been contextualised as one of violations resulting from a situation of non-

---

96   Oellers-Frahm (n 16 above).
97   *African Commission v Libya*, Provisional Measures Order, Application 4/2011, 25 March 2011 (*Libya Provisional Measures* case).
98   Para 2.

international conflict, thus allowing for the application of IHL. Setting out the factual background, the Court refers to the description by the AU PSC of the situation as being characterised by violations of human rights and IHL. In a similar vein, the UN Security Council denounced the 'systematic attacks'. The closest the Court came to taking this route was when it placed the 'present situation' of loss of life in the context of 'on-going conflict'.[99]

3.3   Future evolution of the African Court and the increased role of IHL

Although the African Union Constitutive Act foresaw the creation of two separate continental courts – the African Human Rights Court and the African Union Court of Justice – the AU Assembly decided, mainly for reasons of cost-saving, to amalgamate these two Courts to form the African Court of Justice and Human Rights (ACJHR). According to the Protocol creating the two-chambered Merged Court, the ACJHR would have a broader jurisdiction than the African Human Rights Court. Under the Protocol, which is not yet in force, the ACJHR would have two chambers or 'sections', one dealing mainly with inter-state issues (the general affairs section), and another chamber dealing with human rights cases (the human rights section). Under this arrangement, the Court's jurisdiction *ratione materiae* would not explicitly include IHL but would extend to 'general principles of law'.[100] In line with the African Commission's finding in the *DRC* case, IHL standards such as the Geneva Conventions should be considered to be part of these 'general principles of law'. One of the sections (the general affairs section, most probably) could in other words be most likely to decide IHL violations, for example in an inter-state case in which alleged situation of international armed conflict is at issue.

However, in the meantime, the AU has proposed an alternative structure to the ACJHR, possibly to be inaugurated in the future. A Protocol (Protocol on Amendments to the Protocol on the Statute of the African Court of Justice and Human Rights (Amending Protocol) and the Statute annexed thereto) was adopted by the AU Assembly in terms of which a three-chambered court (the African Court of Justice and Human and Peoples' Rights) would be established.[101] In addition to a general affairs and human rights sections, the proposed Court would also have a chamber dealing with individual criminal responsibility. Its proposed title is the 'African Court of Justice and Human and Peoples' Rights' (here referred to as the three-chambered Merged Court). This name is a misnomer, because it does not capture the essence of the three-chambered

---

99   Para 13.
100   Art 31(d) of Protocol on the Statute of the African Court of Justice and Human Rights.
101   Adopted by AU Assembly on 27 June 2014.

court, which represents the addition of the unprecedented element of individual criminal jurisdiction to the mandate of a regional court.

Without going into the merits of the arguments in favour of or against such a three-chambered court, one of the most positive features of the proposed African criminal chamber is that it would have a much broader and expansive substantive jurisdiction than the International Criminal Court (ICC). In addition to all the ICC crimes (genocide, crimes against humanity, war crimes and the crime of aggression), the proposed court is set to deal also with a long list of additional crimes. Featuring on this list are the following: piracy, terrorism, mercenarism, the 'crime of unconstitutional change of government',[102] the 'crime of aggression',[103] corruption, money laundering, trafficking in persons, trafficking in drugs, trafficking in hazardous wastes and illicit exploitation of natural resources.[104] From this perspective, extending the jurisdiction of the Court to determine individual criminal responsibility simultaneously entails extending the Court's jurisdiction to find violations of both IHRL (such as massive violations amounting to crime against humanity or genocide) and IHL (in the form of war crimes). If established, the three-chambered Court would provide a regional forum for the enforcement and direct application of IHL, something that does not exist anywhere in the world today. However, the fact that the Amending Protocol does not explain the relationship between the African Criminal Court and the ICC is problematic, particularly because the complementarity foreseen under the ICC Statute is between national courts – rather than regional courts – and the ICC.[105]

The possibility of approaching any of the three sections of the Court could result in conflicting outcomes resulting from overlapping jurisdiction if the different sections deal with the same substantive issue at the same time. Take as an example the *DRC* case. In so far as the case dealt with human rights, the Human Rights Section of the three-chambered Merged Court would, similar to the African Commission, have been able and competent to find violations of the African Charter. The General Affairs Section of the Merged Court would have been able to find violations of the Geneva Conventions, if the argument is correct that they fall under the scope of article 3(1) of the African Human Rights Court Protocol. And the International Criminal Section would have had jurisdiction to preside over

---

102 Art 28E of the Amending Protocol.
103 Art 28M of the Amending Protocol defines the crime as follows: 'use, intentionally and knowingly, of armed force or any other hostile act by a state, a group of States, an organization of States or non-State actor(s) or by any foreign or external entity, against the sovereignty, political independence, territorial integrity and human security of the population of a State Party, which, by its character, gravity and scale, constitutes a manifest violation of the Charter of the United Nations or the Constitutive Act of the African Union.'
104 These crimes are covered in art 28 of the Amending Protocol.
105 See Preamble, ICC Statute, par 10, emphasising that the ICC is 'complementary to national criminal jurisdictions'.

the prosecution of those responsible for crimes ranging from war crimes, and other violations of IHL, to the exploitation of the environment. It seems advisable that the Human Rights and General Affairs sections should hear cases jointly, or defer to the section under whose jurisdiction the matter predominately falls. To allow two sections to decide a case in respect of the same respondent state on different legal regimes makes little sense from both a practical and doctrinal point of view. However, it seems less objectionable that criminal proceedings pertaining to the same situation may be simultaneously on-going in the third section, given that the major difference is that the first two sections will be dealing with state responsibility, and the last with individual criminal responsibility.

The Amending Protocol foregrounds IHL in one particular way, and that is by its inclusion as the requisite qualification for judges on this Court. The Statute attached to the Amending Protocol stipulates that judges must have competence and experience in 'international law, international human rights law, *IHL* or international criminal law'.[106] The corresponding provision in the Protocol of the ACJHR refers to competence and experience in 'international law and/or human rights law',[107] and in the African Human Rights Court Protocol, reference is made only to required competence and experience 'in the field of human and peoples' rights'.

It remains to be seen whether the three-chambered court will eventually be established and, if so, how this will impact on the interplay between international human rights and humanitarian law.

## 3.4	Advisory Opinion to galvanise art 4(h) of the AU Constitutive Act

States and AU organs, including the Peace and Security Council, may approach the Court for advisory opinions.[108] Pending the Court's determination of the issue, it remains unclear if NGOs may submit such requests to the Court.[109] Even if NGOs may not direct such requests to the Court, it is clear that the African Commission may refer situations arguably revealing massive violations, for a determination if such a situation reveals instances of genocide, crimes against humanity or war crimes and therefore trigger the invocation, by the AU Assembly, of intervention under article 4(h) of the AU Constitutive Act. The

---

106	Art 3 of the draft Statute of the Court; the corresponding provision in the Protocol of the ACJHR refers to 'international law and/or human rights law' (art 4), and in the African Human Rights Court Protocol, reference is made to 'in the field of human and peoples' rights' (art 11(1)).
107	Art 4 of the draft Statute of the Court.
108	Art 4(1) of the Protocol of the ACJHR.
109	See arguments and amicus curiae brief in the Request for Advisory Opinion 0001/ 2013 *Socio-Economic Rights and Accountability Project* (SERAP), submitted to the African Court, yet to be decided at the time of writing.

Commission has however not yet used its competence to request advisory opinions from the Court.

4 African Children's Rights Committee

The competence of the second quasi-judicial treaty body in the African human rights system, the African Children's Rights Committee, clearly includes IHL. This is so because article 22 of the African Children's Charter places an obligation on states to respect the rules of IHL in so far as they pertain to children.

The position in respect of child soldiers under the African Children's Charter deviates from that pertaining to the UN Convention on the Rights of the Child. By stipulating unequivocally that states must ensure that no child (any person under the age of 18 years) takes direct part in hostilities, and must not recruit any child,[110] the African Children's Charter pre-empts changes that had later been incorporated under the 2000 Optional Protocol to the CRC on the Involvement of Children in Armed Conflict. However, these changes did not fully bring the protection under the CRC to the level of the African instrument. Although the compulsory recruitment (conscription) age is set at a minimum of 18, the door is still left open for voluntary recruitment of those younger than 18.[111] There is therefore no absolute prohibition on the direct participation in hostilities of children (under 18); instead, states are required to take all 'feasible measures' to ensure that children do not take part in such hostilities.[112]

The Committee has taken some steps to indicate an awareness of the importance of children's protection in armed conflict, and the need for states to respect IHL. The African Children's Rights Committee established a Focal Person on Children's Rights in Armed Conflict. Acting on an instruction of the AU Executive Council,[113] the Committee in 2014 met with the AU Peace and Security Council (PSC) to forge a closer collaborative relationship as far as children in pre-conflict, conflict and post-conflict situations are concerned. Although the Committee is not mentioned explicitly in the Protocol Relating to the Establishment of the PSC as a collaborative partner,[114] the two organs agreed that the PSC should in future assist the Committee in the exercise of its mandate in so far as it concerns children in armed conflict. At the very least, the PSC

---

110   African Children's Charter, art 22(2).
111   Arts 2 and 3 of the Optional Protocol.
112   Art 1 of the Optional Protocol.
113   Executive Council Decision EX.CL/Dec.712 (XXI), adopted in June 2012, at its 21st Ordinary Session.
114   Art 19 of the PSC Protocol only refers to the African Commission.

resolved to hold an annual 'open session' devoted to children in conflict situations in Africa.[115]

The African Children's Charter provisions relating to child soldiers have been invoked in a case pending before the Children's Rights Committee relating to the Lord's Resistance Army in Northern Uganda.[116] This case deals with the Ugandan government's failure to protect children against being forcibly conscripted into the Lord's Resistance Army, submitted to the Committee in June 2005, and declared admissible on 23 March 2011.[117] Although the communication does not allege the violation of IHL instruments, as such, it does so through article 22 of the Children's Charter, which requires the state (Uganda, in this case) to ensure respect for the IHL rules applicable in armed conflicts affecting children. In addition, the violations of African Children's Charter rights such as the right to education, as well as the right to life, survival and development, are contextualised against the background of an armed conflict. These prevailing circumstances had an impact on the admissibility finding, related both to the security concerns 'due to impact of relevant state institutions in the region'.

5   Conclusion

Although the African continent has experienced its fair share of armed conflict, in particular non-international armed conflict, since the emergence of the African regional human rights system in the 1980s, the institutions comprising this human rights system have only on rare occasions dealt squarely with human rights violations in this context. Adopting an institutional approach, this contribution focuses on the mandate and case law of the African Commission, African Human Rights Court and African Children's Rights Committee. The small number of relevant cases is partly explained by the dearth of cases submitted to and decided by these bodies, more generally. By highlighting that the operation of the three treaty-based bodies under consideration depends on the jurisdictional scope provided for under their founding treaties, a reason is provided for their lack of reference to IHL.

---

115 African Union Peace and Security 'Press statement of the 420th meeting of the PSC on the Rights and Welfare of the Child (ACERWC)': http://www.peaceau.org/en/article/press-statement-of-the-420th-meeting-of-the-psc-on-the-rights-and-welfare-of-the-child-acerwc#sthash.dMsViSye.dpuf (accessed 22 October 2014).

116 *Lord's Resistance Army v Uganda*, submitted by the Centre for Human Rights, University of Pretoria, invoking the right of children to be protected from being involved in armed conflict (art 22 of the African Children's Charter).

117 See the Committee's admissibility decision 001/Com/001/2005 (Decision on the admissibility of the communication submitted by Mr Michelo Hansungule and Others (on behalf of children in Northern Uganda) on the alleged violations of the rights of children *in the context of armed conflict*) (emphasis added) 3 (typed version on file with author).

In the instances in which the African Commission dealt with such cases, it unequivocally held that the Charter's protection extends to situations of war or other forms of armed conflict. One of the major reasons for this position is the absence from the Charter of a derogations clause, suggesting a blurring of the distinction between non-international armed conflict and situations of insurrection or disturbances. Although restrictions of rights would always be possible, the Commission requires that all restrictions of rights be justified with reference to a limitations exercise involving a proportionality test. In the only inter-state case it has ever decided, the Commission invoked IHL in the context of an international armed conflict. In this case (the *DRC* case) the African Commission reiterated the co-existence of IHL and IHRL, but refrained from finding any violations of IHL. Instead, the Commission used relevant IHL treaty standards as interpretive *lex specialis* to animate and substantiate its findings related to Charter violations. However, in another case (the *Darfur* case), involving non-international armed conflict, the Commission made no mention of IHL standards. This decision not only contrasts with its approach in the *DRC* case, but also with the report of its 2004 fact-finding mission to Darfur. Although there is no explicit reference to IHL in the *Darfur* case, both cases confirm that human rights law is applicable in situations of armed conflict. It is recommended that the Commission should develop a more consistent approach, building on the approach in the *DRC* finding. In the *DRC* case, the Commission also confirmed that the Charter applies extra-territorially, at least in situations of international armed conflict.

As the Commission's protective mandate is not restricted to the African Charter, it may well in the future place more reliance on IHL, even as the source of violations, in respect of treaties over which it has jurisdiction, such as the Women's Protocol and IDP Convention, because IHL standards are textually integrated into the relevant treaties. It should also explore the value of relying on IHL standards, alongside African Charter provisions, in the execution of its promotional mandate, for example in its country and thematic reports.

The massive and serious violations procedure under article 58 of the Charter has not been an avenue through which IHL has entered the Commission's jurisprudence. Rather than referring such cases to the Assembly, the Commission should in future use its collaborative relationship with the PSC to bring situations of armed conflict to the attention of the PSC organs. The PSC has an explicit mandate to ensure respect for IHL, and is better suited to address the root causes of complex and highly politicised situations. It is through on-site protective missions and the activities of its special procedures, especially, that the Commission would obtain information of this nature. In appropriate cases, where the information reveals that the threshold triggering intervention under article 4(h) of the AU Constitutive Act has been reached, the PSC should recommend that the Assembly invokes that provision to mandate the use of force to protect persons experiencing grave human rights violations.

The African Court also did not, in the one case where it was possible, refer to IHL. Although its jurisdictional scope is arguably wide enough to cover IHL standards, it has not placed reliance on these norms in its provisional order in the *Libya Provisional Measures* case. With the future transformation of the Court into the African Court of Justice and Human Rights (with or without criminal jurisdiction) its competence to base findings on IHL will be enhanced.

The African Children's Rights Committee has a clear textually-based competence to decide cases based on IHL standards. Some potential for integrating human rights and IHL can be discerned from one of the communications pending before the Committee.

Despite the constraints of their protective mandates being anchored principally in African human rights treaties, and their inability to find violations in respect of non-state actors, there is much potential and promise that the three institutions making up the African regional human rights system may find ways of strengthening the interaction and complementarity between IHL and IHRL in their application to situations of conflict in Africa.

14

The European Court of Human Rights

Karin Oellers-Frahm

1 Introduction

International human rights law and international humanitarian law have seen an impressive development during the last century. However, only the development of human rights law (IHRL) was accompanied by the creation of means and mechanisms concerning judicial implementation and enforcement which are so essential for the effectiveness of legal obligations. International humanitarian law (IHL) still lacks adequate implementation procedures.

There is no question that the rules on state responsibility apply to violations of humanitarian law,[1] but they do not provide for particular instances of enforcement. This deficiency led to the highly controversial attempt by Italian courts to find an overall solution for the enforcement of violations of IHRL and IHL in armed conflict by admitting individual claims against foreign states before their national courts. The price to be paid for opening this way of redress was the denial of state immunity in cases of grave violations of IHRL and IHL, a highly problematic and controversial finding that was finally brought before the International Court of Justice (ICJ), where the Court did not find in Italy's favour.[2] Admitting individual claims before national courts against foreign states

---

1 ILC Draft Articles on the Responsibility of States for internationally wrongful acts, UN Doc A/CN.4/L.602/Rev.1 of 26 July 2001.
2 *Jurisdictional Immunities of the State (Germany v Italy: Greece intervening)* ICJ Judgment (3 February 2012) http://www.icj-cij.org/docket/index.php?p1=3&p2=3&case=143 &p3=4 (accessed 23 October 2014); K Oellers-Frahm 'State immunity vs human rights: Observations concerning the judgment of the ICJ in the *Jurisdictional Immunities of States Case (Germany v Italy)*' in D Hanschel et al *Mensch und Recht.: Festschrift für Eibe Riedel zum 70 Geburtstag* (2013); C Tomuschat 'The international law of state immunity and its development by national institutions' (2011) 44 *Vanderbilt Journal of Transnational Law* 1105; for the opposite view cf M Bothe 'The question of state immunity before national courts in cases of massive violations of human rights and of international humanitarian law' Legal Expert Opinion written for Amnesty International (2011).

would in fact have offered a promising means of redress in cases of IHRL and IHL violations, but nevertheless the ICJ was absolutely right in not giving its blessing to such remedy, because this would have overturned the basic principles of international law and would not have constituted merely an innovative, value-oriented interpretation of customary international law, but a change of paradigm. It is thus not surprising that, *faute de mieux,* human rights bodies which originally were not meant to tackle violations of IHL,[3] as in particular the regional human rights courts, have been instrumentalised in order to seek enforcement of IHL and redress in case of IHL violations.[4] However, as these courts' competence is limited to ensure the observance of engagements undertaken by the High Contracting Parties in the relevant Convention, in the case of the ECtHR the interpretation and application of the rights guaranteed in the European Convention on Human Rights (ECHR) and the Protocols thereto (article 32 ECHR) the extent to which these provisions can also be applied to cases resulting from armed conflicts (specifically the aspect of convergence of IHRL and IHL) becomes relevant. With special regard to the question of adjudicating cases resulting from armed conflict through the ECtHR the core issues to be addressed are: whether or to what extent IHL has to be considered as *lex specialis* and thus not directly applicable by the ECtHR *ratione materiae* (Part 2); and what the limits of the jurisdiction of the ECtHR *ratione personae* under article 1 of the ECHR, in particular with regard to the extraterritorial application of the Convention (Part 3), are. Special attention must then be given to the role of IHL in the Court's jurisprudence on the merits (Part 4) and the impact of the jurisprudence of the ECtHR on IHL (Part 5). This will be followed by some concluding remarks (Part 6).

2   The *lex specialis* character of IHL

2.1   Exclusiveness of IHL?

IHL and IHRL are two different branches of law of which IHL is much older. Therefore, it is not surprising that according to the opinion prevailing during the last century[5] there was a clear distinction between the

3   G Malinverni *Le droit humanitaire rattrapé par les droits de l'homme ? In La conscience des droits : Mélanges en l'honneur de Jean-Paul Costa* (2011) 401 403.

4   K Watkin 'Controlling the use of force: A role for human rights norms in contemporary armed conflict' (2004) 98 *American Journal of International Law* 1 2, who rightly underlines that the highly developed system of IHRL has much to offer in terms of limiting the impact of some forms of violence, especially when compared to the still evolving accountability framework under IHL, but that the application of human rights principles becomes relevant in particular during situations more closely associated with governance than direct combat with the enemy force.

5   Cf F Berber *Lehrbuch des Völkerrechts, vol II* (1969) 64; A Verdross *Völkerrecht* (1937) 293; R Kolb 'Human rights and humanitarian law' in *Max Planck Encyclopedia of Publiic International Law,* online (2012), in particular MN 4-15 and MN 28; J Chevalier-Watts 'Has human rights law become *lex specialis* for the European Court of Human Rights in

law of war and the law of peace,[6] in that either the one or the other applied. This opinion is evidently still underlying article 4(2) of the International Covenant on Civil and Political Rights (ICCPR) which does not explicitly provide for any derogation from the right to life in armed conflict, but only refers to derogation in public emergency threatening the life of the nation, a fact that can only be understood in the sense that during armed conflict the Covenant was considered not to be applicable.[7] The ECHR does not follow this model; it provides in article 15(1) of the ECHR:

> In time of war or other public emergency threatening the life of the nation any High Contracting Party may take measures derogating from its obligations under this Convention to the extent strictly required by the exigencies of the situation, provided that such measures are not inconsistent with its other obligations under international law.

Paragraph 2 of this article then spells out the rights which do not allow for such derogation, namely: article 2, the right to life, from which, however, deaths resulting from lawful acts of war are excluded; article 3, prohibition of torture or inhuman or degrading treatment or punishment; article 4(1), slavery; and the principle *nulla poena sine lege* laid down in article 7 of the Convention. From the mere existence of this provision it has to be concluded that the ECHR is, in principle, also applicable 'in time of war', so that the first question concerning the overall *lex specialis* character of IHL, that is a strict distinction and exclusive application of either IHRL or IHL, has to be answered in the negative.[8]

This is in line with the meanwhile general opinion according to which IHRL has still its place also in armed conflict.[9] This opinion has been confirmed by the ICJ which had several times to take position on this point.[10] The most detailed findings in this context were made in the Advisory Opinion on the *Legal Consequences of the Construction of a Wall in*

---

right to life cases arising from internal armed conflicts?' (2010) 14 *The International Journal of Human Rights* 584 585f.

6 C Tomuschat 'Human rights and international humanitarian law' (2010) 21 *European Journal of International Law* 21 15 16; J-P Costa & M O'Boyle 'The European Court of Human Rights and international humanitarian law' in D Spielmann (ed) *La Convention européenne des droits de l'homme, un instrument vivant: Mélanges en l'honneur de Christos L Rozakis* (2011) 107 110.

7 Tomuschat (n 6 above) 16.

8 Cf C Johann *Menschenrechte im internationalen bewaffneten Konflikt* (2012) 125 *et seq*, with rich bibliographical references. In the opinion of Johann (183 *et seq*), norm collisions between IHL and IHRL requiring the application of the *lex specialis* rule are rather difficult to imagine due to the fact that IHL does not contain rules explicitly allowing acts that are forbidden under IHRL. IHL rather contains exceptions to IHRL prohibitions so that a true conflict between obligations under IHL and IHRL does not exist or only in very rare situations.

9 Cf Draft Articles of the ILC on 'Effect of armed conflicts on treaties' 2011, UN Doc A/CN.4/L.777.

10 Cf in particular the Advisory Opinion on *Legality of the Threat or Use of Nuclear Weapons* ICJ Reports (1996) 226.

the Occupied Palestinian Territory[11] where the ICJ stated that the protection of the conventions on human rights does not cease in case of armed conflict, but then distinguished three situations, namely those where only IHL applies, those where exclusively IHRL applies and others where both branches of international law apply.[12] As the ICJ did not give any further explanations this distinction was considered 'utterly unhelpful',[13] so that it will be interesting to look at the stance taken by the ECtHR, in particular whether its jurisprudence helps to clarify in which situations we are concerned with violations which have to be judged first and foremost by applying international humanitarian law as *lex specialis* falling outside the jurisdiction of the ECtHR *ratione materiae.*

2.2   The derogation clause in article 15 of the ECHR

The statement just made, namely that the ECtHR is, *in principle,* only empowered to apply the Convention and the Protocols thereto, indicates that there are exceptions to that rule and that, under particular circumstances, the ECtHR may also apply IHL. These particular situations and the preconditions for this exception are provided for in article 15 of the ECHR which reads:

(1)   In time of war or other public emergency threatening the life of the nation any High Contracting Party may take measures derogating from its obligations under this Convention to the extent strictly required by the exigencies of the situation, provided that such measures are not inconsistent with its other obligations under international law.

(2)   No derogation from article 2, except in respect of deaths resulting from lawful acts of war, or from articles 3, 4 (paragraph 1) and 7 shall be made under this provision.

(3)   Any High Contracting Party availing itself of this right of derogation shall keep the Secretary General of the Council of Europe fully informed of the measures which it has taken and the reasons therefor. It shall also inform the Secretary General of the Council of Europe when such measures have ceased to operate and the provisions of the Convention are again being fully executed.

---

11   *Legal Consequences of the Construction of a Wall in the Occupied Palestinian Territory* ICJ Reports (2004) 136.

12   *Wall* case (n 11 above) 178 para 106; cf also *Armed Activities on the Territory of the Congo* ICJ Reports (2005) 168, confirming the view in the *Wall* case, and *Application of the International Convention on the Elimination of all Forms of Racial Discrimination,* Provisional Measures of 15 October 2008, available at http://www.icj-cij.org/docket/files/140/14801.pdf (accessed 23 October 2014), where the distinction made in the *Wall* case is no longer upheld which may, however, be explained by the fact that we are only concerned with an order on the provisional measures request. Cf also Tomuschat (n 6 above) and V Gowlland-Debbas 'Harmonizing the individual protection regime: Some reflections on the relationship between human rights and international humanitarian law in the light of the right to life' in A Constantinides & N Zaikos (eds) *The Diversity of International Law* (2009) 399 400 406-407.

13   'Expert meeting on the right to life in armed conflicts and situations of occupation' The University Centre for International Humanitarian Law, International Conference Centre, Geneva (1-2 September 2005) 19.

According to this provision, the states concerned have to respect 'other obligations under international law' even if use is made of the derogation option which opens the way for the Court to review whether violations of human rights under the Convention are justified by IHL and thus to apply it. When the Convention was elaborated the term 'war' clearly referred only to *international* armed conflicts.[14] Since the Second World War we are however increasingly confronted not with 'wars' in the traditional sense of an inter-state armed conflict, but with non-international armed conflicts to which IHL is applied in a manner eroding progressively the frontier between international and non-international armed conflicts by applying the more detailed law on *international* armed conflict.[15] This situation has advantages with regard to the protection of civilians,[16] who all become entitled to the same – maximal – protection under IHL, but which – and that is evidently a disadvantage – still lacks appropriate enforcement mechanisms. With regard to IHRL the acceptance of this unique standard of armed conflicts under IHL leads to the indiscriminate application of article 15 to international as well as non-international/internal armed conflicts and thus to a more coherent approach, in particular with a view to article 15(2). Although the first alternative of article 15(1) only relates to international armed conflicts, derogations were, however, always admissible also in internal armed conflict; they are addressed under the second alternative, namely 'public emergency' which clearly also covers internal armed conflicts.[17] In both cases the consequences are in principle identical, namely that the ECtHR may decide whether derogations from the Convention are consistent with IHL, irrespective of whether the armed conflict is of an international or internal character. Thus, for example, in the case of *Northern Ireland v United Kingdom*, the ECtHR did, in fact, examine whether the derogation of some Convention rights was consistent with other treaty obligations, namely whether British law in Northern Ireland was in compliance with the Geneva Conventions, what demonstrates that the Court was aware of the applicability of IHL besides IHRL. This issue was, however, not examined in more detail because the Irish Government did not provide any relevant material.[18]

An academic discussion has, however, developed concerning the consequences of derogation with regard to international and non-international/internal armed conflicts when it comes to the 'non-derogable

---

14　Chevalier-Watts (n 5 above) 589; Johann (n 8 above) 106-108; Costa & O'Boyle (n 6 above) 115.

15　Cf *Prijedor, Prosecutor v Tadić (Dusko)* Decision on the Defence Motion for Interlocutory Appeal on Jurisdiction, Case No IT-94-1-AR72 (1996) 35 ILM 32, ICL 36 (ICTY 1995), 2nd October 1995, Appeals Chamber (ICTY) 58 para 119.

16　Kolb (n 5 above) MN 25.

17　JA Frowein & W Peukert *Europäische MenschenRechtsKonvention* (3 ed 2009) art 15 422, MN 6/7.

18　*Ireland v United Kingdom* App no 5310/71 ECHR (18 January 1978) para 222; cf H-J Heintze *Europäischer* Menschenrechtsgerichtshof und Durchsetzung der Menschenrechtsstandards des humanitären Völkerrechts (2000) 12 *Zeitschrift für Rechtspolitik* 508 511.

rights' according to article 15(2). Different views are voiced in particular with regard to the right to life, which allows exceptions exclusively for deaths resulting from lawful acts of war. According to a widespread opinion only when a state has made a derogation referring to time of war, that is in case of an *international* armed conflict in the traditional sense, the otherwise non-derogable right to life allows for the exceptions provided for under IHL. This follows from the fact that 'lawful acts of war', according to this view, cannot be carried out with regard to a state's own citizens, thus in internal armed conflict.[19] In *internal* armed conflicts where exceptions to the provisions of the Convention are generally admitted under the alternative of 'other public emergency', 'deaths resulting from lawful acts of war' in the sense explained above, are thus not included in the derogation. This means that even if use is made of the derogation option, violations of the right to life in *internal* armed conflicts can be assessed by the ECtHR exclusively under article 2 (2)(c). According to this provision deprivation of life is not considered as a violation of article 2 'when it results from the use of force which is no more than absolutely necessary: ... (c) in action lawfully taken for the purpose of quelling a riot or insurrection'.[20] This standard is clearly much stricter than the humanitarian law applicable in international armed conflicts so that comparable acts are differently assessed depending on whether they occurred in international or non-international armed conflict, a consequence that raised criticism in particular with regard to two aspects. The first concern relates to the fact that according to this view states would be prevented from lawfully targeting rebels or others who have lost their protected status, because state action cannot be justified as lawful acts of 'war'. The assimilation of international and internal armed conflicts would, in fact, be helpful to overcome this concern.[21] But despite the advantages of such assimilation it nevertheless is not uncontroversial and leaves a grey zone between non-international armed conflicts which can be assimilated to international armed conflicts and those which simply cannot. Instead the solution gaining support in practice refers rather to a broader definition of 'international' armed conflict in the sense that besides a situation of armed conflict between two different states, the assistance to – or more precisely the overall control over – rebel groups from outside is also assimilated to an international conflict.[22]

---

19   H Krieger 'Die Verantwortlichkeit Deutschlands nach der EMRK für seine Streitkräfte im Auslandseinsatz' (2002) 62 *ZaöRV* 669 692. Cf in the same sense Frowein & Peukert, (n 17 above), art 15 MN 6, 422. But see also TH Irmscher 'Menschenrechtsverletzungen und bewaffneter Konflikt: Die ersten Tschetschenien-Entscheidungen des Europäischen Gerichtshofs für Menschenrechte' (2006) 33 *Europaische grundrechte zeitschrift* 11 16, n 64, who – with good reason – does not share this opinion due to the fact that the law of international armed conflict is increasingly also applied to non-international armed conflict.
20   Cf ECtHR in cases regarding the Chechen conflict: *Isayeva v Russia* App no 57950/00 ECtHR (6 July 2005) para 180.
21   Irmscher (n 19 above).
22   Cf *Tadić* case (n 15 above) para 119 & para 137.

The second problem resulting from the view that article 15(2) is not applicable to internal armed conflicts concerns the risk of conflicting jurisdiction depending on whether cases resulting from the same conflict are brought before the ECtHR or before international criminal courts: The ECtHR would rather consider a conflict as non-international in order to apply the stricter provision, article 2, to deaths committed in the conflict, while international criminal courts would tend to assimilate as far as possible an internal conflict to an international one in order to apply the more detailed rules on IHL applicable to international armed conflicts.[23] This situation clearly bears potential for conflicting decisions, although the assimilation of international and non-international conflicts can also not solve this problem in a satisfactory manner. The only possible solution in such cases of conflicting jurisdiction seems to be respect for decisions of other courts and tribunals and self-constraint in tackling such cases.

This discussion concerning possible consequences of derogations under article 15(1) and its repercussions for the applicability of article 15(2), in non-international armed conflicts, has until now been merely an academic one, because practical experience is lacking. Nevertheless, the ECtHR is aware of the problem and does consider IHL in particular in cases concerning violation of the right to life.[24] However, until now the ECtHR never considered that IHL had to be applied as *lex specialis* in the case at stake, in other words that the killing of a rebel fighter was justifiable under IHL, but not under article 2, which would have led to the consequence that the case had to be dismissed as not covered by its jurisdiction *ratione materiae*. The Court did, however, recently embark on this road, although not in the strict way of dismissing a case after finding that IHL is applicable. The relevant case is the *Hassan v The United Kingdom* case which was, however, not concerned with the right to life and which will be considered more in detail below.

The lack of any precedent of Convention organs clarifying the contemporary understanding of the term 'deaths resulting from lawful acts of war' according to article 15(2) is, as already mentioned, due to the simple reason that there was no case where a party to the ECHR had made a derogation to that effect opening the way to the Court to apply IHL.[25] It is interesting to mention the reason invoked by the Court in order to explain this situation: in the view of the Court a contracting state did not make use of the derogation option concerning 'time of war' because it did not believe 'that its actions abroad constituted an exercise of jurisdiction'

---

23   More in detail infra 5.
24   Cf *Chechen* cases (n 20 above); cf Irmscher (n 19 above).
25   P Rowe 'Non-international armed conflict and the European Court of Human Rights: Chechnya from 1999' (2007) 4 *The New Zealand Yearbook of International Law* 205 207. There are, however, derogations concerning 'public emergency', which usually have been accepted by the Court. Cf H Krieger 'Kapitel 8: Notstand' in R Grote & T Marauhn (eds) *EMRK/GG, Konkordanzkommentar zum europäischen und deutschen Grundrechtsschutz* (2006) 389, MN 17; Frowein & Peukert (n 17 above) 422, MN 6/7.

in the sense of article 1.[26] This statement raises the question whether article 15(2) could have been applied if the Court had found that the relevant actions constituted an exercise of jurisdiction under article 1 or if it would have required a derogation notice according to article 15(3). This leads to the question whether a derogation notice constitutes a precondition for the Court to apply IHL, that is to assess whether the state's measures derogating from the ECHR were 'not inconsistent with its other obligations under international law' or whether the Court has to decide *proprio motu* whether a situation of war was present and thus whether IHRL could be derogated and IHL be applied.

2.3   The relevance of a formal derogation notice under article 15(3) of the ECHR

The question whether article 15 can be applied even if no formal notice has been made of a derogation has not yet been answered clearly by the Court.[27] In the *Northern Ireland* case the Court explicitly confirmed that Great Britain had made such a notification;[28] in the case *Cyprus v Turkey* the Commission required that the people concerned should be informed in a clear manner by some official act of the measures derogating from the Convention,[29] while two members of the Commission were of the opinion that article 15 is in any case applicable in an armed conflict.[30] This separate opinion evidently did not gain ground because the Court's decision in the *Isayeva* case has generally been understood in the sense that an explicit and formal derogation notice is required, since the Court stated in this case that where a state did not officially derogate, the military operations had to be 'judged against a normal legal background'.[31]

---

26   *Banković et al v Belgium and 16 Other Contracting States* App no 52207/99 ECtHR Grand Chamber, Decision on Admissibility (12 December 2001) para 62. The Court referred to the derogations made with regard to certain internal conflicts (in south-east Turkey and Northern Ireland, respectively), which in its view did not constitute a basis 'upon which to accept the applicant's suggestion that art 15 covers all "war" and "public emergency" situations generally ...'; cf MJ Dennis 'Application of human rights treaties extraterritorially during times of armed conflict and military occupation' ASIL Proceedings 2006, 86-90, 88; cf also Frowein & Peukert (n 17 above), art 15, 422, MN 6/7.
27   Krieger (n 25 above), MN 34, 399.
28   *Ireland v United Kingdom* (n 18 above) para 223.
29   Report of the Commission in the case *Cyprus v Turkey* (10 July 1976) European Human Rights Reports 4, para 527, 482-582, No 313.
30   *Cyprus* case (n 29 above), separate opinion of G Sperduti and S Trechsel stating in the last paragraph of their opinion: 'It can be said ... that measures which are in themselves contrary to a provision of the European Convention but which are taken legitimately under the international law applicable to an armed conflict, are to be considered as legitimate measures of derogation from the obligations flowing from the Convention.'
31   *Isayeva v Russia* App no 57950/00 ECtHR (24 February 2005) para 191; cf also Gowlland-Debbas (n 12 above) 414. But see also Johann (n 8 above) 257, who argues, with good reason, that the *Isayeva* case would allow for a different interpretation since here the Court explicitly mentioned that the acts happened 'outside wartime' so that a different conclusion may be possible for the formal derogation requirement in time of war.

In the case *Georgia v Russia II*[32] still pending before the Court for the decision on the merits, this question will become highly relevant since Russia explicitly objected to the competence of the ECtHR, because according to its view the case has to be decided under IHL only. As neither Georgia nor Russia have made use of the derogation option the question of the applicability of article 15 in cases where the Secretary General of the Council of Europe has not received notice of the derogation, has to be addressed by the Court. In this decision the Court will thus have to take position on the understanding of article 15(3), because it seems rather unrealistic that the case may be 'judged against the normal legal background', meaning merely on the basis of the Convention law albeit by referring to – but not applying – IHL. Furthermore, this case may become the leading case with regard to the definition of the extent of the *lex specialis* character of IHL and thus the limits *ratione materiae* of the Court's jurisdiction in international armed conflict. Whether and to what extent the new approach of the Court in the *Hassan* case which concerned the derogable right of liberty laid down in article 5 will be helpful in the *Georgia v Russia II* case has to be seen.

2.4 Legal relevance of the declaratory or constitutive character of the derogation notice

Although at first sight the question of the declaratory or constitutive character of the derogation notice may seem somehow marginal, it nevertheless has significant implications. As stated above, article 15 is the basis for extending the law applicable by the ECtHR, and thus the competence of the Court *ratione materiae*. While under normal circumstances only the Convention and its Protocols are applicable, leading to the consequence that the Court has to dismiss a case for lack of competence if it cannot be decided on the basis of the Convention law, article 15 allows the Court to apply IHL. In such a case the Court has the power to decide whether the acts committed by the state concerned were 'strictly required by the exigencies of the situation' and whether such measures were 'not inconsistent with its [the state's] other obligations under international law', thus also IHL.

In cases resulting from armed conflict where no derogation has been made, the Court can at most 'take into account' IHL, article 31(3)(c) of the Vienna Convention of Law and Treaties (Vienna Convention), but not apply it. Article 31(3)(c) of the Vienna Convention provides that in interpreting a treaty provision the relevant rules of international law in force between the parties have to be taken into account. They are thus a means to fully assess the legal relations between the parties. If, however, such rules turn out to be plainly governing the situation as *lex specialis*, it is

---

32 *Georgia v Russia II* App no 38263/08 ECtHR (11 August 2008).

no longer the treaty provision at stake that is applicable, but the special rule.[33] In *Georgia v Russia II* this would lead to the consequence that if IHL were to be applied as *lex specialis* because the acts at stake cannot be judged by merely applying the ECHR and the Protocols thereto the Court would have to dismiss the case due to the fact that no use was made of the option of derogation; in the case of a formal derogation, however, the Court has the power to decide whether the measures taken by Russia were consistent with IHL. Thus, the effect of a derogation notice lies in the extension of the Court's competence which as any competence of international courts and tribunals depends upon the consent of the states. Consequently, the notice of derogation according to article 15(3) amounts to the consent of the state concerned to accept the special or extended power of the Court to apply not only the law enshrined in the ECHR, but also IHL.

With a derogation notice having this effect, it seems consistent with international law to attribute constitutive and not only declaratory character to the notice. As the ECtHR is a Court conceived under the special regime of human rights under the Convention, it cannot be taken for granted that states that have not made use of the derogation option will leave it to the Court to find whether an armed conflict of either international or non-international nature is taking place. Such determination by the Court would not only be difficult to make due to the problem to adequately assessing the situation, but would also be highly problematic for political reasons,[34] in particular if the state concerned denies that there is a situation of armed conflict. Furthermore it may not be assumed that states, without explicit consent, will accept that the ECtHR decides on whether the state's measures were consistent with IHL or not. IHL is not the field of law which belongs to the original competences of the Court so that a decision on the basis of IHL requires prior consent of the state concerned.

The most recent practice of the Court[35] to decide cases resulting from armed conflict merely on the basis of the Convention by extending the applicability of IHRL to its extremes may and should encourage states to seriously consider making use of the derogation clause under article 15. By doing so despite the 'political costs' to concede the existence of a conflict situation they would prevent IHRL becoming sort of *lex specialis*[36] in armed conflict cases setting aside IHL. With a view to the terms of article 15 it must, however, be mentioned that even such formal derogation could have a rather limited effect because it is restricted to situations 'threatening the life of the nation' and 'to the extent strictly required by the exigencies of

---

33   Cf infra 4.1.
34   N Quénivet *'Isayeva v the Russian Federation* and *Isayeva, Yusupova and Bazayeva v the Russian Federation:* Targeting rules according to art 2 of the European Convention on Human Rights' (2005) 18 *Humanitäres Völkerrecht* 219 221; Heintze (n 18 above) 510.
35   Infra 3.1.
36   Chevalier-Watts (n 5 above) 699.

the situation'. Whether the condition concerning the threat to the life of the nation is presumed to exist or has to also be proved 'in time of war' is not clear; however, there are good reasons in favour of such a presumption.[37]

On the basis of the foregoing considerations it can be concluded that the application of IHL, specifically the recognition of the *lex specialis* character of IHL, does not play a significant role in the practice of the ECtHR. According to the Court's previous jurisprudence – at least the jurisprudence until the decision in the case *Hassan v The United Kingdom*[38] – it would require a formal derogation under article 15. The *Hassan* decision was not concerned with the right to life, but the derogable right to liberty, in particular the taking of prisoners of war and the detention of civilians posing a threat to the security. The Court did no longer insist on a *formal* derogation, but nevertheless found that it can interpret and apply the provisions of the Convention, in that case article 5, 'in the light of the relevant provisions of international humanitarian law only where this is specifically pleaded by the respondent State'.[39] This statement is problematic as it opens the way for expanding the jurisdiction *ratione materiae* of the Court merely on the basis of the Government's request. Even so, it does nonetheless at least maintain the requirement of some, even informal form of derogation and confirms that the Court cannot *proprio motu* interpret and apply the provisions of the Convention in the light of IHL. In essence therefore, even after the *Hassan* case it remains true that in the absence of a derogation (even an informal one made during the pleadings), the Court decides all cases resulting from either international or non-international armed conflicts 'against the normal legal background',[40] that is the Convention law. This does, however, not mean that IHL is of no relevance at all in the jurisprudence of the ECtHR.[41]

---

37   Johann (n 8 above) 242 et seq; W Abresch 'A human rights law of internal armed conflict: The European Court of Human Rights in Chechnya' (2005) 16 *European Journal of International Law* 741 745, n 12; A-L Svensson-McCarthy *The international law of human rights and states of exception: With special reference to the Travaux Preparatoires and the case-law of the international monitoring organs* (1998) 290.
38   *Hassan v United Kingdom* App no 29750/09 ECtHR (16 September 2014).
39   *Hassan* case (n 38 above) para 107
40   See n 30 above.
41   Cf JA Frowein 'The relationship between human rights regimes and regimes of belligerent occupation' (1998) 28 *Israel Yearbook on Human Rights* 1 16; cf also infra 4.

3   The practice of the ECtHR concerning the question of jurisdiction under article 1 of the ECHR

3.1   International armed conflicts and extraterritorial application of the ECHR

In the context of declaring the ECHR applicable and thus opening the way for the Court's jurisdiction in *international* armed-conflicts, the initial problem to be solved before coming to the question of interplay between IHL and IHRL, concerns the territorial reach of the Convention. According to article 1: 'The High Contracting Parties shall secure to everyone within their jurisdiction the rights and freedoms defined in Section I of this Convention'. The central issue is thus the meaning of the term 'within their jurisdiction' which never was understood as being limited to the territory of the state concerned, but to include any exercise of sovereign power as provided for and limited by international law. Accordingly, acts of state organs in foreign countries, such as acts of diplomatic or consular representatives, are undoubtedly acts 'within the jurisdiction' of the state.[42] The answer is, however, not so clear with regard to acts committed in an international armed conflict on the territory of another state which is itself a party or not a party to the ECHR.

3.1.1   The Cyprus v Turkey *cases*

The question of the extraterritorial application of the Convention became relevant for the first time in the complaint of Cyprus against Turkey in the context of the occupation of Northern Cyprus by Turkish troops in 1974. In this case the Commission found that the rights of the Convention are guaranteed to all persons *under the authority and responsibility* of the Contracting Party including its ships and airplanes as well as diplomatic and consular representatives and armed forces even outside the national territory. Therefore the Turkish armed forces in Northern Cyprus which were under the command of the Turkish Government exercised Turkish jurisdiction over individuals and goods in the sense of article 1.[43] This jurisprudence was confirmed by the Court in the later cases resulting from the occupation of Northern Cyprus, for example, the *Loizidou v Turkey* case, where the Court found that the loss of property of the applicant was

---

42   For details cf Frowein & Peukert (n 17 above) art 1, MN 17 *et seq.*
43   Interstate applications to the Commission 6780/74 and 6950/75 (Report 2, 1125) and 8007/77 (Report 13, 85) and interstate application to the Court 25781/94, Judgment para 169; cf Frowein & Peukert (n 17 above) art 1, MN 5; V Coufoudakis 'European human rights law and Turkey's violations in the occupied areas of Cyprus' in A Constantinides & N Zaikos (eds) *The diversity of international law: Essays in honour of Professor Kalliopi K Koufa* (2009) 302-318.

a direct consequence of the occupation of Northern Cyprus by the Turkish troops in 1974;[44] the same reasoning was applied in the case *Cyprus v Turkey*[45] where the Court had to decide on the situation in Northern Cyprus since the military operation in July 1974 and the division of the territory and where the Court found that numerous articles of the Convention had been violated; finally this jurisprudence was confirmed in the *Varnava and others v Turkey* case[46] which concerned the disappearance of members of the Greek-Cypriote forces during the conflict in 1974 and where the Court decided that there was a violation of article 2 of the Convention because Turkey had not conducted the necessary investigation on the fate of the victims disappeared in 1974. In all these cases the question of the exercise of extraterritorial jurisdiction was rather uncontroversial because the Turkish troops acted under the direct command of the Turkish Government and thus exercised 'effective control' in the area. Furthermore, it was also relevant that both states, Cyprus and Turkey, were parties to the ECHR.[47]

3.1.2 The espace juridique *principle in the* Banković *case*

The latter aspect, namely the status as a party to the Convention, became essential in the *Banković* case relating to the NATO bombing of a radio/ television station in Belgrade, Yugoslavia, which was at that time, 1999, not a party to the ECHR.[48] With regard to the extra-territorial application of the Convention the Court found that article 1 did not have the effect that 'anyone adversely affected by an act imputable to a Contracting State, wherever in the world that act may have been committed or its consequences felt, is thereby brought within the jurisdiction of that State for the purpose of art 1'.[49] It stated that the Convention was operating 'in an essentially regional context and notably in the legal space (*espace juridique*) of the Contracting States'[50] and thus declared the case inadmissible. This decision, which was widely criticised,[51] was refined in the later jurisprudence of the Court, in particular with regard to the *espace juridique* argument which – strictly applied – would have led to the result that human rights obligations would lose their binding character when a

---

44   *Loizidou v Turkey* App no 15318/89 ECtHR (23 March 1995) paras 61-64; cf Frowein & Peukert, (n 17 above) 16 f, MN 5; cf Gowlland-Debbas (n 12 above) 399-418.
45   App no 25781/94 ECtHR (20 May 2001).
46   *Varnava et autres v Turkey* App nos 16064/90, 16065/90, 16066/90, 16068/90, 16069/ 90, 16070/90, 16071/90, 16072/90 and 16073/90 ECtHR, GC (18 September 2009) para 185.
47   L Doswald-Beck *Human rights in times of conflict and terrorism* (2011) 21.
48   *Banković* case (n 26 above), paras 67 *et seq.*
49   Para 75 of the decision.
50   Para 80 of the decision.
51   Doswald-Beck (n 47 above) 20; Gowlland-Debbas (n 12 above) 403 ff; C Mallory 'European Court of Human Rights *Al-Skeini and others v United Kingdom* (Application no 55721/07) Judgment of 7 July 2011' (2012) 61 *International & Comparative Law Quarterly* 301 303; R Lawson 'The life after *Banković*: On the extraterritorial application of the European Convention on Human Rights' in F Coomans & MT Kamminga (eds) *Extraterritorial application of human rights treaties* (2004).

state party to the Convention is acting in a non-member state.[52] On the other hand the argument referred to above, namely that the Court could not be competent to review all military actions of the contracting parties all over the world, was also not convincing as a general guideline due to the admitted far-reaching convergence of IHL and IHRL and furthermore was not in line with the Court's previous jurisprudence in the *Cyprus v Turkey* cases. Therefore, it is not surprising that post *Banković* decisions did not follow the very restrictive approach of this case, but developed a rather wide acceptance of the extraterritorial scope of human rights instruments in the exceptional circumstances of effective control or authority exercised over a foreign territory particularly in situations of occupation.[53] This jurisprudence does, however, not need a more detailed examination in the present context,[54] because the Court has 'restated' the requirements for the extraterritorial application of the Convention in the recent *Al-Skeini* case which now replaces *Banković* as the leading Strasbourg authority on the interpretation of article 1 ECHR.[55]

3.1.3　The 'exercise of public powers principle' in the Al-Skeini case

In the *Al-Skeini* case the Grand Chamber of the Court clearly and definitely departed from the argument of the 'Convention legal space' in the *Banković* case by relying on and by refining the aspect of state and state agent authority and effective control and thus imputability. The Court interpreted the term 'within its jurisdiction' in article 1 as comprising not only 'the control exercised by the Contracting State over the buildings, aircraft or ship in which the individuals were held' but moreover as also comprising 'the exercise of physical power and control over the person in question'.[56] This jurisprudence marks a clear departure from *Banković* where exactly this consequence was dismissed,[57] due to the *espace juridique* argument governing the applicability of the Convention. This finding constitutes the logical development already enacted in former decisions

---

52　D Richter 'Humanitarian law and human rights: Intersecting circles or separate spheres?' in T Giegerich (ed) *A wiser century? Judicial dispute settlement, disarmament and the laws of war 100 Years after the Second Hague Peace Conference* (2009) 257 282.

53　Gowlland-Debbas (n 12 above) 404, referring to *Ocalan v Turkey* App no 46221/99 ECtHR (12 May 2005), IV Reports as well as *Issa and others v Turkey* App No 31821/96 ECtHR (16 November 2004) para 17, where the ECtHR accepted that a state could be held accountable for a violation of Convention rights extraterritorially if the complainants were found to be under the state's authority and control through its agents operating in the other state; Richter (n 50 above) 282-283.

54　Cf for the development of the ECtHR's jurisprudence M Milanovic '*Al-Skeini* and *Al-Jedda* in Strasbourg' (2012) 23 *European Journal of International Law* 121 124; Johann (n 8 above) 70 *et seq*.

55　*Al-Skeini v United Kingdom* App no 55721/07 ECtHR (7 July 2011) http://cmiskp.echr.coe.int/tkp197/viewhbkm.asp?sessionId=92671623&skin=hudoc; cf Mallory (n 49 above).

56　Para 136 of the judgment.

57　Cf the statement of the Court in *Banković* (n 49 above) para 75, that not 'anyone adversely affected by an act imputable to a Contracting State, wherever in the world that act may have been committed or its consequences felt, is thereby brought within the jurisdiction of that State for the purpose of art 1'.

which may be considered as the necessary reaction to the odd consequences resulting from the *Banković* case, namely that a state bound by the ECHR could violate its obligations when exercising power in a state not party to the Convention. The Court thus not only restated the earlier jurisprudence of the Commission and the Court in the *Cyprus v Turkey* cases,[58] but extended it irrespective of the *espace juridique* to all situations where a contracting state or its organs exercise 'some of the public powers normally to be exercised by a sovereign government'.

In the *Al-Skeini* case the Court found that the United Kingdom 'assumed authority and responsibility for the maintenance of security in South East Iraq' so that the security operations of its soldiers established 'a jurisdictional link between the victims and the United Kingdom for the purposes of article 1 of the Convention' (para 149). From this jurisprudence it follows that the *espace juridique* no longer plays a decisive or even any role under article 1 ECHR; what is decisive according to this jurisprudence is the effective control over the individual, but only if the state or its agents exercise some kind of public powers, which leads to accepting – in derogating from paragraph 75 in the *Banković* case – that the Convention rights can be 'divided and tailored' (para 137). Where such domination over the territory or the person is established, 'it is not necessary to determine whether the Contracting State exercises detailed control over the policies and actions of the subordinate local administration' (para 138). Whether these requirements, which were again confirmed by the Court in the decision on preliminary objections in the case *Georgia v Russia II* and *Hassan v The United Kingdom*,[59] are fulfilled in a given case has to be assessed by the Court on the basis of the relevant evidence, an assessment which is so closely linked to the merits of the case that it cannot be made in the context of a decision on objections concerning the admissibility of a case. It may therefore be stated that *Banković* has been overruled with regard to the *espace juridique* requirement, but remains in force in so far as acts are concerned which do not reflect 'authority and control as exercise of public powers'. Thus, specifically drone operations would be excluded from the purview of the ECHR in conformity with the *Banković* decision for lack of effective control although constituting clearly an exercise of public power.[60]

On the basis of the *Al-Skeini* judgment the fact that the acts occurred in the context of an *international* armed conflict becomes secondary at least for the question of admissibility of the claim and jurisdiction of the Court *ratione personae*. As to the merits of a case, the jurisdiction *ratione materiae*,

58   P-F Laval 'A propos de la juridiction extraterritoriale de l'État. Observations sur l'arrêt *Al-Skeini* de la Cour Européenne des droits de l'homme du 7 Juillet 2011' (2012) *Revue Générale de Droit international Public* 61 76 ; M Jankowska-Gilberg 'Das Al-Skeini Urteil des Europäischen Gerichtshofs für Menschenrechte- eine Abkehr von Bankovic?' (2012) 50 *Archiv des Völkerrechts* 61.
59   *Georgia v Russia II* (n 32 above); *Hassan* case (n 38 above)
60   Milanovic (n 54 above) 130.

only the ECHR, and not IHL, is the applicable law, at least where a state has not explicitly derogated from Convention obligations under article 15(1). Where such derogation has been made the scope of the Court's mandate, the applicable law, is broader,[61] and the Court would be competent to decide whether human rights violations, in particular the death of persons, resulted from 'lawful acts of war', and thus to decide by applying IHL.

The fact that the derogation option is rarely used and that consequently the Court is restricted according to article 32 ECHR to only apply the ECHR in deciding a case on the merits – a situation that may change after the *Hassan* case which allows for non-formal derogation – explains the Court's reluctance to refer explicitly to IHL in its decisions. This has led to the development of what has been termed a 'Convention law of armed conflict',[62] namely a rigid IHRL approach in deciding cases resulting from armed conflict. This development clearly differs from the general trend and in particular the practice of international criminal courts, which rather tend to bring in line non-international armed conflicts and international armed conflicts in order to apply the more detailed IHL applicable to international armed conflict to internal armed conflicts as well. The jurisprudence of the ECtHR follows the opposite approach, namely to apply as far as possible IHRL irrespective of the character, international or non-international, of the conflict in order to open the way to the Court.[63]

3.2 Non-international armed conflicts

The applicability of the Convention and consequently access to the ECtHR to enforce humanitarian law violations is in general less problematic in non-international armed conflicts because the relevant acts occur on the territory of a Contracting Party raising no problem under article 1 of the Convention. Even in the absence of effective control over parts of the territory the ECtHR has found in favour of a positive obligation under article 1 of the Convention insofar as this is in the power of the state concerned.[64] It is, thus, not surprising that in non-international armed conflicts the ECtHR saw no problem concerning its jurisdiction *ratione personae*.

With regard to the applicable law, however, the situation does not differ from that of cases relating to international armed conflicts, because the Court is limited to apply only the ECHR and the Protocols thereto

---

61 A Paulus 'The protection of human rights in internal armed conflict in Europe – Remarks on the *Isayeva* decisions of the European Court of Human Rights' (2006) *The Uppsala Yearbook of East European Law* 61 68; *supra* 2. 2.
62 Richter (n 52 above) 306.
63 Malinverni (n 3 above) 406.
64 *Ilascu and others v Moldova and Russia* App no 48787/99 ECtHR (8 July 2004) para 331.

whenever no derogation was made under article 15 of the Convention. In such cases the Court did apply the Convention law without examining the question of *lex specialis,* in other words whether the Convention law or whether exceptionally only IHL was applicable.[65] This approach of admitting large convergence between human rights law and IHL has proved particularly helpful in internal armed conflicts for which the applicable IHL is by far not as detailed as that applying to international armed conflicts.[66] While the question concerning access to the Court may be considered as settled after the *Al-Skeini* case, the question of the role of IHL in the decisions of the Court is still open, in particular with regard to the extent of the convergence between IHRL and IHL and thus the question in which situations exclusively IHL is applicable as *lex specialis.*

4 The role of IHL in the decisions of the ECtHR on the merits

4.1 Interpretation of IHRL in the light of IHL

The fact that the ECtHR can decide a case only by applying the ECHR as long as no derogation is made does, however, not mean that IHL does not play any role before the ECtHR. In this context the statement of the Court in the *Loizidou* case referring to the general principles of treaty interpretation under international law is decisive, namely that the Court has to interpret the ECHR in respect of article 31(3)(c) of the Vienna Convention, in taking into account 'any relevant rules of international law applicable in the relations between the parties',[67] thus also IHL. Accordingly, in its case-law the Court did, in fact, refer – although mostly not explicitly – to IHL,[68] but has consistently (and rightly so) refused to apply it.[69] It has also never recognised that in a particular case it was to be

---

65 Malinverni (n 3 above) 407 *et seq,* referring to the case law of the Court.
66 Abresch (n 37 above) 747. To mention just one example: In general, the only applicable treaty law with regard to the right to life is common art 3 of the 1949 Geneva Conventions which is rather imprecise, in any case less detailed than IHRL. The same is true for Protocol II, which is more extensive than art 3, but does not provide any guidance on the legality of attacks that are likely to kill persons not taking part in the combat. In these circumstances there is in fact considerable room for the application of IHRL which can fill the gaps of IHL in helping to develop the law applicable to the conduct of hostilities in internal armed conflicts.
67 This general principle of treaty interpretation is explicitly repeated also in art 15(1) which contains the derogation clause. Also compare the statement of the ICJ in its Advisory Opinion *Legality of the Threat or Use of Nuclear Weapons* (n 10 above) para 25.
68 Cf *Engel and others v Netherlands (Merits)* App nos 5100/71, 5101/71, 5102/72 ECtHR (8 June 1976) para 72; *Cyprus v Turkey* App nos 6780/74 and 6950/75 ECtHR (26 May 1975).
69 R Otto *Targeted killings and international law* (2012) 180, referring to the *Isayeva* cases, paras 168-199, where common art 3 of the 1949 Geneva Conventions was invoked before the Court, but where the Court stuck strictly to human rights; *Isayeva* (n 31 above); *Isayeva, Yusupova and Bazayeva v Russia* App nos 57947/00, 57948/00 and 57949/00 ECtHR (24 February 2005); Quénivet (n 34 above) 220.

considered as the applicable *lex specialis*,[70] which may raise concern with regard to article 31(3)(c) of the Vienna Convention. This practice may seem problematic in particular with regard to *international* armed conflicts, due to the fact that they are governed by a rather specific and detailed branch of applicable law.[71] In internal armed conflicts this attitude seems less problematic, although not completely unproblematic, because here the relevant IHL is less specific and may therefore more easily justify the application of IHRL.[72] In this context it is interesting to note that particularly in cases concerning the right to life the Court, although applying article 2 of the ECHR, used the vocabulary of humanitarian law such as 'incidental loss of civilian life', 'choice of means and methods', 'legitimate military targets', 'disproportionality in the weapons used' and resorted to the cardinal principles of IHL, namely limitations of means and methods of combat, the principle of distinction and the principle of proportionality.[73] In other cases, namely the Chechen cases,[74] which generally were considered as resulting from full-fledged internal armed conflict and thus regulated by common article 3 of the Geneva Conventions, Protocol II and customary law, the Court only applied article 2, although this article differs largely from the rules of IHL concerning the right to life. Article 2 of the Convention covers everything from riots to genuine armed conflict; it does not contain the principle of distinction known from IHL, but protects civilians and combatants alike; it justifies lethal force only where capture is too risky, and applies also where loss of life is an unintended outcome of the legal use of force.[75] Despite these differences, the decision in the concrete case, *Isayeva and others v Russia*, would not have differed if the Court had applied IHL because the acts committed clearly constituted not only a violation of IHRL but also a violation of IHL,[76] a situation that may not always be present in cases resulting from armed conflict.

---

70 A borderline situation was met in the *Cyprus v Turkey* case where the Commission examined the treatment of the prisoners by Turkey under the Third Geneva Convention coming to the conclusion that on the basis of that examination it was not necessary to examine the question of a breach of art 5 of the ECHR. This conclusion can only be understood in the sense that here IHL, the Third Geneva Convention, was the only applicable law, however without expressing clearly its *lex specialis* character. Cf *Cyprus v Turkey* (n 68 above) 108 *et seq*; cf Frowein (n 41 above) 10.

71 Gowlland-Debbas (n 12 above) 416.

72 Malinverni (n 3 above) 412; Abresch (n 37 above) 747.

73 *Ergi v Turkey* App no 23818/94 ECtHR (28 July 1998), IV Reports of Judgments and Decisions, para 79; cf Gowlland-Debbas (n 12 above) 414; Quénivet (n 34 above) 226.

74 *Khasheiyev and Akayeva v Russia* App nos 57942/00 and 57945/00 ECtHR (24 February 2005); *Isayeva* case (n 31 above); *Isayeva, Yusupova and Bazayeva* case (n 69 above).

75 *Isayeva, Yusupova and Bazayeva* case (n 69 above) para 169; Gowlland-Debbas (n 12 above) 415.

76 Cf also Irmscher (n 19 above) 18.

4.2 The principle of proportionality and necessity in the jurisprudence of the ECtHR

The situation was more difficult in the other two Chechen cases,[77] where the application of the substantive provisions included aspects of proportionality and necessity, principles that are also relevant in IHL. But again, the standards governing the application of these principles are different in IHL and IHRL, namely with regard to article 2, where they are much stricter and more compelling than under IHL.[78] While under IHL the primary aim of an operation is the elimination, by capture or killing, of the adversary's combatants and machinery of war referring only to a balance of military advantage with potential loss of civilian life,[79] IHRL permits no more use of force 'than [is] absolutely necessary' to achieve the aims permitted in article 2(2)(a-c).[80] While the killing of an enemy combatant by a combatant does not contradict IHL, it may do so under IHRL. With regard to the use of force against civilians not directly participating in the hostilities, article 27 of the Fourth Geneva Convention only requires 'respect for their persons, their honor and their family rights' and article 51(2) of Protocol I and article 13(2) of Protocol II merely provide that civilians 'shall not be the object of attack' which is clearly less demanding than the requirement of 'use of force which is no more than absolutely necessary' under article 2 of the ECHR. Thus, in IHL necessity does not require that the use of force be the means of last resort, but the decisive issue is whether the force has been used against a 'military object' so that under IHL liability for an attack causing incidental civilian damage is governed by a less strict proportionality test than that applicable under the ECHR.[81]

Despite these significant differences in the wording and in particular in the requirements for assessing proportionality and necessity between IHL and IHRL it is nevertheless the principle of proportionality and necessity that opens the door to considerations of IHL in cases before the ECtHR.[82] One of the most instructive examples in this context is the *Ergi v Turkey* case[83] which was so manifestly connected to IHL that the Court could not avoid analysing the extent of the human rights obligations in the light of IHL. By commenting on what constitutes a legitimate target of attack and whether the predicted risk for the civilian population can be measured

77   *Isayeva* (n 31 above) and *Khasheiyew and Akayeva* (n 72 above).
78   D Kaye 'Comment on European Court of Human Rights: Decisions of February 24, 2005' (2005) 99 *American Journal of International Law* 873 873; Paulus (n 61 above) 74.
79   Art 51, para 5(b); art 57, para 2 (a)(iii); and art 57(b) of Protocol I.
80   *Suleymanova v Russia* App no 9191/06 ECtHR (10 May 2010) para 76.
81   Kaye (n 78 above) 880.
82   Irmscher (n 19 above) 17.
83   *Ergi* case (n 73 above), 1751 which concerned the killing of a woman uninvolved in the fighting when a military officer decided to launch an ambush.

against the military advantage the Court reverted to IHL,[84] but did not go so far as to admit that it was confronted with an armed conflict requiring the application of IHL as *lex specialis*. Considerations of IHL also played a relevant role in the proportionality test of the Court in the recent Chechen cases. In the *Isayeva v Russia*[85] case which resulted from the occupation of the village of Katyr-Yurt by Chechen fighters preventing civilians from leaving the area and thus becoming victims of the aerial bombardment, the Court did not find that the military operation itself, but rather the manner of its performance was illegitimate,[86] because it did not adequately respect the need to protect human lives. In the case *Abuyeva v Russia*[87] which resulted from the same incident, the Court confirmed this conclusion. It is, however, interesting to note that in this case the exclusive application of article 2 without any reference to IHL was commented on in the concurring opinion of Judge Malinverni (joined by Judge Rozakis), who regretted the fact that the Court had:

> [M]ade no mention whatsoever of the principal rules governing the conduct of combatants in situations such as that dealt with in this case, namely the rules of international humanitarian law. In addition to article 3 of the Fourth Geneva Convention … the conduct of combatants in a non-international armed conflict such as the one in question here is governed *first and foremost* by the Protocol Additional to the Geneva Conventions (Protocol II).[88] (emphasis added)

This statement may be understood as an admonition not to extend the application of the ECHR too far, but to recognise in particular situations the *lex specialis* character of IHL.

The Court took a similar position in the *Isayeva and others v Russia* case where it admitted that the air strike could presumably be a legitimate response to the attack of the illegal insurgents, but that it lacked proportionality because the authorities knew or should have known that the road was full of civilians and that they should have alerted officers to the need of extreme caution.[89] The reference to the need of precaution clearly recalls the regulation in Protocol I of 1977.[90] In this case, however, the Court explicitly referred to the fact that the acts occurred 'outside

---

84　H-J Heintze 'The European Court of Human Rights and the implementation of human rights standards during armed conflict' (2002) 45 *German Yearbook of International Law* 60 73-74.

85　*Isayeva* case (n 31 above).

86　*Isayeva* case (n 31 above) para 39, where the Court limited its finding to stating that 'the situation that existed in Chechnya at the relevant time called for exceptional measures' and that 'those measures could presumably include the deployment of army units equipped with combat weapons, including military aviation and artillery'.

87　*Abuyeva and others v Russia* Appl no 27065/05 ECtHR (2 December 2010).

88　*Abuyeva* case (n 87 above) para 3 of the concurring opinion.

89　*Isayeva and others* case (n 69 above) paras 180 *et seq*.

90　*Isayeva* case (n 31 above) paras 189-191; *Isayeva and others* case (n 69 above); in these cases the Court found that the use of military aviation and artillery and the bombing of a civilian convoy by air force was not executed with the necessary care for civilians. Cf

wartime' and that no derogation was made under article 15 so that not IHL but IHRL was applicable (para 191). Also in the cases *Khatsiyeva and others v Russia*[91] and *Taysumov v Russia*[92] the Court admitted the existence of a special situation allowing for exceptional measures, but found again that the measures taken were not proportionate to the achievements of the aims provided for in article 2.[93] The application of article 2 in these cases in the light of the established Convention standards such as legitimacy of aim, necessity and proportionality allowed the Court to reach an outcome which might be considered to be consonant with both IHRL and IHL because in these cases the lawfulness of the acts under IHL was also questionable.

This approach, namely the implicit application of standards of IHL in cases concerning armed conflicts in guise of the categories of legitimacy, necessity and proportionality known under the Convention law[94] may secure a sound legal outcome under both IHRL and IHL. It contributes at the same time to supervise the margin of appreciation left to states involved in an armed conflict and not only to define but also refine how and in what manner legal military operations have to be conducted. In the Chechen cases this approach was acceptable because there was a clear violation of IHL, however, 'hard' cases may arise where the application of the strict proportionality and necessity test under the Convention may contradict IHL.[95] In fact, such 'hard' case is pending before the Court at the time of writing: the question of the *lex specialis* character of IHL in international armed conflicts is crucial in the case *Georgia v Russia II*, which was already declared admissible by the Court.[96]

In this context it is worthwhile to refer at least briefly to the *Al-Jedda* case,[97] which was not concerned with the right to life, but with the right to liberty (article 5). The case resulted from the fact that the applicant had been detained in Iraq after the occupation phase and thus neither under humanitarian law nor under criminal law, but under the authority to detain preventively arguably granted to the United States and the United

A Orakhelashvili 'The interaction between human rights and humanitarian law: Fragmentation, conflict, parallelism, or convergence?' (2008) 19 *European Journal of International Law* 161 173; Quénivet (n 34 above) 224.

91 App no 5108/02 ECtHR (17 January 2008).
92 App no 21810/03 ECtHR (14 May 2009); cf in the same line of argument *Khamzayev and others v Russia* App no 1503/02 ECtHR (3 May 2011) and *Kerimova and others v Russia* App no 17179/04 ECtHR (3 May 2011).
93 Cf Chevalier-Watts (n 5 above) 592-593.
94 Cf in this context to Richter (n 52 above) 314, who speaks of 'reverse proportionality' with regard to the Court's willingness to implement human rights in armed conflict without compromising them by 'more specific' humanitarian law.
95 Kaye (n 76 above) 881.
96 *Georgia v Russia II* (n 32 above).
97 *Al-Jedda v United Kingdom* App no 27021/08 ECtHR: GC (17 July 2011); cf also J Pejic 'The ECtHR's *Al-Jedda* judgment: Implications for IHL' (2011) 14 *Yearbook of International Humanitarian Law* 237; Milanovic (n 54 above) 133 ss; F Naert 'The European Court of Human Rights' *Al-Jedda* and *Al-Skeini* judgments: An introduction and some reflections' (2011) 50 *Military Law and the Law of War Review* 315.

Kingdom under Security Council Resolution 1546 of 8 June 2004. The applicant argued that his detention was in violation of article 5 which in the absence of a derogation under article 15 does not allow for preventive security detention and even more so if no judicial review is available. The question was thus first whether the detention was attributable to the United Kingdom or to the United Nations, and second – and more relevant in the present context – whether Resolution 1546 could be considered as a lawful derogation or qualification to article 5 justifying detention in circumstances not usually covered by article 5.

In this case the Court stated in a first step that Security Council Resolution 1546 did not contain the required 'clear and explicit language [that] would be used were the Security Council to intend States to take particular measures which would conflict with their obligations under international human rights law' (para 102). In a second step the Court examined whether there were other reasons, in the absence of express provision in Resolution 1546, for the applicant's detention which could operate to disapply the requirements of article 5(1). The Court found (para 107) that even:

> [A]ssuming that the effect of Security Council Resolution 1546 was to maintain, after the transfer of authority from the Coalition Provisional Authority to the Interim Government of Iraq, the position under international humanitarian law which had previously applied, this did not establish 'that international humanitarian law places an obligation on an Occupying Power to use indefinite internment without trial.

In coming to this conclusion the Court interpreted specific IHL, namely the Fourth Geneva Convention, however in a way that seems at least problematic, if not even erroneous, with regard to the spirit and letter of IHL.[98] The Court found in fact that there was a breach of article 5(1), because the Fourth Geneva Convention does not provide for an 'obligation' to use indefinite internment without trial. The fact that detention for imperative reasons of necessity is explicitly allowed under IHL in international armed conflict and thus does amount to an authorisation – which is in fact even preferable to an obligation – to detain persons as long as is necessary for security reasons was not considered by the Court. According to the *Al-Jedda* decision states parties to the Convention may not intern civilians unless there is a binding Security Council Resolution mandate or a derogation to article 5 on the basis of article 15.[99]

This case offered, more clearly than even some of the Chechen cases, an occasion to admit the *lex specialis* character of IHL because no derogation notice was made. The outcome of the decision and the

98   Pejic (n 97 above) 252.
99   As above.

interpretation of IHL by the Court in this case plainly support the reluctance of the ECtHR to state that it is confronted with an armed conflict – which is to a certain degree understandable under political aspects – and to admit in particular situations the applicability of the *lex specialis* principle in favour of IHL, what may lead to rather problematic judgments. This case demonstrates in a particularly clear manner that the decision of cases resulting from armed conflict 'against the normal legal background', namely the Convention law, cannot be considered as a panacea applicable whenever no derogation was made, but that it can only work where a violation of both, IHRL and IHL is present or where the standards of the proportionality and necessity test under both branches of law lead to the same result. In addition this case may be taken as a negative experience with regard to the application of IHL by the ECtHR enhancing rather than diminishing the reluctance of states to make use of the derogation option in article 15 and thus supporting the requirement to admit the *lex specialis* character of IHL in particular situations. This question will become crucial in the case *Georgia v Russia II* where the *lex specialis* character of IHL and consequently the lack of competence of the ECtHR were invoked by Russia as an objection to the admissibility of the case. In its decision on admissibility the Court found that 'the question of the interplay between the provisions of the Convention and the rules of international humanitarian law, applied to the circumstances of the case, is to be decided when the case is examined on the merits'.[100] It is to be hoped that the Court will use this opportunity to discuss more in detail the limits of convergence between IHRL and IHL and thus its competence in cases resulting from armed conflict, in particular in the context of international armed conflicts.

Meanwhile the Court has in fact taken a decision which may contribute to solving the problem. Although it was not the case *Georgia v Russia II*, the findings of the Court will be very relevant when that case has to be decided on the merits. The case marking a new approach is the already mentioned *Hassan* case, which has to be considered in close relation to the *Al-Jedda* case. The *Al-Jedda* case and *Hassan* cases did not concern the right to life, but the right to liberty, in particular the detention of civilians posing a threat to the security. In the *Hassan* case –where the situation was somehow different from the *Al-Jedda* case in which Security Council Resolution 1546 of 8 June 2004and not the Third and Fourth Geneva Conventions were considered as the legal basis for detention – the Court stated explicitly that 'it would not be appropriate for the Court to hold that this form of detention falls within the scope of article 5§1(c)'.[101] It then referred to the option of derogating from article 5 according to article 15 ECHR, an option that the United Kingdom had, however, not used in the present case. The United Kingdom had, instead, requested the

---

100 *Georgia v Russia II* (n 32 above) para 74.
101 *Hassan* case (n 38 above) para 97

Court 'to disapply its obligations under art 5 or in some other way to interpret them in the light of the powers of detention available to it under international humanitarian law'.

Referring to its consistent practice of interpreting the Convention in the light of article 31 of the Vienna Convention on the Law of Treaties, the Court reconfirmed that 'even in situations of international armed conflict, the safeguards under the Convention continue to apply, albeit interpreted against the background of the provisions of international humanitarian law'.[102] It further stated that 'by reason of the coexistence of the safeguards provided by international humanitarian law and by the Convention in time of armed conflict, the ground of permitted deprivation of liberty [set out in article 5 ECHR] should be accommodated, as far as possible with the taking of prisoners of war and the detention of civilians who pose a risk under the Third and Fourth Geneva Conventions'.[103]

In more precise terms this means that the question whether IHRL has been breached is determined by considering whether the powers granted under IHL have been respected. In the *Hassan* case the Court came to the conclusion that IHL had not been breached and that consequently there was also no violation of article 5 of the ECHR. The Court thus applied IHL in order to find whether Convention law has been breached. This 'accommodation' of both branches of law is, in fact, highly problematic as the partly dissenting judges explain convincingly. However, the Court does seem to be aware of this problem when it finds that in the case where no formal derogation is lodged:

> [T]he provision of article 5 will be interpreted and applied in the light of the relevant provisions of international humanitarian law only where this is specifically pleaded by the respondent State. It is not for the Court to assume that a State intends to modify the commitments which it has undertaken by ratifying the Convention in the absence or a clear indication to that effect.[104]

This is a new approach which, despite of the well-reasoned critics by the dissenters, has to be welcomed in so far as it is at least required that the state concerned expressly requests the Court to interpret the Convention in the light of IHL. Although article 15 ECHR may thus be circumvented by a simple pleading of the state during the proceedings – which seems highly problematic, under both national and international law – the Court has at least acknowledged that it cannot consider whether acts of states are consistent with IHL without some sort of consent of the state concerned. For the *Georgia v Russia II* case this may have the consequence that the Court has to dismiss the case, if Russia persists in objecting to the

---

102   *Hassan* case (n 38 above) para 104
103   *Hassan* (n 38 above) para 104
104   *Hassan* (n 38 above) para 107.

competence of the Court with the argument that the case can only be decided by applying IHL.

4.3   The relevance of procedural obligations

Besides aspects of proportionality procedural obligations under the ECHR also offer a possibility to assess acts committed in armed conflict which do not constitute a substantial violation of a right guaranteed in the ECHR. The most instructive practice yet again concerns the right to life, where the Convention requires states not only to secure the right to life, but also to 'secure a system of adequate and effective safeguards against arbitrariness and abuse of force and even against avoidable accident'.[105] On this basis the Court found a violation of article 2 in cases where individuals were killed in an armed conflict and the state concerned had not ensured 'that an effective, independent investigation is conducted into deaths arising out of clashes involving the security forces'.[106] In the *Varnava and others v Turkey* case[107] which concerned disappearances during military operations of Turkey in Northern Cyprus in 1974 the Court found a violation of article 2 on the sole basis that procedural obligations had not been fulfilled, namely effective investigations on the fate of the victims.[108] Such procedural safeguards are not provided for in IHL, but are suited to enforce the human rights standards in international and non-international armed conflicts because even legal use of force and military necessity cannot 'displace the obligation under article 2 to ensure that an effective, independent investigation is conducted into deaths arising out of clashes involving the security forces'.[109] While the incorporation of human rights principles of accountability can have a positive impact on the regulation of the use of force during armed conflict, its practicability in large scale application of lethal force seems rather questionable, because not every death can be subject to the exhaustive review process normally associated with the application of human rights in peace time.[110]

From the above considerations it follows that the ECtHR, which is increasingly seized with cases resulting from armed conflict, has seen no problem in admitting and adjudging these cases under Convention law as long as no derogation is made under article 15. The Court applies only the ECHR because, with due respect to the particularities of armed conflict and thus IHL,[111] in the view of the Court 'the Convention should so far as possible be interpreted in harmony with other rules of international law of

---

105   *Suleymanova* case (n 80 above) para 77.
106   *Kaya v Turkey* App no 158/1996/777/978 ECtHR (19 February 1998) para 91.
107   *Varnava* case (n 46 above).
108   Cf Malinverni (n 3 above) 417.
109   *Kaya* case (n 106 above) para 91; cf in this context L Doswald-Beck 'The right to life in armed conflict: Does international humanitarian law provide all the answers?' (2006) 88 *International Review of the Red Cross* 881 888-889.
110   Watkin (n 4 above) 33-34.
111   Paulus (n 59 above) 79.

which it forms part'.[112] It thus contributes to fill in gaps in IHL, in particular the law governing internal armed conflict and with regard to situations concerning rather governance than direct combat with an enemy force, as well as to concretise aspects of proportionality and procedural obligations from a human rights perspective. In particular the concretisation of procedural obligations may lead to the outcome that the same military operation may be in violation of provisions of the ECHR but not of the relevant norms of IHL. This may appear unusual, but actually reflects the differences between the two branches of law, in particular the fact that IHL is incomplete with regard to procedural rules which thus may be defined by IHRL.[113] The fact that IHL and IHRL are still different systems of law – at least to a certain diminishing degree – should lead the Court to be more attentive to reach solutions consonant with both IHRL and IHL or, otherwise, to admit that it is confronted with a situation of armed conflict requiring the application of IHL as *lex specialis*. Such caution is in particular advisable for the reason that the jurisprudence of the ECtHR – in cases resulting from armed conflict – is not without significant implications for IHL and its enforcement.

5　The impact of the Court's jurisprudence on IHL

The most significant consequence of the Court's jurisprudence in armed conflict cases results clearly from the individual rights-centred approach which leads to a refinement of the obligations of states under IHL. This is of particular significance in the context of what is called 'collateral damage' under IHL. The decisions of the Court in the Chechen and Turkish cases demonstrate that the strict human rights standards apply to lethal force in legal armed operations submitting the circumstances and conditions of such operations to IHRL. States therefore have to be more attentive to collateral damage of lawful armed operations and have to be prepared for victims seeking redress before the ECtHR. Although this may be considered as a means to make armed conflict more 'humane', there are borderline situations, for example, the *Isayeva and others* case from which it has to be concluded that the use of air power against rebels does not satisfy the requirements under article 2, namely that the military cannot attack the rebels first or, if it can, it cannot use certain weapons, a finding that will hardly be accepted under IHL, because it leaves open the question of military necessity.[114] The same is true with regard to the consequences of the *Al-Jedda* case concerning detention of civilians.

But there are other more general implications resulting from the human rights approach in deciding cases resulting from the use of force.

112　*Al-Adsani v United Kingdom* App no 35763/97 ECtHR (21 November 2001) para 55
　　referred to in *Georgia v Russia II* (n 32 above) para 72.
113　Cf also Costa & O'Boyle (n 6 above) 129.
114　*Isayeva and others* (n 69 above); cf also Orakhelashvili (n 90 above) 173.

On the one hand it may be asked whether the ECtHR is at all the right organ to deal with massive and widespread violations on an individual basis[115] and whether in such cases individual redress is the adequate solution, in particular with a view to the possible extreme high number of complaints resulting from armed conflict.[116] Raising this question already points to the implied difficulties, but also to the fact that with a view to the lack of implementation mechanisms in the field of IHL, the use of human rights bodies will be increased as until now it is at least a second-best solution.

Another and highly substantial concern with regard to the enforcement of IHL violations through the ECtHR refers to the fact that the ECHR mechanism for implementing human rights violations is limited to cases where rights are violated by a *state*. If non-state actors commit violations of IHRL and converging IHL the Court lacks jurisdiction.[117] As modern armed conflicts are mostly of an internal character opposing armed (rebel) groups and military forces of the state, the situation of victims and their prospects for redress depends on whether state forces or non-state forces committed the violation of their rights.[118] Non-state forces can only be made liable under national or international criminal law which is not comparable to the means of redress by human rights mechanisms. The use of human rights bodies in seeking redress from violations having occurred in armed conflict thus leads to a different status of victims [and perpetrators] according to the author of the violation and may thus affect the whole system of IHL. This is due to the fact that human rights bodies can only decide if the violation is committed by state-forces; they do not have the competence to deal with situations where the human rights violations were committed by non-state actors. IHL constitutes, however, a legal regime providing for rights and obligations of both parties to a conflict; one-sided implementation and redress mechanisms are in clear contradiction to the underlying principle of equality of parties that informs IHL as a body of law.

With a view to these problematic consequences the optimal solution would evidently consist in the creation of a special implementation mechanism under IHL,[119] the realisation of which seems, however, rather unrealistic for the foreseeable future. Thus, the enforcement of IHL through the ECtHR or other human rights organs can only be considered as an alternate or second best solution, in particular with a view to the

---

115 Irmscher (n 19 above) 18; Watkins (n 4 above) 2.
116 Heintze (n 84 above) 77; cf also ICJ *Jurisdictional immunities* (n 2 above); cf also Tomuschat (n 2 above) 1135.
117 This situation shows that in principle only the application of IHL would be promising in this context. Cf Heintze (n 18 above) 517 and JK Kleffner 'Improving compliance with international humanitarian law through the establishment of an individual complaints procedure' (2002) 16 *Leiden Journal of International Law* 237 242.
118 Kleffner (n 117 above) 242.
119 Kleffner (n 117 above) 242 et seq.

inequality of the victims' position following from the fact that only violations of human rights committed by states can be brought before the ECtHR. A way out of this dilemma would be a stronger use of IHL by the ECtHR in the sense of giving more room to the *lex specialis* rule even at the expense of dismissing a case.

The dilemma of going too far in subordinating IHL to IHRL in order to decide cases resulting from armed conflict or in the alternative to leave the case without redress is not peculiar only to the ECtHR, but has seen a parallel development in the practice of the Inter-American human rights organs. While the Inter-American Commission for Human Rights did in fact apply IHL directly in a first phase, it used it in later cases only as means for interpretation of the American Convention on Human Rights.[120] The Inter-American Court of Human Rights in contrast was, at the outset, of the opinion that IHL cannot be applied directly, but only be referred to as a means of interpreting the Convention.[121] Thus, like the ECtHR, the Inter-American human rights organs have also consolidated the standards of IHL and IHRL on the basis of 'complementation' and 'convergence' by considering IHL, according to article 31(3)(c) of the Vienna Convention, as a source for the interpretation of IHRL.[122]

The only way to empower the ECtHR to decide cases by directly applying IHL would consist in enhancing the readiness of states to make use of the derogation clause in article 15 despite the political implications of admitting the existence of an armed conflict situation. There are, however, serious doubts as to whether states will be prepared to take this step and these doubts even find some support in the practice of the Court with regard to the understanding of IHL.[123]

6   Concluding remarks

The practice of the ECtHR has significantly contributed to developing IHL more in line with IHRL, with, as one author put it, 'contemporary mores'.[124] In the view of another author, it is even the IHRL which becomes the *lex specialis,* at least in non-international armed conflicts.[125] This development is in line with the contemporary trend to give more weight to community interests, in particular individual interests, than to

---

120 *Abella v Argentina* App no 11.137, Report of the Inter-American Commission no 55/97, OEA/Ser.L/VII.9, doc 6 rev P 161 (1998) and *Franklin Guillermo Alsalla Molino (Ecuador v Colombia),* Report no 1112/10, admissibility, Inter-state Petition IP-02, 21 October 2010; cf Watkin (n 4 above) 23.

121 *Las Palmeras,* Preliminary Objections, Judgment of 4 February 2000, Series C, no 66, homepage of the IACtHR; cf Kleffner (n 117 above) 240 *et seq.*

122 For the case-law of the American Commission and Court cf Richter (n 52 above) 298 *et seq.* and 311.

123 *AL-Jedda* case (n 97 above).

124 Gowlland-Debbas (n 12 above) 417.

125 Chevalier-Watts (n 4 above) 599; see also Richter (n 52 above) 306.

state interests, which for a long time dominated international law. This development is to be welcomed, in particular in the context of armed conflict where the human rights impact is particularly evident. Nevertheless it must be asked whether the reconciliation of IHL with IHRL, sometimes even the subordination of IHL to IHRL, in the practice of the ECtHR could not in 'hard cases' – and the *Al-Jedda* case may be considered as an example of such situation – lead to different outcomes by applying the ECHR rather than IHL.

In the Chechen cases the Russian responsibility also under IHL seemed clear; but there may be situations where a strict assessment of governmental decisions related to the use of force under Convention law may contradict IHL,[126] a question which the Court cannot avoid in the case of *Georgia v Russia II*. The Court should therefore in cases arising from armed conflict, in particular international armed conflict, give more attention to the *lex specialis* principle even where no formal derogation has been made under article 15. As the ECtHR noted in the *Loizidou* case the ECHR has to be construed in line with article 31(3)(c) of the Vienna Convention, namely in the context of 'any relevant rules of international law applicable in the relations between the parties', thus also obligations of IHL. IHL, not IHLR, is still the *lex specialis* in armed conflict and takes precedence over human rights treaties in so far as it may constitute a special justification in armed conflict for interference with rights protected under human rights treaties.[127]

As the jurisprudence of the ECtHR demonstrates, such situations will in fact be the exception because in particular in non-international armed conflicts the treatment of civilians according to IHRL is widely accepted. The provisions applicable to internal armed conflicts, in particular common article 3 of the Geneva Conventions or the second preambular paragraph of Additional Protocol II are not only 'embryonic', but refer explicitly to the international conventions on human rights.[128] As the use of military force in internal armed conflict often appears as an escalation of police action the submission of these cases to IHRL seems adequate.

With regard to international armed conflicts the practice of the ECtHR demonstrates that the Court was not yet called upon to decide on the legality of military action as such, but rather on human rights violations in occupation situations or on procedural obligations concerning, for example, the investigation obligations in the case of disappearance of persons where the applicability of IHRL is meanwhile generally accepted. A grey zone and thus the most critical issues relate to the so-called collateral damage where an interpretation in the sense of 'complementation' of IHRL and IHL seems rather problematic. In such

---

126   Kaye (n 78 above) 881; Pejic (n 97 above) 248 *et seq.*
127   Frowein (n 41 above) 16; Irmscher (n 19 above) 18; Pejic (n 97 above) 251.
128   Richter (n 52 above) 312.

cases, as for example the Chechen cases, the ECtHR has the difficult task to find the adequate parameter for applying merely IHRL, as it has done until now, or to recognise the *lex specialis* character of IHL. The Court will have to take a clear position on this question in deciding the merits of the case *Georgia v Russia II,* where the issue of the applicable law, IHRL or IHL, is one of the most relevant problems. If the Court comes to the conclusion that in this case IHL is the *lex specialis*, it would have to dismiss the case – as no derogation was made by Georgia or Russia. Otherwise it could at most come to the conclusion that 'in any case' it cannot find that a violation of the ECHR has occurred because IHL is applicable without, however, taking a decision on whether *in concreto* IHL justifies the violation of the ECHR.

The fact that situations which require the partial displacement of ECHR rights and the application of IHL as *lex specialis* as a justification for IHRL violations will increasingly become the exception, may have the odd result of contributing to the fragmentation of international law with regard to the practice of international criminal tribunals. The jurisprudence of these tribunals, in particular the *ad hoc* Tribunals for Yugoslavia and Rwanda, which were the forerunners of the permanent International Criminal Court, shows, as already shortly mentioned, a development opposite to that of the ECtHR. Before these organs, the difference between international and non-international armed conflicts plays only a subordinate role in that the more special and detailed provisions of *international* armed conflicts are largely applied also to internal conflicts,[129] while the ECtHR applies Convention law to both kinds of armed conflict in order to open a means for redress. This may lead to inconsistent case-law, because the ECtHR may find a human rights violation occurred in a situation where a criminal court does not, specifically with regard to the killing of a combatant or even a civilian due to the principle of military advantage. This concern is not without substance even though not states, but only individuals may be brought before international criminal courts. The fact that the context of the individual crime, namely the situation of internal or international armed conflict, is defined by the criminal court may lead to inconsistent decisions because the criminal courts will apply IHL while cases resulting from the same situation may be decided by the ECtHR on the basis of IHRL. This means that in cases resulting from fully-fledged armed conflict the ECtHR should be extremely sensitive to the issue of the *lex specialis* character of IHL.

In a nutshell the result of the above considerations may be summarised in the sense that, with regard to access to the ECtHR the jurisprudence of the Court can be fully shared, in particular after the *Al-Skeini* decision which rightly declared the Convention applicable in the sense of article 1

129　Cf *Tadić* case (n 15 above) para 119.

to all acts of states and state organs occurring during the exercise of some sort of state power wherever it takes place.

With regard to the law applicable to the decision on the merits, the ECtHR has not yet found an all-encompassing, convincing, distinction between 'police action' or 'security measures' and proper acts of armed conflict which should be decided on the basis of IHL. It should therefore be less reluctant to consider the *lex specialis* character of IHL or at least to refer more openly to IHL and to use it explicitly as a source of interpretation what is not only admissible in cases governed by article 15, but is moreover required by the general principle of treaty interpretation laid down in article 31(3)(c) of the Vienna Convention.[130] Nevertheless it must be admitted that such proceeding is of course not satisfactory for effectively improving the supervision of compliance with IHL rather than IHRL,[131] however it is at least a possibility to contribute to the supervision of the implementation of IHL. By referring more explicitly to IHL and eventually admitting its speciality in particular, although exceptional cases that may justify violations of IHRL, the ECtHR would contribute to define the limits between IHRL and IHL[132] in consonance with the accepted principle that IHRL applies also in armed conflict because the individual remains the same in all situations. In this context the *Hassan* case may be of relevance in that the Court, even where nor formal derogation is made under article 15, will treat more openly its consideration/application of IHL if the respondent state makes a request to this effect. On the other hand, the Court will meet high hurdles in drawing a line between a mere interpretation of Convention law in harmony with IHL on the basis of article 31(3)(c) of the Vienna Convention on the Law of Treaties and an application of IHL as parameter for 'accommodating' IHL and IHRL requiring some sort of consent of the state concerned.

---

130 Irmscher (n 19 above) 17, referring to the statement of the ICJ in the Advisory Opinion on the *Legality of the Threat or Use of Nuclear Weapons* (n 10 above) para 25.
131 Kleffner (n 117 above) 241.
132 H-P Gasser 'International humanitarian law and human rights law in non-international armed conflict: Joint venture or mutual exclusion?' (2002) 45 *German Yearbook on International Law* 149.

15

Inter-American Human Rights System

*Dinah Shelton**

1 Introduction

For more than fifty years, the Inter-American human rights system of the Organisation of American States (OAS) has operated in a hemisphere suffused with internal armed conflicts, terrorism, violent organised crime, and militias or death squads supported or condoned by repressive governments. The two organs of the system that seek to promote and protect human rights in this context are the Inter-American Commission on Human Rights (IACHR or Commission), created in 1959 by Resolution VII of the Fifth Meeting of Consultation of Ministers of Foreign Affairs[1] and the Inter-American Court of Human Rights (Court), established upon the entry into force on 18 July 1978 of the American Convention on Human Rights.

Only five years after its creation, the IACHR conducted its first on-site inquiry with respect to a violent conflict in the Dominican Republic.[2] Since that time, the IACHR has repeatedly carried out its mandate to promote and protect human rights in the context of internal armed conflicts in OAS member states. It has6 also dealt with cross-border military operations, including incursions by the United States into Panama and Greneda, and Colombia into Ecuador,[3] as well as transnational death squads such as 'Operation Condor', created by Latin American military

---

*   Manatt/Ahn Professor of Law (emeritus), The George Washington University Law School; member of the Inter-American Commission on Human Rights (2010-2014). The views expressed in this article are those of the author and are not to be attributed to the Inter-American Commission.

1   Resolution VII of the Fifth Meeting of Consultation of Ministers of Foreign Affairs Santiago, Chile, Final Act, OEA/Ser. C/II.5 (1959) 10-11.
2   See Report on the Activities of the IACHR in the Dominican Republic, June 1 to Aug 31, 1965, OAS Doc, OAS/Ser.L/V/II.13, Doc 14, Rev. (15 October 1965); AP Schreiber & PSE Schreiber 'The Inter-American Commission on Human Rights in the Dominican Crises' (1968) 22 *International Organization* 508.
3   See *Franklin Guillermo Aisalla Molina v Colombia* (Admissibility) Report No 112/10, Inter-State Petition IP-02 OEA/Ser.L/V/II.140, Doc 10 IACHR (21 October 2010).

juntas in order to assassinate political opponents.[4] More recently, the IACHR has received numerous petitions from states where increasing levels of violence, including extra-judicial killings, are linked to disputes over natural resources or organised crime. In addition to responding to petitions, the IACHR has issued country reports on internal conflicts and prepared thematic reports on terrorism and human rights[5] and on citizen security.[6] In all of these activities, the IACHR and, more recently, the Court have had occasion to apply humanitarian law to interpret or fill gaps in the human rights guarantees when the situation warrants.

In considering the relationship between the human rights norms they monitor and the international humanitarian law (IHL) norms that govern armed conflicts, the Commission and Court have addressed the scope of their jurisdiction to apply IHL, the threshold of violence that triggers application of IHL norms, and the content of the relevant norms. States sometimes object to and at other times support the application of IHL. Moreover, the Commission and Court have not always agreed about the scope of their jurisdiction. The jurisprudence to date on these matters forms the subject matter of this contribution. It begins by examining the legal framework, including the question of subject matter jurisdiction and the legal rationales given for the application of IHL in the Inter-American system. It then reviews those cases in which the IACHR or Court have deemed the levels of violence to rise to a level governed by IHL. The remaining sections discuss how IHL norms have been interpreted and applied by the Inter-American institutions.

2   The legal framework

International human rights law and IHL, although different in scope, are complementary to each other and concern the rights of all persons affected by a conflict.[7] Although much of the corpus of IHL predates human rights law and was designed specifically to protect persons who are not (or are no longer) participating in hostilities and to restrict the means and methods of warfare, it is now widely recognised that human rights obligations continue to apply in these situations as well. In Resolution 2005/63, the former UN Commission on Human Rights examined the relationship between the two bodies of law and determined that 'human rights law and international humanitarian law are mutually reinforcing', with the

---

4   See, eg: JP McSherry *Predatory states: Operation Condor and covert war in Latin America* (2005).

5   *Report on terrorism and human rights* OEA/Ser.L/V/II.116 Doc 5 rev 1 corr IACHR (22 October 2002)

6   *Report on citizen security and human rights* OEA/Ser.L/V/II. Doc 57 IACHR (31 December 2009).

7   See: UN Office of the High Commissioner for Human Rights *International legal protection of human rights in armed conflict* (2011) 1; Human Rights Council res 9/9 (referring to human rights law and IHL as complementary and mutually reinforcing).

protection provided by human rights law continuing in armed conflicts, 'taking into account when international humanitarian law applies as *lex specialis*'. Conduct that violates international humanitarian law, including grave breaches of the Geneva Conventions or Protocol I, may at the same time constitute a gross violation of human rights. The Trial Chamber of the International Criminal Tribunal for the former Yugoslavia found the 'basic underpinning' for this common core of human rights and IHL obligations in the idea of human dignity.[8] As discussed herein, the scope of guaranteed rights may be limited through properly declared and implemented temporary suspensions according to the terms of derogations clauses, but human rights treaties as a whole are not suspended during armed conflicts.

IHL traditionally has been formulated in terms of obligations of states and organised armed groups, while human rights law sets forth a list of guaranteed rights as well as the obligations of states. The IHL principle that distinguishes combatants from civilians and other protected persons is one important difference between the two bodies of law. Combatants may be attacked until they are *hors de combat* while civilians are protected from attack unless they directly participate in hostilities, and are further protected by the principles of proportionality and precaution.

There are several relevant international agreements accepted by most states in the Western Hemisphere, all of them being members of the OAS.[9] Twenty-four of the thirty-five OAS member states adhere to the American Convention on Human Rights[10] and all but three[11] of them have accepted the jurisdiction of the Inter-American Court. All OAS member states adhere to the 1949 Geneva Conventions; only the United States is not a party to Protocol I and all states except Mexico and the United States are parties to Protocol II. All OAS states are also parties to the International Covenant on Civil and Political Rights.

Until recently, no OAS human rights instrument addressed the special context of armed conflict. This changed with the adoption of article 15(2) of the Inter-American Convention on Forced Disappearances,[12] a

---

8　*Prosecutor v Anto Furundzija* Case No IT-95-17/1-T ICTY (10 December 1998) para 183.

9　The OAS member states are Antigua and Barbuda, Argentina, Bahamas, Barbados, Belize, Bolivia, Brazil, Canada, Chile, Colombia, Costa Rica, Cuba, Dominica, Dominican Republic, Ecuador, El Salvador, Grenada, Guatemala, Guyana, Haiti, Honduras, Jamaica, Mexico, Nicaragua, Panama, Paraguay, Peru, Saint Kitts and Nevis, Saint Lucia, Saint Vincent and the Grenadines, Suriname, Trinidad and Tobago, United States, Uruguay, and Venezuela.

10　Argentina, Barbados, Bolivia, Brazil, Chile, Colombia, Costa Rica, Dominica, Dominican Republic, Ecuador, El Salvador, Grenada, Guatemala, Haiti, Honduras, Jamaica, Mexico, Nicaragua, Panama, Paraguay, Peru, Suriname, Uruguay, and Venezuela. Trinidad and Tobago was a party, but on 26 May 1998, the government denounced the American Convention. Venezuela announced its decision to denounce the Convention on 10 September 2012.

11　Dominica, Grenada and Jamaica.

12　9 June 1994, 33 ILM1429 (1994), OASTS 1994 A-60, entered into force 28 March 1996.

provision inserted at the initiative of the United States government. The paragraph excludes from the Convention's application international, but not internal, armed conflicts. It provides:

> This Convention shall not apply to the international armed conflicts governed by the 1949 Geneva Conventions and their Protocol, concerning protection of wounded, sick, and shipwrecked members of the armed forces; and prisoners of war and civilians in time of war.

More generally, the derogations provisions of the American Convention, like those of the ICCPR, permit temporary suspension of derogable rights[13] as necessary during periods of emergency, which would presumably include international and internal armed conflicts.[14] Any derogation is subject to strict requirements: a public emergency must threaten the life of the nation and the measures taken must be 'strictly required by the exigencies of the situation', consistent with other obligations under international law, necessary and proportional, temporary, non-discriminatory, and subject to judicial guarantees.

The canons and principles the Inter-American organs use to interpret human rights instruments facilitate recourse to IHL. Since its first cases, the Court has referred to 'the special nature of the American Convention in the framework of International Human Rights Law',[15] which includes that the Convention and other human rights treaties are:

> [I]nspired by higher shared values (focusing on protection of the human being), they have specific oversight mechanisms, they are applied according to the concept of collective guarantees, they embody obligations that are essentially objective, and their nature is special vis-à-vis other treaties that regulate reciprocal interests among the States Parties.[16]

As such, the institutions of the system must:

---

13 See *Colombia* (Merits) Report No 26/97, Case No 11.142 IACHR (30 September 1997) para 171; *Argentina* (Merits) Report No 55/97, Case No 11.137 IACHR (22 December 1997) para 158. The ICCPR rights not subject to derogation are article 6 (right to life), article 7 (prohibition of torture or cruel, inhuman or degrading punishment, or of medical or scientific experimentation without consent), article 8, paras 1 and 2 (prohibition of slavery, slave trade and servitude), article 11 (prohibition of imprisonment due to inability to fulfill a contractual obligation), article 15 (no ex post facto laws), article 16 (recognition of legal personality) and article 18 (freedom of thought, conscience and religion). See Committee on Human Rights, General Comment No 29 (2001) para 7.

14 See ICCPR, art 4, and ACHR, art 27.

15 See *Case of Baena Ricardo* (Competence)Ser C No 104 IACHR (28 November 2003) para 96; *Case of Hilaire* (Preliminary Objections) Ser C No 80 IACHR (1 September 2001) para 94; *Case of the Constitutional Court* (Competence) Ser C No 55 IACHR (24 September 1999) para 41, and *Case of Ivcher Bronstein* (Competence) Ser C No 54 IACHR (24 September 1999) para 42.

16 *Case of Mapiripán Massacre v Colombia* Ser C No 134 IACHR (15 September 2005) para 104.

[A]pply and interpret their provisions in accordance with their object and purpose, so as to ensure that the States Party guarantee compliance with them and their *effet utile* in their respective domestic legal systems.[17]

The Court has also pointed out that human rights treaties are living instruments, whose interpretation must go hand in hand with evolving times and current living conditions. It has concluded that this evolutive interpretation is consistent with the directives contained in article 29[18] of the American Convention, as well the general rules of interpretation set forth in the Vienna Convention on the Law of Treaties.[19] In sum, the Court has reached the important conclusion that when interpreting the Convention:

[I]t is always necessary to choose the alternative that is most favorable to protection of the rights enshrined in said treaty, based on the principle of the rule most favorable to the human being.[20]

More generally, the Court holds that the Convention constitutes a *lex specialis* within the international law of state responsibility, in view of the Convention's special nature as an international human rights treaty. Within this special human rights regime of state responsibility, IHL provides a subset of *lex specialis* with respect to human rights and obligations during armed conflicts.

3   Jurisdiction *rationae materiae*

Despite the silence of the American Declaration and Convention about IHL, the Commission and Court have concluded that they must apply IHL when the facts show the existence of an armed conflict. Over time there has been a shift in the manner and the extent to which they invoke IHL. The Commission has taken the opportunity in several individual cases to assert

17   *Mapiripán Massacre* (n 16 above)para 105, citing *Case of the Indigenous Community Yakye Axa* 12 para 101; *Case of Lori Berenson Mejía* (Merits, Reparations and Costs) Ser C No 119 IACHR (25 November 2004) para 220; *Case of the Serrano Cruz Sisters* (Preliminary Objections) Ser C No 11 IACHR (23 November 2004) para 69; and *Case of Hilaire, Constantine and Benjamin et al*, Ser C No 94 IACHR (21 June 2002) para 83.

18   Article 29(b), the so-called 'most-favorable-to-the-individual clause', provides that no provision of the American Convention shall be interpreted as 'restricting the enforcement or exercise of any right or freedom recognized by virtue of the laws of any State Party or another convention to which one of said states is a party'.

19   See *The right to information on consular assistance in the framework of the guarantees of the due process of law* Advisory Opinion OC-16/99 (1 October 1999) Ser A No 16, para 114; *Case of the Gómez Paquiyauri Brothers* Ser C No 110 IACHR (8 July 2004) para 165; *Case of Juan Humberto Sánchez* (Interpretation of the Judgment on Preliminary Objections, Merits and Reparations, art 67 American Convention on Human Rights) Ser C No 102 IACHR (26 November 2003) para 56; *Case of the Mayagna (Sumo) Awas Tingni Community* Ser C No 79 IACHR (31 August 2003) paras 146 to 148; and *Case of Barrios Altos*, Ser C No 75 IACHR (14 March 2001) paras 41-44.

20   *Mapiripán Massacre* (n 16 above)para 106, citing *Case of Ricardo Canese* Ser C No 111 IACHR (31 August 2004) para 181; *Case of Herrera Ulloa* Ser C No 107 IACHR (2 July 2004) para 184, *Case of Baena Ricardo et al* Ser C No 72 IACHR (2 February 2001).

that the text of the American Convention, its own case law, and the jurisprudence of the Court supports its competence to apply or consult humanitarian law rules directly,[21] noting that:

> [T]he American Convention contains no rules that either define or distinguish civilians from combatants and other military targets, much less, specify when a civilian can be lawfully attacked or when civilian casualties are a lawful consequence of military operations. Therefore, the Commission must necessarily look to and apply definitional standards and relevant rules of humanitarian law as sources of authoritative guidance in its resolution of this and other kinds of claims alleging violations of the American Convention in combat situations.[22]

Apart from the principle of distinction referred to by the Commission, IHL 'definitional standards and relevant rules' are only really detailed for international armed conflicts. Common article 3 is less specific than most human rights instruments and is not necessarily more humane. Protocol II to the Geneva Conventions is more detailed with respect to civilians than common article 3, and includes the principle of distinction, but still omits regulation of many aspects of internal armed conflicts.

The Commission has generally relied on Convention article 29(b) as the basis for applying IHL norms, stating that article 29(b) of the American Convention necessarily requires it to take due notice of and, where appropriate, give legal effect to applicable humanitarian law rules. The language and the interpretation given to this provision, however, would seem to direct the application of IHL only if the IHL norms are more protective of human rights than are Inter-American human rights texts. The Commission seemed to suggest this in its decision in *Abella*, for example when it cited Convention article 29 in concluding that:

> [W]here there are differences between legal standards governing the same or comparable rights in the American Convention and a humanitarian law instrument, the Commission is duty bound to give legal effect to the provision of that treaty with the higher standard applicable to the right or freedom in question. If that higher standard is a rule of humanitarian law, the Commission should apply it.[23]

The Commission further explained that:

> Due to their similarity and the fact that both norms are based on the same principles and values, international human rights law and IHL may influence and reinforce each other, following as a interpretative method that enshrined

---

21 See, eg, *Colombia* Report No 26/97, Case No 11.142 IACHR (30 September 1997) par 175; *Abella v Argentina* Report No 55/97, Case No 11.137 IACHR (22 December 1997) para 162.
22 *Abella v Argentina* Report No 55/97, Case 11.137, OEA/Ser.L./V/II.9, doc 6 rev IACHR (1998) para 161.
23 *Abella* (n 22 above) para 165.

in article 31.3.c of the Vienna Convention on the Law of Treaties, which establishes that in interpreting a norm 'any relevant rules of international law applicable in the relations between the parties'[24] may be considered. The foregoing shows that international human rights law may be interpreted in the light of IHL and the latter may be interpreted in the light of international human rights law, as required.[25]

In subsequent cases, nonetheless, the Commission has rarely made an explicit comparison of the relevant texts to determine which body of law affords the greater protection, especially in the context of detainees.

Until recently, the Court's application of IHL generally has been more restrained and indirect than that of the Commission, perhaps because of strong government objections to the application of IHL. New decisions and judgments of both bodies suggest, however, a convergence of approach less assertive than past IACHR decisions, but more expansive than early Court judgments. In *Las Palmeres,*[26] the first case before the Court to discuss IHL, the Court accepted a preliminary objection submitted by the government of Columbia challenging the Court's jurisdiction to make any direct finding that it violated a treaty other than the American Convention. The case concerned an armed operation by members of the national police force that resulted in extrajudicial killings and injuries to civilians, including children. The forces then engaged in a cover-up of the deaths. These acts were alleged to violate both American Convention article 4 and common article 3 of the Geneva Conventions.

The government of Colombia filed a preliminary objection submitting that neither the IACHR nor the Court 'have the competence to apply international humanitarian law and other international treaties',[27] but can only pronounce on the rights and obligations contained in the American Convention. The Commission countered with a declaration of principle, that the case should be decided in the light of 'the norms embodied in both the American Convention and in customary international humanitarian law applicable to internal armed conflicts and enshrined in article 3, common to all the 1949 Geneva Conventions'.[28] The Commission noted that Colombia had not objected to the Commission's characterisation of the situation as an internal armed conflict nor had it contested that the situation corresponded to the definition of an internal armed conflict contained in common article 3.[29] In support of its position, the Commission invoked a passage from the International Court of Justice Advisory Opinion on *the Legality of the Threat or Use of Nuclear Weapons*:

24　Vienna Convention on the Law of Treaties, 1969, art 31.3 (c).
25　*Coard et al v the United States* Report No 109/99, Case 10.951 (Merits) IACHR, (29 September 1999).
26　*Case of Las Palmeras v Colombia* (Preliminary Objections) Ser C No 67 IACHR (4 February 2000).
27　*Las Palmeras* (n 26 above) para 28.
28　*Las Palmeras* (n 26 above) para 29.
29　As above.

In principle, the right not arbitrarily to be deprived of one's life applies also in hostilities. The test of what is an arbitrary deprivation of life, however, then falls to be determined by the applicable *lex specialis*, namely, the law applicable in armed conflict that is designed to regulate the conduct of hostilities.[30]

The IACHR pointed to the IHL principle of distinction, noting that the American Convention does not contain any rule to distinguish lawful killing of combatants from unlawful targeting of protected persons, therefore, the Geneva Conventions should be applied as *lex specialis* because they do make such distinctions. Therefore, to determine during an internal conflict whether a state has violated American Convention article 4, prohibiting arbitrary deprivations of life, the IACHR and the Court had first to assess the facts under common article 3 of the Four Geneva Conventions, as permitted under the rules of interpretation contained in Convention article 29. The Commission considered that this approach constitutes part of its mandate as an organ entrusted with ensuring observance of the fundamental human rights of all persons under the jurisdiction of the states parties. Such a

> justified pro-active interpretation of the mandate of the organs of the system, [is] consistent with the purpose and goal of international human rights law and, at the same time, essentially respectful of the rule of consent and the importance of existing norms of international law.[31]

The Court took a more restrained approach, finding itself competent to determine only whether any act or norm of domestic or international law applied by a state, in times of peace or armed conflict, is compatible or not with the American Convention. The result of the Court's analysis will always be limited to an opinion on whether or not that norm or that act is compatible with the American Convention, because the text of the Convention has only given the Court competence to determine whether the acts or the norms of the states parties are compatible with the Convention itself, and not with the 1949 Geneva Conventions. The Court thus accepted Colombia's position, one that permits the indirect use of IHL to interpret the rights in the Convention, but excludes direct application of IHL norms.

Colombia reasserted its challenge to the use of IHL by the IACHR in the first inter-state case to be declared admissible.[32] Ecuador alleged that on 1 March 2008, Colombian armed forces bombed a camp of the Colombian Revolutionary Armed Forces (FARC) in Ecuador as part of its 'Operation Phoenix', killing 25 civilians and guerrillas, among them

---

30   International Court of Justice *Legality of the Threat or Use of Nuclear Weapons* Advisory Opinion, ICJ Reports (1996), 226 240, para 25.
31   *Las Palmeras* (n 26 above)para 31.
32   *Franklin Guillermo Aisalla Molina (Ecuador – Colombia)* Report No 112/10 (admissibility), Inter-state Petition IP-02, OEA/Ser.L/V/II.140, Doc 10 IACHR (21 October 2010) (hereinafter Ecuador/Colombia).

Ecuadoran national, Franklin Guillermo Aisalla Molina. Ecuador maintained that the results of autopsies 'showed the practice of extra-judicial executions of individuals who were defenseless'. Ecuador thus maintained that Colombia violated, inter alia, the right to life contained in article 4 of the American Convention in relation to article 1.1.[33]

Colombia's preliminary objections asserted a lack of jurisdiction, inter alia by reason of the place and by reason of subject matter. Colombia maintained that article 45 of the American Convention only permits the IACHR to examine inter-state communications dealing with violations of the rights contained in the Convention and that Operation 'Phoenix' was governed by international humanitarian law. Colombia argued that IHL, as *lex specialis*, derogates the more general law, in this case international human rights law and only through IHL may it be 'established whether or not the deprivation of the right to life of an individual resulting from hostilities associated with a military operation which in turn unfolded in the context of an armed conflict, was arbitrary'.[34] Therefore, according to Colombia, the Commission lacked competence *ratione materiae* to examine the inter-state petition.

The Commission responded by restating its view about the interrelationship between international human rights law and IHL, as well as the legal basis for the IACHR to interpret the relevant provisions of the American Convention by reference to the rules of IHL. It noted first that:

> In common with other universal and regional human rights instruments, the American Convention and the 1949 Geneva Conventions share a common core of non-derogable rights and the mutual goal of protecting the physical integrity and dignity inherent in the human being.[35]

Specifically, common article 3 of the Geneva Conventions as well as article 4 of the American Convention protect the right to life and, consequently, prohibit extrajudicial executions under any circumstances. Therefore, any complaint alleging arbitrary deprivation of the right to life, attributable to state agents, is 'clearly within the Inter-American Commission's jurisdiction'.[36] Once the existence of an armed conflict has been established, it becomes indispensable to refer to IHL as *lex specialis*, a source of authorised interpretation which permits the American

---

33　Article 1(1) contains the generic obligations of states parties to the Convention: 'The States Parties to this Convention undertake to respect the rights and freedoms recognized herein and to ensure to all persons subject to their jurisdiction the free and full exercise of those rights and freedoms, without any discrimination for reasons of race, color, sex, language, religion, political or other opinion, national or social origin, economic status, birth, or any other social condition'. Any violation of the one of the rights in the Convention generally also constitutes a violation of this provision.

34　Communication of the State of Colombia, DVAM.DIDHD.GOI No 31461/1312 dated 10 June 2010, received by the IACHR on 14 June 2010, para 82.

35　Ecuador/Colombia (n 32 above) para 117, citing *Abella* (n 22 above)para 158.

36　Ecuador/Colombia (n 32 above) para 118.

Convention's application with due consideration to the particular set of circumstances of the situation.[37]

The IACHR cited the jurisprudence of the ICJ and the Inter-American Court in support of its jurisdiction to apply IHL. In particular, the Commission quoted from the International Court of Justice in the Advisory Opinion on the *Wall in Palestine*:

> More generally, the Court considers that the protection offered by human rights conventions does not cease in case of armed conflict, save through the effect of provisions for derogation of the kind to be found in article 4 of the International Covenant on Civil and Political Rights. As regards the relationship between international humanitarian law and human rights law, there are thus three possible situations: some rights may be exclusively matters of international humanitarian law; others may be exclusively matters of human rights law; yet others maybe matters of both these branches of international law. In order to answer the question put to it, the Court will have to take into consideration both these branches of international law, namely human rights law and, as *lex specialis*, international humanitarian law. [38]

The Commission also noted that the IA Court in particular has repeatedly invoked 'other treaties relating to the protection of human rights' in its decisions and reports.[39] The IACHR concluded that were it to decline jurisdiction in cases of armed conflict, it would risk leaving certain fundamental rights without protection, in contravention of the mandate entrusted to it.[40] The fact that the resolution of a complaint arises in the context of an armed conflict and may require a reference to another treaty does not remove the IACHR's jurisdiction.

Following intermittent efforts in 2011 and 2012 to resolve the matter through negotiations, the two states reached a friendly settlement. On 29 August 2013, the Ecuador advised the IACHR about the 'agreement for social and economic development and reparations and investment for social compensation along the border'. The government indicated that:

> [S]ince that agreement satisfies the claims of the victims and the State of Ecuador raised in case 12.779, the Ecuadorian State, pursuant to the provisions of article 41 of the Rules of Procedure of the IACHR, informs the

37   Ecuador/Colombia (n 32 above) para 120, citing *Gregoria Herminia, Serapio Cristián and Julia Inés Contrera v El Salvador* Report No 11/05 (Admissibility), Petition 708/03 IACHR (23 February 2005) para 20.
38   Ecuador/Colombia (n 32 above) para 124 quoting ICJ *Legal Consequences of the Construction of a Wall in the Occupied Palestinian Territory* Advisory Opinion (9 July 2004) para 106, available at: http://www.icj-cij.org/homepage/sp/advisory/advisory_2004-07-09.pdf (accessed 4 December 2014).
39   *'Other treaties' subject to the advisory jurisdiction of the Court* (art 64 American Convention on Human rights), Advisory Opinion OC-1/82, Series A No 1 IACHR (24 September 1982) para 43.
40   *Coard* (n 25 above) para 43.

Honorable Commission [...] of its withdrawal of the claim lodged against the State of Colombia.[41]

Based on the petitioning government's request, the IACHR decided to archive the case on 4 November 2014.

The US government has also opposed application of IHL by the IACHR, noting that the American Declaration contains no interpretive provision similar to article 29. The IACHR statute identifies the American Declaration as the source of the appropriate human rights standards for OAS member states, like the United States, who are not parties to the American Convention. The Commission replied to the US objection in a communication of 23 July 2002, stating that:

> [T]he Commission remains of the view that it has the competence and the responsibility to monitor the human rights situation of the [Guantanamo] detainees and in doing so to look to and apply definitional standards and relevant rules of international humanitarian law in interpreting and applying the provisions of the Inter-American human rights instruments in times of armed conflict.[42]

On the specific matter before it, the Commission interpreted IHL to conclude that the US could not unilaterally and unreviewably designate detainees as unlawful combatants, leaving them without any legal protection for the duration of a possibly interminable armed conflict.

The debate over jurisdiction continues, but the objections mounted by some of the member states appear to have had an impact in reducing the application of IHL. Although the Court and the Commission continue to apply IHL in appropriate cases, in *Bámaca-Velásquez v Guatemala*, the Court suggested that IHL norms function only as subsidiary 'elements for the interpretation of the American Convention'.[43] In another case against Guatemala, the *Plan de Sánchez Massacre*,[44] the Court did not discuss the application of IHL, but it commented on allegations concerning genocide in a manner that echoes its doctrine on the application of IHL:

> With respect to the issue of genocide mentioned both by the Commission and by the representatives of the victims and their next of kin, the Court notes that in adjudicatory matters it is only competent to find violations of the American Convention on Human Rights and of other instruments of the inter-American system for the protection of human rights that enable it to do so. Nevertheless, facts such as those stated, which gravely affected the members of the Maya

---

41 *Decision to Archive* Inter-State Case 12.779 (*Ecuador v Colombia*), Report No 96/13 IACHR (4 November 2013) para 14.
42 Communication to the Center for Constitutional Rights, 23 July 2002, containing the text from the Commission to the US government.
43 *Bámaca-Velásquez v Guatemala* (Merits and Judgment) Ser C No 70 IACHR (25 November 2000) 209.
44 *Case of Plan de Sánchez Massacre v Guatemala* (Merits) Ser C No 105 IACHR (29 April 2004).

achí people in their identity and values and that took place within a pattern of massacres, constitute an aggravated impact that entails international responsibility of the State, which this Court will take into account when it decides on reparations.[45]

Taking this with the other cases, the Court appears to have concluded that it cannot directly find violations of IHL or other treaties, but it can and sometimes must use them to determine whether or not the state has violated the Convention or another inter-American instrument. Further, in some instances the facts and context may result in a determination that the state has committed an 'aggravated' violation that requires additional measures of reparation.

The Commission's functions extend well beyond receiving and deciding on petitions allleging human rights violations. In on-site visits, public hearings, and country and thematic reports, IHL has had a significant place, in fact, the Commission first referred to IHL law in its notable 1978 Report on the Situation of Human Rights in Nicaragua.[46] The IACHR Report concluded that the Somoza government was responsible for 'serious attempts against the right to life, in violation of the international humanitarian norms', citing excessive and disproportionate force used to suppress an insurrection in the country and indiscriminate bombing of towns, without prior evacuation of the civilian population. The Commission also noted the existence of post-combat summary and collective executions, including of children. The government was held to have obstructed the humanitarian work of the Red Cross during the combat, including care for the wounded, and was found responsible for the death of two Red Cross workers. Torture and other physical abuses were inflicted on numerous detainees, many of whom were held in arbitrary detention. The OAS member states overwhelmingly supported the IACHR report, voting in the Meeting of Consultation of Ministers of Foreign Affairs to impose sanctions on the Somoza government to bring an end to the conflict.[47]

A more recent and lengthy exposition of the Commission's views on the relationship between IHL and HRL appears in the 1999 Colombia Report, Chapter IV of which is entitled 'Violence and Violations of International Human Rights and Humanitarian Law'. The Commission first acknowledges that when organised private groups take up arms to overthrow an elected government, the state has a right under domestic and international law to use legal and appropriate military force to put down such insurrection in order to defend its citizenry and the constitutional

---

45 *Plan de Sánchez Massacre* (n 44 above) para 51.
46 *Report on the situation of human rights in Nicaragua,* OAS Doc OEA/Ser.L/II.45, doc 16, rev 1 IACHR (17 November 1978) 77-78.
47 Resolution II, Seventeenth Meeting of Consultation of Ministers of Foreign Affairs, Washington DC, approved at the Seventh Plenary Session, 21 June 1979, OAS Doc OEA/Ser.F/II.17, Doc 40/79, rev 2 (23 June 1979).

order. At the same time, the government will be held responsible for serious violations of the fundamental rights guaranteed in the American Convention and Declaration during military operations. In order to properly judge the specific claims raised as a result of such operations, the Commission necessarily has either directly to apply rules of international humanitarian law or to inform its interpretations of relevant provisions of the American Convention by reference to these rules.

In the thematic report on terrorism and human rights,[48] the Commission notes that terrorist activities may take place in situations that call for application of different legal regimes, from the application of ordinary human rights law, to the law on states of emergency, to IHL. In all instances, states must afford individuals the most favourable standards of protection available under the applicable law. In the report, IACHR identifies the minimum standards of protection under the various legal regimes, noting that the greatest convergence in norms is found in the obligations of humane treatment,[49] including the prohibition of torture and other mistreatment of detainees. In addition, the Commission identifies an 'absolute and overriding prohibition against discrimination of any kind'.[50] IHL and human rights law also share many of same tests of due process and fair trial, including the requirement of an independent and impartial tribunal, a requirement that generally prohibits the use of ad hoc, special, or military tribunals or commissions to try civilians for any crimes and restricts military tribunals to judging offences of military discipline: 'Military courts may not, however, prosecute human rights violations or other crimes unrelated to military functions, which must be tried by civilian courts'.[51]

In sum, the IACHR and Court appear to have wavered at times in their views about the direct applicability of IHL, although they are in agreement that alleged violations of the Declaration or Convention must be assessed during armed conflicts in the light of IHL norms as *lex specialis*. It is not clear that there would be any difference in the outcome of the cases should the bodies opt for direct application of IHL norms, especially if they analyse and apply the relevant IHL and HRL norms consistent with the principle that the petitioning individuals or groups are entitled to protection of the rule most favourable to them. As noted, however, analysis of which rule is actually the most favourable is not often undertaken; instead IHL is use to determine whether or not human rights have been violated, once it is determined that an armed conflict is underway.

---

48 'Report on terrorism and human rights' IACHR (2002) 374, available at: http://www.cidh.org/terrorism/eng/toc.htm (accessed 4 December 2014).
49 Report on terrorism (n 48 above) para 11.
50 Report on terrorism (n 48 above) para 15.
51 Report on terrorism (n 48 above) para 18.

4 State and non-state responsibility

The Convention and Declaration impose obligations only on states and state actors to respect and ensure the human rights contained therein. Despite this clear norm, some governments have objected to IACHR findings of violations by the state, precisely because the decisions fail to also condemn human rights violations committed by non-state actors, such as the *Sendero Luminoso* in Peru. The jurisdiction of the IACHR and the Court is limited, however, to petitions brought against states and neither body can hear petitions alleging non-state responsibility or made determinations thereof.

Country reports of the IACHR, however, allow consideration of responsibility for IHL violations by both state and non-state actors during internal conflicts because such reports are not limited by the in *personem* jurisdictional limits of the petition process, but can assess the overall human rights situation within a country. By taking into account humanitarian law rules governing internal hostilities, rules that apply equally to and expressly bind all the parties to the conflict, the Commission has a set of accepted legal standards that enable it to assess the conduct not only of the state's security forces, but of non-state actors as well. In practice, the Commission has referred to international humanitarian law in preparing country reports and the OAS General Assembly has requested the Commission to do this analysis on several occasions, recommending that the Commission 'refer to the actions of irregular armed groups' in reporting on the human rights situation in the member states of the inter-American system.[52]

Given the lack of jurisdiction over non-state actors in the petition procedure, it is perhaps understandable that both the Commission and the Court appear to have expanded the scope of state responsibility in order to afford some redress to victims of violations and ensure that the state carries out its due diligence obligations to prevent, investigate, prosecute and punish non-state violations as well as those committed by state agents. In a series of cases against Colombia, the Court has held the state responsible for the acts of paramilitary groups the government had helped create and allowed to operate before declaring them illegal. In addition to noting the evidence of complicity in the cases, the Court determined that the government failed to act diligently to protect civilians from the paramilitaries and, due to this omission, was therefore responsible for

---

52   See 'Strengthening of the OAS in the area of human rights' Resolution adopted at the eleventh plenary session of the twenty-first regular session of the General Assembly, Santiago, Chile, 3-8 June 1991, AG/RES. 1112 (XXI-O/91), OEA/Ser.P/XXI.O.2 (20 August 1991) volume 1, 78; 'Annual Report of the inter-American Commission on Human Rights' Resolution adopted at the eighth plenary session of the twenty-second regular session of the General Assembly, Nassau, The Bahamas, 18-23 May 1992, AG/RES. 1169 (XXII-O/92), OEA/Ser.P/XXII.O.2, (21 June 1992) volume 1, 62.

violations of the rights of the affected persons. In the case of *Mapiripán Massacre v Colombia*,[53] for example, in addition to finding complicity between the government and the paramilitary groups deemed responsible for a major part of the human rights violations,[54] the Court discussed the state's duty to protect under IHL (para 114):

> [W]ith regard to establishment of the international responsibility of the State in the instant case, the Court cannot set aside the existence of general and special duties of the State to protect the civilian population, derived from International Humanitarian Law, specifically article 3 common of the August 12, 1949 Geneva Agreements and the provisions of the additional Protocol to the Geneva Agreements regarding protection of the victims of non-international armed conflicts (Protocol II). Due respect for the individuals protected entails passive obligations (not to kill, not to violate physical safety, etc.), while the protection due entails positive obligations to impede violations against said persons by third parties. Carrying out said obligations is significant in the instant case, insofar as the massacre was committed in a situation in which civilians were unprotected in a non-international domestic armed conflict.

Although Colombia objected to attribution to the state of acts by the paramilitary, the Court found these acts attributable to the state '*insofar as they in fact acted in a situation and in areas that were under the control of the State*'.[55]

The case of the *Pueblo Bello Massacre v Colombia*,[56] similar to the *Mapiripán Massacre* case, involved forced disappearances and extrajudicial executions, allegedly as an act of private justice by paramilitary groups. The Court found that the state had encouraged the creation of the groups and by doing so had 'objectively created a dangerous situation for its inhabitants and failed to adopt all the necessary or sufficient measures to avoid these groups continuing to commit acts such as those of the instant case'. It was not enough to declare the groups illegal; in addition the state should have adopted 'sufficient and effective measures to avoid the consequences of the danger that had been created'. So long as the danger situation subsists, the state has:

---

53 *Mapiripán Massacre* (n 16 above).
54 See Report by the United Nations High Commissioner for Human Rights on the human rights situation in Colombia, E/CN.4/2005/10 (28 February 2005) para 8, and Report by the United Nations High Commissioner for Human Rights on the human rights situation in Colombia, E/CN.4/2001/15 (20 March 2001) paras 29-30.
55 *Mapiripán Massacre* (n 16 above) para 120 (emphasis added). The Court pointed to the facts that the incursion by the paramilitary in Mapiripán was an act planned several months before the date of the massacre, carried out with full knowledge, logistic preparations and collaboration by the Armed Forces, who enabled the paramilitary to act in areas that were under its control, and left the civilian population defenceless during the days of the massacre by unjustifiably transferring the troops to other places. The military also acted to cover up the facts to seek impunity for those responsible.
56 *Case of the Pueblo Bello Massacre v Colombia* (Merits, Reparations and Costs) Ser C No 140 IACHR (31 January 2006).

[S]pecial obligations of prevention and protection in the zones where the paramilitary groups were present, as well as the obligation to investigate diligently, the acts or omissions of State agents and individuals who attack the civilian population.[57]

Even though it was not proved that the state authorities had any specific prior knowledge of the attack on the population, the state's declaration of the illegality of the paramilitary groups implied that it would direct its control and security operations against them, and not only against guerrilla groups. The Court called the obligations of prevention and protection of the inhabitants 'of cardinal importance within the framework of the obligations established in article 1(1) of the Convention'.[58] The Court concluded that the state did not adopt, with due diligence, all the necessary measures with respect to a zone that had been declared 'an emergency zone, subject to military operations'; such a declaration placed the state in a special position of guarantor, owing to the situation of armed conflict in that zone.[59]

As may be evident from these cases, neither the Court nor the Commission consider the state and armed dissident groups to have equal responsibilities with regard to human rights. The state has a unique status with specific rights and obligations under international law. Each party to the American Convention or other human rights treaty has freely assumed the sole responsibility and basic duty of respecting and ensuring the human rights protected in these instruments to all persons subject to its jurisdiction, including during civil strife or any other emergency. The IACHR has reiterated[60] that a state will incur responsibility for the illegal acts of private actors when it has permitted such acts to take place without taking adequate measures to prevent them or, subsequently, to punish the perpetrators. The state also incurs in responsibility when the acts of private parties are committed with the support, tolerance or acquiescence of state agents. At the same time, the Commission has recognised that in situations of conflict the state cannot always prevent, much less be held responsible for, the harm to individuals and destruction of private property occasioned by the hostile acts of its armed opponents.

In respect to military or police activities outside a state's territory, the IACHR holds the state accountable whenever it exercises control over a specific person or situation, without a requirement of occupation or territorial control where the event occurred. The Inter-American Commission's 2002 *Report on terrorism and human rights* expresses the Commission's:

57   *Pueblo Bello Massacre* (n 56 above) para 126.
58   *Pueblo Bello Massacre* (n 56 above) para 134.
59   *Pueblo Bello Massacre* (n 56 above) para 139. See also: *Case of the Rochela Massacre v Colombia* (Merits, Reparations and Costs) Series C No 163 IACHR (11 May 2007).
60   *Third report on the human rights situation in Colombia* OEA/Ser.L/V/II.102, Doc 9 rev 1 IACHR (26 February 1999).

[W]ish to emphasize ... the overriding significance of the principles of necessity, proportionality, humanity and non-discrimination in all circumstances in which states purport to place limitations on the fundamental rights and freedoms of persons under their authority and control.[61]

In sum, human rights law remains connected to the law of state responsibility. In addition to absolute responsibliity for the acts of state organs and agents, the failure, through a lack of due diligence, to prevent, investigate, prosecute and punish violations by non-state actors, including violations of IHL, will violate human rights obligations. The non-state actors may independently be held accountable under domestic or international law, including for breaches of IHL, potentially allowing prosecution by other tribunals.

5   Lex specialis

While IHL and human rights law are largely complementary, there are certain circumstances in which the norms may diverge, such as with respect to the permissible use of deadly force. Determining the proper rule to follow may be governed by the principle *lex specialis derogat legi generali*, according to which the more specific rule is applied in preference to the more general one when the rules conflict. The International Law Commission has indicated that 'for the *lex specialis* principle to apply it is not enough that the same subject matter is dealt with by two provisions; there must be some actual inconsistency between them, or else a discernible intention that one provision is to exclude the other'.[62] This suggests that the more precisely delimited rule should have priority even if it results in applying lower standards of protection. This result would seem inconsistent with the inter-American choice of law principle that calls for invoking the higher standard of protection when different norms may govern. Despite this seeming inconsistency, the IACHR and Court have never declined to apply IHL as *lex specialis* on the grounds that it affords less protection than human rights law, nor have they examined in detail which body of law provides the stronger guarantee in a given case. The reason for this may perhaps be found in the ILC statement above, which refers to inconsistent norms concerning 'the same subject matter'. The human rights tribunals may deem that IHL and human rights law broadly govern similar subject matter, but the existence of an armed conflict gives rise to a separate set of circumstances than those obtaining in peacetime and hence IHL regulates a different subject matter at least in part.

---

61   *Report on terrorism and human rights* (n 48 above) 374 (emphasis added). See also: *Rafael Ferrer-Mazorra et al v United States*, Case 9903, Report No 51/01, OEA/Ser.L/V/II.111 Doc 20 rev IACHR (2000) 1188.
62   See *Fragmentation of international law: Difficulties arising from the diversification and expansion of international law* Report of the Study Group of the International Law Commission, A/CN.4/L.682, paras 56-57.

Some rules of IHL are *lex specialis*, in particular the regulation of the right to life during armed conflict. As the Commission pointed out in its *Third report on the human rights situation in Columbia*,[63] the Inter-American Convention on Human Rights lacks standards on the principles of distinction and proportional use of force during armed conflicts. For matters of fair criminal proceedings, in contrast, the rules of human rights law such as ICCPR article 14 and American Convention article 8 are more detailed than those of common article 3. Moreover, many violations of human rights are not the direct result of hostilities and can and should be resolved by applying international human rights law. Thus, the identification of which body of law should apply depends on examination of the facts and particular rules that may be relevant.

The IACHR has indicated that IHL as *lex specialis* may extend to questions of evidence. The Commission has accepted that the peculiar and confusing conditions frequently attending combat may make it impossible to ascertain 'with clinical certainty' crucial facts relating to situations arising in the context of hostilities.[64] Accordingly, the Commission has stated that the appropriate standard for judging the belligerent actions of those engaged in hostilities must be a reasonable appreciation of the overall situation prevailing at the time the action occurred and not simply speculation or hindsight. The results may not always be conclusive. In particular, where the attending circumstances are unclear or unknown, it may not be possible for the Commission, in good faith, to attribute responsibility for the claimed violation to the proper party. Thus, a human rights body may have to abstain from reaching a conclusion regarding the alleged violation.

In the *Bamaca-Velasquez* case,[65] both the state of Guatemala and the Commission agreed that the Court, based on article 29 of the American Convention, could use the Geneva Conventions and provisions of Common article 3 as *lex specialis*. The Court agreed, finding it proven that, at the time of the facts of the case, an internal conflict was taking place in Guatemala. Due to the existence of the conflict, the Court held that the state must, 'as established in article 3 common to the Geneva Conventions of August 12, 1949', 'grant those persons who are not participating directly in the hostilities or who have been placed *hors de combat* for whatever reason, humane treatment, without any unfavorable distinctions'. The Court reiterated that its function is to determine violations of the American Convention and other inter-American treaties, but added that it can observe that certain acts or omissions also violate other international instruments for the protection of the individual, such as the 1949 Geneva Conventions and, in particular, common article 3, instruments which were applicable to the situation in Guatemala at the time. The Court ordered the

---

63   OEA/ser.L./V/II.102, doc 9 rev 1 IACHR(1999) chap 4, para 12.
64   Third Report on Colombia (n 63 above) chap IV, para 15.
65   *Bámaca-Velásquez v Guatemala* (n 43 above).

Guatemalan state to adopt all legislative or other measures necessary to adapt the Guatemalan legal framework to international human rights and humanitarian law norms and to fully implement those norms on the domestic level.

6　The system's interpretation of IHL

Until the establishment of international criminal courts with jurisdiction to try individuals for war crimes, IHL lacked international tribunals that could develop jurisprudence on the application and interpretation of IHL norms. These norms, like those in human rights instruments, are often written in broad terms, making interpretation a necessary concomittant to exercising jurisdiction to apply IHL. In fact, the IACHR and Court have interpreted and given content to some IHL norms in the cases that have come before them. They have had to determine when levels of violence reach the point of being governed by IHL, what the rights of detainees during armed conflict are, and what human rights norms may be imported into IHL to fill gaps therein, or vice versa. As such the inter-American human rights tribunals have not only applied IHL, they have helpd to develop it.

6.1　Qualifying the level of violence

Humanitarian law applies when certain objective conditions are met, distinguishing several different levels of conflict to which different rules apply. Article 2 common to the Geneva Conventions states that:

> In addition to the provisions which shall be implemented in peacetime, the present Convention shall apply to all cases of declared war or of any other armed conflict which may arise between two or more of the High Contracting Parties, even if the state of war is not recognized by one of them. The Convention shall also apply to all cases of partial or total occupation of the territory of a High Contracting Party, even if the said occupation meets with no armed resistance.

Protocol I to the Geneva Conventions extends the situations covered by common article 2 to include 'armed conflicts in which peoples are fighting against colonial domination and alien occupation and against racist regimes in the exercise of their right of self-determination'.[66] The term 'armed conflict' is not defined. The Commentary to the Geneva Conventions indicates that:

> [A]ny difference arising between two States and leading to the intervention of members of the armed forces is an armed conflict within the meaning of article 2, even if one of the Parties denies the existence of a state of war. It

---

66　Art 1.4.

makes no difference how long the conflict lasts, or how much slaughter takes place.[67]

Yet, there remains uncertainty about whether IHL applies to low-intensity military confrontations such as border incidents or skirmishes. According to the ICJ, for example, not every use of force constitutes an 'armed attack' for purposes of the right of self-defence.[68]

Within countries, sporadic low level disturbances fall within normal law enforcement and human rights law.[69] More intense internal conflicts are covered by common article 3,[70] while Protocol II governs those conflicts in which the armed groups are 'under responsible command' and exercise control over a part of the state's territory, 'so as to enable them to carry out sustained and concerted military operations'. Thus, common article 3 represents the lowest threshold of armed conflict, below which IHL does not apply, but common article 3 contains no definition or criteria for an 'armed conflict not of an international character.' The ICTY has declared that an armed conflict exists for purposes of common article 3 whenever there is 'protracted armed violence between governmental authorities and organized armed groups or between such groups within a State'. Despite this holding, no central authority exists to make determinations about the level of violence and applicable law, so it has fallen to the IACHR and Court to determine when the various thresholds are met in cases presented to them.

In its report on terrorism and human rights, the Commission addressed the question of what level of violence triggers the application of IHL. According to the IACHR, IHL applies to armed conflicts between states and armed confrontations between state authorities and organised armed groups or between such groups within a state.[71] In all cases, the determination as to the existence and nature of an armed conflict is an objective one, based upon the nature and degree of hostilities, irrespective of the purpose or motivation underlying the conflict or the qualification by parties to the conflict.[72] The IACHR report comments that while

---

67   Jean Pictet et al (eds) *Geneva Convention I for the amerlioration of the condition of the wounded and sick in armed forces in the field, Commentary* (1952) 32. See also *Prosecutor v Dusko Tadić*, case No IT-94-1-A, Decision on the defence motion for interlocutory appeal on jurisdiction, ICTY (2 October 1995) para 70 ('an armed conflict exists whenever there is a resort to armed force between States').
68   *Military and paramilitary activities in and against Nicaragua (Nic v USA)* Merits, judgment, ICJ Rep (1986).
69   In addition to the human rights treaty provisions that apply to law enforcement operations, the UN has approved 'Basic principles on the use of force and firearms by law enforcement officials' adopted at the Eighth United Nations Congress on the Prevention of Crime and the Treatment of Offenders in 1990.
70   *Prosecutor v Dusko Tadić* IT-94-1, Appeals Chamber, Decision on the Defence Motion for Interlocutory Appeal on Jurisdiction (2 October 1995) para 70.
71   Report on terrorism (n 48 above) para 59. See: *Abella* (n 22 above) para 152. See similarly International Criminal Tribunal for the Former Yugoslavia, *Tadić* (n 70 above) para. 70.
72   Report on terrorism (n 48 above).

Additional Protocol II is applicable in a more narrowly defined category of internal armed conflicts than common article 3,

> certain of its provisions, including the fundamental guarantees under articles 4, 5 and 6, are considered to develop protections prescribed in common article 3 and should therefore likewise be considered to apply in all non-international armed conflicts.[73]

The IACHR was confronted with the threshold question in the controversial decision of *Abella*[74] when it examined the legality of the state's response to an armed attack by forty-two militants against military barracks in the province of Buenos Aires. A state security force numbering approximately 3500 supported by tanks and helicopters killed a majority of the militants. The Commission first addressed the question of whether the incident involved a mere 'internal disturbance or tension' or instead constituted a non-international or internal armed conflict. The answer would determine whether the Commission would apply IHL or human rights principles on the use of force. Concluding that the *Abella* incident could not be properly characterised as a mere internal disturbance, the Commission held that IHL would supply the relevant proportionality standard to judge whether the state violated the rights of the individuals killed. Debate continues over whether the IACHR properly characterised the incident as an internal armed conflict rather than a law enforcement response to a criminal act, but the locus of the action, the use of the armed forces to respond, and the heavy military equipment employed seem to have been important factors. The resulting characterisation would appear to favour the state in assessing the legality of the use of force.

In its 1999 Colombia report, the Commission avoided the difficult threshold issue, noting that it was not required to determine whether the nature and level of the domestic violence in Colombia constitute an internal armed conflict or to identify the specific humanitarian law rules governing the conflict, because the state had openly acknowledged the factual reality of its involvement in such a conflict and the applicability of article 3 common to the four 1949 Geneva Conventions and other customary law rules and principles governing internal armed conflicts. The Commission also noted that the armed dissident groups had referred to IHL and one group specifically declared that it considered itself bound by the Geneva Conventions and Protocol II.[75]

In another highly controversial decision, the IACHR seemed to pull back from its approach in *Abella,* as it sought to determine state responsibility for deaths that occurred during a military operation to rescue

---

73　Report on terrorism (n 48 above)para 63.
74　*Abella* (n 22 above) 271.
75　See, eg, Constitutional Court Decision No C-574, 28 October 1992, considered itself to be bound by the 1949 Geneva Conventions and Protocol II.

hostages being held by members of the Túpac Amaru Revolutionary Movement [MRTA] in the Japanese Embassy in Peru.[76] In the end, whether the IACHR applied IHL or human rights law may not have affected the outcome, because the Commission found on the evidence that the individuals killed were no longer combatants, if they ever had been, having surrendered their arms and given themselves up to the Peruvian Army. If so, under either IHL or human rights law, the deaths might have to be classified as summary executions or extra-judicial killings.[77]

However, even on these facts different results might obtain under the two bodies of law because human rights law and IHL have somewhat different formulations of proportionality, with IHL authorising states to target enemy fighters and/or military objectives, provided that collateral damage to civilians is not manifestly 'excessive'. When attacks on military targets pose a risk of collateral civilian casualties, states must take 'all reasonable precautions to avoid losses of civilian lives' and must ensure that unintended civilian casualties are not 'excessive in relation to the concrete and direct military advantage related'. The principles of distinction and proportionality do not generally shield combatants from the use of force within an international armed conflict; states are free to target enemy combatants, provided that their chosen means and methods of attack are lawful and the targets are not incapacitated by injury or attempting to surrender.[78] Human rights law prohibits all extra-judicial killings except in self-defence or when lethal force is necessary to protect the life of another.[79] Human rights tribunals tend to apply human rights proportionality standards, as happened in this case, but other international tribunals have applied IHL standards as *lex specialis*.[80]

76   *Eduardo Nicolás Cruz Sánchez et al v Peru* (Merits) Report No 66/10, Case 12.444 IACHR (31 March 2011).

77   The IACHR observed that the state had not provided a consistent explanation of the way in which Peceros Pedraza and Meléndez Cueva were killed. Based on the evidence in the case file, the Commission found it reasonable to believe that Peceros Pedraza and Meléndez Cueva were neutralised by military agents, begged for their lives, and nonetheless were extrajudicially killed, receiving multiple bullet wounds to vital parts of their bodies that were intended to eliminate them.

78   Additional Protocol I to the Geneva Conventions of 12 August 1949, Relating to the Protection of Victims of International Armed Conflicts art 51(5)(b) (8 June 1977) 1125 U.N.T.S. 3 [hereinafter Additional Protocol I]. In *Prosecutor v Tadić*, the International Criminal Tribunal for the Former Yugoslavia found that international armed conflict principles represented 'customary rules' that apply equally 'in civil strife'.

79   See UN Human Rights Council 'Report of the Special Rapporteur on extrajudicial, summary or arbitrary executions' UN Doc A/HRC/14/24/Add.6 (28 May 2010) (prepared by Philip Alston) [hereinafter UN Report on Targeted Killing] (Lethal force under human rights law is legal if it is strictly and directly necessary to save life); International Human Rights Committee 'Compilation of general comments and general recommendations adopted by human rights treaty Bodies', General Comment No 6, HRI/GEN/1/Rev.7 (2004) 3 ('[T]he law must strictly control and limit the circumstances in which a person may be deprived of his life by [state] authorities.').

80   See *Prosecutor v Boskoski* Case No IT-04-82-T, Int'l Crim Trib for the Former Yugoslavia (10 July 2008), where the ICTY recognised a conflict between doctrines of proportionality. See also: M Sassòli & LM Olson 'The relationship between international humanitarian and human rights law where it matters: Admissible killing

In characterising the action as an 'anti-terrorist operation', the IACHR applied the rules governing the use of lethal force in law enforcement. It cited the jurisprudence of the inter-American Court in this regard, noting that while law enforcement officials may legitimately use lethal force in the performance of their duties, this use must be defined by exceptionality and must be planned and proportionally limited by the authorities so that force or coercive means may only be used once all other methods of control have been exhausted and have failed. Its exceptional use must be determined by the law and restrictively construed so that it is used to the minimum extent possible in all circumstances and never exceeds the use which is 'absolutely necessary' in relation to the force or threat to be repelled. Whenever excessive force is used, any resulting deprivation of life is arbitrary. Applying this stricter standard to the facts of the case, the IACHR recalled that:

> States must not use force against individuals who no longer present a threat ... such as individuals who have been apprehended by authorities, have surrendered, or who are wounded and abstain from hostile acts ... The use of lethal force in such a manner would constitute extra-judicial killings in flagrant violation of article 4 of the Convention and article I of the Declaration.

At only one point does the IACHR mention IHL, and it is an odd reference. The Commission states that the kidnapping of diplomats and civilians violates the basic principles of international humanitarian law, without assessing the circumstances or the level of violence involved in the kidnappings. Clearly not all kidnappings trigger the application of IHL and it is unclear why the takeover of the Embassy triggered IHL but the rescue of the hostages did not.

6.2　Rights of detainees

Neither human rights law nor IHL precludes a state from prosecuting and punishing members of dissident armed groups for the commission of crimes under its domestic or international law. Criminal trials, however, must afford defendants the due process safeguards set forth in applicable human rights and/or IHL treaties.

The IACHR and Court are increasingly skeptical of the use of military courts to try any offences other than ones related to military discipline, despite the traditional use of such courts to prosecute war crimes. The inter-American Court decision in the *Castillo Petruzzi*[81] case and the

---

and internment of fighters in non-international armed conflicts' (2008) 90 *International Review of the Red Cross*599 613 (hypothesising that an unarmed insurgent commander shopping in a grocery store outside an active zone of combat could be targeted under IHL proportionality but only apprehended and arrested under human rights law).

81　*Case of Castillo Petruzzi et al v Peru* (Merits) Ser C No 34 IACHR (3 November 1997).

Commission's 2002 *Report on terrorism and human rights*[82] indicate that military courts cannot be considered independent or impartial for the purpose of ensuring accountability for human rights violations by the military.

In the *Peruvian Hostages* case, the Commission reiterated that when state agents use lethal force, the state must conduct an independent and impartial investigation to establish whether that use of force adhered to the principles of legality, necessity and proportionality. Military jurisdiction may only be applied in conjunction with an offence against a military criminal legal interest associated with the specific duties of defence and security of the state, and never to investigate human rights abuses. Human rights violations must be investigated, tried, and punished in keeping with the law by the ordinary criminal courts. The IACHR has repeated the underlying rationale for this strict approach:

> The military criminal justice system has certain peculiar characteristics that impede access to an effective an impartial remedy in this jurisdiction. One of these is that the military jurisdiction cannot be considered a real judicial system, as it is not part of the judicial branch, but is organized instead under the Executive. Another aspect is that the judges in the military judicial system are generally active-duty members of the Army, which means that they are in the position of sitting in judgment of their comrades-in-arms, rendering illusory the requirement of impartiality, since the members of the Army often feel compelled to protect those who fight alongside them in a difficult and dangerous context.

The Commission further observed that a military court cannot be an independent and impartial organ to investigate and try human rights violations because the Armed Forces have a 'deep-seated esprit de corps' which is sometimes misinterpreted as requiring them to cover up crimes committed by their fellow soldiers. Similarly, the IACHR considers that impartiality is compromised when military authorities prosecute actions whose active subject is another member of the Army, since investigations into the conduct of members of the security forces carried out by other members of those same forces generally serve to conceal the truth rather than to reveal it.

The Court has agreed that, taking into account the nature of the crime and the juridical right damaged, military criminal jurisdiction is not the competent jurisdiction to investigate, prosecute and punish the authors of violations of human rights. The case of *Ana, Beatriz, and Cecilia Gonzalez Perez v Mexico*[83] provides detail on the requirements of justice. The case involved the gang rape of three indigenous women in Chiapas shortly after

---

82 *Report on terrorism* (n 48 above).
83 *Ana, Beztriz and Cecilia Gonzalez Perez v Mexico* Case 11.565, Report No 53/01, OEA/ser.L/V/II.111, doc, 20 rev IACHR (2000) 1097.

the start of an armed rebellion.[84] The Commission found that any internal investigation and trial in the military justice system for criminal conduct against civilians is inconsistent with a democratic rule of law, reiterating that 'military courts do not meet the requirements of independence and impartiality imposed under article 8(1) of the American Convention'.[85]

6.3　IHL and the scope of other human rights

The Court has used provisions of the Geneva Conventions and Additional Protocol II in interpreting the rights to freedom of movement,[86] property, private and family life,[87] and rights of the child. The last mentioned topic arose in the case of *Vargas Areco v Paraguay*[88] in which the Court condemned as a violation of article 19, on the rights of the child, the recruitment of child soldiers, referring to IHL, the UN Convention on the Rights of the Child, various reports and recommendations, and the Statute of the International Criminal Court.

In the *Mapiripan Massacre* case, the Court similarly held that the content and scope of Convention article 19 (rights of the child) must be specified, in cases of internal armed conflict, by taking into account the pertinent provisions of the Convention on the Rights of the Child and of Protocol II to the Geneva Conventions. The Court found that these instruments and the American Convention are part of 'a very comprehensive international *corpus juris* for protection of children, which the States must respect'. The Court called attention to the specific consequences of the violations on the boys and girls in the case, who were victims of violence, partially orphaned, displaced and suffered damage to their physical and psychological integrity. The Court pointed to the special vulnerability of boys and girls in a situation of domestic armed conflict, since they are least prepared to adapt or respond to said situation and consequently suffer in a disproportionate manner.[89] The Court held that the specific facts of the case demonstrated the lack of protection for children before, during and after the massacre and deemed that the state did not create the conditions or take the necessary steps for the children to have and develop a decent life, but rather exposed them to a climate of

---

84　This case is also notable for its treatment of rape as a form of torture under international law, citing other inter-American instruments as well as decisions of the ICTY and UN documents.
85　*Perez* (n 83 above) para 81.
86　*Mapiripán Massacre* (n 16 above) para 167-169; *Case of the Ituango Massacres v Colombia* Ser C No 148 IACHR (1 July 2006) paras 201-235.
87　*Mapiripán Massacre* (n 16 above)169-200.
88　*Vargas-Areco v Paraguay* (Merits, Reparaitons, and Costs) Ser C No 155 IACrtHR (26 September 2006) paras 111-134.
89　The Court quoted other sources in support of this conclusion, including statements of the United Nations High Commissioner for Human Rights, the United Nations Committee on the Rights of the Child and the Special Representative of the Secretary General of the United Nations in charge of the issue of children in armed conflicts.

violence and insecurity, constituting a breach of article 19 of the Convention.[90]

The problem of abduction of children during armed conflict arose in the case of the *'Las Dos Erres' Massacre v Guatemala.*[91] The Court observed that within the context of an internal armed conflict, the state's obligations toward children are defined in article 4(3) of the Geneva Conventions' Additional Protocol II, which establishes that: 'the children will be provided with the care and help they need, and, particularly: [...] b) the timely measures to facilitate the reunion of the temporarily separated families will be taken [...]'.[92] The Court referred to the 'special gravity' of being able to attribute to a state party to the Convention the charge of having applied or tolerated within its territory a systematic practice of abductions and illegal retention of minors.[93]

In respect to internal displacement of civilians, the Court has found it necessary to define the content and scope of article 22 (freedom of movement) in a context of internal armed conflict with reference to the Guiding Principles on Internal Displacement issued in 1998 by the Representative of the Secretary General of the United Nations and the regulations on displacement included in Protocol II to the 1949 Geneva Conventions:

Specifically, article 17 of Protocol II prohibits ordering the displacement of civilian population for reasons related to the conflict, unless this is required by the safety of civilians or for imperative military reasons, and in the latter case 'all possible measures shall be taken in order that the civilian population may be received under satisfactory conditions of shelter, hygiene, health, safety and nutrition'. In this regard, in a 1995 judgment, the Constitutional Court of Colombia deemed that:

> [I]n the Colombian case, application of these rules by the parties in conflict is also especially imperative and important, because the country's armed conflict has severely affected the civilian population, as shown by the alarming data on forced displacement of persons.

Using these sources and '[t]hrough an evolutive interpretation of article 22 of the Convention, taking into account the applicable provisions regarding

---

90 In the case of the *Ituango Massacres v Colombia* (n 86 above) para 246, the Court referred to the 'aggravated responsibility' of the state due to the consequences of the brutality visited on the children..

91 *'Las Dos Erres' Massacre v Guatemala* (Preliminary Objection, Merits, Reparations and Costs) Ser C, No 211 IACHR (24 November 2009).

92 *'Las Dos Erres' Massacre* (n 91 above) para 191. According to the International Committee of the Red Cross, this obligation has been defined as follows: 'the parties to the conflict should do everything possible to reestablish family ties, that is, not only allow the members of the dispersed families to search for their next of kin, but also facilitate this search'.

93 *'Las Dos Erres' Massacre* (n 91 above) para 199.

interpretation and in accordance with article 29(b) of the Convention', the Court held that article 22(1) of the Convention protects the right to not be forcefully displaced within a state party to the Convention.[94]

The *Case of the Ituango Massacres v Colombia*,[95] also resulted in the Court making specific use of more detailed standards from humanitarian law to interpret a right in the American Convention, in this case the right to property (Convention article 21). Like other cases from Colombia this one concerned state responsibility for acquiescence in or collaboration with paramilitary groups that caused killings of civilians, forced displacement, and loss of property, acts for which the state accepted its responsibility. In response to allegations concerning violations of the right to property, based on the theft of livestock in the context of the internal armed conflict, the Court made the following analysis (at 179):

> When examining the scope of the said article 21 of the Convention in this case, the Court considers it useful and appropriate, in keeping with article 29 thereof, to use international treaties other than the American Convention, such as Protocol II of the Geneva Conventions of August 12, 1949, relating to the protection of victims of non-international armed conflicts, to interpret its provisions in accordance with the evolution of the inter-American system, taking into account the corresponding developments in international humanitarian law. Colombia ratified the Geneva Conventions on November 8, 1961. On August 14, 1995, it acceded to the provisions of the Protocol II to the Geneva Conventions.

In this regard, the Court observes that articles 13 (Protection of the civilian population) and 14 (Protection of the objects indispensable to the survival of the civilian population) of Protocol II of the Geneva Conventions prohibit, respectively, 'acts or threats of violence the primary purpose of which is to spread terror among the civilian population', and also 'to attack, destroy, remove or render useless, for that purpose, objects indispensable to the survival of the civilian population'.

The Court held that the theft of livestock and setting fire to the houses in El Aro constituted grave violations because they involved objects essential to the population, within the terms of Protocol II.[96] The effect of the destruction of the homes was the loss, not only of material possessions, but also of the social frame of reference of the inhabitants, some of whom had lived in the village all their lives. In addition, the destruction of their homes caused the inhabitants to lose their most basic living conditions; this means that the violation of the right to property in this case was deemed particularly grave.

---

94 *Mapiripán Massacre*, (n 16 above) para 188.
95 *Ituango Massacres* (n 86 above).
96 *Mapiripán Massacre*, (n 16 above) paras 182-183.

7   Conclusions

The Inter-American system has become a forum for the enforcement of IHL due to the number of cases presented and reports prepared that concern states in which internal armed conflicts exist. Unlike the European Court of Human Rights, the IACHR and Court have not been reticent about making reference to the Geneva Conventions and Protocols[97] instead of judging operations according to the standards on the use of force developed in the context of law enforcement.[98] The *Peruvian Hostage* case may mark a turning point in this respect, although as of mid-2013 the Court had not yet decided the matter.

In the decisions, reports and judgments they have issued the inter-American organs have contributed to the development of IHL, as well as human rights law. They have assessed the threshold for applying IHL and given content to specific norms. Whether the same results would be reached in a global tribunal or another region is uncertain because few human rights tribunals hear such cases and the international criminal tribunals judge only individual liability and not state responsibility. The inter-American system has thus emerged as one of the most significant in developing jurisprudence on the interrelationship between IHL and human rights law.

The situation may change as other human rights tribunals receive cases arising from internal or international armed conflicts. While it is to be expected that regional bodies will sometimes come to different conclusions about the scope of rights contained in the specific regional human rights instruments, the risk of divergent application of global IHL norms should not be overlooked. It is not at all clear that other human rights bodies would come to the same conclusions as the IACHR or the Court in the *Peruvian Hostage* case or about cattle stealing in Colombia as a violation of IHL.

In the absence of a global IHL forum it is perhaps inevitable that human rights bodies will have to apply IHL and give its norms content as has been done with human rights guarantees over more than half a century, but the risk of global norms being applied differently in one regional or another is certainly present. With appropriate references and knowledge of the jurisprudence of the various systems, a consistent body of developed jurisprudence may emerge. The use of IHL experts in presenting the cases could benefit the tribunals in achieving this goal, since more commissioners and judges are not specialists in IHL. Many tribunals have the power to call or appoint their own experts for cases and should do

---

97   See W Abresch 'A human rights law of internal armed conflict: The European Court of Human Rights in Chechnya' (2005) 16 *European Journal of International Law* 741.
98   Abresch (n 97 above) 742.

so. Otherwise, applicants may also seek to have experts testify in those tribunals that have oral proceedings. As IHL standards are commonly considered to be customary international law and the Geneva Conventions are the most widely ratified treaties in the world, a common understanding and application of IHL norms is a goal worth pursuing.

International Court of Justice and International Criminal Courts

*Gentian Zyberi**

1 Introduction

Besides the International Court of Justice (ICJ) with broad jurisdiction and the two military tribunals for Germany (the Nuremberg Tribunal) and the Far East (Tokyo Tribunal), for a long time there were no international courts and tribunals (ICs) operating in the fields of human rights and humanitarian law. That situation changed radically after the 1990s with the establishment of the two ad hoc tribunals for Yugoslavia and for Rwanda in 1993 and 1994 respectively (ICTY and ICTR) and the International Criminal Court (ICC) in 1998. This trend was followed by the establishment of a number of hybrid tribunals in the early 2000s, as the Bosnian War Crimes Chamber, the Kosovo Mixed Panels and the Special Panels for Serious Crimes in East Timor, the Special Court for Sierra Leone (SCSL) and the Extraordinary Chambers in the Courts of Cambodia (ECCC).[1] International human rights and humanitarian law stand at the basis of international criminal law, as applied before a number of ICs.[2] In the last 20 years many ICs have been closely involved in interpreting and developing international human rights and humanitarian law rules and principles. The role and contribution of these ICs to interpreting and developing human rights and humanitarian law and more generally international law has attracted considerable attention.[3] While national courts and the regional human rights courts have had to deal with

*   Associate Professor of International Law, Norwegian Centre for Human Rights, University of Oslo. Comments and suggestions are welcome at gentian.zyberi@gmail.com.
1   See Cesare PR Romano et al (eds) *Internationalized criminal courts: Sierra Leone, East Timor, Kosovo and Cambodia* (2004).
2   See inter alia M Sassòli 'Humanitarian law and international criminal law' in A Cassese et al (eds) *The Oxford companion to international criminal justice* (2009) 111-120.
3   See inter alia R Goy *La Cour Internationale de Justice et les Droits de l'Homme* (2002); SRS Bedi *The development of human rights law by the judges of the International Court of Justice* (2007); R Higgins 'Human rights in the International Court of Justice' (2007) 20

a number of cases involving the application of international humanitarian and human rights law, they are not dealt with in this chapter.[4]

International courts are an important component of the operating system of international law,[5] which exercise an increasing influence on interpreting and developing the normative content of human rights and humanitarian law. These international judicial mechanisms provide the necessary forums for ensuring the peaceful solution of inter-state disputes concerning human rights and humanitarian law violations, or for prosecuting individuals alleged to have committed mass atrocity crimes, such as genocide, war crimes and crimes against humanity. In dealing with a number of selected topics this chapter shall draw extensively on the case law and activity of the main ICs, namely the ICJ, the two ad hoc tribunals, and the ICC. The ICJ is a court of general jurisdiction settling inter-state disputes and advising the UN's main organs and specialised agencies, whereas the ad hoc tribunals and the ICC are concerned with ensuring individual criminal responsibility for mass atrocity crimes.

As ICs take on ever more important functions and influence, different aspects of their work have come under scrutiny, including the expertise and election procedures of the judges, their role on the bench and their independence.[6] In discussing the legal methodology of international

---

Leiden Journal of International Law 745-751; G Zyberi *The humanitarian face of the International Court of Justice: Its contribution to interpreting and developing international human rights and humanitarian law rules and principles* (2008); S Sivakumaran 'The International Court of Justice and human rights' in S Joseph & A McBeth (eds) *Research handbook on international human rights law* (2010) 299-325; G Zyberi 'Human rights in the International Court of Justice' in M Baderin & M Ssenyonjo (eds) *International Human Rights Law: 60 Years after the UDHR* (2010) 289-304; B Simma 'Human rights before the International Court of Justice: Community interest coming to life' in CJ Tams & J Sloan (eds) *The development of international law by the International Court of Justice* (2013) 301-325; R Wilde 'Human rights beyond borders at the World Court: The significance of the International Court of Justice's jurisprudence on the extraterritorial application of international human rights law treaties', (2013) 12 *Chinese Journal of International Law* 639. See also H Lauterpacht *The development of international law by the International Court* (1958) reprinted 1982; G Boas & WA Schabas (eds) *International criminal law: Developments in the case law of the ICTY* (2003); L van den Herik *The contribution of the Rwanda Tribunal to the development of international law* (2005); S Darcy & J Powderly (eds) *Judicial creativity at the international criminal tribunals* (2010); CJ Tams & J Sloan (eds) *The development of international law by the International Court of Justice* (2013); N Boschiero et al (eds) *International courts and the development of international law: Essays in honour of Tullio Treves* (2013); S Darcy *Judges, law and war: The judicial development of international humanitarian law* (2014).

4   For a detailed discussion of the contribution of the three regional human rights courts see chapters 13, 14, and 15 by F Viljoen, K Oellers-Frahm and D Shelton respectively, in section D (Judicial Perspectives) of this book. For a detailed discussion of the application of IHL by national courts see generally S Weill *The role of national courts in applying international humanitarian law* (2014).

5   For a discussion of the relationship between the normative system and the operating system of international law see inter alia PF Diehl & C Ku *The dynamics of international law* (2010) 28.

6   D Terris et al (eds) *The international judge: An introduction to the men and women who decide the world cases* (2007); D Zimmermann *The independence of international courts: The adherence of the international judiciary to a fundamental value of the administration of justice* (2014).

adjudication, Paulus notes that this methodology requires a process of three steps: a 'positivist' regard for the confines of the judicial task of interpreting existing legal rules; a Dworkinian examination of the foundational principles of an international legal order allowing for legal decisions standing on principle; and a postmodern view of the element of choice involved in any legal interpretation that enables the judge to consciously and transparently apply her own reasoned judgment, subject to the constraints of the law in force.[7] Albeit interesting, issues concerning consistency or a lack thereof in these ICs case law, the issue of law-making or judicial activism, and issues concerning their legitimacy and effectiveness, have been dealt with in detail elsewhere.

First, this chapter will place within a broader perspective the role of ICs in interpreting and developing the relationship between IHRL and IHL by explaining briefly ICs multifaceted functions in the contemporary international legal order. Second, a number of selected topics are dealt with in more detail on the basis of the case law and other relevant activities of ICs. These topics, which are central to both these bodies of law, include the ICs emphasis on fundamental shared values as human dignity and humanity; the extension of legal protection for certain categories of persons against internationally recognised crimes; the issue of reparations for serious violations of human rights and humanitarian law; and, the role of ICs in preventing such serious violations. Finally, a reflection on the contribution of ICs to clarifying the issue of the relationship between human rights and humanitarian law is provided.

2 The function of international courts and tribunals within international law

The prohibition of aggression, genocide, war crimes and crimes against humanity can be said to constitute a shared common interest of the international community, which has been codified in a number of international treaties and has also become part of customary international law. While in terms of primary rules there is a plethora of international human rights and humanitarian law instruments providing protection for individuals, the operating system of international law is lagging behind in terms of ensuring their enforcement. In that sense, ICJ's finding that whether or not states accept its jurisdiction, they remain in any event responsible for acts attributable to them that violate international law, including international humanitarian law and human rights,[8] is little more than cold comfort. The institutional and other limitations of ICs need to be

---

7   A Paulus 'International adjudication' in S Besson & J Tasioulas (eds) *The philosophy of international law* (2010) 207.
8   See inter alia G Zyberi 'Provisional measures of the International Court of Justice in armed conflict situations' (2010) 23 Leiden Journal of International Law (2010) 579. See respectively *Legality of use of force (Yugoslavia v Belgium)*, Provisional Measures

taken into account when discussing their contribution to clarifying the relationship between human rights and humanitarian law. Before looking closely at the contribution of ICs in clarifying the relationship between human rights and humanitarian law, it is important to briefly place their contribution within the broader framework and development of international law, including the law of international responsibility.[9]

The role of ICs is multifaceted and their activity exercises considerable influence not only on international relations and politics, but also at a national level. International courts serve as guardians of community interests and values,[10] which are embedded in many international human rights and humanitarian law treaties, norms of customary international law and general principles of law.[11] While the first and foremost function of ICs remains that of dispute-settlement, as they have expanded both in terms of numbers and scope of jurisdiction, other functions have also been pointed out. Bogdandy and Venzke have discerned four functions for ICs, namely settling disputes, stabilising normative expectations, making law, and controlling and legitimating public authority.[12] Looking at current ICs, Alter distinguishes the following functions: international dispute settlement, international administrative review, international law enforcement and international constitutional review.[13] And, Alvarez points to the dispute-settlement function, the fact-finding function, the law-making function and the governance function.[14] International criminal courts and tribunals play an important, even if symbolic role, in post-conflict societies affected by serious violations of human rights and

Order of 2 June 1999, ICJ Reports 1999, para 48; *Armed activities on the territory of the Congo (New Application: 2002)* (*Democratic Republic of the Congo v Rwanda*), Provisional Measures Order of 10 July 2000, 249, para 93; *Armed activities on the territory of the Congo (New Application: 2002)* (*Democratic Republic of the Congo v Rwanda*), ICJ Reports 2006, 53 para 127.

9   See inter alia NHB Jørgensen *The responsibility of states for international crimes* (2003); BI Bonafè *The relationship between state and individual responsibility for international crimes,* (2009); A Ollivier 'International criminal responsibility of the state' in J Crawford et al (eds) *The law of international responsibility* (2010) 703-715; Elies van Sliedregt *Individual criminal responsibility in international law* (2012); GI Hernández *The International Court of Justice and the judicial function* (2014).

10   See inter alia FO Raimondo 'The International Court of Justice as a guardian of the unity of humanitarian law' (2007) 20 *Leiden Journal of International Law* 593.

11   On the issue of community interests see B Simma 'From bilateralism to community interest in international law' *Recueil des Cours (Collected courses of the Hague Academy of International Law) Vol 250 (1994)* (1997). See also S Villalpando 'The legal dimension of the international community: How community interests are protected in international law' (2010) 21 *European Journal of International Law* 387; U Fastenrath et al (eds) *From bilateralism to community interest: Essays in honour of Bruno Simma* (2011); O Spijkers *The United Nations: The evolution of global values and international law* (2011).

12   A von Bogdandy & I Venzke 'On the functions of international courts: An appraisal in light of their burgeoning public authority' (2013) 26 *Leiden Journal of International Law* 49.

13   KJ Alter *The new terrain of international law: Courts, politics and rights* (2014) 161.

14   JE Alvarez 'What are international judges for? The main functions of international adjudication' in KJ Alter et al (eds) *Oxford handbook of international adjudication* (2014) 158.

humanitarian law.[15] Nollkaemper has categorised international courts themselves as an intermediate public good, which contributes towards the provision of 'final global public goods',[16] as the judicial protection of individuals from mass atrocity crimes. While the discerned functions of ICs might be somewhat different, these authors acknowledge ICs broader role as important actors of the international legal system and international governance.

The activity of ICs in the fields of human rights and humanitarian law should be seen in the context of three inter-related, though not necessarily mutually reinforcing, ongoing processes of international law, namely *humanisation, judicialisation,* and *cosmopolitan justice.* Meron and Cançado Trindade have spoken about the process of *humanisation* of international law.[17] Meron has pointed out that values of humanity must gain dominance if barbarism is to be contained, if not vanquished.[18] For Cançado Trindade this new *jus gentium,* international law for humankind, stems from human conscience, and is erected upon ethical foundations incorporating basic human values, shared by the entire international community and humankind as a whole.[19] On her part, Teitel points out a process of evolution of sources, content, institutions, and agents of international law towards a humanity law.[20] For her, the law of humanity is a framework that spans the law of war, international human rights law, and international criminal justice.[21]

In its first case, the ICJ has evaluated state conduct on the basis of 'elementary considerations of humanity'.[22] On its part, the ICTY has explained a decades-long shift in international law by noting that: 'A State-sovereignty-oriented approach has been gradually supplanted by a human-being-oriented approach.'[23] While these findings should not be taken out of their legal and historical context, they relate these courts' awareness about fundamental values underpinning international law. The process of *judicialisation* is expressed in the multiplication of ICs within a relatively short period and the increased importance of judicial findings in guiding or at least influencing the behaviour of different actors at both the international and the national level. In the context of this discussion, the process of *cosmopolitan justice* is related to the role of ICs within the project

15   G Zyberi 'The role of international courts in post-conflict societies' in I Boerefijn et al (eds) *Human rights and conflict: Essays in honour of Bas de Gaay Fortman* (2012) 367.
16   A Nollkaemper 'International adjudication of global public goods: The intersection of substance and procedure' (2012) 23 *European Journal of International Law* 783.
17   T Meron *The humanization of international law* (2006); AAC Trindade *International law for humankind: Towards a new jus gentium* (2010).
18   Meron (n 17 above) 88-89.
19   Trindade (n 17 above) 637.
20   RG Teitel *Humanity's law* (2011).
21   Teitel (n 20 above) 4.
22   *Corfu Channel Case, (UK v Albania),* (Merits), ICJ Reports 1949, 22.
23   *Prosecutor v Duško Tadić,* Case No IT-94-1-AR72, Decision on the Defence Motion for Interlocutory Appeal on Jurisdiction, 2 October 1995, para 97 (*Tadić Interlocutory Appeal*).

of cosmopolitan law and the human-centred approach that both human rights and humanitarian law embody and which is central to cosmopolitan law.

3   The relationship between human rights and humanitarian law from the perspective of international courts

Much has been written on the nature and scope of the relationship between human rights and humanitarian law over the last decades.[24] While international human rights and humanitarian law have different historical and doctrinal roots, both share the aim of protecting all persons and are grounded in the principles of respect for the life, well-being and human dignity of the person.[25] The ICJ has identified three possible situations concerning the relationship between international human rights and humanitarian law, namely some rights may exclusively be matters of international humanitarian law; others may exclusively be matters of human rights law; yet others may be matters of both these branches of international law.[26] This general finding simply states that the applicable law will depend on the particular situation and the circumstances.

Similar to the three ICJ situations, a group of authors have noted three models of interaction between human rights and humanitarian law, namely the Displacement Model, whereby humanitarian law displaces human rights law entirely in the zone of armed conflict; under the

---

24   For more information see inter alia R Provost *International human rights and humanitarian law* (2002); H Krieger 'A conflict of norms: The relationship between humanitarian law and human rights law in the ICRC customary law study' (2006) 11 *Journal of Conflict and Security Law* 265; R Arnold & N Quénivet (eds) *International humanitarian law and human rights law: Towards a new merger in international law* (2008); A Orakhelashvili 'The interaction between human rights and humanitarian law: Fragmentation, conflict, parallelism, or convergence?' (2008) 19 *European Journal of International Law* 161; O Ben-Naftali (ed) *International humanitarian law and international human rights law: Pas de deux* (2011); A Müller *The relationship between economic, social and cultural rights and international humanitarian law: An analysis of health-related issues in non-international armed conflicts* (2013); Sir D Bethlehem QC 'The relationship between international humanitarian law and international human rights law in situations of armed Conflict' (2013) (2) *Cambridge Journal of International and Comparative Law* 180; C Kreß 'The international court of justice and the law of armed conflicts' in CJ Tams & J Sloan (eds) *The development of international law by the International Court of Justice* (2013) 263. For more information see also the ICRC 'IHL and human rights': http://www.icrc.org/eng/war-and-law/ihl-other-legal-regmies/ihl-human-rights/index.jsp (accessed 24 October 2014).
25   UN Office of the High Commissioner for Human Rights 'International legal protection of human rights in armed conflict' (New York and Geneva, 2011) 7: http://www.ohchr.org/Documents/Publications/HR_in_armed_conflict.pdf (accessed 24 October 2014).
26   *Legal Consequences of the Construction of a Wall in the Occupied Palestinian Territory* Advisory Opinion, ICJ Reports (2004) 178 para 106 (*Wall* Advisory Opinion). See also *Armed Activities on the Territory of the Congo (Democratic Republic of the Congo v Uganda)*, Judgment, ICJ Reports (2005) 242-243 para 216 (*Armed Activities* case).

Complementarity Model, the two bodies of law both apply in armed conflict and are interpreted harmoniously; and under the Conflict Resolution Model, the two bodies of law may both apply in armed conflict but when that is not possible, there are three possible decision rules for choosing between the two bodies of law.[27] These authors argue for the specificity rule, in which the choice between applying human rights law or humanitarian law depends on which is deemed most specific to the given situation.[28] Betlehem has aptly noted that this interaction between human rights and humanitarian law could take a number of forms:

(1) HRL might act as a gateway for the application of IHL by way of *renvoi*;
(2) HRL might give effect to a relevant but otherwise inapplicable provision of IHL;
(3) HRL might inform the interpretation of IHL, including possibly by supplementing or completing the IHL rule;
(4) HRL might prevail over inconsistent IHL;
(5) HRL might fill in the gaps in circumstances in which there is no relevant IHL provision;
(6) HRL might augment IHL through HRL procedural and accountability mechanisms.[29]

These six different possibilities highlight the complex interaction between these bodies of law.

The interplay between human rights and humanitarian law has received some attention in ICTY's case law. This tribunal has pointed at the convergence between human rights and humanitarian law by noting that: 'The laws of war do not necessarily displace the laws regulating a peacetime situation; the former may add elements requisite to the protection which needs to be afforded to victims in a wartime situation.'[30] Following that line of reasoning, the ICTY has added that:

Because of the paucity of precedent in the field of international humanitarian law, the Tribunal has, on many occasions, had recourse to instruments and practices developed in the field of human rights law. Because of their resemblance, in terms of goals, values and terminology, such recourse is generally a welcome and needed assistance to determine the content of customary international law in the field of humanitarian law. With regard to certain of its aspects, international humanitarian law can be said to have fused with human rights law.[31]

---

27 OA Hathaway et al 'Which law governs during armed conflict? The relationship between international humanitarian law and human rights law' (2012) 96 *Minnesota Law Review* 1883-1944 1942-1943.
28 Hathaway et al (n 27 above) 1943.
29 Bethlehem (n 24 above) 195.
30 See *Prosecutor v Dragoljub Kunarac, Radomir Kovac and Zoran Vukovic*, Case No IT-96-23& IT-96-23/1-A, Appeals Chamber Judgment, 12 June 2002, para 60 (*Kunarac Appeals Judgment*).
31 ICTY, *Prosecutor v Dragoljub Kunarac, Radomir Kovac and Zoran Vukovic*, Case No IT-96-23& IT-96-23/1-T, Judgment, 22 February 2001, para 467 (*Kunarac Trial Judgment*).

While the ICTY has used human rights to inform the interpretation of IHL, including possibly by supplementing or completing the IHL rule, it has also noted two crucial structural differences between human rights and humanitarian law, namely:

(i) Firstly, the role and position of the state as an actor is completely different in both regimes.
(ii) Secondly, that part of international criminal law applied by the Tribunal is a penal law regime. It sets one party, the prosecutor, against another, the defendant. In the field of international human rights, the respondent is the state.

On the one hand the ICTY has noted the vertical relationship between an individual and the state under international human rights law, and on the other hand it has emphasised that international humanitarian law purports to apply equally to and expressly bind all parties to the armed conflict.[32] With regard to the second structural difference the ICTY has noted that this has been expressed by the fact that human rights law establishes lists of protected rights whereas international criminal law (ICL) establishes lists of offences.[33] IHL has a dual nature, in that like ICL it establishes a list of offences with its system of grave breaches, while at the same time, just like human rights it also establishes a list of protected rights. The structural differences between these closely related branches of international law add many nuances to their relationship.

In situations of armed conflict, and more specifically with regard to the conduct of hostilities between the parties to an armed conflict, the *lex specialis* is IHL. The ICJ has dealt with the concurrent application of IHRL and IHL in the context of an armed conflict in a number of cases. Thus, in dealing with the relationship between the International Covenant on Civil and Political Rights (ICCPR) and IHL concerning the right to life, the ICJ has found that:

> In principle, the right not arbitrarily to be deprived of one's life applies also in hostilities. The test of what is an arbitrary deprivation of life, however, then falls to be determined by the applicable *lex specialis*, namely, the law applicable in armed conflict which is designed to regulate the conduct of hostilities. Thus whether a particular loss of life, through the use of a certain weapon in warfare, is to be considered an arbitrary deprivation of life contrary to article 6 of the Covenant, can only be decided by reference to the law applicable in armed conflict and not deduced from the terms of the Covenant itself.[34]

The approach to the right of life is an area where human rights and humanitarian law probably differ the most, in that the first generally

---

32   *Kunarac Trial Judgment* para 470.
33   As above.
34   *Legality of the Threat or Use of Nuclear Weapons*, Advisory Opinion, ICJ Reports 1996, 240 para 25 (*Nuclear Weapons* Advisory Opinion).

applies a law-enforcement paradigm, whereas the second generally applies the combatant's privilege and fundamental principles of IHL.

With regard to the applicability of the International Covenant on Economic, Social and Cultural Rights (ICESCR) the ICJ has found this Covenant as applicable to occupied territories which are subject to a State's territorial jurisdiction as the Occupying Power.[35] Furthermore, the Court has noted that the Occupying Power would be under an obligation not to raise any obstacle to the exercise of such rights in those fields where competence has been transferred to national authorities.[36] Other human rights treaties found applicable in a situation of occupation are the Convention on the Rights of the Child,[37] the 2000 Optional Protocol to the Convention on the Rights of the Child on the Involvement of Children in Armed Conflict,[38] and the African Charter on Human and Peoples' Rights.[39] The ICJ has concluded that international human rights instruments are applicable 'in respect of acts done by a State in the exercise of its jurisdiction outside its own territory' particularly in occupied territories.[40] Partly, by taking into account this case law, the International Law Commission (ILC) has taken the position that, amongst others, treaties for the international protection of human rights continue in operation, in whole or in part, during armed conflict.[41] Non-derogable provisions of human rights treaties apply *during* armed conflict.[42] Moreover, there is a growing consensus that derogable provisions may apply as well.[43] The following subsections discuss a number of areas where ICs have contributed to clarifying or enhancing understanding of the relationship between human rights and humanitarian law, namely human dignity and humanity; the extension of legal protection for certain categories of persons against internationally recognised crimes; the issue of reparations for serious violations of human rights and humanitarian law; and the role of ICs in preventing such violations.

---

35 *Wall* Advisory Opinion 181 para 112.
36 As above.
37 *Wall* Advisory Opinion 181 para 113; *Armed Activities* case 244 para 217.
38 *Armed Activities* case 244 para 217.
39 As above.
40 *Wall* Advisory Opinion 178-181 paras 107-113. For a detailed discussion see Wilde (n 3 above).
41 See article 7 of the Draft Articles on the Effects of Armed Conflicts on Treaties and the Annex with the indicative list of treaties referred to in article 7, in Yearbook of the International Law Commission, 2011, vol. II, Part Two.
42 Secretariat Memorandum 'The effect of armed conflict on treaties: An examination of practice and doctrine' UN Doc A/CN.4/550 and Corr.1, para 32 (footnotes omitted, emphasis in original): http://legal.un.org/ilc/sessions/57/57docs.htm (accessed 24 October 2014).
43 Secretariat Memorandum (n 42 above) para 34.

3.1　Human dignity and humanity as core values and means of interpretation

Two core values underpinning both human rights and humanitarian law norms are those of human dignity and humanity. The principle of humanity is oftentimes cited as a general principle of international humanitarian law, which finds expression in many IHL provisions whether they regulate international or non-international armed conflicts.[44] These core values have been used by ICs to interpret treaties and specific provisions of human rights and humanitarian law. The ICJ has developed the law of international responsibility by using a vague test of 'elementary considerations of humanity' in assessing state conduct vis-a-vis other states, both in peace-time or in a situation of armed conflict.[45] A couple of years later, in dealing with the issue of reservations to the 1948 Genocide Convention the ICJ noted that the object of this Convention 'is to safeguard the very existence of certain human groups and ... to confirm and endorse the most *elementary principles of humanity*'.[46] In contrast to these findings, the ICJ has also held that humanitarian considerations are not sufficient in themselves to generate legal rights and obligations.[47] Although in a cursory manner, the Court has tried to draw a distinction between moral principles and rules of law which create legal rights and obligations.[48] While it is difficult to say whether the ICJ considers *'elementary considerations of humanity'* and *'elementary principles of humanity'* as the same concept, both appear to have a basis in customary international law.

In the *Kupreškić* case, an ICTY Trial Chamber referred to the 'progressive trend towards the so-called "humanisation" of international legal obligations ...' and in particular, to the Martens Clause, which, as a minimum, enjoins reference to the 'principles of humanity' and 'the dictates of public conscience (...) and dictates any time a rule of international humanitarian law is not sufficiently rigorous or precise: in those instances the scope and purport of the rule must be defined with reference to those principles and dictates.'[49] According to Chetail, arguably, the Martens Clause enables one to look beyond treaty law and

---

44　See inter alia S Vité 'Typology of armed conflicts in international humanitarian law: Legal concepts and actual situations' (2009) 91 *International Review of the Red Cross* 69. There have been calls for a single definition of armed conflict; see inter alia JG Stewart 'Towards a single definition of armed conflict in international humanitarian law: A critique of internationalized armed conflict' (2003) 85 *International Review of the Red Cross* 313.

45　*Corfu Channel Case, (UK v Albania)*, (Merits), ICJ Reports 1949, 22.

46　*Reservations to the Convention on the Prevention and Punishment of the Crime of Genocide* (Advisory Opinion), ICJ Reports 1951, 23 (emphasis added).

47　*South West Africa Cases (Ethiopia v South Africa; Liberia v South Africa)*, Second Phase, Judgment, ICJ Reports 1966, 34 para 49.

48　*South West Africa Cases* (n 47 above) 49-50.

49　*Prosecutor v Kupreškić et al* Case No IT-95-16-T, Judgment, 14 January 2000, paras 518 and 525 (*Kupreškić Trial Judgment*).

customary law, and to consider *principles of humanity* and the dictates of the public conscience as separate and legally binding yardsticks.[50] While generally ICs are attuned to public opinion, it is not easy to construe or translate the dictates of the public conscience into clear legal obligations, as Chetail seems to suggest. The approach suggested by the ICTY in *Kupreškić*, that is, using these basic concepts as subsidiary means of interpretation for filling in legal gaps, contributes to the progressive development of international law.

The application of 'elementary considerations of humanity' has been extended by the ICTY to interpreting and applying loose international rules on precautions in attack as spelled out in articles 57 and 58 of the First Additional Protocol of 1977, on the basis that they are illustrative of a general principle of international law.[51] The same humanitarian considerations are applied to prohibited means of warfare by the ICTY Appeals Chamber in *Tadić*. Thus, the Appeals Chamber has found that:

> Indeed, elementary considerations of humanity and common sense make it preposterous that the use by States of weapons prohibited in armed conflicts between themselves be allowed when States try to put down rebellion by their own nationals on their own territory. What is inhumane, and consequently proscribed, in international wars, cannot but be inhumane and inadmissible in civil strife.[52]

In bridging the gap between international and non-international armed conflict and enhancing protection, the ICTY Appeals Chamber has found that, 'Principles and rules of humanitarian law reflect "elementary considerations of humanity" widely recognized as the mandatory minimum for conduct in armed conflicts of any kind'.[53] Through these broad findings international courts have helped bridge the protection gap between international and non-international armed conflicts.

The ICTY has defined persecution as 'the gross or blatant denial, on discriminatory grounds, of a fundamental right, laid down in international customary or treaty law, reaching the same level of gravity as the other acts prohibited in article 5 [of the ICTY Statute]',[54] which deals with crimes against humanity. However, the ICTY has also noted that, '[a]lthough the realm of human rights is dynamic and expansive, not every denial of a human right may constitute a crime against humanity'.[55] These differences relate amongst others also to the gravity threshold which makes crimes against humanity and war crimes different from domestic crimes.

---

50 V Chetail 'The contribution of the International Court of Justice to international humanitarian law' (2003) 85 *International Review of the Red Cross* 258.
51 *Kupreškić Trial Judgment*, para 524.
52 *Tadić Interlocutory Appeal*, para 119.
53 *Tadić Interlocutory Appeal*, para 129.
54 *Kupreškić Trial Judgment*, para 621.
55 *Kupreškić Trial Judgment*, para 618.

Depriving civilians or prisoners of war of relief will in many cases be contrary to the principle of humanity and therefore constitute inhuman treatment and a violation of human dignity.[56] The ICTY has emphasised this in the following words:

> It is unquestionable that the prohibition of acts constituting outrages upon personal dignity safeguards an important value. Indeed, it is difficult to conceive of a more important value than that of respect for the human personality. It can be said that the entire edifice of international human rights law, and of the evolution of international humanitarian law, rests on this founding principle.[57]

The overall protection that the general principle of humanity grants under IHL is threefold: first, non-combatants enjoy general protection against the effects of hostilities in that they must be spared and treated humanely; second, combatants are protected from unnecessary suffering and superfluous injury; and third, there is the continuing general protection under the Martens Clause, providing that civilians and combatants remain under the protection and authority of the principles of international law derived from the principles of humanity. The general guarantee of humane treatment based on elementary considerations of humanity is a commonly shared foundation for both human rights and humanitarian law, which international courts have used to strengthen the protection accruing to individuals as human beings in situations of armed conflict.

3.2　Specific protection for certain categories of persons and against serious crimes

An important area of ICs contribution is that of clarifying and laying down the standards of treatment of certain categories of persons and by the same token, of the conduct of parties to armed hostilities. By and large, this function of ICs relates to what Bogdandy and Venzke have noted as

---

56　See inter alia C Rottensteiner 'The denial of humanitarian assistance as a crime under international law' (1999) 81 *International Review of the Red Cross* 555.

57　ICTY, *Prosecutor v Zlatko Aleksovski*, Case No IT-95-14/1-T (25 June 1999) para 54. See also paras 50-51 providing (footnotes omitted): '50. The International Court of Justice held, in the Nicaragua case, that common article 3, though conventional in origin, has crystallised into customary international law and sets out the mandatory minimum rules applicable in armed conflicts of any kind, constituting as they are "elementary considerations of humanity". 51. The general proscription in common article 3 is against inhuman treatment. It is instructive to take account of the elements of the offence proposed by the International Committee of the Red Cross ("the ICRC") to the Preparatory Commission for the International Criminal Court to assist the latter in its efforts to elaborate the elements of the crimes under paragraph 2 (a) of article 8 of the Rome Statute of the International Criminal Court, being the statutory provision recognising the grave breaches regime of the Geneva Conventions. After analysing the results of its extensive research into the "sources of law", the ICRC determined that the material element of inhuman treatment is satisfied when the act or omission of the perpetrator caused serious physical or mental suffering or injury upon the person or constituted a serious attack on human dignity. As for the mental element, the ICRC noted that it is satisfied when the perpetrator acted wilfully.'

stabilising normative expectations and making law. The large number, as well as the depth and breadth of the case law of ICs, allows only for highlighting a limited number of important findings of these ICs. Some of these international legal norms, such as the prohibition of genocide, have attained the status of peremptory norms of international law or *jus cogens*.[58] Notably, the ICJ has emphasised two cardinal principles contained in the texts constituting the fabric of humanitarian law, namely the *principle of distinction* between civilians and combatants and that of *prohibition of unnecessary suffering to combatants*.[59] In laying down a standard of conduct with regard to the protection of civilians, this court has found that: 'States must never make civilians the object of attack and must consequently never use weapons that are incapable of distinguishing between civilian and military targets.'[60] Under the second cardinal principle, it is prohibited to cause unnecessary suffering to combatants: it is accordingly prohibited to use weapons causing them such harm or uselessly aggravating their suffering.[61] In application of that second principle, the ICJ has noted that states do not have unlimited freedom of choice of means in the weapons they use.[62] Also, the ICJ has found that the rules included in common article 3 of the 1949 Geneva Conventions constitute a minimum yardstick, in addition to the more elaborate rules which are also to apply to international conflicts; and they are rules which reflect what the Court in 1949 called 'elementary considerations of humanity'.[63] The ICTY has extended protection to persons under IHL not only based on the nationality requirement, but also based on 'substantial relations' of allegiance rather on 'formal bonds' of nationality.[64] Taken together, these findings lay down a basic level of protection under IHL for both civilians and combatants.

In a recent case, the ICJ noted three categories of violations of humanitarian law committed by German forces in Italy during the Second World War (WWII), namely large-scale *killing of civilians* in occupied territory as part of a policy of reprisals, the *deportation of civilian population* from Italy to what was in substance slave labour in Germany, and *denial* to members of the Italian armed forces *of the status of prisoner of war*, together with the protections which that status entailed, to which they were entitled and who were similarly used as forced labourers.[65] The ICJ considered

---

58   *Armed Activities on the Territory of the Congo (New Application: 2002) (Democratic Republic of the Congo v Rwanda)*, ICJ Reports 2006, 32 para 64.
59   *Nuclear Weapons* Advisory Opinion, 257 para 78.
60   As above.
61   As above.
62   As above.
63   *Military and Paramilitary Activities in and against Nicaragua (Nicaragua v United States of America)*, (Merits), ICJ Reports 1986, 113-114, paras 218-219 (*Nicaragua* case).
64   *Tadić Appeals Judgment*, para 166; *Aleksovski Appeals Judgment*, paras 149-152; *Blaškić Appeals Judgment*, paras 174-182: http://icty.org/action/cases (accessed 25 October 2014). See inter alia L Vierucci 'Protected persons' in Cassese et al (eds) (n 2 above) 473-474.
65   *Jurisdictional Immunities of the State (Germany v Italy: Greece intervening), Judgment*, ICJ Reports 2012, 121 para 52 (*Jurisdictional Immunities* case).

that the acts in question could only be described as displaying a complete disregard for the 'elementary considerations of humanity' and that such conduct was a serious violation of the international law of armed conflict applicable in 1943-1945.[66]

With regard to detention of civilians, an ICTY Trial Chamber in the *Kordić* case has held their imprisonment would be unlawful where:

- civilians have been detained in contravention of article 42 of the Geneva Convention IV, i.e. they are detained without reasonable grounds to believe that the security of the Detaining Power makes it absolutely necessary;
- the procedural safeguards required by article 43 of the Geneva Convention IV are not complied with in respect of detained civilians, even where initial detention may have been justified; and
- they occur as part of a widespread or systematic attack directed against a civilian population.[67]

This finding of the ICTY has provided some clarification regarding an issue which has been particularly problematic in the context of the armed conflicts in the former Yugoslavia.

Finally, ICTY findings have also been important with regard to firmly establishing the prohibition of torture under international law as a *jus cogens* norm. Thus, the ICTY has found that the presence of a state official or of any other authority-wielding person in the torture process is not necessary for the offence to be regarded as torture under international humanitarian law.[68] This finding expands the protection accruing to individuals under human rights, respectively under article 1 of the 1984 Convention Against Torture. In the *Obligation to Prosecute or Extradite* case, the ICJ noted that the prohibition of torture is also part of customary international law and it has become a *jus cogens* norm.[69] In a finding of a general nature, the ICTY has held that most norms of international humanitarian law, in particular those prohibiting war crimes, crimes against humanity and genocide, are also peremptory norms of international law or *jus cogens*, that is, of a non-derogable and overriding character.[70] While Kreß has noted the reluctance of the ICJ to recognise the *jus cogens* character of the core of the law of armed conflicts,[71] the ICTY seems to have covered this ground in its case law.

---

66   As above.
67   *Prosecutor v Dario Kordić and Mario Čerkez*, Case No IT-95-14/2-T, (26 February 2001) (*Kordić Trial Judgement*) para 303.
68   *Kunarac Trial Judgment*, para 496. See also *Prosecutor v Miroslav Kvočka, Mlađo Radić, Zoran Žigić, Dragoljub Prcać*, Case No IT-98-30/1-A (28 February 2005) para 284 (*Kvočka Appeals Judgement*).
69   *Questions Relating to the Obligation to Prosecute or Extradite (Belgium v Senegal)*, Judgment, ICJ Reports 2012, 457 para 99 (*Obligation to Prosecute of Extradite*).
70   *Kupreškić Trial Judgment*, para 520.
71   Kreß (n 24 above) 296.

3.3 Reparations for serious violations of human rights and humanitarian law

The issue of reparations for violations of human rights and humanitarian law is very important not only for the individual victims, but also for the society and the international community more generally. While considerable progress has been made in this regard as a matter of substantive law, the practice of awarding reparations remains quite limited. In the *Case Concerning the Factory at Chorzów* (the *Chorzów Factory* case), the Permanent Court of International Justice found that:

> The essential principle contained in the actual notion of an illegal act ... is that reparation must, as far as possible, wipe out all the consequences of the illegal act and re-establish the situation which would, in all probability, have existed if that act had not been committed.[72]

The ICJ has made a number of relevant findings concerning reparations for violations of human rights and humanitarian law.[73] Thus, in the *Wall* Advisory Opinion, the ICJ found that Israel was under an obligation to make reparation for the damage caused to all the natural or legal persons affected by the construction of the wall in the Occupied Palestinian Territory.[74] This was the first time that the court indicated reparations directly for natural or legal persons. The court referred to restitution as first amongst essential forms of reparation under customary law, and if that would prove materially impossible to the obligation to compensate the persons concerned for the damage suffered.[75] In the *Armed Activities* case, the ICJ made an explicit finding for the first time in the *dispositif* of a judgment about a state having violated its obligations under international human rights law and international humanitarian law and being under obligation to make reparation for the injury caused.[76] The court has also clarified that in ruling on reparation claims it must ascertain whether, and to what extent, the injury is the consequence of wrongful conduct with the consequence that the respondent party should be required to make

---

72 *Case Concerning the Factory at Chorzow*, Merits, PCIJ Series A No 17 (1928) 47.
73 See respectively the *Nicaragua* case 149 para 292; *Wall* Advisory Opinion 197-198 paras 147-153; *Armed Activities* case 82 para 259; *Application of the Genocide Convention* case, pp. 233-234 paras 461-462.
74 *Wall* Advisory Opinion 198 para 152.
75 *Wall* Advisory Opinion paras 152-153.
76 *Armed Activities* case 280-281 paras 345(3) and (5). In paragraph 3 the court found that: 'Uganda, by the conduct of its armed forces, which committed acts of killing, torture and other forms of inhumane treatment of the Congolese civilian population, destroyed villages and civilian buildings, failed to distinguish between civilian and military targets and to protect the civilian population in fighting with other combatants, trained child soldiers, incited ethnic conflict and failed to take measures to put an end to such conflict; as well as by its failure, as an occupying Power, to take measures to respect and ensure respect for human rights and international humanitarian law in Ituri district, violated its obligations under international human rights law and international humanitarian law.'

reparation for it.[77] The court has required the establishment of a sufficiently direct and certain *causal nexus* between the wrongful act and the injury suffered (consisting of all damage of any type, material or moral), based the case as a whole and with a sufficient degree of certainty that the violation would in fact have been averted if the state had acted in compliance with its legal obligations.[78] Requiring such a strict causal nexus when it comes to establishing state responsibility to make reparations for mass atrocity crimes does not promote responsible state behaviour.

Another important aspect of the topic of reparations for serious violations of human rights and humanitarian law is that of state immunity from legal proceedings in foreign domestic courts. In a recent case, the ICJ upheld state immunity from civil claims in foreign domestic courts based on violations of international humanitarian law.[79] At the same time, the court drew a distinction between the question of whether a state is entitled to immunity before the courts of another state and whether the international responsibility of that state is engaged, including the obligation to make reparation for such violations.[80] The court found no basis in the state practice from which customary international law is derived that international law makes the entitlement of a state to immunity dependent upon the existence of effective alternative means of securing redress.[81] These findings of the ICJ reflect the unsatisfactory international legal framework when it comes to ensuring individual reparations for serious violations of human rights and humanitarian law.

The ICC has been entrusted with ensuring reparations for serious violations of human rights and humanitarian law, in the situations where it is involved.[82] A ground-laying judgment in this regard is that rendered by the ICC in the *Lubanga Dyilo* case.[83] There the ICC laid down the principles and modalities of reparations, including the principles of

77　*Application of the Genocide Convention* case 233 para 462.
78　As above.
79　*Jurisdictional Immunities* case 154-155 para 139(1) and (3).
80　*Jurisdictional Immunities* case 143 para 100.
81　*Jurisdictional Immunities* case 143 para 101.
82　See arts 75 (Reparations to victims) and 79 (Trust Fund) of the ICC Statute. For a commentary see WA Schabas *The International Criminal Court: A commentary on the Rome Statute* (2010) 878–883 and 909-917. For more information see also the ICC Trust Fund for Victims: www.trustfundforvictims.org/homepage (accessed 25 October 2014).
83　*The Prosecutor v Thomas Lubanga Dyilo*, Case No ICC-01/04-01/06, Decision Establishing the Principles and Procedures to Be Applied to Reparations (7 August 2012) especially paras 217-250, listing restitution, compensation, rehabilitation and other modalities of reparations (*Lubanga Dyilo* case).

dignity, non-discrimination and non-stigmatisation.[84] An important finding of the Trial Chamber is that reparations can be directed at particular individuals, as well as contributing more broadly to the communities that were affected.[85] That legal finding has a basis on Rule 97(1) of the ICC Rules, whereby 'the Court may award reparations on an individualized basis or, where it deems it appropriate, on a collective basis or both'. Notably, the Chamber has emphasised that it shall treat the victims with humanity and it shall respect their dignity and human rights; that reparations shall be granted to victims without adverse distinction; and, that reparations should avoid further stigmatisation of the victims and discrimination by their families and communities.[86] Importantly, the ICC has found that in accordance with article 21(3) of its Statute, the implementation of reparations:

> [M]ust be consistent with internationally recognized human rights and be without any adverse distinction founded on grounds such as gender ... age, race, colour, language, religion or belief, political or other opinion, national, ethnic or social origin, wealth, birth or other status.[87]

Article 75 of the ICC Statute lists restitution, compensation and rehabilitation as forms of reparations, but as the Chamber has held in *Lubanga*, this list is not exclusive and would include also other types of reparations, for instance those with a symbolic, preventative or transformative value, as appropriate.[88] Although the ICC can tailor reparations to fit the circumstances of the cases brought before it, its possibilities are limited since the funds available for that purpose are made available to the Trust Fund on a voluntary basis.

While possible under its Rules of Procedure and Evidence (RPE), so far the ICTY has not ordered any reparations for victims.[89] In October 2000, the judges of the ICTY, through their President, suggested to the UN Security Council that the appropriate UN organs should consider creating a special mechanism for reparations in the form of a claims commission for

---

84 For a detailed discussion of this topic see inter alia C McCarthy 'Reparations under the Rome Statute of the International Criminal Court and reparative justice theory' (2009) 3 *International Journal of Transitional Justice* 250–271; L Zegveld 'Victims' reparations claims and International Criminal Courts: Incompatible values?' (2010) 8 *Journal of International Criminal Justice* 79-111; S Zappala 'The rights of victims v the rights of the accused' (2010) 8 *Journal of International Criminal Justice* 137-164.
85 *Lubanga Dyilo* case, para 179.
86 *Lubanga Dyilo* case, paras 187-193.
87 *Lubanga Dyilo* case, para 184.
88 *Lubanga Dyilo* case, para 222. See also paras 222-241.
89 Rule 105 of the ICTY Rules of Procedure and Evidence provides for the restitution of property and Rule 106 provides for compensation to victims. These rules are yet to be used.

the former Yugoslavia.[90] In the Completion Strategy Reports submitted to the Security Council from November 2009 to November 2012, the President of the ICTY called upon the Security Council to take action and establish a trust fund for victims of crimes falling within the tribunal's jurisdiction, to complement the tribunal's criminal trials by providing victims with the resources necessary to rebuild their lives.[91] A similar request was made by the ICTY President during his address to the UN General Assembly in November 2011.[92] The tribunal has acknowledged that other remedies must complement the criminal trials, if lasting peace is to be achieved, including providing adequate reparations to the victims for their suffering.[93] However, the political will on the part of the UN or the states directly concerned to address this issue in a comprehensive manner is clearly lacking. While these ICs established to investigate and prosecute serious violations of human rights and humanitarian law can award reparations both on an individual and collective basis (as appropriate), that part of their activity seems subject to considerable limitations, both of a legal and practical nature. The lengthy legal proceedings before these courts mean that victims of these serious crimes will have to wait for several years and there is no certainty that there will be sufficient funds to address the serious harm suffered by them.

3.4   The role of international courts in preventing serious violations

Besides their function of settling inter-state disputes and investigating and prosecuting individuals for violations of human rights and humanitarian law, ICs have the potential to help in the prevention of violations of human rights and humanitarian law. This potentially preventive effect is exercised either directly in the course of their judicial activity, or through the indirect effect that the mere possibility of being subjected to judicial proceedings has on the behaviour of states or non-state actors. Arguably, provisional

---

90   See the letter addressed to the UN Secretary-General by the President of the ICTY, UN Doc S/2000/1063 (dated 12 October 2000), in Appendix 'Victims' compensation and participation', 18 para 48. President Jorda stated that the judges, prosecutors, defence counsel and legal officers at the Tribunal agreed that the need, or even the right, of the victims to obtain compensation is fundamental for restoration of the peace and reconciliation in the Balkans.

91   See respectively the following Completion Strategy Reports: S/2009/589 (13 November 2009) paras 57-58; S/2010/270 (1 June 2010) paras 69-70; S/2010/588 (19 November 2010) para 78; S/2011/316 (18 May 2011) paras 89-90; S/2011/716 (16 November 2011) paras 58-59; S/2012/354 (23 May 2012) paras 61-62; and S/2012/847 (19 November 2012) paras 60-61.

92   'President Robinson's address before the United Nations General Assembly' Press Release VE/MOW/PR1460e (11 November 2011): www.icty.org/sid/10850 (accessed 25 October 2014).

93   ICTY Completion Strategy Report, S/2012/847 (19 November 2012) para 61.

measures by the ICJ,[94] and preliminary investigations and statements by the ICC Prosecutor carry the potential to change the behaviour and actions of states or non-state actors involved in activities that might violate human rights and humanitarian law. The UN Secretary-General has noted that threat of referrals to ICC can undoubtedly serve a preventive purpose.[95]

Rosenne has pointed out that, as a time honoured attribute of the judicial mission courts should, within the limits of the judicial function, do what they can to prevent the escalation of the conflict between the litigating parties.[96] In several armed conflict situations the ICJ has indicated provisional measures, which call on the parties to a dispute to respect human rights and humanitarian law obligations.[97] These provisional measures could prove important in the long term, despite the unsatisfactory record of compliance with them and a little-developed procedure and possibilities for the ICJ to effectively monitor such compliance.

4   Concluding remarks

As de Wet and Kleffner have noted at the introduction of this book, human rights and humanitarian law provide the most pertinent regulatory framework for the conduct of non-international armed conflicts, belligerent occupation and peace operations. The contribution of ICs to clarifying the relationship and the similarities and differences between human rights and humanitarian law and their relationship in the context of the conduct of non-international armed conflicts, belligerent occupation and peace operations is manifold. Fulfilling these manifold functions is not an easy task for ICs, given the challenges involved in the interpretation and

---

94   On the issue of provisional measures see inter alia L Collins 'Provisional and protective measures in international litigation' *Recueil des Cours de la Académie de Droit International de la Haye, Volume 234, 1992-III* (1992); R Bernhardt (ed) *Interim measures indicated by international courts* (1994); S Rosenne *Provisional measures in international law: The International Court of Justice and the International Tribunal for the Law of the Sea* (2005); C Brown *A common law of international adjudication* (2007) 119-151; CB Herrera *Provisional measures in the case law of the Inter-American Court of Human Rights* (2010); E Rieter *Preventing irreparable harm: Provisional measures in international human rights adjudication* (2010); Zyberi (n 8 above) 571-584.

95   UNSG Report 'Responsibility to protect: Timely and decisive response' (July 2012) UN Doc A/66/874-S/2012/578, 25, para 29.

96   S Rosenne 'A role for the International Court of Justice in crisis management' in Kreijen et al (eds) *State, sovereignty, and international governance* (2002) 181.

97   See inter alia the provisional measures in the *Application of the Convention on the Prevention and Punishment of the Crime of Genocide* (*Bosnia and Herzegovina v Serbia and Montenegro*) (Provisional Measures), ICJ Reports 1993 3; *Armed Activities on the Territory of the Congo* (*Democratic Republic of Congo v Uganda*), (Provisional Measures) ICJ Reports 2000 111; *Application of the International Convention on the Elimination of All Forms of Racial Discrimination* (*Georgia v Russian Federation*) (Provisional Measures) ICJ Reports 2008 353; *Certain Activities Carried Out by Nicaragua in the Border Area* (*Costa Rica v Nicaragua*) (Provisional Measures) ICJ Reports 2011 6; *Request for Interpretation of the Judgment of 15 June 1962 in the Case concerning the Temple of Preah Vihear* (*Cambodia v Thailand*) (Provisional Measures) ICJ Reports 2011 537.

application of international law in view of the legal and social fragmentation of the contemporary legal order.[98] A significant limitation to the role of ICs in enforcing and interpreting human rights and humanitarian law obligations is imposed by existing jurisdictional hurdles,[99] the potential for conflicting decisions, the incremental nature of judicial findings and issues concerning the legitimacy of ICs in pushing the boundaries of international law. That notwithstanding, the case law of the ICs has contributed to what Meron has defined as the humanisation of international law.[100] Simma has pointed at the process of mainstreaming of human rights by the ICJ into the body of general public international law.[101] Thus, besides the immediate aim of settling inter-state disputes or prosecuting individuals for mass atrocity crimes, their judicial activity has laid down standards of conduct for states, individuals and non-state actors more generally.

Largely, the case law of the ICs with regard to the relationship between IHRL and IHL and the fundamental values of these branches of international law seems to reflect a cautious methodological approach, whereas when dealing with specific issues some ICs, and especially the international criminal courts and tribunals, have adopted a progressive development approach. If one were to make a broad comparison with the methodology employed by the International Law Commission (ILC), the methodological approach of ICs has fluctuated between that of 'codification', where ICs have endorsed existing mainstream legal opinion, and progressive development, where ICs have developed under-regulated areas of international law, especially the law concerning non-international armed conflict. Through their case law and other activities, including outreach activities and engagement in a dialogue with other courts and international institutions, ICs have helped clarify the relationship between human rights and humanitarian law, as well as contributed to their enforcement.

---

98   See inter alia Report of the Study Group of the International Law Commission, finalised by M Koskenniemi 'Fragmentation of international law: Difficulties arising from the diversification and expansion of international law' UN Doc A/CN.4/L.682 (13 April 2006). The fears of such fragmentation were played down by the Presidents of the ICJ and the ICTY. See respectively, Speech by HE Judge Rosalyn Higgins, President of the International Court of Justice, to the General Assembly of the United Nations, 26 October 2006: http://www.icj-cij.org (accessed 25 October 2014); and President Pocar's speech to the United Nations General Assembly presented on 9 October 2006: http://icty.org (accessed 25 October 2014).

99   *Armed Activities on the Territory of the Congo (New Application: 2002)(Democratic Republic of the Congo v Rwanda)*, Jurisdiction and Admissibility, Judgment, ICJ Reports 2006, 52 para 125. There the ICJ deemed it necessary to recall that 'the mere fact that rights and obligations *erga omnes* or peremptory norms of general international law (*jus cogens*) are at issue in a dispute cannot in itself constitute an exception to the principle that its jurisdiction always depends on the consent of the parties'. It must be noted also that out of the 194 Member States of the UN only 122 are members to the ICC Statute.

100   Meron (n 17 above) 58.

101   See Simma (n 3 above) 323-325.

This author has pointed out a threefold function of the ICJ with regard to IHL, namely (1) first and foremost, the ICJ clarifies and develops rules and principles of IHL through deciding cases brought before it; (2) it integrates international humanitarian law concepts and principles within the wider framework of international law; (3) it contributes to maintaining the unity of international humanitarian law and its uniform application by international judicial bodies operating in this field.[102] International courts have interpreted the meaning of primary rules as well as secondary rules of international human rights and humanitarian law. As Raimondo has noted, the most notable contribution of the ICJ to humanitarian law is the determination of customary rules that express the 'fundamental' or 'cardinal' general principles of humanitarian law, as the Court called them, namely the rules mentioned by article 3 common to the four 1949 Geneva Conventions, the obligation to respect and to ensure respect for these conventions, the principle of distinction between civilians and combatants, the prohibition of causing unnecessary suffering to combatants, and the Martens Clause.[103] By and large, these contributions point towards a significant role of ICs as moulders, builders and guardians of human rights and humanitarian law norms, alongside other important stakeholders, as states and international and regional organisations.

While pointing out their common fundamental values, ICs have also noted a number of structural differences between these branches of international law. Notably, ICs have to struggle to harmonise state interests with individual interests, since even if the ultimate justification for 'state values' is grounded in 'human values' such as rights, diversity, or efficiency, international legal sources continue to be based on the aggregation of human interests in and by states, whose perceived self-interest may clash with rights accorded to inviduals.[104] Kreß has noted that by connecting the law of armed conflicts with 'elementary considerations of humanity', by declaring an 'intrinsically humanitarian character that permeates the entire law of armed conflict', and by trying to establish a relationship of complementarity – rather that exclusion – with international human rights law, the ICJ reconceptualised the traditional 'laws and customs of war, the codification of which was driven to a significant extent by a utilitarian calculation of State interests, as an integral humanitarian legal regime designed, above all, to ensure respect for the human person'.[105] Indeed, by and large, ICs have interpreted human rights and humanitarian law in a manner so as to grant the maximum possible protection to affected individuals.

The ad hoc tribunals and the ICC have widened the scope of protection accruing to both civilians and combatants under these branches

---

102 Zyberi (n 3 above) 332.
103 Raimondo (n 10 above) 610.
104 Paulus (n 7 above) 211.
105 Kreß (n 24 above) 295-296 (footnotes omitted).

of law. Despite their wide powers and judicial creativity,[106] however, not all conflicts between human rights and humanitarian law norms can be resolved through a process of interpretation by ICs. Some of these conflicts are irreconcilable, and the substantive, procedural and institutional gaps in protection cannot be filled through judicial interpretation, but through the adoption or amendment of specific international instruments, especially with regard to problematic areas as the law of occupation, detention, and *jus post bellum*. Finally, while ICs constitute important tools for resolving inter-state disputes and for investigating and prosecuting individuals for serious violations of human rights and humanitarian law, their effective contribution to enforcing the relevant legal obligations depends on state cooperation and sustained political and institutional support.

---

106   See inter alia S Darcy & J Powderly (eds) *Judicial creativity at the international criminal tribunals* (2010).

Permissions

All chapters in this book were first published in CCHRIHLMO, by Pretoria University Law Press (PULP) by Erika de Wet and Jann Kleffner; hereby published with permission under the Creative Commons Attribution License or equivalent. Every chapter published in this book has been scrutinized by our experts. Their significance has been extensively debated. The topics covered herein carry significant information for a comprehensive understanding. They may even be implemented as practical applications or may be referred to as a beginning point for further studies.

We would like to thank the editorial team for lending their expertise to make the book truly unique. They have played a crucial role in the development of this book. Without their invaluable contributions this book wouldn't have been possible. They have made vital efforts to compile up to date information on the varied aspects of this subject to make this book a valuable addition to the collection of many professionals and students.

This book was conceptualized with the vision of imparting up-to-date and integrated information in this field. To ensure the same, a matchless editorial board was set up. Every individual on the board went through rigorous rounds of assessment to prove their worth. After which they invested a large part of their time researching and compiling the most relevant data for our readers.

The editorial board has been involved in producing this book since its inception. They have spent rigorous hours researching and exploring the diverse topics which have resulted in the successful publishing of this book. They have passed on their knowledge of decades through this book. To expedite this challenging task, the publisher supported the team at every step. A small team of assistant editors was also appointed to further simplify the editing procedure and attain best results for the readers.

Apart from the editorial board, the designing team has also invested a significant amount of their time in understanding the subject and creating the most relevant covers. They scrutinized every image to scout for the most suitable representation of the subject and create an appropriate cover for the book.

The publishing team has been an ardent support to the editorial, designing and production team. Their endless efforts to recruit the best for this project, has resulted in the accomplishment of this book. They are a veteran in the field of academics and their pool of knowledge is as vast as their experience in printing. Their expertise and guidance has proved useful at every step. Their uncompromising quality standards have made this book an exceptional effort. Their encouragement from time to time has been an inspiration for everyone.

The publisher and the editorial board hope that this book will prove to be a valuable piece of knowledge for students, practitioners and scholars across the globe.

List of Contributors

Erika de Wet

Jann Kleffner

Iain Scobbie

Bonita Meyersfeld

Bruce 'Ossie' Oswald

Michelle Lesh

Andrea Carcano

Marten Zwanenburg

André R Smit

Daphna Shraga

Peter M Olson

James Ross

Blaise Cathcart

Frans Viljoen

Karin Oellers-Frahm

Dinah Shelton

Gentian Zyberi

Index

Lightning Source UK Ltd.
Milton Keynes UK
UKHW022116070922
408517UK00001B/3